Financial Accounting
CONCEPTS AND PRACTICES

Financial Accounting

CONCEPTS AND PRACTICES

MORTON BACKER
University of Massachusetts, Emeritus

PIETER T. ELGERS
University of Massachusetts

RICHARD J. ASEBROOK
University of Massachusetts

Harcourt Brace Jovanovich, Publishers

San Diego   New York   Chicago   Austin   Washington, D.C.
London   Sydney   Tokyo   Toronto

Copyright © 1988 by Harcourt Brace Jovanovich, Inc.

All rights reserved. No part of this publication may be reproduced or transmitted in any form or by any means, electronic or mechanical, including photocopy, recording, or any information storage and retrieval system, without permission in writing from the publisher.

Requests for permission to make copies of any part of the work should be mailed to: Permissions, Harcourt Brace Jovanovich, Publishers, Orlando, Florida 32887.

ISBN: 0-15-527371-X

Library of Congress Catalog Card Number: 87-81140

Printed in the United States of America

Preface

Orientation

Financial Accounting, Concepts and Practices is an introductory financial accounting text intended for MBA students and upper-level undergraduates. It is also well suited to programs for undergraduate accounting majors in which a conceptual and decision-oriented approach to the subject is desired. Individual chapters may be used effectively in management training courses and investment analysis seminars. The book is organized to offer considerable flexibility in course content and sequence. A single-semester introductory course would generally cover all twelve chapters. An introductory course taught on the quarter system would utilize the first eight chapters; the second quarter would cover the contemporary issues presented in Chapters 9 through 12.

This textbook is oriented primarily to business managers and the users of financial statements. It seeks to provide readers with an understanding of the ways in which financial reports influence decisions by managers and by investors, creditors, government regulators, and others outside the firm. Students are encouraged to regard choices concerning accounting methods and disclosures as significant policy decisions by managers and accounting regulators that may affect the value of the firm's debt or equity securities.

Features

Distinctive features of the book include the following:

- Discussion of alternative accounting methods and disclosures in the light of the potential economic consequences of accounting policy decisions by managers and regulatory bodies.

- Substantial attention to contemporary accounting issues (such as business combinations, consolidation policies, foreign operations, pensions, and leases) of concern to corporate managers.

- Extensive use (both within chapters and in end-of-chapter materials) of financial statements and disclosures of major corporations familiar to most students.

- Emphasis on information efficiency in securities markets as an aid in identifying substantive areas of choice (both by managers and by accounting regulators) among alternative accounting methods.

- Careful introduction of new terminology and inclusion of an extensive glossary in recognition of the fact that financial accounting courses commonly function to introduce students to business terminology, practices, and financial instruments.

- A variety of challenging end-of-chapter materials (varying in scope from "single concept" discussion questions and exercises to complex integrative case problems designed to elicit an interpretive and evaluative response). The end-of-chapter materials contain approximately 300 discussion questions and over 300 exercises and problems.

Organization of the Book

The twelve chapters are organized under four broad headings: Foundations, Financial Reports, Contemporary Issues, and Accounting Analysis.

The two chapters in Part I provide theoretical, environmental, and procedural foundations. Chapter 1 describes the financial reporting environment in the United States, giving special emphasis to the possible economic consequences of accounting numbers and to the relationship between accounting numbers and securities prices. Chapter 2 focuses on the accounting process, showing how individual transactions and events are ultimately reflected in the financial statements. The appendix to Chapter 2 discusses the use of a worksheet in the preparation of financial statements.

Part II examines the three primary financial statements: the income statement, the balance sheet, and the statement of cash flows. Chapter 3 contains a conceptual discussion of income and its measurement and covers the major sections and overall organization of the income statement for three different types of business enterprises. The appendix to Chapter 3 examines absorption costing versus variable costing of inventories. Chapter 4 discusses three components of net income in detail. The first two sections focus on alternative inventory cost flow assumptions and depreciation patterns permitted by generally accepted accounting principles. The chapter's last section considers issues in accounting for income tax expense. Chapters 5, 6, and 7 are devoted to the major elements of the balance sheet: assets, liabilities, and owners' equity. Recent balance sheets of two U.S. firms (UAL, Incorporated and Apple Computer, Incorporated) are presented to provide the frame of reference for balance sheet discussion. The appendix to Chapter 5 covers the basics of compound interest, including the use of present value and maturity value tables. Chapter 8 covers the statement of cash flows, with discussion based on the FASB's recent Exposure Draft concerning this topic.

Part III (Chapters 9 through 11) treats six contemporary topics in financial accounting: intercorporate investments, segment reporting, leases, defined-benefit pension plans, changing prices, and the translation of foreign operations. The appendix to Chapter 9 examines financial reporting for segments of a business.

Part IV contains one chapter devoted to financial statement analysis. The treatment consists of a synthesis of the ideas developed in preceding chapters and is intended to be a capstone discussion concerning the uses and limitations of financial accounting disclosures. The appendix to this chapter examines the consolidation of finance and insurance subsidiaries and demonstrates the effects of such consolidations on the recalculation of financial ratios.

Ancillary Materials

Resource materials that are available for use in conjunction with the textbook include a Solutions Manual and a Test Book. The Solutions Manual provides detailed answers to all discussion questions, exercises, and problems that appear at the end of chapters — over 600 responses. The Test Book offers over 300 true/false and multiple choice questions, covering each of the twelve chapters.

Acknowledgments

Anyone who sets out to write a textbook accumulates many debts in the course of such a project. We would like to extend our thanks to some of those people without whose help this book would not have been completed.

A number of reviewers read the manuscript for this book at various stages and offered valuable editorial suggestions. In this regard we wish to thank Robert Bloom, John Carroll University; Dennis Daly, University of Minnesota; James Reeve, University of Tennessee; Richard Simpson, University of Massachusetts; and Mikal Tiller, Indiana University. We give special thanks to Professor Reeve for providing additional, detailed review.

We are indebted to the American Institute of Certified Public Accountants, the Financial Accounting Standards Board, and a number of corporations for granting permission to reprint excerpts from their publications and financial reports.

The staff at Harcourt Brace Jovanovich has been extremely helpful and understanding in the preparation of this book. We wish to acknowledge Ken Rethmeier, acquisitions editor; Helen Triller, manuscript editor; Amy Dunn and Karen Lenardi, production editors; Diane Pella, designer; and Lynne Bush, production manager. Special thanks are due Helen Triller for her tireless efforts on the project.

Many of our students at the University of Massachusetts have provided us with editorial assistance over the course of this project. Our thanks are due to Brenda Anderson, Patricia Canavan, Martha Finkel, Gordon Fitzgerald, Chiann-I Jang, Ellen Ku, May Hwa Lo, and Eva Lohrer.

Finally, we received valuable assistance in the typing of the manuscript from Anne Asebrook, Jennifer Asebrook, Alice Bonsignore, Deborah Koziol, and Christine Kubin. Jackie Wisneski also played a critical role in the typing of the manuscript.

To all of the individuals and institutions mentioned above, we offer our sincere gratitude.

Morton Backer
Pieter Elgers
Richard Asebrook

Contents

Preface

PART II   FINANCIAL REPORTING

**Chapter 3 Income Measurement and the Income
Statement**   102

PART III   CONTEMPORARY ISSUES IN ACCOUNTING

Chapter 9   Intercorporate Investments and Business Combinations   422

FOUNDATIONS

Chapter

Chapter

1

The Financial Reporting Environment

This chapter defines financial accounting, describes the financial reporting environment of companies in the United States, and discusses accounting policy issues (specifically, choices among reporting alternatives) from the perspectives of those who establish accounting standards and of those who use financial accounting reports to make decisions. In addition, special emphasis is given to the possible economic consequences of accounting numbers and to the relationships between accounting numbers and securities prices.

FINANCIAL ACCOUNTING DEFINED

Accounting is the measurement and reporting of economic events to provide relevant information to decision makers. Accounting information is divided into two categories: financial accounting and managerial accounting. The information generated by **financial accounting** is directed to decision makers *outside* the firm (investors, creditors, customers, suppliers, government regulators, and other significant groups). Such individuals are not normally in a position to request information that is tailor-made for them; therefore, they must accept information provided by the firm in the form of general purpose financial reports. As a consequence, various "ground rules" are created to ensure a certain level of uniformity in the preparation of financial reports for use by those outside the firm. This set of rules and conventions is referred to as **generally accepted accounting principles,** or **GAAP**, and much of this chapter discusses how these rules are established.

Managerial accounting information is aimed at decision makers *inside* the firm. Managers require information for planning and controlling the firm's operations. For example, managers need information to help them decide whether or not a certain product line should be dropped, a new piece of machinery should be purchased, or operations to date are costing more or less than planned. Managerial accounting reports are tailor-made to provide information relevant to the decision at hand and are not governed by GAAP. Therefore, managers can set their own "ground rules" regarding the amount and type of accounting information to be used inside the firm. Depending on the expected benefits and the costs of preparing the information, different sets of information are prepared for different purposes.

Although it is useful to contrast financial and managerial accounting, the distinction should not be overemphasized. Managers are constantly alert to the potential impact of all their decisions on published financial accounting reports. It is through these financial reports that managers reveal the wisdom or the folly of their decisions. Financial reports are a primary means by which managers communicate with investors, creditors, and others outside the firm.

DECISIONS AND ACCOUNTING INFORMATION

There is no self-contained "art" or "science" of accounting. Accounting is a service function whose product — information — must be relevant to decision makers. Consequently, the products of the accounting profession should be expected to vary in content and form as the information requirements of the decision makers change. An economist would say that the demand for accounting reports is a *derived* demand. This means that accounting reports are not desired for their own sake but because of the benefits (greater command over goods and services) users hope to derive indirectly from their use. Thus, the production of costly accounting reports should be justified by expected improvements based on the resulting decisions. This view of accounting information as an economic good suggests that we address the following questions in order to explain current financial reporting practice:

1. Who are the main users of accounting information?
2. For what types of decisions are accounting numbers used?
3. What accounting information is relevant to these types of decisions?

After we have answered these questions, we consider how to design accounting reports that will provide the most relevant information to decision makers.

The Users of Financial Reports

As indicated earlier, a firm directs its financial reports to outside groups such as the following:

1. Investors
   a. Equity shareholders, primarily owners of common stock in the firm
   b. Bondholders
   c. Investor advisors
2. Lenders, such as banks and other financial intermediaries that provide funds directly to borrowing firms
3. Current and prospective customers and suppliers
4. Labor organizations
5. Government taxing and regulatory agencies
6. Economic planners

Decisions Based on Accounting Reports

Each of the groups using financial reports has specific objectives. Thus, the accounting information that one group requires in order to make the decisions that best fulfill its objectives will probably differ from the information required by another group. Consider the following examples:

- Investors may be concerned mainly with the risks involved in and the returns available from owning the firm's outstanding stocks and bonds.
- Lenders may focus on the ability of the firm to pay its debts as they come due.
- Customers may emphasize the stability of the firm as a continuing source of supply.
- Suppliers may be alert to the firm's growth prospects and credit worthiness.
- Labor organizations may use information about productivity and profitability variances in negotiating new wage contracts.
- Government regulators and planning agencies may wish to examine trends in industry concentration, profitability, pricing, productivity, and other matters related to the functioning of the economy.

This diversity among users of financial information would present no special difficulty if financial accounting reports were designed specifically to suit the information requirements of each separate user group. Current financial reporting practice, however, rests on a presumption that a single set of general purpose financial accounting reports should serve all users. This implies that at least one of three assumptions holds true: (1) the information needs of all groups are quite similar (which we have already stated is not likely to be the case), (2) the data contained in financial reports are sufficiently broad that each group can extract the information required for its own purposes, or (3) a single group is primary. There is wide agreement among accounting regulators and academics that investors as a group comprise an important, and perhaps the primary, audience for published financial accounting reports. For this reason, it is useful for us to attempt to identify the types of accounting information relevant to the investment decision.

Investor Uses of Accounting Reports

Investment entails the postponing of current consumption in return for securities (stocks and bonds, for example). Securities are claims to future, uncertain cash flows. The investor must decide on the overall allocation of funds between (1) current consumption and (2) investment. In the case of investment, the investor must decide how to invest funds among the various available securities. These decisions depend on the expected amounts, timing, and uncertainty of the future cash flows. An investor requires information that will improve the assessments of these future cash flows. Subject to the cost of the information, "better" accounting information will facilitate better prediction of investment cash flows.

Thus far we have spoken of "the investor" as though all investors were similar. In fact, investors are a diverse group, varying in attitudes toward risk, access to financial information, skills in the interpretation and analysis of financial reports, and approaches to risk diversification and portfolio management. For example, the relatively unsophisticated investor may prefer highly abbreviated financial reports with few critical indicators of a firm's wealth, performance, or future prospects. Such an investor may be concerned solely with a "bottom-line" amount, such as the profit during a recent period. A highly skilled financial analyst, on the other hand, would place less weight on any one "bottom-line" summary measure and prefer to assess the investment value of the firm based on a more thorough knowledge of economic events affecting the firm. A sophisticated user would in all likelihood prefer detailed reports with breakdowns of the firm's major product lines, customers, types of expenses, and so on. In addition, a skilled investor might desire information concerning management's plans and forecasts (capital spending plans, impending financial decisions, sales and profit forecasts, cash projections, and other future-oriented information).

Sophisticated and unsophisticated users alike make their decisions based in part on the information generated as the basic product of financial accounting — a set of financial statements and related narrative disclosures that are described in the following section.

FINANCIAL ACCOUNTING STATEMENTS

Financial accounting statements focus on three major dimensions of the firm: (1) wealth, (2) performance, and (3) liquidity. A separate financial statement is prepared to provide information on each of these three dimensions. The basic purpose of each statement is identified in this section, and the form and content of these statements are discussed extensively in Part II of this text.

Measuring Wealth: the Balance Sheet

The financial statement that provides information about the wealth of the firm is the statement of financial position, or the **balance sheet.** The balance sheet lists a firm's valuable resources, or assets, as well as its obligations, or liabilities, at a specific point in time. The amount by which total assets exceed total liabilities is the owners' equity at that date.[1]

The upper part of Exhibit 1-1 shows the September 28, 1985, balance sheet of Apple Computer, Incorporated, in summary form; the lower part shows the balance sheet of Apple Computer on that date in the degree of detail actually used in the firm's annual financial report.

An asset must have certain characteristics to be included on a firm's balance sheet. **Assets** are usually defined as resources that are expected to provide economic benefits. However, not all resources one might consider to be assets from a broad economic perspective are classified as accounting assets. In order for a resource to qualify as an accounting asset, several criteria must be met: (1) the resource must be expected to benefit the firm's future cash flows, (2) the firm must have an identifiable claim to obtain and control the benefits, (3) the event giving rise to the firm's ownership or control of the benefits must have already occurred, and (4) the benefits must be measurable in units of money.[2]

To illustrate the distinction between an asset in the broad economic sense vis-à-vis the more narrow accounting definition, consider the interstate highway system from the standpoint of a national trucking firm. Without question, the interstate highway system is an asset to the firm from an economic point of view. It is a resource that enhances the firm's future cash flows. However, the interstate highway system is not shown on the firm's financial statements as an asset. One reason is that the company cannot control the benefits of using the

---

[1]In financial accounting, the term "owners' equity" (or "shareholders' equity") represents the wealth of the firm from an owners' perspective in a very limited sense. Dollar amounts assigned to assets and liabilities on the balance sheet are often quite different from the corresponding current market values. Accordingly, the arithmetic difference between assets and liabilities, or owners' equity, does not generally reflect the economic value of the owners' interest.

[2]*Statement of Financial Accounting Concepts No. 6*, "Elements of Financial Statements of Business Enterprises" (Stamford, CT: FASB, 1980). The Financial Accounting Standards Board is described later in this chapter (see page 16).

Exhibit 1-1
Balance Sheet (Summary Form)

Apple Computer, Incorporated
Consolidated Balance Sheet
September 28, 1985
(in thousands)

Assets		Liabilities and Shareholders' Equity	
Current assets	$822,065	Current liabilities	$295,425
Property, plant, and equipment	90,446	Deferred income taxes	90,265
Other assets	23,666	Shareholders' equity	550,487
Total	$936,177	Total	$936,177

Balance Sheet (Detailed Form)

Apple Computer, Incorporated
Consolidated Balance Sheet
September 28, 1985
(in thousands)

Assets

Current assets:

Cash and temporary cash investments	$337,013
Accounts receivable, net of allowance for doubtful accounts of $16,209 ($10,831 in 1984)	220,157
Inventories	166,951
Prepaid income taxes	70,375
Other current assets	27,569
Total current assets	822,065

Property, plant, and equipment:

Land and buildings	23,621
Machinery and equipment	78,725
Office furniture and equipment	38,551
Leasehold improvements	34,738
	175,635
Accumulated depreciation and amortization	(85,189)
Net property, plant, and equipment	90,446
Other assets	23,666
	$936,177

Liabilities and Shareholders' Equity

Current liabilities:

Accounts payable	$ 74,744
Accrued compensation and employee benefits	25,595
Income taxes payable	27,800
Accrued marketing and distribution	75,934
Accrued cost of consolidation of operations	20,173
Other current liabilities	71,179
Total current liabilities	295,425
Deferred income taxes	90,265

Commitments and contingencies
Shareholders' equity:

Common stock, no par value, 160,000,000 shares authorized; 61,849,802 shares issued and outstanding in 1985 (60,535,146 shares in 1984)	234,625
Retained earnings	320,324
Accumulated translation adjustment	414
	555,363
Notes receivable from shareholders	(4,876)
Total shareholders' equity	550,487
	$936,177

Source: Apple Computer, Incorporated, *Annual Report*, 1985.

system. Although the firm indeed receives benefits from the use of the highway system, it cannot prevent competing trucking firms from receiving like benefits (criterion 2). Also, it is very difficult to objectively measure in units of money the benefits accruing to the firm from the use of the interstate system (criterion 4).

In a similar fashion, liabilities must have certain characteristics before they are included on the balance sheet. A **liability** is an obligation to transfer economic resources from the reporting entity to another business, person, or governmental unit. For financial accounting purposes, a liability must (1) involve a probable future outflow of resources, (2) be the specific obligation of the reporting firm, (3) be the result of an event that has already occurred, and (4) be measurable in units of money. A firm would not show as a liability on the balance sheet an obligation to pay an employee wages according to a union contract for work to be performed next week. This is because the critical event, the performance of work, has not yet occurred (criterion 3).

As noted earlier, **owners' equity** in financial accounting is the arithmetic result of subtracting total liabilities from total assets. Thus, the meaning of owners' equity depends on the methods by which the firm's individual assets and liabilities are measured. The conventional accounting methods of measuring assets and liabilities are discussed in detail in the next five chapters. At this point, we merely reiterate the fact that in most cases assets and liabilities are not listed on the balance sheet at current market values. (In Exhibit 1-1, the dollar amount of owners' equity [$550,487,000] does not necessarily indicate the economic value of the stockholders' interest in the firm's assets.) Consequently, the dollar amount of owners' equity is not necessarily related to the current market value of the ownership interest in the firm.

Measuring Profitability: the Income Statement

The **income statement** is a financial statement that presents information about a firm's profitability over a given period of time. The income statement shows **revenues** (inflows of net assets from the sale of goods and services) and **expenses** (the consumption of net assets in the process of generating revenues). The difference between revenues and expenses is either the net income or the net loss from the operations of the period.[3]

The upper part of Exhibit 1-2 shows the income statement of Apple Computer, Incorporated, for the year ended September 28, 1985, in summary form; the lower part shows the income statement for that same period in the degree of detail actually used in the Apple Computer annual financial report.

In Exhibit 1-2, the dollar amount of net income ($61,223,000) represents an inflow of net assets from operations during the period. This amount also in-

---

[3]In addition to revenues and expenses, an income statement may contain other elements such as gains and losses. Revenues and expenses relate to the central operating activities of the firm; gains and losses relate to the firm's peripheral activities. Each of these elements is defined in Chapter 3, pages 108–109.

Exhibit 1-2
Income Statement (Summary Form)

Apple Computer, Incorporated
Consolidated Income Statement
For the Year Ended September 28, 1985
(in thousands)

Net sales	$1,918,280
Costs, expenses, and unusual items	1,798,235
Income before income taxes	120,045
Provision for income taxes	58,822
Net income	$ 61,223

Income Statement (Detailed Form)

Apple Computer, Incorporated
Consolidated Income Statement
For the Year Ended September 28, 1985
(in thousands)

Net sales	$1,918,280
Costs and expenses:	
Cost of sales	1,117,864
Research and development	72,526
Marketing and distribution	470,588
General and administrative	110,077
	1,771,055
Operating income before unusual item	147,225
Unusual item — provision for consolidation of operations	(36,966)
Interest and other income, net	9,786
Income before income taxes	120,045
Provision for income taxes	58,822
Net income	$ 61,223
Earnings per common and common equivalent share	$ .99

Source: Apple Computer, Incorporated, *Annual Report,* 1985.

creases the owners' equity reported on the balance sheet. In fact, the change in owners' equity during a particular period of time would be exactly equal to the period's income or loss if there were no additional owner investments (such as the sale of additional ownership shares by the firm) and no distribution of assets to owners (such as dividends to shareholders).

The income of the firm depends on how the net asset inflows and outflows due to revenues and expenses are measured. These measurement rules are discussed extensively in Chapters 2–7. It is worth noting at this point that accounting income may differ substantially from the economic concept of income. In economic theory, income denotes an increase in "well-offness" during a period of time and is usually measured by an increase in wealth. One reasonable measure of the increase in the wealth of the firm's owners may be the increase in the market value of the outstanding stock. **Accounting income,** however, is unlikely to correspond to changes in the value of the firm's equity shares.

Measuring Changes in Liquidity: the Statement of Cash Flows

The **statement of cash flows** provides information about changes in a firm's liquidity. This statement classifies cash receipts and payments by operating, investing, and financing cash flows, and serves to emphasize the distinction between profitability and liquidity. An otherwise profitable firm may fail or be forced into bankruptcy because of a shortage of the cash needed to sustain its operations. Although income is defined as the increase in net assets during a period, some or all of the increases in net assets may not be available in *liquid*, or spendable, form. A firm may have large inflows or outflows of cash that are not directly related to the revenues and expenses of the period. Common examples include inflows of cash from new borrowings, stock issuances, or sales of assets, and outflows of cash for new capital spending, repayments of debts, or dividends paid to shareholders.

The statement of cash flows presented in Exhibit 1-3 is one of several illustrative statements included in the FASB's Exposure Draft, "Proposed Statement of Financial Accounting Standards: Statement of Cash Flows."

The three basic statements presented in Exhibits 1-1, 1-2, and 1-3 interrelate. Together, the income statement and the statement of cash flows indicate changes in owners' equity and liquidity over a period of time, whereas the balance sheet indicates financial position at a specific point in time.

Footnotes

In addition to the information included in the body of the three basic statements, accounting reports contain sets of footnotes that are an integral part of the financial statements. **Footnotes** are generally of three types: (1) detailed explanations concerning management's choices of accounting methods in areas such as consolidation policy, valuation of inventories, accounting for leases and pension plans, and expensing of the costs of long-lived assets; (2) breakdowns and analyses of broad captions in the financial statements, such as details about the composition of property, plant, and equipment; maturity dates for the firm's long-term debt; rights and priorities of debt and equity securities outstanding; and information about major customers and lines of business of the firm; and (3) supplemental information, such as the effects of general inflation and changes in current costs on the firm's financial position and operating results; possible effects of pending litigation or other types of contingent liabilities; and effects of events subsequent to the balance sheet date. Several foot-

Exhibit 1-3
Statement of Cash Flows

Cash Flows from Operating Activities		
Cash received from customers	$10,000	
Dividends received	700	
Cash provided by operating activities		10,700
Cash paid to suppliers and employees	6,000	
Interest and taxes paid	1,750	
Cash disbursed for operating activities		7,750
Net cash flow from operating activities		2,950
Cash Flows from Investing Activities		
Purchases of property, plant, equipment	(4,000)	
Proceeds from disposals of property, plant, and equipment	2,500	
Acquisition of Company ABC	(900)	
Purchases of investment securities	(4,700)	
Proceeds from sales of investment securities	5,000	
Loans made	(7,500)	
Collections on loans	(5,800)	
Net cash used by investing activities		(3,800)
Cash Flows from Financing Activities		
Net increase in customer deposits	1,100	
Proceeds of short-term debt	75	
Payments to settle short-term debt	(300)	
Proceeds of long-term debt	1,250	
Payments on capital lease obligations	(125)	
Proceeds from issuing common stock	500	
Dividends paid	(450)	
Net cash provided by financing activities		2,050
Effect of exchange rate changes on cash		100
Net increase (decrease) in cash		$ 1,300

Source: *Proposed Statement of Financial Accounting Standards (Exposure Draft)*, "Statement of Cash Flows" (Stamford, CT: FASB, 1986), p. 28.

Note: Cash flow from operating activities is reported directly. Noncash transactions are reported in a separate schedule.

note disclosures are specifically required by GAAP; others are indirectly required by the general guideline that financial statements contain sufficient disclosures so as not to be misleading. Some footnote information is voluntarily disclosed by management in an effort to improve the quality of information available to investors.

ASSUMPTIONS AND CONVENTIONS IN FINANCIAL ACCOUNTING

In order to understand the accounting methods included in GAAP, it is helpful to begin with a set of assumptions and conventions that underlie present practice. Be aware at the outset, however, that financial accounting is not a rigidly logical system, and that it is not always possible to proceed in a deductive fashion from underlying assumptions to the explanation of acceptable methods of accounting for particular events. Acceptable accounting practices are rarely deduced by logical analysis from underlying assumptions; rather, general principles are often inferred from existing practice in an attempt to codify accounting methods.

The following paragraphs briefly define a set of seven basic assumptions and conventions underlying current financial accounting practice. The list is not exhaustive, and the items included have been selected because they are critical to an understanding of the basic techniques of accounting discussed in Part II of this text. Each of these concepts will be explained in more detail as it is encountered in later chapters, and the list of assumptions will be expanded as appropriate.

1. **Accounting entity.**   In financial accounting the entity is the business enterprise whose economic activities are reflected in the financial statements. Unless such an entity can be identified and its economic activities specified, it would not be meaningful to speak of accounting for its activities. The corporation is a business entity that is also a legal entity distinct from its owners or other securities holders. In many cases the notions of a legal entity and an accounting entity coincide, such as when financial statements are prepared for a corporation that has no investment in the stock of other companies. Often a corporation owns substantial amounts of stock in other companies. These intercorporate investments frequently bring several companies, each a distinct legal entity, under common control. In such a case it may be necessary, for financial accounting purposes, to look beyond the legal definitions and to define the accounting entity as a set of economic resources under common control. Financial statements that combine operating results and financial positions of multiple legal entities under common control are referred to as consolidated financial statements.

2. **Going concern.**   The accounting entity is assumed not to be liquidating in the foreseeable future unless there is evidence to the contrary. The assumption of going concern is often cited to justify listing the firm's assets at cost and provides the rationale for not listing those assets at liquidating or market values. Liquidating values would be appropriate, however, if the assumption is that the firm is going out of business in the foreseeable future.

3. **Time periods.**   In order to provide information about the firm's progress on an interim basis, it is useful to divide the lifetime performance of the firm into shorter time periods, such as a year. Because economic processes rarely fall neatly into a series of predefined time intervals, the assignment of operating results to time periods entails estimating and approximating. The time period convention requires a tradeoff between precision and timeliness.

4. **Money measurement.**   Measurement in terms of money is useful in describing the assets, liabilities, and performance of the accounting entity. It is necessary to identify an attribute that is common to all the elements in the financial statements, if those elements are to be added, subtracted, or compared in any other fashion. In an environment of stable prices and economic values, the concept of money measurement may be quite useful. However, in the context of significant general inflation and widely varying rates of price change for individual assets and liabilities, the money measurement convention may well be misleading.

5. **Exchange price.**   Financial accounting measurements of assets and liabilities are based on the prices inherent in the exchanges from which they originated. The exchange price concept explains why, in most cases, accounting assets and liabilities appear in financial statements at their initial or historical costs rather than at their current values. The primary justification given for focusing on historical exchange prices is that historical costs are objective and easily verifiable.

6. **Recognition and realization.**   If revenues of the firm are to be assigned to specific time periods shorter than the firm's life, criteria are needed to establish when to recognize such revenues. These criteria stipulate that (1) the revenues should have been earned, in the sense that most of the firm's performance obligations (the functions of production and selling) are complete and (2) the amount of revenue should be measurable with reasonable objectivity. Objective measurement of revenue involves the concept of realization. Until an economic resource has been sold or exchanged in a transaction between two independent parties (an arm's-length transaction), changes in its value may not be reflected in the financial statements. For example, revenue is not measurable with reasonable objectivity if there remains substantial uncertainty about the amount or timing of the economic resources to be received.

7. **Matching.**   As noted earlier, income is defined essentially as recognized revenue less all expenses entailed in producing that revenue during a period. The matching concept refers to the relationship between expenses and revenues. In particular, the matching concept requires that once specific revenues have been recognized in a given period, all applicable expenses incurred to generate those revenues must be "assigned" to that same period. Thus, the timing of expense recognition depends on the timing of revenue recognition. Of course, application of the matching concept requires some compromises because it is often difficult to establish a direct link between revenues and expenses. Consider, for example, the cost of a plant building or other long-lived asset that will be consumed over a number of accounting periods. The expense of using this asset may be difficult to identify with specific accounting periods. Instead, accountants will adopt some reasonable, though arbitrary formula, such as assigning equal amounts of expense to each period of asset use.

8. **Conservatism.**   There are situations in financial accounting in which alternative accounting valuations are possible. In these cases, accountants have historically preferred the alternative that results in the lower valuation of net income and net assets. Stated another way, accountants have generally pre-

ferred that possible measurement errors be in the direction of understatement of net income and net assets, rather than overstatement of these amounts. Nonetheless, conservatism is not intended to connote deliberate, consistent understatement of net income and assets. Recently, the Financial Accounting Standards Board has attempted to modify what is meant by conservatism so that it is more synonymous with *prudence.* Specifically, the FASB has defined conservatism to be "a prudent reaction to uncertainty to try to ensure that uncertainty and risks inherent in business situations are adequately considered."[4]

FINANCIAL REPORTING AND FINANCIAL STATEMENTS

As indicated in Figure 1-1, accounting reports comprise just one portion of the total body of information available to investors. The information that is rele-

Figure 1-1

The Investment Information Set

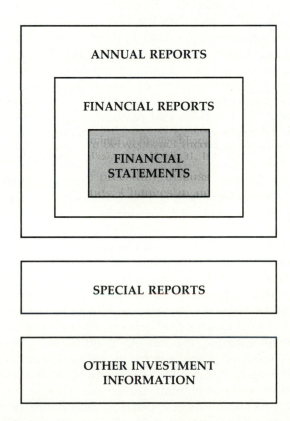

[4]*Statement of Financial Accounting Concepts No. 2,* "Qualitative Characteristics of Accounting Information" (Stamford, CT: FASB, 1980).

vant to investors may be financial or nonfinancial; the financial information may be accounting or nonaccounting in nature; and the accounting information *may* be contained in the basic financial statements or may be supplemental to them. The following types of information are most commonly available to investors:

- Financial Statements
  Statement of Financial Position (Balance Sheet)
  Statement of Revenues and Expenses (Income Statement)
  Statement of Cash Flows
- Financial Reports
  Financial Statements (as above)
  Auditor's Report
  Footnotes: Required and Voluntary
  Historical Summaries
- Annual Reports
  Financial Reports (as above)
  Contents of annual reports in addition to accounting reports (for example, President's letter; projected new capital spending; planned capital structure changes; impending acquisitions or divestitures; environmental and social welfare activities; human capital and other intangible resources; labor relationships; research and development; new product plans; and other financial events).
- Special Reports
  Prospectuses; annual reports to the Securities and Exchange Commission; other required and voluntary releases of information by the firm.
- Other Investment Information
  Financial Reports (as above)
  Economic reports
  Industry reports
  Nonfinancial information: macroeconomic events and forecasts; changes in fiscal or monetary policy; technological changes; management changes; government regulations; and other nonfinancial information.

Even from this partial listing of information available to investors, it is evident that financial reports provide only a portion of the information that may affect the price of securities. Investors do consider these disclosures to be informative, as evidenced by the fact that securities prices change at about the dates of accounting reports. In particular, the securities prices of smaller firms appear to fluctuate more than do those of larger firms, suggesting that accounting reports are a relatively more important source of investor information for smaller firms. A substantial portion of the information contained in accounting reports does appear, however, to be anticipated by the market prior to the issuance of the accounting reports. This suggests that accounting disclosures may overlap with information available from nonaccounting sources, especially for larger firms. An income statement, for example, is not the only source of information regarding a firm's profitability. Other types of information, which may be publicly available before the income statement is presented, include earnings forecasts by professional analysts, sales backlog data (orders for a firm's products that cannot be filled immediately), and earnings forecasts by the company itself. All of this financial information and a myriad of other financial and nonfinancial events have the potential to affect the prices of securities.

Decisions concerning the types and amount of data to be included in accounting reports are termed **accounting policy decisions.** Some accounting policy decisions are made by managers, while others are made by regulatory groups outside the firm. The next section describes various parties involved in formulating or influencing accounting policies.

FINANCIAL ACCOUNTING POLICY DECISIONS

Financial accounting policy decisions include the choices among alternative methods of accounting as well as decisions about the overall level of disclosure. Accounting policy decisions made by managers entail discretionary choices among a variety of generally accepted methods of accounting and decisions about voluntary supplementary disclosures in footnotes or elsewhere in the financial reports. (Discretionary accounting policy decisions made by managers will be considered later in this chapter.) Accounting policy decisions made by regulators, on the other hand, entail changes in generally accepted accounting principles. Such changes may narrow or expand the range of accepted accounting methods, increase or diminish the overall level of required financial disclosure, or alter the frequency of financial accounting requirements. This section describes the various policy-making groups that determine such nondiscretionary or mandatory changes in financial reporting practice.

Mandatory financial reporting practices are established either in the private sector by the **Financial Accounting Standards Board** (**FASB**), or in the public sector through the influence of the **Securities and Exchange Commission** (**SEC**), **Congress**, and the **Internal Revenue Service** (**IRS**).

Financial Accounting Standards Board (FASB)

The FASB was created in 1973 and consists of seven voting members having extensive experience in the public accounting profession, industry, government, or academe. The Board is autonomous in the sense that the members serve on a full-time basis, having severed all other employment relationships. Moreover, no other private-sector body is empowered to overrule or modify FASB pronouncements.

The end product of a FASB policy decision is a **Statement of Financial Accounting Standards** (**SFAS**). To date more than ninety have been issued. The standard-setting process begins with the publication of a discussion memorandum, which attempts to identify alternative points of view concerning the various possible courses of action on a particular accounting issue. All parties interested in the issue are invited to submit position papers. Subsequently, public hearings are scheduled in which persons seeking to influence the Board's thinking present oral arguments. On major accounting issues, the hearings often include presentations by representatives of affected industries, financial institutions, investor advisors, regulators, professional accounting firms and associations, academics, and other groups. The Board considers these arguments and may also commission its own research. An exposure draft of a proposed standard is then prepared and circulated widely among interested persons. Responses to the exposure draft are considered. This may lead to the preparation and dissemination of a final pronouncement, or it may result in further rounds of public hearings and exposure drafts. The length of the standard-setting process may extend from a few months to several years, depending upon the perceived significance of the topic and the tractability of the issues.

Since FASB pronouncements constitute generally accepted accounting principles, firms must comply with FASB statements to be able to represent that their financial statements are in accord with GAAP. For various public financial reporting purposes (such as filings with the Securities and Exchange Commission and annual reports to shareholders), managers must obtain an independent auditor's report that attests the financial statements and other related disclosures conform to GAAP.

In several important areas, such as business combinations, earnings per share, and income tax effects, the FASB has made no substantial policy decisions. In such cases the sources of GAAP are pronouncements of the FASB's predecessor, the **Accounting Principles Board** (**APB**), other professional groups, academic journals and textbooks, prevailing industry practices, and other sources of "authoritative" support. At various points later in this text, we will discuss some of the controversial areas in financial reporting upon which the FASB has made no definitive statements to date.

Securities and Exchange Commission (SEC)

The SEC was created by the United States Congress in 1934 to administer the Securities Act of 1933 and the Securities Exchange Act of 1934, both of which were intended to protect the investor. The Securities Act of 1933 requires that issuers of securities make full disclosure of material facts about the securities. (The concept of materiality is discussed later in this chapter.) These disclosures are accomplished by filing a registration statement and prospectus for SEC approval prior to the sale of securities. In subsequent periods a number of documents must be filed with the SEC; these include Forms 10-K (annual filing of financial statements by firms with publicly traded securities), 10-Q (quarterly financial report), and 8-K (report of unscheduled material events, corporate changes, and so forth, deemed important to investors).

By law the SEC may dictate the accounting principles to be used in these documents, but as a matter of policy the SEC is generally supportive of private-sector (FASB) rule making. In fact, in 1973 the SEC issued a special Accounting

Series Release stating that FASB statements constitute substantial authoritative support for management's choice of accounting methods used in SEC filings. For registration statements and 10-K reports, however, the SEC requires accounting disclosures that are generally more extensive than those specified by GAAP.

The SEC has sometimes issued pronouncements that have effectively reversed or modified FASB statements. Recent examples include accounting for the effects of changing prices and accounting by oil and gas companies. In these cases, the financial press and professional accounting organizations have expressed concern about the possible damage to the FASB's prestige and authority and have debated the relative merits of public versus private establishment of accounting standards. For the present, the SEC supports the continued existence of the FASB, at least as the nominal rule-making body in financial reporting. The FASB serves a useful function in identifying important accounting issues, conducting theoretical and empirical research on those issues, and providing (through its publications and hearings) a thorough airing of the frequently conflicting positions of various affected parties. Accordingly, the FASB, which is supported by private-sector funds, is a valuable resource for the SEC.

Congress

In practice, Congress has delegated its authority to establish accounting principles for publicly held companies to the SEC. However, Congress occasionally chooses to intervene in the standard-setting process. For example, in 1971 Congress considered reinstating a federal subsidy for qualified business investment known as the "investment tax credit." Congress feared that the accounting treatment being considered by the APB (then the private sector policy-making body) would soften the economic stimulus created by the tax credit. For this reason, the legislation included a provision that no taxpayer could be required to use one particular method of accounting for the investment credit to the exclusion of all other methods. A similar intervention by Congress occurred in 1975 in the area of accounting for companies that produce crude oil or natural gas. While such interventions in the standard-setting process are infrequent and are typically confined to areas of substantial economic importance, they do show that the ultimate source of power in public financial reporting resides effectively in the public sector and only nominally in the FASB.

Internal Revenue Service (IRS)

Public financial reporting aims to serve the information needs of investors and other decision makers outside the firm. IRS (or tax) reporting, by contrast, is governed by rules aimed at achieving the objectives of fiscal policy, such as providing incentives or disincentives for various types of business activity, creating subsidies and transfer payments, achieving equity, and encouraging savings. Since the basic purposes of IRS reporting and public financial reporting are quite different, the IRS has little direct influence on public financial reporting.[5] Generally, there is no necessary correspondence between the accounting methods used in public financial reports and those used in tax reports. This basic distinction is overlooked by some financial writers who draw attention to significant differences between the amounts of taxable income and financial accounting income for certain firms. A comparison between these two amounts is not meaningful because they come from different reports prepared for dissimilar purposes.

There may be various indirect relationships between tax law and financial accounting. For example, firms may desire to simplify record keeping by using the same set of accounting records for financial reporting and tax purposes. The main difficulty here is that the accounting methods that best reflect the performance of the firm from an investor standpoint may differ from the accounting methods that serve to minimize taxes.

THE ADEQUACY OF DISCLOSURE

Are the financial disclosure policies of United States firms adequate to serve the needs of investors and other users for external financial reports? This issue has been widely debated in the accounting profession, and the views of professionals vary from the position that financial disclosures are woefully inadequate to the position that financial disclosures are excessive and should be curtailed. The question requires an understanding of the meaning of disclosure adequacy. In this context it is not instructive to define "adequate" as "fair," "full," or "complete." Rather, adequacy can most meaningfully be defined here only in terms of the information needs of a specific user group, and then only if the members of that group have reasonably similar uses for accounting information.

With reference to equity investors as a representative user group, disclosure adequacy can be expressed in terms of the completeness, frequency, and timeliness of financial reporting. Each of these dimensions should be assessed by considering both the costs and the benefits of changes in disclosure policy.

1. *Completeness.* The completeness of financial information involves both the amount and the type of data presented. Issues such as the level of detail provided, the accounting methods employed, the formats and groupings of data in the financial statements and exhibits, the amount of historical and future-oriented information, and the extent of supplementary and interpretive information (in footnotes, for example) must all be considered in assessing the completeness of financial data. Whether financial disclosures of United States corporations are sufficiently complete is a moot question. Relatively unskilled investors often object to the massive amount of data included in financial reports, while surveys of securities analysts and other investment advisors invariably indicate a desire for more extensive disclosures.

---

[5]One notable exception (often referred to as the "LIFO conformity rule") in the area of inventory costing is discussed in Chapter 4.

These different views of the completeness of financial disclosure under-score the fact that disclosure adequacy can only be assessed with respect to a specific decision model. A naïve investor may seek a single number to indicate the earning power or the value of the firm and see the morass of other detail as superfluous. A sophisticated analyst, on the other hand, may look to financial reports to aid in uncovering the basic structure of the firm and to assist in the evaluation of the firm's probable future cash flows. For such a user, the inter-pretations and aggregations of events entailed in preparing the conventional accounting statements may cause a substantial loss of information.

An additional problem in assessing the completeness of accounting disclo-sures concerns the question of cost. From the perspective of many users of published financial information, accounting data may be viewed as a "free good" because there is no direct charge to consumers for the accounting re-ports. In an economic sense, however, disclosures should not be expanded be-yond the point at which the additional costs of providing and interpreting the information equal the additional benefits to be derived from its use. Unfortu-nately, it is difficult to assess either the costs or the benefits associated with changes in the level of financial disclosure. The problem is especially acute when, as in the United States, accounting disclosures are regulated rather than allowed to respond to market forces of supply and demand.

2. *Frequency.*   The most thorough financial reports of U.S. firms are pre-pared once each year in annual reports to investors and to the SEC. Partial fi-nancial data, usually confined to selected income statement amounts, are published on a semiannual and quarterly basis. For special events, such as reg-istration and sale of new securities, special prospectuses and registration state-ments report a variety of historical and projected (pro forma) financial data.

Is such reporting frequency suitable to the needs of investors? Or, should U.S. firms be required to report monthly, weekly, or at some other time inter-val? Should reporting frequency be governed by the occurrence of major events, such as the gain or loss of important customers, or revisions in man-agement's plans or estimates, rather than by the passage of time? The basic is-sues are the same as those considered in discussing the completeness of disclosure, and the answers again depend on user decision models, the result-ing information requirements, and a balancing of overall costs and benefits.

3. *Timeliness.*   From an investor standpoint, information is timely only if it can be used in making investment decisions. In making decisions to buy or sell securities, investors seek to anticipate securities price changes. If financial re-ports change investor assessments of future cash flows, then securities prices would be affected.

Corporate financial reports are typically available to investors within thirty to ninety days after the period covered by the report. A number of studies of securities markets indicate, however, that common stock price changes may oc-cur before the statements are released to the public. As noted earlier, a sub-stantial portion of the information included in financial reports appears to be reflected in common stock prices prior to the publication of those reports. The variability of securities returns increases at about the date that financial reports are released, which suggests that investors find these reports informative. Corporate managers and auditors frequently assert that the time lag between the end of the reporting period and the publication of the financial report is needed to ensure that the information is accurately presented and competently reviewed before publication. This contention poses another basic question in the area of disclosure adequacy: is financial disclosure "fair" if investors without access to inside (prepublication) information are unable to profit from the analysis of published information?

Again, dealing with the underlying issues is difficult. First, it is not clear whether such financial accounting information has been selectively disseminated to certain investors prior to its formal publication, or whether the financial accounting information is simply redundant in repeating information that was previously available to investors through other sources. Refer again to Figure 1-1, which shows financial reports as a subset of the broader information set available to investors. At present we do not know the extent to which the information contained in financial reports complements or overlaps the other information available. Second, assuming that securities prices have reacted to selectively disseminated accounting numbers rather than to other information sources, it is no easy task to ensure that all investors have simultaneous access to financial reports. Information may be acted upon very quickly by investors who have the resources (and the talent) to do so. Therefore, differences of even a few hours may not be acceptable if "equal access" is the objective.

No meaningful concept of disclosure has been specified to date in either FASB or SEC statements. There is general agreement that, as a minimum, financial reports should disclose enough information to ensure that they are not misleading. The concept of potentially misleading accounting disclosures is inextricably tied to the idea of materiality in financial reporting.

MATERIALITY IN FINANCIAL REPORTING

Financial accountants consider an item to be material if its disclosure or method of presentation might reasonably be expected to affect an investor's decisions. Superfluous information is irrelevant to investor decisions, and thereby immaterial; and adequate disclosure implies the publication of all material information. Because an understanding of materiality depends upon a usable definition of disclosure adequacy and because accountants have been unable to state a meaningful concept of disclosure adequacy, it is not surprising that materiality has been labeled the "mystery concept" in financial accounting.

Although there are definitional problems, accountants often assure investors and other users of financial reports that published financial statements do not contain material errors or omit material disclosures. As a working rule of thumb, accountants often cite ten percent of income as a material dollar amount. Consequently, if an error or omission is ten percent of income or larger, it is likely to be deemed material.[6]

---

[6]Several regulatory standards offer qualitative and other quantitative guidelines for determining a material item. For example, some SEC disclosures are based on five percent of income, and some of the APB's rules for computing earnings per share depend on variations of just three percent of income per share.

EVALUATING ALTERNATIVE ACCOUNTING METHODS

To identify better accounting methods, accounting policymakers need a criterion by which to evaluate possible alternatives. Several criteria have been suggested for this purpose. They include stewardship, economic income, predictive ability, and economic consequences.

Stewardship

As the ownership of firms became separated from the management of firms, the notion of stewardship emerged as an important orientation in financial accounting. **Stewardship** focuses on the performance of hired managers in preserving owners' capital and in generating profits. Managers are seen as stewards to whom investors have entrusted their financial resources. While a stewardship point of view is compatible with many different methods of accounting, there is some consensus among accounting writers that stewardship orients financial reports toward the reporting of historical events and prompts a strong emphasis on objective data. For example, the valuation of assets at historical exchange prices is often argued to be consistent with a stewardship point of view.

Economic Income

Under the economic income approach, accounting alternatives are evaluated based on the ability of accounting measures of income and value to approximate economic income and value. **Economic income** is defined as the change in the value of the firm over a given period of time after appropriate adjustments for changes in owner investments and in dividend distributions to owners have been made. The economic value of the firm is also the present value of the firm's future cash flows, after adjusting for futurity and risk.

An attempt to apply the concept of economic income to the assessment of alternative accounting methods encounters some basic difficulties. First, accountants are unwilling to accept the change in the market value of a firm's outstanding securities as a measure of economic income because accounting numbers are intended to be used in valuing securities. In other words, accounting information aims to be an input into securities valuation rather than an output derived from changes in securities values. If accountants are unwilling to accept the market values of the firm's securities for the purpose of measuring income, it then becomes necessary to develop other independent measures of the value of the firm and to demonstrate that in some sense these measures are superior to securities market values. Accountants have not made much progress in developing such alternative measures.

Second, inasmuch as there presumably also is some value created by the way in which assets are combined, the value of the firm is quite different from the sum of the values of the separate assets that comprise the firm. Yet the accounting methods that a policymaker must evaluate generally involve accounting for changes in individual assets or groups of assets. It is not clear how changes in the total value of the firm can be used to determine changes in the values of individual assets.

These basic difficulties, and others not discussed here, preclude the use of economic income as a standard for assessing accounting methods. Yet the discussion here of economic income has accompanied a shift in perspective from historical to future cash flows and has led to the notion of predictive ability as a criterion for evaluating accounting methods.

Predictive Ability

The **predictive ability** criterion ranks accounting alternatives on the basis of their usefulness in prediction. A better accounting method, by this criterion, permits more accurate prediction of economic events of interest to decision makers. As an example, accounting numbers are sometimes used in statistical models to predict bankruptcy. If the bankruptcy predictons were made using numbers obtained from the application of several different accounting methods, the "best" accounting method would be the one most successful in forecasting bankrupt and nonbankrupt firms.

Like the other criteria discussed above, the predictive ability criterion has problems in application. First, it is necessary to identify the different decisions to be made using financial information and then to specify the types of predictions upon which the decisions will be based. There will probably be a large number of different prediction models, and the accounting method that appears best suited for one type of prediction may not be the best for another. Second, in many cases it is not clear how to define predictive accuracy without fairly detailed knowledge of the costs of prediction errors. Consider the apparently straightforward case of bankruptcy prediction mentioned above. Two types of prediction errors are possible: (1) classifying a bankrupt firm as solvent and (2) classifying a solvent firm as bankrupt. If the first type of error is committed, the most likely result is that a loan would be made to a firm unable to repay the loan in full. If the second type of error is made, a loan would probably not be granted to a firm that could pay its debts. The costs of these two types of errors are not likely to be equal; the first type is usually more serious (and costly) than the second. Aside from this generalization, little is known about the varying costs of different prediction errors. Unfortunately, such knowledge is prerequisite to the use of the predictive ability criterion in ranking accounting policy alternatives.

Economic Consequences

The emergence of **economic consequences** as a criterion in assessing alternative accounting methods is discussed in some detail in the next section. Broadly, this criterion encourages the groups to be affected by an accounting standard to argue before the FASB on the basis of economic self-interest. Economic effects, such as changes in securities prices; changes in costs or availability of capital; and likely reactions by regulators, taxing authorities, customers, suppliers, competitors, and others to changes in a firm's accounting methods, are considered in making an accounting policy decision. Alternative accounting methods might, therefore, be ranked according to the desirability of their expected economic consequences, rather than by the use of the other criteria discussed above.

This section has briefly described four criteria that are often suggested as useful for evaluating accounting policy alternatives. None of these has achieved prominence, and all are cited on occasion as partial justification for the choice of specific accounting methods. Each has limitations, and there is little likelihood that all would result in the same ranking of a group of alternative accounting methods.

ECONOMIC CONSEQUENCES OF FINANCIAL REPORTS

There is growing concern on the part of managers and regulators about the "economic consequences" of accounting standards. The economic consequences of accounting standards consist of the effects of accounting standards on the decision-making behavior of managers, investors, creditors, and other users of financial reports. This section considers possible economic consequences of financial accounting standards as a result of direct actions by managers and investors.

Effects on Management Decisions

Managers often predict economic consequences of financial accounting standards in written and oral submissions to the FASB, in essays in the business press, and during meetings with shareholders and financial analysts. A sampling of such arguments might include the following:

1. *Mergers.*   In the late 1960s, the APB considered abolishing a popular method of accounting for business combinations (the "pooling-of-interests" method), and many managers objected on the grounds that the merger wave of the 1960s would then come to a sudden halt. Managers adopted the position that mergers that appeared to be justified under the pooling of interest concept would not be justified under the alternative "purchase" method of accounting, even though the accounting method selected would have no direct effects on business tax payments or other cash flows. (A more detailed discussion of these concepts is contained in Chapter 9.)

2. *Leases.*   The FASB questioned whether various long-term lease agreements were in substance more like purchases than rentals of business assets. Managers claimed that reporting of leased assets and liabilities would substantially increase borrowing costs and reduce the use of leased assets.

3. *Research and development.*   The FASB proposed that costs of research and development activities be expensed as incurred because of the difficulty in identifying the time periods that are benefitted by such costs. Managers argued that such a policy would cause a substantial reduction in research and development activity with a consequent decline in technological progress.

4. *Foreign currency.*   The FASB adopted the position that for firms with assets or liabilities in foreign currencies, changes in exchange rates entail gains or losses. Managers responded that accounting recognition of such gains or losses would lower their securities prices, increase capital costs, cause them to engage in uneconomical hedging transactions, and impair the United States' balance of trade.

5. *Tax subsidy.*   The APB argued that federal government subsidies of the cost of new equipment should be treated as a reduction in the cost of such equipment. Managers (and Congress) objected on the grounds that such a treatment would spread the subsidy over the life of the equipment and, therefore, reduce management's incentive to undertake new investment.

Whether the predicted economic consequences did in fact occur (or would have occurred in cases where the managers' arguments prevailed) is a moot point. For example, the merger wave of the 1960s did decline considerably for several years after the APB changed the accounting rules. Yet many other developments in the financial markets in the early 1970s could also be alleged to have slowed the merger movement. Similarly, it is difficult to determine whether changes in accounting methods have affected business decisions in areas such as leasing, research and development, foreign currency transactions, or capital spending. In a dynamic economy it is rarely possible to identify one event (such as a change in a financial reporting standard) as the one responsible for another event (such as a change in aggregate business spending on research and development).

Notice that the management arguments stated above are not couched in terms of "theoretically sound" methods of accounting (such as which method would provide the best measure of economic income or wealth). Rather, the arguments are stated candidly in terms of "whose ox gets gored." An open admission by parties to accounting debates that they are motivated primarily by economic self-interest is a recent development, and it has been described by some writers as a veritable revolution in the policy-making process.

Is it reasonable to predict that financial accounting standards will bring the types of economic consequences predicted by managers? Keep in mind that in most areas of financial accounting policy there is no direct link between the accounting numbers and the firm's cash flows. In many cases the changes in accounting methods are "cosmetic." That is the case when information that previously appeared in footnotes to financial statements (a discussion of the firm's lease commitments, for example) is instead moved up to the body of the financial statements. A change in location should not affect the substantive issues being revealed. If managers argue that cosmetic changes in accounting methods cause investors to reassess the riskiness or value of the firm's securities, they are assuming implicitly that investors use financial statement information naïvely and fail to consider other publicly disclosed information.

Yet there are at least two types of cases for which changes in accounting standards may have significant economic consequences. The first case involves firms having contracts or agreements defined in terms of financial accounting numbers. For example, long-term borrowing agreements often set lower limits on various accounting-based measures of a firm's liquidity, and violation of these debt agreements may cause the firm serious difficulty. Assume, for instance, that the debt agreement required the company to maintain assets of at least a certain dollar amount to prevent the long-term debt from being payable immediately. It is possible that a change from one acceptable accounting method to another might cause the assets to be valued below this threshold amount, thus forcing immediate repayment of the debt. Unless such agreements are carefully worded, an otherwise cosmetic change may cause the firm to violate its debt agreements.

The second case involves accounting standards that change the amount of financial disclosure. When new information is disclosed, it may cause investors, creditors, customers, and others to alter their decisions. Recent examples of accounting standards that increase the amount of financial disclosure include reporting for segments of a business enterprise, disclosures of information about major customers, and reporting of current costs of certain assets.

Effects on Securities Prices

A second major category of economic consequences involves the indirect effect of accounting numbers on securities prices. If investors use financial accounting numbers to assess investment risk and return, and if such assessments are affected by changes in either the amount of information disclosed or the accounting methods employed, then securities prices are likely to be influenced by accounting policy decisions. (Recall that if financial reports change investor assessments of the amount, timing, and/or certainty of future cash flows, securities prices would be affected.) The overall level of securities prices and the prices of individual firms' securities may be indirectly affected by changes in accounting standards. As a consequence, the costs of capital to individual firms, the distribution of wealth among investors, and even total savings and investment in the economy might conceivably be influenced by accounting policy decisions. The quality and quantity of financial information may affect investor views of the overall level of uncertainty associated with saving as opposed to consumption, and thereby affect the availability and cost of funds to all users. From this perspective, changes in financial accounting standards may have direct and indirect effects on many different groups and may, to some extent, involve reducing the wealth of one group while increasing the wealth of another.

In addition to the possible effects of accounting standards on management decisions and on securities prices, other economic consequences may result from changes in methods of financial accounting. For example, changes in the amount of detail provided in accounting reports concerning business segments or product lines may affect the competitive position of the firm, or may change the views of economic regulators concerning industry concentration or profitability. Changes in the definition or timing of business profits may affect a firm's negotiations with union representatives, suppliers, customers, and others. Changes in the amount or the format of required disclosure also may shift the costs of preparing or assembling financial information between firms and investment analysts. For example, if firms are required to disclose detailed information about product-line performance, securities analysts may avoid the cost of obtaining this information from other sources.

Economic Consequences as a Standard-setting Criterion

Is it appropriate for accounting policy decisions to be influenced by expected economic consequences? Or is it preferable (as some accounting writers urge) to base policy decisions on a theory of accounting? Stated differently, should accountants focus on reporting the "economic facts" in as neutral a fashion as possible and leave it to others to deal with economic consequences? In addressing these questions, it is important to recognize that, by definition, significant areas of accounting policy cannot be economically neutral. If a change from one method of accounting to another is expected to have no economic effects, it is implied that the two methods are equivalent, and the choice between them is unimportant.

Once it is recognized that accounting policy decisions may have economic consequences, the proper role of accounting theory in deciding policy issues must be addressed. Even a casual reading of the professional accounting literature reveals that impressive theoretical arguments can be advanced to support an array of conflicting positions in virtually any area of accounting dispute. This is so because there are widely varying views on the criteria to be used in assessing the preferability of different methods of accounting, disparate assumptions about user information needs, and little agreement about how economic concepts of capital and income should apply to the content of financial accounting reports. As a result, appeals to "accounting theory" often fail to be persuasive in accounting policy debates. As the authority of accounting theory is questioned, increasing attention is given to the economic effects of different financial accounting standards.

The FASB has responded to the increased prominence of economic consequences in accounting policy debates in several ways. The Board has established elaborate procedural machinery for increasing the degree of interaction between the policymakers and those affected by policy decisions. The Board itself is composed of members of various constituencies—representatives from professional accounting, academe, government, and industry. Likewise, the discussion memorandum that precedes public hearings on each major issue is prepared by a task force drawn from different interest groups. Virtually all of the formal meetings of the FASB are open to the public. In addition, the Board has commissioned several empirical studies on the economic consequences of earlier policy decisions (notably in the areas of research and development, foreign currency translation, and oil and gas accounting). The FASB also has identified "probable economic or social impact" as an important quality of useful financial information.

Several of the possible economic consequences of financial accounting reports that have been discussed here depend on how accounting information affects securities prices. In recent years accounting regulators, investors, analysts, and others have given a good deal of attention to the manner in which securities prices respond to changes in information. These studies have several implications for accounting policy.

INFORMATION EFFICIENCY IN SECURITIES MARKETS

The extent to which publicly available information affects securities prices is based on the information efficiency of securities markets. The evidence available from the many recent studies of this issue suggests that common stock prices fully reflect publicly available information, and that new information is reflected very quickly. If securities markets are information efficient, there are important implications for investors, managers, and policymakers with respect to the production and use of accounting reports.

For investors, an **information-efficient securities market** implies that there is little to be gained from attempting to find overvalued or undervalued securities by the analysis of published financial reports. Unless the investor has privileged access to information prior to its public release (inside information) or superior skill in the analysis and interpretation of public information, information efficiency suggests that the investor should act as a price taker. As a price taker the investor would presume that the present trading prices of securities are unbiased estimates of their true values. The investor would then concentrate upon managing the risk of his or her investment portfolio rather than attempting to earn superior returns by finding mispriced securities.

For managers, information efficiency of securities markets has implications for choices among alternative accounting methods, changes in accounting methods, and decisions about the amount and placement of information in accounting reports (placement, for example, in footnotes or in the body of the financial statements). In choosing among alternative accounting methods, managers have traditionally projected the effects of differing accounting methods on the level and variability of income and the accounting valuation of assets. The underlying presumption is that securities prices are sensitive to the choice of accounting method. In an information-efficient securities market, all public information is reflected in securities prices, and this public information includes any information disclosed concerning management's choice of accounting methods. This implies that securities prices will not be affected by accounting methods, provided that there is public information about the accounting methods in use by a given firm, *and* that there is also adequate public information (in footnotes, SEC reports, and so forth) to allow investors to recast the firm's financial statements using other accounting methods.

Similar reasoning applies to changes in methods of accounting. Generally, changes in accounting methods have no direct effect on a firm's cash flows; and, given sufficient public information about the accounting methods employed, we would expect no effect on securities prices. Management's *decision* to change accounting methods, however, may be new information to investors. Analysts will attempt to understand management's motives in changing accounting methods and may infer changes in management's plans or expectations. For example, a change in the methods used to value inventories may reveal previously nonpublic information about expected changes in replacement costs, technological changes, or production plans.

The placement of information in accounting reports should also have little impact in an information-efficient securities market. The substantive issues concern what is disclosed rather than the mere geography of its disclosure. With this view, the placement of information in footnotes as opposed to the body of financial statements should have no impact on securities prices.

For accounting regulators such as the FASB and the SEC, information efficiency implies that disclosed information is more important than the placement of the disclosure within the financial reports. Moreover, the traditional concern of accounting regulators for the naïve or unsophisticated investor may be misplaced. Rather, it may be preferable to inform naïve investors that analysis of published financial information is unlikely to be profitable and to gear the quality of financial disclosures to professional securities analysts.

In an information-efficient securities market, accounting regulators may need to reassess the role of accounting reports. Does the apparent inability of investors to profit from the postpublication analysis of accounting reports imply that the accounting reports are useless? In view of the fact that accounting reports are just one among several available sources of public information, to what extent is accounting information redundant? Are there types of disclosures for which accounting reports represent a comparative economic advantage compared to other ways of obtaining the same information? Even if accounting reports are not timely in the sense that the information contained therein is already reflected in securities prices, does the quality of the other information sources depend upon the eventual publication of an accounting report? These are difficult questions to be grappled with by accounting regulators in deciding issues of financial disclosure.

SUMMARY

This chapter has defined financial accounting, described the financial reporting environment, and discussed the main issues involved in the choice of accounting policies by regulators and managers. Much of the discussion in later chapters is based on the important elements of the framework established here.

Financial accounting has been defined as a service profession that is continually evolving in response to changes in the information needs of investors and others outside the firm. The adequacy of the current set of generally accepted accounting principles (GAAP) is difficult to assess, however, because not enough is known about the information needs of the users of financial reports, the role of accounting numbers as a part of the total information set available to users, and the costs and benefits associated with changes in GAAP.

Accounting regulators must decide on the relative desirability of alternative accounting methods, yet lack any well-articulated criterion for assessing desirability. Criteria such as stewardship, economic concepts of income and value, predictive ability, and economic consequences are vaguely stated and present problems in implementation.

Mandatory accounting rules formulated by regulators and discretionary accounting choices made by managers may have economic consequences in terms of effects on securities prices, the cost and availability of capital, and aggregate levels of savings and investment. Arguments based on expected economic consequences have become increasingly prominent in accounting policy deliberations due to the alleged importance of these economic consequences and to the absence of any other convincing method of assessing accounting policy alternatives.

Securities markets appear to be information efficient in the sense that securities prices seem to reflect all publicly available information. This suggests that the substantive questions in financial accounting concern what information should be disclosed rather than the geography of its disclosure. Moreover, managers should view accounting methods as policy variables over which they may have some control. Managers make discretionary choices among accounting alternatives included in GAAP. In addition, they may influence accounting regulators (the FASB and the SEC) through arguments and evidence presented at public hearings, written submissions (to the FASB), and through the business press. The positions adopted by managers in such instances should reflect an understanding of the implications of information efficiency in securities markets and the possible economic consequences of alternative accounting standards.

QUESTIONS

1. The terms listed below were introduced in this chapter. Define or explain each of them.

   accounting entity
   Accounting Principles Board
   balance sheet
   economic income
   financial accounting
   Financial Accounting Standards Board
   generally accepted accounting principles
   going concern assumption
   income statement
   information-efficient securities market
   managerial accounting
   matching principle
   realization
   Securities and Exchange Commission
   statement of cash flows

2. Define accounting. Distinguish between financial accounting and managerial accounting.

3. List and briefly describe the main audiences for financial accounting information.
4. List and discuss several of the major types of decisions that require the use of accounting numbers.
5. Financial statements focus upon three major dimensions of a business firm: wealth, profitability, and liquidity. Define each of these dimensions and discuss which financial statement focuses most directly on it.
6. Distinguish between an economic asset and an accounting asset. What are the essential characteristics of an accounting asset?
7. "The accounting concept of net income varies substantially from the economic concept of net income." Do you agree or not? Explain.
8. Briefly discuss each of the following basic assumptions underlying present accounting practice:

   a. accounting entity
   b. going concern
   c. time period assumption
   d. money measurement
   e. exchange price
   f. recognition and realization
   g. matching

9. Distinguish between financial reporting and financial statements.
10. What is the function of the Financial Accounting Standards Board?
11. What is the function of the Securities and Exchange Commission? What is the relationship, if any, between the FASB and the SEC?
12. What authority, if any, does the United States Congress have in the setting of financial accounting standards?
13. Discuss the concept of materiality as it relates to financial accounting.
14. Briefly discuss each of the following criteria that might be used to evaluate alternative accounting methods:

    a. stewardship
    b. economic income
    c. predictive ability
    d. economic consequences

15. What are the advantages and disadvantages of using the predictive ability criterion to evaluate alternative accounting methods?
16. Is it appropriate for accounting policymakers to be influenced by expected economic consequences of their actions? Discuss.
17. List two different types of economic consequences that could result from the issuance of a given accounting standard or rule.
18. Describe what is meant by the phrase "information efficiency in the securities markets."
19. Should the format used to disclose information in the financial statements have any impact in a so-called "information-efficient market"?
20. What is a "change in an accounting principle"?

21. List the three primary financial statements and provide a brief description of each. Which of these statements measure change over a period of time? Which measures financial status at a point in time?

EXERCISES AND PROBLEMS

22. *Meaning and Importance of the Bottom Line.*   The following comments appeared in Robert Metz's column in the *New York Times* (May 11, 1974):

In Wall Street there is a feeling that the earnings-per-share figure posted by a corporation is almost holy. And if a growing corporation falters, posting a decline in earnings in a given quarter, the market may react violently and the shares may never recover fully. But there is a colossal irony in this because the bottom-line figure is filled from the spigot of subjectivity. One cynical corporate lawyer who had watched the accountants at work for many a year once said: "They can come up with any number they want down there — within reasonable limits." . . . What then does all of this mean? It means that worshipped attention to the bottom line is often misplaced. It means that management eager for a rising earnings curve has a lot of room to maneuver.

REQUIRED

(a) Provide several examples of management's ability to "shape" the bottom-line figure.
(b) What controls can the accounting profession establish that limit management's latitude in "shaping" the bottom-line figure?
(c) Why isn't accounting completely standardized?
(d) Do you agree that the importance of the bottom line has been "misplaced"?

23. *The Search for Accounting Principles.*   At the first meeting of the newly formed (hypothetical) Accounting Standardization Board, the following discussion took place:

CHAIRMAN: Needless to say, the accounting profession is under very great pressure and unless we find a satisfactory method for resolving the conflicting issues and the mounting criticisms, there is a grave threat that the setting of accounting standards will shift from the private to the public sector.

MR. ECO: Of course, and there is only one logical solution to the problem, and that is to adopt an economic model, at least to the extent that is realistically attainable.

MR. TRADIT: Nonsense. Accounting should be primarily concerned with the stewardship function and that is best achieved with the traditional model.

MR. UTILIT: Accounting is only a system of measurements designed to assist report users to make correct decisions. We must study users' decisions and shape our financial reports to best accommodate these report users.

MR. EMP RESEARCH: I agree, and if we use sound research techniques, we can establish accounting standards that best serve the needs of these report users.

MR.COMPROM: I suppose, in a sense, I agree with all of you. Why can't we assume that these different views all come together when a consensus is reached among the contending interests?

REQUIRED   Discuss the views of each member of the ASB and your solution to the standard-setting problem.

24. *The Matching Concept.*   The determination of business income by accountants follows the matching concept. In this chapter (page 13), it was stated that

> Income is defined as the revenue recognized during a period, less all expenses entailed in producing that revenue. Of course, application of the matching concept requires some compromises. For example, it is often difficult to establish a direct linkage between revenues and expenses . . .

REQUIRED   Indicate how each of the following transactions should be accounted for under the matching concept of income determination. Provide reasons for your answer.

(a) An advertising expenditure of $100,000 is made this period. The company's advertising agency estimates that three-fourths of the expected increase in sales will take place this period but that there will be a delayed effect and one-fourth of the increase in sales attributable to the advertising outlay will occur next period.

(b) The company sustained a fire loss this period (in excess of insurance proceeds) of $180,000.

(c) Research outlays amounting to $80,000 this period are believed to be patentable and will increase revenues in the future.

(d) A machine is purchased for $10,000 that is expected to have a ten-year life. Each period is expected to benefit equally from the machine's output. In the first period the machine operated according to expectations. However, in the second period, because of a recession, the machine was idle.

(e) At the end of a period, salaries and wages for services performed were unpaid in the amount of $25,000.

(f) The company is faced with a pending lawsuit. The company's attorneys refuse to predict the outcome of the case but indicate the damages could conceivably be as high as $400,000.

(g) At the end of the period, accounts receivable from sales to customers amounted to $190,000. Based on past experience it is estimated that $6,000 of this amount will have to be written off as bad debts.

(h) Estimated pension expense for employees applicable to this period is $95,000. The pensions will only be payable to workers still employed by the company at the time of their retirement.

(i) The bill for property taxes will not be received until the beginning of next period. However, it is expected that the property tax will amount to $30,000, of which three-fourths applies to this period.

(j) A fire insurance premium is paid on the first day of this period. The premium covers three periods.

25. *Costs and Values.* The Frisco Company purchased a machine with a ten-year life for $10,000.

REQUIRED In each of the following cases indicate what accounting recognition (if any) you believe should be given to reflect the facts. Consider each case separately. Support your answer.

(a) Immediately after the acquisition, the Frisco Company learns that it could have purchased an identical machine from another supplier for $9,000.

(b) The company estimates that the net value of the output of the machine over its estimated life, discounted to the present at the prevailing long-term interest cost to the company, is $20,000.

(c) The company estimates that the machine could have been constructed internally for $8,500.

(d) Three years after the purchase, the net book cost of the asset is $7,000 (that is, after depreciation). However, due to inflation, the replacement cost is $8,000.

(e) Five years after acquisition, the net book cost is $5,000. However, because a technologically superior machine is now available, the present machine can only be sold for $2,000.

(f) The same facts apply as in (e) except that the machine is actually sold for $2,000.

26. *Accounting Conservatism.* The chief executive officer of a corporation commented to his auditor as follows:

Last year, you made us write-down our inventory to its lower replacement cost. This year the replacement cost of our inventory is significantly higher than our book cost, yet you will not permit us to write-up the inventory. It seems to me that this is unfair and inconsistent. Apparently, accounting is a one-way street.

REQUIRED

(a) Do you think this is a common point of view held by corporate executives?

(b) What would be the reaction of a typical commercial banker to this manifestation of conservatism?

(c) If you were a stockholder, would you prefer to see the management of the company in which you invested subscribe to this practice of writing-down inventories?

(d) As an economist would you be more or less apt to support this doctrine of conservatism?

27. *Materiality.*   The concept of materiality underlies the data disclosed in financial statements. The accounting literature contains numerous references to such terms as "significant," "substantial," "material," and "of consequence."

The following statement appears in the introduction to *Accounting Research Bulletin No. 43* issued by the AICPA—the American Institute of Certified Public Accountants (which is the national professional organization of the public accounting profession):

The committee contemplates that its opinions will have application only to items material and significant in the relative circumstances. It considers that items of little or no consequence may be dealt with as expediency may suggest. However, freedom to deal expediently with immaterial items should not extend to a group of items whose cumulative effect in any one financial statement may be material and significant.

The SEC's statement on materiality appears in *Regulation S-X:*

The term "material," when used to qualify a requirement for the furnishing of information as to any subject, limits the information required to those matters about which an average prudent investor ought reasonably to be informed before purchasing the security registered.

REQUIRED

(a) Do you believe that materiality should be left to the realm of judgment or that guidelines should be established?
(b) If the latter, indicate what kind of guidelines you favor and how they should be determined.

28. *The Monetary Convention.*   Apart from a few nominal shares held by his wife and son, Robert Preston is the sole owner of Ancal Corporation. After receiving the certified income statement for the current year, he commented to his auditor as follows:

The income statement for Ancal, which you certify is in accord with GAAP, shows a profit of $100,000. However, it matches $500,000 of revenues in current dollars with a combination of expenses that consist of $250,000 in current dollars (for example, salaries, advertising, supplies) and $150,000 of depreciation expense based on the value of the dollar at the time the applicable plant and equipment were acquired. Since the date of acquisition of these assets the purchasing power of the dollar has declined by 100%. It would take twice as many dollars to acquire the same assets today. Therefore, it seems to me that depreciation really should be $300,000 and that we had a loss of $50,000 rather than a profit of $100,000.

REQUIRED   Evaluate Preston's comments.

29. *Adequacy of the Accounting Model under Changing Economic Conditions.*

REQUIRED   Can the traditional accounting model provide equally useful information to financial report users under the following circumstances? Consider each separately.

(a) An economic depression such as occurred in the early 1930s.
(b) Double-digit inflation.
(c) Sharply rising real estate values in Florida.
(d) A wave of mergers and takeovers.
(e) Labor negotiations.

30. *Resolution of a Controversial Issue.*   One of the most controversial accounting issues arose out of the inclusion of an investment tax credit in the Revenue Act of 1962. The credit was intended by Congress to stimulate capital investments in qualified assets. Taxpayers were allowed a tax credit (with certain limitations) of 10% of the capital expenditure.

Two methods were adopted by companies to account for the investment credit. While these methods did not alter the amount of taxes paid, they did affect the amount of income reported during the estimated life of the asset. Under the "flow-through" method, the credit was used to reduce the tax expense during the year of the expenditure, thus increasing income during that year. Under the "deferral" method, the credit was spread over the life of the asset, increasing the income during each of those years. These methods did not alter the amount or timing of income taxes paid. The procedures differed only with respect to the period in which income was affected and the amount.

In 1962, the Accounting Principles Board in its *Opinion No. 2* sanctioned the deferral approach. Since this was contrary to the procedure favored by the majority of companies, it evoked vigorous criticism and a number of CPA firms stated that their clients would not abide by this pronouncement. One month later, the Securities and Exchange Commission indicated that it would accept *either* method in reports filed with it. In view of these circumstances, the APB in 1964 issued a new opinion in which it indicated that either method would be acceptable.

REQUIRED

(a) What contrary arguments do you think were put forth by advocates of these two methods?
(b) Suppose you were a member of the APB. Which method would you have endorsed? Why?
(c) Do GAAP provide a conceptual basis for resolving this issue? If so, what is it?
(d) Do you think the SEC should have taken a contrary position to that of the APB? Why?

(e) Why do you think most companies preferred the "flow-through" method? Do you feel that the APB should have supported this majority viewpoint?

(f) What do you think was the most important factor in the final solution of this issue by the APB in 1964? Do you regard this as a satisfactory solution?

31. *Reporting on the Value of Corporate Property.*   In an article in *Fortune* (August 1967), William S. Rukeyser commented about tender offers made to stockholders of Kern County Land Company by Occidental Petroleum and Tenneco as follows:

What made Kern especially attractive was that the market appeared to be undervaluing its stock. Since the bidder in a tender offer normally has to offer a substantial premium over the market, he must be confident that the stock is worth, at least to him, more than the market says it's worth. In this instance, undervaluing was pretty clear. Kern's balance sheet wildly understated the current value of its assets. Most of its California acreage was acquired in 1890 and is carried on the books at cost. Shortly before Occidental made its tender offer, when Kern stock was still selling in the low sixties, Dean Witter & Co., broker, estimated the true current value of Kern shareholders' equity at $442 million, or $102 a share.

REQUIRED

(a) What principle of accounting condoned the accounting treatment of its acreage by Kern County Land Company?

(b) What would be your reaction to these principles if, as a stockholder of Kern County Land Company, you had sold your shares at $60 immediately prior to the tender offers?

(c) What action do you think the accounting profession could or should take to provide report users with more useful information about such undervalued assets?

32. *Recognition of a Loss.*   The following statement appeared in the August 29, 1983 issue of *Business Week*:

At an August 12 meeting with his board of directors and top operating executives, Martin S. Davis, Gulf & Western Industries Inc.'s chief executive, abruptly ended the era of his wheeling-dealing predecessor, Charles G. Bludhorn. In four hours, Davis and his lieutenants mapped out a dramatic restructuring of G&W that was announced two days later. Business representing 20% of the company's $5.3 billion in sales was written down and put on the block, resulting in a $470-million charge to earnings.

This means that instead of posting a 58% rise in income for its fiscal year ended July 31, G&W will report a $215-million loss. The $470-million write-off is based on the difference between the assets' book value and G&W's estimate of the price they will fetch . . .

REQUIRED

(a) Why would a new chief executive consider it desirable to incur so large a write-down of book assets?

(b) Suppose the reverse of the write-down of book assets was accomplished; that is, G&W's assets were written up 20% based "on the difference between the assets' book value and G&W's estimate of the price they will fetch." Would this have been permitted by G&W's auditors?

(c) Do you think it is proper for a company to recognize a loss of this size in the absence of an actual transaction?

(d) What accounting principles or conventions underlie the recognition of this loss? Describe these principles and provide other examples of them. Do you feel that these principles of accounting are justified? If so, why?

(e) Should the management of G&W and their auditors have been aware of and recognized this loss in prior years?

(f) How do you think the stock market reacted to the announcement of this considerable loss?

33. *Reporting on the Wealth of an Individual.* On August 18, 1964, the following excerpt appeared in the *New York Times:*

According to *Life* magazine the L. B. J. family has accumulated a fortune in radio and television stations, Texas real estate, and other properties worth nearly $14 million. This estimate exceeds by nearly $10 million the value placed on the Johnson family property by A. W. Moursund, the principal trustee for the family. Mr. Moursund's figures are based on a report prepared by a certified public accountant (Albert W. Caster & Co.). . . . The *Life* article uses the estimated resale value of the various properties, whereas Mr. Moursund's estimates were based largely on their so-called "book value," which is used for accounting purposes.

Two days later, on August 20, 1964, the *New York Times* stated:

President Johnson and his immediate family own property and liquid assets valued at slightly less than $3.5 million, an independent accounting firm certified today. . . . Haskins and Sells said that the method of accounting was in accord with accepted accounting procedures and was not intended to indicate the values that might be realized if the investments were sold. . .

The method of valuation of the Johnson-family holdings was immediately attacked by Dean Burch, the chairman of the Republican National Committee. . . . He said that the estimate was incredibly low, like the City of New York listing the value of Manhattan Island at $24, the price paid according to legend to its original Indian residents by the first white settlers.

On September 22, 1964, the *New York Times* reported that Touche, Ross, Bailey, and Smart, another large firm of CPAs, used a different method to calculate the net worth of Hubert H. Humphrey:

Because of the nature and purpose of this presentation, the statement of value of household goods and of financial condition of the principal has been prepared on the basis of present market value of their assets, which basis of reporting we believe to be appropriate in the circumstances.

REQUIRED

(a) Which CPA firm acted in accordance with GAAP?

(b) Identify the applicable principle of accounting involved here and discuss whether you believe that it is appropriate today.

(c) In terms of economic reality, which CPA firm's attest statement was more meaningful? Why?

(d) Do you perceive any difference between the application of GAAP to General Motors or to private individuals?

34. *Events Recognition.* Accountants conventionally recognize certain events and ignore others. For each of the following eventualities, indicate whether you believe the item or event should be recognized (that is, reflected in the accounts and financial statements) or ignored, and give the reasons for your answer.

a. The company has been notified in writing that its bid of $500,000 for the manufacturing of uniforms for the Defense Department has been accepted.

b. You are advised by your attorneys that there is an excellent likelihood that a lawsuit for infringement of your patent in the amount of $250,000 will be successful.

c. Receipt of an order from a customer in the amount of $3,000.

d. A bona fide offer of $75,000 for real estate that the company originally purchased for $60,000.

e. The estimated net proceeds from a new drug developed by your research department.

f. The estimated expense to the company this period in connection with the ultimate retirement of employees under the company's pension plan.

g. The estimated value of the company's human resources.

h. Shipment of a customer's order at a sales price of $800.

i. Stored output of a gold mine that cost $300,000 to produce has a sales value of $600,000.

j. A decline in the market price of 1 million outstanding shares of common stock from $50 to $45, attributed to the death of the company's president.

k. Estimated unsaleable inventories on hand (due to style changes) amounting to $35,000.

l. Estimated loss on outstanding accounts receivable, $48,000.

m. Market value of securities owned $80,000; cost $70,000.

n. Market value of securities owned $70,000; cost $80,000.

o. Advertising expenditure made in December expected to increase sales by 5% in December and 3% in January.

35. *Uniformity versus Flexibility in Accounting Methods.*   One of the most controversial issues facing accountants is the extent to which alternative procedures should be permitted. For example, companies may use different methods to match the cost of inventories sold with the revenue derived from their sale or to assign the expired costs of long-lived assets (that is, depreciation) against period revenue. These disparate methods may have a material impact on reported income.

At one extreme are those who believe that variations in accounting methods should be eliminated. They contend that there is insufficient justification for these accounting differences and that uniform methods should be adopted. At the other extreme are those who argue that company managements should not be restricted in their selection of accounting methods that they consider to be appropriate under the circumstances.

REQUIRED

(a) What arguments can you offer in support of uniformity in accounting methods?
(b) What arguments can you offer in support of flexibility?
(c) As an investor, which of the positions would you favor?
(d) As president of a large corporation, which of the two arguments do you favor?
(e) What would be your attitude toward this problem if you were a member of the Financial Accounting Standards Board?

36. *Relevance of General Purpose Financial Statements to Report Users.*   A well-known critic of financial statements commented as follows:

Accountants prepare general-purpose financial statements on the mistaken notion that they are equally beneficial to different report users. However, the informational needs of trade creditors, commercial bankers, investment bankers, stockholders, labor negotiators, rate regulators, tax authorities, internal managements, and various governmental agencies are substantially different. Why don't accountants prepare special reports that have greater relevance to each of these classes of report users?

REQUIRED   What is your reaction to this statement?

37. *Future Forecasts.*   The Report of the Study Group on the Objectives of Financial Statements included the following statement:

An objective of financial statements is to provide information useful for the predictive process. Financial forecasts should be provided when they will enhance the reliability of users' predictions.

Traditionally, the AICPA and the SEC have been opposed to the inclusion of profit forecasts. However, in recent years this position has been reversed and the SEC came very close to requiring companies to include profit forecasts in financial statements filed with the Commission.

REQUIRED

(a) What reasoning do you think supported this shift in attitude?
(b) If corporate management issued forecasts, how might this affect the role of professional securities analysts?
(c) What problems might this present to managements?
(d) Assuming that CPAs were required to attest to such forecasts, what problems might this present to CPAs?

38. *The Efficient Market Hypothesis and Financial Reporting.*   In its pure form, the efficient market hypothesis maintains that securities prices behave as if the information about earnings contained in financial reports and other corporate announcements is already known by the market and is impounded in the existing price of a security.

REQUIRED   Explain the following news item from the *New York Times* News Service on October 19, 1983, in terms of the efficient market hypothesis.

The stock market, reacting swiftly to unfavorable earnings projections by a leading computer manufacturer, plunged Tuesday in accelerated trading. At the end of the session the Dow Jones industrial average was off 17.89 points. . . . The pressure in the market started at about 2 p.m. when Digital Equipment announced that its fiscal first-quarter earnings ended October 1 would be down 25 cents to 35 cents a share from the $1.02 a share netted in the year before period. . . . The depressing profit news sent Digital Equipment's stock as well as many of the other technology issues reeling. Digital Equipment topped the most active list and was the session's biggest loser.

39. *Accounting for Social Responsibility.*   The report of the AICPA Study Group on the Objectives of Financial Statements includes the following statement:

An objective of financial statements is to report on those activities of the enterprise affecting society which can be determined and described or measured and which are important to the role of the enterprise in its social environment.

REQUIRED

(a) What is your interpretation of the meaning of this statement?
(b) Do you think that reports can be developed that will disclose a company's social performance?

2

The Financial Accounting Process

Accounting is defined in Chapter 1 as the measurement and reporting of economic events to provide relevant financial information to decision makers. This chapter concentrates on the financial accounting process traditionally used in this endeavor. In contrast to other chapters, much of the discussion here deals with procedural matters to show how individual transactions and events are ultimately reflected in financial statements.

We begin by considering the key elements and relationships in financial statements. Next, we demonstrate these relationships by means of an illustrative case that also highlights the effects of common business transactions on elements of the financial statements.

The remainder of the chapter is concerned with the **accounting cycle**—the series of steps repeated each accounting period by which financial statements are constructed from selected economic events. To show the logic of this process, we discuss the accounting cycle within the context of a *manual* accounting system, wherein each of the successive steps is done by hand. In fact, virtually all financial accounting operations are now done with the aid of computers. Yet, the basic steps (analyzing, recording, and summarizing events, and preparing the financial statements) are common to all methods of processing accounting information.

While this chapter concentrates on the overall process by which financial statements are prepared, it does not contain a detailed discussion of each of the financial statements. Such discussion is provided in later chapters, as follows:

- Income statement   Chapters 3 and 4
- Balance sheet   Chapters 5, 6, and 7
- Statement of cash flows   Chapter 8

Treatment of the mechanics of financial accounting is important, even in a textbook that is primarily conceptual in nature. Accounting techniques and devices (debit-credit rules, T accounts, and the like) provide a concise and effective way to summarize an otherwise overwhelming mass of financial data and to communicate relationships within that data.

KEY ELEMENTS AND RELATIONSHIPS IN FINANCIAL STATEMENTS

The basic set of financial statements, as discussed in Chapter 1, consists of (1) the balance sheet; (2) the income statement; and (3) the statement of cash flows. Exhibit 2-1 shows the key elements of each of these statements.

The financial statements in Exhibit 2-1 are presented in condensed (highly summarized) form, and it will soon be necessary to present and examine more detailed statements. Before doing so, however, it is useful to consider some important and basic relationships among the elements shown in these condensed financial statements.

The Balance Sheet and the Income Statement

The balance sheet reflects a basic relationship in financial accounting:

$$\text{Assets} = \text{Liabilities} + \text{Owners' Equity}$$

This equation is affected by *every* transaction or event that is recorded in the financial accounting system; for this reason, it is called the **fundamental accounting equation.**

The fundamental accounting equation can be restated as follows:

$$\text{Assets} - \text{Liabilities} = \text{Owners' Equity}$$

Expressing the equation in this form emphasizes the fact that owners' equity is a **residual value**—in this case, the arithmetic difference between total assets and total liabilities. Recall that assets are valuable resources of the firm, while liabilities are the firm's obligations to pay assets to other entities. Since most assets are not recorded at current market values, the residual owners' equity would not be expected to indicate the current market value of the owners' interest.

Assets minus liabilities is referred to as **net assets;** thus, the fundamental accounting equation may also be restated as follows:

$$\text{Net Assets} = \text{Owners' Equity}$$

This way of expressing the fundamental equation makes it easier to see that if the equality stated above is to be maintained, any change in the net assets of the firm must be accompanied by a corresponding change in owners' equity.

Exhibit 2-1
Key Elements of Financial Statements

Balance Sheet

Assets		**Liabilities**	
Cash	$XXX	Accounts Payable	$XXX
Inventory	XXX	Other Liabilities	XXX
Equipment	XXX		
Land	XXX		
Other Assets	XXX	**Owners' Equity**	
		Paid-in Capital	$XXX
		Retained Earnings	XXX
		Total Liabilities and	
Total Assets	$XXX	Owners' Equity	$XXX

Income Statement

Revenues	$XXX
Less: **Expenses**	(XXX)
Net income	$XXX

Statement of Cash Flows

Net Cash Flows from Operating Activities		
Cash Inflows from Revenues	$XXX	
Cash Outflows for Expenses	−XXX	
		$XXX
Cash Flows from Investing Activities		±XXX
Cash Flows from Financing Activities		±XXX
Net Increase (Decrease) in Cash		$XXX

In a corporation, owners' equity consists of paid-in capital (capital received through investment by the owners) and retained earnings (capital earned by the business itself that has not been distributed to the owners). Therefore, we may write the preceding equation as:

$$\text{Net Assets} = \text{Paid-in Capital} + \text{Retained Earnings}$$

Changes in net assets   The balance sheet describes the financial position of a firm at a point in time and is based on the fundamental accounting equation. This equation, or any of the various restatements noted in the preceding discussion, represents a static relationship among three major elements: assets, liabilities, and owners' equity. Business, of course, is not static. Consequently, the composition of each of these three elements and the totals of each often change as business transactions occur and are recorded and processed in the financial accounting system. Since the balance sheet equation holds true for balance sheets at any and all points in time, note that for the period between two specific balance sheets, the following equation would apply.

$$\begin{array}{ccc} \text{Change in} & \text{Change in} & \text{Change in} \\ \text{Net Assets} = & \text{Paid-in Capital} + & \text{Retained Earnings} \end{array}$$

Thus, if the net assets of a firm increase during a period of time, either paid-in capital or retained earnings (or both) increases.

When a corporation sells additional shares of stock to investors, both sides of the above equation must increase.[1] In this situation, the increase in net assets is usually in the form of cash received for the shares of stock and the change in owners' equity is shown as an increase in paid-in capital.

The two primary reasons that retained earnings would change when there is a change in net assets are (1) that the firm has net income (or net loss) for the period and (2) that the firm pays dividends to its owners.

Net income is the increase in net assets over a particular period of time due to a firm's own operations; this increase is measured and communicated by means of the income statement. An increase in net assets due to operations differs from the situation described earlier in which the net assets of the firm increased because of direct investment by the owners. When a firm has an increase in net assets from its own operations, or net income, the compensating increase in owners' equity is shown as an increase in retained earnings.

Revenues and expenses are subcategories of owners' equity used to facilitate the calculation of net income. **Revenues** represent increases in net assets due to operations; **expenses** are decreases in net assets due to operations. The

---

[1]In a corporation, shares of stock are used as evidence of ownership in the business entity, and the owners are referred to as its **stockholders** or **shareholders**. This textbook focuses on the "corporate form" of ownership. Other ownership forms are sole proprietorships and partnerships.

arithmetic difference between revenues and expenses is a measure of the firm's profitability over a period of time. This relationship, which provides the framework for the income statement, is depicted in equation form as follows:

$$\text{Revenues} - \text{Expenses} = \text{Net Income}$$
$$\text{(Increase in net assets from operations)}$$

A corporation may decide to pay out to its shareholders some or all of its net income. Such distributions of past earnings to the owners are called **dividends**, and dividends result in a reduction in both net assets and retained earnings.

To summarize, the changes in retained earnings for a given time period may be stated as follows:

$$\begin{array}{c}\text{Change in} \\ \text{Retained Earnings}\end{array} = \begin{array}{c}\text{Net} \\ \text{Income}\end{array} - \text{Dividends}$$

For a corporation that sells no additional shares of stock during a period, this relationship implies the following:

1. If the firm pays no dividends, the change in net assets will exactly equal the firm's net income for the period.
2. If a firm pays no dividends and incurs a **net loss,** the net assets will decrease by the amount of the loss.
3. If a firm has net income and declares dividends, retained earnings will change by the difference between net income and dividends.

Changes in total assets   The preceding discussion concerned *net* assets, or total assets minus total liabilities. Changes in net assets, by definition, must correspond to changes in owners' equity. However, the *total* assets of the firm may change due to changes in liabilities or changes in owners' equity; that is:

$$\begin{array}{c}\text{Change in} \\ \text{Total Assets}\end{array} = \begin{array}{c}\text{Change in} \\ \text{Liabilities}\end{array} + \begin{array}{c}\text{Change in} \\ \text{Owners' Equity}\end{array}$$

The following situations illustrate this relationship:

1. If a firm borrows money (a change in liabilities), both total assets and total liabilities will increase in equal amounts, with no change in owners' equity.
2. If a firm repays outstanding debts (a change in liabilities), both total assets and total liabilities will decrease in equal amounts, with no change in owners' equity.[2]

---

[2]For the moment we are ignoring interest payments on the debt. Interest expense is identical to other expenses in terms of the effects on net assets and net income.

3. Even if a firm is profitable and declares no dividend, total assets may decrease. This would occur if a firm repaid debt in an amount greater than its increase in owners' equity.

An expanded version of the fundamental accounting equation is presented in Exhibit 2-2. This diagram highlights several of the key relationships just discussed.

Statement of Cash Flows

To complete our treatment of key financial statement relationships, a brief discussion of the statement of cash flows is provided here. The preparation and use of this statement are explained in detail in Chapter 8. The statement of cash flows shows increases and decreases in cash from a firm's operating, financing, and investing activities over a given period of time.

Thus far, the relationships between assets, liabilities, owners' equity, and revenues and expenses have been discussed without considering the specific composition of each of these elements. For example, cash, inventory, buildings, machinery, and land are but a few of the specific items that may make up

Exhibit 2-2

Expansion of the Basic Accounting Equation

Relationships at a Point in Time

Assets − Liabilities

NET ASSETS = OWNERS' EQUITY

Relationships over a Period of Time

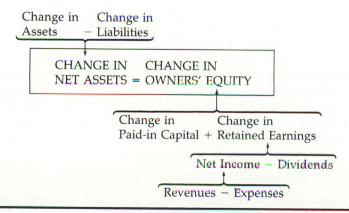

Change in — Change in
Assets − Liabilities

CHANGE IN — CHANGE IN
NET ASSETS = OWNERS' EQUITY

Change in — Change in
Paid-in Capital + Retained Earnings

Net Income − Dividends

Revenues − Expenses

the total assets of a business firm. A firm's specific liabilities might include accounts payable, lease obligations, and bonds payable. To discuss the statement of cash flows, we need a breakdown of total assets into cash and other (non-cash) assets. Accordingly, we will rewrite the fundamental accounting equation as follows:

$$\text{Assets} = \text{Liabilities} + \text{Owners' Equity}$$

$$\text{Cash} + \begin{array}{c}\text{Other}\\\text{Assets}\end{array} = \text{Liabilities} + \begin{array}{c}\text{Paid-in}\\\text{Capital}\end{array} + \begin{array}{c}\text{Retained}\\\text{Earnings}\end{array}$$

Changes in these accounts over a period of time may then be expressed as

$$\begin{array}{c}\text{Change}\\\text{in Cash}\end{array} + \begin{array}{c}\text{Change}\\\text{in Other}\\\text{Assets}\end{array} = \begin{array}{c}\text{Change in}\\\text{Liabilities}\end{array} + \begin{array}{c}\text{Change in}\\\text{Paid-in}\\\text{Capital}\end{array} + \begin{array}{c}\text{Change in}\\\text{Retained}\\\text{Earnings}\end{array}$$

Because the change in retained earnings for a period is equal to the period's net income less dividends, the equation may be restated as follows:

$$\begin{array}{c}\text{Change}\\\text{in Cash}\end{array} + \begin{array}{c}\text{Change}\\\text{in Other}\\\text{Assets}\end{array} = \begin{array}{c}\text{Change in}\\\text{Liabilities}\end{array} + \begin{array}{c}\text{Change in}\\\text{Paid-in}\\\text{Capital}\end{array} + \begin{array}{c}\text{Net}\\\text{Income}\end{array} - \text{Dividends}$$

Finally, in order to focus on the change in cash, we may write

$$\begin{array}{c}\text{Change}\\\text{in Cash}\end{array} = \begin{array}{c}\text{Change in}\\\text{Liabilities}\end{array} - \begin{array}{c}\text{Change}\\\text{in Other}\\\text{Assets}\end{array} + \begin{array}{c}\text{Change in}\\\text{Paid-in}\\\text{Capital}\end{array} + \begin{array}{c}\text{Net}\\\text{Income}\end{array} - \text{Dividends}$$

The last equation allows us to focus on the relationship between (1) changes in cash and (2) net income, dividends, and changes in other asset, liability, and owners' equity accounts. Note in particular that a change in cash is not synonymous with net income. For instance, a firm could have an increase in cash caused by borrowing money (a change in liabilities) or selling new stock (a change in paid-in capital), although neither of these activities directly affects net income. Conversely, it is possible to have net income and not have an increase in cash. Net income is an increase in net assets from operations, but it is not necessary that cash be one of the assets that is increased.

The statement of cash flows presented in Exhibit 2-1 is based on the mathematical equation shown for a change in cash. Of course, a number of additional refinements are needed to prepare a statement of cash flows, and these are developed in Chapter 8.

Nature of Financial Statements: a Summary

Major points made in this section concerning the nature of specific financial statements are listed below.

- The balance sheet is a static statement that presents a firm's assets, liabilities, and owners' equity at a point in time.
- The income statement presents changes in a firm's net assets from operations.
- The statement of cash flows shows increases and decreases of cash from all activities, not just from operations.
- Both the income statement and the statement of cash flows measure changes over a period of time.

ILLUSTRATIVE CASE: THE TANGLEWEB COMPANY

To examine these concepts more closely, consider the activities of the Tangleweb Company, a newly formed corporation that has been organized to conduct investment counseling. Transactions for the firm's first month of operations are listed below; they are numbered (1) through (7). The first transaction occurs on March 31, 1988, and the remainder occur during April 1988. We will analyze the effect of each transaction on the balance sheet equation.

(1)   March 31, 1988: The owners invest $10,000 in cash in exchange for shares of common stock.

ANALYSIS: Increase assets (Cash), increase owners' equity (Capital Stock). The balance sheet of the Tangleweb Company reflects these entries.

Tangleweb Company
Balance Sheet
March 31, 1988

Assets		**Owners' Equity**	
Cash	$10,000	Capital Stock	$10,000

(2)   April 1, 1988: The Tangleweb Company borrows $20,000 in cash from a bank and signs a note to repay the loan in one year at 12 percent interest.

ANALYSIS: Increase assets (Cash), increase liabilities (Notes Payable). An updated balance sheet would show the following:

Tangleweb Company
Balance Sheet
April 1, 1988

Assets		**Liabilities**	
Cash	$30,000	Notes Payable	$20,000
		Owners' Equity	
		Capital Stock	10,000
Total	$30,000	Total	$30,000

(3) April 2, 1988: The Tangleweb Company pays $5,000 for the rental of office space. This expenditure represents a prepayment of rent for five months, beginning April 1 and ending August 31, 1988.

ANALYSIS: Increase assets (Prepaid Rent), decrease assets (Cash). Note that the rental payment is an asset, since the Tangleweb Company has paid for the right to occupy office space for the ensuing five months. Because one asset, cash, has been exchanged for another asset, prepaid rent, the *total* assets of the firm are unchanged. This transaction has no effect, then, on liabilities or owners' equity; only the *composition* of the assets is changed. The balance sheet after this event reflects this change in composition.

Tangleweb Company
Balance Sheet
April 2, 1988

Assets		**Liabilities**	
Cash	$25,000	Notes Payable	$20,000
Prepaid Rent	5,000	**Owners' Equity**	
		Capital Stock	10,000
Total	$30,000	Total	$30,000

(4) April 28, 1988: The Tangleweb Company bills clients $15,000 for counseling services performed during April.

ANALYSIS: Increase assets (Accounts Receivable), increase owners' equity (Retained Earnings). The firm has acquired an asset without a corresponding increase in liabilities, so net assets (assets minus liabilities) have increased. The increase in net assets implies an increase in owners' equity. The increase in owners' equity is not the result of additional shareholder investment (Capital Stock), but is due instead to revenues earned and results in an increase in Retained Earnings.

Tangleweb Company
Balance Sheet
April 28, 1988

Assets		**Liabilities**	
Cash	$25,000	Notes Payable	$20,000
Accounts Receivable	15,000	**Owners' Equity**	
Prepaid Rent	5,000	Capital Stock	10,000
		Retained Earnings	15,000
Total	$45,000	Total	$45,000

(5) First of three transactions on April 30, 1988: The Tangleweb Company pays wages of $12,000 to employees for work performed during April.

ANALYSIS: Decrease assets (Cash), decrease owners' equity (Retained Earnings). The firm has reduced its assets without a corresponding reduction in liabilities, so that both net assets and owners' equity have decreased. Capital Stock is unaffected. Retained Earnings have decreased because the firm has incurred $12,000 of operating expenses.

(6)   Second transaction on April 30, 1988: The Tangleweb Company collects the $15,000 billed to clients in transaction (4).

ANALYSIS: Increase assets (Cash), decrease assets (Accounts Receivable). Only the *composition* of the firm's total assets has changed. Accounts receivable are reduced as cash is received from credit customers. Neither liabilities nor owners' equity is affected by this transaction. The cash receipt does not represent additional revenue to the Tangleweb Company. To recognize revenue at this point would be double counting, because the appropriate revenues were already recognized when owners' equity was increased in transaction (4). Total assets, then, remain unchanged.

(7)   Third transaction on April 30, 1988: The Tangleweb Company distributes $1,000 in cash to the owners of the firm as a dividend.

ANALYSIS: Decrease assets (Cash), decrease owners' equity (Retained Earnings). Note that this transaction, unlike transactions (4) and (5), does not involve either revenues or expenses. Rather, dividends represent a distribution of net income to the owners. Accordingly, dividends do not enter into the calculation of net income, even though dividends reduce retained earnings. After the three transactions on April 30 are recorded, the balance sheet appears as follows:

Tangleweb Company
Balance Sheet (before adjustments)
April 30, 1988

Assets		Liabilities	
Cash	$27,000	Notes Payable	$20,000
Prepaid Rent	5,000	**Owners' Equity**	
		Capital Stock	10,000
		Retained Earnings	2,000
Total	$32,000	Total	$32,000

The balance sheet presented for April 30, 1988 (before adjustments), shows the cumulative effect of all transactions (1–7) affecting the Tangleweb Company since the firm began operations on March 31, 1988. This balance sheet needs additional adjustments, however, in order to reflect the firm's present financial position. A portion of the prepaid rent has expired during April, and it is necessary to account for interest expense on the firm's outstanding note payable. Specifically, the following two adjustments [numbered (8) and (9)] are needed:

(8) April 30, 1988: The Tangleweb Company has occupied the rented offices for one month, so one-fifth of the prepaid rent has been consumed [see transaction (3)]. Thus, rental expense for April 1988 is ⅕ × $5,000, or $1,000.

ANALYSIS: Decrease assets (Prepaid Rent), decrease owners' equity (Retained Earnings). After this adjustment, prepaid rent has a balance of $4,000 ($5,000 − $1,000); this amount reflects prepaid rent, which remains to benefit future periods.

(9) April 30, 1988: The Tangleweb Company has borrowed $20,000 at an annual interest rate of 12 percent, or 1 percent per month [see transaction (2)]; interest expense for April 1988 is 1 percent × $20,000, or $200.

ANALYSIS: Increase liabilities (Interest Payable), decrease owners' equity (Retained Earnings). Note that the interest is paid annually, so that no assets are paid to the lender at the end of April. The Tangleweb Company does have an obligation, however, to pay the interest at a future date for services that have already been received at April 30, 1988.

After adjustments (8) and (9) are made, the firm's balance sheet appears as follows:

Tangleweb Company
Balance Sheet (after adjustments)
April 30, 1988

Assets		**Liabilities**	
Cash	$27,000	Notes Payable	$20,000
Prepaid Rent	4,000	Interest Payable	200
		Owners' Equity	
		Capital Stock	10,000
		Retained Earnings	800
Total	$31,000	Total	$31,000

This balance sheet shows the cumulative effect of all transactions affecting the Tangleweb Company since the firm began operations, plus the effects of the two adjustments made on April 30, 1988, for rent and interest. Exhibit 2-3 summarizes the effects of these transactions and adjustments on the basic accounting equation.

Careful study of Exhibit 2-3 reveals that individual transactions and adjustments may affect the balance sheet in different ways. Consider the following:

1. Transactions (3) and (6) merely affect the composition of total assets; as a result, neither liabilities nor owners' equity is changed by these events.

Exhibit 2-3

Effects of Tangleweb Company's Transactions and Adjustments on the Basic Accounting Equation

	Assets			=	Liabilities		+	Owners' Equity	
Item Description	Cash	Accounts + Receivable	Prepaid + Rent	=	Notes Payable	Interest + Payable	+	Capital Stock	Retained + Earnings
March 1988									
(1) Initial investment	+10,000							+10,000	
April 1988									
(2) Loan from bank	+20,000				+20,000				
(3) Prepayment of rent	−5,000		+5,000						
(4) Revenues earned		+15,000							+15,000 (Revenue)
(5) Expenses incurred	−12,000								−12,000 (Expense)
(6) Receivable collection	+15,000	−15,000							
(7) Payment of dividends	−1,000								−1,000 (Dividend)
(8) Rental expense adjustment			−1,000						−1,000 (Expense)
(9) Interest expense adjustment						+200			−200 (Expense)
Totals	27,000	0	4,000	=	20,000	200		10,000	800
	$31,000 Total Assets				$31,000 Total Liabilities + Owners' Equity				

Transactions

Adjustments

2. Transaction (2) changes total assets and total liabilities by the same amount, so the dollar amount of net assets (and owners' equity) is not affected.
3. Transactions (4) and (5) affect both total assets and owners' equity (retained earnings), because the firm has earned revenue and incurred expenses.
4. Items (8) and (9) also affect both total assets and owners' equity (retained earnings); they are not transactions, but are adjustments to previously recorded transactions.
5. Transaction (7) affects total assets and owners' equity (retained earnings), because the firm has distributed assets to its owners.

Key Relationships in the Tangleweb Company Illustration

Sufficient background information has now been presented to enable us to begin examining relationships between the financial statements of the Tangleweb Company and the elements within these statements. The changes between the firm's balance sheet at March 31 and its balance sheet at April 30 are due to operating flows during April (revenues and expenses), as well as nonoperating flows (other transactions) during that month. Changes during the month are "explained" by means of the two flow statements for the period: the income statement and the statement of cash flows for April. In this section, we will illustrate changes explained by the income statement.

Exhibit 2-4 presents balance sheets for the Tangleweb Company at March 31 and April 30, 1988, as well as the income statement for the month of April. In addition, the exhibit contains a schedule that shows in summary form the changes in retained earnings during April. In particular, observe the paths of the arrows drawn in Exhibit 2-4; they highlight key linkages between the two successive balance sheets and the income statement.

The series of accounting equations presented earlier in this chapter provides the underlying logic for the financial statements presented in Exhibit 2-4. Accordingly, we will first restate certain of these equations using data from the Tangleweb Company illustration to show how each statement is derived. Then we will return to Exhibit 2-4 for a closer look at the relationships shown there.

To begin, a variation of the fundamental accounting equation is used to calculate the dollar amounts for net assets, paid-in capital, and retained earnings for the Tangleweb Company at both the beginning and end of the period.

$$\text{Assets} - \text{Liabilities} = \text{Owners' Equity}$$

$$\text{Net Assets} = \text{Paid-in Capital} + \text{Retained Earnings}$$

At March 31, 1988:

$$\text{Assets} - \text{Liabilities} = \text{Owners' Equity}$$
$$\$10,000 - \quad 0 \quad = \quad \$10,000$$

$$\text{Net Assets} = \text{Paid-in Capital} + \text{Retained Earnings}$$
$$\$10,000 \quad = \quad \$10,000 \quad + \quad 0$$

Exhibit 2-4
Relationships between Income Statement and Balance Sheets

Tangleweb Company
Period from March 31, 1988–April 30, 1988

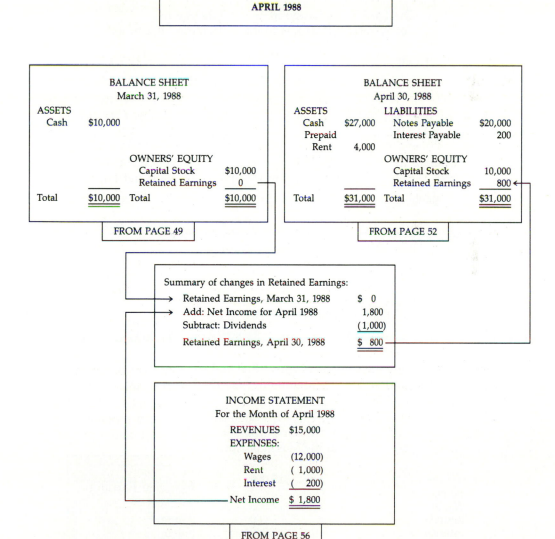

MARCH 31, 1988   **APRIL 30, 1988**

APRIL 1988

BALANCE SHEET
March 31, 1988

ASSETS		
Cash	$10,000	

OWNERS' EQUITY
Capital Stock	$10,000
Retained Earnings	0
Total	$10,000	Total	$10,000

FROM PAGE 49

BALANCE SHEET
April 30, 1988

ASSETS		LIABILITIES	
Cash	$27,000	Notes Payable	$20,000
Prepaid Rent	4,000	Interest Payable	200

OWNERS' EQUITY
Capital Stock	10,000
Retained Earnings	800
Total	$31,000	Total	$31,000

FROM PAGE 52

Summary of changes in Retained Earnings:

Retained Earnings, March 31, 1988	$ 0
Add: Net Income for April 1988	1,800
Subtract: Dividends	(1,000)
Retained Earnings, April 30, 1988	$ 800

INCOME STATEMENT
For the Month of April 1988

REVENUES	$15,000
EXPENSES:	
Wages	(12,000)
Rent	(1,000)
Interest	(200)
Net Income	$ 1,800

FROM PAGE 56

At April 30, 1988:

$$\text{Assets} - \text{Liabilities} = \text{Owners' Equity}$$
$$\$31,000 - \$20,200 = \$10,800$$

$$\text{Net Assets} = \text{Paid-in Capital} + \text{Retained Earnings}$$
$$\$10,800 = \$10,000 + \$800$$

Dollar amounts calculated here for the beginning and end of the period may be used to determine changes during the month of April.

$$\begin{array}{ccc} \text{Change in} & \text{Change in} & \text{Change in} \\ \text{Net Assets} = & \text{Paid-in Capital} + & \text{Retained Earnings} \end{array}$$

During April 1988:

Net Assets	=	Paid-in Capital	+	Retained Earnings
April 30 March 31		April 30 March 31		April 30 March 31
($10,800 − $10,000)	=	($10,000 − $10,000) +		($800 − $0)

$$\begin{array}{ccc} \text{Change in} & \text{Change in} & \text{Change in} \\ \text{Net Assets} = & \text{Paid-in Capital} + & \text{Retained Earnings} \\ \$800 = & 0 + & \$800 \end{array}$$

The equation above shows that the change in retained earnings during the month of April is $800. This amount is due to net income and dividends as follows:

$$\begin{array}{c} \text{Change in} \\ \text{Retained Earnings} = \text{Net Income} - \text{Dividends} \\ \$800 = \$1,800 - \$1,000 \end{array}$$

From the previous equation we know that net income during the month of April is $1,800, and an income statement may now be prepared.

Tangleweb Company
Income Statement
For the Month of April, 1988

		from **Exhibit 2–3**
Revenues	$15,000	Item (4)–transaction
Expenses		
Wages	12,000	Item (5)–transaction
Rentals	1,000	Item (8)–adjustment
Interest	200	Item (9)–adjustment
Net Income	$ 1,800	

Summary of relationships   Careful study of Exhibit 2-4 at this point helps in understanding the relationships between the financial statements of the Tangleweb Company and the elements within these statements. In particular, note the following:

1. The two balance sheets presented reflect the financial position of the Tangleweb Company at two different points in time. These two statements show that the company had net assets of $10,000 on March 31 (assets of $10,000 and no liabilities), and net assets of $10,800 on April 30 (assets of $31,000, less liabilities of $20,200). Hence, the change in net assets during April is $800.
2. The Tangleweb Company's income statement for April shows net income of $1,800. This means that net assets of the Tangleweb Company increased by $1,800 due to operations during the month of April. The income statement does *not* explain *all* changes in net assets during the period. Income statements deal only with those changes in net assets that result from operations.
3. While net income for April was $1,800, retained earnings increased by only $800 during this period. This is because the Tangleweb Company elected not to retain some of its earnings and paid a $1,000 dividend to its owners—an action that reduced cash and retained earnings by $1,000. The net change in retained earnings of $800 is summarized in a schedule included in Exhibit 2-4.
4. The change in cash for the period is not the same as the amount of net income for the period. Cash increased by $17,000 during the month of April ($27,000 cash on the April 30 balance sheet as opposed to $10,000 cash on the March 31 balance sheet), while net income for the period was $1,800.

RECORDING MEDIA AND TECHNIQUES

The Tangleweb Company illustration contains only seven transactions and two adjustments. But what if the firm had seventy transactions during the accounting period? Or seven hundred? In these latter cases, use of the worksheet approach employed in Exhibit 2-3 to keep track of the effects of recorded transactions and adjustments would be cumbersome.

Exhibit 2-5 identifies the major components of the formal accounting system traditionally employed by a business firm when the number of transactions to be recorded and summarized is more than just a few. The sequence of steps shown in this exhibit is called the **accounting cycle.** Recording media and the various techniques that comprise the accounting cycle are discussed in this section.

Economic Events

Economic events provide the basic subject matter from which financial statements are constructed. However, only some of the events that have economic impact on a business entity are proper inputs into its formal accounting system. Generally, events that qualify for inclusion are one of two types: either

Exhibit 2-5
The Accounting Cycle: Economic Events to Financial Statements

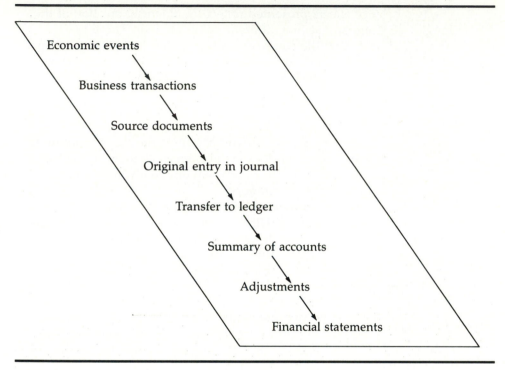

Economic events

Business transactions

Source documents

Original entry in journal

Transfer to ledger

Summary of accounts

Adjustments

Financial statements

(1) *exchanges* of assets or services between the accounting entity and outside parties or (2) events that involve *transfer, use,* or *disposition* of assets within the business itself. Events in the first category, which are referred to as **exchange transactions,** include the buying of inventory from suppliers, the borrowing of money from a bank, the selling of merchandise to customers, and the paying of wages or salaries. Examples of events involving the transfer, use, or disposition of assets within the business include the loss or damage of an asset because of fire and the transfer of raw materials to production for conversion into finished products.

Among the events *not* entered into the accounting system are the gain or loss of key personnel, the bankruptcy of a major competitor, a strike by the labor force, or changes in the general level of interest rates. While these events may indeed have a significant economic impact upon the business entity, they are not transactions for financial accounting purposes.

Data from exchange transactions are usually captured on **source documents** at the time the transactions occur. Sales invoices, checks, payroll time cards, and cash register tapes are all familiar source documents. They aid in the next step in the recording sequence—entering transactions in a journal.

Journal

A **journal** is similar to a diary. More specifically, it is a book in which transactions (expressed in terms of increases or decreases to particular accounts) are listed in chronological order. Because a journal is the first place in which this complete record is formally made, it is often referred to as a **book of original entry.** By providing a complete record of each transaction in a single place, a journal permits users to readily determine those selected economic events that occurred on a given business day.

Exhibit 2-6 shows how the first three transactions from the Tangleweb Company case would be recorded, or **journalized**. You are encouraged to scan Exhibit 2-6 at this point; however, a discussion of the conventions for recording transactions in a journal is deferred until after debit-credit rules are introduced. (A discussion of debit-credit rules begins on page 60, and an illustration of the journalizing of the Tangleweb Company transactions in debit-credit format begins on page 63.)

Ledger

A journal is not useful in answering a question such as, What is the balance of cash at a certain date? This question is answered by referring to the **ledger,** which summarizes the cumulative effects of recorded transactions in separate accounts. This is accomplished by transferring or **posting** information from the journal into appropriate accounts in the ledger. Separate accounts exist in the ledger for various assets, liabilities, and elements of owners' equity (including revenues, expenses, and dividends, which are subcategories of owners' equity). For instance, individual accounts would exist in the ledger for cash, accounts receivable, accounts payable, retained earnings, and so on.

Exhibit 2-6
Tangleweb Company's Journal After the
First Three Transactions Are Recorded

Entry Number	Date	Accounts	Debit (dr.)	Credit (cr.)
	1988			
(1)	March 31	Cash	10,000	
		Capital Stock		10,000
		To record sale of stock.		
(2)	April 1	Cash	20,000	
		Notes Payable		20,000
		To record loan from bank.		
(3)	2	Prepaid Rent	5,000	
		Cash		5,000
		To record prepayment of rent.		

A **ledger account** is a summary device and its simplest form (shown here) is shaped like the letter T and called a **T account.**

Account Title
Debit (dr.) side	Credit (cr.) side

The vertical line in the T divides the account into two sides. The left is called the **debit** side; the right, the **credit** side. The top of the T is used for writing in the appropriate account title.

The nature of the particular account (asset, liability, or owners' equity) determines which side of the account is used for increases or decreases. The rules are as follows:

1. *Assets.* Increases in assets are recorded on the left (debit) side; decreases are on the right (credit) side.
2. *Liabilities.* Increases in liabilities are recorded on the right (credit) side; decreases are on the left (debit) side.
3. *Owners' equity.* Increases in owners' equity (including revenues) are recorded on the right (credit) side; decreases in owners' equity (including expenses and dividends) are recorded on the left (debit) side.

As an example, consider the three increases to cash and three decreases to cash in the Tangleweb Company illustration (see Exhibit 2-3, page 53). These would be recorded and summarized as follows in T-account form in the ledger:

Cash
	(Increases)	(Decreases)	
	10,000	5,000	
45,000	20,000	12,000	18,000
	15,000	1,000	

Ending Balance	27,000	

The account balance here is $27,000—the difference between increases of $45,000 and decreases of $18,000. Observe that a horizontal line has been drawn across the base of the T to separate the ending balance of the account from individual increases and decreases.

Debit-credit rules may be summarized using the fundamental accounting equation as the frame of reference.

Assets		=	Liabilities		+	Owners' Equity	
dr.	cr.		dr.	cr.		dr.	cr.
+	−		−	+		−	+

Note that increase-decrease rules for accounts on the equation's left side (assets) are the opposite of increase-decrease rules for accounts on the right side of the equation (liabilities and owners' equity). Consequently, each entry made to record a transaction in the financial accounting system must consist of at least one account that is debited and one account that is credited, and the total debits recorded for the transaction must equal the total credits. Failure to adhere to these guidelines in recording transactions for accounts would destroy the equality in the fundamental accounting equation.

Use of Temporary Accounts for Revenues and Expenses

In the Tangleweb Company illustration, transactions and adjustments involving revenues and expenses were recorded directly to retained earnings [see items (4), (5), (8), and (9) in Exhibit 2-3]. While technically correct and certainly efficient for determining the ending balance of retained earnings, this procedure does not facilitate preparation of a detailed income statement—that is, one that shows specific sources of revenue and different types of expense.

A scheme that overcomes this difficulty establishes separate accounts for different revenue and expense types. In using this approach, increases and decreases in net assets from operations are assigned initially to these separate revenue and expense accounts, rather than to retained earnings. At the end of the accounting period (after the necessary information is derived for the income statement) the balances in all revenue and expense accounts are transferred, or **closed**, to retained earnings. Since revenue and expense accounts are "closed out" at the end of each period, they are referred to as **temporary accounts.** In contrast, accounts that are not "closed out" at the end of each period—specifically, those that represent balance sheet items—are referred to as **permanent accounts.** Balances in permanent accounts *are* carried forward from one period to the next; balances in temporary accounts are *not* carried forward to the next period.

Debit-credit rules do not change, even though temporary accounts are used. Recall that increases and decreases to any owners' equity account are handled in the following manner:

Owners' Equity

dr.	cr.
−	+

Since revenues and expenses are subcategories of owners' equity, these same rules must apply. Accordingly,

- *instead of crediting retained earnings* to reflect an increase in net assets from operations, an appropriate *revenue account is credited;* and
- *instead of debiting retained earnings* to reflect a decrease in net assets from operations, an appropriate *expense account is debited.*

In sum, revenues reflect increases in owners' equity and thus are recorded as credits, while expenses are decreases in owners' equity and thus are recorded as debits.

A temporary account is sometimes employed for dividends, too. If such is the case, the dividend account is debited in lieu of debiting retained earnings when net assets decrease, because dividends are declared and distributed to the owners.

Closing of Temporary Accounts

All revenue and expense accounts begin every accounting period with a balance of zero. During the period they accumulate values as transactions involving these accounts occur and are recorded. At the end of the accounting period, the balance of each revenue and expense account is transferred to retained earnings. The sum total of these transferred balances constitutes the amount of net income (or net loss) for the period. This transfer process, or **closing**, returns the balances of all revenue and expense accounts to zero. These accounts are then ready to accumulate values for revenues and expenses during the next period. If a separate, temporary account is used for dividends, the balance in this account is also transferred to retained earnings at the end of the period. Closing procedures using the Tangleweb Company data will be demonstrated in the section that follows, which illustrates the entire accounting cycle.

THE ACCOUNTING CYCLE ILLUSTRATED

We are now in a position to integrate information presented thus far into a discussion of the accounting cycle — the series of steps, repeated each accounting period, by which financial statements are constructed from selected economic events. Major steps in the cycle include the following:

A. Sequence during the accounting period
  1. Recording daily transactions in a journal
  2. Posting from journal into accounts in the ledger
B. Sequence at the end of the accounting period
  1. Recording and posting adjusting entries
  2. Preparing financial statements from the ledger
  3. Recording and posting closing entries

Data from the Tangleweb Company illustration will be used to demonstrate these steps.

Recording Daily Transactions in a Journal

This step constitutes the initial input of economic data into the accounting system. Selected events are recorded in the journal to provide a chronological history of the activities of the company.

Exhibit 2-7 shows all daily transactions from the Tangleweb Company case as they would be recorded in the journal. Note the following conventions for journalizing each transaction:

1. The date of each entry is written near the left margin.
2. The debit entry is listed first; the account title is not indented.
3. The credit entry is listed below the debit entry with the account title indented.
4. Amounts are placed in the debit-credit money columns, but no dollar signs are needed.
5. For each entry, debits equal credits.
6. An explanation of each entry is included.

Posting from Journal to Ledger

The next step requires that information be transferred, or *posted*, from the journal to appropriate accounts in the ledger. This clerical function is performed at periodic intervals, perhaps weekly.

Exhibit 2-8 depicts the ledger of the Tangleweb Company after transactions from Exhibit 2-7 have been posted. Permanent accounts appear in the top part of Exhibit 2-8; temporary accounts are in the bottom part.

Posting is a straightforward process and is illustrated by considering the first entry in the Tangleweb Company's journal.

Entry Number	Date	Account Titles	Debit	Credit
	1988			
(1)	March 17	Cash	10,000	
		Capital Stock		10,000

To post this entry, one would turn first to the Cash account in the ledger and enter a $10,000 debit. Next, the Capital Stock account would be located and a $10,000 credit recorded there. A posting reference should accompany each amount as it is entered in the ledger. This allows one to trace the amount back to its source in the journal. In Exhibit 2-8, individual transaction numbers from the journal serve as posting references. They appear in parentheses next to amounts entered in the T accounts.

Recording and Posting Adjusting Entries

As noted in the Tangleweb Company illustration, at the end of each accounting period — after daily transactions are journalized and posted — certain adjustments may be necessary before financial statements are prepared. Adjustments are entered first in the journal and then posted to appropriate ledger accounts. The typical adjusting entry involves one balance sheet account (asset or liability) and one income statement account (revenue or expense) and, with few exceptions, is the result of one of the following:

Exhibit 2-7

Tangleweb Company's Journal

Entry Number	Date	Accounts	Debit (dr.)	Credit (cr.)
	1988			
(1)	March 31	Cash	10,000	
		Capital Stock		10,000
		To record sale of stock.		
(2)	April 1	Cash	20,000	
		Notes Payable		20,000
		To record loan from bank.		
(3)	2	Prepaid Rent	5,000	
		Cash		5,000
		To record prepayment of rent.		
(4)	28	Accounts Receivable	15,000	
		Commissions Revenue		15,000
		To record revenues earned.		
(5)	30	Wages Expense	12,000	
		Cash		12,000
		To record wages paid.		
(6)	30	Cash	15,000	
		Accounts Receivable		15,000
		To record collection of receivables.		
(7)	30	Dividends	1,000	
		Cash		1,000
		To record payment of dividend.		

1. An expenditure that benefits more than one accounting period.
2. The receipt of an asset that will be earned over more than one accounting period.
3. A revenue that is earned but not yet recorded.
4. An expense that has been incurred but not yet recorded.

The first and fourth of these events occur in the Tangleweb Company illustration, resulting in two adjusting entries at the end of the month of April [see items (8) and (9) on page 52]. The first adjustment recognizes that a portion of the prepaid rent has expired during the month:

Entry Number	Date	Account Titles	Debit	Credit
	1988			
(8)	April 30	Rental Expense	1,000	
		Prepaid Rent		1,000

Exhibit 2-8

Tangleweb Company's Ledger After Daily Transactions
Are Posted — Before Adjustments

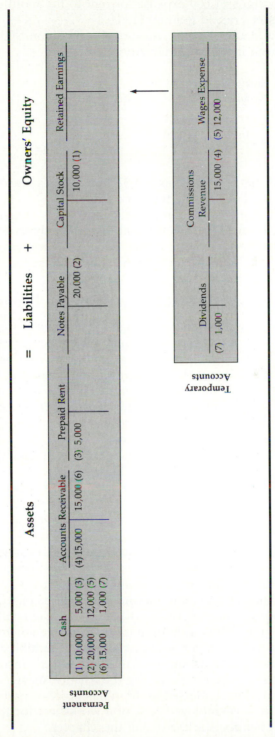

This entry assigns $1,000 expense for rent to the month of April, and also reduces the asset Prepaid Rent by $1,000.

The second adjustment gives formal recognition to the fact that interest expense has been incurred during April:

Entry Number	Date	Account Titles	Debit	Credit
	1988			
(9)	April 30	Interest Expense	200	
		Interest Payable		200

The effect of this entry is to assign $200 interest expense to the month of April and to increase liabilities by the same amount.

Exhibit 2-9 shows the Tangleweb Company's ledger after these adjusting entries have been posted. Notice that in posting these entries, it was necessary to open three new accounts in the ledger that previously had zero balances: Interest Payable, Rental Expense, and Interest Expense.

Preparing Financial Statements from the Ledger

Before financial statements are prepared from balances in the ledger accounts, a trial balance is often prepared to determine whether the ledger accounts balance (that is, if total debits equal total credits). A **trial balance** is a listing of all accounts in the ledger and their corresponding balances entered in the respective debit-credit columns. Actually, a trial balance may be prepared at any point in the accounting cycle, but it is most commonly prepared at the end of the accounting period (usually before adjusting entries, again after adjusting entries, and again after closing entries).

Exhibit 2-10 presents a trial balance for the Tangleweb Company using the ledger balances from Exhibit 2-9. These balances reflect the status of all of Tangleweb's accounts after adjusting entries have been posted but before closing entries are made. This listing of accounts is referred to as a **pre-closing trial balance** because the revenues and expenses have not yet been closed to Retained Earnings.

Financial statements are prepared from balances in the ledger accounts after adjusting entries have been posted, provided that the trial balance shows that total debits equal total credits. Since we have already shown the Tangleweb Company's balance sheet and income statement as of April 30 (see Exhibit 2-4, page 55), they will not be presented again. You may want to confirm, however, that the dollar amounts used in those financial statements agree with the ending balances in the ledger accounts shown in Exhibit 2-9. All temporary accounts, except dividends, are used in preparing the income statement; permanent accounts are used in preparing the balance sheet.

A worksheet is often used to aid in this process, particularly if a manual accounting system is employed. Use of a worksheet for this purpose is demonstrated in Appendix A at the end of this chapter.

Exhibit 2-9

Tangleweb Company's Ledger After Adjusting Entries Are Posted

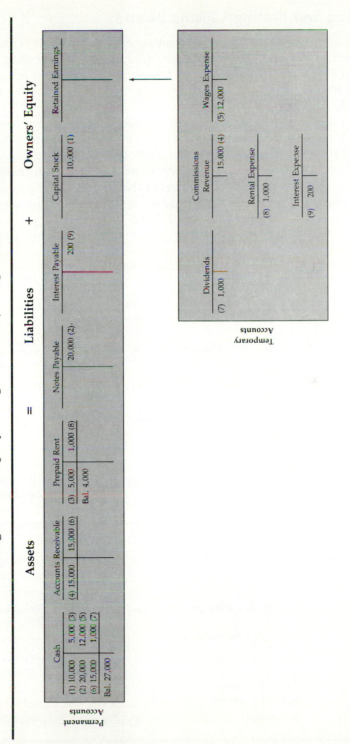

Recording and Posting Closing Entries

The objective of this step in the accounting cycle is twofold: (1) to transfer the net amount of balances in all temporary accounts to the Retained Earnings account and (2) to reset balances of all temporary accounts to zero so that they are ready to measure revenues, expenses, and dividends for the next accounting period.

Any temporary account with a debit balance is closed by crediting that account by the amount of the balance. For example, an account with a debit balance of $200 is closed by crediting it for $200, thus bringing the account balance to zero. In similar fashion, a temporary account with a credit balance is closed by debiting that account by the amount of the balance.

The following journal entries close all revenue and expense accounts for the Tangleweb Company at the end of April:

Entry Number	Date	Account Titles	Debit	Credit
	1988			
(10)	April 30	Commissions Revenue	15,000	
		Revenue and Expense Summary		15,000
(11)	30	Revenue and Expense Summary	13,200	
		Wages Expense		12,000
		Rental Expense		1,000
		Interest Expense		200
(12)	30	Revenue and Expense Summary	1,800	
		Retained Earnings		1,800

Exhibit 2-10
Tangleweb Company's Pre-closing Trial Balance

	Debit	Credit
Cash	$27,000	
Prepaid Rent	4,000	
Notes Payable		$20,000
Interest Payable		200
Capital Stock		10,000
Retained Earnings		0
Dividends	1,000	
Commissions Revenue		15,000
Wages Expense	12,000	
Rental Expense	1,000	
Interest Expense	200	
Totals	$45,200	$45,200

In the entries on page 68, note that the ending balances of revenue and expense accounts are transferred first to the account entitled "Revenue and Expense Summary" [Entries (10) and (11)], and then the balance of Revenue and Expense Summary is closed to Retained Earnings [Entry (12)]. The $1,800 credit to Retained Earnings [Entry (12)] is the amount of the Tangleweb Company's net income for the month of April.

The Dividends account for the Tangleweb Company is closed as follows:

Entry Number	Date	Account Titles	Debit	Credit
	1988			
(13)	April 30	Retained Earnings	1,000	
		Dividends		1,000

This entry brings the balance of the Dividends account to zero and reduces the Retained Earnings account by $1,000.

Exhibit 2-11 shows the Tangleweb Company's ledger after the closing entries have been posted. Observe that all temporary accounts, including Revenue and Expense Summary, now have zero balances. Balances in permanent accounts are carried forward to the next accounting period, at which time the accounting cycle begins anew. The trial balance for the Tangleweb Company at this point is presented in Exhibit 2-12. It is referred to as a **post-closing trial balance** because the revenues and expenses have now been closed to Retained Earnings.

The illustration we have just completed presents a basic outline of the entire accounting cycle. The logic of the sequence of steps in the cycle and the techniques utilized are emphasized by using a small number of transactions. The remainder of this chapter considers one aspect of the cycle—the adjustment process at the end of the accounting period—in greater detail. We will examine several situations where adjusting entries must be made to the ledger accounts before financial statements can be prepared.

ACCRUAL ACCOUNTING AND ADJUSTING ENTRIES

Generally accepted accounting principles (GAAP) mandate the use of the **accrual basis of accounting.** We assumed this basis in recording the transactions in the Tangleweb Company illustration. Under accrual accounting

- revenues are recognized when earned, without regard to the timing of cash receipts, and
- expenses are recognized either (1) in the period in which related revenues are recognized or (2) when incurred, without regard to the timing of cash disbursements.

In Chapter 1 we identified two of the assumptions of financial accounting—realization and matching—that are central to accrual accounting. Realization

Exhibit 2-11

Tangleweb Company's Ledger After Closing Entries Are Posted

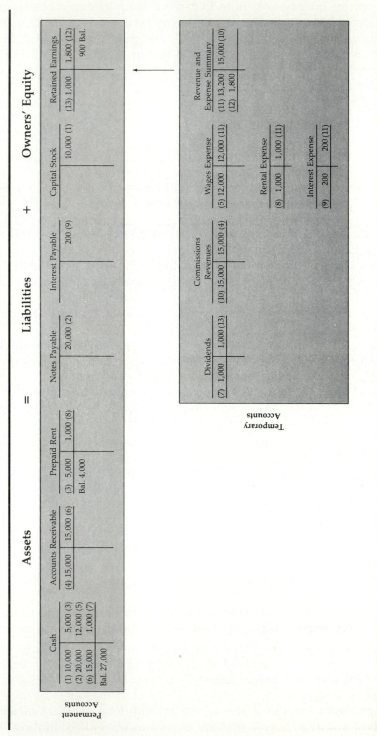

Exhibit 2-12

Tangleweb Company's Post-closing Trial Balance

	Debit	Credit
Cash	$27,000	
Prepaid Rent	4,000	
Notes Payable		$20,000
Interest Payable		200
Capital Stock		10,000
Retained Earnings		800
Totals	$31,000	$31,000

and matching provide guidance to accountants regarding the timing of revenue and expense recognition respectively, and will be discussed in detail in Chapter 3.

A second basis of accounting, but one not supported by GAAP, is the **cash basis.** Unlike the accrual basis, the cash basis links revenue and expense recognition to the timing of cash flows. Specifically, revenue is recognized in the period in which cash is received and expense is recognized at the time cash is disbursed. The cash basis of accounting is objective and relatively easy to use; it is often employed by small businesses and by individuals providing professional services, such as lawyers, dentists, and accountants.

Use of the accrual basis of accounting usually results in a more realistic matching of revenue and expenses than use of the cash basis. Consider, for example, a situation in which a $100,000 cash sale is made in December 1988. The salesman who makes the sale is paid a 20-percent commission in January 1989 (one month later). Assuming that the salesman's company prepares financial statements annually on December 31, the sales revenue and commission expense are assigned to 1988 and 1989 as shown in Exhibit 2-13.

Notice in Exhibit 2-13 that both the sales revenue and the associated commission expense are "matched together" in the same accounting period under the accrual basis but appear in different periods under the cash basis. Because of this failure to match revenues with related expenses, use of the cash basis of accounting in this illustration results in the overstatement of net income by $20,000 in 1988 and the understatement of net income by $20,000 in 1989.

Exhibit 2-13

Comparison of Accrual and Cash Basis

	Accrual Basis		Cash Basis	
	1988	1989	1988	1989
Sales Revenue	$100,000	0	$100,000	0
Commission Expense	20,000	0	0	$20,000

When the accrual basis of accounting is used, adjusting entries are required at the end of the period to record any previously *unrecognized* changes in assets, liabilities, revenues, or expenses. As we noted in the Tangleweb Company case, the purpose of these adjustments is to bring the accounts up to date before financial statements are prepared. Adjusting entries are entered first in the journal and then posted to appropriate ledger accounts. The typical adjusting entry involves one balance sheet account (asset or liability) and one income statement account (revenue or expense).

In the Tangleweb Company example, entries (8) and (9) on page 52 are examples of adjusting entries. In entry number (8) a portion of the prepaid rent was recognized as rental expense; in entry number (9) a liability and expense for interest on notes payable was recorded.

We can identify four general types of situations that usually require adjusting entries prior to the preparation of financial statements:

1. Unrecorded revenues.
2. Unrecorded expenses.
3. Expenditures benefitting more than one accounting period.
4. Revenues received in advance.

An explanation of each of these adjustments is provided below.

1. *Unrecorded revenues.*   At the end of any accounting period, certain earned revenues may not have been recorded during the normal course of events. Common examples include interest earned by the holding of securities during the period (accrued interest revenue); unbilled services performed in the current period (accrued service revenue); and rental fees earned but not yet received from tenants (accrued rental revenue). In each of these cases, cash will be received in a future period for revenue-producing activities of the current period. An adjusting entry is needed in each situation to prevent periodic revenues from being understated. Each entry would include a debit to an asset account (a receivable) and a credit to an appropriate revenue account. Consider the example that follows, which involves accrued interest.

On November 1, 1988, Dennik, Incorporated, invests $5,000 cash in a ten-year government bond. The bond pays 12 percent interest on October 30 of each year. Assume that the company prepares annual financial statements at December 31. Even though the first cash payment for interest is not received until October 30, 1989, interest for the months of November and December is earned in 1988. The amount earned in that year is $100 ($5,000 $\times$ 12% $\times$ $\frac{2}{12}$). Accordingly, the following adjusting entry would be made to the ledger balance at the end of 1988:

Dec. 31   dr.   Interest Receivable   100
            cr.   Interest Revenue   100

Interest Receivable is an asset and appears on the balance sheet. Interest Revenue is an income statement account and affects the determination of net income for 1988. If the above adjusting entry had not been made, assets and income for 1988 would be understated by $100.

2. *Unrecorded expenses.* An expense that has been incurred but not yet recorded is an accrued expense. The expense may not have been recorded, for example, because a bill has not yet been received or because the cash payment is not due until the next period. Since these expenses have not been paid, they represent liabilities at the end of the period. Examples include interest on cash borrowed during the current period that will not be paid until a future period (accrued interest payable); wages earned by employees during the period that will not be paid until the next period (accrued wages payable); and taxes incurred during the current period that will be paid during the next period (accrued taxes payable). Consider the following example involving accrued wages.

The Flagsdale Box Company pays its employees every Friday for a five-day workweek. Assume that the weekly payroll expense is $3,000. The company's fiscal year ends on Tuesday, December 31. Therefore, this adjusting entry is required to record the $1,200 ($\frac{2}{5}$ × $3,000) that the employees have earned, but have not yet been paid.

Dec. 31	dr.	Wages Expense	1,200	
	cr.	Wages Payable		1,200

This entry increases the amount of expenses and liabilities during the current year.

3. *Expenditures benefitting more than one accounting period.* A company must often pay for and record items such as supplies, rent, and insurance in advance of their use in the business. In addition, most firms own property, plant, and equipment items that are expected to last for many years. Expenditures that are expected to benefit more than the current accounting period are recorded by debiting appropriate asset accounts. If, on the other hand, an expenditure is expected to benefit only a single period, it is typically expensed immediately. Costs recorded initially as assets are adjusted at the end of each reporting period to reflect the extent of use or consumption of those assets during the period. This results in a transfer of a portion of the cost from an asset account to an expense account.

Two situations illustrate adjustments for expenditures that benefit more than one accounting period. The first involves the purchase and use of office supplies. The second involves the allocation of the cost of equipment over the period of its estimated useful life (depreciation).

The Central Word Processing Company begins the month of March with $200 in office supplies, and it purchases an additional $300 in supplies on March 17. The company wants to prepare financial statements on March 31, at which time the Office Supplies account in the general ledger reads as follows:

Office Supplies

Beg. Bal.	200	
March 17	300	
	500	

A count of office supplies on March 31 reveals that $375 worth of items remain in stock. Because supplies have decreased by $125 ($500 minus $375) during the period, the following adjusting entry is necessary to record supplies consumption:

    March 31   dr.   Office Supplies Expense   125
                cr.   Office Supplies   125

After this entry is posted to the ledger, the accounts appear as follows:

Office Supplies					Office Supplies Expense		
Beg. Bal.	200				March 31	125	
March 17	300	March 31	125				
March 31	375						

The second illustration of an adjustment for expenditures that benefit more than one accounting period involves depreciation. On January 1, 1988, Central Word Processing purchases an ink-jet printer for $5,000. It is assumed that this equipment will be used at a constant rate over its estimated life of five years. Consequently, $1,000 of expense (⅕ × $5,000) is assigned to each year. The process of allocating the cost of the printer over its estimated useful life is called **depreciation**.

At the end of each of the five relevant years the following adjusting entry would be made in the journal:

    Dec. 31   dr.   Depreciation Expense — Equipment   1,000
               cr.   Accumulated Depreciation — Equipment   1,000

Accumulated Depreciation is a **contra-asset** account, which means that it is subtracted directly from an asset account on the balance sheet. In this case, the ink-jet printer would be reported on the balance sheet at December 31, 1988, as follows:

        Equipment $5,000
        Less: Accumulated Depreciation — Equipment   (1,000) $4,000

In using this format, the financial statements present the original cost of the printer ($5,000), the amount of the cost that has been expensed to date ($1,000), and the unexpired cost applicable to future periods ($4,000).

4. *Revenues received in advance.* A company may receive an advance payment (or unearned revenue) that will be earned over more than one accounting period. Examples include advance payments for rentals, professional fees, and subscriptions. Unearned revenue is considered to be a liability because an obligation exists to perform services in the future. Adjustments are necessary as the revenue is earned. This is illustrated by an example involving subscriptions.

The Canavan Company begins operating in August 1988 and intends to publish a weekly suburban newspaper beginning on the first Saturday in September. As a result of an advertising campaign conducted during August, 100 subscriptions totaling $3,950 are sold. Each subscription runs for 50 weeks. The total of all advance payments on subscriptions is posted to the ledger accounts as follows:

Cash		Unearned Subscription Revenue	
Sept. 1 3,950			Sept. 1 3,950

During September four issues are sent to each subscriber. If financial statements are prepared at the end of September, the following adjusting entry is required in order to record revenue earned during the month:

Sept. 30	dr.	Unearned Subscription Revenue	316	
	cr.	Subscription Revenue		316

The amount earned, $316, is $\frac{4}{50}$ of $3,950. After this adjusting entry is posted to the ledger, the balance in Unearned Subscription Revenue is $3,634.

Unearned Subscription Revenue				Subscription Revenue	
Sept. 30 316	Sept. 1 3,950				Sept. 30 316
	3,634				

SUMMARY

This chapter focuses on the accounting mechanics that lead to the preparation of financial statements. Chapter sections are devoted to (1) key elements and relationships in financial statements, (2) recording media and techniques, (3) the accounting cycle, and (4) accrual accounting and adjusting entries. In addition, relationships in financial statements and the accounting cycle are illustrated by means of a set of common business transactions for a hypothetical firm—the Tangleweb Company.

To reiterate the central relationship in financial accounting (known as the fundamental accounting equation), assets equal liabilities plus owners' equity. This equation forms the basis of the balance sheet, which is used to represent the financial position of a business at a point in time. The other basic financial statements are not static, but measure changes over a period of time. The income statement presents changes in a firm's net assets from operations (net income), while the statement of cash flows shows sources and uses of cash from all activities, not just from operations.

Journals and ledgers are the two major recording media employed in a formal accounting system. Selected events and transactions are recorded initially in a journal to provide a chronological history of activities of the firm. They are then posted from the journal into the ledger, where the cumulative effects of recorded transactions are summarized in separate accounts.

Individual accounts exist in the ledger for various assets, liabilities, and elements of owners' equity (including revenues, expenses, and dividends, which are subcategories of owners' equity). Each ledger account has a left (or debit) side, and a right (or credit) side. Increases to an account are recorded on one side, and decreases on the other. Increase-decrease rules in terms of debits and credits are summarized below, with the fundamental accounting equation serving as the frame of reference.

Assets		=	Liabilities		+	Owners' Equity	
dr.	cr.		dr.	cr.		dr.	cr.
+	−		−	+		−	+

Increase-decrease rules for accounts on the equation's left side are the opposite of those for accounts on the equation's right side.

The accounting cycle is the series of steps, repeated each accounting period, by which financial statements are constructed from selected economic events. Major steps in the cycle include:

A. Sequence during the accounting period
   1. Recording daily transactions in a journal
   2. Posting from journal into accounts in the ledger

B. Sequence at the end of the accounting period
   1. Recording and posting adjusting entries
   2. Preparing financial statements from the ledger
   3. Recording and posting closing entries

Generally accepted accounting principles (GAAP) require the use of the accrual basis of accounting rather than the cash basis. The cash basis of accounting links revenue and expense recognition to the timing of cash flows. In contrast, under the accrual basis revenues are recognized (recorded) when earned, without regard to the timing of related cash receipts, and expenses are recognized when incurred or in the period when related revenues are recognized, without regard to the timing of cash disbursements.

When the accrual basis of accounting is used, adjustments are required at the end of the period to record certain previously unrecognized changes in assets, liabilities, revenues, and expenses. Adjustments are needed to record (1) earned revenues that have not yet been recorded; (2) unrecorded expenses that have been incurred; (3) the portion of the cost of a long-lived asset to be allocated to the current period; and (4) the portion of revenue received in advance that is earned in the current period.

APPENDIX A
USE OF A WORKSHEET IN PREPARING FINANCIAL STATEMENTS

Often when a manual accounting system is used, a worksheet is employed to assist in the preparation of financial statements. This appendix demonstrates the use of a worksheet for this purpose.

The sample worksheet in Exhibit A-1 was compiled using data from the Tangleweb Company illustration in Chapter 2. It consists of three sets of debit-credit columns.

Observe the following features of the worksheet:

1. In the first set of debit-credit columns (labeled "Trial Balance") we have listed balances in the ledger accounts from Exhibit 2-10 (page 68). Exhibit 2-10 contains account balances after adjusting entries were posted at the end of the period. Recall that a trial balance is a listing of all accounts in the ledger and their corresponding balances entered in the respective debit-credit columns. The purpose of preparing a trial balance is to determine whether the ledger accounts balance. In the case of our sample worksheet, both debits and credits equal $45,200.

2. Only the revenue and expense account balances appear in the second set of columns, which are used to prepare the income statement. Note that the total debits equal total credits in this set of columns, but only after a debit entry of $1,800 (representing net income) is entered. Before this is made, the totals of the debit and credit columns are not equal, since revenues (credits) exceed expenses (debits) by $1,800.

3. Only the balance sheet accounts and dividends appear in the worksheet's third set of columns. Total debits and credits are not equal in this last set of columns, however, until the net income of $1,800, as determined in the income statement set of columns, is entered as a credit (increase). The zero dollar amount listed for retained earnings on the worksheet reflects the balance at the beginning of the month, not at April 30. Thus, until net income is entered in the balance sheet set of columns, column totals are unequal. The books have not yet been closed and the Retained Earnings account has not yet been updated. Note also that the balance of $1,000 in the Dividends account is extended to the balance sheet set of columns, but as a debit (decrease). These extensions reflect the fact that revenue and expense accounts, and also dividends, are parts of the Retained Earnings account, and the books will not balance until these amounts are transferred to Retained Earnings. The balance of Retained Earnings at April 30, then,

Exhibit A-1

Tangleweb Company Worksheet

April 30, 1987

Account	Trial Balance (from Exhibit 2-10, page 68) dr.	cr.	Income Statement dr.	cr.	Balance Sheet dr.	cr.
Cash	27,000				27,000	
Accounts Receivable	0				0	
Prepaid Rent	4,000				4,000	
Note Payable		20,000				20,000
Interest Payable		200				200
Paid-in Capital		10,000				10,000
Retained Earnings		0				0
Dividends	1,000				1,000	
Commissions Revenue		15,000		15,000		
Wage Expense	12,000		12,000			
Rental Expense	1,000		1,000			
Interest Expense	200		200			
Totals	45,200	45,200	13,200	15,000		
Net Income			1,800			1,800
			15,000	15,000	32,000	32,000

Retained Earnings, April 30, 1987	=	Retained Earnings, March 31, 1987	+ Net Income − Dividends
	=	0	$1800 − $1000
	=	$800	

is the result of all items in the shaded area in the last set of columns: Retained Earnings, beginning of month, $0; Dividends, $1,000; and net income for April, $1,800.

QUESTIONS

1. The terms listed below were introduced in this chapter. Define or explain each of them.

account
accounting cycle
accrual basis of accounting
adjusting entries
book of original entry

cash basis of accounting
closing entries
contra-asset account
credit
debit

depreciation	post-closing trial balance
dividends	posting
exchange transaction	pre-closing trial balance
expense	residual value
fundamental accounting equation	revenue
journal	source document
ledger	T account
net assets	temporary account
net income	trial balance
permanent account	working capital

2. Identify and briefly describe the three basic financial statements. Which of these statements measures changes over a period of time? Which measures financial position at a point in time?

3. What is the fundamental accounting equation? What is the significance of this equation?

4. Does owners' equity, as shown on the balance sheet, reflect the current market value of the owners' interest in the company? Explain.

5. Is it possible for total assets of a firm to decrease even though the firm has net income for the period and pays no dividends? Explain.

6. Is it possible for a firm to have net income for a period and still experience a decrease in cash? Explain.

7. Distinguish between a journal and a ledger. Explain the function of each.

8. What is the objective of posting?

9. Give two examples of economic events that may have a significant impact on a business firm and yet are not proper inputs into its formal accounting system. What types of events are proper inputs into the financial accounting system?

10. Distinguish between permanent accounts and temporary accounts. Give an example of each.

11. Distinguish between a debit and a credit as the terms relate to sides of a T account in a ledger.

12. "Every journal entry made to the journal in a financial accounting system must have at least one debit and one credit." Do you agree or not? Explain.

13. Summarize the debit-credit rules for increasing and decreasing the following types of accounts:
    a. assets
    b. liabilities
    c. owners' equity
    d. revenues
    e. expenses

14. At what point in the accounting cycle are closing entries made? What is the purpose of closing entries?

15. Describe the major steps in the accounting cycle.

16. Contrast the accrual basis and the cash basis of accounting. Which of the two is required by generally accepted accounting principles?

17. Give two examples of situations that call for an adjusting entry at the end of the accounting period.
18. What function is served in financial accounting by the account entitled "Revenue and Expense Summary"?
19. The Accumulated Depreciation account is a contra-asset account. How is Accumulated Depreciation presented on a firm's balance sheet?
20. On which financial statement would you expect to find the account entitled "Unearned Subscription Revenue"? What type of an account is it?
21. "Increase-decrease rules for accounts on the left side of the fundamental accounting equation are the opposite of increase-decrease rules for accounts on the equation's right side." Do you agree or not? Explain.

EXERCISES AND PROBLEMS

22. *Possible Misconceptions.* A financial reporter overheard the statements listed below in the corporate accounting offices of a major corporation.
    (1) "Recognition of revenue and receipt of cash from a customer are synonymous."
    (2) "In order to prepare historical financial statements it is necessary to make estimates of the future."
    (3) "The balance sheet measures financial position of a business entity at a point in time."
    (4) "Accrual accounting results in a more realistic matching of revenues and expenses than if the cash basis of accounting is used."
    (5) "The primary purpose of adjusting entries is to correct errors in estimates made during the financial accounting process."
    (6) "The only way a company can increase its net assets during a given accounting period is by having net income during that period."
    (7) "Retained earnings represents cash received in prior accounting periods less any dividends paid by the firm."

REQUIRED   For each of these statements, decide if you agree or disagree. Explain fully.

23. *Fundamental Accounting Equation.* The following data represent selected information from the balance sheets of four different companies:

	Firm A	Firm B	Firm C	Firm D
Total Assets	?	$200,000	$500,000	$750,000
Total Liabilities	$ 75,000	?	40,000	400,000
Paid-in Capital	50,000	80,000	?	500,000
Retained Earnings	100,000	(60,000)	425,000	?

REQUIRED   Fill in the missing amounts for each firm. Notice that the dollar amount of Retained Earnings for Firm B is enclosed in parentheses; this represents a negative amount in this account.

24. *Missing Information.* The following data are sets of selected information from the books of three different companies:

1. From Company A
Retained Earnings, 1/1/88	$ 50,000
Retained Earnings, 12/31/88	20,000
Total Assets, 12/31/88	100,000
Dividends for 1988	10,000
Net Income for 1988	?
2. From Company B
   Balances at 12/31/88:
Total Assets	$200,000
Total Liabilities	40,000
Common Stock	130,000
Retained Earnings at 12/31/88	?
3. From Company C
   Balances at 12/31/88:
Long-term Assets	$200,000
Current Liabilities	15,000
Long-term Liabilities	100,000
Common Stock	25,000
Retained Earnings	80,000
Balance in current assets at 12/31/88	?

REQUIRED   Find the missing value in each of these three cases. Show your work.

25. *Relationship between Balance Sheet and Income Statement.* The schedule presented below contains selected information from the financial statements of three different companies.

	Company A	Company B	Company C
Total Assets	$500,000	$1,800,000	?
Total Liabilities	90,000	?	$250,000
Paid-in Capital	100,000	250,000	100,000
Retained Earnings, beginning of the year	350,000	700,000	300,000
Dividends	40,000	?	20,000
Net Income for the year	?	320,000	130,000
Retained Earnings, end of the year	?	900,000	?

REQUIRED   Fill in the missing amounts for each firm.

26. *Relationship between Balance Sheet and Income Statement.* The schedule presented below contains selected information from the financial statements of three different companies. A decrease in a particular category is shown on the schedule by enclosing the dollar amount of the decrease in parentheses.

	Company 1	Company 2	Company 3
Change during the period:			
Assets	$30,000	?	($25,000)
Liabilities	(10,000)	$25,000	5,000
Paid-in Capital	0	10,000	0
Retained Earnings	?	?	?
Total for the period:			
Dividends	5,000	18,000	0
Net Income	?	30,000	?
Revenues	?	50,000	50,000
Expenses	12,250	?	?

REQUIRED   Fill in the missing amounts for each company.

27. *Relationship between Balance Sheet and Income Statement.*   A balance sheet for the Hartford Company at January 1, 1988, is presented below. A partially completed balance sheet for the company at December 31, 1988, is also presented.

Hartford Company
Balance Sheet

	January 1, 1988	December 31, 1988
Cash	$30,000	?
Prepaid Rent	50,000	$40,000
Total Assets	$80,000	?
Notes Payable	0	$20,000
Common Stock	60,000	?
Retained Earnings	20,000	50,000
Total Liabilities and Owners' Equity	$80,000	?

Additional information relating to the period from January 1, 1988, to December 31, 1988:

(1) No cash payments for prepaid expense are made.
(2) Dividends of $10,000 are declared and paid.
(3) $50,000 of new common stock is issued; no common stock is retired.
(4) Market price of common stock is $20 per share on January 1, 1988, and $15 per share on December 31, 1988.
(5) Revenues are $80,000 for the year.
(6) There are three different expense types during the period: rental expense, salary expense, and interest expense; salary expense is $28,000.

REQUIRED

(a) Prepare an income statement for the year ended December 31, 1988, and calculate the values of the missing items in the incomplete balance sheet at December 31, 1988.

(b) Demonstrate that the following equations hold for the data in this problem:

1. Change in
   Retained   Net
   Earnings   = Income − Dividends

2.
   $$\text{Change in Cash} = \text{Change in Liabilities} - \text{Change in Other Assets} + \text{Change in Paid-in Capital} + \text{Net Income} - \text{Dividends}$$

(c) Is the change in cash for the period the same as the amount of net income for the period? If not, why not?

28. *Relationship between Income Statement and Balance Sheet.* Two Acme Company balance sheets (one at January 1, 1988, and the second at December 31, 1988) are presented below.

Acme Company
Comparative Balance Sheets

	January 1, 1988	**December 31, 1988**
Cash	$15,000	$50,000
Building (net of depreciation)	40,000	30,000
Total Assets	$55,000	$80,000
Notes Payable	$10,000	0
Common Stock	20,000	$50,000
Retained Earnings	25,000	30,000
Total Liabilities and Stockholders' Equity	$55,000	$80,000

Additional information:

(1) No buildings were acquired or sold during 1988.

(2) Total amount of revenues for 1988 is $60,000.

(3) Total amount of expense for 1988 is $40,000. There are three different types of expense: depreciation, interest, and salaries; the amount of interest expense is $5,000.

(4) Dividends of $15,000 were declared and paid during 1988.

REQUIRED

(a) Prepare an income statement for the year ended December 31, 1988.

(b) Prepare a schedule that explains the changes in Retained Earnings during the year ended December 31, 1988.

29. *Classification of Accounts.* The following accounts appear in the ledger of the James Company:

(1) Accounts Receivable
(2) Accounts Payable
(3) Advertising Expense
(4) Cash
(5) Commissions Revenue
(6) Common Stock
(7) Dividends
(8) Interest Expense
(9) Notes Payable

(10) Office Supplies
(11) Office Supplies Expense
(12) Prepaid Rent
(13) Rental Expense
(14) Salary Expense
(15) Service Revenue
(16) Unearned Service Revenue
(17) Wages Payable

REQUIRED

(a) Select the proper classification for each account from the following list:

Asset
Liability
Paid-in Capital

Retained Earnings
Revenue
Expense

(b) Specify the normal balance of each account, debit, or credit.

30. *Debit-Credit Rules.* Below is a list of accounts (in alphabetical order) from the ledger of the Seaside Realty Company.

(1) Accounts Payable
(2) Accounts Receivable
(3) Buildings
(4) Cash
(5) Commissions Earned
(6) Common Stock
(7) Dividends
(8) Interest Expense
(9) Interest Receivable

(10) Land
(11) Notes Payable
(12) Office Supplies
(13) Office Supplies Expense
(14) Prepaid Insurance
(15) Retained Earnings
(16) Salaries Payable
(17) Salary Expense
(18) Unearned Interest Revenue

REQUIRED   For each account listed, indicate whether an increase to that account is accomplished by a debit or by a credit.

31. *Missing Information: Journal Entries.*   In the blanks shown below, fill in the account title that you feel would be the "most likely" debit or credit. You may have more than one answer.

	Debit	**Credit**
(1)		Accumulated Depreciation
(2)	Accounts Receivable	
(3)		Capital Stock
(4)		Deferred Revenue
(5)		Accounts Payable
(6)	Salaries Expense	
(7)		Prepaid Insurance
(8)	Interest Receivable	
(9)	Prepaid Rent	
(10)		Retained Earnings

32. *Recording Basic Transactions.*   The following transactions occurred at the Enon Corporation during 1988, the firm's first year of operations:

(1) On January 2—issued 200,000 shares for $5 cash per share.
(2) On January 15—borrowed $80,000 from a bank and signed a note to repay the loan at the end of five years at an interest rate of 10%.
(3) On January 20—purchased a machine and paid $80,000 cash.
(4) During the year, purchased $90,000 of inventory. Of this total amount, $20,000 were cash purchases and the remainder were purchased on credit.
(5) During the year, made payments of $50,000 for inventory that had been purchased previously on credit.
(6) During the year, provided services to its customers. These services generated cash sales amounting to $300,000 and credit sales amounting to $60,000.
(7) During the year, collected $35,000 cash from customers due to credit sales that were previously recorded.

(8) During the year, paid wages of $40,000 in cash.

REQUIRED   Prepare journal entries to record the above transactions.

33. *Journalize Transactions.*   Jane James, Incorporated (a firm that provides accounting services), reports the following events for the month ending January 31, 1988:

1988
⎯⎯

Jan.   1 Ms. James invested $90,000 in the business. Common stock was issued as evidence of ownership.
   2 Purchased office equipment for use in the firm by paying $4,000 in cash and agreeing to pay the remaining $6,000 in 30 days.
   7 The Smith Company offered Ms. James $3,000 to do an audit. Ms. James usually charges $5,000 for an audit of this scope, so she is considering the offer (or the possibility of making a counteroffer).
   8 Completed project for Freeport, Incorporated, and billed that firm $7,000.
  12 Collected $2,000 of the fee billed to Freeport, Incorporated, on January 8.
  15 Paid office rent for the current month, $1,000.
  20 Incurred and paid salaries for the current month, $8,000.
  21 Incurred and paid utility expense, $400.
  24 Paid part of the principal on the note payable, $3,000. (The note was originally recorded on January 2.)
  24 Ms. James purchased a computer for her personal use for $6,000. She wrote a check from her personal checking account for $4,000 and signed a personal note for the difference. The computer was not for business use.
  25 Purchased office supplies on account, $4,000.
  27 Paid $1,000 as partial payment for supplies purchased on account on January 25.
  28 Incurred a repair expense and received a bill for the repairs for $300. Ms. James intends to pay the bill next month.

REQUIRED   Prepare the necessary journal entries for Jane James, Incorporated, to record these transactions.

34. *Identification of Transactions.*   The following entries were made by Baskets, Inc., during the month of October.

		Debit	Credit
(1)	Cash	15,000	
	Common Stock		15,000
(2)	Prepaid Insurance	4,000	
	Insurance Expense	1,000	
	Cash		5,000
(3)	Machinery	7,000	
	Cash		1,500
	Note Payable		5,500
(4)	Accounts Receivable	17,000	
	Sales Revenue		17,000

(5)	Rental Expense	500	
	Cash		500
(6)	Cash	12,200	
	Accounts Receivable		12,200
(7)	Accounts Payable	2,500	
	Cash		2,500

REQUIRED   Give a brief explanation of the transaction that has taken place for each of the entries above.

35. *Identification of Transactions.*   Account balances from the entire ledger of the Newark Company for five consecutive days in May 1988 are presented below.

	Account Balance at the End of:				
	Day 1	**Day 2**	**Day 3**	**Day 4**	**Day 5**
Cash	20,000	15,000	30,000	45,000	40,000
Accounts Receivable	5,000	5,000	5,000	5,000	5,000
Property, Plant, and Equipment	50,000	65,000	65,000	60,000	60,000
Prepaid Insurance	–	–	20,000	20,000	10,000
Notes Payable	10,000	20,000	20,000	20,000	15,000
Accounts Payable	20,000	20,000	20,000	20,000	20,000
Unearned Rent Revenue	5,000	5,000	40,000	40,000	40,000
Capital Stock	25,000	25,000	25,000	30,000	30,000
Retained Earnings	15,000	15,000	15,000	20,000	10,000

REQUIRED   Prepare a brief description of the transaction(s) that most likely took place on each of these days.

36. *Accrual versus Cash Basis of Accounting.*   The Nelson Company began operations on June 1, 1988. The following events took place during the first month of business.

June   1   Owners contributed cash of $20,000 in exchange for capital stock.

       9   Paid rent in the amount of $3,000 for the months of June, July, and August.

    15   Rendered services valued at $3,500 to customers.

    22   Purchased a vacuum cleaner system for $3,000. A down payment of $500 was made and the balance was financed with a loan at a 10% interest rate.

    25   Additional services valued at $2,500 were rendered, of which $1,700 was collected in June.

    27   An insurance bill for $2,000 for the month of June was received. Payment was made on July 3.

    29   Collected $3,300 for services rendered on June 15.

    30   Salaries are paid on a monthly basis. Salaries for the month of June amounted to $4,000 and will be paid on July 1.

REQUIRED

    (a) (1) Prepare the necessary entries to record the above transactions, assuming the company employs the cash basis of accounting.
       (2) Prepare an income statement using the cash basis of accounting.
    (b) Repeat the exercise in (a) above, but assume the accrual basis of accounting.
    (c) Explain the difference between the net income (loss) figures in (a) and (b) above.
    (d) Which basis of accounting provides for the better measurement of performance during the accounting period? Why?

37. *Accrual versus Cash Basis of Accounting.*   The Hatfield Company began its business operations on January 1, 1988. On this date, the owners contributed $50,000 cash to the firm in exchange for stock. The following week, $800 worth of services were rendered to the company's first customer. Payment for these services, however, was not due until February 2, 1988. During January additional services were rendered in the amount of $5,400, of which $2,300 was collected during that month. Expenses for wages, insurance, and rent were incurred and paid during January in the amounts of $1,000, $500, and $700, respectively. Accrued wages at the end of January totaled $300.

REQUIRED

    (a) Prepare the necessary entries to record the above transactions, assuming that (1) the company uses the cash basis of accounting and (2) the company uses the accrual basis of accounting.
    (b) Prepare an income statement, assuming that (1) the company uses the cash basis of accounting and (2) the company uses the accrual basis of accounting.
    (c) Which basis of accounting provides for the better measurement of performance during an accounting period? Why?
    (d) Are both the cash basis and the accrual basis of accounting permissible under generally accepted accounting principles?

38. *Adjusting Entries.*   Computer Skills, Inc., provides students with instruction in the use of various computers. As of the balance sheet dated December 31, 1987, the following information was available:

    (1) Seven teachers are employed by the company. They are paid at the rate of $2,000 per month per person and receive payment on the 16th and 1st of each month for the previous two-week period. At December 31, 1987, nothing has been recorded in regard to wages for the last two weeks.

(2) Two years ago, 20 microcomputers were purchased for a package price of $25,000. The estimated useful life of these microcomputers is five years.

(3) Computer Skills, Inc., rents office and classroom space in a building for $500 per month. Rent is paid on March 1, June 1, September 1, and December 1 of each year for the three-month period following the payment date. The December 1 payment was recorded as follows:

> dr. Rental Expense 1,500
> cr.   Cash   1,500

Nothing has been recorded regarding rental expense since this entry.

(4) Thirty-five students completed a computer course in the last week of December. Payment for this course was not received until January 10, 1988. The per-student charge for the course was $200. As of December 31, 1987, no entry had been made concerning the charges for this course.

(5) Computer Skills, Inc., offers an eight-month course that begins on September 1 and ends on April 30. Students are required to make full payment in advance. The charge per student is $1,200. Ten students enrolled in the course this year. On September 1 the accounting clerk made the following entry:

> dr. Cash   12,000
> cr.   Deferred Tuition Revenue   12,000

Nothing has been recorded regarding tuition revenue subsequent to this entry.

REQUIRED   Prepare the necessary adjusting journal entries for the year ended December 31, 1987.

39. *Adjusting Entries.*   Rug Cleaners, Inc., has just finished its first month of business. The following information was available on January 31, 1988.

(1) On January 1, Rug Cleaners, Inc., made the following entry to record an insurance payment for the first six months of the year:

> dr. Insurance Expense 12,000
> cr.   Cash   12,000

Nothing has been recorded regarding insurance expense since this entry.

(2) Employees are paid on a monthly basis. Payment is made on the first day of the month after the month for which they are being paid.

January salaries amounted to $7,000. Nothing has been recorded regarding these salaries.

(3) On January 1, fifteen rug-cleaning machines were purchased at a cost of $400 each. The estimated useful life of each machine is five years. Depreciation is recorded on a monthly basis.

(4) As of January 31, twelve rugs had been cleaned for a fee of $75 per rug. No customers have made any payments and no entry regarding revenues has been made since Rug Cleaners, Inc., began business operations.

(5) Customers may purchase a twelve-month service contract on any rugs in their home for a price of $400. This fee includes spot cleaning for stains as well as routine cleaning. On January 1, five customers purchased service contracts. At that time the following entry was made:

dr.	Cash	2,000	
cr.	Deferred Cleaning Revenue		2,000

Nothing has been recorded regarding deferred revenues since this entry.

REQUIRED   Prepare the necessary adjusting journal entries at January 31, 1988.

40. *Adjusting Entries.*   The situations described below occurred in the course of the Hanover Company's regular business operations during 1988. The company adjusts and closes its books annually on December 31.

(1) As supplies were acquired during the year, the purchase cost was debited to the Supplies Expense account. At year-end the Supplies Expense account had a $25,000 balance. However, an actual count of the supplies inventory at year-end indicated that there were $5,000 of supplies still on hand.

(2) On January 2, 1988, the firm purchased a machine for $75,000; its estimated useful life was ten years. The firm uses the straight-line depreciation method.

(3) On December 31, 1988, wages earned by workers but not recorded on the books amounted to $8,000. This amount will be paid on the next payday, which is Friday, January 3, 1989.

(4) On January 2, 1988, the Hanover Company signed a service contract with a customer for $90,000. The contract specified that Hanover would service the customer's equipment for the next three years for this fixed fee. The full amount of the fee, $90,000, was received in

cash on the day the contract was signed and was recorded as a debit to Cash and a credit to the Sales Service Revenue account.

(5) On December 1, 1988, the company borrowed $10,000 from the bank at a 12% annual interest rate for a three-month period. The principal of $10,000 plus three month's interest will be repaid to the bank on March 1, 1989.

REQUIRED   Prepare the journal entries needed to adjust the books at December 31, 1988.

41. *Identification of Adjustments.*   The data shown below were extracted from the books of the Stockton Company before and after adjusting entries were posted. The adjusting entries were made on December 31, 1988 — the last day of the fiscal year.

	Balance before Adjustment	Balance after Adjustment
(1) Accrued Interest Revenue	$ 0	$ 1,500
(2) Wages Payable	12,500	12,900
(3) Prepaid Rent	1,000	0
(4) Unearned Subscription Revenue	1,800	1,200
(5) Accumulated Depreciation	24,000	30,000
(6) Interest Payable	2,600	3,000

REQUIRED   For each item above, prepare the adjusting entry that in all probability explains the change in the account listed.

42. *Journalize Transactions and Adjusting Entry.*   Jill Smith, Incorporated, an accounting firm, reports the following transactions for October:

1988

Oct. 1 Jill Smith deposited $150,000 cash in a bank account in the name of the business. Common stock was issued to Jill Smith.
      2 Purchased land for $30,000, with $10,000 paid in cash and $20,000 due in 60 days.
      3 Incurred and paid office rent for October, $600.
      4 Purchased office equipment for cash, $8,400. The equipment has a ten-year life.
      5 Billed customers for accounting fees, $20,000.
     15 Incurred and paid salaries of $5,000.
     18 Sold a one-year contract for accounting work to the Apple Company for $12,000 cash; the work is to begin on November 1, 1988.
     22 Collected $15,000 cash from customers billed on October 5, 1988.
     30 Paid $12,000 of the $20,000 liability incurred on October 2 to purchase land.

REQUIRED   Journalize the October 1988 transactions listed above. Also, prepare the adjusting entry to record depreciation for October.

43. *Journalize Transactions and Adjusting Entries.* Chapter 2 identified four general types of situations that usually require adjusting entries at the end of the reporting period. Several examples of each situation are described below. The examples pertain to activities of the Atlanta Corporation during 1988. The firm closes its books annually on December 31.

A. An expenditure benefiting more than one period—(an asset becomes an expense).

   1. Prepaid insurance.
      On November 20, purchased a three-year insurance policy, paying $3,600 in cash. The insurance coverage begins on December 1, 1988.

   2. Office supplies.
      On May 10, purchased office supplies on account, $600. This was the only purchase of office supplies during the year. The beginning balance in the Office Supplies account was $200, and, per count, the cost of supplies on hand at December 31 was $125.

   3. Prepaid rent.
      On December 1, 1988, paid rent for December and January in the total amount of $2,000.

B. Revenues received in advance—(unearned revenue turns into revenue).

   4. Unearned fees.
      On December 10, 1988, fees of $10,000 were collected. These fees relate to services to be performed during December, 1988 and January, 1989. By December 31, $4,000 of the fees have been earned.

   5. Unearned rent.
      On December 2, 1988, rent was collected in the amount of $6,000. This was for the three-month period beginning December 1, 1988.

C. Unrecorded expense—(an expense [and liability] has been incurred but is not yet recorded).

   6. Accrual of interest payable.
      On December 1, 1988, borrowed $1,000 cash from a local bank. As evidence of this transaction, a $1,000, 12%, two-month note payable was issued.

   7. Accrual of wages.
      The firm's weekly payroll totals $75,000. Employees are paid each Friday evening for the current week's work. December 31, 1988, is a Tuesday.

   8. Depreciation.
      On January 2, 1988, purchased a machine for $105,000. The machine has a ten-year estimated life and a zero salvage value. Straight-line depreciation is to be used. No depreciation has been recorded yet.

D. Unrecorded revenue—(a revenue [and asset] has been earned but is not yet recorded).

9. Fees earned.

At December 31, 1988, $8,000 of fees had been earned because of services performed, but not yet recorded.
10. Accrual of interest revenue.

On December 1, 1988, received a $2,000, 12%, two-month note receivable as evidence of a cash loan made to an employee on that date.
11. Accrual of rent revenue.

By December 31, 1988, $5,000 of rent revenue earned in December had not been recorded or collected.

REQUIRED   For each of the preceding situations, do the following: (a) record the event that took place during the period (if any) that gives rise to a year-end adjustment and (b) record the proper adjusting entry at December 31.

44. *Journalize Transactions and Adjustments (new business).*   The New England Trucking Company was formed on May 2, 1988. During its first month of operations, the following transactions took place:

May   1   Issued 10,000 shares of common stock in exchange for $300,000 cash.
       2   Paid $7,500 for the rental of a furnished office for the months of May, June, and July; in addition, a $1,000 security deposit was made.
      2   Purchased four trucks from Mass Motors at a cost of $20,000 each. A cash down payment of $30,000 was made, with the balance to be paid in 90 days.
      4   Purchased office supplies for cash, $800.
    11   Billed customers $12,000 for trucking services performed by the company through May 10.
    14   Collected $10,000 in cash for services billed to customers.
    15   Paid salaries for the first half of the month, $3,000.
    22   Billed customers $23,000 for trucking services performed during the period from May 11–May 20.
    24   Collected $15,000 in cash for services billed to customers.
    26   Paid $10,000 cash to Mass Motors on amount still due on trucks purchased on May 2.
    28   Collected $12,000 in cash for services billed to customers.
    30   Received $1,200 cash from a customer as a prepayment for certain trucking services to be performed in June.
    31   Paid salaries for the second half of the month, $3,200.
    31   Billed customers $25,000 for trucking services performed during the period from May 21–May 31.

Additional information: The trucks purchased on May 2 from Mass Motors have an estimated useful life of five years. Depreciation charges are to be rounded to the nearest month. Also, a count of office supplies on May 31 shows that $500 of supplies have not yet been consumed.

REQUIRED

(a) Prepare journal entries to record each of the transactions for May listed above.

(b) Prepare any adjusting entries that are necessary at May 31, assuming that financial statements are to be prepared on that date for the month of May.

45. *Journalize Transactions and Adjusting Entries.*   Listed below are selected transactions and events affecting the Apple Company during the year ended December 31, 1988.

   (1) An insurance policy covering a two-year period was acquired for $1,800 on March 1, 1988. The policy covers the period March 1, 1988, to February 28, 1990.

   (2) At December 31, 1987, the Office Supplies account totaled $250. On June 2, 1988, office supplies were purchased on account, $800. At December 31, 1988, the office supplies remaining were counted and costed at $300.

   (3) A one-year service contract was sold to the B Company for $960 cash on August 1, 1988. The contract period extends from August 1, 1988, to July 31, 1989.

   (4) On November 1, 1988, rent of $12,000 was paid for the period from November 1, 1988–April 30, 1989.

   (5) On December 1, 1988, rent was collected in the amount of $24,000 for the period from December 1, 1988–March 31, 1989.

   (6) On November 1, 1988, a $5,000, 24%, three-month note payable was issued for cash. The principal and interest are due on the maturity date of the note.

   (7) At December 31, 1988, accrued wages amounted to $400. On January 4, 1989, the employees were paid $1,000, which included the accrued wages.

   (8) By December 31, 1988, fees amounting to $10,000 had been earned but had not been collected or recorded. These fees were subsequently collected on January 15, 1989.

   (9) On September 1, 1988, a $20,000, 12%, six-month note receivable was received for services performed; these services were billed on September 1, 1988. The principal and interest are to be collected on the note's due date.

  (10) By December 31, 1988, $3,000 of rent revenue had not been collected or recorded, even though it had been earned.

REQUIRED   Journalize the above transactions. Also, prepare any adjusting entries needed at December 31, 1988; the company closes its books annually on December 31.

46. *Journalize Transactions and Adjusting Entries.*   The following are transactions involving the Grape Company during the year ended December 31, 1988:

   (1) An insurance policy covering a one-year period was acquired for $6,000 cash on April 1, 1988. The policy covers the period from April 1, 1988–March 31, 1989.

(2) A one-year service contract was sold to the D Company for $48,000 cash on October 1, 1988. The contract period is from October 1, 1988–September 30, 1989.

(3) Accrued wages at December 31, 1988, amounted to $800. On January 2, 1989, the employees were paid $1,200, which included the accrued wages.

(4) The Office Supplies account began the period (January 1, 1988) with a $200 balance. On August 5, 1988, $400 of office supplies were purchased for cash. Per a count, $250 of office supplies remain on hand at December 31, 1988.

(5) By December 31, 1988, $12,000 of fees had been earned but not collected or recorded.

REQUIRED

(a) Prepare journal entries for all transactions described above that took place during the year.

(b) Prepare adjusting entries needed at December 31, 1988; the firm closes its books annually on December 31.

47. *Closing Entries.*   The following is a list of account balances at December 31, 1988, after adjustments, for the Truro Company:

Land	$400	Service Revenue	$270
Cash	360	Rental Expense	50
Interest Revenue	30	Retained Earnings,	
Supplies Expense	10	January 1, 1988	700
Supplies	40	Dividends	60
Wages Expense	80	Common Stock	100
Accounts Receivable	100		

REQUIRED   Record closing entries for the Truro Company on this date.

48. *Closing Entries.*   A listing of all the accounts in the Brattleboro Corporation's ledger along with accompanying balances on the last day of the accounting period are presented below. Accounts are listed in alphabetical order, even though they are in a different sequence in the ledger.

	Debit	Credit
Accounts Receivable	$ 35,000	
Accumulated Depreciation on Building		$ 40,000
Building	500,000	
Cash	20,000	
Common Stock		300,000
Depreciation Expense	20,000	
Dividends	7,000	
Insurance Expense	2,000	
Interest Expense	5,000	

	Debit	Credit
Prepaid Insurance	$4,500	
Prepaid Rent	1,500	
Rental Expense	6,000	
Retained Earnings		$142,500
Salary Expense	9,500	
Service Revenue		110,000
Unearned Service Revenue		18,000

REQUIRED

(a) Does the balance shown above for Retained Earnings represent the balance at the beginning of the period or at the end of the period? Explain.

(b) Prepare necessary year-end closing entries.

(c) What is the amount of Brattleboro Corporation's net income for the current period?

(d) What is the proper balance of Retained Earnings after closing entries have been posted?

49. *Analysis of Transactions, Adjustments, and Financial Statements (business already started).* Presented below is the trial balance for Company Z for the month ended November 30, 1988.

	Debit	Credit
Cash	$ 60,000	
Accounts Receivable	90,000	
Prepaid Insurance	25,000	
Equipment	150,000	
Accumulated Depreciation		$ 25,000
Accounts Payable		75,000
Accrued Taxes Payable		20,000
Common Stock		100,000
Retained Earnings		105,000
Totals	$325,000	$325,000

During the month of December, the following events took place:

Dec. 1 Received $18,000 cash in the mail for payment on previous month's sales.

7 Paid taxes in the amount of $20,000. These taxes were previously accrued in November.

10 Paid $20,000 on outstanding accounts payable.

11 Paid rent in the amount of $8,000. This payment represents rental expense for the period December–March.

14 Paid wages for the first two weeks of December in the amount of $5,000.

15 Purchased a new copy machine for $12,000. A down payment of $2,000 was made at the time of purchase, while the balance was financed with a loan at a 12% interest rate per year.

19 Received and paid a utility bill for the month of December in the amount of $800.

21 Billed customers for $15,000 of December services rendered to date.
28 Paid wages for the last two weeks of December in the amount of $5,000. December 28, 1988, was a Friday. Employees do not work weekends. An accrual for wages of $500 incurred on December 31, 1988, (a Monday) is necessary.
31 Declared and paid dividends in the amount of $.05 per share on 100,000 outstanding shares of capital stock.

Additional information:

(1) The existing equipment at November 30, 1988, has an estimated useful life of ten years.
(2) The new copy machine has an estimated useful life of five years.
(3) Prepaid insurance at November 30, 1988, represents a payment made in November for the period December 1–April 30.

REQUIRED

(a) Open up T accounts to show the beginning balances at December 1, 1988.
(b) Record the appropriate general journal entries in these T accounts.
(c) Prepare the necessary adjusting journal entries at December 31, 1988, and post them to the T accounts.
(d) Prepare a balance sheet and income statement at December 31, 1988.

50. *Preparation of Financial Statements.*   Presented below is the post-closing trial balance as of September 1, 1987, for the Tutor Consulting Company.

	Debit	Credit
Cash	$14,480	
Accounts Receivable	23,720	
Office Supplies	2,550	
Prepaid Rent	2,700	
Accrued Wages Payable		$ 1,700
Note Payable		25,000
Interest Payable		250
Paid-in Capital		10,000
Retained Earnings		6,500
Totals	$43,450	$43,450

The following transactions occurred during the month of September, 1987.

Sept. 2 Billed customers $1,950 for services performed.
3 Received fees for services not yet performed, $2,500.
8 Payment for $2,030 made for insurance policy effective October 1, 1987–September 30, 1988.
8 Purchased office supplies in the amount of $360.
9 Received payments on account, $9,640.
15 Paid dividends of $500 to owners.

15 Paid wages of $7,000; this includes $1,700 accrued wages payable from August 1987.
15 Received cash for performed services, $3,050.
20 Sold additional shares of stock to investors for $7,500.
21 Billed customers $10,750 for services performed.
22 Made principal payment of $2,000 on note payable.
22 Paid interest due of $250.
25 Received $5,440 payment on account.
30 One-sixth of prepaid rent expired.
30 A count of office supplies on hand reveals that $2,370 worth of items remain in stock.
30 Paid wages of $5,500 for work performed between September 16 and September 30.

REQUIRED

(a) Open T accounts from beginning trial balance.
(b) Record September transactions, opening T accounts as needed.
(c) Make any adjusting entries necessary.
(d) Prepare balance sheet and income statement as of September 30, 1987.

APPENDIX PROBLEMS

51. *Worksheet and Preparation of Financial Statements.* Company B had the following balances in its accounts at the close of business on June 30, 1988. Adjusting entries for June have not yet been made.

Cash	Accounts Receivable	Prepaid Insurance	Buildings
45,000	11,000	15,000	60,000

Accumulated Depreciation	Accounts Payable	Note Payable	Capital Stock
5,000	6,800	36,000	65,000

Rental Expense	Commissions Revenue	Wage Expense	Utilities Expense
15,000	36,700	3,000	500

Additional Information:

(1) The balance in the Prepaid Insurance account represents payment for the months of June, July, and August.

(2) Company B plans to purchase a new building in the month of July for
$100,000. It will be financed with a loan at 14%. The estimated useful
life of the building is 15 years.

(3) The estimated useful life of the building currently owned is 12 years.
Depreciation is recorded on a monthly basis.

(4) The note payable was financed at a 10% interest rate. Interest is paid
quarterly. The last interest payment was made on May 31, 1988.

(5) Wages were last paid on June 26; wages earned by employees for the
period from June 27 to June 30 is $400.

REQUIRED

(a) Prepare all necessary adjusting entries and post to T accounts.
(b) Using the T accounts, prepare a worksheet as shown on page 78 in
Appendix A.
(c) Prepare all necessary closing entries.

52. *Worksheet, Closing Entries, and Financial Statements (net income for period).*
Listed in alphabetical order on the worksheet below are titles of all accounts in the general ledger of the C Company. To the right of each account title in parentheses is the account's balance on the last day of the
fiscal year, after adjusting entries for the year have been posted.

C Company
Worksheet
For the Year Ended December 31, 1988

Account	Adjusted Trial Balance		Income Statement		Balance Sheet	
	dr.	cr.	dr.	cr.	dr.	cr.
Accounts Receivable ($25,000)						
Accumulated Depreciation ($5,000)						
Buildings ($55,000)						
Cash ($12,000)						
Common Stock ($62,000)						
Depreciation Expense ($2,500)						
Interest Expense ($800)						
Interest Payable ($800)						
Notes Payable ($10,000)						
Rental Expense ($8,000)						
Retained Earnings ($7,500)						
Revenue from Services Performed ($23,000)						
Unearned Revenue ($1,000)						
Wages Expense ($6,000)						

REQUIRED

(a) Complete the worksheet for the C Company. The first step is to write in balances in the adjusted trial balance set of columns. Assume all balances are normal balances.

(b) Prepare closing entries for the company.

(c) From the completed worksheet, prepare an income statement for the year ended December 31, 1988, and a balance sheet at December 31, 1988.

53. *Worksheet, Closing Entries, and Financial Statements (net loss for period).* Listed in alphabetical order on the worksheet below are titles of all accounts in the general ledger of the Timeweek Publishing Company. To the right of each account title in parentheses is the account's balance on the last day of the fiscal year, after adjusting entries for the year have been posted.

Timeweek Publishing Company
Worksheet
For the Year Ended December 31, 1988

Account	Adjusted Trial Balance		Income Statement		Balance Sheet	
	dr.	cr.	dr.	cr.	dr.	cr.
Accounts Receivable ($20,000)						
Accumulated Depreciation ($10,000)						
Cash ($40,000)						
Common Stock ($80,000)						
Depreciation Expense ($10,000)						
Interest Expense ($2,000)						
Interest Payable ($500)						
Notes Payable ($40,000)						
Printing Equipment ($60,000)						
Rental Expense ($10,000)						
Retained Earnings ($5,500)						
Revenue from Subscriptions ($30,000)						
Salary Expense ($25,000)						
Unearned Subscription Revenue ($1,000)						

REQUIRED

(a) Complete the worksheet for the Timeweek Publishing Company. The first step is to write in balances in the adjusted trial balance set of columns. Assume all balances are normal balances.

(b) Prepare closing entries for the company.

(c) From the completed worksheet, prepare an income statement for the year ended December 31, 1988, and a balance sheet at December 31, 1988.

FINANCIAL REPORTING

Income Measurement and the Income Statement

Chapter 3 is divided into two parts. The first part contains a conceptual discussion of income and its measurement. This discussion includes coverage of the reasons that we measure income, the distinction between economic and accounting income, the elements of the income statement, and the criteria for recognizing revenue and expense.

The second part of the chapter focuses on three main sections of the income statement: reporting of recurring operations, reporting of nonrecurring operations, and earnings-per-share disclosures. Three different types of business enterprises (a merchandising firm, a manufacturing firm, and a service firm) are used to illustrate the reporting of income from recurring operations.

REASONS FOR MEASURING INCOME

Information concerning the composition and amount of periodic income is used in a variety of decisions relating to the business enterprise.

- Managers use income numbers in evaluating the success of past efforts; in negotiating with labor; in determining corporate dividend policy; and in planning future financing, investing, and operating strategies.
- Governmental agencies rely on income numbers as a basis for taxation and regulation.
- Creditors consider the level and volatility of income in making lending decisions.
- Investors use income numbers in assessing securities risk and return.

Income serves both as a measure of past performance and as a primary information source in predicting cash flows. The importance of cash flow prediction — and its relationship with income — has been emphasized by the FASB in its Conceptual Framework Study. With regard to the overall objectives of accounting, the FASB has stated that "... financial reporting should provide information to help investors, creditors, and others assess the amounts, timing, and uncertainty of prospective net cash inflows to the related enterprise."[1] Some accounting theorists see a potential conflict between this future-oriented objective and the objective of using income as a measure of past performance. This is because a variety of different income measures may be computed using generally accepted accounting principles, and the income measure that seems most useful in cash flow prediction will not necessarily be the one most useful in assessing past performance.

Given the wide relevance of income numbers, it should not be surprising that the concept of income means different things to different people. The next section contrasts economic income and accounting income.

ECONOMIC INCOME AND ACCOUNTING INCOME

From a theoretical perspective, most analysts (including accountants) agree that the concept of economic income is superior to that of accounting income. Application of the economic income concept in the business world, however, poses serious measurement problems. Since economic income depends on estimates of future cash flows, its calculation is often very subjective. Consequently, different people may arrive at very different estimates of the firm's economic income. The measurement of accounting income, on the other hand, is usually defended as being more objective. Knowing what is meant by economic income should provide a better frame of reference for understanding the strengths and limitations of accounting income.

---

[1] *Statement of Financial Accounting Concepts No. 1,* "Objectives of Financial Reporting by Business Enterprises" (Stamford, CT: FASB, 1978), pp. 17–18.

Economic Income

Economists define income as an increase in wealth (or well-offness) during a period of time. In applying this notion to a business entity, one might define income as the maximum amount of net assets or capital that a firm could distribute to its owners during a period while maintaining the same amount of capital it had at the start of the period. This definition assumes no changes in paid-in capital and no dividend declarations during the period; such changes are called **capital transactions,** and adjustment must be made for them if they occur. If the business entity has no changes in paid-in capital and declares no dividends, income is equal to the increase in net assets during the period.

To apply this general concept of economic income, agreement must be reached on two rules: (1) how to value net assets and (2) how to define capital maintenance. Asset valuation rules and capital maintenance rules are subjects of considerable controversy among economists as well as among accountants. Much of the disagreement stems from the fact that different rules for valuing assets and/or maintaining capital will produce different measurements of income.

Valuing net assets   The economic value of net assets depends on the future cash flows expected to be earned by those assets. Because cash flows expected at future dates are worth less today due to uncertainty and the time value of money, it is necessary to discount the future cash flows in order to compute their *present values.*[2] The economic value of net assets may then be defined as the present value of these future cash flows.

Practical application of this asset valuation rule presents several problems. As we mentioned earlier, assessing the present value of future cash flows is very subjective; different people, because of differing expectations and aversions to risk, are likely to arrive at markedly dissimilar valuations. In addition, the present value of the firm's net assets is not simply the sum of the present values of the firm's individual assets and liabilities. We would expect, given that there is economic justification for the firm's existence, that the present value of the net assets in combination is greater than their separate present values.

Maintaining capital   Income is the result of an increase in the value of net assets during a period, after adjustment for capital transactions. Thus, the value of net assets, or capital, used in a firm's operations, must first be maintained before it is possible to have income. This general concept is referred to as **capital maintenance.**

---

[2] The time value of money and the related concept of present value will be developed in Chapter 5, but a simple example should suffice at this point. Assume you deposit $100 in a bank today and earn interest on that money at an annual rate of 5 percent. At the end of one year you would have earned $5 in interest ($100 × 5%) and your balance would be $105. The fact that $100 invested today can grow to more than $100 in the future illustrates the time value of money. Moreover, in this example, the present value of $105 one year from now is $100; that is the amount of money that must be invested in the present at 5 percent interest to have $105 at one year from the present.

A specific capital maintenance rule is needed, however, because of changing prices. If all prices were stable, the difference between the value of net assets at the beginning and end of the period, exclusive of capital transactions, would be a valid measure of the period's income. But prices are not stable; both the *general* level of prices and the *relative* prices of individual goods and services change over time. This gives rise to various possible capital maintenance rules. Three popular alternatives are presented below:

1. **Dollar capital.**   Under this rule, capital is maintained as long as the dollar value of the firm's net assets has not diminished during the period.
2. **General purchasing power of capital.**   Under this rule, capital is maintained as long as the general purchasing power of the firm's net assets has not diminished during the period.
3. **Replacement cost of capital.**   Under this rule, capital is maintained as long as the net assets at the end of the period are sufficient to replace, at current costs, the firm's beginning-of-the-period net assets.

To illustrate the effect of these alternative capital maintenance rules on the calculation of periodic income, consider the following case. Hicks Company's net assets were valued at $20 million on January 1, 1988, and at $24 million on December 31, 1988; there were no paid-in capital changes and no dividends to shareholders during the year. The rate of inflation in the general level of prices was 8 percent, but the replacement cost of the specific net assets owned by Hicks at January 1, 1988, decreased by 5 percent during the year.

Each of the three capital maintenance rules described above will produce a different income measure, as shown in Exhibit 3-1.

This case demonstrates that income measurement requires both a net asset valuation rule and a capital maintenance rule. Here, the net asset valuation rule was the same for all three cases. However, different capital maintenance rules produced different earnings numbers. Many economists may agree on how to value net assets and yet fail to reach agreement on how to measure maintenance of capital.[3] If so, they are unlikely to agree on how to measure income.

Accounting Income

Accountants must also adopt both an asset valuation rule and a capital maintenance rule in order to measure the income of an enterprise. While a number of different asset valuation rules are used in financial accounting, most assets are valued at their historical cost. A discussion of asset valuation rules included in GAAP is presented in Chapter 5. Accountants understand that the economic value of net assets is derived from expected future cash flows. Yet in most

---

[3]In other words, the method used to value assets is not necessarily the method to be used in maintaining capital. For example, constant dollar adjustments can be used with dollar capital maintenance or replacement capital maintenance. These ideas are developed in Chapter 11.

Exhibit 3-1

Calculation of Net Income Using Different Capital Maintenance Rules

Hicks Company

1. Dollar capital maintenance rule:

Net assets, January 1, 1988	$20,000,000
Net assets, December 31, 1988	24,000,000
Increase in net assets, or net income	$ 4,000,000

2. General purchasing power capital maintenance rule:

Net assets, January 1, 1988	$20,000,000
Adjustment factor for inflation	× 1.08
	$21,600,000
Net assets, December 31, 1988	24,000,000
Increase in net assets, or net income	$ 2,400,000

3. Replacement cost capital maintenance rule:

Net assets, January 1, 1988	$20,000,000
Adjustment factor for replacement cost	× .95
	$19,000,000
Net assets, December 31, 1988	24,000,000
Increase in net assets, or net income	$ 5,000,000

cases economic values that exceed historical costs are not entered in the accounting records. The reason is that such changes in value have not been captured, or **realized**, by the firm. On the other hand, when economic values decline below historical costs, accountants will often apply a **lower of cost or market value** (**LCM**) rule and reduce the accounting valuation of the assets affected. These accounting conventions are often defended as being objective and conservative.

The capital maintenance rule adopted by accountants is maintenance of dollar capital. Generally, neither changes in the general level of prices nor changes in the replacement costs of a firm's assets enter into the calculation of periodic accounting income. Rather than rely primarily on direct valuation of net assets at the beginning and end of the period (as we did in calculating economic income), changes in net assets are measured throughout the period as transactions take place and are recorded. Those transactions that result in revenue, expense, gain, and loss are used in determining accounting income. Generally, the **exchange price,** or historical cost, agreed on between independent parties to a transaction is used to represent the value of the inflow or outflow of assets and is accepted as the proper measure of the revenue or expense involved in the transaction. Exhibit 3-2 shows the major steps in the sequence followed in using a **transaction-oriented approach** to calculate accounting income.

Exhibit 3-2

**The Transaction-oriented Approach to
Measuring Accounting Income**

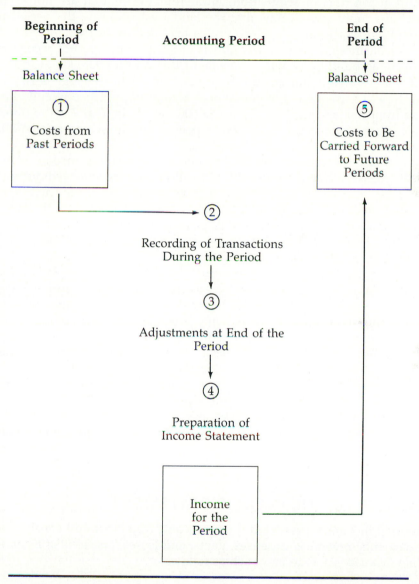

Accountants realize that changes in the value of net assets take place when economic events other than transactions occur. Nevertheless, these "other events" are generally ignored because the amount of the value change is usually not based on objective, verifiable evidence, as is the case with completed exchange transactions.

Consider, for instance, a situation in which land is purchased by a realtor for $10,000 at the beginning of Year 1 and sold at the end of Year 2 for $18,000. The purchase price in the initial exchange transaction, $10,000, is used to value the land at the time of acquisition. Numerous events that are not exchange transactions could conceivably alter the land's value during the period under consideration. For example, interest rates may decline or the land may be re-zoned for business purposes. The effects of such events are not recognized in measuring accounting income. The sale of the land for $18,000 at the end of Year 2 *is* an exchange transaction, however, and a value change is recognized at that time. Consequently, conventional accounting practice would show no income from the land for Year 1, and $8,000 income in Year 2—the difference between the historical cost of $10,000 (expense) and the selling price of $18,000 (revenue).

It should be clear from this illustration that accounting income is not de-signed to measure changes in wealth (or well-offness) experienced during a pe-riod of time. The realtor may very well have been better off at the end of the first year than at its beginning due to appreciation in the value of the land. Yet, because no exchange transaction took place during Year 1 after the land was purchased, increases in the land's value were not recorded, and accounting in-come for Year 1 was reported as zero.

Accountants do not have a conceptual definition of income, only an opera-tional one: accounting income is the excess of recorded revenues and gains over expenses and losses for a period. The key to understanding what is meant by accounting income, then, is knowing the rules used for recognizing reve-nue, expense, gain, and loss. Recognizing revenue customarily precedes recog-nizing expense. Once revenues are recognized for a particular period, attempts are made to assign to that same period the expenses incurred in generating those revenues. The objective is to present efforts (expenses) and related ac-complishments (revenues) in the same reporting period. Revenue recognition is guided by the realization principle, and expense recognition is based upon the matching principle. After a discussion of the nature of revenues, expenses, gains, and losses, the principles of realization and matching will be examined more closely.

ELEMENTS OF THE INCOME STATEMENT

Accounting income is presented on the income statement and consists of four basic elements: revenues, expenses, gains, and losses. *Statement of Financial Ac-counting Concepts No. 6* defines each as follows:

REVENUES—Inflows or other enhancements of assets of an entity or settlements of its liabilities (or a combination of both) during a period from delivering or producing goods, rendering services, or other activities that constitute the entity's ongoing major or central operations.

EXPENSES—Outflows or other uses of assets or incurrences of liabilities (or a combination of both) during a period from delivering or producing goods, rendering services, or carrying out other activities that constitute the entity's ongoing major or central operations.

GAINS—Increases in equity (net assets) from peripheral or incidental transactions of an entity and from all other transactions and other events and circumstances affecting the entity during a period except those that result from revenues or investments by owners.

LOSSES—Decreases in equity (net assets) from peripheral or incidental transactions of an entity and from all other transactions and other events and circumstances affecting the entity during a period except those that result from expenses or distributions to owners.[4]

Consideration of the timing of recognition of these elements, how they should be measured, and how they should be displayed is purposely omitted from the above definitions. This allows one to concentrate on the *nature* of each element. Notice that revenues and expenses relate to the entity's central and ongoing operations, while gains and losses are associated with peripheral activities. Revenues and gains are similar in that both represent increases in net assets. Expenses and losses, in contrast, represent decreases in net assets.

While revenues and expenses relate to the major profit-directed activities of the enterprise, they may take many forms. Some common types of revenues are sales, fees, rents, dividends, and interest earned. Common expenses include costs of goods sold, depreciation, salaries, rent, interest incurred, and taxes.

An example of the peripheral activities associated with the gains and losses of the firm is the sale of a used delivery truck by a furniture store. The store's primary objective is to generate income from the sale of furniture, not from disposing of its used equipment. If the delivery truck is sold for more than its value on the books, a gain is recorded; if it is sold for less than book value, there is a loss.

REVENUE AND EXPENSE RECOGNITION

Generally, revenue is "earned" in stages as the joint result of an entire series of operating activities. Examples of such activities include purchasing, manufacturing, selling, delivering and servicing goods, and collecting cash from sales. This series of income-related activities is referred to as the **earnings process.** In a broad economic sense, each activity in this process contributes to the generation of revenue.

It is important to understand, however, that there is a difference between (1) what revenue is and (2) the rules established in financial accounting for determining when revenue is to be recognized. Even though the nature of revenue is such that it is "earned" in a more or less continuous manner throughout the earnings process, accountants have traditionally recognized revenue at a single point, or critical event, within this process. In accordance with the

---

[4]*Statement of Financial Accounting Concepts No. 6,* "Elements of Financial Statements of Business Enterprises" (Stamford, CT: FASB, 1985), paragraphs 78, 80, and 82–83.

realization principle, *both* of the following conditions must be met before revenue is recognized:

1. Substantially all of the effort (and cost) necessary to generate the revenue should be complete.
2. The net amount to be received (the exchange value) should be measurable with reasonable objectivity.

While there may be disagreement over the actual application of the principle of realization in certain situations, a strict interpretation is as follows: until an economic resource has been sold or exchanged in a transaction between two independent people (that is, in an arms-length transaction), changes in its value may not be reflected in the financial statements.

Revenue Recognition at the Point of Sale

Under the accrual basis of accounting, the critical point at which the two conditions listed above are usually met is the point of sale, which of course need not coincide with the time that cash is collected.

For a firm selling goods, recognizing revenue at the time of sale has many desirable attributes. At the time of sale, title passes to the buyer and the goods are transferred. Apart from collectibility of receivables and possible obligations for guarantees, there is no longer any doubt about the revenues and expenses associated with the sale. In sum, the earnings process is virtually complete.

Unlike the sale of merchandise, the rendering of services (medical, legal, and the like) does not involve the delivery of goods or the transfer of title. In such cases, a transaction is said to be complete after the particular service is rendered and is billable.

Expense Recognition: the Matching Process

Once revenues are recognized for a particular period, the related expenses must also be recognized; this process is termed **matching**. If all related expenses are not matched against revenues, reported income for the period is overstated. All recorded costs must eventually become expenses (or losses) to be matched against revenues on the income statement. As a result, an overstatement of income in one period would eventually cause an understatement of income in some other period(s).

Exhibit 3-3 shows the two possible paths that costs may take in the matching process. The first path is followed when a cost is incurred that will benefit more than one accounting period, such as the purchase of a multi-year insurance policy. In this case, the cost is not recognized immediately as an expense but is **capitalized** and deferred initially as an asset. The second path is more direct; the cost becomes an expense when it is incurred.

Regardless of which path is followed, the basis for determining cost is the same; it is the amount of cash or cash equivalent given up in an arms-length

Exhibit 3-3

**Possible Paths that Costs Take in
the Matching Process**

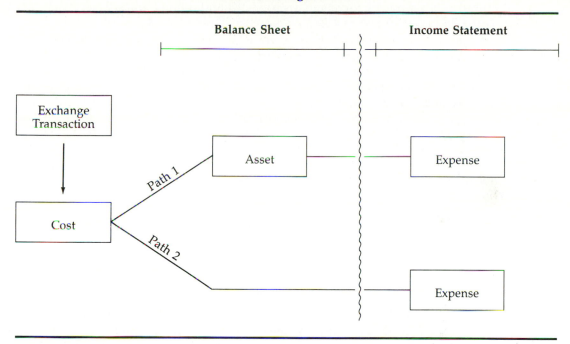

exchange transaction.[5] This is referred to as the **cost principle,** and it will be discussed again in conjunction with asset valuation in Chapter 5.

Expenses of a particular period are expired costs that can be directly associated with revenue of the period; can be associated with the period but not related directly to revenue recognized in the period; or cannot be associated, as a practical matter, with any future period. Costs that fall into the first two classifications are often recorded initially as assets; those costs in the third category are normally expensed immediately.

The FASB has identified three bases for recognizing expenses. These bases are labeled associating cause and effect, systematic and rational allocation, and immediate recognition.

Associating cause and effect   Under this classification there is a direct association between certain expenses and revenues. An example is the relationship between sales revenue and cost of goods sold. It is clear in this case that both the expense and revenue belong in the same period.

---

[5]Sometimes the consideration given up in an exchange transaction is not cash, but a noncash item such as property or stock. In such cases, the cash equivalent is the amount of cash that would be required if cash had in fact been used instead of the property or stock.

Systematic and rational allocation   Some costs clearly benefit more than one period but are not directly associated with specific revenues. Even though a direct relationship does not exist, it is often reasonable to allocate such costs to a number of periods by means of a systematic and rational formula. An example is the allocation of the cost of a delivery truck over the period of its useful life; this process of cost allocation is referred to as **depreciation**. The straight-line method of depreciation is the simplest formula. Under straight-line depreciation an equal amount of the cost of the delivery truck is allocated to each year of the truck's estimated useful life. Straight-line depreciation is based on the assumption that the truck is responsible for generating approximately an equal amount of revenue each period. (A detailed treatment of depreciation methods is included in Chapter 4.)

Immediate recognition   Some costs fall into neither one of the two categories examined in the preceding paragraphs. These costs are expensed in the period in which they are paid or incurred. Examples include virtually all selling, administrative, and general expenses. The principle of immediate recognition also applies to costs from previous periods carried in asset accounts and deemed to have no future value. An example is a patent that is determined to be worthless because of some new invention.

Revenue Recognition at Other than the Time of Sale

The strict interpretation of the realization principle presented on page 110 states, in effect, that revenue should be recognized only when validated by a sale. However, because of extenuating circumstances, such as the need for timely information or the existence of unusual uncertainties, revenues may be recognized at points in the earnings process other than the time of sale. Strict adherence to the realization principle, for instance, might adversely affect the timeliness of reported information for companies that undertake long-term construction contracts.

The main alternatives to "other than the time of sale" are to recognize revenue (1) during production, (2) at the end of production, or (3) at the time of collection. The following illustrations present circumstances that justify each of these alternatives.

Revenue recognition during production   In 1982 the then-aging cable-car system in San Francisco was shut down for two years for extensive repairs. Should the company responsible for this long-term project have been forced to wait until the project's completion before recognizing any revenue? From a pragmatic standpoint, the answer is no; to wait would have made quarterly or annual income statements for this firm of little use to investors, creditors, and other interested parties. Accordingly, departure from a strict interpretation of the realization principle is recommended here, with revenues recognized on a percentage-of-completion basis, provided the remaining costs to complete and the percentage of completion to date can be estimated with reasonable accuracy. This procedure is demonstrated later in this section.

Revenue recognition at the end of production   In some cases, the remaining costs to complete a project or the amount of sales revenue to be realized cannot be estimated with reasonable accuracy until the project is completed and approved by the customer. If such circumstances exist, revenue recognition should be deferred until the end of the production process.

Revenue recognition at the time of collection   Another special case occurs when unusual uncertainties surround the earnings process. When goods are sold on credit, revenue is normally recognized at the point of sale, because the likelihood of collection of the receivable can be estimated with reasonable certainty. Suppose, however, that the receivables from credit sales are to be collected over an extended period and there is no reasonable basis for estimating collectibility. In this *exceptional* case, revenue should be recognized over the period in which the cash is collected, rather than at the point of sale.

ILLUSTRATIVE CASE: NETWORK SYSTEMS, INCORPORATED

To demonstrate revenue recognition at various points in the earnings process, consider the projected revenues and costs for the manufacture and installation of a computerized taxi-dispatch system, as described in Exhibit 3-4. The manufacturer, Network Systems, Incorporated, developed the system after extensive research and development activities performed during 1985 and 1986. A contract was signed with Blackguard Taxi Company in December 1986 for a system to be built during the period from 1987 through 1989, and installed during the first quarter of 1990. The system will be paid for in installments during 1989 and 1990, and Network Systems provides a five-year warranty for parts and labor, which expires in December 1994.

The earnings process described in Exhibit 3-4 has several distinct elements:

1. Research and development, or R&D (1985 and 1986)
2. Contract signing, or point of sale (1986)
3. Manufacture (1987–1989)
4. Installation (1990)
5. Collection of sales proceeds (1989 and 1990)
6. Warranty service (1990–1994)

Excluding the cost of R&D, the contract with Blackguard Taxi is projected to earn net income of $320,000 for Network Systems ($1.2 million in revenues, less $880,000 in total expenses). Because immediate expensing of research and development costs is required by the FASB, Network Systems' R&D costs were expensed as incurred during 1985 and 1986. The company expects to earn sufficient income on subsequent contracts, however, to justify these R&D expenses.

Network Systems will incur costs each year from 1987–1994, as the system is manufactured, installed, and maintained pursuant to the warranty. Cash proceeds from sales will be received during 1989 and 1990. Since the firm must

Exhibit 3-4

**Blackguard Taxi Company Contract:
Projected Costs and Revenues**

Contract price		
Collection schedule:		
$300,000 each six months,		
beginning on June 30, 1989,		
and ending on December 31, 1990		$1,200,000
Projected expenses		
Manufacturing costs:		
$300,000 during 1987, $180,000 during 1988, and		
$120,000 during 1989	$(600,000)	
Installation costs:		
January through March, 1990	(130,000)	
Warranty services:		
$30,000 each year, 1990		
through 1994	(150,000)	
Total expenses		(880,000)
Projected profit*		$ 320,000

*Research and development expenses charged to expense during 1985 and 1986 totaled $960,000 and are not considered above in calculating projected profit of $320,000. Network Systems expects to contract with other taxi companies for similar installations in the future, which will help to off-set these R&D expenses.

prepare financial statements at various dates during this earnings process, it must decide when to reflect the projected income on the income statement. We will consider the recognition of income at the time of (1) contract signing, (2) manufacture, and (3) collection of sales proceeds.

Recognize income when the contract is signed   Advocates of the view that income be recognized when the contract is signed would argue that the critical event for Network Systems is a successful project proposal resulting in a signed contract. As long as the revenues are fixed by contract, and the contract's expenses are reasonably predictable, these advocates would maintain that earnings should be recognized at the time of signing.

Various firms, including health clubs, computer-leasing companies, and real estate development firms, used this method to record earnings on long-term contracts, and during the 1960s the practice came to be known as **front-loading.** In many of these cases it became apparent with the passage of time that the earnings projections were too high, and the firms were forced to record large losses in subsequent years. If Network Systems used this approach, their entire projected earnings would be included in net income for 1986 by the following entry:

Dec. 31   dr.   Accounts Receivable (Blackguard Taxi)   1,200,000
            cr.   Estimated Completion Costs on
                     Existing Contracts   880,000
            cr.   Operating Income   320,000

On the 1986 financial statements, the account receivable would appear as an asset; the estimated completion costs would appear as a liability; and the entire operating income would be included in earnings for 1986.

As we have seen, proponents of this method of recognizing income argue that the "critical event" in the earnings process is the signing with a customer. They maintain that since the revenues are fixed by contract and the expenses can reasonably be estimated, there is no need to postpone recognition of earnings.

Those who oppose this method counter that the selling firm has substantial performance obligations in periods subsequent to the contract signing, so that the critical event has not yet been completed. Moreover, critics argue that uncertainties may exist concerning estimated costs of fulfilling the contract, and/or the ultimate collectibility of the contract revenues.

Recognize income as the system is being manufactured   The second method, termed **percentage of completion,** recognizes income while work on a contract progresses. The completion percentage is usually computed based on the costs incurred to date as a percentage of total estimated contract costs. If, for instance, 40 percent of the total estimated contract costs have been incurred to date, then it is assumed that the project is 40 percent complete. The FASB prefers the percentage-of-completion approach for construction-type contracts, as long as there are reasonably dependable estimates of the costs to complete and of the total costs incurred to date.

To apply the percentage-of-completion method to the Blackguard Taxi contract, the contract costs must be summarized by accounting period. Using Exhibit 3-4, the following summary is prepared:

	(1) Estimated Manufacturing Costs	(2) Percent of Total Costs	(3) Cumulative Percent
1987	$300,000	50%	50%
1988	180,000	30%	80%
1989	120,000	20%	100%
	$600,000	100%	

It is common practice for equipment manufacturers to exclude warranty and installation costs in computing completion percentages. Accordingly, the total estimated manufacturing costs for the project are $600,000. Percentages listed in column (2) above are calculated by dividing the manufacturing costs for each year by the total estimated manufacturing costs for the project (in this case, $600,000). These percentages represent the portion of the project completed in each given year. Percentages listed in column (3) (labeled "Cumulative Percent") represent the portion of the project completed since the beginning of the manufacturing process.

Applying the completion percentages for individual years to the Blackguard Taxi contract results in an allocation of the total earnings of $320,000 to the three years during which the taxi dispatch system was manufactured—1987–1989. Thus, using the percentage-of-completion approach, $160,000 (50 percent of $320,000) of total earnings would be recognized in 1987, $96,000 (30 percent of $320,000) would be recognized in 1988, and $64,000 (20 percent of $320,000) would be recognized in 1989. This is summarized as follows:

	(1) Estimated Manufacturing Costs	(2) Completion Percentage	(3) Allocation of Total Earnings of $320,000
1987	$300,000	50%	$160,000
1988	180,000	30%	96,000
1989	120,000	20%	64,000
	$600,000	100%	$320,000

When the contract is completed, the firm would record a liability for installation and warranty services, based on the estimated costs of those activities.

Revision of estimated costs to complete   In the preceding illustration, there was no change in the estimated earnings during the manufacturing period. Often, however, estimates of costs or revenues are changed as construction progresses, and the resulting change in estimated earnings is assigned to the current and future periods.

To illustrate, assume that Network Systems realizes in 1988 (the second year of the three-year production process) that its original estimate of manufacturing costs for the project was too high. While its original estimate of the project's total manufacturing costs was $600,000, in 1988 its revised estimate of total manufacturing costs is only $560,000. This change in estimate by year is summarized below.

	Manufacturing Costs		
	Original Estimate	Revised Estimate	Difference
1987	$300,000	$300,000	0
1988	180,000	156,000	$24,000
1989	120,000	104,000	16,000
	$600,000	$560,000	$40,000

As a result of this $40,000 cost revision, the actual profit on the project is now estimated to be $360,000, rather than the $320,000 originally projected.

If this cost revision and resulting increase in estimated earnings on the project of $40,000 could have been foreseen from the beginning, a different amount of profit would have been recognized on the company's books in 1987 than was actually recorded. For financial accounting purposes, however, changes in accounting estimates do *not* result in retroactive changes to previously issued financial statements. Instead, such changes in estimates are handled prospectively—that is, in the current and future periods. Accordingly, the $160,000 profit that was recognized prior to 1988 is *not* changed for reporting purposes. However, the $200,000 profit on the project not previously recognized (revised estimate of total profit of $360,000 less $160,000 profit recognized in 1987) is allocated to the current and future periods of the project.

The revised cost estimates for 1988 and 1989 are used in making this allocation. New completion percentages are calculated by dividing revised estimates of manufacturing costs for each remaining year of the project by the total manufacturing costs estimated for all remaining years [see column (2) below]. Assuming no additional changes in estimates, the remaining earnings on the project ($200,000) are allocated by multiplying $200,000 by these new completion percentages.

	(1) Remaining Manufacturing Costs	(2) Percent of Total Remaining Manufacturing Costs	(3) Allocation of Remaining Earnings of $200,000
1988	$156,000	156/260 = 60%	$120,000
1989	104,000	104/260 = 40%	80,000
	$260,000	100%	$200,000

Recognize income as revenues are collected   The third approach, termed the **installment sales method,** recognizes earnings based on the total revenues collected to date. For the Blackguard Taxi contract, projected net income of $320,000 would be divided equally between the years 1989 and 1990, because half of the proceeds are to be received in each of those years. This approach gained popularity due to its acceptability in certain cases for federal income tax calculations. Firms using the installment sales method for financial accounting argued that uncertainty regarding the ultimate collectibility of contract proceeds justified the approach. However, with certain exceptions, GAAP do not allow the use of the installment sales method for purposes of income recognition. Appropriate methods of allowing for uncollectible accounts are presented in Chapter 5.

The preceding discussion has considered three potential patterns of income recognition for the Blackguard Taxi contract, and a number of alternatives might be suggested with some justification. For example, it may seem unrealistic to assign no portion of the income to the research and development (R&D) phase of the earnings process. Prior to 1974, many research-active firms would record R&D costs as an asset, or **capitalize** these costs in order to match them against their expected future benefits. This practice was disallowed by the FASB because of the difficulty in predicting the amount and timing of future benefits.

It is well to recognize that any attempt to assign income to an accounting period shorter than that of the full earnings cycle must be arbitrary to some extent. There are many situations in financial accounting when a single result, such as net income, must be apportioned among multiple causes, such as stages in the earnings process. The problem is shown schematically in Exhibit 3-5.

As depicted in Exhibit 3-5a., net income is a single output from multiple inputs. There is no problem in assigning net income to the entire set of inputs, but difficulties arise when we need to assign income to *individual* inputs.[6] A similar problem is depicted in Exhibit 3-5b., where the cost of a single input (for example, a long-lived asset, such as a building or a piece of equipment) must be assigned to many individual outputs (accounting periods, in this case). Both of the situations shown in Exhibit 3-5 create a need for allocations that cannot be based on strict cause and effect relationships. The allocation problem underlies many areas of dispute in financial accounting, and we will return to the topic at numerous points in this text.

INCOME REPORTING

The first part of this chapter discusses economic and accounting concepts of income, and general criteria for recognizing revenues and expenses. Now we will apply the accounting concepts discussed thus far to the reporting of income on the income statement.

REPORTING OF RECURRING OPERATIONS

Exhibit 3-6 shows the major sections and overall organization of the income statement and provides the frame of reference for the discussion of income reporting. Observe that the shaded portion of Exhibit 3-6 refers to the reporting of recurring operations. Recurring operations are reported separately from nonrecurring operations to aid in the prediction of future events, particularly future earnings and cash flows. The discussion in this section will concentrate on the reporting of recurring operations for three major types of business enterprise: a merchandising firm, a manufacturing firm, and a service firm.

Income of a Merchandising Firm

Merchandising firms sell goods in essentially the same form in which they are acquired. Examples of such firms include department stores, specialty shops, wholesalers, and distributors.

Income statements of merchandising firms contain the following main components: sales revenue; cost of goods sold; gross margin; selling, general, and administrative expenses; and income taxes. While the income statements

---

[6]This assumes that we have agreed on asset valuation and capital maintenance rules, as discussed earlier in this chapter.

Exhibit 3-5

The Allocation Problem

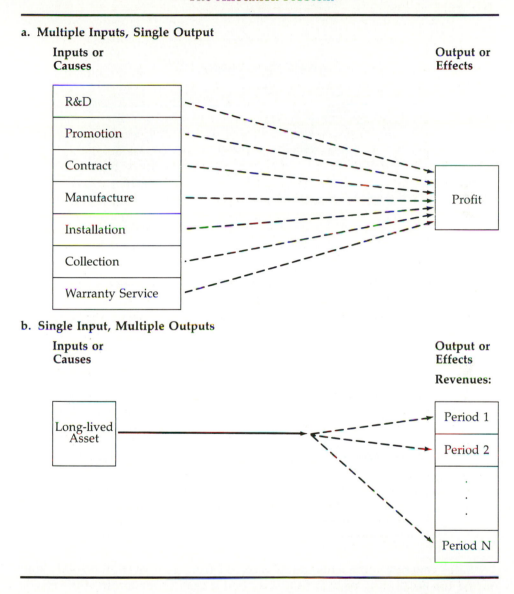

a. Multiple Inputs, Single Output

Inputs or Causes

Output or Effects

R&D
Promotion
Contract
Manufacture
Installation
Collection
Warranty Service

Profit

b. Single Input, Multiple Outputs

Inputs or Causes

Output or Effects

Revenues:

Long-lived Asset

Period 1
Period 2
. . .
Period N

of virtually all merchandising firms include these components, there is some variation in the format and terminology used. The income statement included in the 1985 annual report of the Walgreen Company is representative of such statements and is reproduced in Exhibit 3-7. The Walgreen Company operates a chain of drugstores in the United States and Puerto Rico.

Exhibit 3-6

Sections of the Income Statement

Recurring Operations

A. Revenues and expenses from principal operations
Sales revenue
Cost of goods sold
Gross margin
Selling, general, and administrative expenses
B. Revenues and expenses from secondary activities, and gains and losses that are infrequent or unusual, but not both
Other revenues and gains
Other expenses and losses
C. Income tax expense related to the above activities

INCOME AFTER TAX FROM RECURRING OPERATIONS

Nonrecurring Operations

D. Revenues, expenses, gains, and losses from nonrecurring activities or situations (all shown net of income tax)
Discontinued operations
Extraordinary items
Cumulative effect of changes in accounting principles

NET INCOME

E. Earnings-per-share disclosures

Sales revenue represents assets received from customers for goods sold during the accounting period. Sales may be for cash or on credit. If the sale is for cash, the entry is as follows:

    dr.   Cash   XXX
          cr.   Sales   XXX

If the sale is on credit, the entry is

dr. Accounts Receivable XXX
   cr. Sales XXX

Note in Exhibit 3-7 that sales revenue in Walgreen Company's income statement is labeled "Net Sales" and totals $3,161,935 (in thousands).

Cost of goods sold represents the cost to the seller of items sold to customers during the period. Cost of goods sold is calculated as follows:

Inventory at beginning of period	$XXX
Plus: Additions to inventory during the period	XXX
Cost of goods available for sale	$XXX
Less: Inventory at end of period	(XXX)
Cost of goods sold	$XXX

Exhibit 3-7

Income Reporting for a Merchandising Firm

Walgreen Co. and Subsidiaries
Consolidated Statement of Earnings
For the Year Ended August 31, 1985

(in thousands, except per-share data)

Net Sales		$3,161,935
Costs and Deductions	Cost of sales	2,192,367
	Selling, occupancy, and administration	791,697
		2,984,064
Other Expense (Income)	Interest expense	5,922
	Interest income	(1,751)
	Gains from sale of assets	–
		4,171
Earnings	Earnings from U.S. operations before income taxes	173,700
	Income taxes	79,531
	Earnings from U.S. operations	94,169
	Equity in net earnings of Mexican operations	–
	Gain on sale of equity investments in Mexican operations, net of income taxes	–
	Net earnings	$ 94,169
Net Earnings per Common Share		$ 1.53

Source: Walgreen Company, *Annual Report*, 1985.

Cost of goods sold for the Walgreen Company (in thousands of dollars) is shown in Exhibit 3-7 as $2,192,367 and is labeled "Cost of sales." Relevant data (in thousands) for this calculation not shown in Exhibit 3-7 include inventory at the beginning of the period, $406,190; inventory purchases during the period, $2,245,435; and inventory at the end of the period, $459,258. The computations are presented below.

	(in thousands)
Inventory at beginning of period	$ 406,190
Plus: Purchases	2,245,435
Total available for sale	$2,651,625
Less: Inventory at end of period	(459,258)
Cost of goods sold	$2,192,367

Gross margin is the difference between reported sales revenue and cost of goods sold. It is the seller's "buffer" from which other expenses must be met before it is possible to have net income. In Exhibit 3-7, the Walgreen Company does not show gross margin on a separate income statement line. However, Walgreen Company's gross margin of $969,568 can be determined easily by subtracting reported cost of goods sold ($2,192,367) from reported net sales ($3,161,935).

The percentage relationship between gross margin and sales revenue is termed the **gross margin percentage,** and is computed as follows:

$$\text{Gross Margin Percentage} = \frac{\text{Gross Margin}}{\text{Sales}}$$

The Walgreen Company's gross margin percentage in 1985 is 30.7 percent ($969,568/$3,161,935). Declines in the gross margin percentage may indicate reductions in sales prices, increases in unit costs for goods purchased, or changes in the sales mix (selling proportionately more goods possessing low gross margin percentages and/or less goods with high gross margin percentages). The ability of a merchandising firm to meet its selling, general, and administrative expenses, and to earn a profit, depends on the firm's earning sufficient gross margin on sales.

Selling, general, and administrative expenses represent all expenses, other than cost of goods sold and income taxes, related to the primary recurring activities of the firm.

Income tax expense represents the tax expense associated with the financial accounting income reported on the current period's income statement. If the firm's financial accounting income and its taxable income are the same, the amount of tax expense is equal to the amount of taxes paid (or owed) to the taxing authorities for income of the current period.[7]

---

[7]For reasons that we will discuss in Chapter 4, financial accounting income and taxable income rarely coincide. When these two amounts differ, the amount of tax expense shown on the income statement will not necessarily be equal to the amount of taxes paid (or owed) for the period, and an accounting technique called interperiod tax allocation will be used. This technique is demonstrated in Chapter 4.

Net income represents the firm's earnings for the period, after matching the appropriate expenses against recognized revenues. Recall that in this section we are considering only those transactions resulting from a firm's ongoing, or *recurring,* operations; a later section of this chapter discusses *nonrecurring* events that affect net income.

As a gauge of the efficiency of a firm's operations, analysts often compute **return on sales (ROS),** which is the percentage relationship of net income to sales.

$$\text{ROS} = \frac{\text{Net Income}}{\text{Sales}}$$

Walgreen Company's ROS in 1985 is 3.0 percent ($94,169/$3,161,935). In effect, each dollar of sales has produced, on average, three cents of net income. Analysts would want to know how this compares with the firm's performance in the past and perhaps with the performance of other companies, particularly the firm's direct competitors. The return-on-sales ratio should not be used by itself, however, because it does not give consideration to the amount of capital invested to generate net income or to the dollar amount of assets employed. Discussion of measures of return on assets employed is deferred until Chapter 12, which is devoted entirely to financial statement analysis.

Income of a Manufacturing Company

A manufacturing company buys materials from other firms and converts those materials into finished products for sale to customers. Manufacturing costs are classified as direct materials, direct labor, and manufacturing overhead. These classifications are defined as follows:

- **Direct materials** are resources that are included in and are easily traceable to the finished product. Cloth used in the manufacture of dress shirts is an example of direct material.

- **Direct labor** is the cost of services provided by employees who work directly on the products being manufactured. An example is the cost of the labor of a seamstress sewing a shirt.

- **Manufacturing overhead** includes all manufacturing costs not classified as direct materials or direct labor. Accordingly, this category includes all indirect manufacturing costs. Some examples are indirect materials (for example, factory supplies); indirect labor (wages of foremen, materials handlers, inspectors, and storeroom clerks); and other factory expenses (repairs, depreciation, and utility costs for buildings and equipment used in the manufacturing process).

Manufacturing costs are sometimes referred to as **inventory** (or **product**) **costs.** This is because all manufacturing costs, as they are incurred, are assigned initially to inventory accounts. Inventories, of course, are assets, and costs assigned to inventory accounts do not become expenses until the period in which the inventories are sold. In contrast, nonmanufacturing costs — such as those for selling and administrative activities — are not assigned to inventory accounts and are usually expensed in the period in which they are incurred. Accordingly, such costs are referred to as **period costs.**

A manufacturing company classifies inventory into three accounts according to stage of completion:

1. **Raw materials:** materials on which no work has been performed to date
2. **Work in process:** partially completed goods
3. **Finished goods:** goods awaiting sale to customers

Exhibit 3-8 depicts the flow of manufacturing costs through these three inventory accounts to cost of goods sold. Notice that the costs of direct materials used, direct labor, and manufacturing overhead are all added initially to Work in Process. When goods are completed, the cost of these goods is transferred out of Work in Process and into Finished Goods. At the point of sale, the cost of the goods sold is transferred out of Finished Goods and into the Cost of Goods Sold account. A detailed illustration of the flow of manufacturing costs through the accounting system will be provided shortly.

Income statements of merchandising and manufacturing firms are basically the same. The major difference is that the cost-of-goods-sold component is more complex for a manufacturing company, particularly with reference to the determination of additions to inventory during the period. In a merchandising firm, additions to inventory result from purchases of items already in saleable form, whereas additions in a manufacturing firm involve conversion of raw materials into completed products.

Recall the general method for calculating cost of goods sold:

Inventory at beginning of period	$XXX
Plus: Additions to inventory during the period	XXX
Cost of goods available for sale	$XXX
Less: Inventory at end of period	(XXX)
Cost of goods sold	$XXX

In a manufacturing firm, cost of goods sold is calculated as follows on page 126 after Exhibit 3-8.

Exhibit 3-8

Flow of Manufacturing Costs through the Accounting System

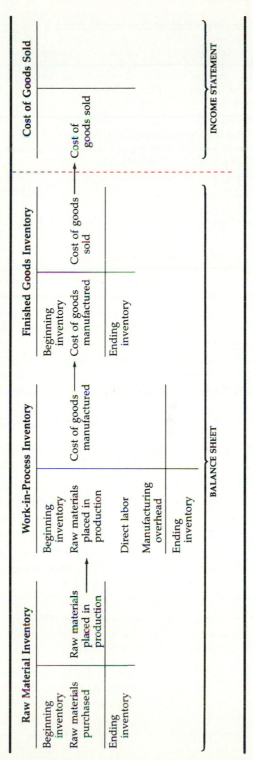

Finished goods inventory, beginning of period $XXX

Additions to finished goods inventory, that is, goods completed during the period:		
Direct materials used	$XXX	
Direct labor	XXX	
Manufacturing overhead	XXX	
Total manufacturing costs for period	$XXX	
Plus: Work-in-process inventory, beginning of period	XXX	
Less: Work-in-process inventory, end of period	(XXX)	
Cost of goods manufactured		XXX

Cost of goods available for sale $XXX
Less: Finished goods inventory, end of period   (XXX)
Cost of goods sold $XXX

Observe in the computations above that the determination of the additions to finished goods inventory during the period is shaded, and that the total cost of these additions is referred to as **cost of goods manufactured.**

The total manufacturing costs incurred during the period provide the starting point for calculating cost of goods manufactured. Work-in-process inventory at the beginning of the period is added to the period's total manufacturing costs because these goods may be completed (and thus, become saleable) during the period. Work-in-process inventory at the end of the period is subtracted because these goods cannot be sold since, by definition, they are not yet complete. Cost of goods manufactured, then, represents the cost of all goods completed during the period, regardless of when they were placed into production.

An illustration: the Jedi Manufacturing Company To examine these concepts more closely, consider the following activities of the Jedi Manufacturing Company for the month of January, 1988:

1. Raw materials purchased amounted to $23,500.
2. Raw materials valued at $20,500 were placed in production as direct materials.
3. Direct labor charges amounting to $12,000 were incurred.
4. Total indirect manufacturing costs incurred were $16,000, which consist of $7,000 in indirect labor, $6,000 in depreciation on factory buildings and equipment, $2,000 in utilities for the factory, and $1,000 in insurance on factory buildings and equipment.
5. The cost of goods completed was $48,000.
6. The cost of inventory sold was $47,000.

Also, assume the following beginning balances on January 1 for each of the firm's inventory accounts: Raw Material Inventory, $1,000; Work-in-Process Inventory, $1,500; and Finished Goods Inventory, $6,000.

Journal entries to record activities during January are summarized in Exhibit 3-9. The recorded entries in Exhibit 3-9 are also presented graphically in

Exhibit 3-9

Recording and Flow of Manufacturing Costs

Jedi Manufacturing Company
For the Month of January, 1988

(1) Raw Materials Inventory	23,500	
Accounts Payable		23,500
To record purchase of raw material on credit.		
(2) Work-in-Process Inventory	20,500	
Raw Materials Inventory		20,500
To record cost of direct materials placed in production.		
(3) Work-in-Process Inventory	12,000	
Wages and Salaries Payable		12,000
To record direct labor cost.		
(4) Work-in-Process Inventory	16,000	
Wages and Salaries Payable		7,000
Accumulated Depreciation		6,000
Utilities Payable		2,000
Prepaid Insurance		1,000
To record indirect manufacturing overhead cost.		
(5) Finished Goods Inventory	48,000	
Work-in-Process Inventory		48,000
To record transfer of completed goods to finished goods inventory.		
(6) Cost of Goods Sold	47,000	
Finished Goods Inventory		47,000
To record the manufacturing cost of the units sold.		

Exhibit 3-10, which depicts the typical flow of costs through the manufacturing cycle. Observe that manufacturing costs flow first through the three inventory accounts, which are balance sheet items. They do not affect the measurement of net income on the income statement *until the period in which the finished goods are sold.*

An income statement for the Jedi Manufacturing Company is presented in Exhibit 3-11. Beginning balances for the three inventory accounts at January 1 were given above, sales during January are $60,000 and nonmanufacturing costs are as follows: selling and administrative expenses, $10,000; income tax expense, $1,200. All other dollar amounts on the January income statement are the result of manufacturing activities presented in Exhibits 3-9 and 3-10.

Assigning manufacturing costs to inventories　Manufacturing costs, as they relate to the level of production, are of two types: fixed and variable. **Fixed manufacturing costs** are those that do not change in total in response to short-

Exhibit 3-10

Flow of Manufacturing Costs through the Ledger

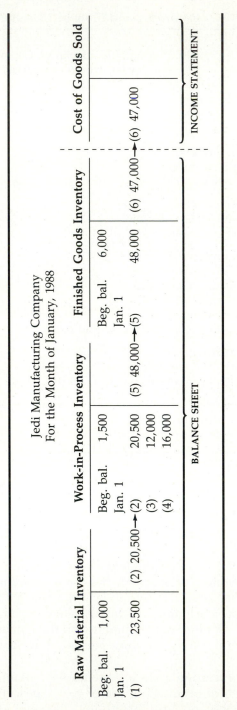

Jedi Manufacturing Company
For the Month of January, 1988

Exhibit 3-11

Income Reporting for a Manufacturing Firm

Income Statement
Jedi Manufacturing Company
For the Month Ended January 31, 1988

Sales			$60,000
Cost of Goods Sold:			
Finished Goods Inventory, January 1		$ 6,000	
Raw materials Used	$20,500		
Direct Labor	12,000		
Manufacturing Overhead	16,000		
Manufacturing Costs for January	$48,500		
Plus: Work in Process, January 1	1,500		
Less: Work in Process, January 31	(2,000)		
		48,000	
Goods Available for Sale		$54,000	
Less: Finished Goods Inventory, January 31		(7,000)	
Cost of Goods Sold			$47,000
Gross Margin			$13,000
Less: Selling and Administrative Expenses			(10,000)
Income before Taxes			$ 3,000
Less: Income Tax Expense			(1,200)
Net Income			$ 1,800

run changes in production levels; thus, with higher levels of production, such costs decrease on a per-unit basis as the fixed amount of cost is spread over more units. Examples are supervisory salaries, property taxes, and fire insurance premiums. In contrast, **variable manufacturing costs** remain the same on a per-unit basis with production level changes, but they vary in total as different levels of output are multiplied by a constant unit cost. The cost of raw materials used in the production process is an example of a variable manufacturing cost. Assigning fixed manufacturing costs to individual units of production is a complicated process because fixed manufacturing costs change per unit as production levels change.

The **absorption** or **full costing** method, which is required by generally accepted accounting principles, was used in the Jedi Manufacturing Company illustration to assign manufacturing costs to inventory accounts. Under absorption costing, *all* manufacturing costs—both fixed and variable—are assigned to each unit of production. What this means is that cost of goods sold (and thus, the amount of reported net income) is influenced not only by the sales level in a particular period, but also by the level of production in that period. This topic is covered in greater detail in the appendix to this chapter.

Income of a Service Firm

In service companies, such as legal firms, banks, advertising agencies, and commercial baseball teams, the costs of human effort and related expenses are linked with the fees derived from such services.

Arthur D. Little, Inc., is an international technology and management consulting firm. This service firm's 1985 income statement is presented in Exhibit 3-12. Notice that the classifications on this income statement are fewer in number than those for the typical merchandising or manufacturing firm. As an example, cost of goods sold does not appear on Arthur D. Little's income statement because the firm derives revenue from selling services, rather than from selling inventory.

Exhibit 3-12
Income Reporting for a Service Firm

Arthur D. Little, Inc.
Consolidated Statement of Income
For the Year Ended December 31, 1985
(in thousands, except per-share data)

	1985
Revenues	
Professional service income	$229,486
Royalties and venture income	3,103
	232,589
Costs and Expenses	
Salaries, wages and other employment costs	124,511
Other operating expenses, net	45,589
Reimbursable costs for materials, travel and other charges to clients	50,160
	220,260
Income from operations	12,329
Income from short-term investments	1,042
Interest expense	(766)
Other income (charges), net (Note G)	(1,549)
Income before taxes on income	11,056
Provision for taxes on income (Note H)	5,072
Net Income	$ 5,984
Earnings per share*	$ 2.35

Source: Arthur D. Little, Inc., *Annual Report*, 1985.

*Per-share amounts have been computed based on the weighted average number of shares outstanding, which was 2,541,232 for the year ended December 31, 1985.

REPORTING OF NONRECURRING OPERATIONS

The discussion now turns to the second major section of the income statement, which concentrates on the reporting of nonrecurring operations. Exhibit 3-13 presents the major sections and overall organization of the income statement. Observe that the shaded portion of Exhibit 3-13 refers to the reporting of non-recurring operations. This section of the income statement may contain as many as three different types of items: (1) discontinued operations, (2) extraordinary items, and (3) changes in accounting principles. These items are reported separately from results of recurring operations because this format is

Exhibit 3-13

Sections of the Income Statement

Recurring Operations

A. Revenues and expenses from principal operations
   Sales revenue
   Cost of goods sold
   Gross margin
   Selling, general, and administrative expenses
B. Revenues and expenses from secondary activities, and gains and losses that are infrequent or unusual, but not both
   Other revenues and gains
   Other expenses and losses
C. Income tax expense related to the above activities

INCOME AFTER TAX FROM RECURRING OPERATIONS

Nonrecurring Operations

D. Revenues, expenses, gains, and losses from nonrecurring activities or situations (all shown net of income tax)
   Discontinued operations
   Extraordinary items
   Cumulative effect of changes in accounting principles

NET INCOME

E. Earnings-per-share disclosures

believed to be more useful to financial statement readers, particularly with re-gard to the prediction of future earnings and cash flows.

In addition to being presented in a separate section, each of the three types of items reported as the result of nonrecurring operations is shown net of re-lated **income tax effects.** The income tax effect of a transaction is the change (increase or decrease) in income taxes payable that results from including that transaction in the determination of taxable income. To illustrate, assume an in-dividual receives a cash bonus of $5,000 at the end of an accounting period. As-sume also that the bonus is subject to income taxes at a 40-percent rate. The tax effect of this $5,000 bonus is an increase in taxes of $2,000 ($5,000 × 40%), and the gain, net of tax, is $3,000. This is summarized below.

Taxable gain (bonus)	$5,000
Less: Tax effect of gain	(2,000)
Gain, net of tax	$3,000

Allocating tax effects to major sections of the income statement is called **in-trastatement income tax allocation.** In effect, total income tax for the period is first allocated between the section of the income statement dealing with recur-ring items and the section dealing with nonrecurring items. Then, a further allocation takes place within the nonrecurring section as discontinued operations, extraordinary items, and the cumulative effect of accounting changes are shown net of income tax effects.

Discontinued Operations

A **discontinued operation** is a segment of a business that ceases to exist. To qualify for separate reporting, however, the segment must represent a separate major line of business or class of customer. Also, the assets, operations, and ac-tivities of the segment must be distinguishable from the rest of the entity. The decision by a company that produces clothing, automobiles, and cement to dis-pose of all operations involving the manufacture of clothing is an example of a situation that qualifies for separate reporting. In contrast, the decision by a clothing manufacturer to drop its line of sweaters would not qualify. In this lat-ter case, the firm is still deemed to be in the clothing business, and the results of its operations as a clothing business would not be classified in the nonrecur-ring section of the income statement.

The suggested income statement format for discontinued operations is pre-sented in the shaded section of Exhibit 3-14. Note that this section consists of two disclosures: (1) results of operations of the segment being discontinued and (2) the gain or loss upon disposition.

The portion of Exhibit 3-14 that is not shaded is included to highlight the fact that transactions and events from recurring operations are reported sepa-rately from transactions and events dealing with discontinued operations. Ob-serve that disclosures relating to discontinued operations are shown net of their related tax effects, and that Income Tax Expense related to income from recurring operations is not affected by the tax effects of the nonrecurring items.

Exhibit 3-14

**Income Statement Presentation
of Discontinued Operations**

Income from recurring operations, before income taxes	$XXX	
Less: Income tax expense	(XXX)	
Income from recurring operations		$XXX
Discontinued operations:		
Income from operations of discontinued segment, less related tax effects	$XXX	
Gain (loss) on disposal of discontinued segment, less related tax effects	XXX	XXX
Net income		$XXX

(As noted previously, the procedure whereby each major section of the income statement is assigned its own tax effects is called intrastatement income tax allocation.)

Extraordinary Items

Extraordinary items are transactions or events that meet both of the following criteria:

1. Unusual nature: the underlying event or transaction should possess a high degree of abnormality and be of a type clearly unrelated to, or only incidentally related to, the ordinary and typical activities of the entity, taking into account the environment in which the entity operates.
2. Infrequency of occurrence: the underlying event or transaction should be of a type that would not reasonably be expected to recur in the foreseeable future, taking into account the environment in which the entity operates.[8]

In determining whether an event or transaction meets the above criteria, one must consider the environment in which the business operates. The company's geographic location, the extent of government regulations, and the characteristics of the industry need to be examined. Thus, an event may be unusual for one company but not for another, because of their different environments. For example, the effects of an earthquake might be considered an

---

[8]Accounting Principles Board *Opinion No. 30*, "Reporting the Results of Operations" (New York: AICPA, 1973), par. 20.

extraordinary item if the earthquake took place in New York, but not if it took place in California.

Items that commonly meet the criteria for being an extraordinary item include the following:

1. Effects of major casualties (if rare in their geographic area)
2. Expropriation of assets by a foreign government
3. Effects of prohibition under a newly enacted law or regulation

Exhibit 3-15 illustrates proper disclosure of extraordinary items on the income statement. Note that such items would be shown net of related income tax effects.

Change in an Accounting Principle

A **change in an accounting principle** results from switching from one acceptable accounting method to another. Certain disclosures are required in the financial statements for the period in which a change in an accounting principle occurs. These disclosures include the nature of the change, justification for the change, and the effect of the change on the period's net income. Changes in an accounting principle may occur either as a result of a management decision or as the result of a new FASB statement. If the change results from a management decision, it is expected that management has reason to believe that the new method will improve the usefulness of the financial statements.

Virtually all changes from one acceptable accounting method to another are reported by using the so-called **current** or "**catch-up**" **approach.** This approach does not require retroactive adjustment; that is, it does not affect the financial statements of prior periods. Instead, the income statement for the period that contains the change in an accounting principle shows the cumulative net of tax

Exhibit 3-15

**Income Statement Presentation
of Extraordinary Items**

Income from recurring operations, before income taxes	$XXX	
Less: Income tax expense	(XXX)	
Income from recurring operations		$XXX
Extraordinary gain, less related tax effects		XXX
Extraordinary loss, less related tax effects		(XXX)
Net income		$XXX

effect of the change on earnings of prior periods.[9] Reporting the cumulative effect on earnings in the current period's income statement allows appropriate balance sheet accounts to "catch up" and reflect dollar amounts *as if* the newly adopted accounting principle had been used all along. There are areas in financial accounting, such as the depreciation of fixed assets, in which more than one acceptable method exists. Switching from one acceptable depreciation method to another is an example of a change in the use of an accounting principle. Alternative depreciation methods are covered in Chapter 4.

EARNINGS-PER-SHARE DISCLOSURES

Earnings per share (EPS) must be disclosed on the face of published income statements by all publicly held corporations. EPS measures probably receive more attention in the investment community than does any other single accounting disclosure. The information is commonly used in developing projections of future market prices and dividends per share.

This section will consider the EPS calculation for firms having a **simple capital structure.** A firm has a simple capital structure for purposes of computing earnings per share if during the period it has no securities outstanding (or agreements to issue securities) that in the aggregate reduce earnings per outstanding common share. Chapter 7 considers EPS calculations for firms with more complicated capital structures. For firms having a simple capital structure, the formula to compute EPS is as follows:

$$\text{Earnings per Common Share} = \frac{\text{Net Income for the Period}}{\substack{\text{Weighted Average of Number} \\ \text{of Shares Outstanding} \\ \text{During the Period}}}$$

Weighting, used in calculating the denominator, allows for the fact that a different number of shares may be outstanding for different portions of the accounting period. For example, assume that at the beginning of a year (January 1) the Bloom Corporation has 10,000 shares outstanding, and that it issues an additional 10,000 shares for cash on October 1. In this case, there are 10,000 outstanding shares for nine months of the year ($9/12$) and 20,000 outstanding shares for the year's remaining three months ($3/12$). The weighted average for the whole year is 12,500 shares outstanding, which is calculated as follows:

---

[9]The cumulative effect of a change in an accounting principle is the difference between (1) the amount of retained earnings at the beginning of the period of the change and (2) the amount that would have been reported for retained earnings at that date if the newly adopted accounting principle had been applied retroactively for all prior periods that would have been affected by the change.

Number of Shares	Fraction of Year Outstanding	
10,000 shares × 9/12 (January–September)	=	7,500
20,000 shares × 3/12 (October–December)	=	5,000
Weighted average of shares outstanding		12,500

If reported income for the year is $25,000, earnings per common share would be $2.00 ($25,000/12,500).

In the Bloom Corporation example, the $25,000 net income was generated by employing resources, or invested capital, available during the period. However, cash from the October 1 stock issue was available for only one-fourth of the year. This is the reason for using the weighted average to calculate the denominator in the EPS ratio. In effect, the 10,000 shares outstanding during the whole year are given a weight of 1, and the additional 10,000 shares issued on October 1 are given a weight of 0.25.

Whenever a company has extraordinary gains or losses, its income statement should include separate disclosures for (1) income before extraordinary items; (2) the extraordinary items, net of related tax effects; and (3) net income. Likewise, reporting of EPS data should be consistent with this income statement presentation. To illustrate, suppose Bloom Corporation's $25,000 net income included a $4,000 extraordinary gain, net of tax. The bottom portion of the income statement would appear as follows:

Income before extraordinary items	$21,000
Extraordinary gain, net of tax	4,000
Net income	$25,000
Earnings per share:	
Income before extraordinary items	$1.68
Extraordinary gain, net of tax	0.32
Net income	$2.00

SUMMARY

This chapter consists of two parts. The first part contains a conceptual discussion of income measurement, and the second part illustrates income reporting for three different types of business enterprises: merchandising, manufacturing, and service firms. An income statement has three major sections: recurring operations, nonrecurring operations, and earnings-per-share disclosures. Each of these income statement sections is examined in the second part of the chapter.

Reported earnings numbers are used by managers, government agencies, creditors, investors, and others in making many different types of decisions. Certain decisions involve assessing past performance, and others are future-oriented—such as the prediction of a company's future earnings and/or cash flows.

The concepts of accounting and economic income are not the same. Economists define income as an increase in wealth during a period of time, and they rely on direct valuation of net assets at the beginning and end of the period to measure changes in wealth. In contrast, accountants use a transaction-based approach to measure income, and they report the income on the income statement. The four basic elements of the income statement are revenues, expenses, gains, and losses. Accounting income is the excess of recorded revenues and gains over expenses and losses for a particular period. Generally, the exchange price agreed on between independent parties to a transaction is used to value the inflow or outflow of assets and is accepted as the proper measure of the revenue or expense.

The timing of revenue recognition on the income statement is guided by the principle of realization. This principle states, in effect, that revenue should not be recognized until the earnings process is complete and the amount of earnings can be measured with reasonable certainty. Generally, this occurs at the point of sale. Expense recognition is guided by the matching principle. The objective here is to present efforts (expenses and losses) and related accomplishments (revenues and gains) in the same reporting period.

Income reporting is least complicated for a service firm, which has no inventories to sell. Merchandising and manufacturing firms do sell inventories and must account for the cost of the inventory items sold in determining income for the period. Income statements of merchandising and manufacturing firms contain the following main sections: sales revenue, cost of goods sold, gross margin, selling and administrative expenses, and income tax expense.

A merchandising firm buys inventory ready for sale, while a manufacturing firm converts raw materials into finished products for sale to customers. A manufacturing firm classifies inventory into three accounts according to stage of completion:

1. Raw materials: materials on which no work has been performed to date
2. Work in process: partially completed goods
3. Finished goods: goods awaiting sale to customer

Manufacturing costs flow through these three inventory accounts, which are presented as assets on the balance sheet. Costs assigned to inventory accounts do not become expenses until the period in which the inventory is sold.

The section of the income statement used to report results of nonrecurring operations may contain as many as three different types of items: (1) discontinued operations, (2) extraordinary items, and (3) changes in accounting principles. Each of these items is reported net of income tax effects.

All publicly held corporations must disclose earnings-per-share measures on the face of published income statements. Earnings per share is calculated by dividing the firm's net income for the reporting period by the weighted average of the number of shares outstanding during the period.

APPENDIX B
ABSORPTION VERSUS VARIABLE COSTING

The term **absorption costing** is used to describe the convention of assigning all manufacturing costs (both variable and fixed) to inventory. Under this costing method, all factory costs, whether variable or fixed with production, must be assigned to cost of goods sold and ending inventory in a reasonable manner. To illustrate, consider the following information concerning the first year of operations of the Idle Notion Company:

	Units
Beginning Inventory	0
Production	12,000
Sales	(8,000)
Ending inventory (all complete)	4,000

Factory costs	Total	Per Unit (for 12,000 units)
Variable factory costs:		
Direct Materials	$ 18,000	$ 1.50
Direct Labor	36,000	3.00
Variable Factory Overhead	12,000	1.00
Total variable costs	$ 66,000	$ 5.50
Fixed factory overhead cost	60,000	5.00
Total factory costs	$126,000	$10.50

The Idle Notion Company has a unit cost of production of $10.50 ($126,000/12,000 units produced). The inventory and cost of sales amounts are

Cost of goods sold	$ 84,000 (8000 units @ 10.50)
Ending inventory	42,000 (4000 units @ 10.50)
Total costs	$126,000

In this example the total factory cost of $126,000 has been accounted for—$84,000 appears on the income statement as an expense (cost of goods sold), and $42,000 appears on the balance sheet as an asset (inventory).

Notice that manufacturing overhead consists of *both* fixed and variable overhead. **Fixed overhead** includes manufacturing costs that do not change in response to short-run changes in production levels. Examples include depreciation, supervisory salaries, certain taxes, and so on. **Variable overhead** costs by definition change with production levels. Examples include indirect materials and supplies, indirect factory labor, certain utilities, maintenance, and so on. Since some factory costs are fixed, the cost per unit of production will vary with the production volume in a given period. The earlier example assumed that Idle Notion produced 12,000 units of output; consider how the inventory costs would differ for other levels of output:

Production Level (units)	Total Factory Costs Fixed + Variable* = Total	Unit Factory Costs Fixed + Variable = Total
8,000	$60,000 + 44,000 = $104,000	$7.50 + 5.50 = $13.00
10,000	$60,000 + 55,000 = $115,000	$6.00 + 5.50 = $11.50
12,000	$60,000 + 66,000 = $126,000	$5.00 + 5.50 = $10.50
15,000	$60,000 + 82,500 = $142,500	$4.00 + 5.50 = $ 9.50

*(Production level) × ($5.50 variable unit cost). We assume that per-unit variable costs are constant.

The illustration reflects the fact that fixed costs are spread over a larger number of units as output increases. If we continue to assume that 8,000 units are sold, then the level of production will affect Idle Notion's cost of sales as follows:

Production Level (units)	Total Factory Costs	Ending Inventory Units × Cost = Total	Cost of Goods Sold
8,000	$104,000	0 × $13.00 = 0	$104,000
10,000	115,000	2000 × $11.50 = 23,000	92,000
12,000	126,000	4000 × $10.50 = 42,000	84,000
15,000	142,000	7000 × $ 9.50 = 66,500	75,500

For a given level of sales, higher levels of production result in a lower cost of goods sold. This occurs because the amount of fixed costs assigned to the ending inventory increases with higher levels of production. In the example above, if Idle Notion produces and sells 8,000 units, then all of the period's fixed costs are included in cost of goods sold because none of the fixed costs are assigned to ending inventory. If, instead, Idle Notion produces 12,000 units and sells 8,000 units, then $20,000 of fixed costs (4000 units × $5.00 unit fixed cost) is assigned to the ending inventory. For this reason, cost of goods would be $20,000 lower and gross margin would be $20,000 higher.

Analysts of the financial statements of manufacturing firms are well aware of the fact that with absorption costing, differences between the levels of production and sale will affect the reported cost of goods sold, as well as the cost amount assigned to inventories. When a firm has beginning and ending inventories, analysts will often correct for the change in inventory fixed costs in order to make meaningful comparisons over time or among different firms.

It is sometimes alleged that managers have deliberately manipulated the amount of reported profits by altering the number of units produced. This argument has led some accounting theorists to suggest that only variable production costs be assigned to inventories. If this were done, the total factory fixed costs would appear as an expense on the income statement each period, and differences in production levels would not affect the reported cost of goods sold. Opponents of this approach argue that variable costing of inventories is inconsistent with the historical cost concept, since fixed factory costs are a necessary part of total manufacturing costs. At present, variable costing of inventories is not acceptable for external financial accounting reports.

QUESTIONS

1. The terms listed below were introduced in this chapter. Define or explain each of them.

absorption (full) costing	gross margin percentage
arms-length transaction	income tax expense
capital maintenance	installment sales method
capital transaction	intrastatement tax allocation
change in an accounting principle	inventory (or product) costs
cost of goods manufactured	losses
cost of goods sold	lower of cost or market rule
cost principle	manufacturing overhead
direct labor	matching principle
direct materials	percentage-of-completion method
discontinued operation	period costs
dollar capital	present value
earnings per share	raw materials inventory
exchange price	realization principle
expenses	replacement cost of capital
extraordinary item	return-on-sales ratio
finished goods inventory	revenues
fixed manufacturing costs	sales revenue
front-loading	selling, general, and administrative
gains	expenses
general purchasing power of capital	variable manufacturing costs
gross margin	work in process inventory

2. Individuals use reported income numbers in making a variety of different decisions. List several of these different types of decisions that utilize reported earnings numbers.

3. How would an economist value assets? What are some of the difficulties in valuing assets using the economic approach to valuation?

4. Is the present value of a company's net assets when considered in the

aggregate equal to the sum of the present value of the firm's individual assets less liabilities? Why or why not? (Hint: Is it possible for the value of the whole to be greater than the sum of its parts?)

5. In order to calculate economic income, it is necessary to first select a specific capital maintenance rule. List and describe the three different capital maintenance rules outlined in the chapter. Which of these rules has been adopted by the accounting profession?

6. Distinguish between (a) a change in the general level of prices and (b) a change in the relative prices of individual goods and services.

7. List three examples of revenue items. List three common expenses.

8. "Accounting income is not designed to measure changes in wealth (or well-offness) during a period of time." Do you agree or not? Explain.

9. Describe the procedure accountants use to determine the timing of revenue recognition on the income statement. Describe the procedure used to determine the timing of expense recognition.

10. What is the difference between revenues and gains? Between expenses and losses?

11. There is a difference between (a) what revenue is and (b) the rules established in financial accounting for determining when revenue is to be recognized. Explain this difference.

12. What two conditions must be met before revenue is to be recognized?

13. Why are some costs expensed as incurred while others are capitalized?

14. Typically revenue is recognized at the point of sale. However, in certain situations revenues may be recognized at points in the earnings process other than the time of sale. Describe these situations.

15. What is the percentage-of-completion method of income (revenue and expense) recognition? How does it differ from the installment sales method?

16. What are the main components of the income statement for a merchandising firm?

17. What is cost of goods sold? How is it calculated?

18. What is gross margin? How is the gross margin percentage calculated? List several factors that might cause a decline in the gross margin percentage from one period to the next.

19. What are the three components of manufacturing costs? Give an example of each.

20. What is manufacturing overhead?

21. How would you classify the cost of fire insurance for a manufacturing plant?

22. What are the three inventory accounts used by manufacturing firms?

23. What is the difference between cost of goods available for sale and cost of goods sold?

24. What is the difference between cost of goods sold and cost of goods manufactured?

25. What is the difference between a fixed cost and a variable cost? Give an example of each.

26. What is absorption costing?
27. Describe the format used to report nonrecurring items (such as discontinued operations and extraordinary items) on a company's income statement.
28. Would the decision by a company that manufactures power tools to cease producing a certain type of saw be properly reported on the firm's income statement as a discontinued operation? Explain.
29. What are the two criteria that must be met before a transaction or event may be properly classified as an extraordinary item?
30. Is a loss due to a tornado in Kansas properly classified as an extraordinary item? Explain.
31. Give an example of a change in an accounting principle.
32. Describe the effects on the financial statements of using the so-called current or "catch-up" approach to account for a change from one generally accepted accounting principle to another.
33. Earnings per share is calculated by dividing net income for a period by the number of shares outstanding for the period. Why is the denominator in this ratio calculated on a weighted-average basis?
34. Describe the recommended format to use in presenting earnings-per-share data, assuming an extraordinary item is included in the determination of net income.

EXERCISES AND PROBLEMS

35. *Different Capital Maintenance Rules: Single Asset Valuation Rule.* The net assets of Price Company were valued at $50,000 on January 1, 1988, and at $60,000 on December 31, 1988. No dividends were paid to stockholders during the year, nor was any of the company's stock (paid-in capital) issued or retired; that is, there were no capital transactions during 1988. Assume that the general rate of inflation was 6% during 1988, and the replacement cost of Price Company's net assets at January 1, 1988, actually decreased by 2% during the year.

REQUIRED   Calculate net income for Price Company for calendar year 1988 using each of the following capital maintenance rules:

(a) Maintenance of dollar capital
(b) Maintenance of general purchasing power
(c) Maintenance of replacement cost of capital

36. *Different Capital Maintenance Rules: Single Asset Valuation Rule.* The net assets of Ku Company were valued at $70,000 on January 1, 1989, and at $78,400 on December 31, 1989. No dividends were paid to stockholders during the year, nor was any of the company's stock (paid-in capital) is-

sued or retired; that is, there were no capital transactions during 1989. Assume that the general rate of inflation was 12% during 1989, and the replacement cost of Ku Company's net assets at January 1, 1989, increased by 14% during the year.

REQUIRED   Calculate the amount of income or loss for Ku Company for calendar year 1989 using each of the following capital maintenance rules:

(a) Maintenance of dollar capital
(b) Maintenance of general purchasing power
(c) Maintenance of replacement cost of capital

37. *Capital Maintenance Rules and Performance Evaluation.*   Business managers and investment analysts frequently use return on owners' equity (net income divided by average owners' equity) in order to gauge the firm's profitability. Owners' equity values at the beginning and the end of 1988 are presented below for Achilles Company and for Patrocles, Inc. Both firms use nominal dollars to measure net assets, and neither firm had any changes in paid-in capital or paid any dividends during 1988. Assume the general rate of inflation was 8% during 1988, and in that year the replacement cost of Achilles' net assets increased by 4% and the replacement cost of Patrocles' net assets decreased by 2%.

	Net Asset Valuation (in millions)	
	December 31	
	1987	**1988**
Achilles Company	$30	$35
Patrocles, Inc.	$20	$25

REQUIRED   Compare the profitability of Achilles and Patrocles during 1988 using the return on owners' equity measure, and using the capital maintenance rule that you consider appropriate. Justify your choice of capital maintenance rules.

38. *Revenue Recognition.*   GAAP require that revenue not be recognized until (1) the earnings process is substantially complete and (2) earnings can be measured with reasonable objectivity.

REQUIRED

(a) Give an example in which the earnings process is substantially complete, but cannot be measured at present with reasonable objectivity.
(b) Give an example in which the amount of earnings can be measured currently, but the earnings process is not substantially complete.

39. *Revenue Recognition.*   The following transactions occurred during 1988 for the Boulder Garden Company:

Cash sales	$120,000
Credit sales	80,000
Cash collected from credit sales	50,000

REQUIRED

(a) What is the total amount of cash inflow from these transactions during 1988?
(b) What is the total amount of revenue that should be recognized from these transactions during 1988?
(c) Explain the difference in amounts between (a) and (b) above, if any.
(d) Is it possible in this problem for cash collected from credit sales to exceed $80,000 during 1988? Explain.

40. *Expense Recognition.*   All recorded costs eventually become expenses (or losses) to be matched against revenues on the income statement. The list below contains certain costs related to the operations of the Bakersfield Company.

(1) Depreciation of furniture used in the sales office
(2) Utilities (lighting and heat) for factory buildings
(3) Commissions earned by the company's sales force
(4) Loss on sale of a used delivery truck
(5) Bonus earned by the company's president
(6) Wages for production control personnel
(7) Wages for clerical staff in the home office
(8) Wages earned by personnel who work on the company's assembly line
(9) Insurance premiums on manufacturing equipment
(10) Depreciation of manufacturing machinery
(11) Cost of goods sold
(12) Interest on outstanding loans
(13) Cost of raw materials used in the production process
(14) Inventory that becomes worthless due to changes in customer demand
(15) Costs of delivering goods sold to customers

REQUIRED   Three bases have been identified by the FASB for expense recognition: (1) associating cause and effect, (2) systematic and rational allocation, and (3) immediate recognition. For each cost listed above, select the expense recognition base that you believe is most appropriate. Explain all answers.

41. *Revenue Recognition: Different Points in the Earnings Cycle.*   On October 1, 1988, the Norton Company signed a contract with Computer Installations, Inc., for the installation of a computerized accounting system at the home office, as well as at ten of the Norton Company's satellite offices. The work was to commence on April 30, 1990. The following facts about the contract are available:

Total Contract Price: $1,800,000
Projected Expenses:
    Consulting charges   340,000
    Installation charges   820,000

Collections of $300,000 will be made at the end of each quarter in 1989 and 1990, beginning with March 31, 1989, and ending with June 30, 1990.
    The contract cost summary by accounting period is shown below:

Cost Element	1988	1989	1990	Total
Consulting charges	140,000	125,000	75,000	340,000
Installment charges	5,000	600,000	215,000	820,000

REQUIRED

(a) Calculate the total projected profit on the contract.
(b) Show the date(s) and amount of profit recognized if Computer Installations, Inc., were to recognize the profit on the contract under each of the three methods listed below.

 (1) Date(s) and profit at the time the contract was signed
 (2) Date(s) and profit under the percentage of completion method
 (3) Date(s) and profit under the installment sales method

(c) Which is the best method for the recognition of profits on this contract? Why?

42. *Revenue Recognition.*   Piet Moss, a local artist with an entrepreneurial bent, is offering limited-edition woodcuts to investors and art lovers at a price of $400 each. Moss offers the following guarantee with each unit sold: if the purchaser is not satisfied with the unit for any reason at the end of three years, the unit may be returned for a full refund. Moreover, returned units will be destroyed in order to enhance the market value of the remaining units. Each unit costs Moss a total of $200 to produce, frame, and ship. Moss estimates that about 50% of the units sold will be returned at the end

of three years. Assume that Moss's entire edition of 10,000 units is sold early in 1988.

REQUIRED

(a) Determine the amount of income to be recognized by Piet Moss in each of the years 1988, 1989, and 1990.

(b) Determine the amount of cash to be received and paid each year by Piet Moss, and the total cash effect over the three-year period, if in fact 50% of the units sold are returned at the end of three years.

(c) Based on your answer to (b), is it sensible for Piet Moss to offer additional woodcuts at the same selling price and with the same refund guarantee if his costs stay the same? Explain.

43. *Revenue Recognition and Income Statement Preparation.*   The Deltoid Health Club began operations on January 2, 1983, and has offered annual membership at a fee of $300. In an effort to expand its membership, the club began to offer lifetime memberships in 1988 at a fee of $2,000, payable in advance. As a result, club membership expanded from 4,000 in 1987 (all annual memberships) to 4,500 in 1988 (3,500 annual memberships and 1,000 lifetime memberships). Operating results for 1987 are shown below. (Assume that the club's cost structure will remain the same in the future.) Les Biceps, the club manager, believes that the typical lifetime member will continue to use the club's facilities for about ten years.

1987 Operating Results

Revenues (4,000 members @ $300)	$1,200,000
Expenses:	
Variable (4,000 members @ $200)*	800,000
Fixed (depreciation, salaries, and so forth)†	250,000
Total	1,050,000
Net income	$ 150,000

*Variable costs are assumed to vary directly and proportionately with the number of active members.
†Fixed costs do not vary with the number of members.

REQUIRED   Prepare an income statement for the Deltoid Health Club for the year ended December 31, 1988.

44. *Revenue Recognition: Percentage-of-completion versus Completed Contract Method.* In November 1987, the Guido Construction Company enters into a contract with a large university to build a steam-generating plant on campus. The contract specifies that the Guido Construction Company is to receive $1 million for this long-term construction project. Work begins in January 1988, and is expected to take about three years to complete. The project is finished in November 1990, at an actual cost of $800,000. The schedule below

shows (1) construction costs incurred to date and (2) estimated costs to complete at December 31 for the years 1988–1990, respectively.

	1988	1989	1990
Costs incurred as of year-end	$200,000	$350,000	$800,000
Estimated costs to complete	550,000	450,000	0
Total estimated costs	$750,000	$800,000	$800,000

REQUIRED

(a) Prepare a schedule showing how much revenue (and profit) should be recognized by the Guido Construction Company in each of the three years of the contract. Assume the completed contract method is used.

(b) Prepare a schedule showing how much revenue (and profit) should be recognized by the Guido Construction Company in each of the three years of the contract. Assume the percentage-of-completion method is used.

(c) Which method used above for recognizing the timing of income do you believe provides the most useful information to users of the financial statements? Explain.

45. *Revenue Recognition: Percentage-of-completion Method.* The Smith Construction Company uses the percentage-of-completion method of accounting for long-term construction contracts. In 1989, Smith Construction began work on Contract #215, which provided for a contract price of $2 million. Other details follow:

	1989	1990
Costs incurred during the year	$ 400,000	$1,300,000
Estimated costs to complete, as of December 31	1,100,000	0

REQUIRED

(a) How much of the $2-million contract price should be recognized as earned revenue in 1989?

(b) How much of the $2-million contract price should be recognized as earned revenue in 1990?

(c) At December 31, 1989, the cost estimate to complete the project was $1.1 million. The project was completed the next year, but at a cost of $1.3 million. How should this $200,000 difference be treated in financial statements of 1988 and 1989?

(d) Describe briefly the procedure for handling changes in estimates required by generally accepted accounting principles.

46. *Changes in Estimates: Percentage-of-completion Method.* The Jones Construction Company uses the percentage-of-completion method of accounting for long-term construction contracts. In 1988, Jones Construction began work on Contract #512, which provided for a contract price of $1 million. Other details follow:

	1988	1989	1990
Costs incurred during the year	$400,000	$300,000	$110,000
Estimated costs to complete, as of December 31	500,000	100,000	0

REQUIRED

(a) What is the amount of total costs actually incurred on Contract #512 over the three-year period?
(b) Did the company's estimate of total costs to be incurred on Contract #512 change over the three-year period? If so, prepare a schedule showing the firm's estimate of total costs for the project at the end of each year.
(c) Describe briefly the procedure required by generally accepted accounting principles for handling changes in estimates.
(d) How much of the $1-million contract price did the company recognize as earned revenue in its annual income statement for each of the three years, 1988–1990?

47. *Economic Events and Income Recognition.* The events listed below had an economic impact upon Surface Beauty Products, Inc., a distributor of cosmetics.

(1) The firm's assistant treasurer announced that she had successfully completed an MBA program at State University.
(2) The U.S. Congress passed an income tax reform bill that will increase the firm's tax rate beginning next year.
(3) A recent newspaper article reveals that area water quality and air pollution levels are deemed hazardous, and are deteriorating.
(4) A competing beauty products firm has just announced a patent on a new product that it expects to "garner a major share of the market."
(5) The market value per share of the firm's common stock has increased by a substantial amount over the past few weeks.
(6) A nationwide chain of department stores has contracted to carry the firm's line of beauty products, which is expected to double sales levels over the next few years.

REQUIRED For each of the items listed above, determine if that item is a proper input in preparing the income statement for Surface Beauty Products, Inc. Explain your answer for each item.

48. *Economic Events and the Recognition of Revenues and Expenses.*   The transactions and events listed below occurred during 1988. In one way or another, each item had an economic impact on the Ware Company, a publisher of maps.

    (1) The general level of prices rose 12% during the year.
    (2) Ware Company paid a cash dividend to its stockholders.
    (3) The company had a loan outstanding for the entire year. The principal and all interest are due to be paid on December 31, 1990.
    (4) The firm purchased some old maps at an auction; none of the maps had been sold by year-end.
    (5) Ware Company had a fire in one of its many warehouses. All of the contents were destroyed, but they were fully insured.
    (6) The company paid for a purchase made on credit during 1987.
    (7) The firm printed and delivered a large order of maps to a major university. A receivable is still outstanding at year-end for this sale.
    (8) The company sold additional shares of stock to raise capital.
    (9) The company signed a labor contract with its workers, agreeing to give them an across-the-board raise beginning July 1, 1988.
    (10) The firm sold a parcel of land that it owned to a real estate developer for more than the original cost of the land.
    (11) Ware Company signed a contract with the U.S. Government to print 100,000 maps of downtown Bayonne. Printing is scheduled to begin in January 1989.
    (12) The company painted the president's home.

REQUIRED   For each of the items listed above, determine if that item is a proper input in preparing the Ware Company's income statement for the year ended December 31, 1988. Explain your answer for each item.

49. *Recognition of Revenues and Expenses.*   The events listed below relate to the operations of the NTS Company. Unless stated otherwise, all of the events occurred during 1987.

    (1) The firm contracted to purchase 12,000 tons of refined sugar at a total cost of $4.8 million, to be delivered in early 1988.
    (2) When NTS's chief accountant suggested that depreciation expense for 1987 for the firm's building be recorded, the president responded that the market value of the building had actually increased during the year.
    (3) Carrie Products Corporation began merger negotiations with NTS, causing both firms' stock prices to increase substantially.
    (4) The Federal Trade Commission announced the initiation of a thorough study of pricing practices in the sugar industry.

(5) Supply shortages in the raw sugar market caused market prices to increase. In fact, the value of the sugar that NTS contracted to buy in (1) above rose to $7.5 million. (NTS will pay just $4.8 million, as agreed.)

REQUIRED Indicate how (if at all) each of the events listed above would affect the 1987 net income of the NTS Company.

50. *Relationship between Income Statement and Balance Sheet.* Two balance sheets for the Santa Fe Corporation are presented below: one at January 1, 1989, and the second at December 31, 1989.

Santa Fe Corporation
Comparative Balance Sheets, 1989

	January 1	December 31
Cash	$15,000	$58,000
Building (net of depreciation)	40,000	30,000
Total Assets	$55,000	$88,000
Notes Payable	$10,000	0
Common Stock	20,000	$50,000
Retained Earnings	25,000	38,000
Total Liabilities and Stockholders' Equity	$55,000	$88,000

Additional information:

(1) No buildings were acquired or sold during 1989.
(2) Total amount of revenues for 1989 is $40,000.
(3) Total amount of expense for 1989 is $22,000. There are three different types of expense: depreciation, interest, and salaries. The amount of interest expense is $5,000.
(4) Cash dividends were declared and paid during 1989.

REQUIRED

(a) Prepare a detailed income statement for the Santa Fe Corporation for the year ended December 31, 1989.
(b) Is the change in cash for the year the same as the amount of net income for the year? If not, why not?
(c) Prepare a schedule that explains the changes in Retained Earnings during the year ended December 31, 1989.

51. *Accounting Income and Cash Flows.* Jack King owns a bicycle shop, which is just beginning its second year of existence; the business started operations on January 1, 1988. Using the company's checkbook, Mr. King prepared the following statement of income as of December 31, 1988:

Statement of Profit
For the Year Ended December 31, 1988

Cash collected from customers and deposited in the bank	$35,000
Expenses paid by check	32,000
Profit	$ 3,000

You have recently been hired to serve as Mr. King's accountant and financial consultant. In one of your first conversations with him, he offers the following:

"This business is fantastic. I never expected to make a profit until the second or third year of operations, but not once during the past year did we ever overdraw our checking account."

The items listed below come to your attention during your first few weeks on the job.

(1) On December 31, 1988, customers owed $2,500 from the sale of bicycles on credit.
(2) Mr. King has not paid his rent since September 30, 1988. Monthly rental on the building is $1,000.
(3) Mr. King financed the business with a $10,000, five-year loan from his father. The terms of the agreement call for a lump-sum payment of $12,500 on December 31, 1992 (repayment of principal: $10,000; interest: $2,500).

REQUIRED

(a) Based on Mr. King's statements and actions, how do you think he would define the term "profit"?
(b) Did Jack King violate generally accepted accounting principles in preparing his statement of profit? Explain.
(c) Prepare an income statement for the year ended December 31, 1988, that is in accordance with generally accepted accounting principles.

52. *Cash Flows, Revenues, and Expenses.*   Listed below are items that relate to the 1988 operations of the Spokane Company.

(1) Cash collected from customers during 1988 totaled $15 million and accounts receivable decreased $3 million during the year.
(2) Cash paid to suppliers totaled $9.5 million, supplier accounts payable decreased by $2 million, and inventories increased by $3 million during the year.
(3) Cash payments for insurance premiums totaled $1.5 million and prepaid insurance increased by $0.2 million during the year.

(4) The net carrying value (cost less accumulated depreciation) of equipment increased by $4.2 million. No equipment was sold or retired and $6 million of new equipment was purchased during the year.

(5) Unearned revenue decreased by $1.5 million and cash advances from customers totaled $7 million.

(6) Wage payments to employees totaled $23 million and salaries payable increased by $4.5 million.

REQUIRED   For each of the items above, determine the amount of revenue or expense that should be recognized for the year ended December 31, 1988.

53. *Cash Flows, Revenues, and Expenses.*   Listed below are items that relate to the 1988 operations of the Tacoma Company.

(1) Credit sales amounted to $320 million and accounts receivable increased by $28 million during the year. (Assume no accounts are uncollectible.)

(2) Cost of goods sold amounted to $145 million, inventories increased by $40 million, and supplier accounts payable increased by $25.5 million during the year.

(3) Insurance expense totaled $2.5 million and prepaid insurance decreased by $1.1 million during the year.

(4) The net carrying value (cost less accumulated depreciation) of equipment increased by $60 million. No equipment was sold or retired and equipment depreciation expense was $12.5 million during the year.

(5) Wages expense was $122 million and wages payable decreased by $12 million during the year.

REQUIRED   For each of the above items, determine the amount of 1988 cash inflows or cash outflows for the Tacoma Company.

54. *Intrastatement Tax Allocation.*   The following information pertains to the 1987 and 1988 income statements of Wilbur Mills, Inc.

	(in millions)	
	1988	**1987**
Operating income before tax	$220.0	$180.0
Other recurring incomes and expenses	60.0	55.0
Extraordinary loss	88.0	
Operating loss, discontinued operations	22.0	
Gain on sale of discontinued operations	27.0	
Income tax expense	71.7	94.0

Income tax expense in 1988 was determined as follows:

	(in millions)
Tax effect* of:	
Operating income before tax	$88.0
Other recurring income and expenses	24.0
Extraordinary loss	(42.0)
Operating loss, discontinued operations	(8.8)
Gain in sale of discontinued operations	10.5
Total income tax expense	$71.7

*This case assumes that different effective tax rates may apply to the various elements of taxable income.

REQUIRED Prepare the portion of the 1988 income statement from "Operating income before tax" through "Net income" for Wilbur Mills, Inc., reflecting intrastatement allocation of income tax expense.

55. *Income Statement Relationships: Merchandising Firm.* Each of the following cases presents partial information related to the income statement of a merchandising firm.

	Case A	Case B	Case C
Sales	$1,000	$2,000	?
Net income (after tax expense)	$ 60	?	?
Gross margin percentage	25%	30%	20%
Income tax rate	40%	40%	40%
Change in inventory	$ 75	$ 100	?
Merchandise purchases	?	?	$2,500
Cost of goods sold	?	?	?
Selling and administrative expenses	?	?	$ 600
Income tax expense	?	$ 80	$ 200

REQUIRED Provide the missing information wherever possible.

56. *Estimating Merchandise Inventory.* The Lynn Corporation is a retail firm. It recently experienced a devastating fire in its only warehouse; the building was completely destroyed, along with all its contents. All merchandise inventory was stored in this building. Financial data available from the accounting records, which are current through the date of the fire, include the following:

Beginning inventory	$ 6,000
Purchases during the period	18,000
Sales during the period	30,000
Gross margin percentage	40%

REQUIRED Estimate the dollar amount (historical cost) of merchandise inventory that was on hand on the day of the fire. Show all work.

57. *Interfirm Comparisons: Pricing Strategies.* Listed below are data selected from the accounting records of two different retail firms in the same small

town. The two firms are direct competitors, but they are managed in markedly different ways. The data relate to the year ended December 31, 1988.

	Firm A	Firm B
Beginning inventory (1/1/88)	$ 200,000	$ 500,000
Ending inventory (12/31/88)	100,000	400,000
Purchases during the year	2,000,000	1,000,000
Sales	3,200,000	2,200,000

REQUIRED

(a) Prepare partial income statements (through the calculation of gross margin) for each company.
(b) Based on the partial income statements you have prepared, compare the pricing policies of the two firms.
(c) One of the two companies is a downtown department store, and the other is a discount store located just outside of town. Which firm do you believe is the downtown department store? Explain your reasoning.

58. *Expense Recognition: Product Costs versus Period Costs.*   In financial accounting, manufacturing costs are assigned initially to inventory accounts and are referred to as product costs. In contrast, the nonmanufacturing costs of doing business (general, administrative, selling, and so on) are not assigned to inventory accounts and are called period costs.
     A list of costs incurred by the Reno Company follows:

(1) Wages for an inspector in the assembly department
(2) Depreciation of office equipment
(3) Salary of the vice-president of marketing
(4) Overtime pay for a punch press operator
(5) Raw materials used in production
(6) Property taxes on the factory buildings
(7) Property taxes on the land held for future development
(8) Supplies used by the factory maintenance staff
(9) Office supplies used
(10) Salary of the company president
(11) Depreciation on autos used by sales force
(12) Heating costs of factory buildings
(13) Insurance premiums on factory machinery
(14) Wages of assembly-line workers

REQUIRED

(a) Classify each of the above as either a product cost or a period cost.
(b) Do all product costs flow through to the income statement in the period incurred? Explain.

(c) Would the caption "Depreciation expense on factory buildings" ever appear on the income statement of a manufacturing firm? Explain.

59. *Basic Journal Entries for a Manufacturing Firm.* During October 1987, the Defiance Manufacturing Company completed the following transactions regarding its manufacturing operations:

(1) Purchased $250,000 of raw materials on account from its suppliers.
(2) Placed $230,000 of raw materials into the production process.
(3) The payroll for manufacturing personnel for the month consisted of 4,000 hours of direct labor at $12 per hour and 500 hours of indirect labor at $15 per hour.
(4) Depreciation on factory buildings and equipment for the month was $20,000.
(5) Cost of utilities (heat, lighting, and so on) for manufacturing buildings and equipment for the month was $10,000.
(6) Completed production of inventory with a total manufacturing cost of $300,000. Completed units were transferred to the finished goods warehouse.
(7) Finished goods costing $280,000 were sold during the month at a total sales price of $450,000.

REQUIRED   Prepare journal entries to record each of the transactions or events listed above.

60. *Cost of Goods Manufactured.* The following data are contained in the Orlando Company's accounting records for the year ended December 31, 1988:

Direct labor	$ 150,000
Direct material purchased	235,000
Direct materials used	250,000
Finished goods inventory, January 1, 1988	400,000
Finished goods inventory, December 31, 1988	450,000
Manufacturing overhead	750,000
Sales	2,300,000
Work-in-process inventory, January 1, 1988	125,000
Work-in-process inventory, December 31, 1988	100,000

REQUIRED   Calculate cost of goods manufactured.

61. *Income Statement for a Manufacturing Firm.* The Lima Company's accounting records contain the following data for the year ended December 31, 1988:

Direct labor	$ 250,000
Direct materials used	150,000
Finished goods inventory, January 1, 1988	450,000

Finished goods inventory, December 31, 1988	425,000
Manufacturing overhead	650,000
Purchases of direct materials	300,000
Sales	3,300,000
Selling and administrative expenses	330,000
Work-in-process inventory, January 1, 1988	100,000
Work-in-process inventory, December 31, 1988	125,000

REQUIRED   Prepare an income statement for the Lima Company for the year ended December 31, 1988.

62. *Evaluating Past Performance.*   The Whiteman Company regularly prepares forecasted financial statements. The 1988 forecasted income statement, prepared at the beginning of that year, is shown below. Also presented are results actually achieved in 1988, and differences between actual and forecasted items.

	Forecasted	Actual	Difference
Sales	$ 75,000	$ 90,000	+15,000
Cost of goods sold	(37,500)	(40,000)	+ 2,500
Gross margin	$ 37,500	$ 50,000	+12,500
Wages expense	(10,000)	(12,500)	+ 2,500
Depreciation expense	(8,000)	(8,000)	0
Interest expense	(2,000)	(3,000)	+ 1,000
Loss on sale of building	0	(9,000)	+ 9,000
Net income before tax	$ 17,500	$ 17,500	0
Income tax expense	(9,000)	(9,000)	0
Net income (loss)	$ 8,500	$ 8,500	0

Notice that actual net income is exactly as forecasted. Differences do exist, however, between forecasted and actual amounts for individual income statement items.

REQUIRED

(a) In light of the actual and forecasted amounts shown above, evaluate the firm's performance for 1988.
(b) Evaluate the firm's performance for 1988, but assume a detailed forecasted income statement was not prepared. Instead, assume that only "the bottom line" was forecasted; that is, net income was projected to be $8,500 for the period.
(c) In the above case, what specific advantages, if any, do you see in having a detailed income statement (as opposed to a statement that lists only "the bottom line")?

63. *Preparation of a Forecasted Income Statement.*   Assume the current time is November 1988, and that you work as an analyst for the Strock Corpora-

tion. The company's published income statements for the previous three years are presented below.

	1985	1986	1987
Sales	$ 25,000	$ 50,000	$100,000
Cost of goods sold	(12,500)	(25,000)	(50,000)
Gross margin	$ 12,500	$ 25,000	$ 50,000
Wages expense	(10,000)	(15,000)	(25,000)
Depreciation expense	(8,000)	(8,000)	(8,000)
Interest expense	(2,000)	(1,000)	(4,000)
Loss on sale of building	0	0	(9,000)
Net income (loss) before tax	$ (7,500)	$ 1,000	$ 4,000
Income tax expense	0	400	1,600
Net income (loss)	$ (7,500)	$ 600	2,400

The best estimate of Strock Corporation's sales revenue for 1988 is $150,000.

REQUIRED Prepare a forecasted income statement for the year ended December 31, 1988. List all assumptions made in preparing the statement and provide your rationale for each assumption.

APPENDIX PROBLEMS

64. *Inventory Costing: Different Levels of Production.* The following schedule shows quarterly sales, expenses, and production levels for Time, Inc., a watch manufacturer, for the year ended December 31, 1989.

	Quarter			
	1	2	3	4
Costs:				
Factory utility costs	$ 8,000	$ 8,000	$ 8,000	$ 8,000
Direct materials	10,000	18,000	6,000	8,000
Factory insurance costs	3,000	3,000	3,000	3,000
Depreciation of equipment	4,000	4,000	4,000	4,000
Direct labor costs	25,000	45,000	15,000	20,000
Variable factory overhead	15,000	27,000	9,000	12,000
Foremen's salaries	4,000	4,000	4,000	4,000
Number of watches:				
Production level	5,000	9,000	3,000	4,000
Sales level (@ $24.00 each)	1,500	4,000	10,500	2,000

Ending inventory on December 31, 1988, was 2,000 watches with an inventory cost of $24,000. Assume Time, Inc., uses the absorption costing method and that the oldest inventory is sold first.

REQUIRED

(a) Classify the costs incurred by Time, Inc., as either (1) fixed costs or (2) variable costs.

(b) Calculate the costs per watch for each quarter.
(c) Calculate the cost of goods sold and the cost of ending inventory for each quarter.
(d) Explain the change in cost of goods sold from quarter to quarter.

65. *Absorption Costing: Two Years.* Simpson Company is a manufacturer of ball bearings. They are interested in analyzing their income statements for the years ended 1987 and 1988. The following data relate to their operations in those years:

	1987	1988
Number of units produced	1,500	4,000
Number of units sold	1,400	1,400
Sales price	$20 per unit	$20 per unit
Direct labor	$ 2 per unit	$ 2 per unit
Fixed factory overhead	$ 6,000	$ 6,000
Direct materials	$ 4 per unit	$ 4 per unit
Variable factory overhead	$ 2 per unit	$ 2 per unit
Selling and administrative	$ 2,000	$ 2,000

REQUIRED

(a) Prepare annual income statements for Simpson Company for 1987 and 1988, using absorption costing. Assume no beginning inventory in 1987, and show computations of variable and fixed unit costs and cost of goods sold. Each year the oldest inventory available is sold first.
(b) After the two income statements have been prepared, explain the difference between the net income figures for the year ended 1987 and the year ended 1988.

66. *Absorption versus Variable Costing.* Western Liquors, Inc., produces a single product, "Old Hooch." Operating statistics during 1988 were as follows:

Production	18,000 cases
Sales	16,000 cases
Selling price	$120 per case
Inventory, January 1, 1988	2,000 cases
Materials cost per case	$ 28
Direct labor per case	$ 24
Variable factory overhead	$ 16 per case
Fixed factory overhead	$252,000

REQUIRED

(a) Prepare a statement showing the company's gross margin for 1988 under both absorption costing and variable costing. In 1987, variable factory costs amounted to $70 per case, and fixed factory overhead amounted to $15 per case. The oldest inventory is sold first each year.

(b) Account for the differences in gross margin in (a) above under the two methods.
(c) Assume that production in 1988 was as indicated, but that sales were higher than 16,000 cases. What effect, if any, would this have on the gross margin under the two different methods?
(d) Assume that sales in 1988 were as indicated, but that production was higher than 18,000 cases. What effect, if any, would this have on the gross margin under the two different methods?

4

The Income Statement: Extensions

Chapters 3 and 4 of this text focus on the income statement, but from different perspectives. While Chapter 3 covers the major sections and overall organization of the income statement, it does not consider the alternative accounting methods permitted for certain individual elements of that statement.

Chapter 4 is more narrow in scope. It examines three components of net income in greater detail. The first two sections focus on alternative inventory cost flow assumptions and depreciation patterns permitted by generally accepted accounting principles. Choices among alternatives in these areas affect the reported dollar amounts of cost of goods sold and depreciation expense, respectively. The chapter's last section considers issues in accounting for income tax expense.

ALTERNATIVES IN INVENTORY COSTING

A common situation in business is the acquisition over time of similar items of inventory for which different unit prices are paid. For example, a certain item may be purchased early in a period for $2 per unit. Later in the period the price paid for the same item may be $3 per unit. Which unit cost—$2, $3, or some other figure—should be used in assigning a dollar amount to ending inventory? This section examines procedures used in financial accounting to answer this type of question.

As explained in Chapter 3, cost of goods sold is a major component of the income statement for merchandising and manufacturing firms and is computed as follows:

Beginning inventory	$XXX
Plus: Cost of goods purchased or manufactured during the period	XXX
Total cost of goods available for sale	$XXX
Less: Ending inventory	(XXX)
Cost of goods sold	$XXX

The overall effect of this computation is to allocate total cost of goods available for sale between (1) those goods that did not sell during the period (ending inventory) and (2) those goods that did sell (cost of goods sold). Thus, the dollar amount assigned to ending inventory in the above calculation affects both the balance sheet and the income statement. Moreover, the ending inventory in one period is the beginning inventory in the next period, so income in both periods is affected by the cost of inventories.

Four methods for allocating costs between ending inventory and cost of goods sold are generally accepted in financial accounting: (1) specific identification; (2) average cost; (3) first-in, first-out (FIFO); and (4) last-in, first-out (LIFO). These methods are called **cost flow assumptions.** The specific identification method allocates costs according to the physical flow of goods. The other methods assume certain cost flow patterns that may or may not reflect the physical flow of goods.

Specific Identification

The **specific identification** method involves keeping track of the unit cost of each individual item in inventory. The objective is to match the unit cost of the specific item sold with sales revenue. To illustrate, assume an art dealer purchases two seemingly identical pieces of pottery during a period. The first piece is acquired for $2,000 and the second is purchased several months later for $2,500. Assume also that only one of these items is sold by the dealer during the period. The amounts assigned to cost of goods sold and ending inventory would depend on which specific piece of pottery is sold. If the item sold is the first piece of pottery, cost of goods sold is $2,000 and ending inventory is $2,500. On the other hand, if the second piece is the one sold, the numbers would be reversed; that is, cost of goods sold would be $2,500 and ending inventory would be $2,000.

The specific identification method provides a highly objective procedure for matching costs with sales revenue because the cost flow pattern matches the physical flow of the goods. This method is not widely employed, however, because it is time-consuming and costly. Its use is practical only if the inventory consists of relatively few items that are expensive per unit (such as furs, jewelry, automobiles, and art objects). Another limitation of the specific identification method is that its use opens up the possibility of income manipulation. The art dealer in the preceding paragraph could choose to have cost of goods sold of $2,000 or $2,500, depending on which of the virtually identical pieces of pottery he elected to sell to the customer.

Average Cost, FIFO, and LIFO

The other cost flow assumptions—average cost, FIFO, and LIFO—are widely used in the business world and provide a practical basis for the measurement of periodic income. Application of these generally accepted methods will be demonstrated using data presented in Exhibit 4-1. These data relate to the inventory purchases and sales of the Oval Record Company for 1987 (its first year of operations) and 1988.

Observe that the data presented in Exhibit 4-1 show that the unit cost of the firm's purchases has been rising steadily. If unit costs were constant, the cost flow assumptions would all result in the same amounts for inventory and cost of goods sold. When unit costs move steadily in one direction, the differences among the inventory cost flow assumptions may be dramatic. For a majority of U.S. firms, unit costs of inventory purchases have risen steadily over the past two decades.

First we will examine the calculations for inventory and cost of goods sold for Oval Records during its first year. Note in Exhibit 4-1 that the physical flow

Exhibit 4-1
Data for Inventory and Cost of Goods Sold Calculations

Oval Record Company

	1987			1988		
	Units	Unit Cost	Total Cost	Units	Unit Cost	Total Cost
Beginning Inventory	0		0	40		?
First Purchase	20	$10	$200	30	$15	$450
Second Purchase	30	$12	$360	50	$18	$900
Third Purchase	50	$13	$650	20	$21	$420
Available for Sale	100		$1,210	140		?
Units Sold	(60)		?	(110)		?
Units in Ending Inventory	40		?	30		?

of goods in 1987 is already known—of the 100 items available for sale, 60 were sold and 40 remain in ending inventory. Also known is the dollar amount of goods available for sale—$1,210. This amount cannot be allocated between cost of goods sold and ending inventory until the Oval Record Company adopts an inventory cost flow assumption.

Average cost   To use the **average cost** method, the total cost of all goods available for sale during the period is divided by the number of units available for sale. The resulting average unit cost is then used to value both the ending inventory and the cost of goods sold. The average unit cost for Oval Records is computed as follows:

Cost of goods available	$1,210
Units available	100
Average cost per unit ($1,210/100)	$12.10

This unit cost is then used to compute ending inventory and cost of goods sold:

Cost of goods available (100 units)	$1,210
Less: Ending inventory	
40 units @ $12.10	(484)
Cost of goods sold	
60 units @ $12.10	$ 726

First-in, first-out (FIFO)   Under the **first-in, first-out** method, the costs of the earliest purchases are assigned to cost of goods sold and the costs of the most recent purchases are allocated to ending inventory. In many cases, this pattern of cost flow conforms to the physical flow of the goods, particularly when the inventory is susceptible to spoilage or style changes. Nevertheless, FIFO may be adopted by any business, regardless of whether or not the physical flow of goods corresponds to the assumption of selling or using the oldest units in stock first.

The 40 units of ending inventory for the Oval Record Company at the end of 1987 are costed as follows if FIFO is used:

Ending inventory	
(Third purchase) 40 units @ $13	$ 520

And, the cost of goods sold is computed below.

Cost of goods available (100 units)	$1,210
Less: Ending inventory (40 units)	(520)
Cost of goods sold (60 units)	$ 690

Because the cost of the latest (third) purchase ($13) is greater than the average unit cost of $12.10 (computed earlier), FIFO costing resulted in a higher valuation of the ending inventory and a lower cost of goods sold as compared to these amounts under average costing. A schedule showing the calculation of cost of goods sold and ending inventory when FIFO is used is presented in Exhibit 4-2.

Last-in, first-out (LIFO)   The **last-in, first-out** method allocates costs of the latest purchases to cost of goods sold and assigns the oldest costs making up goods available for sale to ending inventory. This cost flow assumption matches the physical flow of the goods only if the most recently acquired goods are sold first. If the Oval Record Company employs LIFO, the 40 units in inventory at the end of 1987 are costed as follows:

Ending inventory		
(First purchase)	20 units @ $10	$ 200
(Second purchase)	20 units @ $12	240
	40 units	$ 440

And, the cost of goods sold is computed below.

Cost of goods available (100 units)	$1,210
Less: Ending inventory (40 units)	(440)
Cost of goods sold (60 units)	$ 770

Because the cost of the oldest inventory available ($10—first purchase, $12—second purchase) is below the average unit cost and the FIFO unit cost computed earlier ($12.10 and $13, respectively), LIFO costing resulted in a lower valuation of the ending inventory and a higher cost of goods sold than did either of the other inventory cost flow assumptions. A schedule showing the calculation of cost of goods sold and ending inventory when LIFO is used is also contained in Exhibit 4-2.

Alternative inventory cost flow assumptions affect the financial statements in different ways. Demonstrated effects in the Oval Record Company's first year of operations include the following:

- In a period of rising prices, FIFO results in the highest valuation of ending inventory, and LIFO results in the lowest valuation. (This is because FIFO assigns the more recent and higher unit costs to ending inventory, while LIFO assigns the older and lower costs to ending inventory.)
- In a period of rising prices, FIFO produces the lowest cost of goods sold, and LIFO produces the highest cost of goods sold. Therefore, everything else being equal, FIFO would result in the highest reported net income, and LIFO would result in the lowest reported net income.
- Use of the average cost method produces financial statement effects that are in between those produced by FIFO and LIFO.

The Oval Record Company's ending inventory and cost of goods sold may now be determined for 1988, the firm's second year of operations. According to the data presented in Exhibit 4-1, 100 items are purchased during 1988 at a total cost of $1,770 ($450 + $900 + $420). The cost of beginning inventory for any period is always the same dollar amount as ending inventory in the previous

Exhibit 4-2
Cost of Goods Sold and Ending Inventory, 1987

Oval Record Company

FIFO	Units	Unit Cost	Total Cost	Units	Unit Cost	Total Cost	Units	Unit Cost	Total Cost
					FIFO Cost of Goods Sold			FIFO Ending Inventory	
Beginning Inventory	0								
First Purchase	20	$10	$200	20	$10	$200			
Second Purchase	30	$12	$360	30	$12	$360			
Third Purchase	50	$13	$650	10	$13	$130	40	$13	$520
Total	100		$1,210	60		$690	40		$520
Less: Cost of Goods Sold	(60)		(690)						
Ending Inventory	40		$520						

LIFO	Units	Unit Cost	Total Cost	Units	Unit Cost	Total Cost	Units	Unit Cost	Total Cost
					LIFO Cost of Goods Sold			LIFO Ending Inventory	
Beginning Inventory	0								
First Purchase	20	$10	$200				20	$10	$200
Second Purchase	30	$12	$360	10	$12	$120	20	$12	$240
Third Purchase	50	$13	$650	50	$13	$650			
Total	100		$1,210	60		$770	40		$440
Less: Cost of Goods Sold	(60)		(770)						
Ending Inventory	40		$440						

period; consequently, the *valuation* of the beginning inventory for the Oval Record Company in 1988 depends on which inventory cost flow assumption was used in 1987. Cost of goods available for sale in 1988 is calculated below using the average cost, FIFO, and LIFO inventory cost flow assumptions.

	Average Cost	FIFO	LIFO
Beginning inventory (40 units)	$ 484	$ 520	$ 440
Purchases (100 units)	1,770	1,770	1,770
Total available (140 units)	$2,254	$2,290	$2,210

To compute the cost of goods sold for 1988, *the ending inventory must be valued using the same cost flow assumption as that used at the end of the previous period.* The computations, which appear in Exhibit 4-3, follow the same logic as that applied in costing the previous year's inventory. Note in Exhibit 4-3 that under FIFO, costs of the most recent purchases are assigned to ending inventory. Under LIFO, the oldest costs comprising goods available for sale are allocated to ending inventory. (The oldest costs comprising goods available for sale are those used to value beginning inventory in 1988; the next oldest, those of the first purchase in 1988, and so on.) Because the Oval Record Company did not increase the number of units of inventory during 1988, the ending inventory includes only unit costs that were included in the beginning inventory. In addition to calculations presented in Exhibit 4-3 for LIFO, Exhibit 4-4 shows in detail the composition of the LIFO inventory at the end of 1988.

Exhibit 4-3 shows the different dollar amounts allocated to ending inventory and cost of goods sold by use of the average cost, FIFO, and LIFO inventory cost flow assumptions. The pattern of differences is the same as in the previous year; that is, FIFO produces the lowest cost of goods sold (and thus,

Exhibit 4-3

Ending Inventory and Cost of Goods Sold, 1988

Oval Record Company

Ending Inventory Calculations

Average Cost	Cost of goods available	$2,254
	Total available units	140
	Average unit cost ($2,254/140)	$16.10
	Ending inventory (30 × $16.10)	483.00

FIFO Cost	From purchases during 1988	
	Third purchase, 1988	20 units @ $21 = $420
	Second purchase, 1988	10 units @ $18 = 180
	Ending inventory	30 units $600

LIFO Cost	From beginning inventory, January 1988	
	First purchase, 1987	20 units @ $10 = $200
	Second purchase, 1987	10 units @ $12 = 120
	Ending inventory	30 units $320

Cost of Goods Sold Calculations

	Average Cost	FIFO	LIFO
Beginning inventory (40 units)	$ 484	$ 520	$ 440
Purchases	1,770	1,770	1,770
Total cost of goods available for sale	$2,254	$2,290	$2,210
Ending inventory (30 units)	(483)	(600)	(320)
Cost of goods sold	$1,771	$1,690	$1,890

Exhibit 4-4
LIFO Cost of Goods Sold and Ending Inventory, 1988

Oval Record Company

	Units	Unit Cost	Total Cost	Cost of Goods Sold Units	Unit Cost	Total Cost	Ending Inventory Units	Unit Cost	Total Cost
Beginning Inventory	20	$10	$ 200				20	$10	$200
	20	12	240	10	$12	$ 120	10	12	120
First Purchase	30	15	450	30	15	450			
Second Purchase	50	18	900	50	18	900			
Third Purchase	20	21	420	20	21	420			
Total	140		$2,210	110		$1,890	30		$320
Less: Cost of Goods Sold	(110)		(1,890)						
Ending Inventory	30		$ 320						

the highest net income), while LIFO produces the highest cost of goods sold (and the lowest net income).

Note, however, that the differences in cost of goods sold in 1988 depend on both the beginning inventory and the ending inventory valuations. To illustrate, the FIFO ending inventory of $600 exceeds the LIFO ending inventory of $320 by $280 ($600 − $320). Yet the FIFO cost of goods sold ($1,690) is less than the LIFO cost of goods sold by $200 ($1,890 − $1,690). These differences can be explained as follows:

FIFO Compared to LIFO Valuation of Inventories	Effect on Cost of Goods Sold
Beginning inventory: FIFO higher by $80 ($520 − $440)	Higher by $80
Ending inventory: FIFO higher by $280 ($600 − $320)	Lower by $280
Net effect	Lower by $200

The same relationship may be restated in another way: the FIFO inventory increased by $80 ($520 beginning inventory and $600 ending inventory), while the LIFO inventory decreased by $120 ($440 beginning inventory and $320 ending inventory). This means that the FIFO cost of goods sold is $80 less than the purchases, while the LIFO cost of goods sold is $120 more than the purchases. The difference in cost of goods sold between FIFO and LIFO is then $200 ($80 + $120).

Use of Different Inventory Costing Methods

Exhibit 4-5 shows the extent to which the various inventory cost flow methods are used by 600 publicly held companies sampled annually by the American Institute of Certified Public Accountants. Notice that in each of the years from 1981–1984, LIFO was the most popular method, followed in order by FIFO and average cost.

While 600 firms are included in the AICPA survey, the number of firms using each method in a particular year exceeds 600. This is because it is permissible for a single firm to use one method for a certain part of the inventory (manufactured finished goods, for example) and a different method for another part of the inventory (purchased repair parts, for instance). The bottom half of Exhibit 4-5 is concerned only with LIFO firms. Although 400 of the 600 surveyed firms used LIFO in 1984, only 26 companies (7 percent of those 400) used LIFO on all inventories, while 215 firms (54 percent of those 400) used LIFO on more than half of their inventories.

LIFO Liquidation

While it is true that during periods of rising prices LIFO usually produces lower reported net income than the other inventory costing methods, an important exception may occur when inventory levels are reduced, or "liquidated." A liquidation means that the number of units sold during the period exceeds the number of units purchased during the period. When this occurs in a period of inflation and LIFO is used, cost of goods sold will consist of the cost of all

Exhibit 4-5
Use Survey of Different Inventory Cost Flow Assumptions

	Number of Companies			
	1984	**1983**	**1982**	**1981**
Methods				
Last-in first-out (LIFO)	400	408	407	408
First-in first-out (FIFO)	377	366	373	371
Average cost	223	235	238	241
Other	54	52	53	52
Use of LIFO				
All inventories	26	31	28	26
50% or more of inventories	215	204	206	210
Less than 50% of inventories	82	93	88	89
Not determinable	77	80	85	83
Companies Using LIFO	400	408	407	408

Source: *Accounting Trends and Techniques* (New York: AICPA, 1985), p. 116.

purchases during the period *plus at least some of the costs assigned to LIFO begin-ning inventory,* which are the older and, by definition, the lower unit costs.

As an example, refer back to Exhibit 4-3. Notice in the cost of goods sold calculations at the bottom of the exhibit that ending inventory of 30 units in 1988 is less than beginning inventory of 40 units. Under LIFO, the 10 units that were liquidated during this period are charged to cost of goods sold from be-ginning inventory at a unit cost of $12, which is well below the unit costs of purchases made in 1988. A detailed breakdown of LIFO cost of goods sold in 1988 is contained in Exhibit 4-4.

While the liquidation of these 10 units made LIFO cost of goods sold lower than would otherwise be the case, it was not so severe as to make cost of goods sold under LIFO less than under the other methods. The LIFO cost of goods sold figure could have been less than those of average cost and FIFO, however, if the reduction in the level of inventory had been more dramatic.

To emphasize this point, consider the results for the Oval Record Company if *all* available goods were sold in 1988 leaving no units in ending inventory. In the case of *complete inventory liquidation,* ending inventory would have a zero balance, and cost of goods sold would be equal to the total cost of goods avail-able for sale. Referring again to Exhibit 4-3, observe that cost of goods available for sale in 1988 is $2,290 if FIFO is being used, and $2,210 if LIFO is being used. Thus, LIFO cost of goods sold would be less than the FIFO cost of goods sold by $80 ($2,290 − $2,210) for 1988, even though prices were rising throughout 1987 and 1988.

Holding Gains

Some analysts argue that the use of FIFO or average cost during a period of ris-ing unit costs results in reported net income that is overstated because it con-tains holding gains (or inventory profits). A **holding gain** exists whenever costs assigned to goods sold are less than the costs of replacing those items. The dif-ference may be large when FIFO is used in a period of rising prices, given that FIFO assigns older and lower unit costs to cost of goods sold. Holding gains are possible under LIFO, but they are not likely to be as large because LIFO as-signs the newer and higher unit costs to cost of goods sold.

To illustrate, assume that a bicycle shop has a beginning inventory of 20 bi-cycles. The bicycles were purchased at $180 each. During the period an addi-tional 20 bicycles are purchased at $220 each. Hence, goods available for sale are calculated as follows:

Beginning inventory	20 @ $180 =	$3,600
Purchases during the period	20 @ $220 =	4,400
Goods available for sale		$8,000

Twenty of the bicycles are sold during the period for cash at $350 each. If the company uses FIFO to value inventory, gross margin on these sales may be computed as shown:

Sales (20 @ $350)	$7,000
Cost of goods sold (20 @ $180)	3,600
Gross margin	$3,400

Due to rising unit costs, the company will spend more to replace the 20 bicycles than the cost of goods sold of $3,600 shown above. Assuming that replacement cost has not risen since the company's last purchase, total replacement cost will be $4,400 (20 @ $220). The holding gain in this instance is $800 ($4,400 − $3,600).

Of the $3,400 gross margin shown in this illustration, $800 is a holding gain; the remaining $2,600 is referred to as the **operating margin** (the difference between selling price and replacement cost). In terms of net cash generated by the sale of the 20 items and their replacement, the company is "better off" only by the amount of the operating margin. Specifically, sale of the bicycles generated $7,000 in cash and cost $4,400 to replace, for a net gain in cash of $2,600. This example shows that one may obtain a distorted view of a firm's operating performance if holding gains are ignored.

Inventory Cost Flow Assumptions and Income Tax Expense

Perhaps the most compelling practical reason for the adoption of LIFO has been its acceptance (for income tax purposes) by the Internal Revenue Service. During periods of inflation, LIFO generally results in lower taxable income than other methods. For some companies, use of LIFO has resulted in a permanent deferral of taxes relative to what would have been paid under other acceptable inventory methods. This deferral, of course, has direct cash flow implications: less cash goes out to the IRS, and more cash remains for reinvestment in the firm. In effect, the tax savings are an interest-free loan from the government.

When a company uses LIFO for tax purposes, the IRS requires that LIFO be utilized in the firm's financial accounting reports as well. This **conformity requirement** does not exist for any other inventory costing method. The LIFO conformity requirement was strictly interpreted for many years, but a somewhat liberalized interpretation was adopted by the U.S. Treasury Department in January 1981. Now, taxpayers using LIFO may disclose income and inventory valuations *as if* the company was using a non-LIFO approach, such as FIFO. The non-LIFO disclosures are permitted in financial statement footnotes or as supplemental information that accompanies those statements. LIFO must still be used, however, in the primary financial statements themselves.

Switches to LIFO were particularly heavy during double-digit inflation periods in the 1970s. While LIFO is the single most popular inventory costing method in practice, a majority of U.S. firms continues to use one or more of the other generally accepted methods. (Refer to Exhibit 4-5, page 168.) For many of these firms, a switch to LIFO would provide considerable savings in income tax payments, yet managers resist changing because of "adverse" financial statement effects, such as lower reported earnings and lower inventory valuation on the balance sheet.

The reluctance of many managers to adopt LIFO in cases where unit costs of inventory are expected to rise is based on the view that investors will react negatively to the lower earnings and asset values reported under LIFO. To test that contention, researchers have studied the securities price performance of firms switching from FIFO to LIFO, and of firms switching from LIFO to FIFO. The issue is especially interesting with regard to the information efficiency of the securities market, because the accounting effects and the economic effects of a switch may be in opposite directions.[1] One well-known study reported the following results:

Change in Inventory Method	Effect on Earnings	Effect on Securities Prices
From FIFO to LIFO	Decrease	Increase
From LIFO to FIFO	Increase	Decrease

These results suggest that financial statement users adjust for the lower reported net income under LIFO and focus on LIFO's positive economic effects.

Of course, one should not conclude that the managers of all non-LIFO firms are acting without reason. In some firms, unit costs of inventory might be expected to decrease, and in that case, LIFO would result in higher taxes than would other costing methods. Also, a series of LIFO liquidations, as described earlier, might produce uneven cash outflows for taxes (high in some years, low in others), which in turn could negatively affect securities prices. In addition, the firm's borrowing agreements or loan indentures may place limits on certain key amounts or ratios, and a shift to LIFO might increase the likelihood that the firm would violate these limits. For example, a loan agreement might specify that a long-term loan must be repaid immediately if the total dollar amount of cash, accounts receivable, and inventory drops below the dollar amount of the loan. Since LIFO ending inventory in a period of rising prices is usually lower than under FIFO, the total dollar amount of relevant assets is more likely to violate the required minimum if LIFO is used.

Inventory Cost Flow Assumptions: Concluding Remarks

As pointed out in Chapter 3, many problem areas in financial accounting involve decisions concerning the proper allocation of costs among different accounting periods. The costing of inventories is a good example of the alternatives involved in cost allocation. The choice here is usually between allocating the most recent costs to inventories that were sold (LIFO) or allocating the most recent costs to inventories that were not sold (FIFO). Stated another way, LIFO is more income statement oriented because it usually assigns the most current costs to cost of goods sold. Conversely, FIFO assigns the most recent costs to ending inventory on the balance sheet. Accordingly, LIFO may

---

[1]At least on the surface, the accounting effects of using LIFO are negative—lower reported net income and lower valuation of ending inventory. In contrast, the economic effects are positive—less dollar outflow to the IRS.

provide a more meaningful measure of cost of goods sold and operating profitability, while FIFO may provide a more useful measure of inventory value in depicting financial position.

Regardless of which method is employed, it is important for the users of financial statements to be able to adjust cost of goods sold and reported net income for differences in inventory cost flow assumptions. To facilitate comparisons with other companies, all publicly held firms that use LIFO disclose in footnotes what reported net income would have been had they used another method, such as FIFO or average cost. Exhibit 4-6 shows recent examples of such disclosures.

The basic alternatives in inventory costing discussed in this section are for illustrative purposes only. In practice, most firms use variations of these methods that are designed to cope with changing prices, changes in product mix, technology, and so on. These derived methods are beyond the scope of our introductory discussion and are developed in any intermediate accounting textbook.

ALTERNATIVES IN ACCOUNTING FOR FIXED ASSETS

Fixed assets are long-lived, tangible assets that are employed by an enterprise in the production or sale of inventory or in the provision of services. Examples include automobiles, buildings, computer hardware, office equipment, machinery, and the like. Two problem areas are discussed in this section: (1) allocating the cost of a fixed asset to individual periods that make up the asset's useful life and (2) accounting for the disposal of a fixed asset.

Nature of Depreciation

In everyday language, the term "depreciation" refers to a decline in the market value of an asset. For example, an automobile costing $10,000 is said to depreciate by $3,000 in its first year of use if its resale value at the end of the year is only $7,000. In this usage, depreciation represents a revaluation of the asset.

In financial accounting, however, depreciation is not used to revalue assets. Rather, **depreciation** is the process of allocating the historical cost of a tangible fixed asset to the reporting periods that benefit from its use. In short, depreciation is a process of cost allocation, not asset valuation.

Elements in the Depreciation Process

In accordance with the matching concept, the total cost of using a fixed asset should be allocated to accounting periods based on the *benefits* expected during those periods. In order to compute the periodic depreciation expense for a fixed asset, it is necessary to determine the following: (1) historical cost, (2) residual value, (3) economic life, and (4) benefit pattern. Each of these elements will be discussed separately.

Exhibit 4-6
LIFO Footnote Disclosure Examples

The Sherwin-Williams Company

	1982	1981	1980
	(thousands of dollars)		
Current assets			
Inventories			
Finished goods	$250,803	$278,114	$173,941
Work in process and raw materials	48,505	56,776	63,458
	$299,308	$334,890	$237,399

Notes to Consolidated Financial Statements

Note 3 — Inventories

Inventories are stated at the lower of cost or market. Cost is determined principally on the last-in, first-out (LIFO) method. The following presents the effect on inventories, net income and net income per share had the company used the FIFO and average cost methods of inventory valuation adjusted for income taxes at the statutory rate and assuming no other adjustments. This information is presented to enable the reader to make comparisons with companies using the FIFO method of inventory valuation.

Thousands of dollars except per share data	Years ended December 31,		
	1982	1981	1980
Percentage of total inventories on LIFO	95%	94%	90%
Excess of FIFO and average cost over LIFO	$56,953	$55,949	$32,424
Effect of LIFO on net income	2,148	12,703	14,150
Effect of LIFO on net income per common share	.10	.64	.72

Malone & Hyde, Inc.

	1982	1981
	(in thousands)	
Current Assets		
Cash	$ 969	$ 832
Notes and accounts receivable		
Notes	8,332	13,042
Trade accounts	54,373	46,746
	62,705	59,788
Less allowance for doubtful accounts	3,511	3,529
	59,194	56,259
Merchandise inventories— Note B	162,836	180,557

Notes to Consolidated Financial Statements

Note A (in part): Summary of Significant Accounting Policies

Inventories

The cost of substantially all inventories is determined using the last-in, first-out method (LIFO). Prior to 1981, wholesale groceries were determined using the LIFO method with the remainder using the first-in, first-out method (FIFO). Management believes that the use of the LIFO method results in a better matching of costs and revenues (see Note B).

Note B—Inventories

If the FIFO method of inventory valuation had been used for determining all inventory costs, inventories would have been approximately $21,355,000 and $17,656,000 higher than amounts reported at June 26, 1982 and June 27, 1981, respectively. Adjusted for income taxes applied at the statutory rates and assuming no other adjustments, net income would have been higher than reported by approximately $1,850,000 ($.23 a share) in 1982, $4,842,000 ($.61 a share) in 1981 and $2,680,000 ($5.35 a share) in 1980. This information is presented to enable a reader to make comparisons with companies using the FIFO method of inventory valuation.

Source: *Accounting Trends and Techniques* (New York: AICPA, 1983), pp. 126–27.

1. **Historical cost** includes all expenditures incurred to prepare an asset for use. In addition to the amount paid to the supplier of the asset, historical cost includes any other expenditures for transportation or installation, as well as start-up costs needed to incorporate the asset into the firm's operations.
2. **Residual value** denotes the net proceeds the firm expects to receive upon disposing of the asset at the end of its economic life. Because the firm may intend to use the asset for a number of years, residual values often are difficult to estimate and may be revised with the passage of time.
3. **Economic life** refers to the length of time that the firm expects to use the asset in its operations. The *physical* life of a fixed asset may not coincide with its *economic* life. For example, the economic life of a passenger aircraft owned by a major airline may be about ten years. At the end of that period of time, however, the craft may be sold to a smaller carrier and continue to serve regional markets for another twenty years or more.
4. **Benefit pattern** indicates the pattern over which net revenues are to be generated by the use of the asset. A wide variety of benefit patterns is plausible, depending on the firm and its industry. Some assets provide fairly steady benefits throughout their economic lives; other assets provide the major portion of their benefits in the earlier years of use. Occasionally, assets provide low initial benefits and, for a time, become more efficient with use. In some cases, the benefits acquired from the use of a fixed asset are related mainly to the passage of time; in other cases the benefits are related to how intensively the asset is used.

The depreciation method used will be the one that allocates depreciation expense to periods in a manner that coincides with the benefit pattern of the asset. For example, a fairly constant benefit pattern suggests that depreciation expense should be allocated in equal periodic amounts. On the other hand, if the major portion of benefits are provided in early years, then the depreciation expense should be *accelerated*—that is, allocated predominantly to these earlier years.

Recording Depreciation Expense

The following adjusting entry is made at the end of an accounting period to record the period's depreciation:

> dr.   Depreciation Expense   XXX
>   cr.   Accumulated Depreciation   XXX

Depreciation expense appears on the income statement and is closed at the end of the period along with all other temporary accounts, as discussed in Chapter 2. **Accumulated depreciation,** on the other hand, appears on the balance sheet as a **contra-asset account**—an account that is subtracted directly from the cost of the related asset. The difference between the cost of an asset and its accumulated depreciation is termed the asset's **book value.** The accumulated depreciation account is not closed at the end of the accounting period. The balance in this account increases over the useful life of the asset, reflecting the cumulative amount of the asset cost depreciated to date.

Depreciation Methods for Financial Reporting Purposes

Although a wide variety of benefit patterns is possible, there are relatively few methods of depreciation in common use. The more popular methods are the following:

1. Straight-line depreciation
2. Sum-of-the-years'-digits depreciation } Time-based methods
3. Double declining-balance depreciation
4. Units-of-output depreciation } Output-based method

The first three methods are based on the passage of time; the last method is based on activity. These different methods will be illustrated using a single example.

Assume that the Nantucket Cycle Company acquires a machine on January 1, 1987. Information pertinent to depreciation calculations for the machine appears in Exhibit 4-7. As shown in that exhibit, the total cost of the machine is $25,000, and the estimated residual value after five years of use is $1,000. As a result, the depreciable cost is $24,000 ($25,000 − $1,000), which is to be charged to expense in a reasonable manner over the five-year estimated useful life of the fixed asset. We will consider each of the four depreciation methods listed in the preceding paragraph with reference to the Nantucket Cycle Company's machine.

Straight-line depreciation   The **straight-line depreciation (SL)** method allocates an equal amount of depreciable cost to each period and is appropriate if the asset is expected to provide approximately equal benefit during each period. The formula used to calculate periodic depreciation using the straight-line method is as follows:

$$\text{Straight-line Depreciation } (SL) = \frac{\text{Cost } (C) - \text{Residual Value } (RV)}{\text{Useful Life } (N)}$$

$$\text{or,} \quad SL = \frac{C - RV}{N} = 1/N \times (C - RV)$$

The straight-line rate is $1/N$, and this rate is multiplied by the depreciable cost, $(C - RV)$, to compute the periodic depreciation. Using this formula, Nantucket Cycle's annual depreciation charge is $4,800.

$$SL = 1/N \ (C - RV)$$
$$= 1/5 \ (\$25,000 - 1,000)$$
$$= \$4,800$$

Sum-of-the-years'-digits depreciation   The **sum-of-the-years'-digits depreciation (SYD)** method allocates greater amounts of depreciation to the earlier years of asset use and lesser amounts to later years. For this reason, SYD is termed an **accelerated depreciation method.** A decreasing fraction of depreciable cost is allocated to each successive period. Each year's fraction is computed as follows:

Number of Years of Remaining Service at Beginning of Current Year
-----
Sum of Digits for Years of Estimated Total Service Life

For an asset with an estimated service life of five years, the *denominator* of the fraction is 15 (5 + 4 + 3 + 2 + 1), and it would not change over the five-year life of the asset. The *numerator* is 5 in the first year and would decline by 1 each succeeding year, reflecting the decrease in the number of years of remaining service. For Nantucket Cycle's machine, the depreciation calculations under SYD for each year are shown on the next page.

Exhibit 4-7

Depreciation Calculation: Costs and Estimates

Nantucket Cycle Company

Costs

Invoice cost of machine	$22,000
Transportation	1,000
Installation, inspection, start-up	2,000
Total	$25,000

Estimates

Useful life — 5 years (through December 1991)
Residual value at December 31, 1991 — $1,000

Expected production:		
	1987	1,500 units
	1988	2,000
	1989	2,500
	1990	4,000
	1991	2,000
	Total	12,000 units

Year	Remaining Life	SYD Fraction	Depreciable Cost $(C - RV)$	Depreciation Expense
1	5	5/15	$24,000	$ 8,000
2	4	4/15	24,000	6,400
3	3	3/15	24,000	4,800
4	2	2/15	24,000	3,200
5	1	1/15	24,000	1,600
Total	15	15/15		$24,000
		(100%)		

Notice that the SYD fraction changes each year to reflect the declining number of years of remaining life, and that the sum of these fractions over the five-year period is 15/15 (or 1.0), so that the entire depreciable cost is expensed over the life of the asset. Compared to straight-line depreciation, the depreciation expense calculated using SYD is higher in the earlier years (Years 1 and 2) and lower in the later years (Years 4 and 5). The total depreciation expense over the useful life of the asset is the same for both methods, however.

Double (200%) declining-balance depreciation   Another accelerated method of depreciation is the **double declining-balance (DDB)** method. If DDB is used, each period's depreciation is determined by multiplying the book value of the asset (total cost less accumulated depreciation taken in earlier periods) by a percentage that is twice (or 200 percent of) the straight-line rate; that is,

$$DDB = 2/N \text{ (book value of asset)}$$

In the above equation, N represents the estimated useful life of the asset. The depreciation rate, $2/N$, is constant over the life of the asset, while the book value decreases each period as the amount of accumulated depreciation becomes larger. Note that the residual value is not involved in this calculation, except that the asset must not be depreciated below the estimated residual value.

Application of the double declining-balance method to the Nantucket Cycle Company's machine is shown below. The appropriate depreciation rate is 40 percent (2/5).

Year	Rate	Beginning Book Value	Depreciation Expense	Ending Book Value
1	.40	$25,000	$10,000	$15,000
2	.40	15,000	6,000	9,000
3	.40	9,000	3,600	5,400
4	.40	5,400	2,160	3,240
5	.40	3,240	1,296	1,944*

*Notice that the book value of the asset does not equal the estimated residual value of $1,000 by the end of the fifth year of service. This is discussed in the next paragraph.

When the DDB method is employed, an adjustment is sometimes made to ensure that the full depreciable cost is allocated to the economic life of the asset.

Note in the Nantucket Cycle calculations above, for example, that the double declining-balance method did not assign all of the depreciable cost of $24,000 over the five-year period of the asset's useful life. In a case such as this, the company might switch from the declining-balance method to the straight-line method at the beginning of year 5 in order to depreciate the asset to its residual value of $1,000. Upon switching to straight-line depreciation, the company would allocate an equal amount of the remaining depreciable cost to each of the remaining periods of the asset's useful life.[2]

Units-of-production depreciation   Unlike the methods just discussed, which are based on the passage of time, the **units-of-production** method is based on the expected lifetime *output* of the asset. The depreciation expense per unit of output for the Nantucket Cycle machine is calculated as follows:

$$\text{Unit Depreciation Expense} = \frac{\text{Cost} - \text{Residual Value}}{\text{Total Lifetime Output}}$$

$$= \frac{\$25,000 - \$1,000}{12,000 \text{ units}}$$

$$= \$2 \text{ per unit}$$

Yearly estimates of units to be produced over the life of the machine were provided in Exhibit 4-7. The annual depreciation charges are shown below.

Year	Expected Production (units)	Unit Depreciation Expense	Depreciation Expense
1	1,500	$2	$3,000
2	2,000	2	4,000
3	2,500	2	5,000
4	4,000	2	8,000
5	2,000	2	4,000
Total	12,000		$24,000

Comparison of Depreciation Methods

Exhibit 4-8 summarizes periodic depreciation expense and resulting accumulated depreciation for the four depreciation methods illustrated in the Nantucket Cycle Company case. Observe that the major difference between the methods is one of timing of annual depreciation expenses. While all methods are designed to allocate the same dollar amount — the depreciable cost of

[2]It is not always the case that the double declining-balance method will fail to fully depreciate the asset over the estimated useful life. As you can verify from the schedule of DDB calculations, if the estimated residual value for Nantucket Cycle's machine was above $1,944, the machine would be fully depreciated after five years.

Exhibit 4-8

Comparison of Depreciation Methods

Nantucket Cycle Company

Year	Straight Line		Sum of the Years' Digits		Double Declining Balance		Units of Production	
	Depreciation Expense	Accumulated Depreciation	Depreciation Expense	Accumulated Depreciation	Depreciation Expense	Accumulated Depreciation	Depreciation Expense	Accumulated Depreciation
1	$ 4,800	$ 4,800	$ 8,000	$ 8,000	$10,000	$10,000	$ 3,000	$ 3,000
2	4,800	9,600	6,400	14,400	6,000	16,000	4,000	7,000
3	4,800	14,400	4,800	19,200	3,600	19,600	5,000	12,000
4	4,800	19,200	3,200	22,400	2,160	21,760	8,000	20,000
5	4,800	24,000	1,600	24,000	1,296	23,056	4,000	24,000
Total	$24,000		$24,000		$23,056		$24,000	

$24,000—over the life of the fixed asset, each assigns different dollar amounts to different time periods. These different expense patterns will be reflected in the timing of net income and the balance sheet valuations (book values) of fixed assets. To illustrate these effects, assume that the Nantucket Cycle Company expects to earn $10,000 each year, before depreciation expenses, using the machine described previously.[3] Exhibit 4-9 compares the effects of the three time-based depreciation methods (SL, SYD, and DDB) on selected financial relationships.

The top row in Exhibit 4-9 depicts a stable pattern of earnings of $10,000 per year before depreciation. The next three rows show net income after depreciation expenses are subtracted for each of the time-based depreciation methods. Net income reflects the difference between earnings before depreciation of $10,000 and depreciation expenses presented in Exhibit 4-8 for each time-based method. Observe that reported net income is constant at $5,200 per year under straight-line depreciation. Reported income is not constant under the accelerated depreciation methods (SYD and DDB), however, but increases in each successive year; that is, in the early years of the asset's economic life reported income is less under the accelerated depreciation methods than under straight-line depreciation, and in later years income is greater under SYD and DDB than under straight line.

Managers and investment analysts are interested in measuring profitability of assets employed in the firm. **Return on assets employed (ROA)** is a ratio used widely for performance evaluation. Also, this ratio is useful in investment analysis, especially in comparing economic units of unlike size. The ratio is calculated as follows:

$$ROA = \frac{Earnings}{Assets\ Employed}$$

ROA calculations for the Nantucket Cycle Company are presented at the bottom of Exhibit 4-9. Dollar amounts used for the numerator (earnings) in these calculations are those of net income after depreciation. Because we are assuming that the machine is the only asset presently being used in Nantucket Cycle operations, the dollar amounts used for the denominator (assets employed) are the Nantucket Cycle machine's reported book values under each of the depreciation methods. Notice in Exhibit 4-9 that return on assets calculated this way increases substantially over the five-year period for all methods of depreciation, although the increases are larger for the accelerated methods. The primary reason for this substantial increase in calculated ROA is the decrease in the ratio's denominator each year as accumulated depreciation gets larger. In fact, the ROA measure would always increase as the denominator gets smaller, unless the numerator declines by an equal or greater percentage.

This phenomenon can lead to underinvestment in new assets if return on assets, as calculated here, is the primary means of judging performance. In

---

[3]This example ignores income taxes, which will be discussed in the next section of this chapter.

Exhibit 4-9

Comparative Effects of Depreciation Methods on Selected Financial Ratios

---

Nantucket Cycle Company

	Year				
	1	**2**	**3**	**4**	**5**
Earnings before depreciation	$10,000	$10,000	$10,000	$10,000	$10,000
Net income*: SL	$ 5,200	$ 5,200	$ 5,200	$ 5,200	$ 5,200
SYD	2,000	3,600	5,200	6,800	8,400
DDB	0	4,000	6,400	7,840	8,704
Percent change in net income					
from previous period SL	N.A.	0.0	0.0	0.0	0.0
SYD	N.A.	80.0	44.4	30.8	23.5
DDB	N.A.	-†	60.0	22.5	11.0
Book value (cost less accumulated					
depreciation) SL	$20,200	15,400	10,600	5,800	1,000
SYD	17,000	10,600	5,800	2,600	1,000
DDB	15,000	9,000	5,400	3,240	1,944
Return on assets‡					
SL	25.7	33.9	49.0	89.9	520.0
SYD	11.7	34.0	89.7	261.5	840.0
DDB	0.0	44.4	118.5	242.0	447.7

---

*Ignoring income taxes. The net income amount for each method equals the difference between $10,000 and the depreciation expense amount shown in Exhibit 4-8.

†Undefined, since prior year has zero net income.

‡Net income divided by book value.

such a situation, a manager could improve the ratio merely by curtailing the level of spending for new assets so as to keep the denominator small. The effect is especially pronounced for older assets (see ROA for Years 4 and 5 in Exhibit 4-9) and may in some cases lead managers to act against the best interests of the stockholders. Indeed, it is often suggested in the business press that the wide use of ROA in assessing management performance has led to chronic underinvestment by U.S. corporations.

There is little compelling evidence to date concerning the securities price effects of depreciation accounting. Researchers have examined the relationship between the market prices and earnings of firms using straight-line and accelerated methods of depreciation. The primary measure examined in these studies is a firm's **price-earnings (P/E) ratio,** which is the market price per share of its common stock divided by the earnings per share of that stock. P/E ratios are usually quoted in the financial press and are used as indicators of expected growth. Generally, firms with high P/E ratios are expected to grow faster than those with lower P/E ratios.

The research findings indicate that firms using accelerated methods of depreciation tend to have higher price-earnings ratios than do firms using straight-line depreciation. This finding is not unexpected. As noted earlier, firms using accelerated depreciation methods tend to have lower reported income than do firms using straight-line depreciation, provided that such firms continue to increase their investments in new assets. (The lower the amount used in the denominator of the price-earnings ratio—everything else being equal—the higher the ratio.) In sum, the results of these studies of securities price behavior and depreciation accounting are consistent with the notion of information efficiency in the securities markets; specifically, users of financial statements seem to adjust for the lower reported earnings that result when a firm uses accelerated depreciation.[4]

Disposals of Fixed Assets

A disposal of a fixed asset at an amount other than its book value gives rise to either a gain or a loss. If the amount received for the disposed fixed asset is greater than current book value, a gain results; if less than book value is received, there is a loss. We will illustrate disposals by referring again to data in the Nantucket Cycle Company case.

Recall that the machine purchased by Nantucket Cycle for $25,000 on January 1, 1987, was expected at that time to have a useful life to the firm of five years (through December 31, 1991). But assume that on January 1, 1990 (the beginning of Year 4), the machine is sold unexpectedly for $8,000 cash. When a fixed asset is sold, it must be removed from the books; that is, its book value must be reduced to zero. Because the book value of the fixed asset in this case is represented in two accounts (Machine and Accumulated Depreciation), both accounts are used in the journal entry to record the disposal. The book value of the Nantucket Cycle machine at the date of disposal depends on the depreciation method being used by the firm. The dollar amount of accumulated depreciation on the date of disposal is given for each method in Exhibit 4-8. (For these entries we are using the amounts shown there for the last day of Year 3; these same amounts are relevant on the first day of Year 4, the date of disposal.) Journal entries to record the disposal on January 1, 1990 (assuming employment of each of the four depreciation methods considered in this chapter) are presented below.

Straight-line depreciation:

dr.	Loss on Disposal of Machine	2,600	
dr.	Cash	8,000	
dr.	Accumulated Depreciation	14,400	
	cr. Machine		25,000

---

[4]This interpretation assumes that the firms in the accelerated sample did, in fact, report depreciation expenses that exceeded the straight-line amounts.

Sum-of-the-years'-digits depreciation:

dr.	Cash	8,000	
dr.	Accumulated Depreciation	19,200	
cr.	Machine		25,000
cr.	Gain on Disposal of Machine		2,200

Double declining-balance depreciation:

dr.	Cash	8,000	
dr.	Accumulated Depreciation	19,600	
cr.	Machine		25,000
cr.	Gain on Disposal of Machine		2,600

Units-of-production depreciation:

dr.	Loss on Disposal of Machine	5,000	
dr.	Cash	8,000	
dr.	Accumulated Depreciation	12,000	
cr.	Machine		25,000

In each case shown above, the recorded gain or loss reflects the difference between the $8,000 received from the sale and the book value (cost less accumulated depreciation) of the machine on the date of disposal. Since the book value of the machine is different under each depreciation method, computed gains or losses are also different. However, the *total* expense of using the asset, including the gain or loss on disposal, is the same for all depreciation methods. This can be shown by a comparison of the total expenses for the straight-line and the sum-of-the-years'-digits methods:

	Straight Line	Sum of the Years' Digits
Depreciation expense, 3 years	$14,400	$19,200
Loss (gain) on disposal	2,600	(2,200)
Total expense	$17,000	$17,000

In other words, over the full "cash out to cash in" cycle, the results are identical even though for individual accounting periods within the cycle, the results may be quite different.

Depreciation System for Tax Purposes

Prior to 1981, most businesses used accelerated methods of depreciation (SYD or DDB, for example) to calculate taxable income. Recall that accelerated methods assign a greater amount of depreciation in the early years of an asset's life and lesser amounts in later years. A result of this depreciation pattern is lower taxable income in these earlier years and a minimization of the present value of income taxes paid (because of the time value of money).

In 1981, a new system of depreciation for tax purposes—the **Accelerated Cost Recovery System (ACRS)**—was introduced. Subsequently, the ACRS was modified by the 1986 Tax Reform Act. As a consequence of the 1986 Tax Reform Act, the original ACRS rules apply to qualifying depreciable assets placed in service between January 1, 1981, and December 31, 1986, and modified ACRS rules apply to qualifying assets placed into service on January 1, 1987, and thereafter.

Original ACRS rules   When the ACRS was introduced in 1981, the objective was to simplify the procedures for tax depreciation and at the same time maintain the tax minimization features of the accelerated methods used prior to ACRS. The main provisions of the original system are listed below.

1. Depending on the type of fixed asset involved (personal or real property), different depreciation periods are required. For qualifying *personal* property, the depreciation periods are three years, five years, ten years, and 15 years. For qualifying *real* property, the depreciation periods are 15 years, 18 years, and 19 years (depending on when the asset is placed into service).[5] The depreciation period specified by ACRS must be used for tax purposes, regardless of the depreciation period used for financial reporting purposes.
2. Residual or salvage value is ignored in calculating the amount of depreciation.
3. ACRS requires that depreciation (or cost recovery) be calculated as a specific percentage of the total asset cost. Exhibit 4-10 shows the statutory percentages to be used for three-year and five-year assets. These percentages are used even if the firm owns the qualifying asset for only a fraction of a given year. For example, the 25-percent factor shown in Exhibit 4-10 for the first year of a qualifying three-year asset would be used regardless of whether the asset was placed into service at the beginning of the year, in the middle of the year, or late in the year.

With very few exceptions, the cost recovery periods permitted under ACRS are shorter than the estimated economic lives used for financial reporting purposes. Under the original ACRS rules, for example, automobiles, light trucks, and certain tools are classified as three-year assets for depreciation purposes and most machinery, equipment, and office furniture are classified as five-year assets.

To illustrate the use of ACRS for qualifying property placed into service *before* January 1, 1987, consider the purchase of office furniture by the Northampton Company on January 1, 1986. Assume that the office furniture costs $25,000

---

[5]Generally, the depreciation period for real property placed in service before March 16, 1984, is 15 years. If placed in service after March 15, 1984, and before May 9, 1985, the asset has an 18-year depreciation period. And, if placed in service after May 8, 1985, and before January 1, 1987, the asset has a 19-year depreciation period.

Exhibit 4-10

Accelerated Cost Recovery System: Annual Depreciation Percentages

Year	Three-year Asset	Five-year Asset
1	25%	15%
2	38	22
3	37	21
4	–	21
5	–	21
Total	100%	100%

and has a zero residual value. For tax purposes, the office furniture qualifies under ACRS as five-year property. The schedule below (which uses appropriate statutory percentages for five-year assets as presented in Exhibit 4-10) shows the calculation of depreciation for each year under ACRS.

Year	Calculation	Depreciation
1986	15% × $25,000	$ 3,750
1987	22% × $25,000	5,500
1988	21% × $25,000	5,250
1989	21% × $25,000	5,250
1990	21% × $25,000	5,250
Total		$25,000

The entire cost of $25,000 is recovered for tax purposes after five years.

Modified ACRS rules   The 1986 Tax Reform Act caused numerous changes to the Accelerated Cost Recovery System. The original ACRS rules still apply, however, for assets placed into service before January 1, 1987. The modified ACRS rules apply to assets placed into service on January 1, 1987, and thereafter.

It is beyond the scope of this text to provide a comprehensive treatment of the ACRS rules as modified by the 1986 Tax Reform Act. Nonetheless, two changes in ACRS rules merit consideration here.

1. The modified ACRS rules contain six different categories regarding the number of years in the depreciation period (three, five, seven, ten, 15, and 20 years). For certain assets, the required depreciation period has been extended. For instance, certain three-year assets under the original rules are reclassified as five-year assets under the modified rules; certain five-year assets are reclassified as seven-year assets, and so on.
2. The 1986 Tax Reform Act requires the use of the declining balance method of depreciation (as opposed to the use of statutory percentages

illustrated above). The 200-percent declining balance method (double declining balance) is required for qualifying assets in the three-year, five-year, seven-year, and ten-year categories, and a 150-percent declining balance method is required for qualifying assets in the 15-year and 20-year categories.[6]

INCOME TAX EXPENSE AND INTERPERIOD TAX ALLOCATION

Firms do not necessarily use the same methods of accounting for financial reporting that they use for tax purposes. For financial reporting purposes, a firm is required to apply the revenue recognition and expense matching criteria described in Chapter 3. From a tax standpoint, however, a company should attempt to minimize the present value of its future tax payments. With few exceptions, this is done by postponing the payment of taxes for as long as possible.[7] Postponement of taxes is accomplished by recognizing revenues at the latest point permitted by tax laws, and by recognizing expenses at the earliest time permitted.

Whenever a transaction affects the determination of net income for financial accounting purposes in one reporting period and the computation of taxable income in a different period, a **timing difference** arises. GAAP require that a special technique be used to account for income taxes whenever timing differences exist between financial accounting income and taxable income. Timing differences and accounting for such differences are illustrated in the balance of this chapter.

Timing Differences

To understand what is meant by a timing difference, consider the following data related to a delivery truck acquired by the Vineyard Company:

1. The truck was purchased on January 1, 1986, for $15,000. (Note: Since the truck was purchased *before* January 1, 1987, the original ACRS rules apply.)
2. The truck has an estimated useful life of five years, with an estimated residual value of zero.
3. For tax purposes, the truck qualifies under ACRS as having a three-year life.

---

[6]When using the double declining-balance method, the straight-line rate is doubled (or multiplied by 200 percent); when using the 150-percent declining-balance method, the straight-line rate is multiplied by 150 percent. The double declining-balance method was explained and demonstrated on page 177.

[7]When tax rates are expected to *increase* in later periods, firms may desire to postpone expense recognition or to recognize revenues as early as possible.

Assume that the Vineyard Company uses the straight-line method of depreciation for financial reporting purposes. The annual depreciation expense for the truck is $3,000, or $15,000 divided by 5 years. Regardless of what depreciation method is used for financial accounting purposes, a company *must* use ACRS for tax purposes. ACRS depreciation charges for each of the three years are $3,750 (1986), $5,700 (1987), and $5,550 (1988).[8] The following schedule, which summarizes depreciation charges under both the straight-line method and ACRS, also shows the resulting timing differences.

	Depreciation Charges		
	(1)	(2)	(3) **Timing Differences**
	Straight Line	**ACRS**	**(1) minus (2)**
1986	$ 3,000	$ 3,750	$ (750)
1987	3,000	5,700	(2,700)
1988	3,000	5,550	(2,550)
1989	3,000	0	3,000
1990	3,000	0	3,000
Totals	$15,000	$15,000	0

Observe that there is no difference in total depreciation charges between columns (1) and (2) over the estimated useful life of the asset (the total is $15,000 under both methods of depreciation), but there are differences in individual years, as shown in column (3). These are referred to as timing differences. Note also that these timing differences total zero over the full five-year period.[9]

Timing differences are generally of two types. The first type arises when the tax law requires cash-basis reporting instead of the accrual accounting used under GAAP. Examples of the circumstances under which this type of timing difference might occur include the following:

- Installment sales are reported for financial accounting purposes when the sales transaction occurs, although the sale is reported for tax purposes only as the cash is received.

- Warranty costs are accrued currently on the books, but for tax purposes they may be deducted only as paid.

- Rents received in advance are taxable income when received, but are recognized as financial accounting income when the services are performed.

---

[8]ACRS depreciation charges are calculated as follows: 1986—$15,000 × 25% = $3,750; 1987—$15,000 × 38% = $5,700; 1988—$15,000 × 37% = $5,550. (The annual cost recovery percentages used here were taken from Exhibit 4-10 on page 185.)

[9]In column (3) above the timing differences for the first three years all have the same sign and are termed originating differences. Timing differences in the fourth and fifth years have the opposite sign, and are called reversing differences. For the timing difference to fully reverse, the sum of the originating differences ($750 + $2,700 + $2,550) must equal the sum of the reversing differences ($3,000 + $3,000).

The second type of timing difference is a consequence of government policy. For example, to promote new capital investment the tax laws allow an accelerated system of depreciation (ACRS) for tax purposes, while straight-line methods are generally used for financial accounting purposes. As illustrated in the Vineyard Company case, the pattern of expense may differ between tax and financial accounting reports, but the total expense over the life of the asset is the same in both cases.

Interperiod Tax Allocation

There is little, if any, disagreement that in the long run the cumulative amount of reported income tax expense should be equal to the cumulative amount of income taxes due the government. In the short run, however, there are controversies regarding the amount of income tax expense to be assigned, or allocated, to an individual year.

The special technique required to account for income taxes when timing differences exist between financial accounting income and taxable income is known as **interperiod tax allocation.** As currently mandated by GAAP, interperiod tax allocation requires that the amount of income tax expense allocated to a particular year be related to the revenues and expenses recognized that year for financial accounting purposes. In contrast, income tax payable, as shown on the firm's balance sheet, should be based on taxable income for the period. If differences exist between pretax accounting income and taxable income, the tax effects of those differences are recorded in the Deferred Taxes account.

The model journal entry to account for income taxes when timing differences exist is as follows:

dr.	Income Tax Expense (Pretax Accounting Income × Tax Rate) XXX	
	cr. Income Tax Payable (Taxable Income × Tax Rate)	XXX
	cr. Deferred Taxes (Difference between Pretax Accounting Income and Taxable Income × Tax Rate)	XXX

Observe that the debit to Income Tax Expense is determined by multiplying pretax accounting income by the tax rate, and that the credit to Income Tax Payable is determined by multiplying taxable income by the tax rate. The difference between pretax accounting income and taxable income (the timing difference) is multiplied by the tax rate to determine the amount debited or credited to the Deferred Taxes account.

The assumption is being made in the model journal entry shown here that income tax expense is greater than income taxes payable. When this occurs, the Deferred Taxes account is credited. If income tax expense is less than income taxes payable, the Deferred Taxes account is debited. In either case, the dollar amount recorded for deferred taxes is equal to the timing difference for a particular period multiplied by the tax rate.

Accounting for Income Taxes

Recall that the Vineyard Company purchased a delivery truck on January 1, 1986, for $15,000. The truck has a five-year estimated life with a zero residual value and is considered a three-year asset according to ACRS.

Exhibit 4-11 shows the Vineyard Company's summary income statements and tax reports for the five-year period of operations (1986–1990), assuming a 40-percent tax rate and earnings before depreciation (and taxes) of $10,000 each year. The exhibit shows that over the entire five-year life of the asset, the company reports the *same total pretax income* ($35,000) for both financial reporting and tax purposes. However, the taxable income reported on the firm's tax returns for individual years during the five-year period differs from the pretax accounting income reported on the income statements for those years. This is because of timing differences resulting from the use of the two different depreciation methods.

In order to match income tax expenses against the appropriate revenues, the Vineyard Company will report income tax expense each year equal to

Exhibit 4-11
Projected Income Statements and Tax Reports, 1986–1990

Vineyard Company

Financial Accounting Income

	1986	1987	1988	1989	1990	Total 1986–1990
Earnings before depreciation and taxes	$10,000	$10,000	$10,000	$10,000	$10,000	$50,000
Depreciation expense	3,000	3,000	3,000	3,000	3,000	15,000
Pretax accounting income	$ 7,000	$ 7,000	$ 7,000	$ 7,000	$ 7,000	$35,000
Income tax expense (40%)	2,800	2,800	2,800	2,800	2,800	14,000
Net income	$ 4,200	$ 4,200	$ 4,200	$ 4,200	$ 4,200	$21,000

Income for Tax Purposes

	1986	1987	1988	1989	1990	Total 1986–1990
Earnings before depreciation and taxes	$10,000	$10,000	$10,000	$10,000	$10,000	$50,000
Depreciation expense	3,750	5,700	5,550	0	0	15,000
Taxable income	$ 6,250	$ 4,300	$ 4,450	$10,000	$10,000	$35,000
Income tax due (40% × taxable income)	$ 2,500	$ 1,720	$ 1,780	$ 4,000	$ 4,000	$14,000

40 percent of pretax accounting income. The income taxes payable, however, will reflect the actual amount of tax due the government, as shown on the tax return for the year. The difference between income tax expense and income taxes payable is termed "deferred tax." The entry to record the firm's income taxes for 1986 is as follows:

dr.	Income Tax Expense	2,800	
	cr. Income Tax Payable		2,500
	cr. Deferred Taxes		300

The deferred tax credit of $300 may be interpreted as a liability, since in later years the timing differences will reverse and the firm will pay taxes in excess of the income tax expenses recorded in those years.

Exhibit 4-12 displays the journal entries to record the income tax expense for the years 1986–1990 and also shows the resulting ledger balances in the Deferred Taxes account. Notice that after the timing differences completely reverse (in this case, after five years), the balance in the Deferred Taxes account is zero.

Rationale for Interperiod Tax Allocation

To better understand the reasons for interperiod tax allocation, consider what would happen in the Vineyard Company case if tax allocation had not been used. An alternative advocated by some analysts is to report the amount of taxes due for a particular period as that period's income tax expense. This approach, which is not permitted by GAAP, is referred to as the **flow-through** method.

Exhibit 4-13 contrasts the Vineyard Company's income statements over the five-year period presented earlier, using tax allocation and without tax allocation. The top half of this exhibit duplicates the income statements for the Vineyard Company already shown in Exhibit 4-11, in which interperiod tax allocation is employed. The bottom half of Exhibit 4-13 shows how the same financial statements would appear if no allocation was employed (the flow-through method).

Notice in Exhibit 4-13 that when interperiod tax allocation is employed, the relationship between reported income tax expense and pretax accounting income remains constant at the tax rate of 40 percent in each of the five years. This is because interperiod tax allocation is designed to show the tax effect of each revenue and expense item recognized for financial accounting purposes in a given year in reported income tax expense for that year. Proponents of this approach believe it to be consistent with the matching concept discussed in Chapters 1 and 3.

In contrast, when the flow-through method is used, the reported amount of income tax expense is not related directly to financial accounting income for the period, but is related instead to the amount of taxes due the government for the period. A likely consequence of use of the flow-through method is that the relationship between income tax expense and pretax accounting income

Exhibit 4-12
Deferred Taxes: Journal Entries and Account Balances, 1986–1990

Vineyard Company

Journal Entries

1986:	dr.	Income Tax Expense	2,800	
	cr.	Deferred Taxes		300
	cr.	Income Tax Payable		2,500
1987:	dr.	Income Tax Expense	2,800	
	cr.	Deferred Taxes		1,080
	cr.	Income Tax Payable		1,720
1988:	dr.	Income Tax Expense	2,800	
	cr.	Deferred Taxes		1,020
	cr.	Income Tax Payable		1,780
1989:	dr.	Income Tax Expense	2,800	
	dr.	Deferred Taxes	1,200	
	cr.	Income Tax Payable		4,000
1990:	dr.	Income Tax Expense	2,800	
	dr.	Deferred Taxes	1,200	
	cr.	Income Tax Payable		4,000

Account Balances

Deferred Taxes

	1986:	$ 300	
		$ 300	Balance, December 31, 1986
	1987:	1,080	
		$1,380	Balance, December 31, 1987
	1988:	1,020	
		$2,400	Balance, December 31, 1988
1989: $1,200			
		$1,200	Balance, December 31, 1989
1990: $1,200			
		0	Balance, December 31, 1990

may vary widely over the period of a timing difference. As shown at the bottom of Exhibit 4-13, this range is quite wide in the Vineyard Company illustration (from a low of 24.6 percent in 1987 to a high of 57.1 percent in 1989 and 1990). This situation may be confusing to some who question why there should be a difference in income tax expense each year when the amount of pretax accounting income remains constant at $7,000 in each of the five years in the illustration. Many who argue against the flow-through method contend that

Exhibit 4-13
Comparison of Projected Income Statements
With and Without Interperiod Income Tax Allocation,
1986–1990

Vineyard Company

Income Statement — WITH Interperiod Tax Allocation

	1986	1987	1988	1989	1990	Total 1986–1990
Earnings before depreciation and taxes	$10,000	$10,000	$10,000	$10,000	$10,000	$50,000
Depreciation expense	3,000	3,000	3,000	3,000	3,000	15,000
Pretax accounting income	$ 7,000	$ 7,000	$ 7,000	$ 7,000	$ 7,000	$35,000
Income tax expense (40%)	2,800	2,800	2,800	2,800	2,800	14,000
Net income	$ 4,200	$ 4,200	$ 4,200	$ 4,200	$ 4,200	$21,000
Income tax expense as a percentage of pretax accounting income	40%	40%	40%	40%	40%	40%

Income Statement — WITHOUT Interperiod Tax Allocation

	1986	1987	1988	1989	1990	Total 1986–1990
Earnings before depreciation and taxes	$10,000	$10,000	$10,000	$10,000	$10,000	$50,000
Depreciation expense	3,000	3,000	3,000	3,000	3,000	15,000
Pretax accounting income	$ 7,000	$ 7,000	$ 7,000	$ 7,000	$ 7,000	$35,000
Income tax expense	2,500	1,720	1,780	4,000	4,000	14,000
Net income	$ 4,500	$ 5,280	$ 5,220	$ 3,000	$ 3,000	$21,000
Income tax expense as a percentage of pretax accounting income	35.7%	24.6%	25.5%	57.1%	57.1%	40.0%

basing the amount of reported income tax expense on the timing of cash out-flows is a violation of the matching principle and is potentially misleading to financial statement users.

Other Timing Differences

The Vineyard Company case, which we have just discussed, involves a timing difference caused by employing different methods of depreciation for tax and financial accounting purposes. There are numerous other situations in which similar timing differences give rise to deferred income tax credits. These situations occur when revenues are reported later, or expenses are reported earlier, for tax purposes than for financial accounting purposes.

Although the Vineyard Company illustration resulted only in deferred income tax credits, it is also possible for a timing difference to result in a *debit balance* in the Deferred Tax account. This would happen if revenues are reported earlier, or expenses reported later, for tax purposes than for financial accounting purposes. To demonstrate, assume that on January 1, 1987, the Block Island Company rents a vacant warehouse to another firm for a three-year period at a cost of $6,000. Block Island receives the entire $6,000 payment in advance. Because the cash has been received, the tax code requires that all of the $6,000 be included on the current period's tax return. However, GAAP require that revenues be recognized when they are earned—GAAP do not link revenue recognition to the period in which cash is received. Accordingly, for financial accounting purposes, $2,000 of rental revenue would be recognized in each of the three years of the contract. The schedule below summarizes this timing difference and the effects on income taxes.

	(1) Financial Accounting Income	(2) Taxable Income	(3) Timing Difference (1) minus (2)	(4) Tax Effect (3) × 40%
1987	$2,000	$6,000	($4,000)	($1,600)
1988	2,000	0	2,000	800
1989	2,000	0	2,000	800
Totals	$6,000	$6,000	0	0

Exhibit 4-14 displays journal entries for the Block Island Company to record income taxes for these years, assuming a 40-percent tax rate. Note that the Deferred Taxes account is *debited* at the end of the first year of the timing difference. A debit balance in the Deferred Taxes account is presented on the asset side of the balance sheet, usually as a deferred charge.

Permanent Differences

Differences that arise from transactions or events that affect financial accounting income but *never* affect taxable income, or vice versa, are called **permanent**

Exhibit 4–14
Deferred Taxes: Journal Entries, 1987–1989

Block Island Company

1987:	dr.	Income Tax Expense	800	
	dr.	Deferred Income Taxes	1,600	
	cr.	Income Tax Payable		2,400
1988:	dr.	Income Tax Expense	800	
	cr.	Deferred Income Taxes		800
1989:	dr.	Income Tax Expense	800	
	cr.	Deferred Income Taxes		800

differences. For example, to encourage private investment in our nation's cities, interest earned on municipal bonds is exempt from federal income tax. Nonetheless, such interest must be included as revenue in determining financial accounting income. Interest earned on municipal bonds represents a permanent difference, then, because it is a component of financial accounting income and never a component of taxable income.

Interperiod income tax allocation does *not* apply to permanent differences—only to timing differences. There is no reason to show income tax expense for an item included in pretax accounting income that will never be subject to income tax.

SUMMARY

Chapter 4 examines three components of net income in detail. The first two sections focus on alternative inventory cost flow assumptions and depreciation patterns. Choices from among alternatives in these areas affect the reported dollar amounts of cost of goods sold and depreciation expense, respectively. The last section of the chapter considers issues in accounting for income tax expense.

Four inventory cost flow assumptions are generally accepted in financial accounting for allocating costs between ending inventory and cost of goods sold: (1) specific identification, which matches the unit costs of specific items sold with sales revenue; (2) average cost, which assigns the average unit cost of goods available for sale to each unit sold and each unit of ending inventory; (3) first-in, first-out (FIFO), which assigns the costs of the earliest purchases to cost of goods sold; and (4) last-in, first-out (LIFO), which assigns the costs of the latest purchases to cost of goods sold. Regardless of which inventory cost flow assumption is selected, that method must be applied consistently from year to year.

The use of alternative inventory cost flow assumptions affects the financial statements in different ways. Normally, in a period of rising prices, the use of FIFO results in the highest reported net income, and the use of LIFO results in the lowest reported net income. An important exception may occur, however, in the case of a firm using LIFO. If a firm using LIFO sells more units in a particular period than it purchases or manufactures, cost of goods sold may drop and net income may increase. This situation is referred to as a LIFO liquidation.

A holding gain exists whenever costs assigned to goods sold are less than the costs of replacing those items. Holding gains are normally largest if FIFO is used. During periods of inflation, LIFO generally results in lower taxable income than the other methods. If a company uses LIFO for tax purposes, however, the Internal Revenue Service requires that LIFO be used for financial reporting purposes as well. This rule is called the LIFO conformity requirement.

Fixed assets are long-lived, tangible assets that are employed by an enterprise in the production or sale of inventory or in the provision of services. Depreciation is the process of allocating the historical cost of a tangible fixed asset to the reporting periods that benefit from its use. Depreciation is recorded each period by debiting depreciation expense and crediting accumulated depreciation. The difference between the historical cost of an asset and its accumulated depreciation is the asset's book value.

Periodic depreciation expense is calculated based on the asset's historical cost, residual value, economic life, and benefit pattern. Four popular depreciation methods are widely used: (1) straight line, which allocates an equal amount of the depreciation to each period; (2) sum of the years' digits, which allocates greater amounts of depreciation to early periods of asset use and lesser amounts to later periods; (3) double declining balance, which has a depreciation pattern similar to sum of the years' digits; and (4) units of production, which assigns depreciation in relation to the extent of use of the asset in a particular period. Depending on which of these depreciation methods is used, there may be wide variations in the timing of depreciation expense. These different expense patterns affect the timing of net income on the income statement and also the book values shown on the balance sheet.

Disposal of a fixed asset at an amount other than its book value gives rise to either a gain or a loss. If the amount received is greater than current book value, a gain results; if less than book value is received, there is a loss.

In 1981 a new system of depreciation for tax purposes, the Accelerated Cost Recovery System (ACRS), was introduced. ACRS maintains the tax minimization features of the accelerated methods used prior to its introduction. ACRS was modified by the 1986 Tax Reform Act.

Whenever a transaction affects the determination of net income for financial accounting purposes in one reporting period and the computation of taxable income in a different period, a timing difference is created. There are many different types of timing differences. Two examples are discussed in this chapter. The first involves the use of straight-line depreciation for financial accounting purposes and ACRS for income tax purposes. The second example involves the immediate recognition of a prepayment of rental income for tax purposes, and recognition of the rental income in a later period for financial accounting purposes.

Generally accepted accounting principles require that a technique known as interperiod tax allocation be used to account for income taxes whenever timing differences exist between financial accounting income and taxable income. When using interperiod tax allocation, the calculation of income tax expense is based on pretax accounting income and the amount of income taxes payable is based on taxable income. If a difference exists between pretax accounting income and taxable income, the tax effect of that difference is recorded in a deferred taxes account. GAAP require that the amount of income tax expense allocated to a particular year be related to the revenues and expenses recognized during that year for financial accounting purposes. There are also cases in which transactions affect either financial accounting income or taxable income, but not both. These cases represent permanent differences, not timing differences. Interperiod income tax allocation does not apply to permanent differences.

QUESTIONS

1. The terms listed below were introduced in this chapter. Define or explain each of them.

accelerated depreciation	holding gain
accumulated depreciation	income tax effects
average cost	interperiod income tax allocation
benefit pattern (fixed asset)	last-in, first-out (LIFO)
book value (fixed asset)	LIFO conformity requirement
contra-asset account	LIFO liquidation
cost flow assumption	operating margin
deferred income tax	price-earnings ratio (P/E)
depreciation	residual value (fixed asset)
double declining balance	return on assets employed (ROA)
economic life (fixed asset)	specific identification
first-in, first-out (FIFO)	sum of the years' digits
fixed asset	taxable income
historical cost	units-of-production depreciation

2. What function (purpose) does an inventory cost flow assumption serve in the preparation of financial statements?
3. List and define the four inventory cost flow assumptions discussed in this chapter.
4. Would there be any difference between using LIFO or FIFO if unit costs of inventory purchased remained constant over time? Explain.
5. What are the main advantages and disadvantages of using the LIFO inventory cost flow assumption? Your answer should focus on both income statement and balance sheet effects.
6. What are the main advantages and disadvantages of using the FIFO inventory cost flow assumption? Your answer should focus on both income statement and balance sheet effects.
7. "In a period of rising prices, LIFO results in a higher reported amount of net income than does FIFO." Do you agree or disagree? Explain.
8. What is a LIFO liquidation?
9. Are holding gains on inventory more likely under FIFO than under LIFO? Explain.
10. Do generally accepted accounting principles permit a firm that uses LIFO in its financial statements to provide additional disclosure in those statements indicating what net income (and ending inventory) would have been if the firm had used a different cost flow assumption (such as FIFO)?

11. What are the effects of using LIFO as opposed to using FIFO in terms of income tax expense and cash outflow to the Internal Revenue Service?

12. "As used in financial accounting, the term 'depreciation' refers to a process of cost allocation, not asset valuation." Do you agree or not? Explain.

13. Before it is possible to calculate annual depreciation expense for a particular asset, it is necessary to know the historical cost of that asset. What other factors must be known or determined before one can calculate the dollar amount of depreciation expense for the period?

14. List and describe the four depreciation methods discussed in this chapter.

15. Contrast straight-line depreciation with accelerated depreciation in terms of the effects of each on reported net income.

16. Is it permissible to use a different method of depreciation for financial reporting purposes than for tax purposes?

17. What advantage, if any, does an accelerated method of depreciation provide in terms of cash outflow to the taxing authorities?

18. Describe the effect that the depreciation process has on the return on assets ratio. (Assume net income and total assets, as reported in the financial statements, are used to calculate this ratio.)

19. Distinguish between intrastatement and interperiod income tax allocation.

20. Distinguish between a permanent difference and a timing difference as they relate to interperiod income tax allocation.

21. What is meant by the "income tax effect" of a transaction? What is the income tax effect of a tax deductible item of $4,000, assuming the tax rate is 40%?

EXERCISES AND PROBLEMS

22. *Statements to Ponder.*   The following statements relate to several controversial issues discussed in Chapter 4:

    (1) (*President to Controller*) "In view of constantly rising prices, I can understand all this talk about abandoning historical costs in favor of replacement costs. However, in our company, we have adopted LIFO, which produces the same results as replacement costs. Instead of arguing about whether or not to use replacement costs, why not require all companies to adopt LIFO and accelerated depreciation?"

    (2) (*Student to professor*) "If as you say, depreciation doesn't represent a decline in the value of a fixed asset, what is it? What is the meaning of a balance sheet that reports an offsetting Accumulated Depreciation that doesn't denote the decline in value of the related fixed asset?"

    (3) (*Young economist to class*) "In recent years, greater emphasis is being placed on cash flow. For example, if you add the cash flow derived from depreciation to the loss reported by Eastern Airlines, you get a picture of a healthy company able to move into the future with a strong positive cash flow."

    (4) (*CEO to member of trade association*) "I can't understand why all companies don't adopt LIFO. Our industry is undergoing intense

competition from the Japanese largely because of an undervalued yen. With double-digit inflation, we can increase our cash flow about 15% by using LIFO. This goes a long way toward overcoming this dollar–yen problem."

(5) (*Bank officer to loan applicant*) "I am puzzled about the Deferred Tax Liability account on your balance sheet that just keeps getting larger each period. Although your company had only a small increase in profits this year, there was a substantial increase in this account. This is having an adverse effect on the liquidity ratios that I calculate and may severely limit your borrowing capacity."

REQUIRED   Comment on each of these statements.

23. *Effects of Inventory Errors.*   The Salt Lake Company prepared income statements that reflected net income of $42,000 for 1987 and $30,000 for 1988. An audit of the financial statements revealed the following independent errors in the inventory accounts:

	Amount Reported	Correct Amount
Ending inventory, 1987	$17,000	$15,000
Ending inventory, 1988	$11,000	$12,500

REQUIRED   Calculate the correct amount of income for each year, ignoring income tax implications.

24. *Inventory Cost Flow Methods.*   Data regarding beginning inventory and purchases of inventory for the Toledo Company during the current year are shown below.

January 1	Beginning inventory	120 items @ $10 each
April 15	Purchase	400 items @ $12 each
August 20	Purchase	400 items @ $11 each
November 25	Purchase	100 items @ $14 each

A physical count shows that 150 items of inventory are on hand at December 31.

REQUIRED   Determine the dollar amount to be assigned to ending inventory at December 31 under each of the following inventory cost flow methods:

(a) First-in, first-out (FIFO)
(b) Last-in, first-out (LIFO)
(c) Average cost

25. *Inventory Cost Flow Assumptions: Three Years.*   The Branch Tool Company was organized in January 1987 to sell a particular type of wrench, known as a "Big Ben." Data concerning units purchased and sold for the three-year

period from 1987–1989 are presented below.

	Items Purchased		Items Sold	
	Number of units	Purchase price	Number of units	Sales revenue
1987	230,000	$172,500	200,000	$250,000
1988	250,000	$225,000	240,000	$312,000
1989	260,000	$234,000	280,000	$378,000

REQUIRED

(a) Prepare a partial income statement (through the calculation of gross margin) for each of the three years assuming that the inventory cost flow assumption used is LIFO. Prepare the same statement using FIFO.

(b) Describe the effect in each year of using FIFO as opposed to using LIFO on the following financial statement items: (1) ending inventory, (2) net income, and (3) total assets.

26. *Comparison of LIFO and FIFO Inventory Methods.* The Dover Company began operations in 1987 and has always used LIFO to value its inventories. Selected information from published financial statements concerning the company's first four years of operation is presented below.

	Income Statement	Balance Sheet	Footnotes
	Net income	Ending inventory (LIFO)	Ending inventory if FIFO had been used
1987	$40,000	$12,000	$13,000
1988	46,000	15,000	20,000
1989	52,000	15,000	23,000
1990	55,000	13,000	23,000

In each of these years, the firm's income tax expense was 40% of income before taxes.

REQUIRED

(a) For each of the years 1987–1990, compute the amount of net income after taxes the company would have reported on its income statement if the FIFO inventory cost flow assumption had been employed instead of LIFO.

(b) Assuming the unit prices of inventory increased every year, identify the year(s) in which (1) the number of units of inventory decreased, and (2) the number of units of inventory remained the same.

(c) What is a LIFO liquidation? Identify the year(s), if any, in which the firm experienced a LIFO liquidation.

27. *Footnote Disclosures Regarding Alternative Cost Flow Assumptions.*   Excerpts from the financial statements of two hypothetical companies regarding inventory cost flow assumptions are presented below.

   (1) Mannino's Apparel Company uses LIFO inventory costing and reports the following footnote information: "If the company had used FIFO, the beginning and ending inventories would have been lower by $600 million and $800 million, respectively."
   (2) Singer Straw Company uses LIFO inventory costing and reports the following footnote information: "The beginning and ending inventories at LIFO cost are $240 million and $300 million, respectively. If FIFO had been used, the inventory costs would have been $240 million and $380 million, respectively."

REQUIRED

   (a) In the Mannino Apparel Company case, how would gross margin be affected by the use of FIFO costing of inventories?
   (b) In the Singer Straw Company case, how would gross margin be affected by the use of FIFO costing of inventories?

28. *Differences between FIFO and LIFO Valuations.*   Toys-U-Must began business on January 1, 1988, and uses FIFO inventory costing. At December 31, 1988, and at December 31, 1989, the inventories would have been $100 million and $150 million lower, respectively, if the firm had used LIFO costing. Assume the income tax rate is 40%.

	Differences, if LIFO had been used	
	1988	**1989**
Inventory, December 31	$100 million lower	$
Working capital, December 31	$ 60 million lower	$
Gross margin	$100 million lower	$
Income tax expense	$ 40 million lower	$
Net income	$ 60 million lower	$
Retained earnings, December 31	$ 60 million lower	$

REQUIRED

   (a) Explain each of the differences shown above for 1988.
   (b) Show how the financial statement elements listed above would have differed in 1989 if the firm had used LIFO.

29. *Inventory Holding Gains.*   The Eugene Company concentrates all of its efforts on selling one basic product, a high-quality racing bicycle. The

following are selected items from the firm's financial statements for the year ended December 31, 1988:

Cost of goods sold	$450,000
Purchases	475,000
Sales	920,000
Inventory, January 1, 1988	80,000
Inventory, December 31, 1988	105,000

Inventory was valued by using the first-in, first-out (FIFO) method. The number of bicycles on hand at the end of the period is the same as at its beginning. Financial statement footnotes disclosed that cost of goods sold would have been $490,000 if calculated on a replacement cost basis.

REQUIRED

(a) Prepare a partial income statement (through the calculation of gross margin) for the year ended December 31, 1988.
(b) Does the amount of gross margin shown on the income statement contain holding gains (inventory profits)? If so, calculate the amount of the holding gains.
(c) What is the dollar amount of the firm's operating margin for the year?

30. *LIFO Liquidation.* The Freeport Company uses LIFO to value its inventories. Data regarding 1988's beginning inventory and inventory purchases up to the current date, which is December 28, 1988, are shown below.

January 1	Beginning inventory	500 items @ $ 2 each
April 15	Purchase	400 items @ $12 each
August 20	Purchase	400 items @ $11 each
November 25	Purchase	100 items @ $14 each

The $2-per-unit cost assigned to beginning inventory (the base "LIFO layer") represents a unit cost that has been carried forward for many years. The year's sales up to December 28 have been unusually strong: 1,300 items sold at $20 per item. Despite these strong sales, however, it appears that net income for the period will be lower than in previous years. Very few additional sales, if any, are expected to be made before December 31. Operating expenses other than cost of goods sold total $12,000 for the year.

REQUIRED

(a) Prepare an income statement for the year ending December 31, 1988, incorporating each of the following assumptions: (1) an additional 400 items of inventory are purchased for $14 each on December 29, 1988, and (2) an additional 400 items of inventory are purchased for $14 each, but the purchase is not made until January 3, 1989.

(b) Why might Freeport's management be motivated to purchase additional inventory on January 3, 1989, rather than on December 29, 1988? Explain fully.

31. *Effects of LIFO Liquidation.* Data regarding beginning inventory and inventory purchased up to December 29, 1988, for the Farry Company are shown below.

January 1	Beginning inventory	150 items @ $ 4 each
March 12	Purchase	300 items @ $10 each
June 18	Purchase	500 items @ $11 each
October 25	Purchase	300 items @ $14 each

The Farry Company uses LIFO to value its inventory. Sales in 1988 have been 1,200 items at $21 per item. No additional sales are expected. Farry's manager is considering whether to purchase 200 items on December 30, 1988, or to purchase 200 items on January 2, 1989. The cost will be $15 per item in either case. Operating expenses other than cost of goods sold total $8,000 for the year. The income tax rate is 40%.

REQUIRED

(a) Prepare two separate income statements for the year ending December 31, 1988, assuming first that Farry Company purchased 200 additional items of inventory on December 30, 1988, and next assuming those 200 items were purchased instead on January 2, 1989.
(b) Compute the income tax savings between these two decisions.
(c) What justification exists for the Farry Company management to decide to purchase the inventory on (1) December 30, 1988, or (2) January 2, 1989?

32. *LIFO Liquidation.* During 1982 many companies found it necessary or desirable to liquidate earlier layers of LIFO inventories acquired at much lower prices. Data are shown below for selected companies for the first nine months of the year.

	Net Earnings First Nine Months	Addition to Net Earnings Due to LIFO Liquidation	LIFO Liquidation as a Percent of Net Earnings
	(in millions)	(in millions)	
General Tire and Rubber	$ 21.0	$ 4.0	20%
Gulf Oil	623.0	200.0	32
Interlake	5.3	1.5	28
Libbey-Owens-Ford	14.0	3.5	24
Mobil	959.0	95.0	10
Standard Oil of California	952.0	165.0	17
Texaco	975.0	315.0	32

REQUIRED

(a) What factors might have motivated the managements of these companies to favor a LIFO liquidation in 1982, which was a recession year?

(b) What balance sheet and income statement relationships were affected by this action?

(c) Assume that in each of these cases the LIFO liquidation occurred as the result of a management decision. Under what circumstances can LIFO liquidation take place as a consequence of events over which management has little or no control?

(d) Are there any disadvantages to a LIFO liquidation?

33. *Factors Involved in a Change from FIFO to LIFO.* The H & G Supply Stores, Inc., is a large company with over 300 stores in various regions throughout the United States. The company also has several manufacturing divisions and its stock and bonds outstanding are listed on a leading securities exchange. Because of its rapid expansion, the company's net cash flow was barely positive in 1981. In 1982, R. J. Hollings, the chief executive officer, is contemplating a change in inventory costing method from FIFO to LIFO.

REQUIRED How might each of the following factors affect Hollings' decision?

(a) The amount of taxes paid in recent years.

(b) Probable or pending tax legislation.

(c) Earnings per share.

(d) Cash flow.

(e) Supply uncertainties and labor unrest.

(f) The consistent price-level rises since World War II and the double-digit inflation of the late 1970s.

(g) Management's product-pricing procedures.

34. *Change in Inventory Cost Flow Assumption.* The Chrysler Corporation reported net income (loss) for the years 1968, 1969, and 1970 as follows:

1968	$290.7 million
1969	$ 88.7 million
1970	$ (7.6) million

In the company's annual report for 1970 the following statement appeared in a footnote:

Inventories are stated at lower of cost or market for the period January 1, 1957, through December 31, 1969. Last-in, first-out (LIFO) method of inventory valuation had been used for approximately 60% of consolidated inventory. Cost of the remaining 40% of inventories was determined using first-in, first-out (FIFO) or average-cost methods. Effective January 1, 1970, FIFO method of inventory valuation has been adopted for inventories previously valued using LIFO method. This results in a more uniform valuation method throughout the corporation and its consolidated subsidiaries and makes financial statements with respect to inventory valuation comparable with those of the other U.S. automobile manufacturers. As a result of adopting FIFO in 1970, net loss reported is less than it would have been by approximately $20.0 million or $.40 a share. Inventory amounts at December 31, 1970, are stated higher by $150 million than they would have been had LIFO been continued.

REQUIRED

(a) Why do you think Chrysler made the change in its inventory costing method in 1969 and not previously?
(b) Do you believe this change was regarded by the market as cosmetic or that it affected the price of Chrysler's shares?

35. *Comparison of LIFO and FIFO Inventory Methods.*   The Sawyer Company commenced business on January 1, 1983. During the year, 220,000 units were sold at an average price of $16 per unit. Purchases were as follows:

1st purchase	50,000 units @ $10
2nd purchase	60,000 units @ $11
3rd purchase	70,000 units @ $12
4th purchase	80,000 units @ $13

The company uses LIFO and at the close of the year, the following financial statements were prepared:

Balance Sheet
December 31, 1983

Cash	$ 90,000	Accounts Payable	$ 302,000
Accounts Receivable	360,000	Other Payables	130,000
Inventory	400,000	Common Stock	2,100,000
Other Assets	1,800,000	Retained Earnings	118,000
Total	$2,650,000	Total	$2,650,000

Income Statement
For the Year Ended December 31, 1983

Sales	$3,520,000
Cost of goods sold	2,640,000
Gross margin	$ 880,000
Less: Other expense	600,000
Pretax income	$ 280,000
Less: Income taxes	112,000
Net income	$ 168,000

Income taxes for 1983 are paid in 1984. The liability on December 31, 1983, is included in Other Payables.

REQUIRED

(a) Suppose the Sawyer Company had decided to use FIFO during 1983. How would the financial statements have differed?

(b) Is cash flow affected by the use of these alternative inventory methods?

(c) Could Sawyer's management have taken action to avoid paying income taxes in 1983? If so, how? What factors would restrain them from such action?

(d) Suppose that a supply shortage developed in 1984 and it was necessary to use all of the December 31, 1983, inventory to meet sales demand—that is, there was no inventory on hand at the end of 1984. How would profits in 1984 have been affected if the company had adopted FIFO instead of LIFO at the start of business?

36. *LIFO versus FIFO in Credit and Investment Decisions.* The New England Oil Company sells home heating oil in a number of towns and small cities in Massachusetts and Connecticut. The firm services approximately 30,000 customers whose heating requirements are computer programmed. Four strategically located storage depots are maintained with an aggregate capacity of 5 million gallons of oil. Although sales have increased at an average annual rate of 15% during the past five years, earnings have risen at an annual rate of only 3%.

The company's president, Sam Chico, is considering taking the company public and has consulted Parker Burroughs, who is associated with a firm of investment bankers. Burroughs is familiar with NEOCO and has advised Chico that the use of LIFO has curtailed the company's earnings performance. He contends that if LIFO is replaced with FIFO, a new issue of common stock could be marketed at a higher price.

The company is on a fiscal year reporting basis, from April 1 to March 31. On April 1, 1988, NEOCO had 3.5 million gallons of oil stored, of which 3 million gallons (base stock) were originally acquired at $.20 a gallon. The remaining 500,000 gallons were acquired at $.70 a gallon. During the year ended March 31, 1989, purchases and sales of oil were as follows:

	Purchases (gals.)	Sales (gals.)
August 1988	1 million @ $ .80	
September	2 million @ $ .85	1.5 million @ $1.20
October	3 million @ $1.00	3.2 million @ $1.35
November	3 million @ $1.05	3.3 million @ $1.35
December	4 million @ $1.10	4.2 million @ $1.45
January 1989	4.5 million @ $1.10	4.8 million @ $1.45
February	4 million @ $1.15	4.6 million @ $1.45
March	3.5 million @ $1.15	3.9 million @ $1.45

Chico has attempted to price his oil at $.30 per gallon over current cost, although this is not always possible because of competition. Selling, storage, delivery, and administrative expenses during the year ended March 31, 1989, were $1.6 million (fixed) plus 15% of sales. Although financial statements for the year have not as yet been prepared, apart from inventory and income tax payable (at a 40% rate), account balances on March 31, 1989, showed current assets of $2.2 million and current liabilities of $1 million.

REQUIRED

(a) Calculate the income for the year ended March 31, 1989, on a LIFO and FIFO basis.
(b) How might a banker considering a 90-day seasonal loan to NEOCO be influenced by the company's use of LIFO (as contrasted with FIFO)?
(c) Do you agree with Burroughs' comments?

37. *Preparation of Financial Statements and Analysis (FIFO versus LIFO).*   The Great Lakes Mercantile Company's balance sheet as of the close of 1988 was as follows:

The Great Lakes Mercantile Company
Balance Sheet
At December 31, 1988

Assets

Cash		$ 86,000
Accounts Receivable		294,000
Inventories (50,000 units @ $4)		200,000
Fixed Assets	$ 4,000,000	
Less: Accumulated Depreciation	(1,600,000)	2,400,000
Total Assets		$2,980,000

Liabilities and Stockholders' Equity

Accounts Payable	$ 270,000	
Income Tax Payable	90,000	
Total Liabilities		$ 360,000
Common Stock	$ 2,400,000	
Retained Earnings	220,000	
Total Stockholders' Equity		2,620,000
Total Liabilities and Stockholders' Equity		$2,980,000

During 1989, the following transactions took place. Assume that purchase costs and selling prices changed on the first day of each quarter.

	Units Purchased	Unit Cost	Units Sold	Selling Price
1st quarter	100,000	$5	80,000	$ 7
2nd quarter	100,000	6	90,000	8
3rd quarter	100,000	7	100,000	9
4th quarter	100,000	8	110,000	10

Additional considerations are as follows:

(1) No fixed assets were bought or sold during 1989. A composite depreciation rate of 10% is used.
(2) On December 31, 1989, cash amounted to $88,400; marketable securities, $150,000; and accounts payable, $300,000.
(3) The income tax rate is 40%.
(4) General and administrative expenses were $350,000.
(5) A cash dividend of $50,000 was declared on December 31, 1989. There were no other transactions affecting stockholders' equity.
(6) The company presently uses FIFO, but because of constantly rising prices, it is considering a change to LIFO as a way to reduce its income tax.

REQUIRED

Part 1
(a) Calculate the firm's tax liability for the year ended December 31, 1989, assuming the FIFO inventory costing method is used.
(b) Prepare an income statement for the year ending December 31, 1989, assuming FIFO is used.
(c) Prepare a balance sheet as of December 31, 1989.

Part 2
(a) Calculate the firm's tax liability for the year ended December 31, 1989, assuming the LIFO inventory costing method is used.
(b) From the information above for the Great Lakes Mercantile Company, prepare an income statement for the year 1989 and a balance sheet as of December 31, 1989, assuming the company changed to LIFO on January 1, 1989.
(c) Do you think this company should change its inventory costing method to LIFO? Why?

38. *Depreciation Methods.* On January 1, 1988, a fixed asset is purchased for $100,000. The asset has an estimated economic life of five years, after which time its residual value is projected to be $10,000.

REQUIRED   Determine the proper amount of depreciation expense for the years 1988, 1989, and 1990 under each of the following methods of depreciation: (1) straight line, (2) double declining balance, and (3) sum of the years' digits.

39. *Depreciation Methods.* On January 2, 1987, the Urbana Company paid $110,000 cash for a delivery truck. This fixed asset had an estimated economic life of five years and an estimated residual value of $10,000.

REQUIRED   Compute depreciation expense for both 1987 and 1988 under each of the following methods: (1) straight line, (2) sum of the years' digits, and (3) double declining balance.

40. *Identification of Depreciation Methods.*   On January 4, 1987, the Champaign Company paid $210,000 cash for a computer. This fixed asset had an estimated economic life of five years and zero residual value. Annual depreciation expenses for 1987 and 1988, using two alternative depreciation methods, are shown below.

	1987	1988
Alternative method 1	$70,000	$56,000
Alternative method 2	$42,000	$42,000

REQUIRED   Identify these two alternative depreciation methods. Show your work.

41. *Depreciation Calculations: Changes in Estimates.*   Hum Lo Corporation purchased a machine on January 1, 1986, at a cost of $240,000, with an estimated useful life of ten years and an estimated residual value of $20,000. The firm uses the straight-line method of depreciation for this machine.

REQUIRED   Determine the amount of depreciation expense to be recorded in 1988, based on the changes in estimates listed below. Assume each change in estimate is made on January 1, 1988. Each case is to be considered independently.

(a) The useful life of the machine is estimated to be six years.
(b) The residual value estimate is revised to $80,000.
(c) The remaining benefit pattern is estimated to decline over time in a manner consistent with double declining-balance depreciation.

42. *Depreciation Methods and Profitability Measurement (Return on Assets Employed).*   On January 1, 1988, the Patti, Maxine, and Laverne divisions of the Andrews Company each acquired an identical machine costing $900,000 with an estimated five-year useful life and zero residual value. Each of the three divisions expects to use the machine to earn $220,000 per year of operating profit *before* depreciation (ignoring taxes). Patti uses straight-line depreciation, Maxine uses sum-of-the-years'-digits depreciation, and Laverne uses double declining-balance depreciation (switching to straight-line depreciation in the last year).

REQUIRED

(a) Determine each division's pretax return on assets employed in 1988 and 1989 (use the year-end book value of the machine in the denominator of your calculations).

(b) Determine each division's rate of profit growth from 1988–1989.

(c) Rank the divisions based on average profit over the five-year period.

(d) Rank the divisions based on average return on assets employed over the five-year period.

(e) Why are your rankings different in items (c) and (d)? Can you suggest a more useful way to assess the profitability of assets across the divisions? Discuss.

43. *Different Depreciation Methods and Effects.* Assume that each of four competing companies (Alpha, Beta, Chi, and Delta) simultaneously purchases a $30,000 machine with an estimated life of five years and no salvage value. The machine is expected to produce 6,000 salable products during Year 1, 8,000 in Year 2, 10,000 in Year 3, 10,000 in Year 4, and 6,000 in Year 5. Each product will yield an incremental income of $1.25 before depreciation expense. Each company uses a different depreciation method, as follows: Alpha — straight line; Beta — sum of the years' digits; Chi — double declining balance; and Delta — production output.

REQUIRED

(a) Calculate the annual depreciation expense and the net book balance of the machine at the end of each year for the four companies.

(b) Calculate the annual pretax income (that is, income after deducting depreciation) for each company.

(c) Calculate the annual return on the average annual net book balance of the machine for each company.

(d) Compare results and discuss your interpretation of these results.

(e) Assume that at the end of the third year each company sells the machine for $9,000. Calculate the respective gains or losses. What is your interpretation of these figures?

44. *Disposal of a Fixed Asset.* On July 1, 1987, equipment was acquired by the Delta Company for $85,000. At the time of purchase, the equipment had an estimated economic life of eight years, with a $5,000 residual value. Six months of depreciation was recorded on December 31, 1987, and thereafter annual depreciation has been recorded on December 31 of each year using the straight-line method. On April 1, 1991, the fixed asset is sold for $30,000.

REQUIRED

(a) Record the necessary journal entry at April 1, 1991 (the date of the sale of the asset).

(b) What was the total net cash expended for the use of this fixed asset, excluding operation expenses and tax considerations?

(c) What was the company's total reported expense (depreciation plus loss on disposal of fixed asset) over the useful life of the asset?

(d) Are your answers to (b) and (c) the same? Should they be? Explain.

45. *Depreciation Methods and Disposal of Fixed Assets.*   The Babara Company purchased a warehouse for $60,000 on January 2, 1986. The estimated economic life of the warehouse is ten years and the estimated residual value, $5,000. On January 1, 1988, the Babara Company decides to sell the warehouse for $35,000 cash.

REQUIRED

(a) Compute the depreciation expense for 1986 and 1987 under each of the following methods: (1) straight line, (2) double declining balance, and (3) sum of the years' digits.

(b) Prepare journal entries required at January 1, 1988, to record the disposal of the warehouse under each of the three depreciation methods.

(c) Compute the total expense of using the asset (including the gain or loss on disposal) for these three depreciation methods.

46. *Various Depreciation Methods and Interperiod Tax Allocation.*   The Leaden Flask Company purchased a machine on January 1, 1986, costing $600,000, with a five-year estimated useful life and an estimated residual value of $100,000.

REQUIRED

(a) Determine the *second* year's depreciation expense, assuming:
   (1) Straight-line depreciation
   (2) Sum-of-the-years'-digits depreciation
   (3) Double declining-balance depreciation

(b) Assume that Leaden Flask uses straight-line depreciation on its financial statements and ACRS to calculate depreciation on its tax return. Because the asset was purchased prior to January 1, 1987, the original ACRS rules apply. Under the original ACRS rules, this asset has a three-year life for tax purposes. The financial statements report $80,000 of income *before* taxes, and the firm is taxed at a rate of 40%. Provide a journal entry to record the firm's income tax expense, income tax payable, and (if necessary) change in its deferred income tax account, for the first and second years that the machine is used.

47. *Interperiod Tax Allocation (one asset; complete reversal).*   The Seattle Company's pretax income statements for three consecutive years are shown below. These statements are in highly summarized form, with all revenues on one line and all expenses (except income tax expense) on the next line.

	1987	1988	1989
Revenues	$140,000	$240,000	$210,000
Expenses (including depreciation)	100,000	200,000	160,000
Net income before taxes	$ 40,000	40,000	$50,000

The company has only one fixed asset, which was purchased on January 2, 1987, for $60,000. The asset has an estimated life of three years and a zero residual value. Assume these estimates apply for both tax and accounting purposes. The company uses straight-line depreciation to prepare its income statement and the Accelerated Cost Recovery System to prepare its tax return. Because the asset was purchased after December 31, 1986, the modified ACRS rules apply. The asset qualifies under these rules as having a three-year life for tax purposes. The company's effective income tax rate is 40%.

REQUIRED

(a) Prepare journal entries that were made by the company each year to record income taxes.
(b) Calculate the balance of the Deferred Income Tax account at the end of each of the three years.

48. *Interperiod Income Tax Allocation.*   Pretax accounting income and taxable income for the Southington Company for the period 1987–1989 are as follows:

	Pretax Accounting Income	**Taxable Income**
1987	$ 80,000	$ 85,000
1988	80,000	77,200
1989	80,000	77,800
Totals	$240,000	$240,000

The difference, if any, between pretax accounting income and taxable income in any given year is due entirely to the use of ACRS for tax purposes and straight-line depreciation for financial reporting purposes. Assume that the company has only one fixed asset. This asset was purchased for $60,000 in January 1987 and has a three-year useful life with a $5,000 residual value. Because the asset was purchased after December 31, 1986, the modified ACRS rules apply. The asset qualifies under these rules as having a three-year life for tax purposes. The firm's effective income tax rate is 40%.

REQUIRED

(a) How much depreciation was taken each year on the company's tax return? Explain.

(b) Prepare the necessary entries to record income taxes for the years 1987–1989.

49. *Deferred Taxes: Continued Investment in New Assets.*   Static Dynamics, Inc., began operations on January 1, 1987. Beginning with the first year of operations, the firm's policy is to purchase one new fixed asset each year for $120,000. Each fixed asset purchased will have an estimated economic life of three years and an estimated residual value of zero. Because all fixed assets in this problem are purchased after December 31, 1986, the modified ACRS rules apply to each of them. For tax purposes, these machines are in the three-year life class under ACRS. Each fixed asset produces operating profits *before* depreciation and taxes each year of $80,000, and the firm's income is taxed at a rate of 40%.

REQUIRED

(a) Determine depreciation expense and the depreciation deduction on the firm's tax return for the first four years of operations.
(b) Record the firm's income tax expense, tax liability, and deferred tax change for the first four years of operations.
(c) Assume that Static Dynamics does *not* use deferred tax accounting, and record the firm's tax expense and tax liability for the first four years of operations.
(d) Contrast the amounts determined for tax expense and tax liability each year in (b) and (c) above. Why do the amounts differ in the first two years? Why are they the same in the third and fourth years?
(e) If the firm were to continue acquiring one new asset each year, would deferred tax accounting be preferable to nondeferred tax accounting after the second year? Explain.
(f) Assume that the firm ceased investing in new assets at the end of 1990. Record the firm's tax expense, tax liability, and deferred tax change in 1991 and 1992.

50. *Calculation of Deferred Tax Credit.*   The Axello Corporation begins operations on January 1, 1987. On that day, it purchases a machine for $15,000. At the beginning of each subsequent year, it purchases an additional identical machine for $15,000. Each machine has an estimated life of five years with no salvage value. The company uses the straight-line depreciation method on its books and ACRS for tax purposes. The asset qualifies under ACRS as having a five-year life. Each machine produces an annual income before depreciation and income taxes of $6,000. The income tax rate is 40%.

During 1991, the company received unearned revenue of $8,000, which properly was treated as a deferred credit in that year, but recognized as revenue in 1992. However, under IRS regulations, this had to be reported as taxable income in 1991.

REQUIRED Prepare a schedule showing income tax paid, income tax expense, income tax deferred, and the balance of the Deferred Tax Credit account for each year, 1987–1991.

51. *Interperiod Income Tax Allocation.* In 1991, after five years of successful operation, the Northington Company went out of business. With one exception, the firm used the same methods to determine pretax accounting income as it used to calculate taxable income. This single exception involved depreciation of fixed assets. The company employed straight-line depreciation for financial reporting, but used ACRS for tax purposes. Assume that all fixed assets were purchased in January 1987 for $90,000. The estimated useful life for both financial accounting and tax purposes was five years, with a zero residual value after that period of time. The company's effective income tax rate is 40%.

Selected income data for Northington's five years of operation are presented below:

Year	Accounting Income before Depreciation and Income Tax Expense	Taxable Income before Depreciation
1987	$ 210,000	$ 210,000
1988	240,000	240,000
1989	260,000	260,000
1990	310,000	310,000
1991	230,000	230,000
Totals	$1,250,000	$1,250,000

REQUIRED

(a) Are all differences between accounting income and taxable income in this case properly classified as timing differences? Explain.
(b) For each of the five years of the company's existence, calculate depreciation expense for financial accounting purposes and depreciation for tax purposes.
(c) Determine pretax accounting income and also taxable income for each year listed.
(d) Prepare the necessary journal entries to record income taxes for each year listed.

52. *Deferred Income Taxes.* The 1982 annual report of the Penril Corporation contained the following information with respect to deferred income taxes:

	1982	1981
Balance Sheet		
Under Current Liabilities		
Taxes on Income		
Current	$ 103,007	$ 578,952
Deferred	46,200	95,000
Under Noncurrent Liabilities		
Deferred Income Taxes (Note 5)	235,000	377,000
Income Statement		
Provision for income taxes		
Current	1,241,400	1,836,700
Deferred	(190,800)	39,000

REQUIRED

(a) What do the differences on the company's balance sheet and income statement between current and deferred income taxes represent?

(b) What does the deferred taxes on income shown under current liabilities represent? Do you agree with this presentation?

5

The Balance Sheet: Assets

Chapter 5 is the first of three chapters devoted to the major elements of the balance sheet: assets, liabilities, and owners' equity. This chapter describes methods of accounting for the assets of the firm. The discussion begins with the Financial Accounting Standards Board's definition of assets. Recent balance sheets of two U.S. firms (UAL, Incorporated, and Apple Computer, Incorporated) are presented, and accounting for each of the major types of assets is discussed in some detail. The chapter ends with a summary and evaluation of alternative valuation methods used in assets reporting.

ASSETS DEFINED

The Financial Accounting Standards Board defines assets as " . . . probable future economic benefits obtained or controlled by a particular entity as a result of past transactions or events."[1] The statement also identifies four essential characteristics of an asset:

1. An asset must contribute to future net cash inflows (or obviate future net cash outflows).
2. The enterprise must be able to obtain the benefit and control access of others to it.
3. The event giving rise to an asset must already have occurred.
4. The future benefit must be quantifiable or measureable in units of money.

The FASB's conceptual framework definitions are not necessarily intended to be descriptive of current practice, but rather to serve as guides in developing future accounting standards. In order to describe the asset section of the balance sheet in light of contemporary accounting standards, we need to refer to a second definition of assets. This definition was fashioned by the now-defunct Accounting Principles Board (APB) and is admittedly circular; it states, in effect, that an item is an asset just because GAAP say it is.

> Assets—economic resources of an enterprise that are recognized and measured in conformity with generally accepted accounting principles. *Assets also include certain deferred charges that are not resources* but that are recognized and measured in conformity with generally accepted accounting principles.[2] (Emphasis added)

The italicized segment of the preceding definition is meant to highlight a major difference between this older definition and the newer one developed by the FASB. GAAP currently permit residuals from the matching process to be included in the asset section of the balance sheet, even though they represent items that are clearly not economic resources. An example is a debit balance in Deferred Income Taxes.[3] Application of the FASB's definition of assets, by contrast, would not permit an item to be included on the balance sheet simply to facilitate the process of income determination.

---

[1] *Statement of Financial Accounting Concepts No. 6,* "Elements of Financial Statements" (Stamford, CT: FASB, 1980), par. 25.

[2] Accounting Principles Board *Statement No. 4,* "Basic Concepts and Accounting Principles Underlying Financial Statements of Business Enterprises" (New York: AICPA, 1970), par. 132.

[3] Interperiod tax allocation for purposes of income reporting was discussed in Chapter 4. This topic is on the current agenda of the FASB.

ASSET REPORTING

Exhibit 5-1 shows the asset sections of the balance sheets of Apple Computer, Inc., at September 30, 1983, and UAL, Inc., at December 31, 1983. The following observations pertain to the exhibit:

1. The assets are classified on the balance sheet as (1) current assets; (2) property, plant, and equipment; and (3) other assets, such as noncurrent investments, intangibles, and so on. These groupings have evolved over the years to provide meaningful summaries of similar assets. They provide the frame of reference for the discussion that follows.

2. UAL's assets consist mainly of operating property and equipment. Over 71 percent of all UAL assets ($3.6 billion of property and equipment divided by $5.1 billion in total assets) consist of these types of noncurrent assets. Apple Computer's assets, on the other hand, are mainly short-term in nature. Apple's current assets comprise over 84 percent of the firm's total assets, and noncurrent assets are less than 16 percent. UAL, Inc.'s asset structure is more **capital intensive** than that of Apple Computer because UAL, Inc., depends more heavily on long-lived assets. Apple Computer's assets, in contrast, are highly liquid; cash, temporary investments, and accounts receivable account for over 50 percent of Apple's total assets.

3. Several different valuation methods are used in valuing assets. For example, GAAP require that temporary cash investments be valued at the lower of historical cost or current market value; that accounts receivable be valued at their expected net cash proceeds; and that inventories be valued at historical cost, but factors such as obsolescence or declines in replacement cost may require a lower carrying value. Generally, the valuation rules for current assets reflect a concern for business liquidity, and current assets are not valued above their expected future cash benefits. Noncurrent assets, on the other hand, are generally valued at original historical cost less accumulated depreciation, amortization, or depletion. Except in cases where the values of noncurrent assets have been permanently impaired (that is, their carrying values are not expected to be recoverable through future profitable operations or resale), these assets continue to be reported at cost. (Each of these different valuation methods, which are sometimes called **measurement bases,** will be explained later in the chapter.)

4. The noncurrent assets of UAL, Inc., include a substantial amount for capital leases. The firm does not have legal title to these assets but signed long-term rental agreements (leases) that the FASB deems to be in substance similar to an installment purchase of assets. (The rules for reporting leased assets in financial statements have provoked sharp debate among accounting policymakers. In order to include a detailed

Exhibit 5-1
Asset Reporting: Two Examples

UAL, Incorporated
Statement Of Consolidated Financial Position

		December 31, 1983
ASSETS	(In thousands)	
Current assets:	Cash	$ 45,789
	Marketable securities	246,357
	Receivables, less allowance for doubtful accounts ($10,809)	766,800
	Aircraft fuel, spare parts and supplies, less obsolescence allowance ($34,351)	138,678
	Prepaid expenses	56,157
		1,253,781
Operating property and equipment:	Owned—	
	Flight equipment	3,845,013
	Advances on flight equipment purchase contracts	87,244
	Other property and equipment	1,786,289
		5,718,546
	Less—Accumulated depreciation and amortization	2,544,649
		3,173,897
	Capital leases—	
	Flight equipment	758,278
	Other property and equipment	159,398
		917,676
	Less—Accumulated amortization	438,609
		479,067
		3,652,964
Other assets:	Receivables and investments	105,752
	Pledged marketable securities	29,098
	Other	92,048
		226,898
		$5,133,643

Apple Computer, Inc.
Consolidated Balance Sheet

September 30, 1983
(Dollars in thousands)

Assets	1983
Current assets:	
Cash and temporary cash investments	$143,284

Current assets (*continued*):

Accounts receivable, net of allowance for doubtful accounts of $5,124	$136,420
Inventories	142,457
Prepaid income taxes	27,949
Other current assets	18,883
Total current assets	468,993
Property, plant and equipment:	
Land and buildings	19,993
Machinery and equipment	51,445
Office furniture and equipment	22,628
Leasehold improvements	15,894
	109,960
Accumulated depreciation and amortization	(42,910)
Net property, plant and equipment	67,050
Other assets	20,536
	$556,579

Sources: UAL, Incorporated, *Annual Report*, 1983; Apple Computer, Inc., *Annual Report*, 1983.

presentation of the issues involved, treatment of leasing has been deferred to Chapter 10.)

The discussion in the following pages illustrates methods of accounting for each of the main types of assets to be found on the balance sheets of U.S. firms. Where possible, reference will be made to the examples in Exhibit 5-1.

ACCOUNTING FOR CURRENT ASSETS

Current assets are cash and other economic resources that can reasonably be expected to be realized in cash or sold or consumed within one year, or within the normal operating cycle, whichever is longer. A firm's **operating cycle** is the average time it takes to convert cash into the firm's major product or service and then back again into cash. For example, the following sequence of activities represents the operating cycle of a typical manufacturer: use of cash for the purchase of raw materials, conversion of raw materials into finished products, sale of these products on account, and collection of cash from the credit sales. For most businesses, the normal operating cycle is less than one year.

Current assets are usually presented on the balance sheet in the order of decreasing liquidity. Since cash is the most liquid of assets, it is shown first. Other current assets in typical order of presentation are temporary investments, receivables, inventory, and short-term prepayments.

Cash and Temporary Investments

Cash includes currency, funds deposited in a bank, checks, money orders, demand certificates of deposit, and bank drafts. At certain times during a business year, a firm may have excess cash. Idle cash produces no revenue and loses purchasing power in a period of rising prices. To protect against such possibilities, idle cash is normally invested, but in a way that it can easily be converted into cash again if needed.

An investment is classified on the balance sheet as a **temporary investment** if two criteria are met: (1) the investment is *readily marketable* (that is, management is able to sell it very quickly), and (2) it is management's *intention* to convert the investment into cash as needed within one year or within the operating cycle, whichever is longer. If *either* criterion is not met, the investment is reported as a long-term investment. For example, Exhibit 5-1 shows that "other" noncurrent assets of UAL, Inc., include certain receivables, investments, and marketable securities. Even though the marketable securities are readily convertible into cash, it is apparently not the intention of UAL management to liquidate these items. For this reason, the items are not expected to provide cash for operating purposes within a year or within UAL's operating cycle.

A portfolio of temporary investments might include the following:

1. **Short-term paper:** interest-bearing instruments such as certificates of deposit and U.S. Treasury bills.
2. **Marketable debt securities:** government and corporate bonds.
3. **Marketable equity securities:** ownership interests in other companies in the form of preferred or common stock.

According to the cost principle, all temporary investments are recorded initially at acquisition price plus other incidental costs (brokerage fees and transfer taxes, for example). Subsequent to acquisition, GAAP prescribe the use of the cost basis for short-term paper and marketable debt securities, and the lower of cost or market basis for marketable equity securities.

We will demonstrate the lower of cost or market rules for marketable equity securities with reference to the example in Exhibit 5-2. The FASB requires that the entire portfolio of temporary (current) investments in marketable equity securities be valued at the lower of aggregate cost or market, using a valuation allowance if market value is below cost.[4] Changes in the valuation allowance are used in the determination of periodic net income.

Consider the current portfolio shown in Exhibit 5-2. Since the portfolio's aggregate market value of $6,200 is below its aggregate cost of $6,500, a valuation allowance of $300 is needed. Assuming that the current balance of the Valuation Allowance account is zero, the following adjustment is made to increase the balance to $300:

dr.	Unrealized Loss, Current Portfolio	300	
	cr. Valuation Allowance, Current Portfolio		300

---

[4]*Statement of Financial Accounting Standards No. 12,* "Accounting for Certain Marketable Securities" (Stamford, CT: FASB, 1975), par. 8–12.

Exhibit 5-2
Portfolio of Temporary Investments

Costs and Market Values
December 31, 1987

Security	Cost	Market Value (December 31)
A	$1,000	$1,800
B	2,500	1,200
C	3,000	3,200
Totals	$6,500	$6,200

Whenever the valuation allowance is increased, as in the case just considered, an unrealized loss is recognized and will reduce net income for the period. The loss is unrealized because the securities have not yet been sold. The valuation allowance is a contra-asset account and is subtracted on the balance sheet from the aggregate cost of the temporary investments to determine the carrying value of the portfolio. Consequently, the portfolio of temporary investments described in Exhibit 5-2 would be described as follows in the December 31, 1987, balance sheet:

Temporary investments in marketable equity securities
of $6,500, less valuation allowance ($300 in 1987) $6,200

At each subsequent financial reporting date, the aggregate cost and the aggregate market value of the current portfolio are determined, and the valuation account is adjusted as necessary. For example, assume the following aggregate cost and market value information for the two subsequent reporting dates:

	Aggregate Cost	Aggregate Market Value
December 31, 1988	$7,200	$6,700
December 31, 1989	8,100	8,500

The December 31, 1988, balance sheet requires a valuation allowance of $500 ($7,200 cost less $6,700 market value). Since the valuation allowance already has a balance of $300 from 1987, the firm must recognize an additional unrealized loss of $200 in 1988 ($500 less $300). At December 31, 1989, however, the investment in marketable equity securities should be valued on the balance sheet at cost, since the aggregate market value of the portfolio exceeds its cost ($8,100 cost, $8,500 market value). In this situation, the valuation allowance is not needed and should be decreased to zero. Whenever the valuation allowance is decreased (debited), the Recovery of Unrealized Loss account is credited and will increase net income for the period. Since the valuation allowance has a credit balance of $500, the following adjusting entry is needed to reduce its balance to zero:

dr.	Valuation Allowance, Current Portfolio	500	
cr.	Recovery of Unrealized Loss, Current Portfolio		500

Note that the carrying value of the portfolio is never increased above the total historical cost of the investments. Unrealized gains above historical cost are not recognized in income. When individual securities are sold, however, any difference between their original cost and the sales proceeds is reported as a realized gain or loss.

These accounting rules do *not* reflect a current value approach to asset valuation, because the securities portfolios are revalued only when aggregate market values are *below* cost. The lower of cost or market rules for marketable equity securities are considered by many to be an improvement over strict historical cost reporting in cases where current market values are substantially below historical costs. Note that the accounting rules for marketable equity securities reflect a weakening of the linkage between realization and income determination, because these rules allow for the reporting of an unrealized loss on certain securities before they are actually sold.

Receivables

Receivables are claims on assets of others or on services to be provided by others in the future. Most receivables are due within one year or within the firm's normal operating cycle, if the cycle is longer than a year. These receivables are properly classified as current assets and are presented on the balance sheet at **net realizable value,** or at the net amount of cash expected to be collected.

For financial statement purposes, trade receivables are usually differentiated from other receivables. **Trade receivables** arise from the credit sale of an enterprise's goods (inventory) or services in the normal course of business. In most cases, trade receivables take the form of an "open account" due in 30–60 days and are called **accounts receivable.** Accounts receivable usually do not involve interest charges, although such charges may be imposed if payments are not made within a certain period of time. Cash due from credit sales to customers is usually the most significant of all receivables. Accounts receivable are important in assessing a firm's liquidity and financial flexibility.

It is inevitable that some credit sales will not be collected. This is explicitly recognized in financial accounting by an adjusting entry made at the end of each accounting period:

dr.	Bad Debt Expense	XXX	
cr.	Allowance for Doubtful Accounts		XXX

Bad Debt Expense is an income statement account, and it reduces the period's net income. **Allowance for Doubtful Accounts** is a contra-asset account that is subtracted directly from Accounts Receivable on the balance sheet. The arithmetic difference between the gross amount of the receivables and the balance of the allowance account is referred to as either the **book value** or the **net realizable value** of the receivables.

Exhibit 5-1 shows that accounts receivable for UAL, Inc., total $766.8 million at December 31, 1983, after deducting an allowance for doubtful accounts of $10.8 million. By comparison, Apple Computer, Inc., has receivables of $136.4 million, net of an allowance for doubtful accounts of $5.1 million. UAL's allowance is about 1.4 percent of its outstanding receivables, while Apple Computer's allowance is about 3.6 percent of its outstanding receivables. The difference in these percentages may reflect differences in customer quality, the average age of outstanding accounts, and other factors.

In accounting for bad debts, dollar amounts are determined by considering either (1) the dollar amount of credit sales for the period or (2) the composition (age) of accounts receivable. Estimating uncollectible accounts as a function of the amount of the period's credit sales is an attempt to match anticipated current expenses with current sales revenue. Specifically, the emphasis is on determining the proper amount to be debited to Bad Debt Expense; thus, the approach is income statement oriented. To illustrate, assume that the Bloom Company has $500,000 of credit sales during 1987, and that in the past approximately 1 percent of credit sales have proven to be uncollectible. The appropriate entry is

dr.	Bad Debt Expense ($500,000 × 1%)	5,000	
cr.	Allowance for Doubtful Accounts		5,000

The second approach to estimating uncollectible accounts is based on the premise that the longer a particular receivable is outstanding, the more likely it is to be uncollectible. This approach, referred to as the **aging method,** analyzes the age of receivables with emphasis on the proper valuation of the Allowance for Doubtful Accounts. Since Allowance for Doubtful Accounts is a contra-asset account, the approach is balance sheet oriented.

Consider another illustration. Assume that on December 31, 1987, the Ruth Company has total accounts receivable of $700,000, and that past experience indicates that the chance of a receivable being uncollectible is related to its age in accordance with the following figures:

Age of Receivable (days outstanding)	Probability of Receivable Being Uncollectible
0–30	1%
31–60	4%
61–90	7%
91 or more	15%

In Exhibit 5-3, the dollar amounts of receivables in each age category are multiplied by the percentages shown above to arrive at an estimate that $18,400 of current receivables will not be collected. Accordingly, the appropriate credit balance for the allowance account at the balance sheet date is $18,400. Assum-

Exhibit 5-3
Estimate of Uncollectible Accounts

Ruth Company
December 31, 1987

Age Category (Days Outstanding)	Dollar Amount in Age Category	Percentage Expected to Be Uncollectible	Amount Expected to Be Uncollectible
0–30	$570,000	1%	$ 5,700
31–60	40,000	4%	1,600
61–90	30,000	7%	2,100
91 or more	60,000	15%	9,000
	$700,000		$18,400

ing that Allowance for Doubtful Accounts already has a $2,000 *credit* balance, the following adjusting entry would be made at the end of the period:

dr.	Bad Debt Expense	16,400	
	cr. Allowance for Doubtful Accounts		16,400

If, instead, the allowance account already has a *debit* balance of $4,000, the proper entry would be the following:

dr.	Bad Debt Expense	22,400	
	cr. Allowance for Doubtful Accounts		22,400

Both of the approaches discussed here for estimating uncollectible accounts deal only with an overall dollar total; they do not require identification of specific receivables as being uncollectible. However, when a particular account is eventually judged to be uncollectible, it is written off as follows:

dr.	Allowance for Doubtful Accounts	XXX	
	cr. Accounts Receivable		XXX

Depending on the circumstances, this entry may be made in the same period as the original credit sale or in a subsequent period. Note that the entry does not result in a change in the total book value of accounts receivable. Both the Allowance for Doubtful Accounts and Accounts Receivable are reduced by a like amount keeping the arithmetic difference between the two the same.

A popular analytical measure involving accounts receivable is a **turnover rate.** This financial ratio is calculated by dividing net credit sales for the period by the average accounts receivable outstanding. For example, assume that the Sardinas Company has annual credit sales of $1 million and an average balance in receivables during the year of $100,000. The firm's accounts receivable turnover rate is 10, which is calculated as follows:

$$\frac{\text{Net Credit Sales}}{\text{Average Accounts Receivable}} = \frac{\$1,000,000}{\$100,000} = 10 \text{ times}$$

This turnover rate can be used to calculate the average number of days necessary to collect receivables:

$$\frac{\text{Number of Days in the Year}}{\text{Receivable Turnover Rate}} = \frac{360}{10} = 36 \text{ days}$$

These ratios are useful in assessing liquidity and efficiency of cash collection. On the average, it takes the Sardinas Company 36 days to turn receivables into cash. If the credit terms are such that payment is expected within 60 days, collection is efficient; if, on the other hand, credit terms demand payment in 10 days, collections are lagging.

Although most receivables are trade receivables, some firms also have substantial amounts of nontrade receivables. **Nontrade receivables** arise from any source *except* credit sales of merchandise inventory or services in the normal course of business. Examples include loans or advances to company officers, deposits for returnable items (containers and the like), interest earned but not yet received, and claims against insurance companies for casualties suffered. Cash inflow from these sources is usually more variable from period to period than inflow from trade receivables.

Inventory

Inventory includes those tangible goods that are held for sale to customers in the ordinary course of business. Such goods are called **merchandise inventory** (or simply, inventory) in a merchandising firm, and **finished goods** in a manufacturing firm. Manufacturing company inventory also consists of (1) materials not yet placed into the production process (**raw materials**) and (2) goods in production but awaiting completion (**work in process**). Generally, more resources are invested in inventory than any other current asset, and the selling of inventory provides the enterprise with its principal source of revenue.

Exhibit 5-1 shows that Apple Computer's inventories are valued at $142.5 million on September 30, 1983, and comprise 30 percent of total current assets ($142.5 million divided by $469.0 million). UAL, on the other hand, is not a merchandising or manufacturing firm, and therefore does not have any substantial inventory investment. The UAL balance sheet does show such items as fuel and spare parts, which will be consumed by UAL in its operations and will not be sold directly to customers.

Three major questions dealing with inventory must be answered in preparing financial statements:

1. What items should be included?
2. What measurement base should be used?
3. What is the proper content and format of financial statement disclosure?

In answer to the first question, an item must be owned before it may be included as inventory. Although this rule is straightforward, at times there are questions involving its application. One example involves inventory on **consignment**. A consignment is an arrangement whereby a firm (the consignor) sends goods to another company (the consignee), but retains title to the goods. The consignee attempts to sell the items for the consignor. In this situation, the items should be included in the inventory of the consignor, even though physical possession is with the consignee.

Another example illustrating what items to include as inventory involves a situation in which a company sells goods but does not ship them immediately. Sold items awaiting shipment are excluded from the inventory of the seller if title has already passed to the buyer. Of course, the goods would be included in the buyer's inventory. Note that physical possession of the inventory is not relevant in either of the two examples just considered, but that ownership is critical.

Once it is determined which items to include in inventory, it is necessary to assign dollar values to those items. Inventories are generally presented on the balance sheet on a lower of cost or market (LCM) basis. In this context, the term "cost" means historical cost determined by applying an appropriate inventory cost flow assumption, and the term "market" means **replacement cost** by purchase or manufacture.

The central idea in applying the LCM rule is that the historical cost principle should be modified if the inventory's future utility, or revenue-producing ability, is no longer as great as its original cost. If this occurs, an expense is recognized during the period of the decline of the asset's utility by the following journal entry:

> dr.   Expense Due to Decline in Inventory Value   XXX
>   cr.   Inventory   XXX

LCM is defended on the basis of conservatism. While indeed conservative from the standpoint of the balance sheet, its use permits a future income statement to show a larger net income than if the inventory was carried forward at cost. LCM allows for the shifting of income among periods; if more cost is allocated to the current period because of an inventory write-down, less remains to be assigned to the period of sale as cost of goods sold.

The third major question to be answered in connection with inventory concerns the content and format of disclosure. The methods and procedures used to account for inventory have significant effects on both the balance sheet and the income statement. This phenomenon was discussed in the section of Chapter 4 dealing with inventory costing. As demonstrated there, alternative cost flow assumptions (FIFO, as opposed to LIFO, for example) may result in markedly different dollar amounts being allocated to ending inventory. Accordingly, the methods and procedures used to cost the inventories must be fully disclosed, usually in a separate section of the financial statements entitled "Summary of Significant Accounting Policies." For instance, Apple Computer's footnote disclosures include the following information:

> Inventories: Inventories are valued at the lower of cost or market. Cost is computed using currently adjusted standards which approximate actual cost on a first-in, first-out basis.

At minimum, the reporting firm must disclose the basis for measuring inventory (cost, LCM, and so forth) and the cost flow assumption used (FIFO, LIFO, or one of the other assumptions). The financial statement reader may assume that the methods and procedures disclosed have not been changed during the current reporting period. If this is not the case, the effects of the change on the financial statements must also be disclosed. Lastly, the FASB encourages disclosure of supplemental current cost information for inventories of certain companies. These disclosures are discussed in Chapter 11.

The average level of inventory and the velocity with which it "turns over" are important factors in predicting cash flow from operations and in evaluating operations efficiency. A commonly used index in this regard is the annual **inventory turnover rate.** To illustrate its use, assume that the Monterey Corporation has cost of goods sold for the year of $600,000 and average inventory of $50,000. The firm's inventory turnover rate is calculated as follows:

$$\frac{\text{Cost of Goods Sold}}{\text{Average Inventory}} = \frac{\$600,000}{\$50,000} = 12 \text{ times}$$

This indicates that the average daily stock of inventory on hand for the Monterey Corporation is sold and replaced twelve times during the year; in other words, inventory is typically on hand for about one month (30 days) before it is sold. This is calculated using the following formula:

$$\frac{\text{Number of Days in the Year}}{\text{Inventory Turnover Rate}} = \frac{360}{12} = 30 \text{ days}$$

Generally, a company attempts to increase the turnover of inventory. Increasing turnover usually means that fewer resources need be tied up in inventory because the average inventory level is smaller. Up to a point, this results in increased profitability (because of lower costs for financing and storage of inventory) and provides a firm with flexibility to employ resources elsewhere. Yet, the highest inventory turnover rate possible would rarely be the optimum. A high turnover rate can be achieved by keeping inventory on hand at extremely low levels, but this may prove to be counterproductive if it results in lost sales, higher ordering costs, and the like.

It is impossible for an outside analyst to know a company's optimum inventory turnover rate; therefore, comparisons are made on a relative basis. Changes or trends may be detected by comparing the company's current rate with its own past performance and with the performance of other firms in the same industry. Depending upon the industry, average turnover rates differ considerably. For example, inventory would be expected to turn over within days in a restaurant but would probably move at a much slower rate for an antique dealer.

If companies use different inventory costing methods, intercompany comparisons are difficult, even within the same industry. A company using LIFO, for instance, will usually show a higher inventory turnover rate than a firm using FIFO. This is explained by the fact that in a period of rising prices, LIFO ordinarily shows higher cost of goods sold and lower inventory than the use of FIFO would yield. The FASB recommends (as part of the new price disclosures that are discussed in Chapter 11 of this book) that firms provide footnote disclosure of the current replacement costs of inventories. As a result of these new disclosures, analysts may now make interfirm comparisons of inventories valued at current costs.

Prepaid Expenses

Prepaid expenses are payments made for certain goods and services in advance of their use or their consumption. Common prepaid items might include insurance premiums, rent, taxes, and office supplies. It is assumed that these items will be consumed (and thus, become expenses) within the coming year. Since specific items in this category are not likely to be material in amount, they are usually presented together on the balance sheet under the caption Prepaid Expenses. (Notice in Exhibit 5-1 that prepaid expenses comprise a relatively minor portion of the assets of both UAL and Apple Computer.)

ACCOUNTING FOR NONCURRENT ASSETS

The remaining sections of this chapter discuss items that are classified in the noncurrent assets section of the balance sheet. These include property, plant, and equipment; long-term investments; natural resources; and intangible assets. For much of the material that follows it is necessary to understand the concept of compound interest. Readers who are unfamiliar with this topic should read Appendix C at this point. A set of present value and future value tables is included in the appendix (Tables C-1 through C-4). These tables will be employed at various points in the following discussion and in several subsequent chapters.

Property, Plant, and Equipment

Long-lived, tangible assets that are employed by the enterprise in the production or sale of inventory or in the provision of services are referred to as **property, plant, and equipment,** or simply as **fixed assets.** Examples include automobiles, buildings, computer hardware, furniture, land, land improvements, machinery, office equipment, and the like. Refer again to Exhibit 5-1. You will note that UAL, Inc., shows over $3.6 billion invested in property, plant, and equipment. Of this total, about 88 percent ($3.17 billion) is owned by the company, and 12 percent ($0.48 billion) is leased from other firms. Apple Computer, by comparison, has a modest ($67 million) investment in property, plant, and equipment.

Fixed assets are presented on the balance sheet at *book value,* which is an asset's total acquisition cost less accumulated depreciation. **Acquisition cost** consists of all necessary expenditures made to prepare the asset for its intended use. These expenditures include the invoice price of the asset, freight charges, and costs incurred for installation and testing. Under certain conditions (to be discussed shortly) interest incurred during construction may also be added to the acquisition cost of a fixed asset. A typical reporting format is shown below for the fixed asset, Buildings.

Buildings	$400,000
Less: Accumulated depreciation, buildings	180,000
	$220,000

Only by coincidence would the $220,000 book value in this example reflect the current market value of the buildings. Recall that in financial accounting, depreciation is a process of cost allocation, not asset valuation. Thus, accumulated depreciation represents the amount of costs that have been matched to date against revenues in determining financial accounting income, and book value represents the historical costs to be carried forward to future periods.

GAAP require that the following information be disclosed, either in the body of the financial statements or in the footnotes:

1. Total depreciation expense for the period
2. Depreciation method(s) used
3. Groupings of acquisition costs of fixed assets, classified by nature or by function
4. Related groupings of accumulated depreciation (to date) for these categories of fixed assets.[5]

The footnote disclosures related to property, plant, and equipment for UAL and Apple Computer are presented in Exhibit 5-4. Note that UAL's footnote discussion is more extensive, reflecting the greater relative importance of property, plant, and equipment in UAL's financial position and operating results. The FASB recommends disclosure by certain companies of supplemental current cost information for property, plant, and equipment (see Chapter 11).

---

[5]Accounting Principles Board *Opinion No. 12,* "Omnibus Opinion–1967" (New York: AICPA, 1967), par. 5.

Exhibit 5-4
Footnote Disclosures Relating to Property, Plant, and Equipment

UAL, Inc.

Operating Property and Equipment

Owned operating property and equipment are stated at cost. Cost includes interest capitalized, where appropriate, on aircraft, hotel and land development acquisition costs.

Leased property under capital leases, and the related obligation for future minimum lease payments, are initially recorded at an amount equal to the then present value of those lease payments, using, primarily, the interest rate implicit in the lease.

Depreciation and Amortization and Retirements

Depreciation and amortization of owned property and equipment are based on the straight-line method over the estimated service lives of depreciable assets. Leasehold improvements are amortized over the remaining period of the lease or the estimated service life of the related asset, whichever is less. Aircraft are depreciated to a nominal salvage value over lives of 10 to 16 years. Buildings are depreciated over lives of 25 to 45 years.

Leased properties under capital leases are amortized on the straight-line method over the life of the lease. Lease terms are 15 to 19 years for aircraft and 10 to 40 years for buildings. Lease amortization is included in depreciation and amortization expense.

Gains or losses on retirements of individual units of owned property and equipment or leased property under capital leases are reflected in earnings.

Maintenance

Maintenance and repairs, including the cost of minor replacements, are charged to maintenance expense accounts. Costs of additions to and renewals of units of property are charged to property and equipment accounts.

Apple Computer, Inc.

Property, Plant and Equipment

Property, plant and equipment are stated at cost. Depreciation and amortization are computed principally by use of declining balance methods over the estimated useful lives of the assets.

Interest capitalization and fixed assets   In the past, there has been considerable controversy regarding the proper accounting for interest costs incurred to finance the construction of a fixed asset. The basic alternatives are (1) to expense such costs immediately as interest expense or (2) to capitalize them, thus adding interest costs to the total acquisition cost of the asset. In the latter case, interest costs are allocated to future periods as expense through the depreciation process.

Because of growing inconsistency among corporations regarding accounting for interest cost, the FASB issued *SFAS No. 34* in 1979. Capitalization of interest is required by this statement for assets that are either constructed for the firm's own use or constructed as discrete projects for sale or lease to others. An example is a long-term construction project such as a real estate development. *SFAS No. 34* does not permit capitalization of interest for all assets, however. The major exception to the capitalization requirement involves inventories that are routinely manufactured or otherwise produced in large quantities on a repetitive basis.[6]

Once assets that qualify for interest capitalization are identified, the next task is to determine the amount of interest associated with those assets. For a given qualifying asset, the amount of interest to be capitalized must be based on the actual amounts borrowed and the costs of these borrowings.

SFAS No. 34 states that the amount to be capitalized "... is intended to be that portion of the interest cost incurred during assets' acquisition periods that theoretically could have been avoided ... if expenditures for the assets had not been made."[7] Thus, the specific amount to be capitalized is the product of the average accumulated expenditures on the asset during the period and the appropriate interest rate(s). If the firm incurs a specific borrowing for a qualifying asset, the interest rate on that borrowing is used. A weighted average of the rates on other borrowings is applied to expenditures not covered by specific new borrowings.

To illustrate, assume that the Washington Company began to construct its own new manufacturing facility during 1987. Expenditures for this project were incurred evenly throughout the year and totaled $1.2 million. The building, which qualifies for interest capitalization, is expected to be completed in 1988. At the beginning of 1987, the company borrowed $400,000 specifically for the construction of this building at an annual interest rate of 15 percent. The company had other interest-bearing liabilities of $2 million outstanding during 1987, with a weighted-average interest rate of 12 percent. As a result of these borrowings, interest charges for 1987 were $300,000.

The amount of interest to be capitalized by the Washington Company for 1987 is determined as follows:

Step 1: *Determine the average accumulated expenditures for the year.* Since expenditures took place evenly throughout the year, the average accumulated expenditures amount is calculated by dividing total yearly expenditures on the project by 2 ($1.2 million/2 = $600,000).

Step 2: *Determine the source of borrowings for the average accumulated expenditures incurred during the year.* Washington Company incurred average accumulated expenditures of $600,000 for the year (Step 1). Since $400,000 was borrowed specifically for this project, the remaining $200,000 is from other borrowings.

---

[6] *Statement of Financial Accounting Standards No. 34,* "Capitalization of Interest Cost," (Stamford, CT: FASB, 1979), par. 9 and par. 10.

[7] *Statement of Financial Accounting Standards No. 34,* "Capitalization of Interest Cost," (Stamford, CT: FASB, 1979), par. 12.

Step 3:   *Multiply the average accumulated expenditures by the appropriate interest rate(s).*

Specific borrowing: $400,000 × 15% = $60,000
Other borrowings: $200,000 × 12% =   24,000
Interest to be capitalized $84,000

Based on the above calculations, $84,000 in interest would be capitalized by means of the following journal entry:

dr.	Building	84,000	
dr.	Interest Expense	216,000	
	cr. Cash (or Interest Payable)		300,000

Observe that of the total interest charges of $300,000 during 1987, $84,000 is added to the asset account Building and the remaining $216,000 is expensed during the current period.

Long-term Receivables and Investments

Exhibit 5-1 (page 218) shows that $105.8 million of the total assets of UAL, Inc., at December 31, 1983, consisted of noncurrent receivables and investments. Companies make investments for reasons ranging from deployment of idle cash to control of another company through ownership of its stock. If recorded investments do not meet the classification criteria for current assets, they are properly assigned to this long-term category.

Long-term investments may take several different forms, including the following:

1. **Debt securities:** loans made in the form of notes and bonds. The investor in debt securities has the legal right to receive interest payments at specified intervals and to collect the principal when the loan matures.
2. **Sinking funds:** cash, securities, or other assets accumulated by means of periodic contributions that have specific restrictions as to their use. For example, sinking funds may be established to provide for the repayment of a loan on its maturity date, or the replacement of certain noncurrent, tangible assets.
3. **Equity securities:** ownership interests in the form of preferred or common stock. The equity investor hopes for appreciation of the market price of the stock, plus the receipt of dividends.

Accounting for debt securities   One way that a firm may extend credit to customers is by accepting a **long-term note receivable** in return for goods or services. These notes may be interest bearing, in which case the rate of interest is stated on the note agreement. The firm will be repaid the amount loaned, plus the interest. Alternatively, the firm may accept a noninterest-bearing note. In that case, the value of the note when received is less than the face amount of the note, and the difference, termed the **note discount,** will constitute the interest on the note. To illustrate the accounting methods for long-term notes receivable, we will discuss two cases. In the first case, we consider a situation in which a long-term noninterest-bearing note is received to replace a past-due account receivable. In the second case, we consider a situation in which a machine is sold to a customer in exchange for a long-term noninterest-bearing note to be paid in installments over several years.

Case 1: *Long-term note receivable with a single payment at maturity.* Assume that on September 1, 1986, Lansing Distributors sells a machine on credit to a customer for $100,000. The customer is unable to pay on the due date, however, because of severe financial difficulties. In an effort to resolve this problem, Lansing Distributors agrees to accept a three-year, noninterest-bearing note from the customer on January 1, 1987, as settlement for the past due account receivable. The principal and all of the interest earned on the note are to be received in one lump sum on its maturity date (December 31, 1989).

Lansing Distributors is willing to accept the noninterest-bearing note only if it can earn a 14 percent annual return on the amount financed over the three-year period. Thus, calculation of the note's maturity value (or face value) requires reference to Table C-3 in Appendix C at the end of this chapter (Maturity Value of $1 Received or Paid at the End of Period). The maturity value is calculated as follows:

Present value of receivable, January 1, 1987	$100,000
Maturity value factor, 3 years at 14% (Table C-3)	× 1.482
Maturity value of noninterest-bearing note	$148,200

The note discount in this illustration is $48,200; this is the difference between the note's present value of $100,000 and its face value of $148,200. The note discount represents the total amount of interest on the note.

The journal entry required on January 1, 1987, to record the replacement of the overdue account receivable with the noninterest-bearing note is as follows:

Jan. 1, 1987   dr.   Long-term Note Receivable   100,000
                cr.   Accounts Receivable   100,000
               To record replacement of overdue account receivable with a
               long-term note receivable.

Exhibit 5-5 shows how the present value of the note increases each year. Notice that by December 31, 1989, the present value of the note has increased to equal the maturity value of the note, $148,200. Exhibit 5-5 also shows how the total interest of $48,200 is allocated over the three-year period.

Journal entries to record the accrual of annual interest income and to record the receipt of the maturity value of the note are presented below. These entries are based on the interest calculations made in Exhibit 5-5 and assume that Lansing Distributors closes its books annually on December 31.

Exhibit 5-5

Long-term Note Receivable and Interest Income: Single Payment at Maturity

---

Lansing Distributors

Face value of note due in three years	$148,200
Present value of note	100,000
Note discount, to be earned as interest income over three years	$ 48,200

Year	Present Value of Note, Start of Year	Interest at 14% of Present Value	Present Value of Note, End of Year
1987	$100,000	$14,000	$114,000
1988	114,000	15,960	129,960
1989	129,960	18,240*	148,200
Total interest income		$48,200	

---

*Multiplying the present value of the note at the start of 1989 by 14% interest ($129,960 × .14) equals $18,194.40. The $45.60 difference between $18,194.40 and the $18,240 used in the exhibit above is due to rounding in initially establishing the face value of the note.

Dec. 31, 1987	dr.	Long-term Note Receivable	14,000	
	cr.	Interest Income		14,000

To record interest earned on note for 1987.

Dec. 31, 1988	dr.	Long-term Note Receivable	15,960	
	cr.	Interest Income		15,960

To record interest earned on note for 1988.

Dec. 31, 1989	dr.	Long-term Note Receivable	18,240	
	cr.	Interest Income		18,240

To record interest earned on note for 1989.

Dec. 31, 1989	dr.	Cash	148,200	
	cr.	Long-term Note Receivable		148,200

To record receipt of face value of note at maturity date.

In reviewing these entries, note that the amount of annual interest income increases each year. This is because the present value of the note receivable also increases as time passes, and interest income is a constant percentage (14 percent) of this increasing value.

Case 2: *Long-term note receivable to be paid in installments.* In the previous example, we assumed that the principal and interest on a long-term note were to be received in a lump sum on its maturity date. It is common practice, however, for firms to sell products in exchange for **installment notes receivable,** which entail payments over several future periods. The amount of sales revenue to be recognized in such cases is determined by the present value of the note receivable at the date of sale. To illustrate, assume that on January 1, 1988, Lansing Distributors sells a machine costing $220,000 to a customer in return for a noninterest-bearing installment note receivable. The note receivable obligates the customer to pay $100,000 at the end of each year for three years (that is, on December 31 of 1988, 1989, and 1990) at an interest rate of 12 percent per year.

The amount of sales revenue to be recognized is determined by the present value of the installments as of January 1, 1988, and is calculated as follows:

Payment to be received at the end of each year	$100,000
Present value of a three-period annuity at 12% (Table C-2)	× 2.402
Present value of installment note receivable	$240,200

The note discount in this illustration is $59,800; this is the difference between the note's present value, $240,200, and its face value of $300,000 ($100,000 per year for three years). The note discount represents the total amount of interest on the note to be recognized over three years as shown in the journal entries below. The amount of profit recorded by Lansing Distributors on the sale of the machine is $20,200, which is the difference between the $240,200 present value of the installment note receivable, and the $220,000 cost of the machine.

Exhibit 5-6 shows how the carrying value of the note receivable changes each year due to interest income and installment payments. Journal entries to record the sale of the machine, the accrual of annual interest income, and the receipts of the installment payments are presented on the following page. These entries are based on the interest calculations made in Exhibit 5-6.

Exhibit 5-6

Long-term Note Receivable and Interest Income: Payments in Installments

Face value of note (three payments of $100,000 per year)		$300,000
Present value of note		240,200
Note discount, to be earned as interest income over three years		$ 59,800

Year	Present Value of Note, Start of Year	Add: Interest at 12% of Present Value	Subtract: Payment at End of Year	Present Value of Note, End of Year
1988	$240,200	$28,824	$100,000	$169,024
1989	169,024	20,283	100,000	89,307
1990	89,307	10,693*	100,000	0

*Rounding adjustment made in the last year of the note to reflect total interest expense for three years of $59,800.

Jan. 1, 1988	dr.	Installment Note Receivable	240,200	
	cr.	Sales		240,200
	dr.	Cost of Goods Sold	220,000	
	cr.	Inventory (Machines)		220,000
Dec. 31, 1988	dr.	Installment Note Receivable	28,824	
	cr.	Interest Income		28,824
	dr.	Cash	100,000	
	cr.	Installment Note Receivable		100,000
Dec. 31, 1989	dr.	Installment Note Receivable	20,283	
	cr.	Interest Income		20,283
	dr.	Cash	100,000	
	cr.	Installment Note Receivable		100,000
Dec. 31, 1990	dr.	Installment Note Receivable	10,693	
	cr.	Interest Income		10,693
	dr.	Cash	100,000	
	cr.	Installment Note Receivable		100,000

In reviewing these entries, note that the amount of annual interest income decreases each year. This occurs because the installment cash payments exceed the interest income each year, so that the carrying value of the receivable declines annually. Because interest income is based on a constant percentage of the carrying value of the receivable (12 percent in this example), interest income must decline also.

Finally, note that the amount of profit attributed to the sale of the machine, $20,200 ($240,200 sales, less $220,000 cost of goods sold) depends on the interest rate used to discount the installment payments. Obviously, if the interest rate was zero, the present value of the installment payments as of January 1, 1988, would be $300,000, and profit attributed to the sale of the machine would be $80,000 ($300,000 sales, less $220,000 cost of goods sold). The higher the interest rate assumed for a given series of installment payments to be received, the lower the amount recorded as sales revenue (equal to the present value of the payments), and the higher the amount recorded as interest income.

Both of the notes receivable just described are **monetary assets** (that is, assets that consist of claims to a fixed amount of dollars). Monetary assets are noncurrent when the claims represent dollars to be received in periods longer than a year or the operating cycle and noncurrent monetary assets are valued on the balance sheet at the present value of the future cash receipts. The carrying value (or book value) of monetary assets is adjusted over time so that successive balance sheets report the present value of the remaining cash flows, and income statements reflect the interest income associated with the increases in present value. The valuation of noncurrent monetary assets at present values differs from the valuation of nonmonetary assets (property, plant, and equipment, for example), which are generally valued at historical cost.

Accounting for sinking funds   Cash and other assets may be accumulated in special funds that are designated for specific purposes. Common objectives in establishing funds of this type are the payment of the face value of a bond at maturity, the retirement of preferred stock, or the replacement of a building or other fixed asset. When restrictive funds are established for these and similar noncurrent purposes, they are referred to as **sinking funds.** Sinking funds are noncurrent assets, and are usually classified in the long-term investments section of the balance sheet.

Many variations exist in administering a sinking fund and in accumulating fund assets. Two important variations are the following:

1. Depending on legal and other circumstances, the fund assets may be (a) managed *internally* by company employees or (b) transferred outside the company and administered *externally* by a trustee, such as a bank or an insurance company.
2. The company may agree to (a) make equal periodic payments to the fund at regular intervals or (b) make payments on a variable basis (for example, relating the amount and timing of each payment to the level of reported earnings for the period).

As an illustration, assume that the Salt Lake Company decides to establish a sinking fund on January 1, 1988, that it will manage internally. The purpose of the fund is to accumulate $50,000 to use in paying the face value of its outstanding bonds when they mature in two years (December 31, 1989). Salt Lake's management decides to accumulate this amount by making equal payments to the fund at the end of each year, beginning December 31, 1988. Assuming that the fund assets will be invested to earn interest at 8 percent, a payment of $24,038.46 at the end of each year is required.[8] A sinking fund accumulation schedule, which shows annual cash payments and interest earned on fund assets, is presented in Exhibit 5-7.

Notice in column (1) of Exhibit 5-7 that there are no earnings on fund assets for 1988. This is because the first cash contribution to the sinking fund does not take place until the last day of that year. Earnings on fund assets for 1989, however, are $1,923.08; this is calculated by multiplying the accumulated fund balance at the beginning of 1989 ($24,038.46) by the interest rate of 8 percent. Also, observe in Exhibit 5-7 that the total accumulated value of $50,000 is

---

[8]The required annual payment of $24,048.46 is determined from Table C-4 as follows:

$$\text{Annual Payment} = \frac{\text{Maturity Value}}{\text{Maturity Value Factor from Table C-4, 2 periods at 8\%}}$$

$$= \frac{\$50,000}{2.080}$$

$$= \underline{\$24,038.46}$$

Exhibit 5-7
Sinking Fund Accumulation Schedule

Salt Lake Company

Year	(1) 8% Earnings on Fund Assets	(2) Cash Payment to Fund, End of Year	(3) Total Increase in Fund for Year	(4) Accumulated Fund Balance, End of Year
1988	0	$24,038.46	$24,038.46	$24,038.46
1989	$1,923.08	24,038.46	25,961.54	50,000.00
Totals	$1,923.08	$48,076.92	$50,000.00	

a combination of $1,923.08 in earnings on fund assets [column (1)] plus $48,076.92 in cash contributions to the fund [column (2)].

Journal entries required to account for the sinking fund on the Salt Lake Company's books are presented below. All dollar amounts are taken from the sinking fund accumulation schedule in Exhibit 5-7, and it is assumed that the company closes its books annually on December 31.

Dec. 31, 1988	dr.	Sinking Fund	24,038.46	
	cr.	Cash		24,038.46

To record cash contribution to fund.

Dec. 31, 1989	dr.	Sinking Fund	1,923.08	
	cr.	Interest Income		1,923.08

To record 8% interest earned on fund assets.

Dec. 31, 1989	dr.	Sinking Fund	24,038.46	
	cr.	Cash		24,038.46

To record cash contribution to fund.

Dec. 31, 1989	dr.	Bonds Payable	50,000.00	
	cr.	Sinking Fund		50,000.00

To record repayment of face value of bond at maturity.

The last entry just presented is used to record payment of the face amount of the outstanding bonds on the day they mature. Notice that after this payment is recorded, the sinking fund has a zero balance.

Accounting for equity securities **Equity securities** are ownership interests in the form of preferred or common stock. The accounting methods to be used for equity securities depend on the percentage of stock owned as well as management's intended holding period for the investment. Special methods of accounting (for example, the equity method, consolidation, and so forth) are required when the ownership interests are significant, and these are discussed in Chapter 9, which deals with intercorporate investments. When ownership interests do not meet the criteria discussed in Chapter 9, the accounting for noncurrent investments in equity securities closely parallels that used for temporary investments; that is, the investments are valued at the lower of cost or market, except that any unrealized loss is not treated as a reduction in net income, but is reflected instead in the shareholders' equity section of the balance sheet.

To illustrate accounting for noncurrent investments in equity securities, consider the noncurrent portfolio shown in Exhibit 5-8. Since the portfolio's aggregate market value of $8,600 is below its aggregate cost of $9,000, a valuation allowance of $400 is needed. Assuming that the current balance of the Valuation Allowance account is zero, the following adjustment is made to increase the balance to $400:

dr.	Unrealized Loss, Noncurrent Portfolio	400
cr.	Valuation Allowance, Noncurrent Portfolio	400

To record decline in aggregate market value of the portfolio of noncurrent equity securities.

Whenever a valuation allowance is increased, an unrealized loss account is increased (debited). Unlike the case discussed previously for the current portfolio, however, the unrealized loss on noncurrent investments does *not* reduce net income for the period. Instead, the unrealized loss is reported as a contra account in the shareholders' equity section of the balance sheet on the presumption that unrealized losses on noncurrent investments are temporary and will be recovered in future periods. The unrealized losses will reduce income in cases where the presumption of future price recovery appears to be unjustified, or when the loss is realized through sale of the noncurrent investments.

Exhibit 5-8
Portfolio of Noncurrent Investments in Equity Securities

Costs and Market Values
December 31, 1987

Security	Cost	Market Value (December 31)
A	$5,000	$3,500
B	$3,000	$4,000
C	$1,000	$1,100
Totals	$9,000	$8,600

Consequently, the portfolio of noncurrent investments described in Exhibit 5-8 would be described as follows on the December 31, 1987, balance sheet:

Noncurrent Investments in Marketable Equity Securities
Less Valuation Allowance ($400 in 1987) $8,600

And the shareholders' equity section of the balance sheet would include the following contra account:

Unrealized Loss, Noncurrent Portfolio $400

At each subsequent financial reporting date, the aggregate cost and aggregate market value of the noncurrent portfolio are determined, and the valuation account is adjusted as necessary. Whenever the valuation account is increased or decreased, the unrealized loss account (contra equity) is also adjusted, leaving net income unaffected. As in the case for the current portfolio, the noncurrent portfolio is *never* increased above the historical cost of the investments, and when individual securities are sold, the income statement reports the amount of realized gain or loss.

Natural Resources

Natural resources include oil reserves and gas deposits, minerals, coal, iron ore deposits, and timber. Since they are depleted or consumed as used, they are often referred to as **wasting assets.** Although similar in many ways to inventories, natural resources are not classified as current assets. Their noncurrent classification reflects the fact that it usually takes many years for the firm to receive economic benefits from ownership.

The cost of a natural resource includes the cost of the land on which it is located, plus certain other costs of development (for example, the building of roads and costs associated with preparation for drilling, mining, or cutting). These costs are capitalized, or debited to an asset account. Then, in a manner similar to depreciation of fixed assets, the capitalized costs are allocated as expenses to the periods that benefit from their use. When dealing with natural resources, this allocation process is referred to as **depletion**. The units-of-production method of depletion is almost always used in these instances. (This method is identical to the units-of-production method described earlier on page 178 for the depreciation of fixed assets.)

Consider a brief illustration of accounting for the depletion of natural resources. Assume that the Cooper Company has acquired certain mineral rights for $800,000. This expenditure gives the Cooper Company the right to explore for and extract copper from a particular parcel of land that is owned by another company. Geologists estimate that the land contains 2,000 tons of copper.

The first step is to calculate the depletion expense rate per ton of copper extracted and sold.

$$\text{Depletion Expense Rate} = \frac{\text{Capitalized Cost of Natural Resource}}{\text{Estimated Number of Units Acquired}}$$

$$= \frac{\$800,000}{2,000 \text{ tons}}$$

$$= \$400 \text{ per ton}$$

At the end of every reporting period the amount of depletion expense would be determined by multiplying the number of tons extracted and sold during that period by the depletion expense rate. If at the end of the first year the Cooper Company had mined and sold 200 tons of copper, it would make the following journal entry:

dr.   Cost of Goods Sold (Depletion Expense—Mineral Rights)   80,000
   cr.   Accumulated Depletion—Mineral Rights   80,000

The $80,000 depletion expense is calculated by multiplying the 200 tons of copper sold by the $400 depletion expense rate. **Accumulated Depletion** is a contra-asset account and is presented on the balance sheet as a subtraction from the account showing the capitalized cost of the natural resource. For the Cooper Company, the mineral rights would be presented as follows at the end of the first year:

Mineral rights	$800,000
Less: Accumulated depletion—mineral rights	(80,000)
	$720,000

Intangible Assets

Intangible assets are noncurrent resources that lack physical substance and are used in the regular operations of a business. Examples of intangibles include patents, copyrights, trademarks, franchises, and goodwill. In accounting for any of these items, the following questions must be considered:

- Should expenditures incurred be capitalized (that is, recorded as assets) or should they be expensed immediately?
- If costs are capitalized, how should these costs be allocated to future periods?

In answering these questions, it is helpful to first classify intangibles on the basis of two dimensions: (1) identifiability and (2) manner of acquisition.

Identifiability   All of the assets listed as intangibles in the preceding paragraph, except goodwill, are said to be specifically identifiable; that is, they may be exchanged individually, apart from the business that owns them. Goodwill lacks specific identifiability because it is inseparable from the business as a whole, and thus it may be exchanged only in connection with the sale of the entire business or a substantial part thereof.

Manner of acquisition   Only two possibilities exist concerning the manner of acquisition of an intangible asset: either an intangible is acquired from an external source, or it is developed within the enterprise itself.

Exhibit 5-9 cross-classifies intangibles on these two dimensions. The resulting table, which is divided into four quadrants, provides a convenient way to summarize the general accounting rules for intangibles. The remainder of this section discusses the four quadrants of the table in greater detail.

Accounting for identifiable intangibles   With a few exceptions, accounting for identifiable intangible assets follows the same general principles as those used for long-lived, tangible assets. The two upper quadrants in Exhibit 5-9 show that identifiable intangibles—whether developed internally or acquired from outside sources—are ordinarily capitalized. They are recorded at historical cost, which includes all incidental expenditures necessary to make them

Exhibit 5-9

Classification of Intangibles with Required Accounting Treatment

		Manner of Acquisition	
		Internally Developed	**Externally Acquired**
Identifiability	**Specifically Identifiable**	*General Rule:* Capitalize and amortize over period estimated to be benefited. The period of amortization, however, may not exceed 40 years. *Example:* Costs incurred for development, protection, and registration of a trademark. *Exception:* All research and development costs should be expensed as incurred.	*General Rule:* Capitalize and amortize over period estimated to be benefited. The period of amortization, however, may not exceed 40 years. *Example:* Franchise purchased from another company.
	Lacking Specific Identifiability	*General Rule:* Expense as incurred. *Examples:* Costs incurred to develop good management through training programs or to develop customer relations through advertising. This is often referred to as "internally generated goodwill."	*General Rule:* Capitalize and amortize over period estimated to be benefited. The period of amortization, however, may not exceed 40 years. *Example:* Purchasing an entire business and paying more for that business than the fair market value of the identifiable net assets acquired.

ready for use (except for related research and development costs, to be discussed shortly).

After acquiring or developing an asset, a company must assign the cost of the asset to future periods that benefit from its use. When dealing with intangible assets, this cost allocation process is called **amortization**. Estimating the pattern and duration of expected benefits from intangibles is usually more difficult than estimating the benefits from tangible assets. The amortization rules are as follows:

1. The straight-line method should be applied unless a firm demonstrates that a different systematic method is more appropriate.
2. The capitalized value of each intangible asset should be amortized on the basis of the estimated life of that specific asset; however, the period of amortization may not exceed 40 years.

There is one major exception to these rules for amortizing intangibles. The rules do not apply to research and development (R&D) costs. **Research** is directed activity aimed at discovery of new knowledge, while **development** is the attempt to integrate research findings or other knowledge into new products or processes. Since 1974, GAAP have required the *immediate expensing of R&D costs,* regardless of the expected benefits from such efforts. The main argument supporting this position is that future benefits from most R&D efforts are uncertain and too difficult to assign to specific future periods. From a pragmatic standpoint, this requirement forces reporting uniformity and minimizes the possibility of income manipulation.

One example of the effects of this immediate expensing rule for R&D costs involves the proper method of accounting for patents. A **patent** is an exclusive right granted by the U.S. Patent Office that gives the owner control of the use or sale of an invention for 17 years. Patents may be purchased from an outside party or may result from activity within the firm. If patents are developed internally, all related R&D costs must be excluded from the capitalized value of the patent.

Accounting for intangibles lacking specific identifiability   Some intangibles that lack specific identifiability are developed internally (see lower left-hand quadrant of Exhibit 5-9). Examples are customer loyalty that has been cultivated by means of a long-term advertising campaign and good management developed through extensive training. Expenditures such as these result in what is referred to in financial accounting as **internally generated goodwill.** While such costs often result in benefits that accrue past the current accounting period, GAAP usually require that these costs be expensed immediately. The rationale used to support this immediate expensing requirement is the same as that used for R&D costs: future benefits in connection with internally generated goodwill are uncertain, and it is too difficult to assign the costs of such goodwill efforts to specific future periods.

Goodwill may be recorded as an asset, however, if it is acquired externally as the result of the purchase of one business by another (see lower right-hand quadrant of Exhibit 5-9). The dollar amount assigned by the purchaser to goodwill in this situation is the difference between the value of the consideration given for the business (its overall market value) and the fair market value of the identifiable assets acquired. If, for example, a business is purchased for $1 million and the fair market value of the identifiable net assets obtained in the exchange transaction is $800,000, then the remaining $200,000 is allocated to goodwill. This is diagrammed as follows:

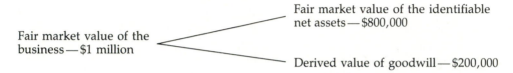

Fair market value of the business—$1 million

Fair market value of the identifiable net assets—$800,000

Derived value of goodwill—$200,000

Note from this example that the $200,000 is a residual amount representing the value of many intangibles lacking specific identifiability (for example, good location, customer loyalty, superior work force, excellent management, and so on) believed to exist when the buyer pays $1 million for an entity having identifiable net assets with a fair market value of $800,000. Measurement of goodwill is discussed more extensively in Chapter 9, which deals with intercorporate investments and business combinations.

The principles for amortizing goodwill that has been capitalized are the same as for amortizing identifiable intangibles. Thus, goodwill is written off over the period of its expected benefit, but this period may not exceed 40 years. Straight-line amortization is generally used.

Other Assets

In addition to the types of assets discussed earlier in previous sections of this chapter, Exhibit 5-1 shows that UAL, Inc., and Apple Computer, Inc., also have investments in "other assets." This catch-all category usually consists of **deferred charges,** which are long-term prepayments that do not fit into any of the other classifications. Examples include organization costs, long-term advances to company officers, and deposits made to secure future contracts.

MEASUREMENT BASES FOR ASSETS

The preceding parts of this chapter have discussed methods used in accounting for the assets of the firm. In the course of that discussion, various bases were used to value different assets. For example, the valuation of monetary assets, which are cash or claims to a fixed number of dollars, depends on whether the assets are current or noncurrent. Current monetary assets (cash and accounts receivable, for example) are valued at their expected cash proceeds. Noncurrent monetary assets (noncurrent notes receivable, for example) are valued at the discounted net present value of their expected cash proceeds. Moreover, measurement rules differ for monetary versus nonmonetary assets: nonmonetary assets, with some exceptions (such as marketable equity securities with cost in excess of market value), generally are valued at unexpired historical cost.

The purpose of the discussion that follows is to evaluate several alternative measurement bases for assets. Exhibit 5-10 provides a summary of these alternatives, including brief descriptions and examples. Each alternative will be discussed here in turn.

Historical Cost

This is perhaps the most familiar and easiest measurement base to understand. **Historical cost** represents the amount of consideration given (usually, cash paid) in an exchange transaction to acquire an asset. The primary justification for focusing on historical exchange prices is that they are objective and easily verifiable.

All nonmonetary assets are initially recorded at historical cost. Subsequent to acquisition, historical costs of nonmonetary assets are allocated to appropriate future periods as the service potential of the asset declines (an example of

Exhibit 5-10
Alternative Measurement Bases for Assets

Measurement Base	Description	Examples
1. Historical cost	Initially, the amount of cash paid to acquire an asset; subsequent to acquisition, the historical amount may be adjusted for depreciation, depletion, or amortization	Plant and equipment Land Patents Inventory, when historical cost is less than replacement cost
2. Current cost	Amount of cash that would have to be paid if the same asset were acquired currently.	Inventory, when replacement cost is less than historical cost
3. Current market value	Amount of cash that could be obtained currently by selling the asset	Marketable equity securities, when market value is less than cost
4. Expected market value in the normal course of business	Amount of cash into which the asset is expected to be converted in the normal course of business, less direct costs necessary to make that conversion	Accounts receivable Inventory, when deemed obsolete
5. Present value of expected cash flows	Present value of future cash inflows into which the asset is expected to be converted in the normal course of business	Long-term receivables

Source: Adapted from *Discussion Memo—Conceptual Framework Project* (FASB, 1976), p. 193.

this allocation procedure is the depreciation process for fixed assets). The reported balance subsequent to acquisition, then, represents that portion of the original historical cost that has not yet been matched against revenues and is to be carried forward to future periods. (Accounting for land is a notable exception to this pattern. Land usually retains its original historical cost valuation until sold.)

One problem with using historical cost is suggested by its name; historical cost deals with the past, while most decisions are future-oriented. When using historical cost, the recorded dollar value of an asset depends on its date of purchase. Of course, prices of goods and services can change rapidly and at times unexpectedly. Consequently, the historical cost of a particular asset may bear little relationship to its value today.

A related problem stems from the fact that a business firm typically holds a mixture of assets acquired at different dates. The recorded dollar amounts, while all in terms of U.S. currency, generally represent units of varied purchasing power. They are aggregated, nonetheless, in preparing a balance sheet. Aggregation of dollars of unlike purchasing power makes comparisons difficult, both among different firms and for the same firm over time.

Current Cost

Current cost is the amount of money (cash or its equivalent) that would have to be given up today to acquire an existing asset. If this measurement base is used, the dollar value of an asset is not anchored to one historical date, but is updated at each balance sheet date to reflect the current cost of replacing that asset. The relevant value is not the list price of a new asset, but the cost of replacing an existing one—one that in all probability has lost some of its service potential to the firm since it was originally acquired.

It may be very difficult to determine current replacement costs objectively. Ideally, there exists an active market with quoted prices for the assets being valued; this would constitute the same type of verifiable evidence that makes the use of historical cost so attractive. Alternatively, one may use specific price indices, which are sometimes available for particular industries or types of assets. If neither of these two approaches is possible, appraisals of individual assets must be employed; this method of determining current replacement cost information may at times be highly subjective.

Under present GAAP, an example of the use of current cost in the preparation of financial statements involves the valuation of inventory. Specifically, this occurs when replacement cost is less than historical cost and the lower of cost or market method is being employed.

Current Market Value

The **current market value** of an asset is the amount of cash or its equivalent that could be obtained by selling an asset in its present condition. This may be determined by direct appraisal or by making reference to quoted market prices for the sale of an asset of a similar type in equivalent condition. A basic assumption in financial accounting is that the reporting entity is a going concern and not in the process of selling its operating assets; accordingly, current market values are not often reported. However, an exception occurs with reporting of marketable equity securities. These are sometimes reported at present market prices when the market value is less than historical cost.

Expected Market Value

The **expected market value** of an asset is often referred to as **net realizable value**—the net cash amount (selling price less direct costs of disposal and collection) into which an asset is expected to be converted in the normal course of business. Under GAAP, most current monetary assets are valued at net realizable value. Current accounts receivable, for example, are reported at the amount of cash expected to be collected from credit sales outstanding. Since some credit sales inevitably turn out to be uncollectible, the net realizable value is rarely the face amount of these credit sales.

Present Value of Expected Cash Flows

The **present value** of an asset is the net amount of discounted cash inflows and outflows pertaining to that asset. The cash flows used to measure an asset's present value are the same as those used to measure its expected market value. However, the time value of money is explicitly considered in measuring the present value of an asset, and for that reason the expected cash flows are multiplied by an appropriate rate of discount. Present value analysis is discussed in the appendix to this chapter. Under GAAP, noncurrent receivables are recorded at their present values.

SUMMARY

Chapter 5 describes and illustrates accounting methods for the types of assets that are commonly reported by U.S. companies. The appendix focuses on compound interest, including the calculation of present and future values.

Assets are defined by the FASB as "... probable future economic benefits obtained or controlled by a particular entity as a result of past transactions or events." In financial accounting assets are classified as being either current or noncurrent. Current assets are cash and other economic resources that are reasonably expected to be realized in cash or sold or consumed within one year or within the firm's normal operating cycle, whichever is longer. In addition to cash, current assets include temporary investments, receivables, inventory, and short-term prepayments.

Cash includes currency, funds deposited in a bank, checks, money orders, and the like. An investment is classified as being temporary if it is readily marketable and if it is management's intention to convert the investment into cash in the short run. Temporary investments in marketable equity securities are reported on the balance sheet at the lower of cost or market value. This allows for the reporting of unrealized losses when the market price of the aggregate portfolio of these investments declines below its cost.

Receivables are claims on assets or services to be provided by others in the future. Most receivables are due within one year or within the firm's normal operating cycle. They are presented on the balance sheet at net realizable value. Since it is inevitable that not all receivables will be collected, accounting procedures exist to account for bad debts. The amount of bad debts for a period is estimated by considering either the dollar amount of credit sales for the period or the composition (age) of the receivables.

Inventory includes those tangible goods held for sale to customers in the ordinary course of business. Inventories are generally presented on the balance sheet on a lower of cost or market basis. In this context, "cost" means historical cost determined by applying the appropriate inventory cost flow assumption, and "market" means replacement cost by purchase or manufacture.

Prepaid expenses are payments made for goods and services in advance of their use or consumption. Prepayments may be made for items such as insurance premiums, rent, taxes, and office supplies.

Noncurrent assets include property, plant, and equipment; long-term investments; natural resources; and intangible assets. Noncurrent assets and current assets are usually reported separately on the balance sheet.

Property, plant, and equipment (or fixed assets) are long-lived, tangible assets that are employed by the firm in the production or sale of inventory, or in the provision of services. Examples include automobiles, buildings, computer hardware, machinery, and office equipment. Fixed assets are presented on the balance sheet at book value, which is an asset's acquisition cost less accumulated depreciation. Acquisition costs consist of all necessary expenditures made to prepare the asset for its intended use. Under certain conditions, interest incurred during construction of a fixed asset may be added to its capitalized acquisition cost.

A firm's long-term investments may include debt securities, sinking funds, and equity securities. In general, investments in noncurrent debt securities are valued on the balance sheet at the present value of future cash receipts. A detailed discussion of reporting standards for equity securities is deferred until Chapter 9.

Natural resources include oil and gas reserves, minerals, coal, and timber. The costs of acquiring and developing natural resources are initially capitalized. Then, in a manner very similar to depreciation of fixed assets, the capitalized costs are allocated as expenses to the periods that benefit from their use. When dealing with natural resources, this allocation process is referred to as depletion.

Intangible assets are noncurrent resources that lack physical substance and are used in the regular operations of the business. Examples include patents, copyrights, trademarks, franchises, and goodwill. With few exceptions, accounting for assets in this category follows the same general principles as those used for long-lived, tangible assets.

Different measurement bases are required by GAAP for different assets. The five measurement bases used in financial accounting are historical cost, current cost, current market value, expected market value, and present value of expected cash flows.

APPENDIX C
COMPOUND INTEREST: MATURITY VALUES AND PRESENT VALUES

The reader is likely to be familiar with many instances of the discounting or compounding of funds. The **present value,** or discounted value, is the value today of a sum of money to be received in the future. Conversely, the **maturity value,** or compounded value, is the future worth of funds available today, assuming that the funds are invested at the prevailing interest rate. The techniques of computing present values and maturity values are essential to the solution of diverse problems in financial accounting, such as those encountered in accounting for noncurrent receivables and payables, pensions, leases, and so forth.

The mechanics of these calculations are straightforward, and it is worth the effort to understand the basic, widely used formulas. The following notation will be employed in the discussion:

PV = present value, or value today, of funds to be received at a future date

MV = maturity value, or future worth, of funds invested at a specified interest rate

R = interest rate

A_t = the amount received or paid at the end of a specific time period (for example, A_2 represents the amount received or paid at the end of period 2)

N = the total number of cash flows to be received or paid in cases involving multiple cash flows (annuities, for example)

Calculating Maturity Value

To illustrate the calculation of maturity value using a savings account as our example, assume an investment of $100 ($A_t$) at an interest rate of 10% (R) for a period of one year compounded annually. The cash flow occurs at the beginning of period 1, and is written as A_0. The maturity value (MV) of the deposit is computed as

$$MV = A_0(1 + R)^t$$
$$= \$100(1 + .10)^1$$
$$= \$110$$

Assume now that the entire $110 remains on deposit a second year. The interest for the second year will exceed $10, since the 10% factor is applied to a greater initial deposit.

$$MV = A_0(1 + R)^t$$
$$= \$110(1 + .10)^1$$
$$= \$121$$

Note that we could have calculated the maturity value of the deposit at the end of the two years directly as

$$MV = A_0(1 + R)^t$$
$$= \$100(1 + .10)^2$$
$$= \$100(1.210)$$
$$= \$121$$

In general, given the expression $MV = A_0(1 + R)^t$, the compound value factor is $(1 + R)^t$ and it can be used to solve for the maturity of any initial deposit by substituting appropriate values for R and t. If we assume our $100 initial deposit is invested at 10 percent for a five-year period, the maturity value is calculated as

$$MV = \$100(1 + .10)^5$$

The calculations for longer time periods can become quite tedious. Fortunately, the widespread use of present value techniques has led to the construction of standard tables for maturity value factors and for present value factors. Portions of such tables are included at the end of this appendix (Tables C-1 to C-4, beginning on page 258). To solve the example above [$MV = \$100(1 + .10)^5$], refer to Table C-3 and read across the fifth row (since $t = 5$) to the 10% (R) column. Note that the maturity value factor is 1.611, which equals $(1 + .10)^5$.

$$MV = \$100(1 + .10)^5$$
$$= \$100(1.611)$$
$$= \$161.10$$

In the preceding examples we have assumed interest is compounded annually. You may be familiar, however, with advertising by banks and other savings institutions that offer "interest at 5% compounded semiannually," or "interest at 4% compounded monthly," or more recently, "interest compounded from day of deposit to day of withdrawal." What effect does the frequency of compounding have on the maturity value of an interest-earning deposit? The answer is clear once we realize that the selection of a full year as the compounding period in our initial example was entirely arbitrary. The convention is to think of interest in terms of annual returns for reasons grounded more in history than in necessity. Essentially, if interest is compounded more than once annually, the amount of annual interest earned rises. A review of the calculations for compounding periods of varying duration will emphasize this point.

Assume that the following three investment opportunities are available:

1. Deposit at Bank A, which earns 8% compounded annually.
2. Deposit at Bank B, which earns 8% compounded semiannually.
3. Deposit at Bank C, which earns 8% compounded quarterly.

Intuition may suggest that the more frequent compounding provides the higher interest rate, and in this case intuition proves reliable — but *how much better* is Bank C than Bank A? Also, can the banks be compared if the quoted annual interest rates are different? To answer these questions, simplify the computations by noting that semiannual compounding breaks the year into two periods (each six months long), and assumes that each period earns interest at one-half the annual rate (one-half of 8% in this example, or 4%). Quarterly compounding breaks the year into four periods and compounds interest each period at one-fourth the annual rate (or 2%, in the present example).

In general, if interest is compounded z times per year, the maturity value is computed as $MV = A(1 + \frac{R}{z})^{zt}$ where z equals the number of compounding periods per year. This does not contradict our earlier expression; in the previous examples we assumed that z equals one. Applying this formula to the interest rates quoted by Bank A, Bank B, and Bank C yields the following comparison:

Bank A: Annual Compounding

$$MV = A_0\left(1 + \frac{R}{z}\right)^{zt}$$

$$= \$100.00\left(1 + \frac{.08}{1}\right)^{1 \times 1}$$

$$= \$108.00$$

Bank B: Semiannual Compounding

$$MV = A_0\left(1 + \frac{R}{z}\right)^{zt}$$

$$= \$100.00\left(1 + \frac{.08}{2}\right)^{2 \times 1}$$

$$= \$100.00(1 + .04)^2$$

$$= \$108.16^*$$

---

*Use of tables at three decimals has caused a slight rounding error.

Bank C: Quarterly Compounding

$$MV = A_0\left(1 + \frac{R}{z}\right)^{zt}$$

$$= \$100.00\left(1 + \frac{.08}{4}\right)^{4\times1}$$

$$= \$100.00(1 + .02)^4$$

$$= \$108.24^*$$

We have used Table C-3 for Banks B and C. Bank B requires the use of the second row (2 periods) and the 4% column. Bank C requires the use of the fourth row and the 2% column. The interest earned in Bank A is 8% of the initial deposit. Bank B provides a return of 8.16% on the initial deposit, and Bank C pays interest of 8.24% on the initial deposit. Clearly, the frequency of compounding increases the true (or effective) interest rate, but note that the benefits of more frequent compounding do not increase in proportion to the number of compounding periods. In fact, if interest were compounded each second, the effective annual rate would increase only to 8.82%.

Calculating Present Value

Present value is the opposite of maturity value; accordingly, the present value factors are the reciprocals of the compound value factors. The present value of a future receipt is computed as follows:

$$PV = A_t \times \frac{1}{(1 + R)^t}$$

Note that $(1 + R)^t$ was termed the maturity value factor, and $1/(1 + R)^t$ will be termed the present value factor. The compounding process reflects the growth of an initial deposit over time, and at any positive interest rate the compounding factor is greater than one. Consequently, as the number of time periods increases, the compounding factor grows larger. The converse is true for the present value factor: if $(1 + R)^t$ exceeds one, then $1/(1 + R)^t$ must be less than one. As the number of periods (t) increases, the present value factor becomes smaller. This is quite sensible, since the present value factor is a discount for futurity. The more distant in time the future receipt is, the less it is worth today. As either the required interest (R) or the number of periods (t) increases, the future receipt is worth less today.

Table C-1 shows present value factors that correspond to the maturity value factors of Table C-3. Each of the elements in Table C-1 is the reciprocal of

*Use of tables at three decimals has caused a slight rounding error.

the corresponding element in Table C-3. As an example, we noted earlier that the maturity value factor for five periods at 10% equals 1.611 (or one dollar invested at 10% will amount to $1.611 at the end of five periods). Conversely, the right to receive $1.611 at the end of five years is worth $1.00 today. The present value of $1.611 over five periods at 10% is $1.00. Applying the formula,

$$PV = A_t \times \frac{1}{(1 + R)^t}$$

$$= \$1.611 \times \frac{1}{(1 + 10)^t}$$

$$= \$1.611 \times \frac{1}{1.611}$$

$$= \$1.00$$

Alternatively, the present value factor from Table C-1 for five periods at 10% is .621.

$$PV = A_t \times \frac{1}{(1 + R)^t}$$

$$= (\$1.611) \times (.621)$$

$$= \$1.00$$

Calculating the Present Value of a Series of Cash Flows

Each of the previous examples treated a single cash inflow in computing present value. Present value calculations are widely employed in cases that involve a series of cash inflows and outflows over a number of periods. However, the techniques developed in the preceding paragraphs are readily applied where a sequence of cash flows is to be evaluated. It is only necessary to compute the present value of each individual cash inflow or outflow, and add the present values to obtain the present value of the entire series of flows (the proposed investment, bond issue, or other "package" of cash flows). If we employ the usual notation for summation, the formula can be expressed as

$$PV = \sum_{t=0}^{N} A_t \times \frac{1}{(1 + R)^t} \quad \text{or} \quad PV = \sum_{t=0}^{N} \frac{A_t}{(1 + R)^t}$$

Note that future cash flows are time dated, and A_t is interpreted as the cash flow occurring at time t. To demonstrate the use of the expression, consider a cash flow of $25,000 per year to be received at the end of each of five years. Because the cash flow occurs at the end of each year, there is no cash flow when $t = 0$ (that is, $A_0 = 0$). The first cash flow will be received after one year, when $t = 1$. The present value of total cash flows of $125,000 computed at 10% is as follows:

End of Year (t)	Cash Inflow (A)		Present Value Factor $\dfrac{1}{(1 + R)^t}$		Present Value
1	$25,000	×	.909	=	$22,725
2	25,000	×	.826	=	20,650
3	25,000	×	.751	=	18,775
4	25,000	×	.683	=	17,075
5	25,000	×	.621	=	15,525
					$94,750

Calculating the Present Value of an Annuity

An annuity is simply a stream of equal amounts paid (or received) at equal intervals. Common examples in business include the interest coupons paid on bonds, pension payments to retired employees, installment accounts receivable from customers, amounts paid on long-term leases, and so on. The previous example evaluated a $25,000 five-year annuity, using simple techniques of present value analysis. Annuities are discussed here as a separate topic merely to introduce a useful economy in calculation. Tables are widely available for computing the present value (and also the maturity value) of an annuity without requiring that each cash flow be evaluated separately, as was the procedure in the previous annuity problem. Recall that for any series of cash flows

$$PV = \sum_{t=0}^{N} A_t \times \frac{1}{(1 + R)^t} \quad \text{or} \quad PV = \sum_{t=0}^{N} \frac{A_t}{(1 + R)^t}$$

By definition, all the A's of an annuity are equal. Also, constants can be moved outside the summation sign. As a result, for annuities

$$PV = A_t \times \sum_{t=0}^{N} \frac{1}{(1 + R)^t}$$

Stated differently, to evaluate an annuity it is necessary to add the appropriate present value factors (or compounding value factors), and multiply the result by the annuity payment. Applying this approach to our previous example,

End of Year (t)	Present Value Factor $\dfrac{1}{(1 + R)^t}$
1	.909
2	.826
3	.751
4	.683
5	.621
Total	3.790

$$\text{Present Value of Annuity} = \text{Cash Inflow} \times \text{Present Value Factor}$$
$$\$94{,}750 = \$25{,}000 \times 3.790$$

Because annuity calculations are required frequently in business, special tables have been constructed that contain the sums of the appropriate present value factors. These tables allow one to directly calculate the present and future values of annuities. Tables C-2 and C-4, which appear at the end of this appendix, are used for the direct calculations of the present values and future values of annuities, respectively. To illustrate the use of Table C-2, the present value of a five-year annuity of $25,000 is computed as follows:

Step 1 Find the present value factor for five periods at 10%, which is 3.790. Notice that Table C-2 is based upon the assumption that all annuity cash flows occur at the end of the period (that is, there is no cash flow at $t = 0$; in our example, the five cash flows occur in periods $t = 1$ through $t = 5$).

Step 2 Multiply the periodic payment of $25,000 by the present value factor ($25,000 × 3.790). The product, $94,750, is the present value of the annuity.

If the annuity cash flows were to occur at the beginning rather than the end of each period, Table C-2 could still be used, with a minor adjustment. If the cash flow will be received for t periods, simply use the cash flow for a $(t - 1)$ period annuity, and add 1.0 to allow for the cash flow at $t = 0$. In our example, if the flows were to occur at the beginning of each period:

Present value factor for four periods at 10% (Table C-2)	3.170
Add 1.0 for the cash flow at $t = 0$	1.000
Present value factor, adjusted	4.170
Multiply periodic payment	× $25,000
Present value of annuity	$104,250

As expected, the present value of the five-period annuity beginning at $t = 0$ ($104,250) is greater than the present value of the five-period annuity beginning at $t = 1$ ($94,750, as shown earlier), because the cash flows occur earlier.

Calculating the Maturity Value of an Annuity

A number of financial problems require the calculation of the compound sum of an annuity. Other problems entail the computation of annuity payments that will equal a specified amount at the end of a given number of periods. For example, companies sometimes make annuity payments to a sinking fund to provide for expenditures at a future date for a new plant and equipment. The annuity must have a maturity value equal to the amount required to purchase the plant and equipment. Sinking funds are usually invested in interest-earning assets, so that the payments to the fund are not idle; as a result, total payments to the fund will be less than the maturity value of the fund.

As noted earlier, the maturity value of a single cash flow after t periods is $MV = A_0(1 + R)^t$. For a series of N periodic cash flows, each occurring at the end of the period, the maturity value is computed as

$$MV = A_1(1 + R)^{N-1} + A_2(1 + R)^{N-2} + \ldots + A_N(1 + R)^{N-N}$$

Note that because the cash flows occur at the end of each period, the first cash flow occurs at the end of period 1, and earns interest for the remaining $N - 1$ periods, and so on. The last cash flow occurs at the end of period N, and so earns no interest (the exponent $N - N$ equals zero). The computation may be written as

$$MV = \sum_{t=1}^{N} A_t(1 + R)^{N-t}$$

If the cash flows are equal in dollar amount, the series is an annuity and the expression is then

$$MV = A \sum_{t=1}^{N} (1 + R)^{N-t}$$

In some cases the cash flows occur at the beginning, rather than at the end, of each period. In these cases the appropriate calculation is

$$MV = A \sum_{t=0}^{N-1} (1 + R)^{N-t}$$

This expression shows that the first cash flow is received at the beginning of the initial period ($t = 0$) and earns interest for the full N periods, and so on; the last cash flow earns interest for just one period (the exponent $N - t$ equals one). Notice that the factors in Table C-4 for the maturity value of an annuity are based on the assumption that the annuity cash flows occur at the end of each period. If the cash flows were to occur at the beginning rather than the end of each period, the factors in Table C-4 would require the following adjustment:

Maturity value factor for $N + 1$ periods, Table C-4	X.XXX
Less 1.0 for the fact that no cash flow is received when $t = N + 1$	−1.000
Maturity value factor, adjusted	X.XXX

In order to illustrate the calculations, assume that a firm will make a series of five annual payments of $1 million to a sinking fund for plant expansion, and that the sinking fund assets are expected to earn interest at 12% per year. If

Table C-2 Present Value of an Annuity of $1 Received or Paid at the End of Each Period

Periods (N)	1%	2%	4%	6%	8%	10%	12%	14%	15%	16%	18%	20%	22%	24%	25%	26%	28%	30%	35%	40%	45%	50%
1	0.990	0.980	0.962	0.943	0.926	0.909	0.893	0.877	0.870	0.862	0.847	0.833	0.820	0.806	0.800	0.794	0.781	0.769	0.741	0.714	0.690	0.667
2	1.970	1.942	1.886	1.833	1.783	1.736	1.690	1.647	1.626	1.605	1.566	1.528	1.492	1.457	1.440	1.424	1.392	1.361	1.289	1.224	1.165	1.111
3	2.941	2.884	2.775	2.673	2.577	2.487	2.402	2.322	2.283	2.246	2.174	2.106	2.042	1.981	1.952	1.923	1.868	1.816	1.696	1.589	1.493	1.407
4	3.902	3.808	3.630	3.465	3.312	3.170	3.037	2.914	2.855	2.798	2.690	2.589	2.494	2.404	2.362	2.320	2.241	2.166	1.997	1.849	1.720	1.605
5	4.853	4.713	4.452	4.212	3.993	3.791	3.605	3.433	3.352	3.274	3.127	2.991	2.864	2.745	2.689	2.635	2.532	2.436	2.220	2.035	1.876	1.737
6	5.795	5.601	5.242	4.917	4.623	4.355	4.111	3.889	3.784	3.685	3.498	3.326	3.167	3.020	2.951	2.885	2.759	2.643	2.385	2.168	1.983	1.824
7	6.728	6.472	6.002	5.582	5.206	4.868	4.564	4.288	4.160	4.039	3.812	3.605	3.416	3.242	3.161	3.083	2.937	2.802	2.508	2.263	2.057	1.883
8	7.652	7.325	6.733	6.210	5.747	5.335	4.968	4.639	4.487	4.344	4.078	3.837	3.619	3.421	3.329	3.241	3.076	2.925	2.598	2.331	2.108	1.922
9	8.566	8.162	7.435	6.802	6.247	5.759	5.328	4.946	4.772	4.607	4.303	4.031	3.786	3.566	3.463	3.366	3.184	3.019	2.665	2.379	2.144	1.948
10	9.471	8.983	8.111	7.360	6.710	6.145	5.650	5.216	5.019	4.833	4.494	4.192	3.923	3.682	3.571	3.465	3.269	3.092	2.715	2.414	2.168	1.965
11	10.368	9.787	8.760	7.887	7.139	6.495	5.988	5.453	5.234	5.029	4.656	4.327	4.035	3.776	3.656	3.544	3.335	3.147	2.752	2.438	2.185	1.977
12	11.255	10.575	9.385	8.384	7.536	6.814	6.194	5.660	5.421	5.197	4.793	4.439	4.127	3.851	3.725	3.606	3.387	3.190	2.779	2.456	2.196	1.985
13	12.134	11.343	9.986	8.853	7.904	7.103	6.424	5.842	5.583	5.342	4.910	4.533	4.203	3.912	3.780	3.656	3.427	3.223	2.799	2.468	2.204	1.990
14	13.004	12.106	10.563	9.295	8.244	7.367	6.628	6.002	5.724	5.468	5.008	4.611	4.265	3.962	3.824	3.695	3.459	3.249	2.814	2.477	2.210	1.993
15	13.865	12.849	11.118	9.712	8.559	7.606	6.811	6.142	5.847	5.575	5.092	4.675	4.315	4.001	3.859	3.726	3.483	3.268	2.825	2.484	2.214	1.995
16	14.718	13.578	11.652	10.106	8.851	7.824	6.974	6.265	5.954	5.669	5.162	4.730	4.357	4.033	3.887	3.751	3.503	3.283	2.834	2.489	2.216	1.997
17	15.562	14.292	12.166	10.477	9.122	8.022	7.120	6.373	6.047	5.749	5.222	4.775	4.391	4.059	3.910	3.771	3.518	3.295	2.840	2.492	2.218	1.998
18	16.398	14.992	12.659	10.828	9.372	8.201	7.250	6.467	6.128	5.818	5.273	4.812	4.419	4.080	3.928	3.786	3.529	3.304	2.844	2.494	2.219	1.999
19	17.226	15.678	13.134	11.158	9.604	8.365	7.366	6.550	6.198	5.877	5.316	4.844	4.442	4.097	3.942	3.799	3.539	3.311	2.848	2.496	2.220	1.999
20	18.046	16.351	13.590	11.470	9.818	8.514	7.469	6.623	6.259	5.929	5.353	4.870	4.460	4.110	3.954	3.808	3.546	3.316	2.850	2.497	2.221	1.999
21	18.857	17.011	14.029	11.764	10.017	8.649	7.562	6.687	6.312	5.973	5.384	4.891	4.476	4.121	3.963	3.816	3.551	3.320	2.852	2.498	2.221	2.000
22	19.660	17.658	14.451	12.042	10.201	8.772	7.645	6.743	6.359	6.011	5.410	4.909	4.488	4.130	3.970	3.822	3.556	3.323	2.853	2.498	2.222	2.000
23	20.456	18.292	14.857	12.303	10.371	8.883	7.718	6.792	6.399	6.044	5.432	4.925	4.499	4.137	3.976	3.827	3.559	3.325	2.854	2.499	2.222	2.000
24	21.243	18.914	15.247	12.550	10.529	8.985	7.784	6.835	6.434	6.073	5.451	4.937	4.507	4.143	3.981	3.831	3.562	3.327	2.855	2.499	2.222	2.000
25	22.023	19.523	15.622	12.783	10.675	9.077	7.843	6.873	6.464	6.097	5.467	4.948	4.514	4.147	3.985	3.834	3.564	3.329	2.856	2.499	2.222	2.000
26	22.795	20.121	15.983	13.003	10.810	9.161	7.896	6.906	6.491	6.118	5.480	4.956	4.520	4.151	3.988	3.837	3.566	3.330	2.856	2.500	2.222	2.000
27	23.560	20.707	16.330	13.211	10.935	9.237	7.943	6.935	6.514	6.136	5.492	4.964	4.524	4.154	3.990	3.839	3.567	3.331	2.856	2.500	2.222	2.000
28	24.316	21.281	16.663	13.406	11.051	9.307	7.984	6.961	6.534	6.152	5.502	4.970	4.528	4.157	3.992	3.840	3.568	3.331	2.857	2.500	2.222	2.000
29	25.066	21.844	16.984	13.591	11.158	9.370	8.022	6.983	6.551	6.166	5.510	4.975	4.531	4.159	3.994	3.841	3.569	3.332	2.857	2.500	2.222	2.000
30	25.808	22.396	17.292	13.765	11.258	9.427	8.055	7.003	6.566	6.177	5.517	4.979	4.534	4.160	3.995	3.842	3.569	3.332	2.857	2.500	2.222	2.000
40	32.835	27.355	19.793	15.046	11.925	9.779	8.244	7.105	6.642	6.234	5.548	4.997	4.544	4.166	3.999	3.846	3.571	3.333	2.857	2.500	2.222	2.000
50	39.196	31.424	21.482	15.762	12.234	9.915	8.304	7.133	6.661	6.246	5.554	4.999	4.545	4.167	4.000	3.846	3.571	3.333	2.857	2.500	2.222	2.000

Table C-3 Maturity Value of $1 Received or Paid at the End of Period

Periods	1%	2%	3%	4%	5%	6%	7%	8%	9%	10%	12%	14%	15%	16%
1	1.010	1.020	1.030	1.040	1.050	1.060	1.070	1.080	1.090	1.100	1.120	1.140	1.150	1.160
2	1.020	1.040	1.061	1.082	1.102	1.124	1.145	1.166	1.188	1.210	1.254	1.300	1.322	1.346
3	1.030	1.061	1.093	1.125	1.158	1.191	1.225	1.260	1.295	1.331	1.405	1.482	1.521	1.561
4	1.041	1.082	1.126	1.170	1.216	1.262	1.311	1.360	1.412	1.464	1.574	1.689	1.749	1.811
5	1.051	1.104	1.159	1.217	1.276	1.338	1.403	1.469	1.539	1.611	1.762	1.925	2.011	2.100
6	1.062	1.126	1.194	1.265	1.340	1.419	1.501	1.587	1.677	1.772	1.974	2.195	2.313	2.436
7	1.072	1.149	1.230	1.316	1.407	1.504	1.606	1.714	1.828	1.949	2.211	2.502	2.660	2.826
8	1.083	1.172	1.267	1.369	1.477	1.594	1.718	1.851	1.993	2.144	2.476	2.853	3.059	3.278
9	1.094	1.195	1.305	1.423	1.551	1.689	1.838	1.999	2.172	2.358	2.773	3.252	3.518	3.803
10	1.105	1.219	1.344	1.480	1.629	1.791	1.967	2.159	2.367	2.594	3.106	3.707	4.046	4.411
11	1.116	1.243	1.384	1.539	1.710	1.898	2.105	2.332	2.580	2.853	3.479	4.226	4.652	5.117
12	1.127	1.268	1.426	1.601	1.796	2.012	2.252	2.518	2.813	3.138	3.896	4.818	5.350	5.936
13	1.138	1.294	1.469	1.665	1.886	2.133	2.410	2.720	3.066	3.452	4.363	5.492	6.153	6.886
14	1.149	1.319	1.513	1.732	1.980	2.261	2.579	2.937	3.342	3.797	4.887	6.261	7.076	7.988
15	1.161	1.346	1.558	1.801	2.079	2.397	2.759	3.172	3.642	4.177	5.474	7.138	8.137	9.266
16	1.173	1.373	1.605	1.873	2.183	2.540	2.952	3.426	3.970	4.595	6.130	8.137	9.358	10.748
17	1.184	1.400	1.653	1.948	2.292	2.693	3.159	3.700	4.328	5.054	6.866	9.276	10.761	12.468
18	1.196	1.428	1.702	2.026	2.407	2.854	3.380	3.996	4.717	5.560	7.690	10.575	12.375	14.463
19	1.208	1.457	1.754	2.107	2.527	3.026	3.617	4.316	5.142	6.116	8.613	12.056	14.232	16.777
20	1.220	1.486	1.806	2.191	2.653	3.207	3.870	4.661	5.604	6.728	9.646	13.743	16.367	19.461
25	1.282	1.641	2.094	2.666	3.386	4.292	5.427	6.848	8.623	10.835	17.000	26.462	32.919	40.874
30	1.348	1.811	2.427	3.243	4.322	5.743	7.612	10.063	13.268	17.449	29.960	50.950	66.212	85.850

Table C-4 Maturity Value of an Annuity of $1 Received or Paid at the End of Each Period

Period	1%	2%	3%	4%	5%	6%	7%	8%	9%	10%	12%	14%
1	1.000	1.000	1.000	1.000	1.000	1.000	1.000	1.000	1.000	1.000	1.000	1.000
2	2.010	2.020	2.030	2.040	2.050	2.060	2.070	2.080	2.090	2.100	2.120	2.140
3	3.030	3.060	3.091	3.122	3.152	3.184	3.215	3.246	3.278	3.310	3.374	3.440
4	4.060	4.122	4.184	4.246	4.310	4.375	4.440	4.506	4.573	4.641	4.770	4.921
5	5.101	5.204	5.309	5.416	5.526	5.637	5.751	5.867	5.985	6.105	6.353	6.610
6	6.152	6.308	6.468	6.633	6.802	6.975	7.153	7.336	7.523	7.716	8.115	8.536
7	7.214	7.434	7.662	7.898	8.142	8.394	8.654	8.923	9.200	9.487	10.089	10.730
8	8.286	8.583	8.892	9.214	9.549	9.897	10.260	10.637	11.028	11.436	12.300	13.233
9	9.369	9.755	10.159	10.583	11.027	11.491	11.978	12.488	13.021	13.579	14.776	16.085
10	10.462	10.950	11.464	12.006	12.578	13.181	13.816	14.487	15.193	15.937	17.549	19.337
11	11.567	12.169	12.808	13.486	14.207	14.972	15.784	16.645	17.560	18.531	20.655	23.044
12	12.683	13.412	14.192	15.026	15.917	16.870	17.888	18.977	20.141	21.384	24.133	27.271
13	13.809	14.680	15.618	16.627	17.713	18.882	20.141	21.495	22.953	24.523	28.029	32.089
14	14.947	15.974	17.086	18.292	19.599	21.051	22.550	24.215	26.019	27.975	32.393	37.581
15	16.097	17.293	18.599	20.024	21.579	23.276	25.129	27.152	29.361	31.772	37.280	43.842
16	17.258	18.639	20.157	21.825	23.657	25.673	27.888	30.324	33.003	35.950	42.753	50.980
17	18.430	20.012	21.762	23.698	25.840	28.213	30.840	33.750	36.974	40.545	48.884	59.118
18	19.615	21.412	23.414	25.645	28.132	30.906	33.999	37.450	41.301	45.599	55.750	68.394
19	20.811	22.841	25.117	27.671	30.539	33.760	37.379	41.446	46.018	51.159	63.440	78.969
20	22.019	24.297	26.870	29.778	33.066	36.786	40.995	45.762	51.160	57.275	72.052	91.025
25	28.243	32.030	36.459	41.646	47.727	54.865	63.249	73.106	84.701	98.347	133.334	181.871
30	34.785	40.568	47.575	56.085	66.439	79.058	94.461	113.283	136.308	164.494	241.333	356.787

QUESTIONS

1. The terms listed below were introduced in this chapter. Define or explain each of them.

   accounts receivable
   accounts receivable turnover rate
   accumulated depreciation
   amortization
   book value
   capital-intensive firm
   current asset
   current cost
   current market value
   debt securities
   deferred charges
   expected market value
   fixed assets
   goodwill
   historical cost

   intangible assets
   inventory turnover rate
   marketable equity securities
   measurement bases
   monetary assets
   net realizable value
   noninterest-bearing note
   operating cycle
   patents
   prepaid expenses
   present value
   replacement cost
   sinking fund
   temporary investment
   trade receivable

2. The FASB's definition of the term "asset" differs from the definition espoused by the Accounting Principles Board. What is the most important difference between these two definitions?

3. Would you expect a major airline company to be more or less capital intensive than a computer manufacturing firm? Explain.

4. List four items that are typically included in the current assets section of the balance sheet. Comment on the order of presentation normally used for listing these items.

5. What criteria must be met before an item may be classified as a temporary investment? If these criteria are not met, how would the investment be classified?

6. Per the cost principle, temporary investments are recorded initially at acquisition price plus incidental costs. List several of these incidental costs.

7. Distinguish between a realized loss and an unrealized loss on marketable equity securities. Is it permissible for a firm to show an unrealized loss on marketable equity securities on its income statement? Explain.

8. Distinguish between marketable debt securities and marketable equity securities.

9. Is the carrying value of the portfolio of marketable equity securities ever increased above the total historical costs of the investments? Explain.

10. Accounts receivable are presented on the balance sheet at net realizable value. Explain what is meant by net realizable value. Why is this measurement base required for accounts receivable?

11. Describe the two methods outlined in the chapter of accounting for bad debts. Include in your description an explanation of why one method is

characterized as being income statement oriented and the other balance sheet oriented.

12. What, if any, is the effect on the book value of accounts receivable of writing off a specific account as a bad debt?

13. What type of account is Allowance for Doubtful Debts? How is this account presented on the financial statements?

14. A firm is considering offering customers a 2% discount for cash payment within ten days of a credit sale. Currently, the average time to collect receivables is 30 days. If instituted, what effect do you think this cash discount plan would have on the accounts receivable turnover rate? Explain.

15. List and describe the three types of inventory presented on the balance sheet of a manufacturing firm.

16. Would knowledge of the inventory turnover rate be more relevant in evaluating Apple Computer or UAL? Explain your reasoning.

17. Inventory is usually valued at the lower of cost or market. When used in this context, explain what is meant by the phrase "lower of cost or market."

18. Valuing inventory at the lower of cost or market is said to shift income among accounting periods. Explain.

19. Per the cost principle, inventory is recorded initially at acquisition price plus "other costs" incurred to get the inventory ready for sale. List several of these "other costs."

20. Generally, a company attempts to increase the turnover of inventory. Yet, the highest rate possible would rarely be the optimum. Why?

21. The industry average is often used as a point of reference in interpreting a firm's inventory turnover rate. What other points of reference might also be used?

22. All other things being equal, would you expect the inventory turnover rate of a firm using LIFO to be higher than that of one using FIFO? Explain.

23. "In financial accounting, depreciation is a process of cost allocation, not asset valuation." Do you agree or disagree? Explain.

24. Contrast accounting for equity securities classified as temporary (current) with those classified as long-term (noncurrent).

25. Give examples of three different intangible assets.

26. Current GAAP require that all research and development expenditures be expensed immediately, even though they may very well have considerable future value. What is the rationale for this rule?

27. Explain the difference between an identifiable and an unidentifiable intangible. Give an example of each.

28. Under what conditions may goodwill be recorded as an asset? Explain.

29. Assume that the market value of the identifiable assets of a firm totals $500,000. Would it necessarily be irrational to offer more than that amount to buy the entire business? Explain your answer.

30. What is the difference between current cost and current market value? Give an example of when each would be used.

31. Explain what is meant by "the time value of money."
32. Explain the difference between compounding (future value) and discounting (present value).

EXERCISES AND PROBLEMS

33. *Balance Sheet: General Questions.*   The balance sheet is often referred to as the statement of financial position, and its primary purpose is to present information that should aid the user in assessing the financial status of a company at a particular date. Specifically, the balance sheet is useful in assessing liquidity, financial flexibility, and profit performance. However, the balance sheet also has several distinct and potentially serious limitations.

REQUIRED

(a) While a balance sheet may be referred to as a statement of financial position, should that title be taken literally; that is, is a balance sheet designed to reflect a particular company's worth? Explain fully.

(b) As a general rule, is a different measurement base used for valuing monetary assets than is used for nonmonetary assets? Explain.

(c) Evaluating two different companies is difficult because of lack of comparability on the balance sheet. Give two separate examples of how the asset section of the balance sheet might differ for two similar companies in the same industry.

(d) It was mentioned in the text that current accounting practice places greater emphasis on the measurement of income than on providing meaningful balance sheet valuations. Give two examples of this phenomenon, particularly as it relates to the measurement of assets on the balance sheet.

34. *Statements to Ponder.*   The following statements relate to several controversial issues discussed in Chapter 5:

(1) (*President to Controller*) "We need additional capital and I would like to issue bonds. Unfortunately, we have a high debt to equity ratio and our investment banker advises me that this will result in a poor bond rating and a high interest rate. However, I believe that the net worth shown on our balance sheet is far too low. At the close of this past year, the market value of all of our outstanding shares was $200 million higher than what we reported in the stockholders' equity section of the balance sheet. This obviously represents goodwill and undervalued tangible assets recognized by the market but not reflected on our books. Why can't we charge goodwill and specific tangible assets and credit stockholders' equity for this amount? This would significantly reduce our debt to equity ratio. You will concede that if our company was purchased, these undervalued assets would be recognized."

(2) (*Board member of Du Pont to Financial Vice President*) "In view of uncertainty about future benefits, I can understand why accountants no longer permit companies to capitalize R&D. However, we spent millions of dollars to develop Nylon. The actual amount can be determined by going over our books. Now that this product has been patented and there is a huge market for it, why don't we capitalize past R&D expenditures for Nylon and amortize it over 40 years, which we are doing with other patents that we purchased?"

(3) (*From a "supposed" old article in a business journal written at the time of the takeover*) "Stockholders of Kern County Land Company agreed yesterday to sell their shares to Tenneco at a 30%-premium over the market price. Was this a good deal for these shareholders? It's hard to say, but one factor that should be considered is that Kern County's balance sheet did not reflect approximately $100 million of current market value of California land owned for many years by the company on which oil subsequently was discovered."

(4) (*Investor to his tax accountant*) "Mind you, I'm not complaining since I received a good price for my shares in Paramount Pictures when Gulf and Western took them over. However, the substantial value of Paramount's old film library (essentially for TV showings) was never reported on its balance sheet. I'd bet that the people at G&W had a darn good idea of the value of these films when they made their stock offer."

(5) (*Economist to accountant*) "Accountants are too conservative. They continue to report fixed assets at historical costs when in many cases current replacement costs may be twice as high. Obviously, this distorts both the balance sheet and the income statement and related financial ratios. Much more meaningful information would be provided if historical costs were adjusted to current replacement costs."

REQUIRED   Comment on each of these statements.

35. *Asset Structures of Firms in Different Industries.*   The selected financial information presented below has been derived from the financial statements of four firms. Each of the firms belongs to one of the following industries: (1) data processing software and services, (2) telephone utility, (3) airline, and (4) broadcast entertainment.

	Firm A	Firm B	Firm C	Firm D
Percentage of total assets in:				
Cash and temporary investments	21%	5%	7%	38%
Receivables	8	23	18	12
Inventories	–	12	2	3
Other current assets	2	3	22	7
Total current assets	31%	43%	49%	60%
Property, plant, and equipment (net)	62	55	24	28
Other noncurrent assets	7	2	27	12
Total assets	100%	100%	100%	100%

Percentage relative to total sales:

Net income	.5%	4%	6%	9%
Cost of goods sold	–	33	1	2
Depreciation, amortization, and depletion	3	8	2	9
Total assets	110	132	120	88

REQUIRED

(a) Which of the firms would be expected to have relatively large investments in receivables? In inventories? In property, plant, and equipment? In other noncurrent assets?

(b) Which firms would have relatively large percentages of sales represented by cost of goods sold? By depreciation, depletion, and amortization?

(c) Which firm appears to be using its assets most effectively? Least effectively?

(d) Based on your answers to (a) through (c) and on your own observations, attempt to identify the industry to which each firm belongs.

36. *Marketable Equity Securities: Journal Entry Sequence.* On December 10, 1988, the Sacramento Company purchased 1,000 shares of stock in the Reno Corporation at $10 per share. These shares were properly classified as marketable equity securities. The shares were the only marketable equity securities owned by the company. The Sacramento Company closes its books annually on December 31.

REQUIRED Prepare journal entries to record the following:

(a) On December 31, 1988, the market value of the shares had declined to $6 per share.

(b) On December 31, 1989, the market value of the shares was $8 per share.

(c) All the shares were sold on January 15, 1990, for $8 per share.

37. *Short-term Portfolio of Marketable Equity Securities.* The Boiler Plate Company began operations early in 1987 and had the following transactions in short-term marketable equity securities during the year:

(1) Bought 500 shares of QED Corporation securities at $60 per share.

(2) Bought 1,000 shares of BYO Corporation securities at $75 per share.

(3) Received dividends of $5 per share on the QED Corporation shares.

(4) Bought 200 shares of ASAP Corporation at $150 per share.

(5) Sold 400 of the BYO Corporation shares at $65 per share.

At December 31, 1987, the shares had the following market values:

Shares	Market Value per Share
QED Corporation	$ 70
ASAP Corporation	140
BYO Corporation	60

REQUIRED

(a) Provide journal entries to record the 1987 transactions described above.
(b) Provide the necessary entry, if any, to provide a valuation allowance for the current portfolio on December 31, 1987.
(c) Summarize the effects of the above transactions on the 1987 income statement and year-end balance sheet of the Boiler Plate Company.

(Note: Exercise 37 must be completed prior to attempting exercise 38.)

38. *Short-term Portfolio of Marketable Equity Securities.*   In 1988, the Boiler Plate Company had the following transactions affecting the current portfolio of marketable equity securities:

(1) Sold 500 BYO Corporation shares at $70 per share.
(2) Sold all of the ASAP Corporation shares for a total of $30,000.

At December 31, 1988, the remaining shares had the following market values:

Shares	Market Value per Share
QED Corporation	$80
BYO Corporation	70

REQUIRED

(a) Provide journal entries to record the 1988 transactions described above, and (if necessary) to adjust the valuation allowance on December 31, 1988.
(b) Summarize the effects of the above transactions on the 1988 income statement and year-end balance sheet of the Boiler Plate Company.
(c) How does your interpretation of the carrying value of the short-term portfolio differ between the balance sheet on December 31, 1987 (Problem 37), and December 31, 1988?

39. *Interest-bearing Note Receivable.*   On April 1, 1988, the Portsmouth Company received a $5,000, 12% interest-bearing note from a customer in lieu of a full cash payment of $5,000 for merchandise sold and delivered on that

date. The customer pays the entire amount due (both principal and interest) on the note's maturity date, which is March 31, 1989. The Portsmouth Company closes its books annually on December 31.

REQUIRED Record the necessary journal entries on the Portsmouth Company's books at the following dates: April 1, 1988; December 31, 1988; and March 31, 1989.

40. *Noninterest-bearing Note Receivable.* On January 1, 1988, the Hillsboro Company received a $2,000, six-month, noninterest-bearing note from Zing Company in settlement of goods sold to Zing. The fair market value of the goods is $1,800. Zing Company pays the note when it is due.

REQUIRED Record the journal entries for the Hillsboro Company on January 1 and on June 30 that pertain to this note receivable.

41. *Noninterest-bearing Note Receivable.* On January 2, 1988, Sunset Auto, Incorporated, sells a car to an MBA student. Instead of paying cash at the time of the sale, the student signs a $14,000 noninterest-bearing note that is due on December 31, 1991. Sunset Auto, Incorporated, had paid $9,000 for the car. Assume that the prevailing interest rate on similar loans is 8%.

REQUIRED

(a) Calculate the present value of the note.
(b) What is the profit on the sale of the car? Show all work.
(c) Prepare the necessary journal entry to record the sale of the car on January 2, 1988.
(d) Prepare the necessary journal entries to record interest for the years 1988 and 1989. Assume that Sunset Auto closes its books annually on December 31.

42. *Interest-bearing versus Noninterest-bearing Notes.* Creative Financing, Incorporated, finances the sale of automobiles using various methods. As an example, it is possible to finance a particular car with a $1,000, 10% note, due in one year. Alternatively, one may finance the same car with a $1,100 noninterest-bearing note, also due in one year.

REQUIRED

(a) If a person purchases the car, are the cash outflows to Creative Financing, Incorporated, the same under each of the alternative financing agreements outlined above? Explain.
(b) Prepare journal entries to account for the financing of the car, assuming the 10% note payable is used.

(c) Prepare journal entries to account for the financing of the car, assuming the noninterest-bearing note payable is used.

(d) Compare the journal entry sequence in (b) and (c) above. Are they the same? Should they be? Explain.

43. *Efficiency of Cash Collection: Accounts Receivable.*   The Cincinnati Corporation had $1 million in sales during the year ended December 31, 1987. Credit sales represent $600,000 of this total amount. Per the general ledger, a $50,000 balance exists in the Accounts Receivable account at December 31, 1987. This balance is believed to be typical; rarely during the year did the amount of accounts receivable vary by more than a few thousand dollars on either side of this $50,000 amount. Terms on all credit sales are such that cash payment in full is required within two weeks of each sale.

REQUIRED

(a) Calculate the company's accounts receivable turnover rate for the past year. Also, calculate the average number of days it took the Cincinnati Company to collect its receivables.

(b) Based upon the ratios computed in (a), comment on the efficiency of cash collection for the company.

44. *Uncollectible Accounts: Allowance Method.*   The Springfield Company has credit sales totaling $800,000 during 1988. While the company's general ledger shows a $60,000 balance in Accounts Receivable at December 31, 1988, some receivables invariably turn out to be uncollectible. An aging of accounts receivable at year end indicates that $3,500 of the total balance is expected to be uncollectible. The allowance for Doubtful Accounts had a $1,900 credit balance on the December 31, 1987 balance sheet. During 1988, $1,800 of accounts receivable were written off as uncollectible.

REQUIRED

(a) Given that the company uses the allowance method to account for bad debts, prepare the necessary adjusting entry at December 31, 1988.

(b) Assume the same facts as in (a), except that Bad Debt Expense is to be determined as a function of the amount of credit sales for the period. In the past, 1/2 of 1% of credit sales have proved to be uncollectible.

(c) Compare your answers in (a) and (b) above. Explain why the dollar amounts are different.

45. *Uncollectible Accounts: Aging Method.*   On December 31, 1988, Golf Company has total accounts receivable of $85,000 on its books. According to

past experience, the chance of a receivable being uncollectible is related to its age. The accounts receivable aging schedule for Golf is as follows:

Age of Receivable (days outstanding)	Percentage Expected to Be Uncollectible	Amount
0–30	1%	$61,000
31–60	3%	10,000
61–90	5%	6,000
91 or more	10%	8,000

The Allowance for Doubtful Accounts had a $1,900 credit balance on the December 31, 1987 balance sheet. During 1988, $1,500 of accounts receivable were written off as uncollectible.

REQUIRED

(a) Prepare the necessary adjusting entry at December 31, 1988, assuming that the aging method is used.
(b) How should Accounts Receivable and its related allowance account be presented on the Golf Company's balance sheet as of December 31, 1988?

46. *Accounting for Bad Debts: Two Methods.* When the allowance method is used to account for uncollectible accounts, it is necessary to estimate the total dollar amount of uncollectible accounts at the end of the accounting period. This dollar amount is estimated as either (1) a function of the period's credit sales or (2) by use of an aging method.

REQUIRED

(a) One of these two methods is said to be more balance sheet oriented; the other, more income statement oriented. Explain.
(b) Regardless of which of the two methods is used, the same accounts are debited and credited in the adjusting entry made at the end of the accounting period. What account is debited, and what is the nature of that account (for example, asset, liability, revenue, and so forth)? What account is credited, and what is the nature of that account?
(c) When the aging method is used, is it necessary to know the amount already in allowance for uncollectible accounts in order to complete the appropriate journal entry at the end of the accounting period? Is your answer the same if uncollectible accounts are estimated as a certain percentage of the period's credit sales? Explain.
(d) What journal entry is made to record the fact that Customer X's account of $1,800 is judged to be uncollectible? What effect, if any, will this journal entry have on the net amount of accounts receivable shown on the company's balance sheet?

47. *Items to Be Included in Inventory.*   Listed below are items that may or may not be classified as inventory in a firm's financial statements:

(1) A desk on display in the showroom of a furniture store.
(2) A desk used by the receptionist in a dentist's office.
(3) Light bulbs that a hardware store received on consignment.
(4) A personal computer sold by a retailer but still in the store awaiting shipment.
(5) A manual typewriter in an office supplies store; the typewriter has been a slow moving item, but is expected to be sold in the next month at a substantial discount.
(6) Inventory sold but currently in transit; title to the inventory does not pass until the goods are received by the buyer.

REQUIRED   In each of the above situations, determine if the item in question should be included in inventory on the firm's current financial statements. Explain all answers.

48. *Lower of Cost or Market: Inventory.*   Generally accepted accounting principles require the use of different measurement bases in different situations. For example, inventory is initially recorded at historical cost, but a value that is lower than historical cost may be required if there is a subsequent decline in the inventory's future utility (revenue-producing ability). Said another way, inventory is generally presented on the balance sheet at the lower of cost or market (LCM).

REQUIRED

(a) What is the meaning of "market" as the term is used in valuing inventory on a LCM basis?
(b) What account is debited and what account is credited if it becomes necessary to record a decline in the revenue-producing ability of the inventory?
(c) The chapter states that "LCM allows for the shifting of income among periods." Explain.

49. *Inventory Turnover Rate: LIFO versus FIFO.*   Data regarding beginning inventory and purchases during the current year are shown below:

January 1	Beginning inventory	100 items @ $10 each
March 28	Purchase	300 items @ $15 each
August 25	Purchase	400 items @ $18 each
October 10	Purchase	300 items @ $20 each

Per a physical count, 100 items of inventory are on hand at December 31.

REQUIRED

    (a) Determine the dollar amount to be assigned to ending inventory under FIFO and under LIFO.

    (b) Calculate the inventory turnover rate for the firm, assuming first that it uses FIFO and then that it uses LIFO.

    (c) Comment on the difference between the two turnover rates calculated above.

50. *Treatment of Excess Inventory Costs (Douglas Aircraft).* Douglas Aircraft is no longer in existence. Subsequent to the time span discussed in this case, the company encountered severe financial difficulties and merged with McDonnell Aircraft Company (now McDonnell Douglas).

During the last quarter of 1965, the first three DC-9's were completed and sold. The actual cost of these planes, which substantially exceeded selling price, was removed from the Work in Process Inventory account and charged to Cost of Goods Sold. Six additional planes were sold in the first quarter of 1966. However, the company changed its accounting procedure, charging Cost of Goods Sold at selling price rather than actual cost, which exceeded the selling price by approximately $4 million. This excess cost was permitted to remain in Work in Process Inventory, and thus did not appear as a charge to income on the income statement distributed to stockholders for the first quarter. The $4 million was equal to approximately $.50 per share of stock. Reported first quarter profits were $.85 per share. Since interim reports were unaudited, the matter was not discussed with the company's auditors. The first quarter report did not disclose the deferral of these excess inventory costs.

Management defended this treatment of the excess inventory costs by claiming that the high cost of producing the first batch of planes was due to a learning experience. For example, the efficiency level in the first quarter of 1966 was 46%. Past experience with learning curves in this and other aircraft manufacturing companies indicated that efficiency would significantly increase with successive batches of planes produced. The first batch of planes, while not experimental, was viewed by management as developmental from a production standpoint. Therefore, management believed it could justify spreading the excess cost over the cost of all future DC-9's to be produced. Management felt that failure to defer these excess costs (termed "smooth" income) would seriously distort reported income for the first quarter of 1966 and give stockholders an erroneous impression of expected earnings for the balance of the year. According to the company's profit plan, which was believed to have been carefully and conservatively prepared, the first quarter was expected to be poor but would be offset by rising profits in succeeding quarters. Actually, manufacturing efficiency did not improve but worsened as unanticipated material shortages (primarily undelivered engines) occurred that seriously upset production schedules.

REQUIRED

(a) Do you think Douglas' treatment of its excess inventory costs was in accord with GAAP? Explain.

(b) Evaluate management's reasons for deferring the excess inventory costs.

51. *Installment Note Receivable.* Patient Company has a long-overdue account receivable in the amount of $300,000 due from Supplicant, Inc. The firms have agreed to restructure the receivable as a long-term installment note, to be paid in equal annual installments at the end of each of the next five years. Assume that the relevant interest rate is 10%.

REQUIRED

(a) Determine the dollar amount of Supplicant's annual cash payments to Patient Company.

(b) Provide journal entries on Patient's books to record the receipt on January 1, 1988, of the installment note in place of the existing account receivable. Also, record the interest income and cash receipts for the first two years.

(c) Provide journal entries on Supplicant's books to record the signing on January 1, 1988, of the installment note in place of the existing account payable. Also, record the interest expense and cash payments for the first two years.

(d) Show how the installment note would appear in the balance sheets of both firms on January 1, 1988 (after the note has been signed), and on January 1, 1989 (after the first payment).

52. *Installment Note Receivable, Operating Profit, and Interest Income.* Fell Company is a retailer that sells machinery to its customers. On January 1, 1987, Fell Company sold a machine to Swoop, Inc., in exchange for an installment note receivable. The note requires Swoop to pay Fell $100,000 at the end of each of the next four years. Fell Company purchased the machine from a manufacturing company for $300,000.

REQUIRED

(a) Assuming that the interest rate is 6%, how would the transaction affect the amount of sales revenue, operating profit, and interest income to be reported by Fell Company in each year through 1990? (Ignore income taxes.)

(b) Assuming that the interest rate is 12%, determine how the transaction would affect the amount of sales revenue, operating profit, and interest income to be reported by Fell Company in each of the four years. (Again, ignore income taxes.)

(c) Explain why the *total* income over the four years is the same in both (a) and (b), while the *yearly* income differs as the discount rate is changed.

53. *Depreciation Expense: Repairs and Improvements.* Wlinski Taxi Company has just spent $2 million for parts and labor for its fleet of taxi cabs.

REQUIRED Indicate how this expenditure is to be accounted for (that is, expensed or capitalized, and the period of amortization) in each of the following alternative cases:

(a) The $2 million was spent primarily for new paint, decals, and other "bells and whistles" to make the cabs more distinctive and attractive to potential riders.
(b) The $2 million was spent primarily to perform maintenance, which had unwisely been deferred by the former operations manager. Maintenance spending was well below standard levels for the past three years.
(c) The $2 million was spent primarily for engine renovations and replacements, which will increase fuel efficiency and extend the useful lives of the vehicles affected.
(d) About half of the $2 million was spent to add display advertising space to the roofs and rear trunk areas of the cabs. The remaining amount was spent to add protective shields and other antitheft devices to the interiors of the vehicles.

54. *Capitalization versus Expensing of Transactions.* The issue of capitalization versus expensing of various costs was discussed in this chapter. If a cost is capitalized, it is debited to an asset account; if expensed, it is debited to an expense account. From a theoretical perspective, all necessary and reasonable costs of preparing the asset for use are capitalized at the time of acquisition. Subsequent to acquisition, regular recurring maintenance and repair costs are expensed. Other costs that have benefits that are longer term in nature may be capitalized.

REQUIRED For each of the situations listed below, determine if the relevant costs should be capitalized or expensed. Also, specify the dollar amount of these costs.

(a) A machine is constructed internally at a cost of $29,000. An identical machine purchased externally would have cost $32,000.
(b) A milling machine is ordered from Germany at a total installed cost of $80,000, broken down as follows:

Invoice price	$76,000
Interest on bank loan to finance purchase	100
Overseas and domestic freight	1,500
Initial installation expense	1,000
Moving and reinstallation expense	1,400
	$80,000

(c) An escalator in a department store required a major overhaul (which will prolong its life) at a cost of $110,000.

(d) A recently constructed warehouse is severely damaged by a tornado. Reconstruction costs amount to $1,600,000. Insurance proceeds amount to $1 million.

(e) A firm has commissioned a construction company to erect a building according to agreed specifications. At the end of the year the building is only partially completed and payments of $3 million have been made as noted below:

Architect	$ 200,000
Cost of land	1,200,000
Land clearance	190,000
Laying of foundation	1,410,000
	$3,000,000

(f) A boiler in a building with a remaining life of 15 years must be replaced at a cost of $80,000. The boiler has an estimated life of 20 years. However, once installed and used, the boiler has no resale value.

(g) A mining company expended $20 million for mineral rights for a mine with an estimated recoverable output of 1 million tons. The breakdown of this expenditure is shown below.

Geological survey	$ 200,000
Mineral rights	17,000,000
Access (roads, shafts, and so forth)	340,000
Legal expense on mineral rights	60,000
Interest on money borrowed to acquire mine	2,000,000
Mining supplies	400,000
	$20,000,000

(h) In order to prolong the life of its blast furnaces, a firm had them relined at a cost of $4.5 million.

(i) A company spent $400,000 on research and development during a particular year, which resulted in a patentable product that is expected to earn revenues for at least ten years.

55. *Interest During Construction.*   The 1985 consolidated financial statements of Air Products and Chemicals, Inc., include the following footnote:

Capitalized interest: As the company is building new plant equipment, it includes in the cost of these new assets a portion of the interest payments it makes during the year. In 1985, the amount of capitalized interest was $5.5 million. In 1984, it was $7.1 million and in 1983, $11.1 million.

REQUIRED

(a) How does the capitalization of interest affect the amount of net income reported by the firm during the periods that the assets are being constructed? How is the carrying value (or book value) of the assets affected?

(b) How does the capitalization of interest payments during the construction of an asset affect the firm's total net income over the entire period from the beginning of construction until the asset is either retired or sold? How does capitalization of interest affect depreciation expense (net of gain or loss on disposal of the asset) during the same period? How does it affect the firm's interest expense?

(c) Assume the company did not incur debt to construct the asset, but instead financed the construction of the new plant and equipment solely by the retention of earnings and the issuance of additional common stock. Under these circumstances, would the cost of the new assets include capitalized interest? Do you believe that the manner in which the firm finances its plant and equipment should affect the carrying value of those assets? Explain.

56. *Interest During Construction.*   Levered, Inc., and Unfettered Corporation have each undertaken the building of new plants and equipment. A summary of expenditures and financing costs is provided below.

	Levered, Inc.	Unfettered Corp.
	(in millions)	
Annual construction expenditure (incurred evenly throughout each year)		
1985	$100	$400
1986	200	200
1987	400	100
Total	$700	$700

Levered, Inc., has financed its building costs by issuing long-term debt, at an interest rate of 12% per year. Unfettered Corporation has financed its building costs by the retention of earnings and the issuance of common stock. Both firms will place their new plants and equipment in service at the beginning of 1988. (Assume that Levered, Inc.'s, interest costs are deemed to be material in amount.)

REQUIRED

(a) Determine the amount of interest cost that will have been capitalized and the carrying value of each firm's assets at the beginning of 1988. Is it sensible to consider Levered, Inc.'s, plant and equipment to be more expensive than that of Unfettered Corporation? Explain your position.

(b) Over the useful life of the assets, which firm will report the higher depreciation expense? (Assume equal disposal values for the assets of both firms.)

(c) Assume that an investor analyst wishes to impute interest cost to the assets of Unfettered Corporation in order to make more meaningful comparisons between the financial statements of the two firms. How would the analyst determine a suitable "cost of capital" for Unfettered Corporation?

(d) Do GAAP permit Levered, Inc., to continue to capitalize interest costs after the assets have been fully constructed and placed in service?

(e) Do you believe that firms should capitalize interest costs incurred to finance investments in other assets such as inventory and accounts receivable? Defend your position.

57. *Sinking Fund for Plant Expansion.*   The management of Eventual Products, Inc., has decided to establish a sinking fund for plant expansion.

REQUIRED

(a) If the firm deposits $10 million at the end of each year and deposits earn interest at 10%, what will be the amount available for plant expansion at the end of five years? Provide journal entries for the first year to show the deposit to the sinking fund.

(b) If the firm deposits $10 million at the beginning of each year and deposits earn interest at 10%, what will be the maturity value of the fund after five years? Provide journal entries for the first year.

(c) If management desires to have $80 million available after five years, and the fund is expected to earn 12% interest each year, what amount must be deposited in the sinking fund at the end of each year?

(d) Assume that a particular building costs $60 million today to construct and that construction costs will increase at the rate of 8% per year. Rather than build today, assume that management plans to begin construction of the building in three years and intends to make a lump sum cash payment for the total market value of the building at that time. Management intends to accumulate this amount by making annual payments at the end of each year to a sinking fund earning 12% annually. The first payment to the sinking fund will be at the end of the current year. What amount should be contributed annually to the sinking fund?

(e) Suppose that the building described in (d) is to be financed by annual sinking fund payments at the beginning of each year, and that the fund is expected to earn interest at 8% per year. What is the required annual sinking fund payment?

58. *Accounting for Research and Development.* During 1987, the Lawnsteen Company incurred research and development expenditures of $500,000 to develop a new product, which was then patented. In December 1987, the Lawnsteen Company sold the patent on this new product to Howard Company for $800,000. The Howard Company estimates that the economic life of the patent is ten years. Amortization of the patent is to begin on January 1, 1988.

REQUIRED

(a) Prepare the journal entries necessary to record research and development expenditures during 1987 for the Lawnsteen Company.
(b) Prepare the journal entries necessary on the Howard Company's books to record the purchase of the patent in 1987 and the appropriate amortization expense for the patent during 1988.
(c) If the Howard Company had developed the patent itself and incurred the same research and development costs as those incurred by Lawnsteen Company ($500,000), would those R&D costs appear on the Howard Company's balance sheet at December 31, 1987? Explain.

59. *Disclosures Regarding Exploration and Production of Oil and Gas Reserves (Getty Oil Company).* The following data was abstracted from Getty Oil Company's 1981 annual report to stockholders:

Total net property, plant, and equipment shown on Getty's December 31, 1981, balance sheet ($6.274 billion) included a net investment in exploration and production of gas and oil of	$4,706,313,000
Number of common shares outstanding at December 31, 1981	81,974,052
Common stockholders' equity at December 31, 1981	$4,773,529,000
Market price per share of common stock at December 31, 1981	64 5/8

The following schedule, which we have labeled Exhibit A, was also presented as a supplemental disclosure:

Exhibit A

Getty Oil Company

Changes in the present value of estimated future net revenues from proved oil and gas reserves for the years ended December 31, 1981, 1980 and 1979, were as follows: [1]

	1981	1980	1979
		(in millions)	
Present value of estimated future net revenues from proved oil and gas reserves at beginning of year	$17,217	$13,931	$ 7,595
Increases			
Additions to proved reserves	1,241	1,164	451
Revisions to estimates of reserves proved in prior years	2,665	4,484	7,202
Expenditures that reduced estimated future development costs	874	559	390
Purchase of reserves in place	8	348	268
	4,788	6,555	8,311
Decreases			
Oil and gas sales less production costs	3,016	2,891	1,875
Present value of estimated future development and production costs	451	378	100
	3,467	3,269	1,975
Present value of estimated future net revenues from proved oil and gas reserves at end of year	$18,538	$17,217	$13,931

[1] The reconciliation of the present values of estimated future net revenues from proved oil and gas reserves was determined in accordance with Securities and Exchange Commission Regulation S-X, Section 210.4-10 (k)(8). The present value of estimated future net revenues should not be construed as the price at which Getty would sell the assets involved.

Note: The present value of net revenues from proved oil and gas reserves was discounted at 10% in accordance with SEC requirements.

Supplemental disclosures in Exhibit A only include proved oil and gas deposits. There are two other classifications of oil and gas deposits— probable and possible—that are excluded from these calculations for reasons of conservatism, but that have considerable potential value.

REQUIRED

(a) What was Getty's "present value of estimated future net revenues from proved oil and gas reserves at end of year"? Would this information be of value to you as a stockholder in the Getty Oil Company? Why?

(b) Assume that you are president of Pennzoil or Texaco and are contemplating a takeover offer of approximately $125 per share to

Getty's common stockholders. Would the estimated present value of Getty's oil and gas deposits be meaningful information? If so, why?

(c) Getty states in a footnote to the schedule that "the present value of estimated future net revenues should not be construed as the price at which Getty would sell the assets involved." Why do you think this statement was made?

(d) What do you think were the major factors resulting in the increase in present value of these resources from $13.9 billion as of December 31, 1979, to $18.5 billion on December 31, 1981?

60. *Determining the Fair Market Value of Oil Property.* (President to Controller) "I am very close to reaching an agreement with Birnie Goodman of Lunanjo to purchase their business. We have agreed on prices for all of their assets except their old West Texas oil wells. They are asking $600,000 for this property. I've requested Grey and Gold to estimate the number of recoverable barrels of crude at West Texas. I also asked them to advise us as to how the fair market value of oil property is established by independent appraisers. Here is the letter I received from Jim Grey (Exhibit A). I want you to calculate the value of this property using the procedure described by Grey and his suggested figures. Fixed assets at the well are fully depreciated both for financial and tax purposes. While the wells are fully depleted on the company's books, for tax purposes you can deduct a charge for depletion equal to 10% of net income before depletion. Assume that our income tax rate will continue at 30%. If we take over Lunanjo, it will be effective as of the beginning of next year."

Exhibit A

Grey and Gold, Inc.
Independent Appraisers
Dallas, Texas

Dear Mr. Preston:

Pursuant to your instructions, our geological survey indicates that there are approximately 220,000 recoverable barrels of crude oil in the West Texas wells owned by Lunanjo Company. With the company's present lifting equipment, we estimate maximum annual production at 40,000 barrels. Assuming that these wells will continue to be operated at maximum, they have a remaining life of six years.

You also inquired how appraisers determine the value of oil property. Apart from technical problems in estimating recoverable oil and gas, the procedure used by independent appraisers is as follows:

1. Determine the net cash flow from each year's production during the expected remaining life of the property. The major difficulty here is forecasting the future well-head price for the type of crude produced. Most experts believe that

crude prices have bottomed out and will rise over the next six years in the range of $4–8 a barrel. We believe that an average crude well-head price of $16 per barrel for West Texas oil during the next six years is sufficiently conservative. We also estimate new "lifting" costs, (that is, total cash costs of production) at Lunanjo's wells to be about $10 a barrel. However, an additional $.50 a barrel royalty must be paid to the original owners of the property.

2. The present value of the forecast net cash flow is calculated by applying an interest rate to give effect to the time value of money. The capitalization rate presently used by independent appraisers is 10%. This is the rate that banks currently are demanding on loans to finance good oil investments.

3. The above procedure will yield the estimated present value of the forecasted cash flow. However, there is a difference between the present value of the cash flow and the fair market value of the property represented by an allowance for risk. As a rule of thumb, market value is equal to 70–80% of the discounted future cash flow. In the case of Lunanjo's West Texas oil property, we believe that fair market value should be equal to 75% of the discounted cash flow.

Enclosed is the bill for our services. If we can be of any further assistance, please contact us.

Very truly yours,
James Grey, President

REQUIRED

(a) Determine the estimated fair market value of the property rounded to the nearest $1,000.
(b) Do you think that the disclosure by oil companies in their annual reports of the estimated fair market value of their oil and gas properties would be useful information to investors? Why?
(c) What limitations are there to such disclosures?

61. *Accounting for Intangible Assets.*   At the beginning of a year, Marion Company purchased a patent for a new product from another company for $250,000. The other company had invested a considerable amount of resources in research to develop the product that it patented. Marion Company estimates the patent will have an economic life of ten years.

REQUIRED

(a) Prepare the journal entries necessary to record the acquisition and amortization for the patent for its first two years.

(b) In contrast to (a), assume that the product was developed internally and the related R&D costs totaled $225,000. In addition, assume that the costs of applying for and receiving the patent were $5,000. Prepare the journal entries to account for the patent and R&D.

62. *Valuation of a Business and Determination of Goodwill.* Congloma, Inc., is negotiating for the purchase of the ARC Corporation. An unresolved issue between the parties is the amount to be paid for goodwill. Exhibit A contains data for ARC relevant to the determination of goodwill.

Two methods for calculating goodwill have been recommended to Peter Gomez, president of Congloma. Ruffem, Pasteim, and Smackum, the company's investment bankers, believe that the market value of the company's common stock should be used as the basis for calculating goodwill. This procedure is outlined in Method 1 below. However, Sweet, Docile, and Kind, the company's appraisers, have indicated that independent appraisers rely on a procedure that capitalizes excess earnings as indicated by Method 2. In the latter instance, Congloma's management considers 10% to be a normal return on investment for a company in ARC's risk category.

Method 1

Net worth per books	XXX
Add: Increase in asset value to reflect replacement cost of assets	XXX
Net worth based on replacement cost	XXX
Value of corporation based on market value of outstanding common stock	XXX
Implied value of goodwill	XXX

Method 2

Net income per books		XXX
Less: Additional depreciation based on replacement cost of assets, net of income tax*		XXX
Net income based on replacement cost		XXX
Less: Normal return on investment		
Net worth per books	XXX	
Add: Adjustment for replacement cost	XXX	
Net worth based on replacement cost	XXX	
Normal percentage return on investment expected	×10%	
Normal return on investment		XXX
Excess of actual return over normal return		XXX
Present value of an annuity of $1 for 5 years at 10%		3.79
Implied value of goodwill		XXX

*Assume effective rate of 30%

Exhibit A
Relevant Data for ARC Corporation

Assets, less allowances, at December 31, 1987	$130,000,000
Liabilities at December 31, 1987	$ 60,000,000
Net income for the year 1987	$ 10,000,000
Increase in net assets based on replacement cost	$ 11,000,000
Increase in depreciation based on replacement cost	$ 800,000
Average number of common shares outstanding during 1987	1,000,000
Average market value of common stock during 1987	$90

REQUIRED

(a) Calculate goodwill under the two methods based on data contained in Exhibit A.
(b) Evaluate the two methods.
(c) What is the effect of recognizing goodwill?
(d) If goodwill exists, why should it be recognized only when the purchase of another business takes place?

63. *Alternative Measurement Bases for Assets.* The Chambers Sterling Company has valued its assets using each of the five measurement bases discussed in the FASB's conceptual framework project (and summarized in Exhibit 5-7). The alternative asset valuations are reported in the following table.

Asset Valuations Using Alternative Measurement Bases

Chambers Sterling Company
(in millions)

	Historical Cost	Current Cost	Current Market Value	Expected Market Value	Present Value of Expected Cash Flows
Current assets					
Cash	$ 3.5	$ 3.5	$ 3.5	$ 3.5	$ 3.5
Temporary investments	2.1	2.9	2.9	3.6	2.9
Accounts receivable (net)	15.4	15.4	14.9	15.4	14.9
Inventory	10.0	8.6	6.2	10.3	9.0
Prepayments, other	4.4	5.2	2.0	5.4	4.8
Total current	$35.4	$ 35.6	$ 29.5	$ 38.2	$ 35.1
Noncurrent assets					
Plant, equipment (net)	32.0	34.0	26.5	41.5	36.6
Land	6.5	14.6	14.2	20.0	14.2
Intangibles, other	5.2	30.0	36.0	49.5	36.0
Total noncurrent	43.7	78.6	76.7	111.0	86.8
Total assets	$79.1	$114.2	$106.2	$149.2	$121.9

REQUIRED

(a) Indicate the asset valuations that would be reported on the firm's balance sheet, assuming that the firm follows GAAP in preparing its financial statements.

(b) Which of the measurement bases best measures the resources under management's control?

(c) Which measurement base is most pertinent in assessing the worth of the company's outstanding debt securities?

(d) Which measurement base is most pertinent in assessing the worth of the firm's common stock?

(e) Is it meaningful for the balance sheet to add together asset values in cases where different measurement bases are used for different assets? Explain.

(f) Should a single measurement base be used for all assets? If so, which of the five bases included in the table presented here should be selected? Explain.

(g) The assets of Chambers Sterling Company consist of some items that eventually will be converted into cash in the normal course of business (for example, temporary investments, accounts receivable, and inventory) and other items that will be consumed and expensed in future periods (prepayments, plant, and equipment, for example). (1) What is meant by the "expected market value" of the latter type of assets (items that will be consumed and expensed in future periods)? How would expected market value be measured? (2) How would the present value of the expected cash flows be measured?

(h) Business assets are often combined to provide cash inflows. Discuss the potential difficulty in valuing individual assets based on expected market values, if the assets must be used in combination with other assets in order to generate cash inflows.

(i) Which asset measurement base produces the most objective valuation? Which is least objective? Is there a relationship between objectivity and usefulness? Explain.

64. *Goodwill.* The balance sheet for the Tame Company on December 31, 1989, is as follows:

Tame Company
Balance Sheet
December 31, 1989

Assets		Liabilities & Stockholders' Equity		
Accounts receivable	$ 70,000	Mortgage payable		$ 10,000
Inventory	50,000			
Building (net of depreciation)	120,000	Common stock	200,000	
Land	40,000	Retained earnings	70,000	270,000
Total	$280,000			$280,000

On this balance sheet date the Tame Company is purchased by Aggressive, Incorporated, for $500,000. A listing of identifiable assets acquired (including fair market values) is shown below:

Identifiable Asset	Current Fair Market Value
Accounts receivable	$ 70,000
Inventory	90,000
Building	100,000
Land	200,000
	$460,000

In addition, Aggressive, Incorporated, agrees to assume responsibility for the mortgage payable on the building; the present value of this liability is $10,000.

REQUIRED

(a) Is it surprising that the fair market value of the net assets acquired differs from the values shown on the balance sheet? Explain your answer.
(b) Is it unreasonable for a company to pay $500,000 for a business with net identifiable assets of $450,000 (assets of $460,000 less liability of $10,000)? Explain.
(c) What is the nature of goodwill (as the term is used in financial accounting)? Is there goodwill in this problem? If so, show how it is calculated.

65. *Use of Different Measurement Bases for Assets.*   Different assets are accounted for by using different measurement bases. Five different measurement bases are recognized by generally accepted accounting principles: historical cost, current replacement cost, current market value, expected market value (net realizable value), and present value.

REQUIRED

(a) Define each of the measurement bases listed above.
(b) For each of the assets listed below, identify the proper measurement base to be used.

   (1) accounts receivable
   (2) building
   (3) cash
   (4) deferred income taxes (debit balance)
   (5) goodwill
   (6) inventory (historical cost greater than replacement cost)
   (7) inventory (replacement cost greater than historical cost)
   (8) land

(9) long-term investment in marketable equity securities
(10) marketable equity securities
(11) notes receivable
(12) patents
(13) prepaid insurance

66. *Alternative Measurement Bases for Assets: Return on Assets.* Stickney Wheel Company has provided the net asset valuations at December 31, 1988, and December 31, 1989, displayed in the following table. The firm had no capital transactions (purchases or sales of stock) and paid no dividends during 1989, so that net income is equal to the change in net assets during the year.

	December 31	
	1988	**1989**
	(dollars in millions)	
Net asset measurement base:		
Historical cost	62	70
Current cost	58	56
Current market value	52	50
Expected market value	75	90
Present value of expected cash flows	70	78

REQUIRED

(a) Compute Stickney Wheel Company's net income and return on assets (net income dividend by average net assets) using each of the net asset measurement bases shown above.
(b) Which of the return on asset measures computed in (a) is most useful as a gauge of management's profitable use of assets?
(c) Which of the return on asset measures is most relevant to a decision by management regarding liquidation of the firm or continuation of current operations?
(d) Which of the return on asset measures is most likely to correspond to the rate of return (dividends and capital gains) earned by investors in the firm's common stock during 1989? If the investor's rate of return does not correspond to the ratio selected, what are likely causes for the difference?
(e) Which of the ratios is most relevant in assessing the likely profitability of additional new asset acquisitions, assuming that the firm's product and service mix remain the same?

67. *Issues in Accounting for Human Capital.* The following comments have been excerpted from recent annual reports of three firms.

In looking to the future, we will build on our strongest assets—our employees. Since the company's inception, the recruitment, motivation, and retention of high quality people has been our top priority.

(Air Products and Chemicals)

Sears is a company of people. Their motivation and professionalism are the resources that make Sears what it is today.

(Sears, Roebuck & Co.)

Alaska Airlines is fortunate to have an outstanding team of professional employees. It is another asset we believe is worth nourishing.

(Alaska Airlines)

REQUIRED

(a) Do a firm's employees constitute assets in an economic sense? Explain.
(b) Do a firm's employees meet the FASB's criteria for inclusion as assets in the balance sheet? Explain.
(c) Should a firm capitalize as assets the amounts that it spends in order to recruit, motivate, and maintain its employees?
(d) Are there other methods of valuation (instead of historical cost) that would provide more useful valuations of a firm's "human capital"? Discuss.
(e) If a firm's human capital were to be reported as assets, would these costs require amortization as operating expenses in future periods? What estimates or projections would be required?
(f) If a firm were to curtail its efforts to maintain or expand its human capital, what would be the short-term effects on asset values and net income? (Assume the financial statements are prepared in accordance with GAAP.) What would be the likely longer-term effects?

APPENDIX PROBLEMS

68. *Compound Interest: Compounding Frequency and Present Values.* Present values are affected by the frequency at which future cash flows are compounded.

REQUIRED   Determine the present value of each of the following cash flows:

(a) $1 million to be received in four years at a discount rate of 12% compounded annually.
(b) $1 million to be received in four years at a discount rate of 12% compounded semiannually.
(c) $1 million to be received in four years at a discount rate of 12% compounded monthly.

69. *Compound Interest: Present Values and Future Amounts.* Both present values and future values are a function of the dollar amount of the cash flows, the timing of the cash flows, and the interest rate.

REQUIRED   Determine the present or future values, as requested, in the following situtations:

(a) What is the present value of a series of ten annual cash payments of $10,000, to be paid at the end of each year if the interest rate is 10% per annum?

(b) What is the future amount, at the end of ten years, of a series of ten annual cash payments of $10,000, to be paid at the end of each year, if the interest rate is 10% per annum?

(c) Consider the future amount determined in (b). What is the present value of that future amount, if the interest rate is 10% per annum? Why is your answer the same as the present value determined in (a)?

(d) How much money must a firm deposit in a bank account at the end of each year in order to have an account balance of $1 million at the end of eight years if the account earns 12% per annum?

70. *Compount Interest: Required Annuity Payments.*   The required amount of an annuity payment is affected by the amount of the cash flows to be accumulated, the frequency with which payments are made, and the relevant interest rate.

REQUIRED   Determine the required cash flows (deposited or withdrawn) in each of the following independent cases:

(a) The amount to be deposited at the end of each year for ten years at an interest rate of 8%, in order to have a maturity value of $12 million.

(b) The amount to be deposited at the beginning of each year for ten years at an interest rate of 8%, in order to have a maturity value of $12 million.

(c) The highest equal annual amount that could be withdrawn at the end of each year for five years, from a bank account having an initial balance of $100,000 earning interest at 6% per year.

(d) The highest equal annual amount that could be withdrawn at the beginning of each year for five years, from a bank account having an initial balance of $100,000 earning interest at 6% per year.

71. *Compound Interest: Present Values and Future Values.*   Present values and future (maturity) values are affected by changes in the amount of the cash flows, the interest rate, and the relevant time period.

REQUIRED   Determine the values of the following cash flows, as requested:

(a) Present value of $600,000 to be received at the end of ten years, at a discount rate of 8% per year.

(b) Present value of $100,000 to be received at the end of each year for eight years, at a discount rate of 10% per year.

(c) Present value of $100,000 to be received at the beginning of each year for eight years, at a discount rate of 10% per year.

(d) Maturity value of $400,000 left on deposit for 20 periods at a periodic interest rate of 6%.

(e) Maturity value of $20,000 per year deposited at the end of each year for 20 years, at an annual interest rate of 12%.

(f) Maturity value of $20,000 per period deposited at the beginning of each period for 20 periods, at an annual interest rate of 12%.

The Balance Sheet: Liabilities

Chapter 5 discusses methods of accounting for the assets of the firm. To invest in assets, financial managers must raise funds from a variety of sources. Basically, funds are raised either by borrowing (liabilities) or by owner investment and retained earnings (shareholders' equity). This chapter discusses the methods used in accounting for liabilities. Chapter 7 discusses accounting for the equity of the firm. Both chapters, therefore, focus on the right-hand or "sources" side of the balance sheet.

LIABILITIES DEFINED

The FASB's *Statement of Financial Accounting Concepts No. 6* defines liabilities as "... probable future sacrifices of economic benefits arising from present obligations of a particular entity to transfer assets or provide services to other entities in the future as the result of past transactions or events."[1] The statement also identifies three essential characteristics of a liability:

1. A liability is a present obligation that entails probable future transfer or use of cash, goods, or services.
2. A liability is an unavoidable obligation of the enterprise.
3. The event causing a liability must already have occurred.

Liabilities represent claims against the firm's resources, and the timing of such claims is important to managers, lenders, and investors. For this reason, liabilities are classified as current or noncurrent. **Current liabilities** are defined as "... obligations where liquidation is reasonably expected to require use of existing resources properly classified as current assets or the creation of other current liabilities."[2] All other liabilities are classified as **noncurrent**.

LIABILITY REPORTING

Exhibit 6-1 shows the liabilities and owners' equity sections of the balance sheets of Apple Computer, Inc., at September 30, 1983, and UAL, Inc., at December 31, 1983 (owners' or shareholders' equity is discussed in Chapter 7). The exhibit reveals the following:

1. UAL, Inc., relies heavily on liabilities as a source of funds: over 68 percent ($3.5 billion in liabilities divided by $5.1 billion in total liabilities and shareholders' equity) of its investment in total assets is provided by borrowed capital. Apple Computer, Inc., on the other hand, relies mainly on shareholders' equity: only 32 percent ($179 million in liabilities, noncurrent obligations, and deferred taxes divided by $556 million in total liabilities and shareholders' equity) of its investment in total assets is provided by borrowed capital. All firms rely on borrowed capital (liabilities) to some extent, although the proportion of total funds represented by liabilities varies widely from one firm to another. Managers and outside analysts pay close attention to this proportion. Financial managers, when financing the firm's investment in total assets, attempt to minimize the cost of capital employed, while assuring the solvency of the firm. Lenders and equity

---

[1]*Statement of Financial Accounting Concepts No. 6*, "Elements of Financial Statements" (Stamford, CT: FASB, 1980), par. 35.

[2]*Accounting Research Bulletin No. 43*, "Restatement and Revision of Accounting Research Bulletins" (New York: AICPA, 1953), ch. 3A, par. 7.

investors attempt to assess the effects of a firm's debt and equity securities. It is widely agreed that the cost of capital to a firm and the riskiness of its outstanding securities are affected by its proportion of borrowed capital.

2. Liabilities include more than simple borrowings from lenders. For example, UAL, Inc.'s liabilities include amounts that must be paid to lenders in cash at specific future dates (for example, notes payable, accounts payable, and currently maturing debt); amounts that require services rather than direct cash payments (advance ticket sales and customer deposits); and amounts that are technically not liabilities at all (deferred income taxes). On the other hand, items sometimes classified as shareholders' equity (redeemable preferred stock, for instance) may in economic substance be more similar to debt than to shareholders' equity.

3. Obligations under capital leases appear on the balance sheets of both firms. In this case, the FASB's three "essential characteristics" of a liability (page 290) appear to have been modified, because these amounts depend on future use of the leased facilities. There is sharp debate among accounting policymakers concerning executory contracts in general and the liability reporting of leases in particular. This issue is discussed in Chapter 10, which deals with leases and pension plans.

The discussion in the following pages illustrates methods of accounting for each of the main types of liabilities that appear on the balance sheets of U.S. firms. Where possible, reference will be made to the examples in Exhibit 6-1.

ACCOUNTING FOR CURRENT LIABILITIES

Current liabilities are short-term debts—those requiring the use of resources classified as current assets. These liabilities are usually one of the following types: an obligation to pay cash or other assets to an outside entity in the form of accounts payable, notes payable, or accrued liabilities; an obligation to deliver goods or services for which cash or other assets have been received in advance; or an obligation under product warranties or guarantees tied to previously recorded revenues. Each of these will be discussed briefly.

Accounts Payable

The most common examples of obligations requiring the payment of cash or other assets to an outside entity involve **accounts payable.** This is because most business transactions with suppliers and customers involve short-term credit, with payment made over short periods (from 30 to 60 days). Chapter 5 discusses accounting for customer accounts receivable; an account receivable of one firm is, of course, an account payable of another firm. To illustrate, assume that a firm purchased inventory costing $250,000. The firm will pay that

Exhibit 6-1
Liability Reporting: Two Examples

UAL, Incorporated
Statement of Consolidated Financial Position
December 31, 1983
(in thousands)

Liabilities and Shareholders' Equity

Current liabilities:	Notes payable and commercial paper	$ 187,940
	Long-term debt maturing within one year	87,647
	Current obligations under capital leases	42,938
	Advance ticket sales and customer deposits	453,232
	Accounts payable	398,084
	Accrued salaries, wages and benefits	536,815
	Other accrued liabilities	227,580
		1,934,236
Long-term debt		691,879
Long-term obligations under capital leases		619,388
Deferred credits and other liabilities:	Deferred income taxes	260,670
	Other	30,125
		290,795
Redeemable preferred stock:	5½% cumulative prior preferred stock, $100 par value	4,929
Nonredeemable preferred stock, common stock and other shareholders' equity:	Preferred stock, no par value; authorized 16,000,000 shares—	
	Series A $.40 cumulative (convertible); issued 514,861 shares in 1983 and 526,422 shares in 1982; involuntary liquidation value $25 per share, aggregating $12,872,000 in 1983	2,574
	Series B $2.40 cumulative (convertible); outstanding 8,000,000 shares in 1983; involuntary liquidation value $25 per share, aggregating $200,000,000	193,234
	Common stock, $5 par value; authorized 50,000,000 shares; outstanding 34,484,544 shares in 1983 and 29,609,734 shares in 1982	172,423
	Additional capital invested	555,427
	Retained earnings	681,383
	Accumulated foreign currency translation adjustments	(10,507)
	Less—454,261 shares of Series A $.40 cumulative (convertible) preferred stock held in treasury	(2,118)
		1,592,416
Commitments and contingent liabilities	(See note on contingencies and commitments)	
		$5,133,643

Apple Computer, Incorporated
Consolidated Balance Sheet
September 30, 1983
(in thousands)

Liabilities and Shareholders' Equity

Current liabilities:

Notes payable to banks	$ –
Accounts payable	52,701
Accrued compensation and employee benefits	15,770
Income taxes payable	–
Accrued marketing and distribution	21,551
Other current liabilities	38,764
Total current liabilities	128,786
Non-current obligations under capital leases	1,308
Deferred taxes on income	48,584

Shareholders' equity:

Common stock, no par value, 160,000,000 shares authorized, 59,198,397 shares issued and outstanding	183,715
Retained earnings	195,046
	378,761
Notes receivable from shareholders	(860)
Total shareholders' equity	377,901
	$556,579

Sources: UAL, Incorporated, *Annual Report,* 1983; Apple Computer, Incorporated, *Annual Report,* 1983.

amount to the supplier in 60 days. The entry to record the purchase would be

dr.	Inventory	250,000	
	cr. Accounts Payable		250,000

The entry made to record the payment 60 days later is

dr.	Accounts Payable	250,000	
	cr. Cash		250,000

Often, suppliers offer **cash discounts** for prompt payment of accounts payable. For example, payment terms of 2/20 net 60 offer a 2 percent discount if the bill is paid within 20 days; otherwise the full amount is due in 60 days. Of course, if a firm foregoes the cash discount and elects instead to pay the account in 60 days, it has in effect borrowed from the supplier for a period of 40 days (60 days less the 20 days in the discount period) at a cost of 2 percent. Financial managers will compare this cost of trade credit with the costs of other types of debt and equity financing in deciding whether to pay bills within the discount period.

To illustrate accounting for cash discounts, assume that the inventory purchase described above entails payment terms of 2/20 net 60. Assume also that management has decided to pay such bills within the discount period. The entry to record the purchase would be

| dr. | Inventory | 245,000 | |
| | cr.   Accounts Payable | | 245,000 |

Note that the inventory is recorded at the net amount to be paid to the supplier ($250,000 less the discount of 2 percent, or $5,000). The entry to record payment within 20 days would be

| dr. | Accounts Payable | 245,000 | |
| | cr.   Cash | | 245,000 |

Notes Payable

Much short-term borrowing in contemporary business entails the signing of a formal **promissory note** with a fixed maturity date and an explicitly stated interest rate. For example, assume that on April 1 a firm borrowed $100,000 from a bank and signed a note promising to repay that amount in three months (90 days) at an interest rate of 18 percent per annum. (Interest expense for 90 days [$\frac{1}{4}$ of a year] at 18 percent per annum is $4,500 [$100,000 \times \frac{1}{4}$ of 18%].) The entry to record the borrowing would be

| dr. | Cash | 100,000 | |
| | cr.   Notes Payable | | 100,000 |

The entry to record payment of interest and principal 90 days later would be

dr.	Interest Expense	4,500	
dr.	Notes Payable	100,000	
	cr. Cash		104,500

Accrued Liabilities

In addition to accounts payable and notes payable, the liability reports included in Exhibit 6-1 show various **accrued liabilities.** These items represent expenses that have been incurred during the period, but have not yet been paid, and are thus liabilities at the end of the period. For example, assume that a firm has a weekly payroll of $200,000 that is paid each Friday. Assume also that December 31, the financial report date, falls on Wednesday. Since as of Wednesday, December 31, the firm has not yet recorded the salaries expense for Monday through Wednesday of that week, the following accrual entry is made prior to preparing the financial statements.

| dr. | Salaries Expense | 120,000 | |
| | cr.   Accrued Salaries Payable | | 120,000 |

The income statement for the year includes the $120,000 of salaries expense ($200,000 weekly payroll × 60%), and the ending balance sheet shows a liability of $120,000 for accrued salaries.

Revenues Received in Advance

Another type of current liabilities involves obligations to deliver goods or services for which cash or other assets have been received in advance. Firms sometimes receive payments from customers before performing services or delivering products. For example, Exhibit 6-1 shows that UAL, Inc., has an obligation to provide future services to customers in order to earn assets already in its possession. When UAL, Inc., receives advance payments or deposits from customers, they are recorded as follows:

dr.	Cash	XXX
	cr. Advance Ticket Sales and Customer Deposits	XXX

Unlike accounts payable, this obligation will not be discharged by the payment of cash to a lender. When UAL, Inc., performs those actions needed to earn the revenues already received, the entry will be

dr.	Advance Ticket Sales and Customer Deposits	XXX
	cr. Passenger Revenues	XXX

To reduce the obligation and report revenues as services are performed.

It is, of course, likely that the firm will incur various expenses in earning these revenues. Moreover, a portion of any income on the transaction will be taxed and paid to the government. The net income after tax will then increase the firm's owners' equity. In effect, revenues received in advance consist of two elements: (1) amounts that will be paid as expenses in earning those revenues and (2) an amount that will be credited to owners' equity.

Warranty Obligations

The last type of current liability to be discussed here involves obligations incurred in connection with product warranties. Companies often guarantee the performance of their products and promise to remedy any deficiencies during a specific period after sale. For example, assume that Major Appliance Company provides customers with a two-year warranty for repair parts and service. The firm's management estimates that over the warranty period the firm will incur warranty costs equal to about 20 percent of the sales price of the product. During 1987, the company's sales of major appliances amounted to $180 million, and the company has spent $10 million providing warranty repairs on appliances sold during that year. The following entries would be recorded in 1987:

| dr. | Accounts Receivable (or Cash) | 180,000,000 | |
| | cr. Sales Revenue | | 180,000,000 |

To record sales of major appliances.

| dr. | Warranty Expense | 36,000,000 | |
| | cr. Warranty Obligation | | 36,000,000 |

To record estimated expense of two-year warranty on 1987 sales—20 percent of $180 million, or $36 million.

| dr. | Warranty Obligation | 10,000,000 | |
| | cr. Cash (or Other Assets) | | 10,000,000 |

To record actual spending on warranty repairs during 1987.

Notice that the full estimated warranty expense of $36 million is recorded in 1987, the period in which the related revenues are recorded. This is necessary in order for revenues and expenses to be properly matched. The estimated warranty expense of $36 million will not provide revenues in future periods; rather, this expense is directly associated with the sales revenue recorded in 1987.

In future periods, as additional warranty costs related to 1987 sales are incurred, the following entry will be made:

| dr. | Warranty Obligation | XXX | |
| | cr. Cash (or Other Assets) | | XXX |

Current Liabilities: a Summary

This section has briefly described accounting for several different types of current obligations: liabilities that require that cash or other assets be disbursed to specific lenders (such as accounts payable, notes payable, and accrued liabilities); revenues received in advance that require that the firm perform certain actions to satisfy the related obligations; and warranty obligations, based on estimated future costs of satisfying product guarantees related to past and present sales. These types of liabilities are similar in obligating the firm to do something in the short-term future, yet dissimilar in terms of the claims that they make against the firm's assets.

ACCOUNTING FOR NONCURRENT LIABILITIES

The remaining sections of this chapter discuss items classified in the noncurrent liabilities section of the balance sheet. Some of these items (long-term commitments and contingent obligations, for example) are technically not debts, even though they may be important in assessing a firm's debt position.

In order to understand accounting for noncurrent liabilities, the reader must be familiar with the concepts of compound interest and present and future values. These concepts are explained and illustrated in Appendix C at the end of Chapter 5. A set of present value tables is also included in that appendix (Tables C-1 and C-2). These tables will be employed at various points in the following discussion.

Long-term Notes

One of several ways that a company may incur noncurrent liabilities is to issue a note payable in exchange for cash or other assets. If the note is interest bearing, the rate of interest is stated on the note agreement, and the lender is repaid the amount borrowed (the principal of the loan), plus the interest. Alternatively, the firm may issue a noninterest-bearing note. In the case of a noninterest-bearing note, the lender pays the borrower less than the face amount of the loan, and the difference (termed the loan discount) constitutes the interest on the note.

To illustrate an **interest-bearing note,** assume that on January 1, 1987, a firm borrows $1 million to be repaid in three years. The note payable has a stated interest rate of 14 percent, payable at the end of each year. The borrowing firm records the obligation as follows

```
dr.   Cash                          1,000,000
      cr.   Noncurrent Note Payable              1,000,000
      Proceeds of note, to be repaid December 31, 1989.
```

At the end of each year, the interest expense ($1,000,000 × 14% interest = $140,000) and payment entry is

```
dr.   Interest Expense        140,000
      cr.   Cash                            140,000
```

To illustrate a **noninterest-bearing note,** assume that the same firm signs a note promising to pay $1 million at the end of three years. Nominally this note does not bear interest. Prospective lenders will insist on earning the current rate of interest on their money, however, which we will assume to be 14 percent per year. Thus, the lender will be willing to loan *the present value* of $1 million to be repaid in three years, discounted at 14 percent per annum.

$1,000,000	(future amount, due in three years)
× .675	(present value factor, three years at 14 percent [Table C-1])
$ 675,000	(present value of loan)

Computing the present value of $1 million, we see that the lender will be willing to loan no more than $675,000, because if this amount is put on deposit for three years at 14 percent compounded annually, it will amount to $1 million at the end of that time ($675,000 × $[1 + .14]^3$ = $1 million). This implies that the borrower's promise to pay $1 million to the lender in three years is worth just $675,000 today. In other words, the note is discounted by $325,000 ($1 million − $675,000) to provide the lender with interest income.

The value of the borrower's note will increase as time passes, and at the end of three years the value of the note will be $1 million, payable on that date. Exhibit 6-2 shows the change over time in the present value of the note. Notice that the interest is larger in each successive year. This occurs because the borrower is not paying the interest at the end of each of the three years. The loan balance increases because the interest not paid is added to the balance payable. Thus, the borrower has higher interest expense in successive years because the interest expense is 14 percent of the new balance. The total interest over the life of the loan is $325,000 ($1 million − $675,000).

The borrower would account for the loan over its three-year term as shown in the entries below. (The interest expense amount in these entries is computed by calculating the 14 percent interest on each year's beginning balance, as shown in Exhibit 6-2.)

Jan. 1, 1987	dr.		Cash	675,000	
	dr.		Note Payable Discount	325,000	
		cr.	Note Payable		1,000,000
Dec. 31, 1987	dr.		Interest Expense	94,500	
		cr.	Note Payable Discount		94,500
Dec. 31, 1988	dr.		Interest Expense	107,730	
		cr.	Note Payable Discount		107,730
Dec. 31, 1989	dr.		Interest Expense	122,770	
		cr.	Note Payable Discount		122,770
	dr.		Note Payable	1,000,000	
		cr.	Cash		1,000,000

Exhibit 6-2
Present Value of Notes Payable at Various Dates

	(1) Balance, Beginning of Year	(2) Interest (1) × 14%	(3) Balance, End of Year (1) + (2)
First year	$675,000	$ 94,500	$ 769,500
Second year	769,500	107,730	877,230
Third year	877,230	122,770*	1,000,000
Total interest		$325,000	

*The actual figure is $122,812.20, and the difference is due to rounding.

Balance sheets prepared by the borrower before the note is repaid would show the note payable less the remaining discount; the discount is a contra account that is subtracted from the face amount of the note. For example, on December 31, 1988, at the end of the second year, the note would be reported as

Note payable	$1,000,000
Less: Unamortized note payable discount	(122,770)
	$ 877,230

In the preceding examples, notes payable were issued for cash. Frequently, notes are issued for noncash considerations such as property or services. In these cases, if the note does not state a rate of interest (or if the stated rate of interest differs from current interest rates), it will be necessary to discount the note at current interest rates in order to determine the cost basis of the property or services received.

Consider this illustration. Assume that on January 1, 1988, Salem, Inc., acquired equipment from Fulcrum Corporation in exchange for Salem's noninterest-bearing note promising to pay $1 million per year at the end of each of the next five years. To record the purchase, it is first necessary to discount the note repayments at an appropriate rate of interest, which we will assume to be 10 percent. As discussed in Appendix C, this note is an annuity (a series of equal amounts paid at equal intervals), and its present value is computed as follows:

$1,000,000	(future payments, each year for five years)
× 3.791	(annuity present value factor, five years at 10 percent [Table C-2])
$3,791,000	(present value of loan)

The cost of the equipment is therefore $3,791,000, because this is the present value of the liability incurred in order to purchase the equipment. The entry to record the equipment purchase on January 1, 1988, is

dr.	Equipment	3,791,000	
dr.	Discount on Installment Note Payable	1,209,000	
	cr. Installment Note Payable		5,000,000

At December 31, 1988, the interest expense (10% × $3,791,000 = $379,100) is recorded:

dr.	Interest Expense	379,100	
	cr. Discount on Installment Note Payable		379,100

And the first installment payment is made and recorded.

dr.	Installment Note Payable	1,000,000	
	cr. Cash		1,000,000

Exhibit 6-3 shows the carrying value (installment note payable less discount) of the installment note and the calculation of interest expense each year. Interest expense is less in each successive year because the loan balance is gradually repaid over the life of the loan. Each year's interest expense is less than the amount of cash repaid to the lender, and the difference is a reduction in the loan balance.

Bonds Payable

Business enterprises frequently sell bonds to investors as one way of issuing noncurrent debt. A **bond** is a promise to pay a sum of money (called the **principal**) at a specified maturity date and to pay interest periodically, usually every six months. These interest payments are made at a specified interest rate on the principal amount of the bond. The rate is referred to as the **coupon rate of interest.**

To illustrate accounting for bonds, assume that on January 1, 1987, Lever, Inc., issues bonds with a principal amount of $100 million to investors. The bonds have a 12 percent coupon rate of interest, paid semiannually. This means that the bonds pay total interest each year of $12 million (12 percent of $100 million), and that the interest payments are made in two $6-million installments—one on June 30 and one on December 31. The Lever, Inc., bonds have a ten-year term to maturity; the principal amount will thus be repaid on December 31, 1996.

Proceeds of the bond issue   The amount that Lever, Inc., will receive for the bonds it issues depends on the prevailing market rate of interest at the time the

Exhibit 6-3
Installment Note Payable and Interest Expense

Salem, Inc.

| | Balance, Beginning of Year | | | (4) Interest Expense | (5) Note | Balance, End of Year | |
	(1) Installment Note Payable	(2) Discount	(3) Net (1) − (2)	(3) × 10%	Repayment	(6) Installment Note Payable	(7) Discount
1986	$5,000,000	$1,209,000	$3,791,000	$379,100	$1,000,000	$4,000,000	$829,900
1987	4,000,000	829,900	3,170,100	317,010	1,000,000	3,000,000	512,890
1988	3,000,000	512,890	2,487,110	248,711	1,000,000	2,000,000	264,179
1989	2,000,000	264,179	1,735,821	173,582	1,000,000	1,000,000	90,597
1990	1,000,000	90,597	909,403	90,940	1,000,000	0	343*

*Due to rounding differences.

bonds are sold. If the market rate of interest equals the coupon rate, the bonds will sell at par—that is, at their principal or face value. This occurs because the interest coupon is sufficient to earn a competitive return for investors. If the market rate of interest exceeds the coupon rate, the bonds will sell at a discount—investors will pay no more than the present value of the bond interest and principal payments, computed at the prevailing market interest rate. The final possibility is that the bonds will sell for more than their face value. If the market rate is less than the coupon rate, the bonds will sell at a premium because the present value of the bond interest and principal payments exceeds the principal amount of the bonds.

The relationship between the coupon rate, the market interest rate, and the proceeds of the bond issue may be summarized as follows:

Interest Rates	Proceeds to Bond Issuer
Coupon rate equals market rate	Principal or face amount
Coupon rate less than market rate	Less than face amount (at a discount)
Coupon rate exceeds market rate	More than face amount (at a premium)

Exhibit 6-4 shows the computations for the present value of the Lever, Inc., bonds described above, assuming three different market interest rates: (a) 12 percent—equal to the 12-percent coupon rate, so that the bonds sell at par value; (b) 16 percent—greater than the coupon rate, so that the bonds sell at a discount; and (c) 8 percent—less than the coupon rate, so that the bonds sell at a premium. Bear in mind that the same set of cash flows is being valued in each case; the bond issue is a promise by Lever, Inc., to repay $100 million in ten years' time, and to pay an additional $6 million every six months for ten years. The *present value* of this set of cash flows depends, however, on the market rate of interest.

The actual amount of interest to be paid by Lever, Inc., is dictated by the market rate of interest (see Exhibit 6-4). The bonds obligate Lever, Inc., to pay a total of $220 million to bondholders (20 semiannual payments of $6 million, plus the principal payment of $100 million). If the bonds sell at par, Lever's interest expense over the ten-year period is $120 million ($220 million in payments less $100 million in proceeds when issued). If the bonds sell at a discount, Lever's interest expense over the ten-year period is $139,592,000 ($220 million in payments less $80,408,000 in proceeds when issued). If the bonds sell at a premium, Lever's interest expense over the ten years is $92,860,000 ($220 million in payments less $127,140,000 in proceeds when issued). In other words, the actual interest expense is equal to the total interest coupons plus the bond discount (or less the bond premium) when the bonds are sold.

Recording the proceeds of the bond issue   Lever, Inc., will increase cash and increase bonds outstanding (a noncurrent liability) when the bonds are

Exhibit 6-4

Present Value of Lever, Inc., Bonds at Various Market Rates of Interest

Description of Bond Issue

$100 million principal amount, 12% coupon interest rate paid semiannually each June 30 and December 31; issued January 1, 1987, maturing in ten years on December 31, 1996.

Case A: Bonds Sold at Par

Coupon interest rate equals the market rate, 12% compounded semiannually. Present value of principal payment due in 10 years (20 six-month periods), at 6% per period

Amount ×	Present Value Factor (Table C-1)	
($100,000,000) ×	(0.312)	= $ 31,200,000

Present value of interest coupon payments due every six months

Amount × Present Value of Annuity Factor (Table C-2)		
($6,000,000) ×	(11.470)	= 68,800,000*

Total present value at issue date		$100,000,000

Case B: Bonds Sold at a Discount

Coupon interest rate is less than the market rate, which is 16% compounded semiannually.
Present value of principal payment due in 10 years (20 six-month periods), at 8% per period

Amount ×	Present Value Factor (Table C-1)	
($100,000,000) ×	(0.215)	= $21,500,000

Present value of interest coupon payments due every six months

Amount × Present Value of Annuity Factor (Table C-2)		
($6,000,000) ×	(9.818)	= 58,908,000

Total present value at issue date		$80,408,000

Case C: Bonds Sold at a Premium

Coupon interest rate exceeds the market rate, which is 8% compounded semiannually.

Present value of principal payment due in 10 years (20 six-month periods), at 4% per period

Amount ×   Present Value Factor (Table C-1)

($100,000,000) ×   (0.456)   = $45,600,000

Present value of interest coupon payments due each six months

Amount × Present Value of Annuity Factor (Table C-2)

($6,000,000) ×   (13.590)   = 81,540,000

Total present value at issue date $127,140,000

---

*Due to rounding in the present value tables, the actual product of $6,000,000 × 11.470 is $68,820,000. For illustrative purposes, the $20,000 rounding difference will be ignored.

sold. The form of the entry depends on whether the bonds sell at par, at a discount, or at a premium. For the three cases shown in Exhibit 6-4, the following entries apply:

Case A: Bonds Sold at Par

dr.	Cash	100,000,000	
	cr. Bonds Payable		100,000,000

Case B: Bonds Sold at a Discount

dr.	Cash	80,408,000	
dr.	Bond Discount	19,592,000	
	cr. Bonds Payable		100,000,000

Case C: Bonds Sold at a Premium

dr.	Cash	127,140,000	
	cr. Bonds Payable		100,000,000
	cr. Bonds Premium		27,140,000

Notice that Case B involves a bond discount account, and Case C involves a bond premium account. These accounts are used to adjust the carrying value of the bonds on the balance sheet. Exhibit 6-5 shows how the bonds would be described on the balance sheet prepared by Lever, Inc., on January 1, 1987 (the date of issue).

Exhibit 6-5

Balance Sheet Reporting of Bonds Payable (at date of issue)

Case A: Bonds Sold at Par

Noncurrent liabilities:

Bonds payable	$100,000,000

Case B: Bonds Sold at a Discount

Bonds payable	$100,000,000
Less: Bond discount	(19,592,000)
Carrying value	$ 80,408,000

Case C: Bonds Sold at a Premium

Bonds payable	$100,000,000
Add: Bond premium	27,140,000
Carrying value	$127,140,000

Recording interest expense   In order to calculate interest expense, the carrying value of the bonds at the beginning of each interest period is multiplied by the market rate of interest when the bonds were sold. For the Lever, Inc., bonds sold at par (Case A), the entries below would be made to record interest expense and payments during 1987. (In each instance, the interest expense is calculated by multiplying the $100-million carrying value by the 6 percent semiannual interest rate.)

June 30	dr.	Interest Expense	6,000,000	
	cr.	Cash		6,000,000
Dec. 31	dr.	Interest Expense	6,000,000	
	cr.	Cash		6,000,000

Since the carrying value of the bonds remains at $100 million over the entire ten-year life of the issue, this same entry would recur each interest period. The interest expense and the interest coupon paid are the same each period.

For the Lever, Inc., bonds sold at a discount (Case B), the entries below would be made to record interest expense and payments during 1987. (The interest expense calculation of carrying value multiplied by the market rate of interest at the time of issuance reflects the higher market rate of interest— .08 × $80,408,000.)

June 30	dr.	Interest Expense	6,432,640	
	cr.	Bond Discount		432,640
	cr.	Cash		6,000,000

As a result of this entry on June 30, the carrying value of the bonds increases because a portion of the bond discount has been amortized. The bond discount, which initially was $19,592,000, has now been reduced to $19,159,360 ($19,592,000 − $432,640). The carrying value of the bonds correspondingly increases to $80,840,640 ($100,000,000 − $19,159,360). Since the carrying value of the bonds has increased, the interest expense will increase in the next interest period also. (The interest expense calculation for the next entry employs the increased carrying value — .08 × $80,840,640.) The entry at December 31, 1987, is

Dec. 31	dr.	Interest Expense	6,467,251	
	cr.	Bond Discount		467,251
	cr.	Cash		6,000,000

Each successive period's interest expense will be higher because the market interest rate when the bonds were sold (16 percent paid semiannually, or 8 percent every six months) is multiplied by a carrying value that increases each period. Exhibit 6-6, Case B, extends the example for additional interest periods.

For the Lever, Inc., bonds sold at a premium (Case C), the interest calculation causes the carrying value of the bonds to decrease in each successive period so that interest expense declines over the life of the issue. The entries to record interest expense and payments for 1987 are shown below. (The interest expense calculation for the first entry is .04 × $127,140,000; for the second — .04 × $126,225,600, reflecting the decreasing carrying value of the bonds.)

June 30	dr.	Interest Expense	5,085,600	
	dr.	Bond Premium	914,400	
	cr.	Cash		6,000,000

Dec. 31	dr.	Interest Expense	5,049,024	
	dr.	Bond Premium	950,976	
	cr.	Cash		6,000,000

Calculations for additional interest periods are given in Exhibit 6-6, Case C.

To recapitulate, each period's bond interest expense is calculated by multiplying the market interest rate when the bonds were issued times the carrying value of the bonds at the start of that interest period. If bonds are sold at par, the carrying value is the same each interest period; as a result, the interest expense is constant from period to period. If bonds are sold at a discount, the carrying value increases each period as the discount is amortized, and the interest expense also increases. If bonds are sold at a premium, the carrying value decreases each period as the premium is amortized, and the interest expense decreases also.

Exhibit 6-6

Bonds Payable Interest Expenses and Amortization of Bond Premiums and Discounts

Lever, Inc.

Case B: Bonds Sold at a Discount
Ten-year bonds with 12% semiannual coupon, sold to yield 16%

Book Value, Start of Period

Period Ending	(1) Principal	(2) Less: Discount	(3) Book Value (1) − (2)	(4) Interest Expense (3) × 8%	(5) Discount Amortization (4) − $6,000,000	(6) Discount, End of Period (2) − (5)
1987: June 30	$100,000,000	$19,592,000	$80,408,000	$ 6,432,640	$ 432,640	$19,159,360
Dec. 31	100,000,000	19,159,360	80,840,640	6,467,251	$ 467,251	18,692,109
1988: June 30	100,000,000	18,692,109	81,307,891	6,504,631	$ 504,631	18,187,478
Dec. 31	100,000,000	18,187,478	81,812,522	6,545,001	545,001	17,642,477
⋮	⋮	⋮	⋮	⋮	⋮	⋮
1996: Dec. 31	100,000,000	1,844,000	98,156,000	7,852,480	1,852,480	8,480*
				$139,592,000	$19,592,000	

Case C: Bonds Sold at a Premium
Ten-year bonds with 12% semiannual coupon, sold to yield 8%

Book Value, Start of Period

Period Ending	(1) Principal	(2) Plus: Premium	(3) Book Value (1) + (2)	(4) Interest Expense (3) × 4%	(5) Premium Amortization $6,000,000 − (4)	(6) Premium, End of Period (2) − (5)
1987: June 30	$100,000,000	$27,140,000	$127,140,000	$ 5,085,600	$ 914,400	$26,225,600
Dec. 31	100,000,000	26,225,600	126,225,600	5,049,024	950,976	25,274,630
1988: June 30	100,000,000	25,274,630	125,274,630	5,010,985	989,015	24,285,615
Dec. 31	100,000,000	24,285,615	124,285,615	4,971,425	1,028,575	23,257,040
⋮	⋮	⋮	⋮	⋮	⋮	⋮
1996: Dec. 31	100,000,000	1,972,000	101,972,000	4,078,880	1,921,120	50,880*
				$92,860,000	$27,140,000	

*Non-zero due to rounding in the present value tables

When bonds are sold at premiums or discounts, the carrying value of the bonds is adjusted each interest period. Be aware, however, that these changes in carrying values are not departures from historical cost and do not constitute attempts to revalue the bond obligations at their current market values. The interest calculations described for Lever, Inc., are designed to charge each period at the interest rate existing when the bonds were issued. Market interest rates change frequently, causing the current market values of outstanding bonds to change as well. However, these changes in market interest rates and current values do not affect the calculation of bond interest expenses or carrying values.

Retirement of bonds prior to maturity   Firms often buy back their outstanding bonds prior to the scheduled maturity date. In most cases, the market value of the bonds differs from their carrying value, due mainly to changes in market interest rates. If market interest rates have risen following bond issuance, the market price of the bonds will be less than their carrying value. If, on the other hand, market interest rates have fallen following bond issuance, the market price of the bonds will exceed their carrying value. Market prices of outstanding bonds fluctuate because investors continually revalue the bonds' contractual cash flows (interest coupons and principal repayment) at current market interest rates. In any event, when a firm buys back its own bonds, any difference between the carrying value of the bonds and the amount paid to reacquire them will be interpreted as a gain or loss.

The FASB specifies the accounting rules for the **early retirement of debt** and requires that material gains or losses be reported as extraordinary items on the income statement.[3] These reporting requirements were imposed because rising interest rates throughout the 1970s caused the market values of corporate bonds to fall well below their carrying values, and many corporations reacquired their outstanding bonds and reported the resulting gains as elements of income from continuing operations. Often, the firms retired existing debt and issued additional debt at the current higher market rates of interest. Some analysts maintained that the retirement of low-interest debt and subsequent issuance of high-interest debt was motivated largely by the resultant accounting gains, rather than by sound financial reasoning. Moreover, it was argued that the inclusion of such accounting gains as income from recurring operations was misleading. Since the gains were not disclosed separately, they made it difficult to assess a firm's operating success. Critics also objected to the considerable discretion permitted management over the timing of business income by the recording of gains or losses when debt was retired. All of this criticism eventually resulted in the drafting of more restrictive reporting requirements.

To illustrate accounting for debt retirement, we will return to the example of the Lever, Inc., bonds described earlier. Assume that the bonds were sold at

---

[3]*Statement of Financial Accounting Standards No. 4*, "Reporting Gains and Losses from Extinguishment of Debt" (Stamford, CT: FASB, 1975), par. 8.

par on January 1, 1987, when the coupon rate and market rate of interest were both 12 percent compounded semiannually. Assume also that two and one-half years later, on June 30, 1989, the market interest rate has risen to 16 percent compounded semiannually, so that the market value of the firm's outstanding bonds has fallen. The market value of the bonds is determined by discounting the remaining contractual cash payments on the bonds (principal amount of $100 million due in seven and one-half years [on December 31, 1996] and fifteen semiannual interest payments of $6 million). The calculations are as follows:

Present value at June 30, 1989, of bond principal

Dollar Amount × Discount Factor (Table C-1) 15 Periods at 8%

$100,000,000 × 0.315   = $31,500,000

Present value at June 30, 1989, of interest coupons

Dollar Amount
  per Period   × Discount Factor (Table C-2) 15 Periods at 8%

$6,000,000 × 8.559   =   51,354,000
                                              $82,854,000

The market value of the Lever, Inc., bonds is $82,854,000 on June 30, 1989, and the carrying value of the bonds for financial accounting purposes is $100 million because the bonds were issued at par value two and one-half years earlier. Lever, Inc., has benefitted economically from the rise in interest rates. The economic benefit occurs as interest rates rise, but it is not recognized for accounting purposes unless (and until) management buys back the outstanding bonds.[4] For this reason, management can control the timing of the effect on income. If the bonds were bought back and retired at June 30, 1989, the entry would be

dr.	Bonds Payable	100,000,000	
	cr. Cash		82,854,000
	cr. Gain on Bond Retirement		17,146,000

To retire bonds with a book value of $100 million, for a cash payment of $82,854,000.

---

[4]If the bonds were to remain outstanding until maturity, the economic benefit would be reflected in the fact that interest expense reported on the income statement would be lower than the prevailing market rate of interest.

If, on the other hand, management should choose not to retire the bonds, there would be no gain recorded in 1989.[5]

In the bond retirement example above it was assumed that the bonds were initially issued at par value, and as a result the carrying value of the bonds was equal to the principal amount of the bonds. If, in contrast, the bonds were not sold at par value and there is unamortized bond discount or premium related to bonds being retired prior to maturity, then the carrying value will differ from the principal amount of the bonds. In such cases, the gain or loss on bond retirement is the difference between the carrying value and the amount paid to retire the bonds.

In some cases, corporations issue convertible debt (debt that may be converted at the investor's option into other securities—usually common stock of the issuing firm). The methods of accounting for convertible debt will be discussed in Chapter 7.

This concludes our discussion of the accounting methods used for corporate bonds. The remaining sections of the chapter deal with additional actual and potential claims against the firm's resources, where the nature of the liability to be reported (if any) is a matter of some controversy.

Contingent Obligations and Commitments

Notice in Exhibit 6-1 that UAL, Inc., includes a caption on its December 31, 1983 balance sheet for "Commitments and Contingent Liabilities." No dollar amount is given; instead, the reader is referred to an explanatory footnote, reproduced here in Exhibit 6-7. The FASB defines **contingencies** as existing conditions that are uncertain as to possible gains or losses, but that will be resolved by the occurrence of future events.[6]

In the example presented in Exhibit 6-7, UAL, Inc., describes in detail the status of a lawsuit in which the firm is involved and states that management is unable to determine whether its effects will materially affect UAL's financial position. The future event that will resolve the contingency is the decision of the trial court hearing the lawsuit. UAL also reports that it is contingently liable as guarantor of certain indebtedness of other firms. The future event leading to resolution in the latter instance is the repayment (or default) on that debt by the other firms.

Different levels of disclosure are required for contingent liabilities, depending on the probability of occurrence and the estimability of the dollar amount involved. In *SFAS No. 5*, the FASB uses the terms *probable, reasonably possible,*

---

[5]Technically, the firm need not buy back its outstanding bonds. In a transaction called *defeasance*, a firm may instead set up a trust and irrevocably fund that trust with government securities (U.S. Treasury Bonds, for example) having interest coupons and maturity value sufficient to repay the debt. Even though the debt is not repurchased, the firm then recognizes gain or loss on any debt that is funded by defeasance.

[6]*Statement of Financial Accounting Standards No. 5,* "Accounting for Contingencies" (Stamford, CT: FASB, 1975), par 1.

Exhibit 6-7

UAL, Inc., Footnote Disclosures of Contingencies and Commitments

---

Contingencies and Commitments

The companies have certain contingencies resulting from litigation and claims incident to the ordinary course of business. Among such contingencies is *McDonald v. United Air Lines, Inc.*, a lawsuit in which the Federal Court has determined that United's "no-marriage rule" for stewardesses violated Title VII of the Civil Rights Act of 1964 and that United is liable for damages. Approximately 1,800 former stewardesses may be eligible for class membership and entitlement to reinstatement to the flight attendant position and/or back pay from the dates of their resignation or discharge to the present time, less an offset of amounts which they earned elsewhere or amounts which they could have earned with reasonable diligence. In 1982, the trial court ruled that all claimants who could prove they left their position with United only because of the no-marriage rule would be entitled to reinstatement. For job-related functions, however, the court accorded them only the actual seniority they accrued as stewardesses. That decision was affirmed by the U.S. Court of Appeals on September 21, 1983; however, a petition for Supreme Court review has been filed by the claimants. A hearing on the amount of classwide back pay was held in November and December 1982, and the trial court's decision is expected sometime in 1984. Hearings on individual claims for class membership began in January 1983 and will likely continue throughout 1984.

Management is unable at this time to estimate the potential amount or range of loss to which United may be subject as a result of the *McDonald* lawsuit and to determine whether its ultimate disposition will materially affect UAL's consolidated financial position. With respect to the remaining contingencies resulting from litigation and claims incident to the ordinary course of business, management believes, after considering a number of factors, including (but not limited to) the views of legal counsel, the nature of the contingencies and the prior experience of the companies, that the ultimate disposition of such contingencies will not materially affect UAL's consolidated financial position.

As of December 31, 1983, certain indebtedness (and related accrued interest) of others amounting to approximately $109,000,000 had been guaranteed by UAL or its subsidiaries. This amount includes $71,000,000 of airport lease revenue bonds guaranteed by UAL.

UAL's consolidated commitments at December 31, 1983 for the purchase of property and equipment, principally aircraft, approximated $1,330,000,000 (after deducting advance payments). An estimated $220,000,000 of these commitments will be spent during 1984, $310,000,000 in 1985, $290,000,000 in 1986, $270,000,000 in 1987 and $240,000,000 in 1988. The major commitments are for 20 B-767 aircraft, five of which are presently scheduled for delivery in each of the years 1985–1988. However, in December 1983 United reached agreements in principle with The Boeing Company and Pratt & Whitney to amend the existing contracts for the purchase of these B-767 aircraft. Under the agreements in principle, delivery would take place from 1987 through 1991. The agreements in principle would also allow United to substitute B-737-300 or other newly developed Boeing aircraft for some or all of the 20 B-767 aircraft or to cancel delivery of all of the aircraft upon payment of a fixed penalty. United's decision to substitute aircraft or cancel delivery would not be required until October 1985. The revised delivery schedule, if agreed to and assuming that there would be no aircraft substitutions or cancellations, would result in revised estimated expenditures of December 31, 1983 commitments as follows: 1984 — $190,000,000; 1985 — $100,000,000; 1986 — $60,000,000; 1987 —

$160,000,000; 1988 — $270,000,000; and after 1988 — $550,000,000. The specific terms (including those affecting the amount of capital commitments) of the agreements in principle are subject to further negotiations.

Source: UAL, Incorporated, *Annual Report*, 1983.

and *remote* to identify three levels of probability of occurrence. The FASB defines the terms as follows:

Probable — Likely to happen

Reasonably possible — More than remote, but less than likely to happen

Remote — Slight chance of occurrence

A contingent liability must be recorded as a charge to an expense only if (1) information available prior to the issuance of the financial statements indicates that it is *probable* that a liability has been incurred *and* (2) the dollar amount can be reasonably estimated. If only one (but not both) of these two conditions is met, then no contingent liability is recorded. Instead, footnote disclosures must describe the nature of the contingency and must include an estimate of the probable loss, or a statement that an estimate cannot be made.

A great deal of diversity exists in the interpretation of such terms as "probable," "reasonably possible," "remote," and "reasonably estimable." Consequently, disclosures firms make concerning contingencies vary considerably in nature and extent.

In addition to contingencies, the footnote shown in Exhibit 6-7 also describes a number of commitments. Generally, these commitments are agreements that have not yet been fully performed and are not reflected in the accounting records because they are not completed transactions. UAL has commitments to purchase substantial amounts of property and equipment.

OFF-BALANCE SHEET FINANCING

The preceding discussion has described and illustrated the major types of liabilities that are reported on the balance sheets of U.S. firms. Footnote disclosures, however, reveal that a significant portion of firms' financing does not appear on the balance sheet. Among the most important components of this additional debt are (1) pension obligations, (2) obligations of unconsolidated subsidiaries, and (3) operating leases. Separate chapters are devoted to these topics later in the text, but it is appropriate to include a brief discussion here.

Pension Obligations

Pension assets and liabilities constitute a major part of the resources of and claims against U.S. firms, but only the *difference* between pension plan assets and liabilities is disclosed on the balance sheet. For example, at the end of 1985 the balance sheet for General Motors Corporation reported total assets of $63.8 billion and total liabilities of $34.3 billion. The ratio of debt to total assets was 53.7 percent ($34.3/$63.8). It was reported in the footnotes, however, that

General Motors' pension plans had assets of over $23.3 billion and liabilities exceeding $25.3 billion.

Many analysts argue that pension assets and liabilities should be included on the sponsoring firm's balance sheet, because the sponsor has effective control over the assets and is ultimately responsible for the payment of pension benefits. In the General Motors case, such pension reporting would increase total assets to $87.1 billion ($63.8 + $23.3) and total liabilities to $59.6 billion ($34.3 + $25.3). The revised ratio of debt to total assets would be 68.4 percent ($59.6/$87.1). Chapter 10 contains an expanded discussion of the issues involved in the reporting of pensions.

Obligations of Unconsolidated Subsidiaries

Many major corporations have established finance subsidiaries, and often separate financial statements are provided for such subsidiaries. The typical finance subsidiary exists primarily to finance the operations of the parent company by extending credit to customers and dealers. Such subsidiary firms are usually more heavily debt-laden (highly leveraged) than a manufacturer or retailer would be. When a firm opts not to consolidate a subsidiary in its financial statements, it must provide summarized information in footnotes about the subsidiary's assets, liabilities, and operating results. The effects can be substantial. At the end of 1985 General Motors Corporation disclosed that General Motors Acceptance Corporation (GMAC), a finance subsidiary, had total assets of over $75.4 billion and liabilities of over $70.3 billion. The subsidiary's debt to asset ratio was 93 percent ($70.3/$75.4). If the finance subsidiary were to be consolidated with the parent company, General Motors' debt percentage would increase from 53.7 percent (computed earlier) to over 75 percent. Chapter 9 contains an expanded discussion of the issues involved in accounting for intercorporate investments.

Operating Leases

Large amounts of business assets are acquired by lease rather than by purchase. If such leases qualify as "operating leases" (using the criteria to be discussed in Chapter 10), then neither the leased asset nor the liability for lease payments appears on the balance sheet. Consider an example involving ITT. At the end of 1985 ITT Corporation reported that the firm's minimum payments under existing noncancelable operating leases were approximately $1.5 billion. This amount, disclosed in a footnote, is equal to about 40 percent of the noncurrent liabilities reported on the firm's balance sheet. Chapter 10 contains an expanded discussion of the issues in accounting for lease obligations.

In summary, the liabilities that appear on corporate balance sheets may comprise just a minor portion of the claims against a firm's resources. Similarly, the assets reported on the balance sheet may represent just a portion of the resources under direct or indirect control of a firm's management. Generally accepted methods of accounting require (in the case of pensions and leases) or permit (in the case of consolidation policy) the omission of these items from the balance sheet. The analyst may often decide to recast the financial statements, based on footnote disclosures and other information, prior to making interfirm comparisons or other analytical judgments.

SUMMARY

This chapter begins with the definition of liabilities contained in the FASB's *Statement of Financial Accounting Concepts No. 6,* and distinguishes between current and noncurrent liabilities. The chapter illustrates accounting methods for the types of liabilities that are typical of publicly reporting U.S. firms. Some liabilities (accounts payable, notes payable, and bonds payable) require that cash be paid to lenders at specific future dates, while other liabilities (revenues received in advance) require that firms deliver goods or render services in order to satisfy an obligation. Noncurrent liabilities are generally reported at discounted present values, using the interest rates in effect when the obligations were incurred. Current liabilities are generally reported at their face amounts (that is, without discounting).

In addition to liabilities that are consistent with the FASB's concepts statement, the chapter also discusses the reporting of commitments (not-yet-completed transactions) and contingencies (potential liabilities, which may or may not obligate the firm, depending upon future events). Contingencies and commitments frequently may be pertinent in permitting an accurate assessment of a firm's borrowing capacity and the riskiness of its outstanding securities. Finally, the chapter discusses the significance of "off-balance sheet financing" through pensions, obligations of unconsolidated subsidiaries, and operating leases. Later chapters provide a fuller discussion of these controversial topics.

QUESTIONS

1. The terms listed below were introduced in this chapter. Define or explain each of them.

accounts payable	current liabilities
accrued liabilities	early retirement of debt
bond	liability
cash discounts	noninterest-bearing note
contingencies	principal
coupon rate of interest	promissory note

2. Distinguish between accounts payable and all other types of payables.
3. What criteria are used to determine if a particular liability should be classified as a current liability or a noncurrent liability?
4. List four items that are typically included in the current liability section of the balance sheet.

5. "All liabilities are satisfied by paying cash or some other asset to the lender in the future." Do you agree or not? Explain.

6. Explain why the receipt of cash in advance of the performance of agreed-upon services results in a liability to the firm receiving the cash.

7. Distinguish between the market rate of interest and a bond's coupon rate of interest. Need they be the same?

8. "If the market rate of interest exceeds a bond's coupon rate of interest, the bond will sell at a premium." Do you agree or not? Explain.

9. "A bond will sell at par (face value) only if its coupon rate of interest equals the market rate of interest." Do you agree or not? Explain.

10. If a bond is sold at discount, the carrying value of that bond increases in each successive year as the bond moves toward maturity. Explain why this is so.

11. Assume that market rates of interest have risen following a particular bond issue. Is the market price of those bonds likely to be greater or less than their carrying value? Explain.

12. Describe the procedure required under GAAP to account for the early retirement of debt.

13. What type of account is Bond Premium? How is this account presented in the financial statements?

14. "At the date of issuance, the carrying value of bonds should be the present value of those bonds." Do you agree or not? Explain.

15. Give examples of two different contingencies that one might find disclosed as part of the financial statements of a major U.S. company.

16. How are contingent obligations disclosed in a company's financial statements?

17. What is meant by "off-balance sheet financing"?

EXERCISES AND PROBLEMS

18. *Criteria for Liability Recognition or Disclosure.* Listed below are seven independent cases that involve possible liabilities under GAAP.

   (1) A firm warrants its products for 60 months following the date of sale, and will repair any manufacturing defect without charge to customers within the warranty period.

   (2) A firm has signed a purchase contract with a key supplier for substantial quantities of inventory to be delivered over the next three years.

   (3) A group of former employees has initiated a class action lawsuit against the firm, alleging that unsafe working conditions have been injurious to their health.

   (4) A firm has received consulting revenues from clients for services to be rendered over the next two years.

   (5) A firm has signed a five-year employment contract with a key executive, and payments will continue for five years even if the

executive's employment is terminated by the firm before the five years have ended.

(6) A new income tax bill is being debated by the U.S. Congress that would substantially increase corporate tax rates. The tax bill appears very likely to become law.

(7) A firm has entered into a long-term rental arrangement for its administrative and sales offices. The arrangement is noncancelable.

REQUIRED For each case, indicate if it qualifies as a liability under GAAP. If a particular case does not meet the criteria for a liability, indicate how it would be reported (if at all) in the financial statements.

19. *Current Liabilities.* Levi Tea Company's current liabilities include the following amounts at December 31, 1988:

Accounts payable to suppliers	$ 700,000
Revenues received in advance	450,000
Warranty obligations	230,000
Total	$1,380,000

Assume that Levi Tea Company satisfied each of these liabilities during 1989 as follows:

(1) Accounts payable were paid in full.
(2) Revenues received in advance were fully earned during 1989; the associated expenses amounted to $280,000.
(3) For merchandise sold prior to 1989, warranty services costing a total of $180,000 were performed during 1989. There are no additional warranty obligations for pre-1989 sales.

REQUIRED Provide journal entries to record the satisfaction of each of these liabilities during 1989.

20. *Current Liabilities: Accounts Payable—Revenues Received in Advance.* The Singer Party Products Company had the following transactions during December, 1989:

(1) Purchased cups and straws on credit for $3,500, to be paid in 60 days.
(2) On December 10 purchased plates and napkins on credit for $5,000, at terms of 2/10, net 60. Singer intends to pay this bill in ten days in order to earn the 2% cash discount.
(3) Received a property tax bill for $2,200, covering the period July 1, 1989–June 30, 1990. The tax bill is due and payable on January 10, 1990.
(4) Received a bill for $15,000 from a building contractor for extensive renovations to Singer's accounting office. The renovations were completed by November 30, 1989.

(5) Received a deposit of $500 for materials to be provided in February, 1990, for a party to be given by Antic Evening, a local social club.

REQUIRED   Prepare journal entries to reflect the above transactions in the December 31, 1989, financial statements of the Singer Party Products Company.

21. *Revenues Received in Advance: Warranty Obligations.*   Ed's Law School received $120,000 in tuition payments on September 1, 1988, for law courses to be taught during the Fall 1988 and Spring 1989 semesters. The first semester lasts from September 30, 1988–January 31, 1989; the second semester begins on February 1, 1989, and ends on June 30, 1989. Sixty students are enrolled for the entire academic year, and each has paid tuition of $2,000.

REQUIRED

(a) On the basis of the information given, provide journal entries to record (1) the receipt of tuition payments, (2) tuition revenues earned during 1988, and (3) tuition revenues earned during 1989.
(b) Upon further inquiry you have learned that Ed's Law School offers students two courses in the Fall 1988 semester and three courses during the Spring 1989 semester. All courses have the same number of meetings and the same estimated costs. How, if at all, does this information affect your answers to item (a) above?
(c) In order to attract additional students, Ed is considering guaranteeing students a rebate of one-half of their tuition if they fail to pass their professional exams within two years after completing his courses. Ed believes that about 75% of his students would pass their professional exams within this period. How would such a guarantee affect your answers to item (a) above?

22. *Warranty Expense and Liability, and Deferred Taxes.*   The Headperson Radio Company provides a three-year warranty on its popular headset radios. Based on past experience, the company provides a charge (debit) equal to 8% of sales each period to the account Estimated Warranty Expense. The entry is as follows:

> dr.   Estimated Warranty Expense   XXX
>   cr.   Estimated Warranty Liability   XXX

The actual expense of servicing warranty claims is charged (debited) against the Estimated Warranty Liability account. For federal income tax purposes, warranty expenses are deductible on the tax return when actually incurred by the firm. The federal income tax rate is 40%. Sales and warranty expenses actually incurred for the years 1987–1990 follow.

	198_
Sales	1,000
Warranty expenses actually incurred	30

REQUIRED

(a) Determine the estimated warranty expense each ye____
year-end balance in the Estimated Warranty Liabilit___
1988, 1989, and 1990.

(b) Determine the increase or decrease in the company's ____
account each year due to the differences between estim___
expense and the warranty expenses actually incurred.

(c) Compare the changes each year in the Deferred Taxes a___
changes in the Estimated Warranty Liability account. Exp___
changes in these two accounts are related.

23. *Warranty Obligation: Revision of Estimates.*   Shortlived Products,____
antees the performance of its products with a two-year warranty____
parts and service. This is the end of the firm's third year of o___
and each year's warranty expense has been estimated at 4% of___
sales. A summary of warranty expenses and actual warranty costs___
vided below.

Year	Product Sales	Warranty Expense (estimated 4% of sales)	Warranty Expendi___ (parts and labor___
1	$20,000,000	$ 800,000	$ 200,000
2	30,000,000	1,200,000	1,100,000
3	45,000,000	1,800,000	1,650,000
Total	$95,000,000	$3,800,000	$2,950,000

of year 3? What adjustment (if any) would be
year 3, assuming that the books have not yet

oblem may be attempted independently of exercise 43 in

Revisited: Revenues Received in Advance; Memberships Sold
. Deltoid Health Club was founded on January 1, 1983,
ness for five years, and has enrolled 1,000 new members at
ch year. The firm offers a five-year membership at a fee of
advance. Les Biceps, the manager, estimates that the annual
pense per member is $100, and that Deltoid Health Club's cost
g is 10% per annum.

rmine the present value at the beginning of a new membership of
five-year series of per-member annual operating expenses. (For
venience, assume that operating expenses are paid in cash at the
d of each year.) Is it profitable for Deltoid to sell memberships at
50?
hat is the lowest price at which Deltoid could sell memberships
without incurring a loss?
Les Biceps desires to offer renewal memberships at a price below that
offered to new members. Assume that Biceps offers a five-year
renewal membership for $300 and that all of the 1,000 charter
members, whose memberships would have expired on December 31,
1987, sign renewal memberships before that date. Determine the
amount of income or loss associated with the renewal memberships.
How (if at all) would Deltoid Health Club's financial statements at
December 31, 1987, report the firm's obligations to initial and renewal
members?

*Note: The following problem is related to exercise 42 in Chapter 3 but may be
attempted independently of that exercise.*

25. *Piet Moss, Revisited: Present Value of Estimated Liability for Refunds; Change in*

REQUIRED

(a) Using present value concepts, determine whether Moss's operations are expected to be profitable.

(b) What is the lowest price that Moss could charge per print if all expectations are correct?

(c) Provide journal entries to record the sale of the new edition and the estimated liability for refunds as of January 1, 1988.

(d) Provide journal entries to record any interest incomes or expenses through December 31, 1992, and to record Moss's payment of cash refunds to customers making returns.

(e) The preceding calculations in (a) and (b) are based on the assumption that half of the prints will be returned for a refund. How high a refund percentage could occur before Moss would incur a loss?

(f) Suppose that by December 31, 1988, the interest rate has fallen to 4% per year. How (if at all) would this affect the amount of income to be reported in 1988 and the carrying value of Moss's estimated liability for refunds at that date?

26. *Discount Note Payable.* Kurtson Products, Inc., borrowed $7,430 from the Marley Bank on January 1, 1987, on a two-year, noninterest-bearing note. The face amount of the note is $10,000 and that amount is to be repaid on December 31, 1988.

REQUIRED

(a) What is the effective annual interest rate on the note?

(b) What is the total interest expense over the two-year term of the note?

(c) How should the interest expense determined in (b) be apportioned between 1987 and 1988?

(d) Provide journal entries to reflect (1) the signing of the note and the receipt of the cash proceeds on January 1, 1987; (2) interest expense for the year ended December 31, 1988, and (3) repayment of the note on December 31, 1988.

27. *Installment Debt Purchase of Equipment: Differing Interest Rates.* Over Bearing Company has just acquired factory machinery in exchange for its promise to pay the supplier $1,000,000 per year at the end of each of the next five years. The equipment is estimated to have a five-year life, no residual value, and is to be depreciated using the straight-line method.

REQUIRED

(a) Determine interest expense and depreciation expense for the first and fifth years, and the amount to be reported as an installment note payable at the end of the first year, assuming that the relevant interest rate is (1) 2%, (2) 8%, and (3) 16%.

(b) Assume that Over Bearing Company judges the operating performance of its managers based partly on ROA (the ratio of income to assets). The machinery described above is expected to earn profits *before* depreciation and interest expenses of $1,400,000. Which of the interest rates shown in item (a) would produce the best ROA (after depreciation and interest expenses) in the first year? Which would produce the highest ROA measure in the last year? Which would show the best rate of ROA growth between the first and second years?

28. *Alternative Debt Financing Arrangements.* The Limpid Pool Company has decided to borrow in order to finance a $10-million expansion of its plant and equipment. The interest rate is 10%, and the following repayment arrangements are being considered by management. The loan takes place on January 1, 1988, and all cash flows occur at the end of the year.

   (1) Repay the loan and interest with a single payment at the end of ten years.
   (2) Pay interest of $1 million per year for ten years and repay the principal at the end of the tenth year.
   (3) Repay the loan and interest by making ten equal annual payments to the lender.
   (4) Repay the loan and interest by making ten equal annual payments to a sinking fund. (The sinking fund is expected to earn interest at the rate of 8% per year.)

   REQUIRED

   (a) For each repayment plan, determine the total dollar amounts of the cash payments to the lender [or to the sinking fund, in arrangement (4)].
   (b) For each repayment plan, indicate the total interest expense to be paid over the ten years. [For plan (4), determine the *net* interest expense after sinking fund interest income.]
   (c) For each repayment plan, show the journal entries of the first and second years to record all cash receipts, cash payments, and interest expense.
   (d) For each repayment plan, indicate how the debt would be described and valued on Limpid Pool's balance sheet. Explain any differences in the carrying value of the debt across the repayment plans.
   (e) Based on your answers to items (a)–(d), which of the repayment plans is best for Limpid Pool?

29. *Basic Present Value Calculations: Single and Annuity Cash Flows.* Present values of future cash flows are affected by the interest rate, plus the timing and amount of the cash flows. Seven different situations involving cash flows are listed below.

REQUIRED   Determine the present value cash flows in each of the following situations:

(a) $1 million to be received at the end of 20 periods, at an interest rate of 6% per period.

(b) $50,000 to be received at the end of each of 20 periods, at an interest rate of 6% per period.

(c) $40,000 to be received at the end of each of 20 periods, at an interest rate of 6% per period.

(d) $60,000 to be received at the end of each of 20 periods, at an interest rate of 6% per period.

(e) A ten-year bond with a principal amount of $1 million and a coupon rate of 10% interest paid semiannually, issued at a market interest rate of 12%. Verify that your answer is equal to the sum of your answers in items (a) and (b).

(f) A ten-year bond with a principal amount of $1 million, and a coupon rate of 12% interest paid semiannually, issued at a market interest rate of 12%. Verify that your answer is equal to the sum of your answers in items (a) and (d).

(g) A ten-year bond with a principal amount of $1 million, and a coupon rate of 8% interest paid semiannually, issued at a market interest rate of 12%. Verify that your answer is equal to the sum of your answers in items (a) and (c).

30. *Basic Present Value and Interest Expense Calculations.*   The Typical Bindery Company intends to borrow $10 million to finance construction of additional facilities. The debt will be incurred on January 1, 1988, and will be repaid in equal annual installments (including interest). The interest rate is 12% per annum.

REQUIRED

(a) Assuming that the debt is to be repaid over five years, (1) determine the required annual repayment; (2) determine the journal entry to record the receipt of the loan proceeds; (3) determine the interest expense for the first and second years; and (4) determine the total interest expense over the term of the loan.

(b) Answer all four questions in item (a) again, but assume that the debt is to be repaid over ten years.

(c) Compare your answers to items (a) and (b). Why is the first year's interest expense the same under both alternatives? Why is the total expense greater for the ten-year repayment period? Which alternative, (a) or (b), should the Typical Bindery Company select?

31. *Bonds Payable: Bond Premium and Bond Discount Amortization.*   The diagram on page 322 shows how the carrying value of bonds payable changes over time for bonds issued at a premium, at par, and at a discount.

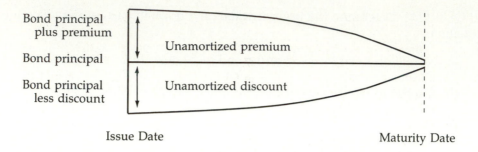

Bond principal
plus premium

Bond principal

Bond principal
less discount

Unamortized premium

Unamortized discount

Issue Date

Maturity Date

REQUIRED

(a) Explain the change in carrying value of the bonds, in terms of the difference between the periodic interest expense and the periodic interest coupon payments to investors.

(b) Explain why the slopes of the lines for unamortized premiums and discounts become *steeper* as the maturity date of the bonds approaches.

32. *Bonds Issued at a Discount: Basic Entries.*   On January 1, 1988, the Watts Crockery Company issued bonds with a principal amount of $5 million bearing a 10% semiannual coupon rate of interest and maturing in 20 years. The market rate of interest was 12% semiannually compounded when the bonds were sold. Interest is payable each June 30 and December 31.

REQUIRED

(a) Determine the proceeds of the bond issue.

(b) Prepare journal entries pertaining to the bond issue for Watts Crockery for the following dates: (1) January 1, 1988; (2) June 30, 1988; and (3) December 31, 1988.

(c) How would the bond, and any related discount or premium, appear on the balance sheet dated January 1, 1988? On the balance sheet dated December 31, 1988?

33. *Bond Financing: Amortization of Discount.*   Perennial Florists, Inc., sold bonds on January 1, 1987, with a principal amount of $5 million and a 10% semiannual coupon rate. At the date of sale of the bonds the market interest rate was 12% compounded semiannually. The bonds have a 20-year life and mature on December 31, 2006. The interest coupons are paid each June 30 and December 31.

REQUIRED

(a) Determine the proceeds to Perennial Florists upon the sale of the bond issue, and provide the journal entry to record the issuance on January 1, 1987.

(b) What will be the total interest expense over the 20-year life of the bond issue?

(c) Record journal entries to provide interest expense and payment on June 30 and December 31, 1987.

(d) Determine the interest expense for the last interest payment period, July 1–December 31, 2006.*

---

*The interest coupon is $250,000 (5% × $5 million), and the interest expense is 6% of the book value of the bonds on July 1, 2006. The book value of the bonds on July 1, 2006, is the present value of the total cash payments to the bondholders on December 31, 2006.

34. *Bond Financing: Amortization of Premium.* The Occasional Bus Company sold bonds on January 1, 1987, with a principal amount of $10 million and a 14% semiannual coupon rate. At the date of sale of the bonds the market interest rate was 12% compounded semiannually. The bonds have a ten-year life and mature on December 31, 1996. The interest coupons are paid each June 30 and December 31.

REQUIRED

(a) Determine the proceeds to Occasional Bus Company upon the sale of the bond issue, and provide the journal entry to record the issuance on January 1, 1987.

(b) What will be the total interest expense over the ten-year life of the bond issue?

(c) Record journal entries to provide interest expense and payment on June 30 and December 31, 1987.

(d) Determine the interest expense for the last interest payment period, July 1–December 31, 1996.*

---

*The interest coupon is $700,000 (7% × $10 million), and the interest expense is 6% of the book value of the bonds on July 1, 1996. The book value of the bonds on July 1, 1996, is the present value of the total cash payments to the bondholders on December 31, 1996.

35. *Bond Financing: Proceeds at Date of Issue (Comprehensive).* Saucer, Inc., intends to sell bonds with a $10 million principal and a 12% semiannual coupon rate on January 1, 1987. The bonds mature in ten years (on December 31, 1996) and pay interest each June 30 and December 31.

REQUIRED

(a) What is the total amount (principal and interest) that Saucer, Inc., will pay to the bondholders over the ten-year life of the bonds?

(b) Determine the proceeds of the bond issue on January 1, 1987, assuming that the market rate of interest at that date is (1) 12% compounded semiannually, (2) 16% compounded semiannually, and (3) 8% compounded semiannually.

(c) Provide journal entries to record the issuance of the bonds and the first year's interest expense, assuming that the bonds were sold to yield (1) 8% to investors, compounded semiannually and (2) 16% to investors, compounded semiannually.

(d) What is the total interest expense over the life of the bonds, assuming that the bonds were sold to yield (1) 12% to investors, compounded semiannually, (2) 16% to investors, compounded semiannually, and (3) 8% to investors, compounded semiannually.

36. *Bond Financing: Early Retirement at a Gain.* On January 1, 1987, the Shell Game Company had long-term debt outstanding with a principal amount of $100 million and a 6% semiannual coupon interest rate. The bonds had a ten-year term remaining to maturity. They were initially sold at par value. Market interest rates have subsequently increased to 12% compounded semiannually, and Shell Game's management is considering retirement of the debt. If retired, the debt would be replaced with an issue maturing in ten years with a 12% semiannual coupon interest rate.

REQUIRED

(a) Determine the market value on January 1, 1987, of the 6% debt presently outstanding.

(b) Assume that management decides to issue new debt in an amount sufficient to retire the old debt. Provide journal entries on January 1, 1987, to record (1) the sale of the new debt issue with a 12% semiannual coupon interest rate and (2) use of the proceeds from the new debt issue to retire the old debt issue.

(c) Discuss the treatment of any gains and losses on these debt transactions in the financial statements of the Shell Game Company.

(d) How would Shell Game's bond refunding affect (1) interest expense for 1987 and (2) the firm's debt-to-equity ratio?

(e) Determine the total cash payments to bondholders and the firm's total interest expense over the next ten years, assuming that (1) the old 6% debt remains outstanding and (2) the old debt is replaced with the new 12% debt. Explain why the total cash payments are higher if the old debt remains outstanding, and also why the total interest expense is higher if the old debt is replaced with the new 12% debt.

(f) What advice would you offer to Shell Game's management concerning the decision to refund the 6% debt?

37. *Bond Refunding Subsequent to Interest Rate Decline.* On January 1, 1980, the CMC Company sold at par $100 million of bonds payable with a 12% semiannual coupon and a 20-year term to maturity. Management is deciding whether to refund the bond issue in late December 1988. The current interest rate on similar debt is 8% compounded semiannually.

REQUIRED

(a) Determine the market value of CMC's bonds on December 31, 1988.
(b) Provide the journal entries on December 31, 1988, necessary to record (1) the issuance by CMC of a new bond issue with a coupon rate of 8% compounded semiannually (in an amount equal to the market value of the old bond issue) and (2) the repurchase and retirement of the old bond issue. (Ignore taxes and transaction costs).
(c) Show the income statement amounts in 1988 and 1989 for interest expense and gain or loss (if any) on early retirement of debt, and the balance sheet liability on December 31, 1988, for bonds payable if (1) the old bonds remain outstanding and (2) the new bond issue is sold and the old bond issue is retired.
(d) Is CMC Company better or worse off as a result of the bond refunding? Explain.

38. *Bond Refunding Subsequent to Interest Rate Decline, with Call Premium.* On January 1, 1985, Tonya Company sold at par $60 million of bonds payable with a 16% semiannual interest coupon. The bonds are callable at 105 plus accrued interest,* and have a ten-year term to maturity. Interest rates have subsequently declined to 8% compounded semiannually, and management is considering whether to refund the bond issue at the end of December 1987.

---

*Callable bonds may be retired prior to their scheduled maturity date at the option of the issuer. In this case, Tonya Company has the right to repurchase the bonds at 105% of face value, plus accrued interest.

REQUIRED

(a) Determine the market value of Tonya's bonds payable on December 31, 1987.
(b) Provide journal entries on December 31, 1987, to record (1) the issuance by Tonya of a new bond issue with a coupon rate of 8% compounded semiannually in an amount equal to the call price of the old bond issue and (2) the repurchase and retirement of the old bond issue (assume no taxes or transaction costs).
(c) Show the amount of interest expense and gain or loss (if any) on early retirement of debt, on the income statements for 1987 and 1988, as well as the balance sheet liability on December 31, 1987 for bonds payable if (1) the old bonds remain outstanding and (2) the new bond issue is sold and the old bond issue is retired.
(d) Is Tonya Company better or worse off as a result of the bond refunding? Is the income statement effect of the refunding consistent with the economic effect? Explain.

39. *Acquisition of Outstanding Bonds.* Convertible subordinated debentures are bonds that can be converted into shares of stock at a stated price. Subordination means that the bonds claim on income is subordinate or junior to that of other debt. During the first quarter of 1982, Hueblein, Inc., purchased (in the open market) 4.5% of its convertible subordinated debentures with a book and face value of $12 million. Hueblein paid $7,273,000.

REQUIRED

(a) What was the market rate of interest for bonds in this category at their original issuance date?
(b) In what way might the low stated interest rate on these bonds at time of issuance have been affected by Hueblein's expected future earnings per share?
(c) Why do you think the market value of these bonds had declined?
(d) What reasons do you think Hueblein's management may have had for acquiring these bonds?
(e) How should the difference between the cost and book value of these acquired bonds be accounted for?

40. *Sinking Fund for Bond Retirement (Use of Future Value Tables).* The management of the Shady Siding Company has decided to establish a sinking fund to retire bonds outstanding with a principal amount of $10 million and a ten-year term remaining to maturity. The company will make equal annual deposits to the sinking fund at the end of each of the next ten years; sinking fund deposits are expected to earn 10% per year, compounded annually.

REQUIRED

(a) What amount must Shady Siding deposit at the end of each year in order to have $10 million on hand at the end of the tenth year?
(b) Assuming the 10% interest is appropriate, what will be the amount on deposit at the end of the fifth year?
(c) If the sinking fund deposits earn only 8% per annum, what will be the amount on hand at the end of ten years?
(d) Provide journal entries for the first and second years to show Shady Siding Company's deposits to the sinking fund and to recognize 10% interest earned on the sinking fund deposits.
(e) Management has suggested that for balance sheet reporting purposes the amount on deposit in the sinking fund should be subtracted from the firm's outstanding bonds payable. How would this subtraction affect the firm's debt-to-equity ratio? Return on assets ratio? Return on equity ratio?
(f) Evaluate management's suggestion, described in item (e) to subtract the amount in the sinking fund from outstanding bonds payable.

41. *Footnote Disclosures Concerning Long-term Debt.* AT&T's 1984 annual report to shareholders includes the following footnote information concerning the company's long-term debt:

Long-term Debt

Interest rates and maturities on long-term debt outstanding at December 31, 1984, were as follows:

Maturities	2⅝% to 6⅞%	7% to 8⅞%	9% to 14.7%	Total
1986	$ 132.0	$ 15.0	$ 7.5	$ 154.5
1987	307.0	15.0	7.5	329.5
1988	7.0	15.0	7.5	29.5
1989	7.0	15.0	407.5	429.5
1990–1999	2,151.0	529.0	1,575.0	4,255.0
2000–2009	500.0	2,408.1	45.0	2,953.1
2010–2019		300.0		300.0
Total	$3,104.0	$3,297.1	$2,050.0	$8,451.1

Source: AT&T, *Annual Report*, 1984.

REQUIRED

(a) Explain why the interest rates on AT&T's long-term debts vary over the range from 2⅝% to 14.7%.
(b) Is the information concerning the timing of debt maturities useful to investment analysts? Explain.
(c) Why do you suppose that AT&T's management classifies its long-term debt in terms of both maturities and interest rates?
(d) AT&T discloses substantially more information about its long-term debt than is excerpted above. List the additional types of information concerning long-term debt that you consider to be useful to investment analysts.

42. *Disclosure of Various Liabilities.* AMR is a holding company for American Airlines and its subsidiaries. Three of the major events reported by AMR involving American Airlines that occurred during 1982 are listed below:

(1) As of December 31, 1982, American Airlines had on order 27 Boeing 767 passenger aircraft, which were contractually scheduled for delivery in 1983–1989 at a total cost of $1.36 billion. Deposits were made toward the purchase of these aircraft in the amount of $89,993,000.
(2) On December 31, 1982, customers had made deposits for future flights on American Airlines in the amount of $305,332,000.
(3) In the notes to its December 31, 1982, annual report, AMR included the following statement, among others, regarding its long-term debt: "In 1982, American acquired $60 million of its floating rate equipment trust certificates with the proceeds from the issuance of

long-term fixed rate promissory notes and a registered bond. The effective interest rate for these new issues is 16%." The trust certificates were listed on the company's books at $57.4 million. The registered bonds had a face value of $23 million and the promissory notes had a face value of $52 million. These obligations were issued on June 30, 1982, and were due on June 30, 1987. They carried a stated interest rate of 9%, payable semiannually. (Note: The data has been modified somewhat to facilitate student solution.)

REQUIRED

(a) How should the company disclose these facts regarding events (1) and (2) in its consolidated financial statements for the year ending December 31, 1982?
(b) Ignoring debt issuance costs, prepare journal entries to record the transactions described in items (1), (2), and (3) above. Round your answer to the nearest $100,000.

43. *Assets Designated for Specific Uses: Right of Offset.*   Managers frequently designate assets for specific uses, such as the repayment of debt. Some analysts suggest that the designated assets should be subtracted from the related debt on the balance sheet. Listed below are five independent cases.

(1) A firm has purchased a portfolio of short-term U.S. Treasury bills that management has segregated to be used solely to pay next period's federal income tax.
(2) Pursuant to its long-term borrowing agreement, a firm has been making annual payments to a sinking fund that will be used to retire its outstanding debt five years hence. The sinking fund is managed by the firm and is currently invested in both debt and equity securities of other firms.
(3) This case is the same as item (2) except that the sinking fund is managed by an independent trustee, and the fund must be used at maturity for retirement of the outstanding debt.
(4) A firm's employment contract with a key executive obligates the firm to pay $500,000 to the executive at her retirement date, four years hence. Moreover, the firm has been funding the obligation by making payments to a sinking fund that is managed by an independent trustee.
(5) A firm's union contract obligates the firm to make annual payments to a fund managed by an independent trustee. As employees retire, the trustee will pay pension benefits from the fund's assets in accordance with the firm's labor contract. As of the balance sheet date, the market value of the fund's investments slightly exceeds the estimated present value of the employee retirement benefits earned to date.

REQUIRED In each of the cases described above, indicate whether you believe that more meaningful balance sheet disclosure information will result if designated assets are offset against their related liabilities. Discuss how each item should be reported in the financial statements.

44. *Accounting Methods to Reduce Reported Debt.* A recent *Wall Street Journal* article bearing the title "Loose Ledgers," contained the following comments:

(1) ...most investors, bankers, and economists aren't sophisticated enough to see off-balance-sheet borrowing tactics. So investors make ill-informed decisions. Banks often don't know that a company seeking a loan is already in hock. And economists misjudge how highly leveraged American business really is.

(2) ...If an oil company...owns less than 50 percent of a pipeline venture, it usually—at most—calls the money borrowed to build the pipeline a "contingent liability" in footnotes. The rules permit that practice on the assumption that the pipeline won't go out of business."

(3) ...Insilco Corp...sells precut lumber for build-it-yourself homes and extends loans to the lumber buyers through a 100-percent owned finance unit, Miles Homes. If Miles' debt had been included on Insilco's balance sheet in 1982, debt would have consumed 80 percent of the parent company's capital. Instead, Insilco reported consolidated debt at 31 percent of capital.

(4) In each of the past three years, Penny has sold to its own finance subsidiary more than $3 billion of receivables. If Penny had consolidated results of its finance subsidiary for its latest fiscal year, ended last January 31, its debt-to-equity ratio would have risen to 1.52 from the .27 reported.

REQUIRED Discuss the propriety of each of the accounting practices described in (1)–(4) above.

45. *Interest Rates and Length of Borrowing.* The Equity Cushion Company is planning to issue $100 million in long-term debt in order to invest in new plant and equipment. Prevailing interest rates for U.S. Government borrowings and for firms with about the same credit standing as Equity Cushion Company are shown below.

	Annual Interest Rate	
	U.S. Government	Comparable Quality Corporate Debt
Length of borrowing (term to maturity)		
Five years	8.2%	11.0%
Ten years	9.8	13.5
Fifteen years	10.2	15.1
Twenty years	10.0	16.0
Thirty years	9.4	14.6

REQUIRED

    (a) Discuss reasons why the current interest rates on corporate debt exceed those for government securities having the same term to maturity.

    (b) Why do interest rates per year differ based on the term to maturity of the loan? In the illustration above, why do interest rates decline as the term to maturity lengthens from 20 to 30 years?

    (c) Which term to maturity is likely to be best for the shareholders of Equity Cushion Company? Explain.

The Balance Sheet: Owners' Equity

This chapter discusses the methods used in accounting for owners' equity (paid-in capital and retained earnings). It begins with the FASB's definition of owners' equity and discusses the characteristics that distinguish owners' equity from liabilities. A variety of transactions that affect owners' equity are then illustrated, including the sale of common and preferred stock; the issuance of stock rights and warrants, and the sale of securities that are convertible into equity shares; the distribution of stock dividends and stock splits; the repurchase of outstanding shares; and the events and appropriations that affect retained earnings. The chapter ends with an illustration of earnings-per-share calculations for firms with simple and complex capital structures.

OWNERS' EQUITY DEFINED

Owners' equity is the difference between a firm's total assets and total liabilities. Thus, the amount reported as owners' equity depends on the methods used to value assets and liabilities. In this sense, owners' equity is a residual amount. It is also a residual in a legal sense: creditors have priority over equity shareholders in the event of corporate liquidation.

The FASB's *Statement of Financial Accounting Concepts No. 6* defines owners' equity as " . . . the residual interest in the assets of an entity that remains after deducting its liabilities."[1] The essential characteristics of owners' equity, according to the statement, center on the conditions for transferring enterprise assets to owners. Generally, a firm is not obliged to transfer assets to owners. (This is not the case, however, if the firm has formally declared its intention to pay a dividend, or if the firm is being liquidated.) Distributions to stockholders are discretionary. In contrast, distributions to creditors are nondiscretionary; once a liability has been incurred, the firm must make future asset transfers, which take precedence over ownership interests.

OWNERS' EQUITY REPORTING

Exhibit 7-1 duplicates Exhibit 6-1 in the previous chapter and shows the liabilities and owners' (shareholders') equity sections of the balance sheets of Apple Computer, Inc., at September 30, 1983, and UAL, Inc., at December 31, 1983. The exhibit reveals the following:

1. The shareholders' equity of Apple Computer consists of (1) paid-in capital from the sale of common stock and (2) retained earnings. In contrast, the shareholders' equity for UAL, Inc. is more complex, consisting of several different types of preferred stock, as well as common stock. The descriptions of the various types of stock include different terms (redeemable, cumulative, convertible, liquidating value, and par value). Each of these terms (all of which will be discussed later in this chapter) offers important information to the analyst about the rights and priorities associated with ownership of the various equity securities.
2. UAL subtracts from shareholders' equity the cost of "preferred stock held in treasury." This means that UAL has repurchased some of its previously issued preferred stock but has not retired those shares.
3. UAL's owners' equity is also reduced by accumulated foreign currency translation adjustments. This indicates that UAL's financial statements consolidate the financial statements of subsidiary firms using the translation method described in Chapter 11. This adjustment is

---

[1]*Statement of Financial Accounting Concepts No. 6*, "Elements of Financial Statements" (Stamford, CT: FASB, 1985), par. 49.

technically neither paid-in capital nor retained earnings, and its economic interpretation is unclear.

The discussion in the following pages illustrates methods of accounting for each of the owners' equity elements normally found on the balance sheets of U.S. firms. Where possible, reference will be made to the examples in Exhibit 7-1.

ACCOUNTING FOR OWNERS' EQUITY

This section illustrates the accounting methods used for transactions affecting owners' equity, including the sale of common and preferred stock; the issuance of stock rights and warrants, and the sale of securities that are convertible into equity shares; the distribution of stock dividends and stock splits; the repurchase of outstanding shares; events and appropriations that affect retained earnings; other elements of owners' equity; and earnings-per-share calculations for complex capital structures.

Issuance of Stock

When a firm is incorporated, the corporate charter includes an authorization to issue a specified number of shares of stock. Individual shares serve as evidence of ownership in the corporation.

Common stock   The voting ownership shares of a firm are called **common stock.** Common stock is issued to investors in return for cash or other considerations (for noncash assets or in payment of liabilities). The issued stock remains outstanding until it is repurchased by the issuing corporation. Firms usually assign a **par value** or **stated value** to each share of stock. Legal requirements mandate the disclosure of this amount in the financial statements, although neither par value nor stated value purports to measure the market value of the stock.[2]

Exhibit 7-1 shows that Apple Computer's common stock has no par value. The dollar amount shown indicates the total proceeds received upon sale of the outstanding shares. By comparison, UAL's common stock has a par value of $5 per share, and the 34,484,544 shares outstanding at the end of 1983 have a total par value of $172.4 million. However, this does not represent the proceeds that UAL received upon the sale of the stock; the proceeds received over and above par value are reported in Exhibit 7-1 as **additional capital invested.**

In order to illustrate accounting for the sale of common stock, assume that Achilles' Tendon Corporation was organized on January 1, 1987, and was authorized to issue 10 million shares of $25 par value stock. One million shares

---

[2]Par value is sometimes important in computing dividend distributions, as will be shown later. An initial issue of stock for less than par value may cause difficulties in the event of corporate liquidation.

Exhibit 7-1
Owners' Equity Reporting: Two Examples

UAL, Incorporated
Statement of Consolidated Financial Position
December 31, 1983
(in thousands)

Liabilities and Shareholders' Equity

Current Liabilities:	Notes payable and commercial paper	$ 187,940
	Long-term debt maturing within one year	87,647
	Current obligations under capital leases	42,938
	Advance ticket sales and customer deposits	453,232
	Accounts payable	398,084
	Accrued salaries, wages and benefits	536,815
	Other accrued liabilities	227,580
		1,934,236
Long-term Debt		691,879
Long-term Obligations under Capital Leases		619,388
Deferred Credits and Other Liabilities:	Deferred income taxes	260,670
	Other	30,125
		290,795
Redeemable Preferred Stock:	5½% cumulative prior preferred stock, $100 par value	4,929
Nonredeemable Preferred Stock, Common Stock and Other Shareholders' Equity:	Preferred stock, no par value; authorized 16,000,000 shares—	
	Series A $.40 cumulative (convertible); issued 514,861 shares in 1983; involuntary liquidation value $25 per share, aggregating $12,872,000 in 1983	2,574
	Series B $2.40 cumulative (convertible); outstanding 8,000,000 shares in 1983; involuntary liquidation value $25 per share, aggregating $200,000,000	193,234
	Common stock, $5 par value; authorized 50,000,000 shares; outstanding 34,484,544 shares in 1983	172,423
	Additional capital invested	555,427
	Retained earnings	681,383
	Accumulated foreign currency translation adjustments	(10,507)
	Less— 454,261 shares of Series A $.40 cumulative (convertible) preferred stock held in treasury	(2,118)
		1,592,416
Commitments and Contingent Liabilities	(See note on contingencies and commitments)	
		$5,133,643

Apple Computer, Incorporated
Consolidated Balance Sheet
September 30, 1983
(in thousands)

Liabilities and Shareholders' Equity

Current liabilities:

Notes payable to banks	$ –
Accounts payable	52,701
Accrued compensation and employee benefits	15,770
Income taxes payable	
Accrued marketing and distribution	21,551
Other current liabilities	38,764
Total current liabilities	128,786
Non-current obligations under capital leases	1,308
Deferred taxes on income	48,584
Shareholders' equity:	
Common stock, no par value, 160,000,000 shares authorized, 59,198,397 shares issued and outstanding	183,715
Retained earnings	195,046
	378,761
Notes receivable from shareholders	(860)
Total shareholders' equity	377,901
	$556,579

Sources: UAL, Incorporated, *Annual Report,* 1983; Apple Computer, Incorporated, *Annual Report,* 1983.

were sold to investors on that date for $60 per share. The entry to record the sale is as follows:

dr.	Cash		60,000,000
	cr.	Common Stock at Par	25,000,000
	cr.	Additional Paid-in Capital	35,000,000

To record sale of 1 million shares at $60 per share.

Preferred stock   Firms also often issue other equity securities that take precedence over common stock in the distribution of dividends and other corporate assets. Such stock is usually designated as **preferred stock.** The number of preferred stock arrangements that is possible is limited only by the securities laws and the imagination of financial managers. For example, Exhibit 7-1 shows that UAL, Inc., has several types of preferred stock outstanding. The first is designated as *Redeemable 5½ percent cumulative prior preferred stock.* Footnote disclosures reveal that this stock may be redeemed at any time at the option of UAL for $100 per share. Moreover, redemption of the shares is required by various dates through June 1995. Using the FASB's conceptual framework definitions, the mandatory redemption feature gives these securities the character of liabilities rather than of equity. Notice that UAL lists these securities between liabilities and owners' equity on its balance sheet, so that the analyst may decide on the appropriate classification. The stock is described as "5½ percent cumulative," which indicates that the shareholders are entitled to an annual dividend of $5.50 per share (5½ percent of the $100 par value). The **cumulative** feature means that if UAL does not declare a dividend of $5.50 per share annually, the dividends are **in arrears,** and the cumulative amount of dividends in arrears must be paid before any dividend distributions are made to the holders of other types of outstanding equity securities.

Other types of preferred stock listed by UAL are designated as *Series A $.40 and Series B $2.40 cumulative (convertible) no par preferred stock; involuntary liquidation value $25 per share.* The preferred dividend is stated here as a per-share amount because these stocks have no par value. A footnote disclosure by UAL includes the following information concerning the conversion feature and liquidating value of these stocks:

> Each share of the Series A preferred stock is entitled to one vote and is redeemable by UAL at $26.05 per share beginning in 1986 and at prices decreasing in each year thereafter to $25.00 per share in 1993. Both the Series A and the Series B preferred stocks are convertible into common stock, the Series A on a share-for-share basis and the Series B on the basis of one share of preferred for .5854 of a share of common, subject in both cases to adjustment in certain events. The Series A and Series B preferred stocks are considered "nonredeemable" because they are redeemable only at the option of UAL.[3]

As the footnote reveals, these preferred shares entitle their holders to vote, and the shareholders may exchange their shares of preferred stock for common shares at specified exchange ratios.

The preceding descriptions of UAL's preferred stock include many of the important terms used to describe the rights and priorities of shareholders. To review, the terms listed below are often encountered in descriptions of preferred stock:

- **Cumulative**—indicates that before any distributions are made to shareholders of common stock, all preferred dividends, including any that were missed in previous years, must be paid. Missed dividends are referred to as **dividends in arrears.**

- **Convertible**—indicates that the preferred stock can be exchanged for a firm's other designated securities (usually common stock) at a specified exchange ratio.

- **Redeemable**—indicates that the issuing firm must repurchase the outstanding preferred shares at a specified price. Preferred shares that are "nonredeemable" may be repurchased at the prevailing market price, if management so decides.

---

[3]UAL, Inc., *Annual Report,* 1983, p. 41.

■ **Callable**—indicates that management has the right, if it so chooses, to redeem the shares at a predetermined price.

■ **Liquidating value**—indicates the amount to which the preferred shareholder is entitled when the firm liquidates (and before any distributions are made to common shareholders).

■ **Participating**—indicates that when dividends to common shareholders equal the preferred dividend percentage, both groups of shareholders share in any further distributions.

To examine accounting for preferred stock (and to cement your understanding of the important related terms), consider the shareholders' equity section of the Cyclops Optical Corporation statement shown in Exhibit 7-2. Cyclops Optical has issued both preferred and common stock, and the directors have decided to declare a dividend of $15 million at the end of 1987. There have been no dividends paid on the firm's preferred or common stocks for the past two years. The apportionment of the total dividend between the preferred shareholders and the common shareholders depends on the provisions of Cyclops Optical's preferred stock arrangement. For illustrative purposes, we will consider three possibilities:

1. *Eight percent noncumulative, nonparticipating preferred stock, $50 million par value.* The preferred dividend is $4 million (eight percent of $50 million); the remaining $11 million of the $15 million to be distributed is paid to the common shareholders.

Exhibit 7-2

Statement Segment for Use in Illustrating Accounting for Preferred Stock

Cyclops Optical Corporation
December 31, 1987

Shareholders' Equity:

Paid-in capital	
Preferred stock, at par value 1 million shares authorized, issued, and outstanding*	$ 50,000,000
Common stock, at par value, 1 million shares authorized, issued, and outstanding	100,000,000
Additional paid-in capital	180,000,000
Total paid-in capital	$330,000,000
Retained earnings	95,000,000
Total shareholders' equity	$425,000,000

*The preferred stock description would include details about preferences in dividend distributions. See text for several alternative assumptions concerning these shares.

2. *Six percent cumulative, nonparticipating preferred stock, $50 million par value.*   The total preferred dividend is $9 million. Of this amount, $6 million represents the dividends in arrears at the start of 1987 (two years × six percent × $50 million), and $3 million is the 1987 dividend (six percent × $50 million). The common stockholders receive the remaining $6 million.

3. *Seven percent noncumulative, participating preferred stock.*   The total dividend of $15 million is equal to ten percent of the total par value of the preferred and common shares (the total par value of the outstanding shares is $150 million—$50 million for the preferred stock and $100 million for the common stock). As a result, the preferred shareholders receive $5 million (ten percent of $50 million par), and the common shareholders receive $10 million (10 percent of $100 million par).

Effects of preferred stock on common stock book value per share and EPS
When firms have issued other equity securities that take precedence over common stock in the distribution of dividends and other corporate assets, that precedence will affect various financial ratios used by investor analysts. To illustrate this point, we will consider the calculations of book value per common share and earnings per share (EPS) for Cyclops Optical Corporation. In order to compute the **book value** of common stock, total shareholders' equity must be reduced by the preferred stockholders' equity. For Cyclops Optical (see Exhibit 7-2), the calculation at December 31, 1987, is

$$\text{Book Value per Share} = \frac{\text{Total Shareholders' Equity,}}{\text{Common Shares Outstanding}}$$

$$= \frac{\$425,000,000 - \$50,000,000}{1,000,000}$$

$$= \$375$$

(Any dividends in arrears on cumulative preferred stock would also be included in preferred stock equity in the above computation.)

The preferred stock's current dividend must likewise be subtracted from net income to obtain the net income available to the common shareholders, that is

$$\text{EPS} = \frac{\text{Net Income, Less Current Period Preferred Dividend}}{\text{Common Shares Outstanding}}$$

Stock Rights and Warrants

Stock rights are agreements that entitle the holders to acquire shares of a particular class of stock in the future at a specified price per share. Stock rights are evidenced by a certificate called a **stock warrant,** which may represent the right to purchase one or more shares of stock. Warrants may be issued for several purposes. They are often included as an "equity sweetener" when other securities, such as bonds, are issued. Warrants may also be given as compensation to underwriters, managers, and employees.

When warrants are issued with other securities, the accounting method to be used in recording pertinent transactions depends on whether the warrant is *detachable*. A **detachable warrant** is a warrant that can be sold separately from the other securities and therefore permits the determination of separate market values for the warrants and the other securities. If the warrants are detachable, the proceeds received for the issuance would be allocated between the warrants and the other securities on the basis of their relative market values. If the warrants are not detachable (as is the case for most convertible bonds), no allocation is permitted.

To illustrate the accounting for stock warrants, consider the balance sheet of Icarus Airlines Corporation shown in Exhibit 7-3. The firm intends to raise additional funds to acquire new aircraft, and management has decided to sell a combination of debt and equity securities.

The current market price of the firm's common stock is $90, but management believes that the stock will rise to about $120 within one or two years. Accordingly, the company's managers have decided to sell warrants to investors that entitle them to purchase 600,000 shares of the company's stock at any time during the next two years for a price of $120 per share. The investor incurs an initial cost to buy each warrant and will pay an additional $120 (the exercise price) upon exercise of the warrant. If the investor later decides not to

Exhibit 7-3

Balance Sheet for Use in Illustrating Accounting for Stock Warrants

Icarus Airlines Corporation
Balance Sheet
December 31, 1986

Total assets	$130,000,000
Current liabilities	$ 11,000,000
Long-term debt	29,000,000
Total liabilities	$ 40,000,000
Shareholders' equity:	
Common stock ($40 par, 1,000,000 shares issued and outstanding)	$ 40,000,000
Additional paid-in capital	28,000,000
Retained earnings	22,000,000
Total shareholders' equity	$ 90,000,000
Total liabilities and equity	$130,000,000

exercise the option, the initial cost of the warrant will not be refunded by the firm and will be a loss to the investor. Investors are often willing to buy a warrant to purchase stock at prices higher than the current market value of the stock because the amount of potential loss is limited to the price paid for the option, while the potential gain may be considerable if the stock price increases. Each of the warrants to be offered for sale by Icarus entitles the holder to purchase one share of common stock.

We will illustrate the methods to be used in accounting for Icarus' warrant sale under three different sets of circumstances. In the first instance, bonds and warrants are sold as separate securities. In the second illustration, bonds are sold with detachable warrants and in the third illustration, bonds are sold with nondetachable warrants (that is, as convertible debt).

Bonds and warrants sold as separate securities   Assume that Icarus bonds with a face value of $60 million and a semiannual interest coupon of 12 percent are sold at par, and the 600,000 warrants are sold for $10 each. The entry to record the sale of the bonds and stock warrants is

dr.	Cash	66,000,000	
	cr. Bonds Payable		60,000,000
	cr. Stock Warrants Outstanding		6,000,000

To record the sale of $60 million of bonds at par value, and warrants at $10 each to purchase 600,000 shares at $120 per share.

In this case, the stock warrants outstanding would be classified as paid-in capital, and the effective interest rate on the bonds would be reported as 12 percent in the firm's financial statements.

Bonds sold with detachable warrants   Assume that instead of selling bonds at face value and warrants at $10, Icarus Airlines decides to sell $60 million of long-term bonds (with a semiannual interest coupon of 12 percent) with detachable warrants to purchase 600,000 shares of the company's common stock. (Each hundred dollars of bond principal includes a detachable warrant for one share of stock.) Assume that the bonds with warrants sell for a total of $63 million.[4] To place a value on the two separate securities, it is necessary to determine the value of the bonds without the warrants, and the value of the warrants without the bonds. These amounts were given earlier as $60 million and $6 million, respectively. The allocation of the $63 million of proceeds would be made on the basis of relative market values, as follows:

---

[4]This differs from the $66 million in proceeds assumed in the previous case above because it is possible that the sum of the market values (bonds and warrants sold individually) will not equal the proceeds of the package (bonds with detachable warrants).

$$\frac{\text{Value of Bonds}}{\text{Value of Bonds} + \text{Value of Warrants}} \times \text{Total Proceeds} = \begin{array}{c}\text{Value Assigned}\\ \text{to Bonds}\end{array}$$

$$\frac{\$60 \text{ million}}{\$60 \text{ million} + \$6 \text{ million}} \times \quad \$63 \text{ million} \quad = \$57.27 \text{ million}$$

The remaining proceeds of \$5.73 million (\$63 million less \$57.27 million) would be assigned to the warrants. The journal entry to record the transaction is

dr.	Cash		63,000,000	
dr.	Discount on Bonds		2,730,000	
	cr.	Bonds Payable		60,000,000
	cr.	Stock Warrants		5,730,000

Bonds sold with nondetachable warrants (as convertible debt) As an alternative to the cases just described, assume that Icarus decides to sell **convertible debt**—bonds that can be exchanged by the investor for common stock at the rate of one share of stock for each \$100 of bond principal. In an economic sense, the convertible debt provides investors with rights very similar to those mentioned in the previous cases (debt with a face value of \$60 million and the right to buy 600,000 Icarus shares at \$120 per share). Assume that the proceeds of the convertible debt sale are \$62 million. The transaction would be recorded as follows

dr.	Cash		62,000,000	
	cr.	Bonds Payable		60,000,000
	cr.	Premium on Bonds		2,000,000

To record the sale of \$60 million of convertible bonds at greater than par value.

In this case, there is *no accounting recognition* that investors, in effect, have paid a portion of the sales proceeds for the right to buy Icarus shares in the future for \$120 per share. Rather, the entire amount of proceeds is attributed to the debt. The resulting bond premium will be amortized as a reduction of bond interest expense over the life of the bonds. Accountants have debated whether it would be preferable to identify a portion of the proceeds of convertible debt as payment for the conversion privilege and to allocate that portion to shareholder equity. APB *Opinion No. 14* focused on the legal form rather than the economic substance of convertible debt, and specified that *none of the proceeds should be attributed to the conversion feature.*[5] For balance sheet purposes, the convertible debt remains classified as debt until converted. This classification is maintained even when market prices of the firm's stock rise above the

---

[5]Accounting Principles Board *Opinion No. 14,* "Accounting for Convertible Debt and Debt Issued with Stock Purchase Warrants" (New York: AICPA, 1969), par. 12.

conversion price, although in such a case it is virtually certain that investors will eventually exchange the bonds for stock.

When convertible debt is actually converted, the firm will decrease outstanding debt and increase shareholders' equity. In most cases, the credit to shareholders' equity is for the carrying value of the debt.[6] For example, assume that on December 31, 1988, the carrying value of the Icarus Airlines bonds is $61.6 million (bond principal of $60 million, plus $1.6 million unamortized bond premium). If all the bonds are converted to common stock at that date, the following journal entry would record the conversion:

dr.	Bond Payable	60,000,000	
dr.	Premium on Bonds	1,600,000	
	cr. Common Stock at Par Value		24,000,000
	cr. Additional Paid-in Capital		37,600,000

To record the conversion of outstanding bonds to 600,000 shares of $40 par value common stock.

The reported ratio of debt-to-shareholder equity of Icarus Airlines will fall as a result of the debt conversion. Interest expense will decrease since the debt has been converted to stock, and net income will increase. The number of common shares also increases, so that the effect of the debt conversion on earnings per share may be positive or negative. The effect depends on EPS before conversion and the following ratio:

$$\frac{\text{Interest Expense on Converted Bonds, after Tax}}{\text{Shares Issued to Retire Bonds}}$$

If this ratio exceeds EPS before conversion, conversion will increase EPS. In the opposite case, EPS will decrease.

Stock Splits and Stock Dividends

Firms frequently distribute shares of stock to existing shareholders as stock splits or stock dividends. A **stock split** is a distribution of additional shares of stock to present shareholders in proportion to their present ownership percentages. A stock split *increases* the number of shares outstanding, and at the same time *reduces* the par value per share so that the total par value of the outstanding shares is unchanged. For example, if a firm with 1 million shares of $100 par value stock were to have a two for one stock split, the 1 million old shares would be replaced by 2 million new shares of $50 par stock. The total par value would be $100 million before and after the split, so that the firm's total paid-in capital and total retained earnings would be unaffected. Managers may split

---

[6]An infrequently used alternative is to credit shareholders' equity at the current market value of the securities with a resultant gain or loss on debt retirement.

stock in order to reduce the per-share trading price of the stock, on the assumption that lower priced shares will appeal to a broader group of investors and be more actively traded. Stock splits do not require formal journal entries, since the dollar amounts appearing in the financial statements are unaffected.

A **stock dividend** is also a distribution of shares to present shareholders in proportion to their ownership interests, but a stock dividend (in contrast to a stock split) does not decrease the par value per share of stock. Accordingly, the total par value of outstanding shares *increases* as the additional shares are issued and retained earnings is reduced by the amount of the dividend. A stock dividend is usually recorded as a debit to retained earnings and a credit to paid-in capital, based on the market value of the firm's shares when the dividend is declared.

dr.	Retained Earnings	XXX	
	cr. Common Stock at Par Value		XXX
	cr. Additional Paid-in Capital		XXX

The journal entry is needed because the dollar amounts appearing in the financial statements are affected by stock dividends. This entry reduces retained earnings and increases paid-in capital, leaving shareholders' equity unchanged.

Managers may pay stock dividends in an effort to reduce the per-share price of company shares. Other reasons firms issue stock dividends include the following:

1. A firm may need its existing liquid assets as working capital—to finance an expansion, to retire debt, or for other purposes. A stock dividend may give the naïve investor the impression that the firm is distributing something of value.
2. A firm may desire to reduce its amount of retained earnings without reducing the net assets employed. A stock dividend reduces retained earnings (the dollar amount is shifted from retained earnings to paid-in capital, as shown in the preceding journal entry). By the simple expedient of declaring a stock dividend, management reduces the retained earnings balance.
3. Managers may use stock dividends as a signal to investors that total dividends to shareholders will be increased in the future. This is more likely if the firm has a tradition of maintaining a given cash dividend per share. In this sense, the declaration of a stock dividend may be an indirect means utilized by managers to communicate their forecasts of higher operating cash flows to investors.

In the case of both stock splits and stock dividends, shareholders receive additional shares in direct proportion to the number of shares they currently own. Thus, *each shareholder's fractional interest in the firm remains unchanged.* Moreover, since the firm receives no new assets and incurs no new liabilities as the result of stock splits and dividends, the net assets and the earning power of the firm should, in theory, remain unaffected. Yet, stock splits and stock dividends receive a good deal of attention in the business press, and there is a prevailing belief among investors that news of these stock distributions will increase the value of their stockholdings.

A number of studies of the effects of stock splits and stock dividends on securities prices indicate that investors react favorably to news of these events. Generally, during the period preceding management's formal public announcement of a stock split or dividend, the shares of the firm involved outperform those of other firms of equivalent risk. This implies that investors in the aggregate believe that such stock distributions have economic substance and affect the total value of the firm. One likely interpretation of the stock price effect is that investors view stock distributions as forecasts of higher future earnings or cash dividends. Some studies have compared the behavior of stock prices for two groups of firms during the period subsequent to a stock distribution. One group experienced improved earnings performance following the stock distribution. Earnings of firms in the second group did not improve. The evidence from these studies suggests that if stock distributions are not followed by improved earnings, the favorable stock price performance associated with stock distributions soon disappears.

Transactions in Treasury Stock

Firms occasionally repurchase shares of their own outstanding stock (which are then termed treasury stock shares). They do this for several reasons, including the following:

1. Managers may believe that the market price of the firm's shares is presently too low and that the shares constitute a good investment.
2. The firm may be obliged to issue common stock pursuant to employee stock option plans or other contractual arrangements and may wish to avoid the expenses associated with issuance of new shares.
3. Managers may attempt to increase the trading price of the firm's shares by reducing the supply of shares outstanding.
4. Shares may be repurchased to alter the voting interests of various shareholders or to concentrate ownership interest among fewer shareholders.
5. Managers may perceive the accounting effects of share repurchases as desirable because (as will be shown) treasury stock repurchases may affect various financial ratios.

To illustrate accounting for treasury shares, assume that on December 31, 1987, Pandora Corrugated Products paid $60 per share to repurchase 200,000 shares of its outstanding stock. The repurchase should be recorded as follows

dr.	Treasury Stock	12,000,000	
	cr. Cash		12,000,000

To record repurchase of 200,000 shares at $60 per share.

The firm's balance sheet after the repurchase appears below.

Pandora Corrugated Products Corporation
Balance Sheet at December 31, 1987
(after treasury stock repurchase)

Net assets	$50,600,000
Shareholders' equity	
Common stock (10 million $25 par value shares authorized, 1 million issued, of which 200,000 are in treasury)	$25,000,000
Additional paid-in capital	35,000,000
Total paid-in capital	$60,000,000
Retained earnings	2,600,000
Less: Treasury stock, at cost	(12,000,000)
Total shareholders' equity	$50,600,000

Treasury stock is not classified as an asset because that would imply that a corporation owns part of itself. Rather, when a firm buys back some of its own stock, it reduces its capitalization. In essence, treasury stock is the same as unissued stock, and a firm's unissued stock is not reported as an asset. Moreover, firms do not recognize gains or losses from dealing in treasury stock. If Pandora were to sell the treasury stock at other than the $60-per-share reacquisition price, the difference between their reacquisition price and their resale price would be treated as an adjustment to paid-in capital. This is consistent with the view that treasury stock transactions constitute adjustments in capitalization and are *not* purchases or sales of assets.

As a result of the treasury stock acquisition described above, the book value per share of Pandora's outstanding stock has increased from $62.60 to $63.25 ($50.6 million total shareholders' equity divided by 800,000 shares outstanding). The change in book value per share occurs because there is a difference between the market price per share and the book value per share at the date of the stock repurchase. As a consequence, the numerator and denominator of the book value per share ratio will change in different proportions. When book value and market value per share are equal, there will be no such effect. When market value exceeds book value, treasury stock repurchases will decrease the book value of the remaining outstanding shares. Throughout much of the past decade, about one-half of the securities traded on the New York Stock Exchange had book values higher than their market values, so that treasury stock repurchases by those firms would have increased the book values of the remaining shares outstanding.

The effect of treasury stock repurchases on EPS depends on the earnings rate on the assets paid to acquire the treasury shares, as well as on the **price-to-earnings (P/E) multiple** of the firm's shares. To illustrate this point, assume that before the treasury stock repurchase, Pandora has a market price of $60. Because EPS is $5, the firm has a P/E multiple of 12 ($60/$5). The reciprocal of the P/E multiple is termed the **earnings yield (E/P).** In this instance, the earnings yield is 8⅓ percent ($5.00 EPS/$60.00 market price). The firm paid $12 million in order to acquire the treasury shares, and it is reasonable to assume that the total net income of Pandora will be lower after paying out those assets.[7] If the after-tax return on those assets is less than the earnings yield, the firm's earnings per share will increase as a result of the treasury stock repurchase. Conversely, if the after-tax return on those assets is greater than the firm's earnings yield, the treasury stock repurchase would decrease earnings per share.

The effects of treasury stock repurchase on the book value and earnings per share of the remaining outstanding shares may be summarized as indicated below.

Book Value and Earnings per Share (EPS) Effects of Treasury Stock Repurchase

Book Value Effects	
Relationship between Market Value per Share (MV) and Book Value per Share (BV) before Repurchase	Effect of Treasury Stock Repurchase on Book Value per Share
If MV is less than BV	BV increases
If MV equals BV	No change in BV
If MV is greater than BV	BV decreases

EPS Effects	
Relationship between After-tax Return on Assets (ROA) and Earnings Yield (E/P) before Repurchase	Effect of Treasury Stock Repurchase on EPS
If ROA is greater than E/P	EPS decreases
If ROA equals E/P	No change in EPS
If ROA is less than E/P	EPS increases

Because firms do not recognize gains or losses from transactions involving their own shares, if Pandora subsequently resells the treasury shares acquired, any difference between the sale proceeds and the cost of the shares will be an adjustment to paid-in capital. For example, assume that Pandora's treasury shares are subsequently resold for $70 per share. The resale would be recorded as follows:

dr.	Cash	14,000,000	
	cr. Treasury Stock		12,000,000
	cr. Excess over Par, Sale of Treasury Shares		2,000,000

To record sale of 200,000 shares at $70 per share.

Retained Earnings Changes

The retained earnings of a firm may change during a given period for any of the reasons discussed in the following paragraphs:

---

[7]Even in the unlikely event that the $12 million was being held as an idle cash balance, there would be opportunity costs involved in not investing the cash or in distributing cash dividends to shareholders.

1. *Net income (or loss)* for the period causes the retained earnings balance to increase (or decrease). As discussed in Chapter 2, periodic net income is closed to the Retained Earnings account by the following entry

dr.	Expense and Revenue Summary	XXX	
	cr. Retained Earnings		XXX

2. *Cash dividends* declared during the period cause the retained earnings balance to decrease and are recorded as follows

dr.	Retained Earnings	XXX	
	cr. Dividends Payable		XXX

Notice that this entry causes a decrease in total owners' equity.

3. *Stock dividends* also reduce retained earnings, but do not cause a decrease in total owners' equity. Stock dividends only change the composition of total owners' equity and are recorded as follows

dr.	Retained Earnings	XXX	
	cr. Paid-in Capital		XXX

Observe that the increase in one owners' equity account is offset by the decrease in another, leaving total owners' equity unchanged.

4. *Prior-period adjustments* may cause the beginning balance of Retained Earnings to be increased or decreased retroactively.

5. *Business combinations* or sales of intercorporate investments may cause increases or decreases in retained earnings. These effects are discussed in Chapter 9, which deals with intercorporate investments.

6. *Appropriations of retained earnings* reduce the amount that is available for the declaration of shareholder dividends. Appropriations may be made to satisfy legal requirements, to comply with bond indenture contracts, or simply to inform investors that financial managers have internal need for the earnings retained and do not plan to distribute them as dividends in the near future. The appropriation is recorded in the following way

dr.	Retained Earnings	XXX	
	cr. Appropriated Retained Earnings		XXX

There is no effect on net assets or paid-in capital due to the appropriation of retained earnings. The effect is merely to divide total retained earnings into two proportions—appropriated and unappropriated.

Some states legally require that retained earnings be appropriated in an amount equal to the cost of treasury shares. This restriction is designed to protect lenders who have relied on shareholder equity as security, in the event that the firm becomes insolvent. For a similar reason, lending agreements (loan indentures) often impose contractual limits on a firm's dividend payments, sometimes through appropriation of retained earnings. Note, however, that the appropriation of retained earnings does not set aside specific assets for debt repayment or other purposes. It is possible that a firm will have insufficient liquid assets to meet its debts as they mature, even though the balance sheet may show ample amounts of appropriated retained earnings. The analyst must look to the asset side of the balance sheet to determine whether the firm has set aside assets to meet its debt or other cash requirements. As discussed in Chapter 5, firms often earmark assets for specific uses by establishing sinking funds.

Other Elements of Shareholders' Equity

Recent FASB statements have created two new elements (in addition to paid-in capital and retained earnings) in shareholders' equity: (1) a provision for temporary declines in the market value of a firm's noncurrent investments in marketable equity securities and (2) translation adjustments for consolidating foreign subsidiaries. Accounting for marketable equity securities is discussed in Chapter 5, and accounting for foreign operations is discussed in Chapter 11. These elements will not be covered here, except to note that they are not compatible with the basic concepts of shareholders' equity because they represent neither paid-in capital nor retained earnings. Rather, their appearance in the shareholders' equity section of the balance sheet reflects compromises by the FASB to avoid the allegedly undesirable economic consequences of previous methods used in accounting for marketable equity securities and foreign operations.

EPS Calculations for Complex Capital Structures

Many firms have simple capital structures consisting only of common stock. The earnings-per-share (EPS) calculation for such firms is straightforward and was illustrated in Chapter 3. To review, the calculation formula is

$$\text{EPS} = \frac{\text{Net Income Available to Common Stockholders}}{\text{Weighted Average of Common Shares Outstanding}}$$

The calculation becomes more intricate when a firm has a complex capital structure. A **complex capital structure** includes one or more of the following types of securities: convertible debt, convertible preferred stock, stock rights, or stock options. Although these securities are not themselves common stock, their conversion or *exercise* allows the holder to acquire shares of the firm's common stock. The major concern is that these securities may have a **dilutive effect** on EPS; that is, if converted or exercised, these securities may reduce EPS.

Firms with complex capital structures must present on the face of the income statement two types of EPS data: **primary earnings per share (PEPS)** and **fully diluted earnings per share (FDEPS)**. The steps used to compute this EPS data are summarized in Exhibit 7-4 and will be illustrated in the discussion that

Exhibit 7-4
Steps in Computing Earnings per Share (EPS)

1. To determine EPS—divide net income available to common stockholders by the weighted-average number of shares actually outstanding during the period.

2. To determine primary earnings per share (PEPS)
   (a) Identify common stock equivalents (CSEs)
   (b) Determine whether CSEs are dilutive
   (c) Include all dilutive CSEs in computation of PEPS

3. To determine fully diluted earnings per share (FDEPS)
   (a) Identify other (non-CSE) potentially dilutive securities
   (b) Determine whether the non-CSEs are dilutive
   (c) Include all dilutive non-CSEs in the computation of FDEPS.

follows here. The exhibit includes a number of technical terms, such as common stock equivalents (CSEs) and dilutive securities, which will be explained in the illustration that follows.

Primary earnings per share (PEPS)   The primary earnings per share figure is based on the weighted-average number of common shares outstanding, plus the effect of any dilutive common stock equivalents. A **common stock equivalent (CSE)** is defined as

> A security that is not, in form, a common stock but that contains provisions to enable its holder to become a common stockholder and that, because of the terms and conditions under which it was issued, is, in substance, equivalent to a common stock.[8]

The essential feature of a common stock equivalent is that its value is derived largely from the common stock to which it is related. Stock rights and options are *always* common stock equivalents; convertible debt and convertible preferred stock are classified as common stock equivalents *if the cash yield to the holder at the time of issuance is significantly below a comparable rate for similar securities without the conversion option.*[9]

To illustrate the calculation of primary EPS, consider the information in Exhibit 7-5 concerning the capital structure and earnings of Medusa Corporation.

---

[8] Accounting Principles Board *Opinion No. 15*, "Earnings Per Share" (New York: AICPA, 1969), par. 25.

[9] The FASB has established an arbitrary measure for making this determination. For practical purposes, a cash yield of less than two-thirds of the yield on high-quality corporate bonds will cause a convertible security to be classified as a common stock equivalent. See *Statement of Financial Accounting Standards No. 55*, "Determining Whether a Convertible Security Is a Common Stock Equivalent" (Stamford, CT: FASB, 1982), par. 7.

Exhibit 7-5

Data for EPS Calculations

Medusa Corporation

Net income, year ended December 31, 1987 $24,000,000

Common shares outstanding (no change during 1987)   6,000,000 shares

Market price per share (essentially unchanged during 1987) $50 per share

Stock options: Employees hold options to purchase up to 1,200,000 shares of Medusa Corporation common stock, at an exercise price of $30 per share, at any time between January 1, 1987, and December 31, 1990.

Convertible bonds: $50,000,000 principal amount of debentures convertible into Medusa Corporation common stock, at a ratio of one share of stock for each $50 of bond principal. The bonds were sold originally at face value to yield 10 percent. At that time, the prevailing market rate on high-quality corporate debt was 14 percent.

Convertible preferred stock: 2,000,000 shares of $100 par, 5 percent cumulative preferred stock, convertible to Medusa Corporation common stock at a ratio of one preferred share for each common share. The preferred stock was sold when the prevailing market interest rate on high-quality corporate debt was 12 percent.

In addition to the shares outstanding, Medusa has three types of potentially dilutive securities: (1) stock options, (2) convertible bonds, and (3) convertible preferred stock. Without considering the potentially dilutive securities, Medusa has an EPS of $2.33, which is calculated below. (The preferred dividend amount in the calculation equals 2 million shares $\times$ $100 $\times$ .05 percent.)

$$\text{EPS} = \frac{\text{Net Income Available for Common Shareholders}}{\text{Weighted Average Common Shares Outstanding}}$$

$$= \frac{\$24,000,000 - \$10,000,000 \text{ (preferred dividend)}}{6,000,000 \text{ shares}}$$

$$= \$2.33$$

After EPS has been calculated, the next step in the primary EPS computation is to identify the common stock equivalents and to determine whether their effects are dilutive. By definition, stock options are common stock equivalents. The status of the convertible debt and convertible preferred stock depends on the **cash yield test.** If the yield is below two-thirds of the market rate of interest on high-quality corporate debt, then the particular security in question is a common stock equivalent.

In the case of the Medusa Corporation's convertible bonds, the cash yield is 10 percent, which exceeds two-thirds of 14 percent (the market rate of high-quality corporate debt on the date the bonds were originally issued). Thus, the convertible bonds are not common stock equivalents.

The cash yield on Medusa Corporation's convertible preferred stock is 5 percent, which is less than two-thirds of the 12-percent market rate of high-quality corporate debt on the date the preferred stock was originally issued. Thus, the convertible preferred stock is a common stock equivalent.

We have determined that common stock equivalents for the Medusa Corporation consist of the stock options and the convertible preferred stock. The next step involves testing the stock options and the convertible preferred stock for possible dilutive effects.

If the stock options were exercised at the beginning of the period, Medusa would receive $36 million (1.2 million shares at the $30 option price) and would issue 1.2 million shares of common stock. Because the $36 million is assumed to be received at the beginning of the period, it is also necessary to make assumptions about how those funds will be used. Rather than allow a variety of subjective judgments about the use of such proceeds, the APB requires in *Opinion No. 15* that firms use the **treasury stock method.** The treasury stock method assumes that the proceeds from the exercise of the stock options are used to buy back the firm's common stock at the current market price. In this case, we have assumed that the current market price is $50. Accordingly, Medusa could purchase 720,000 shares with the stock option proceeds ($36 million/$50 current market price). If this repurchase is made, the net effect would be to increase outstanding shares by 480,000 (1.2 million − 720,000). The resultant EPS would be

$$\text{EPS} = \frac{\$24,000,000 - \$10,000,000 \text{ (preferred dividend)}}{6,480,000 \text{ shares}}$$

$$= \$2.16$$

Exercise of the stock options, given the assumption of use of the proceeds to buy back the firm's own stock at the current market price of $50, would have a dilutive effect on earnings per share: EPS would be reduced from $2.33 to $2.16.

The **"if converted" method** is used to test the effect of conversion of preferred stock on EPS. In the Medusa Corporation case, if the preferred stock is converted at the beginning of the year, an additional 2 million shares of common stock will be outstanding throughout 1987. In addition, conversion of the preferred stock will make the entire $24 million of net income available for the common shareholders, because there would no longer be any preferred stockholders. The resultant EPS would be

$$\text{EPS} = \frac{\$24,000,000}{8,840,000 \text{ shares}}$$

$$= \$2.83$$

As this calculation shows, a conversion of the convertible preferred stock would result in an increase in EPS from $2.16 (assuming no conversion) to $2.83 (assuming conversion). Thus, an assumed conversion of the convertible preferred stock does not have a dilutive effect on EPS.

GAAP require that all common stock equivalents that would have a dilutive effect on earnings if converted or exercised be included in the final calculation of primary EPS. In the Medusa Corporation illustration, only the stock options were common stock equivalents with a dilutive effect on EPS. Thus, primary earnings per share (PEPS) would be presented on the face of Medusa Corporation's income statement as $2.16, which assumes exercise of the stock options. Because the convertible bonds in the Medusa case are not common stock equivalents and because the preferred stock is not dilutive, neither the bonds nor the preferred stock affects the calculation of primary EPS.

Fully diluted earnings per share (FDEPS)   Because Medusa Corporation has other potentially dilutive securities that are not common stock equivalents (the convertible bonds), it is necessary to compute a second per-share amount termed *fully diluted* EPS. If the fully diluted EPS is lower than primary EPS, the firm will report both per-share amounts in the financial statements. The convertible bonds, although not common stock equivalents, still represent potential dilution if converted. The "if converted" method is applied to the bonds to test whether conversion would have a dilutive effect on earnings. If it does, such conversion is assumed in calculating fully diluted EPS; otherwise, conversion is not assumed.

To test for dilution, the bonds are assumed to be converted on the first day of the current reporting period. If the bonds were converted on January 1, 1987, the earnings available to common stockholders would increase by the amount of the bond interest expense, net of any related tax effect. In addition, the number of outstanding shares would increase by 1 million (one share for each $50 of bond principal). Assuming that Medusa's income is taxed at a 40 percent rate, the EPS calculation is

$$EPS = \frac{\$24,000,000 - \$10,000,000 \text{ (preferred dividend)} + \$3,000,000 \text{ (bond interest expense of \$5 million, net of \$2 million tax effect)}}{6,480,000 \text{ shares} + 1,000,000 \text{ shares}}$$

$$= \$2.27$$

Because the effect of including the bonds is not dilutive (that is, EPS would not be decreased), conversion of the bonds is not assumed in calculating fully diluted EPS. In this case in which primary EPS and fully diluted EPS would be the same amount, Medusa Corporation would report only the primary EPS amount of $2.16.

USEFULNESS OF ACCOUNTING-BASED MEASUREMENTS OF SHAREHOLDERS' EQUITY

Although there are many unresolved conceptual issues in accounting for owners' equity, recent empirical evidence suggests that accounting measures of equity may be useful for investment analysis. Researchers have found that financial leverage, computed using accounting-based measures of debt and equity, is closely associated with empirical measures of risk of equity securities, bond interest rate differences among firms, and bond ratings assigned by leading rating agencies. Moreover, accounting measures of financial leverage have been employed successfully in statistical models for predicting events such as corporate bankruptcy and changes in bond ratings.

SUMMARY

This chapter begins with the definition of owners' equity contained in the FASB's *Statement of Financial Accounting Concepts No. 6,* and discusses the characteristics that distinguish owners' equity from liabilities. A variety of transactions affecting ownership equity are explained and illustrated, including issuance of common and preferred stock; payment of cash dividends; distributions of stock splits and stock dividends; sale of stock rights and warrants; repurchase and subsequent resale of treasury shares; and the exchange by debtholders of convertible bonds for equity securities. Earnings-per-share calculations are illustrated for firms with simple and complex capital structures.

The voting ownership shares of a firm are called common stock. The stock is issued to owners for cash or other consideration. Firms usually assign a par value or stated value to shares of common stock. The proceeds received over and above par value are reported as "additional paid-in capital."

Besides common stock, firms might also issue other equity securities called preferred stock. Preferred stock has certain priorities over common stock, usually involving the distribution of dividends and other corporate assets.

Some preferred stock issuances are cumulative. This means that before any distributions are made to common stockholders, all preferred dividends must be paid, including any that were missed in previous years. Preferred stock may also be convertible. Convertible preferred stock can be exchanged for a firm's common stock at a specified exchange ratio. A firm may also issue preferred stock that is redeemable. This means that the issuing firm may, at its option, repurchase the outstanding preferred shares at a specified price. Finally, preferred stock may be participating. The participating feature allows the preferred shareholders to receive dividends in excess of those normally paid.

Stock rights are agreements that entitle the holders to acquire shares of a particular class of stock in the future at a specified price per share. Stock rights are evidenced by a certificate called a stock warrant.

When warrants are issued with stocks or bonds, the accounting method to be used depends on whether the warrant is detachable. A detachable warrant is a warrant that can sell separately from the stocks or bonds. If the warrant is detachable, the proceeds received from the issuance are allocated between the warrants and the other securities based on their relative market values. If the warrants are not detachable, as is the case for most convertible bonds, then none of the proceeds are allocated to the warrants.

Firms frequently distribute shares of stock to existing shareholders as stock dividends or stock splits. A stock split is a distribution of additional shares of stock to present shareholders in proportion to their present ownership percentages; it increases the number of shares outstanding and at the same time reduces the par value per share, so that the total par value of the outstanding shares is unchanged. A stock dividend is also a distribution of shares to present shareholders in proportion to their ownership interests, but in contrast to a stock split, a stock dividend does not decrease the par value per share of stock.

Treasury stock is a firm's own stock that has been issued and subsequently repurchased. It is reported as a subtraction in the stockholders' equity section of the balance sheet. Firms do not realize gains or losses from transactions involving their own shares. Accordingly, if treasury stock is resold, any difference between the sale proceeds and the cost of the treasury shares is an adjustment to paid-in capital. Depending on the circumstances, treasury stock transactions may increase or decrease earnings per share and book value per share.

Firms may appropriate, or restrict, retained earnings. An appropriation of retained earnings does not affect a firm's net assets or paid-in capital. The effect is to divide total retained earnings into two categories: appropriated and unappropriated. The appropriated portion is unavailable for the declaration of dividends to shareholders.

A firm with only common stock has a simple capital structure. Earnings per share for a firm with a simple capital structure is calculated by dividing net income by the weighted-average of the common shares outstanding. If a firm has convertible debt, convertible preferred stock, stock rights, or stock options, it has a complex capital structure. A firm with a complex capital structure must present two types of earnings-per-share data on the face of its income statement: primary earnings per share (PEPS) and fully diluted earnings per share (FDEPS).

A common stock equivalent is a security that is not a common stock in form, but contains provisions that enable its holder to convert it to common stock. If dilutive, common stock equivalents are used in calculating primary earnings per share. Fully dilutive earnings-per-share calculations will include any security (even those not classified as common stock equivalents) that has dilutive effects on EPS.

QUESTIONS

1. The terms listed below were introduced in this chapter. Define or explain each of them.

appropriations of retained earnings	convertible preferred stock
book value of common stock	cumulative preferred stock
cash yield test (EPS)	dilutive effect (EPS)
common stock	earnings yield
common stock equivalent	fully diluted earnings per share
convertible debt	liquidating value (preferred stock)

owners' equity	stated value
par value	stock dividend
participating preferred stock	stock rights
preferred stock	stock split
price-to-earnings multiple (P/E)	stock warrants
primary earnings per share	treasury stock

2. The total dollar value assigned to owners' equity on the financial statements is said to be a residual amount. Explain what this means.

3. Under what circumstances would you prefer to own shares of a company's preferred stock rather than shares of its common stock? Under what circumstances would you prefer common stock to preferred stock?

4. What is the significance of the par value assigned to shares of common stock? Is par value intended to reflect market value of shares of stock?

5. From the perspective of a common stockholder, what is the significance of the firm's having cumulative preferred stock? Is it possible for noncumulative preferred stock to have dividends in arrears?

6. Distinguish between a stock right and a stock warrant.

7. Would an investor be willing to pay for a warrant to purchase stock at a price greater than the current market price of the stock? Explain.

8. Convertible bonds involve (a) debt and (b) the right to convert debt into stock. How should the proceeds of an issuance of convertible debt be allocated between the debt and the conversion feature? Explain.

9. Describe the recommended procedure to account for the conversion of convertible debt into common stock.

10. What is the effect of the exercise of the conversion feature of convertible debt on the ratio of debt to shareholders' equity?

11. What is the effect on the earnings-per-share calculation of the exercise of the conversion feature on convertible debt?

12. Distinguish between a stock split and a stock dividend. Does accounting for stock splits differ from accounting for stock dividends? Explain.

13. Is the total par value of shares outstanding changed as the result of a stock split? Of a stock dividend?

14. Are the net assets of a firm changed by declaring and distributing a cash dividend? A stock dividend? A stock split?

15. List several reasons that a corporation might repurchase shares of its own outstanding stock.

16. Describe the journal entry sequence outlined in the chapter to account for the purchase and subsequent reissuance of treasury stock.

17. Discuss the possible effect(s) of a treasury stock purchase on a firm's earnings per share.

18. List several reasons why a firm's Retained Earnings account might change during any given accounting period.

19. Describe the journal entry sequence outlined in the chapter to account for appropriations of retained earnings. Are net assets of a firm affected by an appropriation of retained earnings? Explain.

20. What purposes are served by appropriating retained earnings?
21. Distinguish between primary earnings per share and fully diluted earnings per share. Do GAAP require that both be reported? Explain.
22. Describe the logic behind the cash yield method used to determine if a particular item is a common stock equivalent.
23. If an item is deemed to be a common stock equivalent, will it always affect the final calculation of primary earnings per share?

EXERCISES AND PROBLEMS

24. *Statements to Ponder.*   The following conversation segments relate to issues discussed in Chapter 7:

    (1) (*Husband to wife*) "We have stock in the Matrix Corporation. Although the company is only a few years old, it has been very profitable and has experienced rapid growth. The company hasn't paid a cash dividend since its inception, but each year there is a stock split, and instead of cash we just get more paper. It looks like we made a bum investment."

    (2) (*Wife to husband*) "I don't understand the figures contained in the Mirage Company's annual report. The income statement shows no improvement in net income for 1987 over 1986, yet earnings per share increased 10%. How is this possible?"

REQUIRED   Comment on each of these conversation segments.

25. *Transactions in Common and Preferred Stock.*   Road Scholars, Inc., is a newly organized firm offering home tutoring in a variety of subjects. On January 1, 1988, the firm received a charter granting the right to issue two classes of stock: 1 million shares of $50 par value 10% cumulative preferred stock, and 1 million shares of $10 par value common stock. During 1988 the following transactions occurred:

    (1) Sold 200,000 shares of common stock to investors at a price of $55 per share.
    (2) Sold 150,000 shares of preferred stock to investors at a price of $75 per share.
    (3) Acquired a building in exchange for 50,000 shares of common stock. On the date of the exchange, the common stock had a market value of $65 per share.
    (4) Declared and paid a cash dividend of $5 per share to the preferred stockholders.
    (5) Declared and distributed a 10% stock dividend to common stockholders. The common stock had a market value of $60 per share on the date that the stock dividend was declared.
    (6) Repurchased 7,000 shares of common stock as treasury stock at $70 per share.

(7) Declared and paid a cash dividend of $4 per share to the common shareholders.

(8) Sold 5,000 of the treasury shares at $72 per share.

(9) Closed the Revenue and Expense Summary, which had a credit balance of $6.5 million to the Retained Earnings account.

REQUIRED

(a) Provide journal entries to record each of the transactions described above.

(b) Prepare the shareholders' equity section of the Road Scholars, Inc., balance sheet at December 31, 1988.

26. *Effect of Owners' Equity Transactions on Elements of Financial Statements.* A list of business transactions and events follows:

(1) Sale of common stock to investors for cash.

(2) Sale of preferred stock to investors for cash.

(3) Declaration of a cash dividend to common shareholders.

(4) Payment of the dividend declared in item (3).

(5) Convertible bonds are converted to shares of common stock.

(6) Convertible preferred stocks are converted to shares of common stock.

(7) Treasury stock is purchased.

(8) Treasury stock is sold at a price in excess of its acquisition cost.

(9) Treasury stock is sold at a price below its acquisition cost.

(10) Options are issued to employees and will become exercisable in two years.

(11) The firm's shares are presently selling for $100, and the firm has sold to investors warrants to purchase shares at a price of $130 at any time over the next two years.

(12) A 5% stock dividend is declared.

(13) A two-for-one stock split is announced.

(14) A portion of retained earnings is appropriated for plant and equipment purchases.

REQUIRED
Indicate how each of the items in the above list would affect (increase, decrease, or cause no change) the following financial statement elements and financial ratios:

(a) Total assets

(b) Liabilities

(c) Shareholders' equity

(d) Common shareholders' equity

(e) Common paid-in capital

(f) Retained earnings

(g) Net income

(h) Earnings per share

(i) Financial leverage (debt-to-equity ratio)

(j) Return on Equity (net income-to-shareholders' equity ratio)

27. *Recording Various Equity Transactions.* Listed below are actual transactions involving stockholders' equity of three different U.S. corporations.

A. *USG Corporation*
    (1) During 1984, the company exchanged 199,753 shares of its $4 par value common stock for $14,350,000 of outstanding debentures (net of unamortized discount of $123,000). The market value of the common stock when these conversions took place averaged $47.654 per share.
    (2) Stock options exercised in 1984 resulted in the issuance of 54,383 shares of common stock at an average price of $47.184 per share.

B. *Hammermill Paper Company*
    (3) 33,657 shares of common stock, par value $1.25, were issued in 1983 in payment of timberland acquisition note obligations amounting to $1,203,000.
    (4) A shareholder (officer) contributed his $557,000 "short-swing" profit on sale of Hammermill's common stock as required under federal securities law.

C. *General Motors*
    (5) In 1984 the company reacquired in the open market 137,350 and 142,000 shares respectively of its $5.00 series and $3.75 series preferred stock, with stated values of $100 per share, at a total cost of $11.8 million.

REQUIRED   Record the appropriate journal entry to reflect each of the transactions described.

28. *Reconstruction of Stockholders' Equity.* As of December 31, 1983, the consolidated balance sheet of U.S. Steel Corporation reported that its stockholders' equity amounted to $5,605 million. A breakdown of stockholders' equity was as follows:

	Shares	Amount (in millions)
Preferred stock		
Adjustable rate (stated value $50)	4,000,000	$ 200
$12.75 convertible (stated value $100)	3,350,000	335
$ 2.75 convertible (stated value $25)	10,000,000	250
$10.75 convertible (stated value $100)*	2,250,000	250
Total preferred outstanding	19,850,000	$1,035

	Shares	Amount (in millions)
Common stock (stated value $20)	104,639,408	2,093
Paid-in capital in excess of par		91
Net income reinvested in the business		2,464
Foreign currency adjustment		(78)
Total stockholders' equity		$5,605

*This issue is subject to mandatory redemption and actually is shown on the balance sheet between long-term liabilities and stockholders' equity.

The following transactions affecting stockholders' equity occurred in 1984:

(1) 150 shares of a new issue of preferred stock (Series A — Money Market) with a stated value of $500,000 per share were sold to the public at a price of $493,333.33 per share.

(2) 1,950 shares of the $2.25 convertible preferred stock were converted into 1,687 shares of common stock.

(3) 714,796 shares of common stock were issued to stockholders under the Dividend Reinvestment Plan at an average price of $25.182.

(4) 1,748,692 shares of common stock were issued in conjunction with employee stock plans at an average price of $26.88.

(5) 88,696 shares of common stock were issued at a market price of $33.711 to acquire an interest in another company.

(6) In 1984 U.S. Steel reported a net income (after taxes) of $493 million and declared dividends as follows:

Preferred stock	(per share)
Adjustable rate	$ 6.49
$12.75 convertible	12.75
$ 2.25 convertible	2.25
$10.75 convertible	10.75
Money market — Series A	6125.00
Common stock (on average number of shares outstanding during the year; that is, 1/2 opening plus closing shares outstanding)	1.00

REQUIRED Determine the balance reported as stockholders' equity on U.S. Steel's December 31, 1984, consolidated balance sheet, showing all supporting details (to nearest million dollars).

29. *Shareholders' Equity: Comprehensive.* The following transactions have affected the shareholders' equity of the Bevelheaded Tool Company since it was founded on January 1, 1988.

(1) On January 1, 1988, the company was authorized to issue 1 million shares of $20 par value common stock and 500,000 shares of 10% $50

par value cumulative, nonparticipating preferred stock. During January 1988, the company sold 400,000 common shares and 200,000 preferred shares for a total consideration of $42 million. The company had net income of $6.5 million during 1988, and declared no dividends.

(2) During January 1989, the company sold an additional 100,000 common shares to investors for consideration of $7.2 million. The company had net income of $13.5 million during 1989, and declared and paid cash dividends of $2.5 million. In addition, a 5% common stock dividend was declared and issued to the common shareholders when the market price per share was $60.

(3) Early in 1990, the company repurchased 50,000 shares of its common stock at an average price of $82 per share. Subsequently, the common stock was split 2 for 1 (and the par value per share was halved). The authorized shares were increased to 2 million. The firm incurred a net loss of $2.6 million for 1990, and paid no dividends. In 1990, management appropriated retained earnings of $10 million, described as "Retained Earnings Appropriated for Plant Expansion."

REQUIRED   Prepare the shareholders' equity section of the Bevelheaded Tool Company's balance sheet at December 31, 1990.

30. *Capital Structure Measurement at Book Value and Market Value.*   You have been provided with the following financial information to aid in assessing the investment worthiness of two firms.

	(in millions)	
	Bert, Co.	Ernie, Inc.
Total assets, December 31, 1988[1]*	$50	$200
Total liabilities[2]	30	120
Shareholders' equity[3]	20	80
Net income, year 1988	5	20
Income tax rate	40%	40%

*Superscripts (1), (2), and (3) correspond to items (1), (2), and (3) below.

(1) Bert uses the LIFO inventory cost flow assumption, and accelerated depreciation for plant and equipment for both book and tax purposes. Ernie uses FIFO inventory costing and straight-line depreciation for book and tax purposes. If Bert had been using FIFO and straight-line depreciation, then Bert's pretax operating income for 1988 would have been higher by $4 million. In addition, the book values of Bert's inventory and plant and equipment at December 31, 1988, would have been higher by $12 million.

(2) Bert's liabilities consist primarily of bonds issued at par in 1985 when the market rate of interest was 10%; the bonds have 20 years to maturity and a market value of $25 million. Ernie's liabilities consist of

bonds issued at par in 1980 when the market rate of interest was 20%; the bonds have 20 years to maturity and a market value of $180 million.

(3) Bert has 1 million common shares outstanding, with a market value of $50 per share on December 31, 1988. Ernie has 2 million common shares outstanding, with a market value of $90 per share on December 31, 1988.

REQUIRED

(a) Determine the ratio of debt to equity (the financial leverage ratio) for both firms at December 31, 1988, using the balance sheet information reported above.

(b) Determine the financial leverage ratios for both firms at December 31, 1988, using the relative market value weights for debt and equity. Are book value or market value weights more suitable in measuring financial leverage?

(c) Discuss likely reasons for the differences between the book values and the carrying values of the debt and equity of both firms.

(d) Determine the relationship between net income and total assets (the return-on-assets ratio) and between net income and shareholders' equity (the return-on-equity ratio) for both firms. How do the differences in inventory costing and depreciation methods affect your calculations of total assets, shareholders' equity, and net income?

31. *Cash Dividend, Stock Dividend, and Stock Split.* The stockholders' equity accounts of the Lurtsema Company have the following balances on December 31, 1988:

Common stock, $20 par, 800,000 shares	$16,000,000
Additional paid-in capital	7,000,000
Retained earnings	5,000,000

REQUIRED

(a) Prepare journal entries for the following events, which occurred after December 31, 1988:

(1) A cash dividend of $2 per share is declared and paid.

(2) A stock dividend of 5% is declared and issued. On the date of the declaration of the stock dividend, the stock has a market price of $40 per share.

(3) A two for one stock split is declared and issued. On the date the stock split is declared, the market price of the stock is $38 per share.

(b) Prepare the stockholders' equity section of the Lurtsema Company's balance sheet after completion of the above transactions.

32. *Preferred Stock Dividend Distributions.* The outstanding stock of Manger Fast Foods, Inc., consists of the following: preferred stock, 8%, $100 par,

1 million shares authorized, 200,000 shares issued and outstanding; and common stock, $50 par, 5 million shares authorized, 2 million shares issued and outstanding.

REQUIRED   Assume that the company will declare and pay a total dividend of $30 million in the current year. Determine how much of this total each class of stock should receive under each of the following conditions:

(a) The preferred stock is noncumulative and nonparticipating.
(b) The preferred stock is cumulative and nonparticipating, and dividends are in arrears for one year.
(c) The preferred stock is cumulative and nonparticipating, and dividends are in arrears for five years.
(d) The preferred stock is noncumulative and fully participating.

33. *Stock Repurchase.*   On January 1, 1989, Humbert Company has 500,000 shares of $20 par common stock outstanding, which were issued for $40 per share. On July 1, 1989, Humbert Company repurchases 50,000 of these shares for $60 per share.

REQUIRED

(a) Provide the journal entry to record the treasury stock transaction.
(b) If there were no other stock transactions during 1989, what was the weighted-average number of common shares outstanding for the year?

34. *Treasury Stock Repurchase: Effects on Selected Ratios.*   The General Ennui Company reports the following amounts in its 1988 financial statements:

Shareholders' equity:
Common stock, $10 par; authorized 1 million shares;

issued 600,000 shares	$ 6,000,000
Additional paid-in capital	9,000,000
Retained earnings	12,000,000
Total	$27,000,000
Net income, year ended December 31, 1988	$ 5,400,000

REQUIRED

(a) Outstanding shares have not changed during 1988. Determine the company's earnings per share (EPS), book value per share, and return on shareholders' equity.
(b) Management is considering the acquisition of 100,000 shares of treasury stock in early January 1989. Indicate the effects on EPS and book value per share for 1989 under the following alternative sets of assumptions. (In all cases, assume that dividends will be equal to net

income during 1989, so that the retained earnings balance will remain at $12 million.)

(1) Treasury stock is purchased at $45 per share, and income declines by $900,000 to $4.5 million.

(2) Treasury stock is purchased at $60 per share, and income declines by $900,000 to $4.5 million.

(3) Treasury stock is purchased at $30 per share, and income declines by $900,000 to $4.5 million.

(4) Treasury stock is purchased at $45 per share, and income declines by $600,000 to $4.8 million.

(5) Treasury stock is purchased at $60 per share, and income declines by $600,000 to $4.8 million.

(c) Based on your answers to item (b), how are treasury stock purchases expected to affect book value per common share?

(d) Based on your answers to item (b), how are treasury stock repurchases expected to affect EPS?

(e) Discuss the probable effect of treasury stock repurchases on (1) the price per share of the remaining outstanding stock and (2) the total market value of the remaining outstanding stock.

35. *Bonds and Warrants.* On January 1, 1987, the Addled Systems Company issued bonds with a face amount of $10 million, which mature in 20 years. The bonds have a 12% semiannual interest coupon rate and detachable warrants giving the bondholders the right to purchase one share of stock for each $100 of bond principal at a cost of $50 at any time in the next two years. The market rate of interest was 12% compounded semiannually when the bonds were sold. The total proceeds of the bonds and detachable warrants was $11,980,000. At the date of sale, the market price of the company's common stock was $38 per share, and each one-share warrant had a market value of $15.

REQUIRED

(a) Explain why the bonds were sold to investors at an amount greater than the face amount, even though the market rate and the coupon rate of interest were the same.

(b) Provide a journal entry to record the sale of the bonds and detachable warrants. (Hint: Proceeds attributable to detachable warrants are treated as paid-in capital.)

(c) Determine the interest expense on the bonds for the year 1987.

(d) Assume that the market interest rate was 16% compounded semiannually when the bonds were sold for $11,980,000. In this case, what portion of the proceeds would be attributed to the detachable warrants?

36. *Straight Debt versus Convertible Debt.* On January 1, 1988, when the market rate of interest was 10%, the Aycee Company issued bonds with a principal amount of $60 million, maturing in ten years, with a 10% semiannual interest coupon. The bonds were sold at face value. On that same date, the Deecee Company, which has a similar credit rating, issued bonds with features identical to the Aycee Company bonds, except that Deecee's bonds were convertible into shares of Deecee's common stock. As a result, the Deecee bonds (which also had a 10% semiannual interest coupon) were sold at an effective rate of 8% compounded semiannually.

REQUIRED

   (a) Determine the proceeds of the Deecee Company's bond issue.
   (b) Provide journal entries to record (1) the proceeds of the bond issue on Aycee's books and (2) the proceeds of the bond issue on Deecee's books.
   (c) Determine the interest expense to be recognized for 1988 by Aycee and Deecee.
   (d) Should the two firms report different amounts of interest expense (for 1988) and bond liabilities at the end of 1988? Discuss.

37. *Conversion of Debt.* The Metamorphic Company has bonds outstanding with a face value of $10 million and a book value of $9,360,000 that are convertible into 80,000 of the company's $10 par common shares at any time, at the option of the bondholders. Assume that the entire debt issue is converted into stock immediately after an interest payment date. At that date, the market value of the debentures was 106 (that is, the entire issue had a market value of $10.6 million).

REQUIRED   Provide a journal entry to record the debt conversion.

38. *EPS Calculations: Effects of Preferred Stock Conversion.* The stockholders' equity of Warsaw Company contains convertible preferred stock with the following charactistics: $100 par, 10%, cumulative. This stock qualifies as a common stock equivalent, and has been outstanding for the entire year.

REQUIRED   For each of the cases listed below, determine the effects (increase, decrease, no effect) on primary EPS of the conversion of the convertible preferred stock.

   (a) EPS before conversion is $7.50. The conversion ratio is 1:1 (one preferred share for one common share).
   (b) Same as item (a), except that the conversion ratio is 2:1.
   (c) Same as item (a), except that the conversion ratio is 1:2.
   (d) Same as item (a), except that EPS before conversion is $3.00.

39. *EPS Calculations: Stock Options.*   The Exec Perk Company has granted certain key employees options to purchase up to 2 million shares of the firm's common stock at an exercise price of $100 per share. Exec Perk's 1986 EPS before considering these options is $12.50, based on a weighted average of 12 million shares outstanding.

REQUIRED   Determine the effect of the following assumptions on the EPS calculation:

    (a) Exec Perk's stock has a market value of $100 per share throughout 1986.
    (b) Exec Perk's stock has a market value of $80 per share throughout 1986.
    (c) Exec Perk's stock has a market value of $120 per share throughout 1986.

40. *Stock Options as Executive Compensation.*   Companies frequently issue stock options to employees as an element of executive compensation. If the option price is at least equal to the market price when the options are granted, the issuing firm does *not* impute any value to the options in recording this transaction. Accordingly, there is no reported compensation expense associated with these stock options. Ken Bland and Barbie Dahl are recent MBA graduates, and early in January 1988 each has been offered a five-year employment contract at Tinsel, Inc. Ken's contract provides him with an annual salary of $100,000. Barbie's contract includes an annual salary of $70,000. In addition, at the start of each year, Barbie will receive options to purchase 3,000 common shares of Tinsel, Inc., stock at the market price per share on that date; the options remain exercisable for five years from the day of receipt. Tinsel's common stock is presently selling at $100, and over the past several years the stock has had a return (dividends and capital gains) of about 15% per annum. Warrants to buy Tinsel, Inc.'s common shares at $100 per share are currently valued by investors at $20.

REQUIRED

    (a) Provide any journal entries required in 1988 to reflect (1) Ken's signing of his employment contract and (2) Ken's salary expense for 1988.
    (b) Provide any journal entries required in 1988 to reflect (1) Barbie's signing of her employment contract; (2) Barbie's receipt of options to buy 3,000 Tinsel shares at $100 per share in January 1988; and (3) Barbie's salary expense for 1988.
    (c) Assume that Tinsel shares have a market value of $120 per share at the end of 1988. How (if at all) would this affect the amount of Barbie's compensation expense reported by Tinsel, Inc.? Which of the two junior executives has received the higher compensation during 1988?
    (d) Assume that Tinsel common shares increase in market value to $200 per share by the end of 1992, the last year of the employment contract. Barbie has accumulated options to buy 15,000 shares (3,000

shares per year for five years) at an average price of $140 per share and exercises all of the options at the end of 1992. Provide the journal entry on Tinsel's books to reflect the exercise of the options.

(e) Based on these facts, what has been the total compensation cost recorded by Tinsel, Inc., for the five years of Ken's contract? For the five years of Barbie's contract? What has been the total income received by Ken? By Barbie? Explain any difference between the compensation expense recorded by Tinsel, Inc., and the compensation income received by Barbie.

41. *EPS Calculations: Effects of Bond Conversion.* Rutland Company has convertible bonds outstanding. These bonds qualify as common stock equivalents and have been outstanding for the entire year. The company's effective income tax rate is 40%.

REQUIRED For each of the items listed below, determine the effects (increase, decrease, no effect) on primary EPS of the conversion of these bonds. Explain.

(a) EPS before conversion is $5.00. The bonds have an interest rate of 12% and are convertible at the rate of 10 shares per $1,000 bond principal.

(b) Same as item (a), except that the bond interest rate is 4%.

(c) Same as item (a), except that the bond interest rate is 15%.

(d) Same as item (a), except that the conversion rate is 20 shares per $1,000 of bond principal.

(e) Same as item (a), except that the conversion rate is 5 shares per $1,000 of bond principal.

(f) Same as item (a), except that EPS before conversion is $2.00.

(g) Same as item (a), except that EPS before conversion is $10.00.

42. *Earnings per Share: Basic Calculations.* Primary earnings per share is influenced by many different factors, including the number of shares outstanding, the amount of preferred dividends in arrears, and the existence of convertible debt. Seven different situations involving various firms are outlined below:

(1) A firm had 5 million common shares outstanding on January 1, 1988. Additional shares were issued on July 1 (1 million shares) and October 1 (2 million shares). Net income was $12.4 million, and there were no other classes of stock or common stock equivalents.

(2) A firm had 10 million common shares outstanding throughout 1988, as well as 4 million shares of 8%, $100 par value cumulative, nonparticipating preferred stock with no dividends in arrears. Net income was $35 million, and there were no common stock equivalents.

(3) Assume that the facts are the same as in item (2), except that the preferred dividends are two years in arrears.

(4) Assume that the facts are the same as in item (2), except that the preferred stock was issued on October 1, 1988.

(5) A firm had 8 million common shares outstanding throughout 1988, as well as convertible debt that was sold at its face value of $20 million to yield 12% per annum. The debt is convertible into 2 million shares of common stock, and qualified as a common stock equivalent at the date issued. Net income (after income tax) was $6.4 million, and the firm's income tax rate was 40%.

(6) Assume that the facts are the same as in item (5), except that the firm's net income was $4 million in 1988.

(7) Assume that the facts are the same as in item (5), except that the firm's tax rate was 25% in 1988.

REQUIRED For each of these situations, determine the amount of primary earnings per share.

43. *EPS, Dilutive Common Stock Equivalents.* Gustav Company has provided the following information relative to the calculation of primary earnings per share for 1989. The firm's income is taxed at 40%.

Net income	$135 million
Number of common shares outstanding (unchanged throughout 1989)	20 million
Market price per common share (stable throughout 1989)	$150

Stock options are held by key employees as follows:
Options to purchase 4 million shares at a price of $90 per share are exercisable at various dates through 1992. Options to purchase 6 million shares at a price of $180 per share are exercisable at various dates through 1996.
Bonds payable of $900 million with a 10% interest coupon were sold at par in 1985 and each bond is convertible into ten shares of common stock. The bonds qualify as common stock equivalents.
Ten million shares of cumulative convertible $100 par value 10% preferred stock are outstanding and are convertible to common stock on a share for share basis. The preferred shares qualify as common stock equivalents.

REQUIRED

(a) Determine whether each of the common stock equivalents considered *individually* has a dilutive effect on EPS.

(b) Which dollar amount will be reported to investors as primary EPS? (Hint: The most dilutive combination of common stock equivalents will be used in the calculation of primary EPS.)

44. *Price-earnings Multiples And Potential Dilution.* Price-earnings ratios differ from firm to firm for various reasons, including differences in risk, expected rates of growth, accounting methods used in measuring income, and potentially dilutive securities. Selected financial information is provided below

for firms A, B, and C. Assume that the firms are in the same industry, have the same expected rates of growth, and are considered to have the same investment risk.

Selected Financial Information, Firms A, B, and C

	Firm A*	Firm B†	Firm C‡
Net income applicable to common stock	$120 million	$360 million	$240 million
Shares outstanding (unchanged during the year)	30 million	90 million	60 million

Tax rate, all firms: 40%

*Firm A has outstanding bonds that are convertible into 5 million common shares. If the bonds are converted, interest expense (before tax) will decline by $25 million.

†Firm B has outstanding options and warrants that enable the holders to purchase 20 million common shares at an average price of $30 per share. B's stock is currently valued at $50 per share.

‡Firm C has convertible cumulative preferred stock with a total annual dividend requirement of $80 million. The preferred stock is convertible into 10 million shares of common stock.

REQUIRED

(a) Assume that the average firm in the industry presently has a price-to-earnings multiple of 10. What would you expect to be the appropriate market value per share of common stock for firms A, B, and C?

(b) On further inquiry you learn that firm C uses LIFO inventory costing and accelerated depreciation of plant and equipment costs. Firms A and B use FIFO costing and straight-line depreciation. If C had used FIFO and straight-line depreciation the current year's after-tax operating income would be higher by $130 million. How (if at all) does this information affect your answer to item (a)?

45. *Alternatives in Financing Asset Acquisitions.* Ursula Products, Inc., a newly incorporated firm, intends to raise $100 million to finance its initial capital spending program. The assets are expected to earn $20 million each year, before interest and taxes, and the firm's income tax rate is 40%. The firm is considering three financing alternatives:

(1) All equity financing—Sell 800,000 shares of $50 par value common stock at a price of $125 per share (800,000 × $125 = $100 million).

(2) Debt and equity financing—Sell $60 million principal amount of long-term debt at an interest rate of 16% per annum and 400,000 shares of $50 par value common stock at a price of $100 per share (400,000 × $100 = $40 million).

(3) Convertible debt and equity financing—Sell $68 million principal amount of long-term convertible debt at an interest rate of 10% per

annum and 400,000 shares of $50 par value common stock at a price of $80 per share (400,000 × $80 = $32 million).

REQUIRED

(a) Verify that each financing alternative provides total cash proceeds of $100 million.
(b) Why is the market price per share of common stock likely to differ across the three financing alternatives?
(c) Why does the expected interest rate on the debt financing differ between alternatives (2) and (3)?
(d) Provide journal entries to record receipt of the $100-million proceeds under each of the three financing alternatives.
(e) Determine the firm's net income and earnings per share under each of the three financing alternatives.
(f) Which financing alternative appears to be best for Ursula Products?

46. *Alternatives in Financing Plant Expansion.* Updike Company intends to raise $200 million to finance plant expansion. The expansion is expected to increase operating income before interest and tax expense by $30 million. The income tax rate is 40%. Pertinent financial information for the period prior to the plant expansion is provided in the table below and management is considering the following financing alternatives:

(1) All equity financing—Raise $200 million by the issuance of common stock at an expected price of $100 per share.
(2) Debt and equity financing—Raise $150 million by the sale of bonds expected to yield 16%, and raise the additional $50 million by the sale of 500,000 shares of common stock at an expected price of $100 per share.

Updike Company
Selected Financial Information
for the Period Preceding Plant Expansion

Total assets	$600 million
Total liabilities	$250 million
Shareholders' equity	$350 million
Number of common shares	5 million
Net income	$ 50 million
Market price per common share	$100

REQUIRED

(a) Determine the effect on Updike Company's net income and earnings per share for the next period assuming in turn that the plant expansion is financed using alternatives (1) and (2). Which financing alternative appears to be best?
(b) Assume that the effect on operating income of the plant expansion is not known for certain. At what level of operating income would earnings per share be the same for alternatives (1) and (2)?

(c) Assume that the effect on operating income of the plant expansion is not known for certain and that the relationship between share price and EPS (the price-to-earnings ratio) will be affected by debt financing in the following manner:

> Alternative (1): price-earnings ratio of 10.
> Alternative (2): price-earnings ratio of 8.

At what level of operating income would the market price per share of common stock be the same for alternatives (1) and (2)? [Note that alternative (2) requires that the firm issue a greater number of common shares in order to raise $50 million. Because the initial market price per share would be $80 rather than $100, the firm would issue 625,000 shares (625,000 × $80 = $50 million).]

47. *Transaction Effects on Selected Financial Ratios.*   On December 31, 1988, the Grass Shirt Company had total assets of $8 million, total liabilities of $3 million, and shareholders' equity of $5 million. The firm had 100,000 shares of common stock outstanding. During 1988, net income was $630,000, and dividends declared were $210,000. The market price per share of stock remained at $126 throughout the year and the firm's income tax rate is 40%.

REQUIRED

(a) Compute the following ratios for the Grass Shirt Company:

   (1) Debt to shareholders' equity
   (2) Book value per share
   (3) Earnings per share
   (4) Dividends per share
   (5) Earnings yield
   (6) Dividend yield
   (7) Price-earnings ratio
   (8) Market value-to-book value ratio

(b) For each of the ratios computed in item (a), discuss the reasons that the Grass Shirt Company's ratios might be either higher or lower than the corresponding ratios for other firms.

(c) Indicate how each of the financial ratios developed in item (b) would be affected by the events listed below. Consider each event independently.

   (1) The firm issues additional shares of stock at $126 per share.
   (2) The firm buys treasury shares at $126 per share.
   (3) The firm buys treasury shares at $150 per share.
   (4) The holders of $1 million of Grass Shirt Company's convertible debt convert their holdings to common stock at a ratio of ten shares of stock for each $1,000 of bond principal. Prior to conversion, the debt is carried on the books at par value, and bears an interest rate of 12% per annum.

8

The Statement of Cash Flows

The preceding five chapters have concentrated on the income statement and the balance sheet. In this chapter, the emphasis shifts to the third of the primary financial statements—the **statement of cash flows (SCF).**

The first part of Chapter 8 describes the statement of cash flows and explains how it relates to the balance sheet and income statement. Also included is an extended example that illustrates how various business transactions and events affect the reporting of cash flows. Both the direct and indirect methods of calculating net cash flows from operating activities are explained and illustrated. In the later sections of the chapter, we demonstrate the mechanics of using a worksheet to prepare a statement of cash flows, and include a discussion of the analytical uses of cash flow information.

HISTORICAL BACKGROUND

APB *Opinion No. 19*, which was published in 1971, required the presentation of a statement of changes in financial position as a basic financial statement. This statement was intended to show the effects of inflows and outflows of a firm's "funds" during the reporting period. APB *Opinion No. 19* allowed management the choice of defining "funds" as cash or as working capital (current assets less current liabilities). At first, most firms prepared the statement of changes in financial position on a working capital basis, but in recent years a majority of firms elected to use the cash basis.

At the time of this writing, the FASB has announced its plans to require companies to replace the statement of changes in financial position with a statement of cash flows. This chapter is based on the FASB's July 1986 Exposure Draft concerning this topic, which is entitled "Proposed Statement of Financial Accounting Standards: Statement of Cash Flows."

THE STATEMENT OF CASH FLOWS, THE BALANCE SHEET, AND THE INCOME STATEMENT

The SCF is related to both the income statement and the balance sheet and is intended to provide cash flow information that these statements do not provide directly. A SCF is included as a basic financial statement for each period in which an income statement is presented.

Both the income statement and the SCF provide links between a firm's balance sheet at the beginning of the period and its balance sheet at the end of the period. The nature of each link is summarized below.

- Income Statement—The income statement focuses on accrual-based revenues and expenses resulting from a firm's operating activities. Stated another way, the income statement explains *all* asset and liability changes between a firm's beginning and ending balance sheets that are due to operations.

- Statement of Cash Flows—This financial statement explains how *one* asset (cash) changes between a firm's beginning and ending balance sheets because of the firm's major operating, financing, and investing activities.

A model SCF is presented in Exhibit 8-1; this illustrative statement is adapted from one contained in the FASB's Exposure Draft.

Observe in Exhibit 8-1 that the statement of cash flows shows a firm's cash inflows and cash outflows from its major operating, investing, and financing activities during the reporting period.[1] The SCF presented in Exhibit 8-1 shows

---

[1] Actually, a SCF measures changes in cash and **cash equivalents.** A cash equivalent is defined as a highly liquid investment that (1) is readily convertible into a known amount of cash and (2) is so near its maturity that it presents negligible risk of change in value because of changes in interest rates.

Exhibit 8-1

Illustration of a Statement of Cash Flows

XYZ Company
Statement of Cash Flows
For the Year Ended December 31, 1988

Cash Flows from Operating Activities

Cash received from customers	$10,000	
Dividends received	700	
Cash provided by operating activities		$10,700
Cash paid to suppliers and employees	$ 6,000	
Interest and taxes paid	1,750	
Cash disbursed for operating activities		7,750
Net cash flow from operating activities		$ 2,950

Cash Flows from Investing Activities

Purchases of property, plant, equipment	$ (4,000)	
Proceeds from disposals of property, plant, and equipment	2,500	
Acquisition of Company ABC	(900)	
Purchases of investment securities	(4,700)	
Proceeds from sales of investment securities	5,000	
Loans made	(7,500)	
Collections on loans	5,800	
Net cash used by investing activities		(3,800)

Cash Flows from Financing Activities

Net increase in customer deposits	$ 1,100	
Proceeds of short-term debt	75	
Payments to settle short-term debt	(300)	
Proceeds of long-term debt	1,250	
Payments on capital lease obligations	(125)	
Proceeds from issuing common stock	500	
Dividends paid	(450)	
Net cash provided by financing activities		2,050
Net increase (decrease) in cash		$ 1,200

Source: *Exposure Draft of Proposed Statement of Financial Accounting Standards,* "Statement of Cash Flows" (Stamford, CT: FASB, 1986), p. 28.

net cash flow from operating activities in the amount of $2,950; net cash used by investing activities in the amount of $3,800; and net cash provided by financing activities in the amount of $2,050. The overall effect is a net increase in cash for the period of $1,200.

CLASSIFICATION OF BUSINESS ACTIVITIES

The first step in the preparation of a SCF is to classify all recorded transactions and events into the three activity categories presented in Exhibit 8-1. The paragraphs that follow describe the guidelines for differentiating among operating, financing, and investing activities.

1. **Operating activities.**   A firm's operating activities include all the typical day-to-day transactions involving the sale of merchandise and the providing of services to customers. Typical cash inflows from operating activities include cash receipts from the sale of goods or services, cash receipts from interest earned on loans, and cash receipts in the form of dividends. Typical cash outflows from operating activities include cash payments for acquisitions of inventory, cash payments to employees, cash payments to suppliers, and cash payments for taxes.

2. **Investing activities.**   Generally speaking, investing activities involve acquiring and disposing of noncurrent assets. Examples include the buying and selling of securities of other companies; the buying and selling of property, plant, and equipment; and the lending of money to other companies and subsequent collection of these loans.

3. **Financing activities.**   There are two sources of financing: creditors and owners. Accordingly, financing activities affect long-term liabilities and certain stockholders' equity accounts. Examples of financing activities involving creditors include the borrowing of resources and the subsequent repayment of those resources. Examples involving owners include the selling of stocks, the repurchasing of some or all of those stocks, and the paying of dividends on shares of stock outstanding.

THE EFFECTS OF SELECTED TRANSACTIONS ON CASH FLOWS: AN ILLUSTRATION

To illustrate the concepts just presented, we will consider the activities of the L. A. Doyle Company, a newly formed corporation organized to sell sporting goods. Assume that the company commenced business on January 1, 1987. Summary transactions and appropriate journal entries (including adjustments) for the year ended December 31, 1987, are listed below. A brief analysis is provided for each transaction. The analysis classifies the transaction according to type of activity and also identifies its cash flow and income statement effects.

Transactions during the Year Ended December 31, 1987

(1)   Issued common stock for $300,000 cash:

dr.	Cash	300,000	
	cr. Common Stock		300,000

ANALYSIS: This is a financing activity that increases cash by $300,000 and has no effect on income.

(2)   Purchased several fixed assets for $240,000 cash:

dr.   Fixed Assets   240,000
   cr.   Cash   240,000

ANALYSIS: This is an investing activity that decreases cash by $240,000 and has no effect on income.

(3)   Borrowed $100,000 cash from the bank (long-term loan):

dr.   Cash   100,000
   cr.   Bank Loan Payable   100,000

ANALYSIS: This is a financing activity that increases cash by $100,000 and has no effect on income.

(4)   Purchased a two-year insurance policy for $20,000 cash:

dr.   Prepaid Insurance   20,000
   cr.   Cash   20,000

ANALYSIS: This is an operating activity that decreases cash by $20,000 and has no effect on income.

(5)   Purchased inventory on credit costing $125,000:

dr.   Merchandise Inventory   125,000
   cr.   Accounts Payable   125,000

ANALYSIS: This is an operating activity that has no effect on cash or on income.

(6)   Paid suppliers $110,000 for inventory purchased in transaction (5):

dr.   Accounts Payable   110,000
   cr.   Cash   110,000

ANALYSIS: This is an operating activity that decreases cash by $110,000 and has no effect on income.

(7)   Sold inventory to customers on credit for $210,000:

dr.   Accounts Receivable   210,000
   cr.   Sales   210,000

ANALYSIS: This is an operating activity that has no effect on cash but increases income by $210,000. [Note: We are assuming that the firm uses the periodic inventory system; thus, cost of goods sold is calculated as a year-end adjustment. See (12) below.]

(8)   Collected cash of $180,000 from credit sales made in transaction (7):

dr.   Cash   180,000
   cr.   Accounts Receivable   180,000

ANALYSIS: This is an operating activity that increases cash by $180,000 and has no effect on income.

(9)   Paid wages of $40,000 in cash:

dr.   Wages Expense   40,000
   cr.   Cash   40,000

ANALYSIS: This is an operating activity that decreases cash by $40,000 and decreases income by $40,000.

(10)   Paid annual interest of $8,000 in cash:

dr.   Interest Expense   8,000
   cr.   Cash   8,000

ANALYSIS: This is an operating activity that decreases cash by $8,000 and decreases income by $8,000.

(11)   Sold for $13,000 cash a fixed asset with a book value of $15,000 (acquisition cost, $16,000; accumulated depreciation, $1,000):

dr.   Cash   13,000
dr.   Accumulated Depreciation — Fixed Assets   1,000
dr.   Loss on Sale of Fixed Assets   2,000
   cr.   Fixed Assets   16,000

ANALYSIS: This is an investing activity that increases cash by $13,000 and decreases income by $2,000.

Adjustments at the End of the Year (December 31, 1987)

(12)   The cost of the inventory sold in transaction (7) is $90,000:

dr.   Cost of Goods Sold   90,000
   cr.   Merchandise Inventory   90,000

ANALYSIS: This adjustment reflects an operating activity that has no effect on cash but decreases income by $90,000.

(13)   The cost of accrued wages (earned but unpaid) at year-end is $1,000:

dr.   Wages Expense   1,000
    cr.   Accrued Wages Payable   1,000

ANALYSIS: This adjustment reflects an operating activity that has no effect on cash but decreases income by $1,000.

(14)   During the year, $10,000 of prepaid insurance expires:

dr.   Insurance Expense   10,000
    cr.   Prepaid Insurance   10,000

ANALYSIS: This adjustment reflects an operating activity that has no effect on cash but decreases income by $10,000.

(15)   Annual depreciation expense for fixed assets is $6,000:

dr.   Depreciation Expense   6,000
    cr.   Accumulated Depreciation—Fixed Assets   6,000

ANALYSIS: This adjustment reflects an operating activity that has no effect on cash but decreases income by $6,000.

The results of the analysis of the L. A. Doyle Company's transactions and adjustments are summarized in Exhibit 8-2. Each transaction's activity type (operating, investing, or financing) is noted in column (1); the income statement effect is shown in column (2); and the cash flow effect appears in column (3). Those transactions with cash flow effects are classified by specific activity category in columns (4), (5), and (6).

The column totals in Exhibit 8-2 indicate that L. A. Doyle's net income for 1987 is $53,000 [column (2)] but that its cash account increased during 1987 by $175,000 [column (3)]. Totals for columns (4), (5), and (6), respectively, show that this $175,000-positive cash flow is the result of endeavors in three areas: operating activities increased cash by $2,000; investing activities decreased cash by $227,000; and financing activities increased cash by $400,000.

It is possible to prepare a statement of cash flows directly from Exhibit 8-2. The data in columns (4), (5), and (6) are particularly useful in this regard. Such a statement is presented in Exhibit 8-3.

CALCULATING AND REPORTING CASH FLOWS FROM OPERATING ACTIVITIES

The statement of cash flows presented in Exhibit 8-3 does not contain sufficient detail to explain how the L. A. Doyle Company increased its cash from operating activities by $2,000 during 1987. This section describes the two approaches

Exhibit 8-2
Summary of Income Statement and Cash Flow Effects

L. A. Doyle Company
Transactions and Adjustments
For the Year Ended December 31, 1987

Transaction or Adjustment	(1) Type of Activity	(2) Income Statement Effect	(3) Cash Flow Effect	Cash Flow Classified by Activity		
				(4) Operating	(5) Investing	(6) Financing
(1) Issued common stock	Financing		300,000			300,000
(2) Purchased fixed assets	Investing		(240,000)		(240,000)	
(3) Borrowed from bank (long-term loan)	Financing		100,000			100,000
(4) Purchased two-year insurance policy	Operating		(20,000)	(20,000)		
(5) Purchased inventory on credit	Operating					
(6) Paid suppliers for inventory purchased in transaction (5)	Operating		(110,000)	(110,000)		
(7) Sold inventory on credit	Operating	210,000				
(8) Collected cash (partial payment) from sales made in transaction (7)	Operating		180,000	180,000		
(9) Paid wages	Operating	(40,000)	(40,000)	(40,000)		
(10) Paid annual interest	Operating	(8,000)	(8,000)	(8,000)		
(11) Sold fixed asset at a loss	Investing	(2,000)	13,000		13,000	
(12) Made adjustment for cost of goods sold	Operating	(90,000)				
(13) Made adjustment for accrued wages	Operating	(1,000)				
(14) Made adjustment for expired insurance	Operating	(10,000)				
(15) Made adjustment for annual depreciation	Operating	(6,000)				
		53,000	175,000	2,000	(227,000)	400,000

Cash Flow from All Activities = 175,000

Exhibit 8-3

Statement of Cash Flows

L. A. Doyle Company
Statement of Cash Flows
For the Year Ended December 31, 1987

Cash Flows from Operating Activities		$ 2,000
Cash Flows from Investing Activities		
Purchase of fixed assets	$(240,000)	
Proceeds from sale of a fixed asset	13,000	
Net cash used by investing activities		(227,000)
Cash Flows from Financing Activities		
Proceeds from issuing common stock	$ 300,000	
Proceeds from incurring long-term debt	100,000	
Net cash provided by financing activities		400,000
Net increase in cash		$ 175,000

Note: All cash outflows are shown in parentheses.

presently being considered by the FASB for calculating and reporting cash flow from operating activities. The FASB refers to these approaches as (1) the direct method and (2) the indirect method. The starting point in both approaches is the income statement. The income statement focuses on the revenues and expenses from operating activities, but not on the cash effects of those transactions.

Direct Method

If the **direct method** is used to calculate and report cash flow, the SCF reports major categories of cash receipts and cash payments from operating activities. The general format for direct-method reporting appears in Exhibit 8-4. The difference between operating cash receipts and operating cash payments is labeled "Net cash flow from operating activities."

The dollar amounts for cash receipts from operating activities and cash payments for operating activities are computed by converting the accrual-based revenues and expenses listed on the income statement to a cash basis. In effect, the end result of this conversion process is an income statement prepared on the cash basis of accounting.

We will use the data from the L. A. Doyle Company case examined earlier to demonstrate the direct method for calculating cash flows from operating activities. To begin, we need (1) a copy of the company's income statement for 1987 and (2) a schedule of changes in all noncash balance sheet accounts for

Exhibit 8-4

**Major Categories in Reporting Net Cash Flow from
Operating Activities: Direct Method**

Cash Receipts from Operating Activities
Cash collected from customers
Cash received from interest and dividends

Cash Payments for Operating Activities
Cash paid to suppliers for inventory
Cash paid to suppliers for other operating expenses
Cash paid to employees for wages
Cash paid to creditors for interest
Cash paid to the government for taxes

Net Cash Flow from Operating Activities

---

the year. The schedule may be constructed by subtracting appropriate values on the beginning-of-period balance sheet from corresponding values on the end-of-period balance sheet. In the L. A. Doyle Company case, however, the beginning-of-period balance sheet contains all zero values because 1987 is the company's first year of operations. Consequently, balances in the end-of-period balance sheet also represent changes in each account for the year (and, of course, all of these changes are increases). L. A. Doyle's income statement for 1987 and its balance sheet at December 31, 1987, are presented in Exhibit 8-5.

We will consider each income statement item in turn, converting each item from the accrual basis to the cash basis of accounting.

1. *Converting sales to cash collected from customers.* When a company only has cash sales, the reported sales revenue equals the amount of cash collected from customers. When sales are made on credit, however, conversion to the cash basis must consider the change during the period in accounts receivable. The relationship between sales revenue and cash collected from customers in cases involving sales made on credit is computed in accordance with the following formula:

$$\text{Cash Received from Customers} = \text{Sales} \begin{cases} + \text{ Decrease in} \\ \quad \text{Accounts Receivable} \\ \quad\quad\quad \text{or} \\ - \text{ Increase in} \\ \quad \text{Accounts Receivable} \end{cases}$$

A decrease in accounts receivable reflects the fact that cash collected from customers during the period exceeds the amount of reported sales; therefore, the decrease is added to reported sales to calculate the amount of cash received

Exhibit 8-5

Financial Statements for Calculating Cash Flows from Operating Activities

L. A. Doyle Company
Income Statement
For the Year Ended December 31, 1987

Sales		$210,000
Expenses		
Cost of goods sold	$ 90,000	
Insurance	10,000	
Wages	41,000	
Interest	8,000	
Depreciation	6,000	
Loss on sale of fixed asset	2,000	
		157,000
Net income		$ 53,000

L. A. Doyle Company
Balance Sheet
December 31, 1987

Assets

Cash		$175,000
Accounts Receivable		30,000
Inventory		35,000
Prepaid Insurance		10,000
Fixed Assets	$224,000	
Less: Accumulated Depreciation	5,000	
		219,000
Total Assets		$469,000

Liabilities and Owners' Equity

Accounts Payable		$ 15,000
Wages Payable		1,000
Bank Loan Payable		100,000
Common Stock		300,000
Retained Earnings		53,000
Total Liabilities and Owners' Equity		$469,000

from customers. Conversely, an increase in accounts receivable reflects the fact that cash collections are lagging behind reported sales, and is thus subtracted from sales in order to determine the amount of cash collected.

Reference to Exhibit 8-5 shows that the L. A. Doyle Company has a $30,000 increase in accounts receivable during 1987. Thus, the amount of cash collected from customers during 1987 is

Sales	$210,000
Less: Increase in accounts receivable	30,000
Cash collected from customers	$180,000

Notice that the $180,000 calculated here agrees with our analysis earlier, which is summarized in Exhibit 8-2. [See transaction (8).]

2. *Converting cost of goods sold to cash paid to suppliers for inventory.* This conversion is a two-step process. The first step is designed to determine the amount of inventory purchases for the period, and the second step determines the amount of cash paid for these purchases. The full relationship is stated below.

$$
\begin{aligned}
&\begin{array}{l}\text{Cash Paid to} \\ \text{Suppliers for} \\ \text{Inventory}\end{array} = \begin{array}{l}\text{Cost of} \\ \text{Goods} \\ \text{Sold}\end{array} \left\{ \begin{array}{c} \textit{Step 1} \\ +\ \text{Increase in} \\ \text{Inventory} \\ \text{or} \\ -\ \text{Decrease in} \\ \text{Inventory} \end{array} \right\} + \left\{ \begin{array}{c} \textit{Step 2} \\ +\ \text{Decrease in} \\ \text{Accounts Payable} \\ \text{or} \\ -\ \text{Increase in} \\ \text{Accounts Payable} \end{array} \right\}
\end{aligned}
$$

In Step 1, an increase in inventory reflects the fact that the cost of purchases made during the period is greater than the cost of goods sold. Accordingly, an increase in inventory is added to the cost of goods sold to determine the amount of purchases for the period. Alternatively, a decrease in inventory would be subtracted from the cost of goods sold to determine the amount of purchases.

In Step 2, a decrease in accounts payable reflects the fact that cash paid for inventory during the period exceeds the amount of purchases. Consequently, a decrease in accounts payable would be added to purchases to determine the amount of cash paid to suppliers for inventory purchases. Alternatively, an increase in accounts payable would be subtracted from purchases to determine the amount of cash paid.

Reference to Exhibit 8-5 shows that the L. A. Doyle Company has a $35,000 increase in inventory during 1987 and a $15,000 increase in accounts payable. Thus, the amount of cash paid to suppliers for inventory during 1987 is calculated as shown below.

Cost of goods sold	$ 90,000
Plus: Increase in inventory	35,000
Less: Increase in accounts payable	15,000
Cash paid to suppliers for inventory	$110,000

Notice that the $110,000 calculated here agrees with our analysis earlier, which is summarized in Exhibit 8-2. [See transaction (6).]

3. *Converting insurance expense to cash paid for insurance.*   In the L. A. Doyle illustration, insurance is an example of a prepaid expense. In order to convert an expense related to a prepaid expense to the cash basis, we must consider the change in the prepaid expense during the period. This relationship is stated as follows:

$$\text{Cash Payment} = \text{Expense} \begin{cases} + \text{ Increase in Related} \\ \quad \text{Prepaid Expense} \\ \quad\quad\quad\text{or} \\ - \text{ Decrease in Related} \\ \quad \text{Prepaid Expense} \end{cases}$$

An increase in a prepaid expense during the period reflects the fact that cash paid for this asset exceeds the amount of the related expense. Accordingly, the increase in the prepaid expense is added to the related expense to calculate the amount of cash paid during the period. Alternatively, a decrease in the prepaid expense is subtracted from the related expense to calculate the amount of cash paid.

Reference to Exhibit 8-5 shows that the L. A. Doyle Company has a $10,000 increase in prepaid insurance during 1987. Thus, the amount of cash paid for insurance during 1987 is

Insurance expense	$10,000
Plus: Increase in prepaid insurance	10,000
Cash paid for insurance	$20,000

Notice that the $20,000 calculated here agrees with our analysis earlier, which is summarized in Exhibit 8-2. [See transaction (4).]

4. *Converting wages expense to cash paid to employees.*   In the L. A. Doyle Company illustration wages expense is an example of an accrued liability. In order to convert an expense related to an accrued liability to the cash basis, we must consider the change in the accrued liability during the period. This relationship is stated below.

$$\text{Cash Payment} = \text{Expense} \begin{cases} + \text{ Decrease in Related} \\ \quad \text{Accrued Liability} \\ \quad\quad\quad\text{or} \\ - \text{ Increase in Related} \\ \quad \text{Accrued Liability} \end{cases}$$

A decrease in an accrued liability during the period reflects the fact that cash paid exceeds the amount of the related expense. As such, the decrease in the accrued liability is added to the related expense to calculate the amount of cash paid during the period. Alternatively, an increase in an accrued liability is subtracted from the related expense to calculate the amount of cash paid.

Reference to Exhibit 8-5 shows that the L. A. Doyle Company has a $1,000 increase in accrued wages payable during 1987. Thus, the amount of cash paid for wages in 1987 is

Wages expense	$41,000
Less: Increase in accrued wages payable	1,000
Cash paid for wages	$40,000

Notice that the $40,000 calculated here agrees with our analysis earlier, which is summarized in Exhibit 8-2. [See transaction (9).]

5. *Converting interest expense to cash paid to creditors.*   In the L. A. Doyle Company illustration, interest expense is an example of a situation in which the amount of cash paid and the amount of expense determined on the accrual basis of accounting coincide. When this occurs, no adjustment is necessary. Thus, the $8,000 in interest expense shown on the income statement in Exhibit 8-5 equals the amount of cash paid for interest during 1987. Notice that this amount agrees with our analysis earlier, which is summarized in Exhibit 8-2. [See transaction (10).]

6. *Eliminating depreciation expense.*   Depreciation expense is eliminated because it does not represent a cash payment. Moreover, the purchase of the fixed assets that gives rise to the depreciation expense is classified as an investing activity, not an operating activity. In the L. A. Doyle Company illustration, the amount of depreciation expense to be eliminated is $6,000. Notice in our earlier analysis (summarized in Exhibit 8-2) that depreciation expense did not affect cash flow from operating activities. [See item (15).]

7. *Eliminating loss on sale of a fixed asset.*   Even though an expense appears on the income statement in Exhibit 8-5 for a loss on the sale of a fixed asset, that item does not represent an operating activity. Accordingly, it is eliminated here because we are attempting to calculate cash flow from *operating activities*. [The item is included in Exhibit 8-2 under the category "Cash Flow from Investing Activities," column (5).] In the L. A. Doyle Company illustration, the amount of loss on the sale of a fixed asset is $2,000, and this amount is eliminated. Notice in our earlier analysis (summarized in Exhibit 8-2) that the loss on the sale of a fixed asset did not affect cash flow from operating activities. [See transaction (11).]

Exhibit 8-6 shows how cash flow from operating activities using the direct method would be presented for the L. A. Doyle Company as a result of the conversion adjustments described above.

Indirect Method

If the **indirect method** is employed to calculate cash flow from operating activities, the SCF reports a reconciliation of reported net income with cash flows from operating activities. Thus, the indirect method begins with net income as reported on the income statement. A series of adjustments is then made to

Exhibit 8-6

Cash Flow from Operating Activities: Direct Method

L. A. Doyle Company
Schedule of Cash Flow from Operating Activities
For the Year Ended December 31, 1987

Cash collected from customers		$180,000
Cash payments for operating activities		
Cash paid to suppliers for inventory	$110,000	
Cash paid for insurance	20,000	
Cash paid to employees for wages	40,000	
Cash paid to creditors for interest	8,000	
		178,000
Net cash flow from operating activities		$ 2,000

convert this amount from an accrual basis to a cash basis.[2] These adjustments involve the same changes in balance sheet accounts used above in illustrating the direct method. However, in using the indirect method, the adjustments are applied to reported net income rather than to the income statement's individual revenues and expenses.

Two types of situations that require adjustments are (1) those in which revenues are earned in one period but collected in another and (2) those in which expenses are incurred in one period but paid in another. Both of these situations result in changes in assets or liabilities during the period.

The rules for adjusting reported net income for changes in assets (except, of course, for changes in the cash account itself) and liabilities are as follows:

- Decreases in noncash assets are added to reported net income and increases are subtracted.

- Increases in liabilities are added to reported net income and decreases are subtracted.

Three examples (two involving assets and one involving a liability) should suffice to explain the underlying logic of these two rules.

Changes in an asset: accounts receivable   An increase in accounts receivable indicates that cash received from customers during the period is less than revenues earned. Since revenues increase the amount of net income, the amount of

---

[2]These adjustments made in preparing a SCF should not be confused with adjusting entries introduced in Chapter 2. The adjustments referred to above are *not* adjusting entries, but are made here only to convert accrual-based numbers to cash basis amounts.

the increase in accounts receivable must be subtracted from net income to reflect the amount of cash received. Conversely, a decrease in accounts receivable must be added to net income to adjust for the fact that reported revenues are less than the amount of cash collected. Similar logic may be applied to changes in all other noncash assets.

Changes in an asset: book value of a fixed asset   The book value of a fixed asset is reduced by the amount of a period's depreciation expense. Depreciation is an example of a reported expense that involves no cash flow in the current period. Because depreciation is subtracted from revenues to calculate net income, it must be added back in order to eliminate its effect on net income. Similar logic may be applied to other expenses that do not involve any cash flow, such as amortization and depletion.

Changes in a liability: wages payable   An increase in wages payable indicates that cash paid to employees during the period is less than the amount of expenses recognized. Since expenses reduce the amount of net income, the amount of the increase in wages payable must be added to net income to reflect the amount of cash paid. Conversely, a decrease in wages payable must be subtracted from net income to reflect the amount of cash paid. Similar logic may be applied to changes in all other liabilities.

One additional type of situation exists that requires adjustments to reported net income under the indirect method. It involves revenues and expenses reported on the income statement that do not relate to operating activities. In such cases, the effects of these transactions must be removed from reported net income.

An example of a situation in which an expense reported on the income statement does not relate to operating activities is the sale of a fixed asset at a loss. As discussed earlier in the L. A. Doyle Company illustration [see transaction (11), page 376], the sale of a fixed asset is not an operating activity. It is, however, an investing activity and the cash effect of such a sale should be reflected in cash flow from investing activities. Because the loss on the sale of a fixed asset is subtracted from revenues to calculate net income, it must be added back in order to eliminate its effect on net income. Similar logic may be applied to a gain on the sale of a fixed asset, except that the gain would be subtracted from (not added to) reported net income.

Exhibit 8-7 shows how cash flow from operating activities under the indirect method would be presented for the L. A. Doyle Company as a result of the types of adjustments described above. A comparison of Exhibits 8-6 and 8-7 indicates that both the direct method and the indirect method produce the same dollar amount for net cash flow from operating activities.

CONSTRUCTING THE STATEMENT OF CASH FLOWS

The SCF can be prepared by analyzing the cash effects of individual transactions, as was done in the L. A. Doyle Company illustration. Because of the

Exhibit 8-7

Cash Flow from Operating Activities: Indirect Method

L. A. Doyle Company
Schedule of Cash Flow from Operating Activities
For the Year Ended December 31, 1987

Net income	$53,000
Add (Deduct) items to convert net income to cash basis	
Increase in accounts receivable	(30,000)
Increase in inventory	(35,000)
Increase in prepaid insurance	(10,000)
Increase in accounts payable	15,000
Increase in accrued wages payable	1,000
Depreciation	6,000
Loss on sale of fixed asset	2,000
Net cash flow from operating activities	$ 2,000

great number of transactions that flow through a company's accounting records during even a short period of time, however, this procedure is rarely used. Instead, the SCF is usually prepared by comparing a firm's beginning and ending balance sheets and analyzing the changes that took place during the period in the noncash accounts.

The purpose of a statement of cash flows is to indicate the nature of the changes in cash that occurred during the period. A change in cash is equal to the net change in all balance sheet accounts other than cash. This can be shown by transforming the basic accounting equation as shown below. The following codes will be used in transforming the equation:

$$C = \text{Cash}$$
$$CAO = \text{Current assets other than cash}$$
$$NCA = \text{Noncurrent assets}$$
$$CL = \text{Current liabilities}$$
$$NCL = \text{Noncurrent liabilities}$$
$$OE = \text{Owners' equity}$$

	Assets	Liabilities	Owners' Equity

Basic Accounting Equation: $(C + CAO + NCA) - (CL + NCL) = OE$

Transformation: $C = OE + CL + NCL - CAO - NCA$

Statement of Cash Flows
(where Δ = change): $\Delta C = \Delta OE + \Delta CL + \Delta NCL - \Delta CAO - \Delta NCA$

The last equation presented above demonstrates that a change in cash (left side of the equation) is equal to the net change in all balance sheet accounts other than cash (right side of the equation). Notice that, except for changes in current assets other than cash and changes in noncurrent assets, each item on the right side of this equation is preceded by a plus sign. The minus sign associated with changes in assets other than cash reflects the fact that changes in these items are opposite in direction from changes in cash. (For example, an increase in investment in securities of another firm results in a decrease in cash.) In contrast, changes in all other items on the equation's right side (owners' equity and liabilities) move in the same direction as do changes in cash.

Most business entities use a worksheet to aid in the preparation of a SCF. To illustrate this approach, we will continue with the L. A. Doyle example from the first section of this chapter. The discussion earlier considered recorded transactions and adjustments for the firm during 1987. Now we will focus on the firm's activities during 1988, its second year of existence. Comparative balance sheets for the L. A. Doyle Company at December 31, 1987 (reproduced from Exhibit 8-5, page 381) and at December 31, 1988, and an income statement for the year ended December 31, 1988 are presented in Exhibit 8-8.

The first step in the construction of a cash flow statement from comparative balance sheets is the compilation of a schedule that shows the period's net change in each balance sheet account other than cash. This schedule for the L. A. Doyle Company appears in Exhibit 8-9. Because both balance sheets must by definition have equal debits and credits, the total debit changes (increases to assets or decreases to liabilities and owners' equity) must equal the total credit changes (decreases to assets or increases to liabilities and owners' equity.) Exhibit 8-9 reveals that L. A. Doyle's cash balance decreased by $90,000 during 1988 (see shaded area in columns labeled "Net Changes during 1988"). The changes in all of the other balance sheet accounts also total $90,000.

The next step in the analysis requires that the year's activity in the noncash asset accounts, the liability accounts, and the owners' equity accounts be reconstructed. This is necessary because the net change in a given account may result from different sources and uses of cash. In order to reconstruct the activity in these accounts, it is necessary to know the specific reasons why the accounts changed during the period. Thus, answers to questions such as the following must be obtained:

- Do changes in the firm's obligations reflect borrowings as well as repayments of debt?
- Do changes in the firm's fixed assets result from acquisitions as well as disposals of fixed assets?
- Do changes in the firm's Accumulated Depreciation account result from disposals of assets as well as the amount of the period's depreciation?
- Do changes in the firm's Retained Earnings account represent changes due to net income only? Or are the changes also affected by dividends, treasury stock transactions, and the like?

In the L. A. Doyle illustration, we assume that in 1988 the firm did not borrow additional funds from banks and did not repurchase any of its own

Exhibit 8-8
Financial Statements for Construction of the Statement of Cash Flows

L. A. Doyle Company
Comparative Balance Sheets
At December 31, 1987, and 1988

	December 31, 1987	December 31, 1988
Assets		
Cash	$175,000	$ 85,000
Accounts Receivable	30,000	87,000
Inventory	35,000	55,000
Prepaid Insurance	10,000	2,000
Fixed Assets	224,000	325,000
Less: Accumulated Depreciation	(5,000)	(35,000)
Total Assets	$469,000	$519,000
Liabilities and Owners' Equity		
Accounts Payable	$ 15,000	$ 32,000
Wages Payable	1,000	500
Bank Loan Payable	100,000	80,000
Common Stock	300,000	325,000
Retained Earnings	53,000	81,500
Total Liabilities and Owners' Equity	$469,000	$519,000

L. A. Doyle Company
Income Statement
For the Year Ended December 31, 1988

Sales		$530,000
Expenses		
Cost of goods sold	$245,000	
Insurance	36,000	
Wages	140,500	
Interest	7,500	
Depreciation	32,500	
		461,500
Net Income		$ 68,500

common stock. Accordingly, the net changes shown in Exhibit 8-9 represent the year's activity in these accounts. It is necessary, however, to reconstruct the activity in the Fixed Assets, Accumulated Depreciation, and Retained Earnings accounts, based on the following information:

Exhibit 8-9
Net Changes in Balance Sheet Accounts

L. A. Doyle Company
Worksheet of Net Changes
For the Year Ended December 31, 1988

	Balance December 31, 1987	Net Changes during 1988 dr.	Net Changes during 1988 cr.	Balance December 31, 1988
Assets				
Cash	175,000		90,000	85,000
Accounts Receivable	30,000	57,000		87,000
Inventory	35,000	20,000		55,000
Prepaid Insurance	10,000		8,000	2,000
Fixed Assets	224,000	101,000		325,000
Less: Accumulated Depreciation	(5,000)		30,000	(35,000)
Total Assets	469,000	178,000	128,000	519,000
Liabilities and Owners' Equity				
Accounts Payable	15,000		17,000	32,000
Wages Payable	1,000	500		500
Bank Loan Payable	100,000	20,000		80,000
Common Stock	300,000		25,000	325,000
Retained Earnings	53,000		28,500	81,500
Total Liabilities and Owners' Equity	469,000	20,500	70,500	519,000
Total Debits and Credits		198,500	198,500	

1. During 1988 the firm had net income of $68,500 and paid dividends on common stock of $40,000.
2. During 1988 the firm sold at book value, fixed assets with an original cost of $52,000 and accumulated depreciation of $2,500.

This information allows us to reconstruct the activity in these accounts as follows:

Retained Earnings

		53,000	Balance, Dec. 31, 1987
Dividends, 1988	40,000	68,500	Net income, 1988
		81,500	Balance, Dec. 31, 1988

Fixed Assets

Balance, Dec. 31, 1987	224,000		
Acquisitions, 1988	153,000	52,000	Disposals
Balance, Dec. 31, 1988	325,000		

Accumulated Depreciation

		5,000	Balance, Dec. 31, 1987
Disposals, 1988	2,500	32,500	Depreciation expense, 1988
		35,000	Balance, Dec. 31, 1988

The analysis of retained earnings shows that the net increase of $28,500 shown in Exhibit 8-9 is the result of net income ($68,500) less dividends ($40,000). In preparing the statement of cash flows, net income will be reconciled to operating cash flow, and dividends paid will be reported as a financing cash flow, as will be shown below.

The analysis of fixed assets and accumulated depreciation shows that the net increase in fixed assets ($101,000 in Exhibit 8-9) is the result of fixed asset acquisitions ($153,000) and disposals ($52,000). Moreover, the book value of the fixed assets at the date of disposition was $49,500 ($52,000 cost less $2,500 accumulated depreciation), and this amount was a source of cash during 1988.[3] The year's depreciation expense, $32,500, is an expense that did not require a cash outflow in the current period.

This reconstruction of the activity in the noncash accounts of the L. A. Doyle Company permits a more useful depiction of the changes between the beginning and ending balance sheets, as shown in Exhibit 8-10. The statement of cash flows will be prepared by appropriately classifying these activities, and this classification is made in Exhibit 8-11 on page 393.

The first two columns of Exhibit 8-11 simply repeat the information from Exhibit 8-10 labeled "Detailed Changes during 1988." This information is then classified in the three right-hand columns according to type of activity (operating, investing, or financing). The net cash flow effects from each of the three activities are shown at the bottom of Exhibit 8-11 and the statement of cash flows may be prepared using this information.

The statement of cash flows prepared for the L. A. Doyle Company using the indirect method appears in Exhibit 8-12, page 394. As can be seen, all of the information in this statement has come from Exhibit 8-11. A schedule of cash flows from operating activities prepared using the direct method appears in Exhibit 8-13, page 395; this schedule is based on income statement information from Exhibit 8-8 and information concerning detailed changes in certain balance sheet accounts from Exhibit 8-10.

---

[3]If the fixed assets had been sold at a gain (or a loss), then the amount of cash received would be correspondingly greater (or less).

Exhibit 8-10
Detailed Changes in Balance Sheet Accounts

L. A. Doyle Company
Worksheet of Detailed Changes
For the Year Ended December 31, 1988

	Balance December 31, 1987	Detailed Changes during 1988		Balance December 31, 1988
		dr.	cr.	
Assets				
Cash	175,000		90,000	85,000
Accounts Receivable	30,000	57,000		87,000
Inventory	35,000	20,000		55,000
Prepaid Insurance	10,000		8,000	2,000
Fixed Assets	224,000	153,000*	52,000[†]	325,000
Less: Accumulated Depreciation	(5,000)	2,500[‡]	32,500[§]	(35,000)
Total Assets	469,000	232,500	182,500	519,000
Liabilities and Owners' Equity				
Accounts Payable	15,000		17,000	32,000
Wages Payable	1,000	500		500
Bank Loan Payable	100,000	20,000		80,000
Common Stock	300,000		25,000	325,000
Retained Earnings	53,000	40,000[‖]	68,500[#]	81,500
Total Liabilities and Owners' Equity	469,000	60,500	110,500	519,000
Total Debits and Credits		293,000	293,000	

*Additions to fixed assets

[†] Disposals of fixed assets

[‡] Accumulated depreciation on disposals

[§] Depreciation expense for 1988

[‖] Dividends on common stocks in 1988

[#] Net income for 1988

ANALYSIS OF CASH FLOW INFORMATION

Financial analysts utilize cash flow information in assessing the liquidity of business firms. Several widely used relationships are listed in Exhibit 8-14 on page 395 and will be discussed in this section.

Cash Flow per Share

Since 1973, the Securities and Exchange Commission has prohibited companies from reporting cash flow on a per-share basis. The SEC believes that investors

Exhibit 8-11

Worksheet Showing Cash Flows Classified by Activity

L. A. Doyle Company
Worksheet of Cash Flow Classifications
For the Year Ended December 31, 1988

Changes Classified by Activity

	Detailed Changes during 1988		Operating		Investing		Financing	
	dr.	cr.	dr.	cr.	dr.	cr.	dr.	cr.
Assets								
Cash		90,000						
Accounts Receivable	57,000		57,000					
Inventory	20,000		20,000					
Prepaid Insurance		8,000		8,000				
Fixed Assets	153,000	52,000			153,000	52,000		
Accumulated Depreciation	2,500	32,500		32,500	2,500			
Total Assets	232,500	182,500						
Liabilities and Owners' Equity								
Accounts Payable		17,000		17,000				
Wages Payable	500		500					
Bank Loan Payable	20,000						20,000	
Common Stock		25,000						25,000
Retained Earnings	40,000	68,500		68,500			40,000	
Total Liabilities and Owners' Equity	60,500	110,500						
Total Debits and Credits	293,000	293,000	77,500	126,000	155,500	52,000	60,000	25,000

Cash Flow Effect:

48,500 (Decrease)	103,500 (Increase)	35,000 (Increase)

Cash Flow from All Activities = 90,000

Exhibit 8-12

Statement of Cash Flows: Indirect Method

L. A. Doyle Company
Statement of Cash Flows
For the Year Ended December 31, 1988

Operating Activities

Net income	$ 68,500
Add (deduct) items to convert net income to cash basis	
Increase in accounts receivable	(57,000)
Increase in inventory	(20,000)
Decrease in prepaid insurance	8,000
Increase in accounts payable	17,000
Decrease in wages payable	(500)
Depreciation	32,500
Net cash flows from operating activities	$ 48,500

Investing Activities

Acquisitions of fixed assets	$(153,000)	
Proceeds from disposals of fixed assets	49,500	
		(103,500)

Financing Activities

Payment of bank loan	$ (20,000)	
Sale of common stock	25,000	
Payment of dividend	(40,000)	
		(35,000)
Net change in cash		$ (90,000)

---

accustomed to seeing earnings-per-share data would be confused and would regard cash flow per share as a measure of earning power. The FASB's current position is as follows:

> Reporting cash flow per share would falsely imply that cash flow, or some component of it, is equivalent to or perhaps superior to earnings as an indicator of performance and an alternative to earnings per share...[4]

An illustration of the relative importance of cash flow vis-à-vis income is contained in the financial statements of Walt Disney Productions Inc. In 1979 the company earned $114 million or $3.51 per share of stock. However, by the close of 1983 income had declined to $93.2 million or $2.70 a share. During the same time period, cash flow generated by operations had increased by 84

---

[4]*Exposure Draft of Proposed Statement of Financial Accounting Standards,* "Statement of Cash Flows" (Stamford, CT: FASB, 1986), par. 74.

Exhibit 8-13

Schedule of Cash Flows from Operating Activities: Direct Method

L. A. Doyle Company
Statement of Cash Flows
For the Year Ended December 31, 1988

Cash collected from customers
(Sales, $530,000 less increase in accounts receivable, $57,000) $473,000

Cash paid for operating activities
Cash paid to suppliers for inventory
(Cost of goods sold, $245,000, plus increase in inventory,
$20,000 less increase in accounts payable, $17,000) $248,000
Cash paid for insurance
(Insurance expense, $36,000, less decrease in prepaid
insurance, $8,000)   28,000
Cash paid for wages
(Wages expense of $140,500, plus decrease in wages
payable, $500)   141,000
Cash paid for interest
(Interest expense, $7,500)   7,500

                                                                                              424,500
Net cash flow from operating activities $ 48,500

Exhibit 8-14

Financial Relationships Based on Cash Flow Information

1. Cash flow per share
2. Free cash flow
3. Cash flow from operations as a percentage of total cash flow
4. Cash flow from operations as a percentage of long-term debt
5. Cash flow from operations as a percentage of capital expenditures

percent and amounted to a record $337.4 million or $9.78 a share in 1983. One reason for this discrepancy is that depreciation on Disney's amusement parks amounted to $88 million and amortization of film library costs totaled $65.6 million (although the properties involved continue to appreciate in value).

Another example of the cash flow/income relationship may be observed in the W. T. Grant bankruptcy case. The company filed a petition of bankruptcy in October 1975. From 1966–1973 Grant's reported income and working capital remained relatively constant. In fact, the price of the company's stock rose from 1966–1971. Yet cash flow generated from operations showed a steady and sharp decline beginning in 1969. It was not until 1972 that the market discovered that Grant's cash flows were not adequate to meet its debt repayment schedules and the price of its stock tumbled.

Limitations to cash flow per share   The increased attention devoted to cash flow per share by securities analysts and investors does not imply that it is replacing income as a basis for measuring corporate performance. Cash flow and income are both important in financial analysis and their relative importance depends on the particular circumstances involved. As we have seen, cash flow generated from operations excludes depreciation and other accrual entries. Consequently, the matching of revenues and expenses achieved under traditional income measurement (which is useful as a starting point for making earnings projections) is absent in the cash flow calculation. Many firms also have negative cash flows during certain years that may not necessarily be indicative of future prospects. High-technology companies, such as IBM and Xerox, generally have negative operating cash flows during their early years of existence (due to heavy research and development expenditures) that may not be representative of future operating cash flows.

Free Cash Flow

In recent years, a number of financial analysts have adopted a method of analysis termed free cash flow (FCF). Although there are some variations in the method of application, generally **free cash flow** represents the amount of cash available from operations after providing for asset replacement and dividends. The residue, or free cash, presumably is available to reduce indebtedness and provide for growth. Recent changes in GAAP are such that the presentation of certain replacement cost data in published financial statements is no longer required, but is voluntary. Accordingly, the financial statements may or may not contain the replacement cost information necessary for the FCF calculation discussed above. (A detailed discussion of accounting for changing prices is presented in Chapter 11.)

An interesting calculation of FCF has been made by Kidder, Peabody, & Co. and reported in *Forbes*.[5] The FCF was determined for 20 of the 30 companies that comprised the Dow-Jones Industrial Average for the period from 1975–1979. The results are presented in Exhibit 8-15. The data in Exhibit 8-15 dramatically depict the difference between FCF and reported income during periods of rapid price increases. While all of the companies examined reported sizeable profits during the years under examination, 15 of the 20 firms had negative cash flows after adjusting income for depreciation based on replacement cost and deducting dividends to stockholders.

There are certain controversial aspects to the use of FCF. It is predicated on the assumption that replacement will be made in kind, when in fact, this may

---

[5]Richard Greene, "Are More Chryslers in the Offing?" *Forbes*, February 2, 1981, p. 70.

Exhibit 8-15
A Comparison of Reported Net Income and Free Cash Flow, 1975–1979

(in millions)

Company	Net Income as Reported	Free Cash Flow*
Alcoa	$ 1,221.1	$ −493.9
American Brands	978.6	−29.1
American Can	533.7	−390.6
Bethlehem Steel	462.6	−2,082.0
Du Pont	2,997.6	−517.0
General Electric	5,345.8	906.8
General Foods	985.1	−268.8
General Motors	13,894.1	−2,127.6
Goodyear	861.7	−1,445.3
Inco	646.3	−986.6
IBM	13,229.3	11,972.1
International Harvester	1,085.1	−475.1
Johns-Manville	430.6	−140.7
Merck	1,451.1	446.2
Owens-Illinois	528.0	−184.7
Procter & Gamble	2,285.5	425.4
Sears, Roebuck	3,786.6	−437.0
Union Carbide	2,158.5	−819.6
US Steel	673.4	−6,622.6
United Technologies	1,030.6	264.5

Source: Kidder, Peabody, & Co. *Financial Quality Profiles,* as reported by Richard Greene, "Are More Chryslers in the Offing?" *Forbes,* February 2, 1981.

*Referred to as "Discretionary Cash Flow."

not be the case. There are also several unresolved accounting issues (discussed in Chapter 11) that are related to the use of replacement costs.

Cash Flow from Operations as a Percentage of Total Cash Flow

When a significantly greater portion of cash flow is derived from sources other than operations (issuance of stock, incurrence of long-term debt, or sale of non-current assets), there is cause for concern about a company's liquidity. For example, in 1981 funds derived from operations for Eastern Airlines constituted only 27.3 percent of the total funds provided from all sources.[6] By contrast, a competitor, Delta Airlines, had a ratio of 83.1 percent in that year. The low portion of Eastern's cash flow derived from operations signaled the grave financial

---

[6]Prior to 1987, companies were permitted to report the effect of resource inflows and outflows on either a cash or a working capital basis. In 1981, many companies, including Eastern and Delta, reported funds flow in terms of working capital rather than cash.

crisis confronting Eastern's management. In fact, in 1983 Eastern was reorganized to avert bankruptcy. Subsequently, it was taken over by Texas Airlines.

Cash Flow from Operations as a Percentage of Long-term Debt

Cash flow from operations as a percentage of long-term debt is commonly referred to as **debt coverage.** It is a key liquidity index applied in bond ratings and term bank loans (loans that extend over one year) and indicates the time required for current cash from operations to liquidate long-term debt. Eastern Airlines' balance sheet showed long-term debt, as of December 31, 1981, to be $1.667 billion, while its cash generated from operations amounted to $167.2 million. Accordingly, the debt coverage was ten years in 1981. By comparison, Delta Airlines' debt coverage at the end of 1981 was the equivalent of two years.

Cash Flow from Operations as a Percentage of Capital Expenditures

In the long run, a company must generate sufficient funds from operations to finance its capital expansion and replacement programs and to compensate its capital providers. Even in the short run, however, when capital expenditures significantly exceed funds derived from operations, a liquidity problem may be surfacing. Eastern's combined capital expenditures during 1980 and 1981 amounted to $1.250 billion, while its funds obtained from operations amounted to $340.6 million, or 27.2 percent of capital spending. In 1981 Delta's funds generated from operations were 87.7 percent of its capital expenditures.

Liquidity and other ratios used in financial analysis are extensively discussed in Chapter 12. A number of researchers have attempted to trace the relationship between financial ratio levels and credit ratings, while others have investigated the ability of financial ratios to predict business failures. The results of such studies are also discussed in Chapter 12.

SUMMARY

The first part of Chapter 8 describes the statement of cash flows (SCF) and explains how it relates to the balance sheet and the income statement. The discussion also includes coverage of both the direct method and the indirect method of calculating cash flows from operations. In the middle section of the chapter we demonstrate the mechanics of using a worksheet to prepare a SCF. The chapter concludes with a discussion of various ways that analysts use cash flow information to assess a firm's liquidity.

The SCF shows a firm's cash inflows and cash outflows from its major operating, investing, and financing activities during the reporting period. It is included as a basic financial statement for each period in which an income statement is presented.

GAAP provide guidelines for differentiating among operating, investing, and financing activities. A firm's operating activities include all the typical day-to-day transactions involving the sale of merchandise and the providing of services to customers. Generally speaking, investing activities involve acquiring and disposing of noncurrent assets. There are two sources of financing: creditors and owners. Accordingly, financing activities affect long-term liabilities and certain stockholders' equity accounts.

Two approaches for calculating cash flow from operating activities are the direct method and the indirect method. If the direct method is used, the SCF reports major categories of cash receipts and cash payments from operating activities. Dollar amounts for operating cash receipts and cash payments are computed by converting the accrual-based revenues and expenses listed on the income statement to a cash basis. If the indirect method is employed, the SCF reports a reconciliation of reported net income with cash flows from operating activities. Thus, the indirect method begins with net income as reported on the income statement. A series of adjustments is then made to convert this amount from an accrual basis to a cash basis.

Most firms find it convenient to use a worksheet to aid in constructing a SCF. Use of a worksheet for this purpose is demonstrated in the middle section of this chapter.

Financial analysts use cash flow information in assessing a firm's liquidity. Commonly used measures include cash flow per share, free cash flow, cash flow from operations as a percentage of total cash flow, cash flow from operations as a percentage of long-term debt, and cash flow from operations as a percentage of capital expenditures.

QUESTIONS

1. The terms listed below were introduced in this chapter. Define or explain each of them.

   cash flow per share
   financing activities
   free cash flow
   investing activities
   operating activities
   statement of cash flows

2. Explain how the statement of changes in financial position differs from the newly proposed statement of cash flows.
3. A statement of cash flows requires that cash effects of operating, investing, and financing activities be separately disclosed. Define each of these different types of activities and give an example of each.
4. "Common cash receipts from financing activities include cash received from interest earned and cash received from dividends." Do you agree or disagree with this statement? Explain.

5. Distinguish between the direct method and the indirect method of calculating cash flow from operating activities.
6. Explain the relationship that exists between sales revenue prepared on the accrual basis of accounting and the amount of cash collected from customers.
7. Explain the two-step process necessary in order to convert cost of goods sold to cash paid to suppliers for inventory.
8. Explain the relationship that exists between an expense determined under the accrual basis of accounting and the change in a related prepaid expense during the period.
9. Explain the relationship that exists between an expense determined under the accrual basis of accounting and the change in a related accrued liability during the period.
10. "A decrease in an accrued liability is added to the related expense to calculate the amount of cash paid during the period." Do you agree or disagree with this statement? Explain.
11. Why is depreciation expense eliminated from reported net income when calculating net cash flow from operating activities?
12. Why is loss from sale of a fixed asset eliminated from reported net income when calculating net cash flow from operating activities?
13. Two situations that require adjustment when using the indirect method to calculate cash flow from operating activities are (1) those in which revenues are earned in one period but collected in another and (2) those in which expenses are incurred in one period but paid in another. Give an example of each situation.
14. List the rules discussed in the chapter for adjusting reported net income for changes in noncash assets and liabilities when using the indirect method to calculate cash flow from operating activities.
15. Why is the so-called worksheet approach used most often in practice in preparing a statement of cash flows?
16. Why has cash flow analysis increased in importance in recent years?
17. What is the FASB's position concerning the reporting of cash flow per share (as opposed to earnings per share)?
18. Discuss some of the limitations to cash flow analysis.
19. List and discuss several ratios involving cash flow that may be used in assessing a firm's liquidity.
20. Describe what is meant by "free cash flow" analysis.

EXERCISES AND PROBLEMS

21. *Classification of Miscellaneous Cash Flow Transactions.* The transactions listed below relate to the business of the Ohio Sales Company.

    (1) Land with an estimated market value of $20,000 received from a stockholder as a donation.
    (2) Issuance of common stock for $500,000 cash.

(3) Loss of $500 on equipment with a net book value of $2,500; the equipment was sold for $2,000 cash.

(4) Holders of convertible bonds with a carrying value of $200,000 exchanged the bonds for common stock.

(5) Income tax expense charged to income amounted to $100,000. Income tax liability accrued during the year was $80,000. The deferred income tax liability increased by $20,000.

(6) Accrued salaries increased by $60,000 during the year.

(7) Stock dividend of $25,000 was distributed during the year.

(8) Purchase of building for $300,000 accomplished by issuing bonds for $300,000.

(9) Obsolete inventory written down by $12,000 during the year.

(10) Trade-in allowance of $5,000 received toward $12,000 price of new automobile purchased.

REQUIRED   Indicate how each of the transactions described above would be reported on a statement of cash flows.

22. *Identification and Classification of Relevant Cash Flow Transactions.*   The items listed below relate to the business of the Houston Sales Company.

(1) Increase in accounts receivable during the period
(2) Net income
(3) Increase in an accrued liability
(4) Expenses paid in cash
(5) Acquisition of stock in another company
(6) Proceeds of bank loan
(7) Increase in deferred income tax account
(8) Dividends paid
(9) Depreciation
(10) Proceeds from sale of machinery
(11) Amortization of patents
(12) Cash sales
(13) Purchase of land
(14) Loss on sale of machinery
(15) Interest expense paid

REQUIRED   For each item listed above, indicate whether it would be reported on a statement of cash flows. If the item would be reported, classify it as one of the following:

(a) Cash flows from operating activities
(b) Cash flows from investing activities
(c) Cash flows from financing activities

23. *Identification of Relevant Cash Flow Transactions.* The items listed below relate to the business of the El Paso Sales Company.

(1) Increase in accounts receivable during the period
(2) Net income
(3) Income tax paid
(4) Amortization of patents
(5) Salaries paid to employees
(6) Acquisition of treasury stock
(7) Cash expenditures to repair building
(8) Credit to deferred income tax liability
(9) Increase in accrued salaries
(10) Cost of addition to building
(11) Purchase of stock in another company
(12) Capitalized cost of computer software
(13) Amortization of deferred computer software cost
(14) Cash dividend distributed
(15) Decrease in accounts payable
(16) Writedown of obsolete inventory
(17) Retirement of bonds
(18) Write-off of uncollectible receivable
(19) Loss on sale of machinery
(20) Increase in accrued bonus to executives

REQUIRED   For each item listed above, indicate whether it would be reported on a statement of cash flows. If the item would be reported, classify it as one of the following:

(a) Cash flows from operating activities
(b) Cash flows from investing activities
(c) Cash flows from financing activities

24. *Classification of Cash Flow Transactions.* The following events and transactions occurred during the current year for Autocomp, Incorporated.

(1) Net income amounted to $100 million.
(2) The company's outstanding stock consisted of 3 million shares of $100 par common stock, of which 500,000 shares were sold during the year at $110 per share.
(3) Aggregate dividends distributed to stockholders during the year were the following:

Stock dividends — 100,000 shares of common stock with a market value of $112 per share

Cash dividends — $20 million

(4) During the year Autocomp recorded the following entry:

dr.	Income Tax Expense	35,500,000	
cr.	Cash		30,000,000
cr.	Deferred Income Tax		5,500,000

(5) Depreciation amounted to $15.2 million. However, the Accumulated Depreciation account showed a net increase of only $14.7 million. The difference represented machinery and equipment that originally cost $800,000 and were sold at a loss of $100,000.

(6) Autocomp purchased certain patent rights for $1.5 million and spent $2 million internally on research that resulted in additional patent rights. Amortization of patents during the year amounted to $400,000.

(7) On January 1, the company sold $40 million of 10% convertible bonds due in ten years at par. The following entries for interest were recorded during the year:

July 1	dr.	Interest Expense	2,000,000	
	cr.	Cash		2,000,000
Dec. 31	dr.	Interest Expense	2,000,000	
	cr.	Accrued Interest Payable		2,000,000

(8) Plant and equipment acquired during the year amounted to $80 million, of which $20 million was paid in cash and $60 million was represented by a mortgage.

(9) In November, the company's Biscayne warehouse was flooded and a loss of $600,000 was sustained. Assume that this warehouse was uninsured.

(10) Accounts receivable was $16 million greater at the end of the year than at the beginning, and accounts payable to suppliers rose by $22 million.

REQUIRED   Indicate how each of the events and transactions listed above would affect Autocomp's statement of cash flows for the current year.

25. *Calculating Effects of Transactions on Reported Earnings and Cash Flow.*   The Collegiate Stress Center was established on April 1, 1988, to provide psychological counseling to students at a large urban university. The journal entries listed in the left-hand column of Schedule A on page 404 reflect *all* transactions that occurred during April 1988, plus any necessary adjustments.

Schedule A
Schedule Contrasting Effects of Transactions on Earnings and Cash Flow

Collegiate Stress Center
For the Month Ended April 30, 1988

	Net Income (Earnings)		Cash Flow		
(1) Journal Entries	(2) Dollar Impact of Transaction on Net Income	(3) Dollar Impact of Transaction on Cash Flow	(4) Cash Flow from Operations	(5) Cash Flow *Not* from Operations
dr. Cash 10,000					
cr. Common Stock 10,000					
dr. Cash 5,000					
cr. Notes Payable 5,000					
dr. Building 6,000					
cr. Cash 6,000					
dr. Cash 2,200					
cr. Counseling Fees Earned 2,200					
dr. Wages Expense 1,000					
cr. Cash 1,000					
dr. Rent Expense 200					
cr. Cash 200					
dr. Depreciation Expense— Building 75					
cr. Accumulated Depreciation— Building 75					
dr. Dividends 300					
cr. Cash 300					
Totals					

REQUIRED

(a) For each recorded journal entry, explain the situation that probably gave rise to the entry.

(b) Complete columns (2)–(5) for each journal entry listed in the schedule.

(c) Calculate and enter totals for columns (2), (3), (4), and (5).

(d) Prepare an income statement from the data in column (2).

(e) Since the dollar amounts in both columns (2) and (4) relate to operations, why are the column totals different? Explain fully.

(f) Prepare a statement of cash flows from the data in columns (3)–(5).

(g) Column (4) is used to calculate "cash flow from operations" on a transaction-by-transaction basis. Calculate "cash flow from operations" by starting at net income for the period and making appropriate adjustments for noncash revenue and/or expenses.

26. *Worksheet for Preparing the Statement of Cash Flows.* Net changes in the noncash balance sheet accounts of the East Asian Import Company during the year ended December 31, 1988, are listed below.

	Increase	Decrease
Current assets other than cash	$ 750,000	
Plant, property, and equipment	1,500,000	
Accumulated depreciation	300,000	
Land		$200,000
Patents		20,000
Current liabilities	180,000	
Noncurrent liabilities	1,000,000	
Stockholders' equity	400,000	
Retained earnings		250,000

Additional facts are as follows:

(1) The company sustained a net loss during 1988 of $200,000, including a loss of $250,000 on the sale of land having a book value of $800,000. No property, plant, or equipment was sold during the year.

(2) One hundred thousand shares of common stock were sold at $4 per share.

(3) A cash dividend of $50,000 was paid. No stock dividends were declared.

(4) No patents were acquired or sold during 1988.

REQUIRED

(a) Complete a worksheet for the year ended December 31, 1988, using the format in Exhibit 8-11 on page 393.

(b) Prepare a statement of cash flows.

27. *Determining Cash Flow from Operations.* The income statement for the Pylon Service Company for the year ended June 30, 1988, appears on page 406.

Pylon Service Company
Income Statement
For the Year Ended June 30, 1988

Sales		$10,000,000
Less: Expenses		
Salaries	$4,000,000	
Supplies	2,900,000	
Utilities	280,000	
Rent	500,000	
Insurance	80,000	
Depreciation	260,000	
Miscellaneous	100,000	
		$ 8,120,000
Operating margin		1,880,000
Plus: Gain on sale of equipment		40,000
Pretax income		$ 1,920,000
Less: Income tax		600,000
Net income		$ 1,320,000

During the period covered by the income statement, increases (decreases) in the following specified accounts took place:

Account Increases/Decreases

Accounts receivable	$50,000
Supplies inventory	(10,000)
Other current assets	4,000
Accounts payable	30,000
Deferred income tax liability	5,000

REQUIRED

(a) Using the information presented above, calculate the net cash flow from operating activities for the Pylon Service Company.

(b) Why is the income statement a good starting point for calculating net cash flow from operating activities?

28. *Cash Flow per Share.*   A research report by a brokerage firm on Inter-Continental Airlines, Inc., contained the following statement:

We recommend buying this company's stock. Because of reported operating losses, the price per share has declined to a level that we consider to be attractive. We believe the market has failed to consider the sharp increase in cash flow per share, as shown below.

	This Year	Last Year
Reported loss	$(30,000,000)	$(20,000,000)
Loss per share	$(30)	$(20)
Reported loss	$(30,000,000)	$(20,000,000)

Plus: Loss on sale of planes	15,000,000	
Depreciation	28,000,000	24,000,000
Operating cash flow	$ 13,000,000	$ 4,000,000
Operating cash flow per share	$13	$4

REQUIRED

(a) Evaluate the recommendation.

(b) Would the importance you attach to cash flow be different for an oil company that has oil wells in a single location? (Recall that a company adds back depletion to reported net income in order to calculate net cash flow from operating activities.)

29. *Preparation of a Statement of Cash Flows.*   The following is a list of increases and decreases to the cash account of the Superior Dairy Company for the year ended December 31, 1987:

	Increase/Decrease
Salaries paid	$(15,000,000)
Customer collections	83,000,000
Interest received from investments in securities	10,000
Miscellaneous expenses	(4,100,000)
Delivery trucks purchased	(180,000)
Loan from Farmers and Merchants Bank	2,000,000
Payments to suppliers	(61,000,000)
Customers' net container deposits	200,000
Note Payable to Farmers and Merchants Bank	(500,000)
Sale of homogenizers	80,000
Taxes paid to Internal Revenue Service	(800,000)
Acquisition of stock in Grassy Meadows Farm	(1,900,000)
Interest paid	(110,000)
Treasury stock acquired	(300,000)
Cash dividends paid to stockholders	(800,000)
Interest on loans to farmers	30,000
Dividend received from Grassy Meadows Farm	40,000
Sale of marketable securities	300,000
Loans to farmers	(400,000)

REQUIRED   From the data presented above, prepare a statement of cash flows for the Superior Dairy Company.

30. *Preparation of a Statement of Cash Flows.*   The Midwest Merchandise Company purchases various household products that it stores in its Gary, Indiana, warehouse. The items are sold to distributors throughout the Midwest by the firm's sales force. The company's income statement for the year ended June 30, 1988, is presented in Exhibit B and its balance sheet in Exhibit A.

Exhibit A

Midwest Merchandise Company
Balance Sheet
At June 30, 1988, and 1987

	1988	1987
Assets		
Current Assets		
Cash	$ 60,000	$ 40,000
Marketable Securities	15,000	12,000
Accounts Receivable	80,000	70,000
Inventories	130,000	110,000
Prepaid Expenses	12,000	14,000
Total Current Assets	$ 297,000	$ 246,000
Fixed Assets		
Land	$ 100,000	$ 90,000
Building	1,000,000	900,000
Allowance for Depreciation	(400,000)	(373,000)
Machinery and Equipment	200,000	160,000
Allowance for Depreciation	(100,000)	(80,000)
Total Fixed Assets	$ 800,000	$ 697,000
Other Assets		
Investment in the Stock of Delta Co.	$ 76,000	$ 70,000
Patents	25,000	20,000
Goodwill	39,000	40,000
Total Other Assets	$ 140,000	$ 130,000
Total Assets	$1,237,000	$1,073,000
Liabilities and Stockholders' Equity		
Current Liabilities		
Accounts Payable for Merchandise Purchased	$ 90,000	$ 77,000
Income Tax Payable	40,000	30,000
Other Current Liabilities	10,000	13,000
Total Current Liabilities	$ 140,000	$ 120,000
Long-term Liabilities		
10%-convertible Debentures	$ 600,000	$ 600,000
Less: Discount	(24,000)	(30,000)
Deferred Income Tax	23,000	20,000
Total Long-term Liabilities	$ 599,000	$ 590,000
Stockholders' Equity		
Common Stock Outstanding	$ 400,000	$ 300,000
Premium on Common Stock	10,000	
Retained Earnings	88,000	63,000
Total Stockholders' Equity	$ 498,000	$ 363,000
Total Liabilities and Stockholders' Equity	$1,237,000	$1,073,000

Exhibit B

Midwest Merchandise Company
Income Statement
For the Year Ended June 30, 1988

Sales		$1,106,000
Cost of goods sold		700,000
Gross profit		$ 406,000
Less: Selling and administrative expenses:		
Selling	$127,000	
Shipping	15,000	
Administrative	80,000	
Total	$222,000	
Other expenses:		
Interest	$ 66,000	
Amortization of patents	5,000	
Amortization of goodwill	1,000	
Total	$ 72,000	294,000
Income before income tax		$ 112,000
Less: Income tax expense		50,000
Net income		$ 62,000

REQUIRED

(a) Answer the following questions related to specific cash flows during the year ended June 30, 1988.

   (1) What amount of cash was spent to expand the size of the warehouse?

   (2) Assuming that no fixed assets were sold, what is the amount of depreciation for the year? (Assume that the depreciation is included under "Selling expenses" in Exhibit B.)

   (3) What amount of cash was spent to acquire patents?

   (4) What amount of cash was paid for income taxes?

   (5) What amount of cash was paid to stockholders as dividends?

   (6) What were the net cash proceeds from the sale of common stock?

   (7) What amount of cash was paid to creditors for interest?

(b) From the information given above, prepare a statement of cash flows for the year ended June 30, 1988.

31. *Preparation of a Statement of Cash Flows.* Balance sheets for the L. C. Canby Corporation at December 31, 1986, and 1985 are presented below.

	1986	1985
Assets		
Current Assets		
Cash	$ 12,000	$ 56,000
Accounts Receivable	80,000	85,000
Inventories	105,000	82,000
Total Current Assets	$197,000	$223,000
Fixed Assets		
Buildings and Equipment	$120,000	$110,000
Accumulated Depreciation	(50,000)	(42,000)
Land	60,000	20,000
Patents	5,000	15,000
Goodwill	18,000	20,000
Total Fixed Assets	$153,000	$123,000
Total Assets	$350,000	$346,000
Liabilities and Stockholders' Equity		
Current Liabilities		
Accounts Payable	$ 39,000	$ 42,000
Income Tax Payable	22,000	20,000
Total Current Liabilities	$ 61,000	$ 62,000
Long-term Liabilities		
Mortgage Payable	40,000	70,000
Total Liabilities	$101,000	$132,000
Stockholders' Equity		
Common Stock Outstanding	$170,000	$150,000
Paid-in Capital in Excess of Par	25,000	25,000
Retained Earnings	89,000	89,000
Treasury Stock	(35,000)	(50,000)
Total Stockholders' Equity	$249,000	$214,000
Total Liabilities and Stockholders' Equity	$350,000	$346,000

Additional information:

(1) Net income for the year is $20,000.
(2) Dividends paid total $10,000 in cash dividends and common stock (at par), $10,000.
(3) Treasury stock costing $15,000 was sold for $10,000. Loss was debited to paid-in capital.
(4) Patents with a book cost of $7,000 were sold for $9,000.

REQUIRED   Prepare a statement of cash flows for the year ended December 31, 1986.

32. *Preparation of a Statement of Cash Flows.*   The data listed below were taken from the financial statements included in the annual report of Amfac, Inc., for the year ended December 31, 1982. All figures given are dollars in thousands. ("Obligations under capital leases" are discussed in Chapter 10. They are to be treated here as a long-term liability.)

Net income	$34,208
Other sources of cash generated from investment activities	965
Cash payment for business acquired	3,016
Decrease in long-term notes receivable	7,743
Sales of property	17,164
Depreciation and amortization	50,196
Cash dividends on capital stock outstanding	21,765
Increase in inventories	24,131
Cash received from investments	69,711
Increase in accounts payable and accrued expenses	6,836
Decrease in current notes payable	12,859
Issuance of common stock for cash	6,744
Decrease in prepaid expenses	1,956
Increase in noncurrent portion of deferred income tax liability	10,661
Increase in other current assets	2,485
Increase in other deferred credits	3,964
Increase in other long-term debt	60,992
Reduction of obligations under long-term capital leases	9,299
Increase in receivables — net	59,295
Increase in current income tax payable	21,513
Reduction of other long-term debt	53,950
Property additions	60,438

REQUIRED   Using the data listed above, prepare a statement of cash flows for Amfac, Inc.

33. *Preparation of a Statement of Cash Flows.*   The Nuts and Bolts Company manufactures hardware that it sells to stores in the western part of the United States. Exhibit A contains a pre-closing trial balance as of December 31, 1987, and a post-closing trial balance as of December 31, 1986.

Exhibit A

Nuts and Bolts Company
Trial Balances
At December 31, 1987, and 1986

	Pre-closing Trial Balance December 31, 1987	Post-closing Trial Balance December 31, 1986
Cash	$ 104,000	$ 88,000
Marketable securities	45,000	
Accounts receivable	530,000	450,000
Inventories	630,000	600,000
Prepaid expenses	55,000	65,000
Building	300,000	300,000
Allowance for depreciation — building	(189,000)	(180,000)
Machinery and equipment	90,000	80,000
Allowance for depreciation — machinery and equipment	(48,000)	(40,000)
Land	50,000	50,000
Patents	75,000	60,000
Stock of Everyone's Hardware stores	110,000	
Accounts payable	(495,000)	(500,000)
Income tax payable	(110,000)	(43,000)
Interest payable	(3,000)	
Mortgage payable	(50,000)	(70,000)
Deferred income tax	(85,000)	(65,000)
Common stock	(700,000)	(600,000)
Retained earnings	(195,000)	(195,000)
Sales	(5,350,000)	
Cost of sales	3,900,000	
Selling and administrative expenses	1,230,000	
Depreciation — buildings	9,000	
Depreciation — machinery and equipment	8,000	
Interest expense	3,000	
Amortization of patents	6,000	
Income tax expense	80,000	
	0	0

REQUIRED   From the information contained in Exhibit A, prepare a statement of cash flows for 1987.

34. *Statement Interrelationships.* Exhibit A contains the balance sheet of Pressed Products, Inc., at January 1, 1986, and Exhibit B contains a statement of cash flows during the year 1986.

Exhibit A

Pressed Products, Inc.
Balance Sheet
At January 1, 1986

Assets

Current Assets		
Cash	$ 60,000	
Accounts Receivable	400,000	
Inventories	500,000	
Other	80,000	$1,040,000
Noncurrent assets		
Machinery and Equipment	$3,000,000	
Less: Allowance for Depreciation	1,400,000	
	1,600,000	
Patents	200,000	1,800,000
Total Assets		$2,840,000

Liabilities and Stockholders' Equity

Current Liabilities		
Accounts Payable	$ 400,000	
Other	100,000	$ 500,000
Noncurrent Liabilities		
Note Payable		300,000
Total Liabilities		$ 800,000
Common Stock Outstanding	$2,000,000	
Retained Earnings	40,000	$2,040,000
Total Liabilities and Stockholders' Equity		$2,840,000

Exhibit B

Pressed Products, Inc.
Statement of Cash Flows
For the Year Ended December 31, 1986

Cash Flows from Operating Activities

Net income		$ 80,000
Noncash expenses, revenues, losses, and gains included in income		
Depreciation	150,000	
Amortization of patents	20,000	
Loss on sale of machinery	5,000	
Increase in accounts receivable	(30,000)	
Increase in inventories	(60,000)	
Decrease in other current assets	5,000	
Increase in accounts payable	50,000	
Increase in other current liabilities	3,000	
Net cash from operating activities		$ 223,000

Cash Flows from Investing Activities

Purchase of building*	$(400,000)	
Proceeds from sale of machinery†	50,000	
Net cash used by investing activities		(350,000)

Cash Flows from Financing Activities

Proceeds from issuance of common stock	$ 300,000	
Dividends paid	(100,000)	
Net cash provided by financing activities		200,000
Net increase in cash		$ 73,000

*On December 31, 1986
†Cost $100,000, accumulated depreciation $45,000

REQUIRED   Prepare a balance sheet at December 31, 1986.

35. *Preparation of a Cash Flow Forecast.*   Assume that you are the financial vice-president of Tandem Computers and must determine how much common stock should be issued early in 1989. The company is a pioneer in fault-tolerant systems and has become a major participant in computer networking. Its growth has been spectacular. Revenues rose from $7.7 million in 1980 to $208 million in 1988 and are expected to increase to $372 million in 1989. Net income is forecast at $41 million for 1989.

The company has been able to finance its growth from internally generated funds and the sale of stock to the public and its employees. As indicated in Exhibit A, there was no long-term debt at December 31, 1988.

Exhibit A

Tandem Computers
Consolidated Balance Sheet
At December 31, 1988
(in millions)

Assets

Current Assets

Cash and Equivalents		$ 89.8
Accounts Receivable		70.7
Inventories		54.5
Prepaid Expenses		5.0
Total Current Assets		$220.0
Property, Plant, and Equipment	$44.3	
Less: Depreciation	8.4	
		35.9
Total Assets		$225.9

Liabilities and Shareholders' Equity

Current Liabilities	$ 43.0
Deferred Income Tax	8.1
Total Liabilities	$ 51.1
Shareholders' Equity	204.8
Total Liabilities and Shareholders' Equity	$255.9

Tandem's management desires to have $73 million in cash available on December 31, 1989. Based on discussions with other company executives, you projected the following dollar amounts:

	(dollars in millions)
For the year 1989:	
Depreciation	8.0
Additions to property, plant, and equipment	40.0
At December 31, 1989:	
Accounts receivable	147.0
Deferred income tax	8.5
Prepaid expenses	9.0
Current liabilities	20.6
Inventories	97.0

REQUIRED Prepare a statement of forecast cash flows for 1989 for Tandem Computers and determine the proceeds required from the issuance of common stock to meet the company's financial goals.

36. *Evaluating a Loan Proposal.*   Fleetair, Inc., is a large international airline. Some relevant operating statistics for the firm for the years 1984–1986 are shown below. (The facts presented in this problem are authentic; Fleetair, Inc., is fictitious.)

	1986	1985	1984
Revenue plane miles flown (in M Miles)			
Domestic	108,000	96,000	88,000
International	26,000	22,000	21,000
Passenger load factor			
Domestic	52.5%	50.3%	51.9%
International	58.3%	52.8%	48.2%
Passenger break-even load factor			
Domestic	50.5%	46.4%	48.5%
International	49.7%	48.3%	45.8%
Average passenger revenue per mile (in cents)			
Domestic	8.9	9.1	8.4
International	8.4	8.8	8.4

Condensed income statements for the years 1984–1986 appear in Exhibit A on page 417 and selected balance sheet items appear in Exhibit B on page 418.

At the close of 1986, Fleetair applied to its principal long-term debtors, a consortium of banks and insurance companies, for additional long-term loans amounting to $409 million. There seemed to be little doubt that the loan request would be granted. (It was, in fact, granted.) The company indicated that it would use the funds as follows:

(1) Reduce long-term debt by $180 million.
(2) Apply the remaining $229 million to the purchase of new planes and other property. These assets are expected to increase in value by $323 million in 1987.

In addition to the $409-million loan, the following transactions affecting cash are projected for 1987:

(1) Long-term prepayments to plant manufacturers and deferred charges will be increased by $29 million.
(2) The company will continue to pay a cash dividend to common stockholders amounting to $7 million.
(3) Fleetair plans to raise $6 million from the sale of used planes that have a net book value of $4 million.
(4) The company intends to recover $37 million from a reduction in equipment-purchase deposits advanced to plan manufacturers.

The following changes in revenues and expenses are projected for 1987:

(1) A 38% rise in total operating revenues.

(2) Airline flying, maintenance, and ground operations, which include fuel, will increase in direct proportion to the expected increase in total operating revenues.
(3) Gasoline and oil prices are expected to rise by $170 million in 1987 over the normal variable increase in this expense, due to greater mileage flown.
(4) Depreciation and amortization is projected at $78 million.
(5) Other operating expenses are expected to be $46 million greater in 1987 than in 1986.
(6) The company estimates that servicing the present and proposed debt will increase its interest expense by $16 million in 1987.
(7) Other nonoperating income of $4 million is anticipated, including gain on sale of planes.

Operations in 1987 are expected to result in a loss. The company will be able to receive a tax credit equal to 46% of the loss. Assume that the Deferred Income Tax account will be reduced in 1987 to $35 million.

Exhibit A

Fleetair, Inc.
Condensed Income Statement
For the Years Ended December 31, 1984–1986
(in millions)

	1986	1985	1984
Operating revenues			
Airline Passengers	$845,000	$678,000	$583,000
Other	127,000	113,000	97,000
Total	$972,000	$791,000	$680,000
Operating expenses			
Airline flying, maintenance, and ground operations	$682,000	$544,000	$468,000
Depreciation and amortization	61,000	56,000	51,000
Other operating expenses	149,000	122,000	102,000
Total	$892,000	$722,000	$621,000
Operating income (loss)	$ 80,000	$ 69,000	$ 59,000
Less: Nonoperating revenues and expenses			
Interest expense	$ 34,000	$ 28,000	$ 26,000
Other	(9,000)	(8,000)	(3,000)
Total	$ 25,000	$ 20,000	$ 23,000
Net income before income taxes	$ 55,000	$ 49,000	$ 36,000
Less: Provision for income taxes	10,000	13,000	9,000
Net income	$ 45,000	$ 36,000	$ 27,000

Exhibit B

Fleetair, Inc.
Selected Balance Sheet Items
At December 31, 1984–1986
(in millions)

	1986	1985	1984
Current Assets	141,000	134,000	113,000
Current Liabilities	155,000	124,000	115,000
Working Capital	(14,000)	10,000	(2,000)
Property, Plant, and Equipment, net	612,000	493,000	467,000
Long-term Debt	349,000	273,000	242,000
Common Stock and Additional Paid-in Capital	57,000	57,000	57,000
Retained Earnings	193,000	155,000	124,000

REQUIRED   As a senior member of your bank's loan committee, you have been asked to evaluate whether the bank should participate in the new loan to the extent of $20 million at a very attractive interest rate. Fleetair presently is not indebted to the bank. Based only on the information provided, prepare a projected income statement and a statement of cash flows for 1987. Assume that there will be no change in current assets and current liabilities other than cash during 1987. Analyze this data and submit a written recommendation to the loan committee.

37. *Investment Decision Based on Cash Flows.*   Horace Grissom is a successful realtor who owns and operates three hotels in Florida. In September 1986, he met with his auditor and commented as follows:

"I have been approached by Andrew Teller, who owns the Excelsior Hotel, which he bought five years ago. The hotel hasn't shown a profit during this period and Mr. Teller has discretely been trying to unload it. He is now willing to sell the assets at net book value of $1.5 million, even though the property has been appraised at $2 million.

Mr. Teller has had no previous experience in the hotel business. I believe that with proper management the Excelsior should be a very good investment. From December 1 to March 31, customers are being turned away. In my judgment, the room rates at the Excelsior are too low compared with similar hotels. I also think Mr. Teller is wrong in closing the hotel during July and August.

As you know, my primary interest is in cash flow. Because it is not a cash flow item, I consider depreciation to be an irrelevant expense. The investment criterion I use is that I must obtain a cash flow of at least double the interest I would be losing by having to sell relatively secure bonds (which are now earning 10%) in order to raise the $1.5 million-purchase price.

Mr. Teller has agreed to let you review Excelsior's books."

An income statement for 1987 prepared by Mr. Teller and his staff is presented in Exhibit A. After reviewing this statement, Mr. Grissom asks his auditor to prepare a statement for 1987 indicating the projected cash flow based on the following assumptions:

(1) Room rentals from December 1 to March 31 would be raised $15, but a 10% reduction in room occupancy is expected.
(2) No change in room rentals or rates are expected from April 1 to June 30 and from September 1 to November 30.
(3) The hotel would remain open during July and August; assume 50 daily rentals at a reduced daily rate of $40.
(4) Variable expenses per room rental would continue as at present.
(5) Advertising expenses would be increased by $20,000.
(6) Fixed salaries would be reduced by $10,000.
(7) Mr. Grissom would not assume the existing loan from First Florida Bank, but would sell bonds if he decided to purchase the hotel.
(8) The income tax rate is 40%.

Exhibit A

Excelsior Hotel
Income Statement
For the Year Ended March 31, 1986

Revenues (total room rentals — 15,000)*		$1,050,000
Less: Variable expenses		510,000
Contribution margin		$ 540,000
Less: Fixed expenses		
Depreciation — hotel	$ 60,000	
Depreciation — equipment, furniture, and fixtures	60,000	
Depreciation — outdoor facilities	30,000	
Fixed portion of utility expenses	20,000	
Property taxes	40,000	
Tennis and pool attendants	30,000	
Building maintenance and security	40,000	
Bookkeeping and front desk	50,000	
Advertising	60,000	
Hotel and room management	60,000	
Legal and auditing	25,000	
Payroll taxes	10,000	
Interest on loans to First Florida Bank	90,000	
Miscellaneous	25,000	
Total		$ 600,000
Net Loss		$ (60,000)

*7,500 room rentals from December 1 to March 31, and 7,500 room rentals from April 1 to June 30 and September 1 to November 30. Room rates are fixed throughout the year at $70.

REQUIRED

(a) Prepare a statement of forecast cash flows for 1987 and determine whether Grissom's investment criterion would be met.

(b) Evaluate Mr. Grissom's investment criterion.

CONTEMPORARY ISSUES
IN ACCOUNTING

9

Intercorporate Investments and Business Combinations

This chapter discusses accounting for a firm's investments in the ownership shares of other corporations. It begins by describing management's motivations for making such intercorporate investments and includes coverage of the various types of ownership relationships that may exist among the firms.

In preparing its financial statements, an investor firm must decide whether or not to *consolidate* or combine its financial statements with those of the firms in which it has invested. If the financial statements are not to be consolidated, the investor firm will account for its investment using either the cost method or the equity method. In general, these decisions (whether or not to prepare consolidated financial statements and whether to use the cost method or the equity method) will depend on the degree of control or influence that the investor firm possesses.

Use of the cost and equity methods for reporting of intercorporate investments and procedures for consolidating the investor and investee firms are described and illustrated in the middle sections of this chapter. In addition, the effects of these different accounting methods on key financial ratios are explored. The chapter's final section treats accounting for business combinations using the pooling-of-interests and purchase methods. An appendix is included that describes reporting standards for segments of a business.

Chapter 9 and its appendix deal with a common theme, but from opposing perspectives. The central question involves the fact that the corporation, as a legal entity, may not be identical to the economic entity that is meaningful to financial statement users. Financial reporting for intercorporate investments generally entails *aggregating* or combining the financial statements of two or more legally separate firms. Segment disclosures, in contrast (the subject matter of the chapter's appendix), entail the reporting of subentity data: total corporate operations are *disaggregated* to reveal the operating results and assets employed in various lines of business.

MANAGEMENT MOTIVATIONS FOR INTERCORPORATE INVESTMENTS

The overriding objective in any business decision is profitability, and the decision to invest in ownership shares of other firms must be judged by the same standard. In order to discuss specific motives for investments in equity securities, it is useful to categorize such investments as either passive or active, as defined below.

Passive Investments

When an investor firm does not intend to exert influence or control over the investee firm, the investment is regarded as **passive**. The percentage of the voting equity securities acquired is usually minor. For practical purposes, an investment of less than 20 percent of the voting shares of the investee firm is usually presumed to constitute a passive investment. Management's motives for making passive investments may involve liquidity considerations or investment returns.

1. *Liquidity considerations.* Managers may temporarily invest cash in equity securities in order to earn a return on otherwise idle cash balances. Because temporary investments usually involve securities that are traded on major stock exchanges, they can be readily converted to cash when the need arises. These securities comprise the firm's *current* portfolio of marketable equity securities. The current portfolio is valued on the balance sheet at the lower of aggregate cost or market value, as described in Chapter 5.
2. *Investment returns.* Managers may make passive investments in the equity securities of other firms in order to earn returns from dividends and capital gains. If management's intended holding period for the investments is longer than the period used to define current assets, these securities comprise the firm's *noncurrent* portfolio of equity securities. On the balance sheet, the noncurrent portfolio is also valued at the lower of aggregate cost or market value.

Active Investments

When an investor firm aims to influence or direct the activities of another firm—a firm that may be a present or prospective supplier, a major customer, or a competitor—the investment is regarded as **active**. There are various reasons that a firm might choose to make active investments in the ownership shares of another firm, rather than undertaking new capital expenditures to acquire similar productive capacity. These reasons may include the following:

1. *Lower required investment.* A firm may control the operations of another firm by acquiring a majority (but not necessarily all) of its voting shares. This usually entails a smaller expenditure than would the direct purchase of the other firm's assets.
2. *Lower cost.* Because of increases in replacement costs of plant and equipment, it may be less expensive for a firm to acquire control of the assets of another firm through stock ownership than to purchase new assets with the same productive capacity.
3. *Limited market size.* A firm may wish to enter a given product market, but management may believe that the total market demand for the product is insufficient to support an additional producer. If so, control of an existing firm that produces the product may be a viable alternative.
4. *Established market.* Introduction of new products and attempts to displace established firms may be risky, and such risks can be avoided by obtaining control of an existing firm through stock ownership.
5. *Tax advantages.* A profitable firm may obtain an unprofitable firm in order to reduce its own income tax expense, because in many cases the losses of the acquired firm may be used to offset the profits of the investor firm on a consolidated income tax return.
6. *Intangible assets.* The firm to be acquired may possess unique management talent, patents, reputation, or other advantages that the investor firm might otherwise be unable to obtain.
7. *Other advantages.* Firms may avoid delays in the construction of new plants, compliance with governmental regulations for new construction, recruiting and training of a competent work force, and other costly undertakings by buying control of existing firms.

ACCOUNTING FOR INTERCORPORATE INVESTMENTS: AN OVERVIEW

An investor firm must decide whether its financial statements will be unconsolidated or consolidated with the financial statements of investee firms. If unconsolidated, an investor firm will account for its investment using either the cost method or the equity method. The circumstances appropriate to the use of each of these methods are summarized in Exhibit 9-1 and discussed in later sections of the chapter.

There are two methods of accounting for unconsolidated intercorporate investments on the separate books of the investor firm: the cost method and the equity method. These methods are *not interchangeable*. One method or the other will apply to a given set of circumstances, depending on whether the investment is active or passive. An ownership percentage of less than 20 percent of the voting shares is generally presumed to be a passive investment, and the

Exhibit 9-1

Accounting for Intercorporate Investments: Methods and Circumstances

Method	Circumstances
1. *Unconsolidated*	
Cost method	Investor lacks significant influence over investee firm (usually, less than 20-percent interest).
Equity method	Investor has significant influence, but not control, over investee firm, *or* investor has control over investee firm (greater than 50-percent interest), but consolidation would impair the usefulness of the financial statements.
2. *Consolidated*	Investor has control over investee firm (greater than 50-percent interest) and consolidation improves the usefulness of the financial statements.

Note: Recall from Chapter 5 that the investor's *portfolio* of investments in marketable equity securities must be valued at the lower of aggregate cost or market. Individual investments, however, are carried at cost.

LCM (lower of cost or market) method is used for such investments. An ownership percentage that equals or exceeds 20 percent is generally presumed to be an active investment, and active investments require the use of the equity method of accounting. (The 20-percent guide is not a hard and fast rule, and the FASB has provided examples where investments exceeding 20 percent might not provide the investor with significant influence over an investee.)

Ownership of less than 50 percent of the voting shares of another firm is referred to as a **minority interest.** The 20-percent ownership guide for use of the equity method recognizes the fact that one firm can substantially influence the decisions of another firm, even when it owns less than a majority of the other firm's voting shares—that is, even when it is in a minority interest position.

In those cases involving a majority ownership of the voting shares (50 percent or more), consolidated financial statements will normally be prepared. Procedures for combining the financial statements of two or more separate legal entities into a set of consolidated financial statements are discussed later in the chapter.

Cost Method

To apply the cost method, investments are recorded at the full cost of acquisition, including any commissions or other costs necessary to obtain the securities. Dividends received by the investor firm are recorded as revenue. The investor firm does *not* reflect the reported income or loss of the investee firm in its own accounting statements. As discussed in Chapter 5, the current and noncurrent portfolios of passive equity investments are valued on the balance sheet at the lower of aggregate cost or market.

To illustrate the cost method, assume that on January 1, 1987, P Company pays $15 million for a passive investment in the equity shares of S, Inc. On October 1, 1987, S pays dividends to P of $1.5 million. As a result of these events, P records the following entries:

Jan. 1, 1987	dr.	Investment in S, Inc.	15,000,000		
	cr.	Cash		15,000,000	
Oct. 1, 1987	dr.	Cash	1,500,000		
	cr.	Dividend Income		1,500,000	

P's 1987 financial statements would be affected as follows: the balance sheet would report the investment at a cost of $15 million (subject to the lower of cost or market rule), and the income statement would reflect the $1.5 million dividend as a revenue.

Equity Method

To apply the equity method, investments are initially recorded at the full cost of acquisition, including any commissions or other costs necessary to obtain the securities. Each time the investee firm reports income or loss, the investor firm records its percentage share of the income or loss, and correspondingly adjusts the carrying value of the investment. When the investee firm pays dividends, these are recorded by the investor as a return of investment. This is done because it would be double-counting to record the investee's income and subsequently to reflect dividends as additional income.

Notice that under the equity method the investor recognizes income of the investee firm *before* it is realized. Income is recognized over the period of time that the investor holds the investment, which seems more reasonable than waiting until the point of sale and reporting the whole gain in income at that time. (Of course, this argument might be extended to justify recognizing other sources of unrealized gains and losses, as discussed in Chapter 3.) At present, the equity method represents a piecemeal relaxation of the realization principle under generally accepted accounting principles.

To illustrate the equity method, we will use the same dollar amounts for the investment and the dividend totals as those presented in the previous example for P Company and S, Inc. The situations, however, are not the same: the earlier case involves accounting for a passive investment, while in the illustration that follows we assume that the investment is active. The same dollar amounts are used in order to emphasize the differences between the cost and equity methods, but we reiterate that these two methods are *not interchangeable*.

Exhibit 9-2 presents the balance sheets of P and S immediately following P's purchase of $15 million of S's outstanding ownership shares. Note that these shares constitute 25 percent of S's voting shares, so that the equity method of accounting is appropriate here (that is to say, the investor firm has

Exhibit 9-2

The Equity Method of Accounting
Balance Sheets at Date of Acquisition
Investment Cost Equals Book Value

P Company
Balance Sheet at January 1, 1987
(in millions)

Assets

Investment in S, Inc.	$ 15.0
Other Assets	335.0
Total Assets	$350.0

Liabilities	$200.0

Owners' Equity

Paid-in Capital	100.0
Retained Earnings	50.0
Total Liabilities and Owners' Equity	$350.0

S, Inc.
Balance Sheet at January 1, 1987
(in millions)

Assets	$100.0

Liabilities	$ 40.0

Owners' Equity

Paid-in Capital	50.0
Retained Earnings	10.0
Total Liabilities and Owners' Equity	$100.0

significant influence, although it does not control the investee firm). In addition, for this illustration, P's investment cost of $15 million coincides with P's share of S's owners' equity — 25 percent of $60 million. Of course, investment costs and underlying book values are rarely equal, and we will soon consider other situations.

During 1987 S earns $8 million, and pays $6 million in total dividends. P earns $20 million *exclusive* of income from the investment in S, and pays no dividends. P's journal entries to account for the investment in S are shown below.

```
dr.   Investment in S, Inc.          2,000,000
      cr.   Income from S, Inc.                  2,000,000
To record share of earnings in S, Inc. — 25 percent of reported
income of $8,000,000.
```

dr. Cash   1,500,000
      cr. Investment in S, Inc.   1,500,000
To record share of dividends of S, Inc. — 25 percent of dividends of $6,000,000.

The resulting balance sheets are shown in Exhibit 9-3. In examining P's balance sheet, you should note two features:

1. The investment in S is carried at $15.5 million, which equals 25 percent of S's shareholders' equity at book value ($62 million). P Company initially bought 25 percent of S at book value, and has recorded 25 percent of the *changes* in S's book value (see entries above) subsequent to the date of acquisition.

Exhibit 9-3

The Equity Method of Accounting
Balance Sheets One Year after Acquisition
Investment Cost Equals Book Value

P Company
Balance Sheet at December 31, 1987
(in millions)

Assets
Investment in S, Inc. (equity method)	$ 15.5
Other Assets	356.5
Total Assets	$372.0

Liabilities	$200.0

Owners' Equity
Paid-in Capital	100.0
Retained Earnings	72.0
Total Liabilities and Owners' Equity	$372.0

S, Inc.
Balance Sheet at December 31, 1987
(in millions)

Assets	$102.0
Liabilities	$ 40.0

Owners' Equity
Paid-in Capital	50.0
Retained Earnings	12.0
Total Liabilities and Owners' Equity	$102.0

2. P's retained earnings have increased by $22 million, which is the sum of its separate earnings of $20 million, and its share of S's earnings of $2 million (25 percent of $8 million).

In effect, P's share of S's shareholders' equity is reflected in one line on P's balance sheet (Investment in S, Inc., $15.5 million), and its share of S's net income will be reflected in one line of P's income statement (Income from S, Inc., $2 million). For this reason, the equity method of accounting is often termed a **one-line consolidation.**

Extensions of the equity method   Adjustments to the equity method are appropriate in cases where the investor pays more or less than the book value of the percentage of shareholders' equity (net worth) acquired, and also in cases where the firms earn profits or losses in transactions with each other. Each of these situations will be discussed in turn.

Cost of investment exceeds book value   In our earlier example, P Company paid $15 million for a 25-percent interest in S. The balance sheet for P Company in Exhibit 9-4 recasts this earlier example to reflect the situation in which P pays $19 million for the 25-percent interest in S. (The balance sheets for S, Inc.,

Exhibit 9-4

The Equity Method of Accounting
Balance Sheets at Date of Acquisition and One Year after Acquisition
Investment Cost Exceeds Book Value

P Company
Balance Sheets at January 1, 1987, and 1988
(in millions)

	Jan. 1, 1987	Jan. 1, 1988
Assets		
Investment in S, Inc.	$ 19.0	$ 19.1*
Other Assets	331.0	352.5
Total Assets	$350.0	$371.6
Liabilities	$200.0	$200.0
Owners' Equity		
Paid-in Capital	100.0	100.0
Retained Earnings	50.0	71.6
Total Liabilities and Owners' Equity	$350.0	$371.6

*Cost of $19 million, plus $2-million share of S's income, less $1.5-million dividend, less $400,000 in amortization.

do not appear in Exhibit 9-4 because they remain the same as those presented in Exhibits 9-2 and 9-3.) In this new example, the investment cost exceeds by $4 million P's interest in the book value of S's shareholders' equity ($19-million cost, less $15-million share in S's shareholders' equity at book value.)

In this instance, P's income from S is less than its percentage of S's net income because, from P's viewpoint, S's assets are more costly: P paid $4 million more than the underlying book value of S's assets and must record additional expense when those assets are consumed by S. If we assume that those assets will be consumed evenly over the next ten years, P's income from S for the current year is computed as follows:

P's share of S's net income (25% of $8,000,000)	$2,000,000
Less: Amortization of excess of cost of investment over book value	
($\frac{1}{10}$ of $4,000,000)	(400,000)
Income from S	$1,600,000

P would make the following entries to record its share of S's net income for the period:

dr.   Investment in S, Inc.   2,000,000
      cr.   Income from S, Inc.   2,000,000
To record 25 percent of S's reported income of $8,000,000.

dr.   Income from S, Inc.   400,000
      cr.   Investment in S, Inc.   400,000
To record amortization of excess of cost over book value
($\frac{1}{10}$ of $4,000,000).

Note that after both of these entries are posted, P has recorded income of $1.6 million ($2 million less 400,000) from its investment in S. The second entry presented above, which amortizes the $4-million excess of acquisition cost over underlying book value, would be required each year for ten years in order to fully amortize this excess.

The $4-million excess of investment cost over underlying book value has two effects: (1) P's earnings from S are less than its percentage of S's net income, because P must amortize this excess cost over the useful life of the related assets and (2) the carrying value of the investment in S will not be the same as P's percentage share of S's shareholders' equity until this excess cost has been completely expensed (ten years, in this example).

With reference to the second effect listed above, observe in Exhibit 9-4 that the carrying value of P's investment in S is $19.1 million. This represents P's percentage interest in S's net worth (shareholders' equity), *plus* any unamortized goodwill. These amounts, which together explain the carrying value of P's investment in S, may be calculated as follows:

■ Note in Exhibit 9-3 that the total shareholders' equity of S is $62 million. Since P owns 25 percent of the voting stock in S, P's percentage interest in S's net worth is $15.5 million (25 percent of $62 million).

- The amount of the excess of cost over book value at acquisition in this case is $4 million. But one-tenth of this cost, or $400,000, has been amortized to date (see P's journal entry on page 430). Thus, the current amount of the unamortized goodwill is $3.6 million ($4 million less $400,000).

These calculations are summarized below:

Percentage interest in S's reported net worth (25% of $62 million, per Exhibit 9-3)	$15,500,000
Plus: Unamortized goodwill	3,600,000
Total carrying value of P's investment in S (see Exhibit 9-4)	$19,100,000

Intercompany profits and losses   Additional adjustments to the equity method are needed when transactions between the investor and investee firms create profits or losses for either firm. From a consolidation perspective, such profits or losses are not the results of transactions between separate economic entities and they often require adjustments to the investor's income from investments, and to the investment's carrying value. Transactions of this nature include intercompany purchases or sales of inventory or other assets, and the acquisition by either firm of outstanding debt securities of the other firm. No numerical examples are given here because the topic of intercompany profits and losses is covered in greater detail in the discussion of consolidations later in this chapter.

Cost and Equity Method: Financial Statement Effects

Either the cost method or the equity method is used to account for less than majority ownership of the equity shares of other firms. Passive investments (usually less than 20 percent) are recorded using the cost method, while active investments require employment of the equity method. The two methods differ as follows in their effects on the financial statements of the investor firm.

- Balance sheet—Under the cost method, the investment account is valued at original cost, subject to the lower of cost or market rule illustrated in Chapter 5. Under the equity method, the investment account is valued at original cost and adjusted for the investor's share in the investee's incomes and losses. In addition, dividends are treated as returns of investment.

- Income statement—Under the cost method, dividends from investments are reported as income. Under the equity method, income includes the investor's share of the investee's income or loss for the period. Dividends do not affect the investor's income.

CONSOLIDATION OF INVESTOR AND INVESTEE FIRMS

Consolidation is the combination of the financial statements of legally separate firms to reflect the fact that they are under common control. Usually a single firm, termed the **parent company,** owns controlling interest in the voting shares of one or more other firms, which are termed **subsidiary companies.** Majority control, evidenced by ownership of more than 50 percent of a subsidiary's voting stock, is a necessary, though not sufficient, condition for consolidation; the usefulness of the resulting financial statements is the essential criterion. After discussing the procedures used in preparing consolidated financial statements, we will discuss the reasons that majority-owned subsidiaries may be excluded from a consolidation. In such cases, the subsidiary is accounted for using the equity method described earlier.

Consolidated financial statements show the assets, liabilities, revenues, and expenses of legally distinct entities *as if* they were in fact a single economic entity under the control of the parent company's shareholders. For the most part, consolidation is a simple adding together of the components of the separate firms' financial statements. Some adjustments are needed, however, for the following financial statement items:

1. The parent company's assets include the costs of investments in the shares of the subsidiaries. From the standpoint of the consolidated group, however, such investments are not assets because they represent a firm's ownership in itself. For this reason, investments in consolidated subsidiaries must be eliminated as a consolidating adjustment. Similarly, shares of the subsidiary firms that are owned by the parent firm are not outstanding from a consolidated perspective, so the shareholders' equity of the subsidiaries must be eliminated in consolidation.

2. Affiliated companies (parent and subsidiaries) often have accounts receivable from and accounts payable to each other, and these receivables and payables must be eliminated from the standpoint of consolidated financial statements. It does not make economic sense for a consolidated firm to be a debtor to or creditor of itself.

3. There are often customer-supplier relationships among affiliated firms, so that one firm's sales are included in another firm's purchases. When the firms are consolidated, these intercompany sales must be eliminated, since they do not represent transactions with outside entities.

4. At the balance sheet date, inventories may be on hand that were purchased from affiliated firms at amounts other than cost. When the firms are consolidated, such inventory profits (or losses) must be removed so that the balance sheet reflects the historical cost of inventory to the consolidated enterprise.

5. Dividends paid by one firm to another firm are not to be interpreted as income or as reductions of consolidated shareholders' equity, if both firms are included in a consolidation.

6. If a firm has acquired outstanding debt of another firm included in the consolidation, then from a consolidated perspective the debt has been retired, and there may be a gain or loss.
7. In many cases the subsidiaries being consolidated are less than 100-percent owned by the parent company. The other (minority) shareholders have an interest in the net assets shown on the consolidated balance sheet, as well as in consolidated revenues and expenses.
8. Whenever the parent firm acquires stock in a subsidiary at a cost that differs from the underlying book value of the parent's percentage interest, the subsidiary's net assets have a cost for the purpose of consolidation that differs from their cost on the subsidiary's separate financial statements. Accordingly, various assets and liabilities may need to be revalued in the process of consolidation.

Examples of many of these consolidation adjustments will be provided in the illustrations that follow. We will continue to designate the investor firm as P Company and the investee company as S, Inc., although the illustrations that follow are not a continuation of the examples presented earlier in this chapter. Exhibit 9-5 shows the balance sheets of P Company and S, Inc., at January 1,

Exhibit 9-5
Balance Sheets Preceding Acquisition of Majority Ownership

P Company and S, Inc.
January 1, 1987
(in millions)

	P Company	S, Inc.
Assets		
Current Assets	$ 500.0	$200.0
Noncurrent Assets	700.0	300.0
Total Assets	$1,200.0	$500.0
Liabilities		
Current Liabilities	$ 100.0	$ 50.0
Noncurrent Liabilities	400.0	150.0
Total Liabilities	$ 500.0	$200.0
Shareholders' Equity		
Paid-in Capital	$ 300.0	$180.0
Retained Earnings	400.0	120.0
Total Shareholders' Equity	$ 700.0	$300.0
Total Liabilities and Shareholders' Equity	$1,200.0	$500.0

1987, immediately preceding P's acquisition of S's equity shares. We will assume that P purchases controlling interest in S in three separate cases and in each case we will prepare the consolidated balance sheet at the acquisition date. The cases are the following:

1. P buys 100 percent of S at book value.
2. P buys 100 percent of S at a cost greater than book value.
3. P buys 80 percent of S at a cost greater than book value.

Case 1: 100-percent Ownership; Cost Equal to Subsidiary's Book Value

Assume that P Company buys all of the outstanding S, Inc., shares from S shareholders on January 1, 1987, at a total cost of $300 million, which is equal to the net worth of S, Inc. This transaction involves P Company and the shareholders of S, Inc.; there is no effect on the financial statements of S, Inc. Exhibit 9-6 shows the post acquisition balance sheets of both firms and the preparation of a consolidated balance sheet at January 1, 1987.

Note in Exhibit 9-6 that P Company's investment in S, Inc., is eliminated by means of worksheet adjustments used to prepare the consolidated balance sheet. Also, note that S's shareholders' equity is eliminated as well. This is done because all of the S shares are owned by P Company. The other assets and liabilities are added together, or consolidated. The shareholders' equity of P Company, consolidated, is the same as the shareholders' equity of P Company, unconsolidated.

Case 2: 100-percent Ownership; Cost Greater than Subsidiary's Book Value

In the second case, we assume that P Company buys all of the outstanding S, Inc., shares at a total cost of $400 million, which exceeds the net worth of S, Inc., by $100 million. P's willingness to pay $400 million indicates that the book values of S's assets and/or liabilities do *not* reflect their current market values. To account for this acquisition, P Company must attempt to identify the specific assets and liabilities that are responsible for this difference between the market value and book value of S's net assets. Assume that an appraisal of S's net assets reveals the following information:

Item	Book Value	Market Value	Difference
Current assets	$200.0	$220.0	$ 20.0
Noncurrent assets	300.0	350.0	50.0
Current liabilities	(50.0)	(50.0)	0.0
Noncurrent liabilities	(150.0)	(140.0)	10.0
Net worth	$300.0	$380.0	$ 80.0
Unassigned to specific items (goodwill)			20.0
Total excess of cost over book value			$100.0

Exhibit 9-6
Post-acquisition Balance Sheets and Consolidation at Acquisition Date
100-percent Ownership; Investment Cost Equals Investee's Book Value

P Company and S, Inc.
January 1, 1987
(in millions)

	P Company	S, Inc.	Consolidating Adjustments		P Company Consolidated
			dr.	cr.	
Assets					
Current Assets	$ 200.0	$200.0			$ 400.0
Noncurrent Assets	700.0	300.0			1,000.0
Investment in S, Inc.	300.0			(1) 300.0	
Total Assets	$1,200.0	$500.0			$1,400.0
Liabilities					
Current Liabilities	$ 100.0	$ 50.0			$ 150.0
Noncurrent Liabilities	400.0	150.0			550.0
Total Liabilities	$ 500.0	$200.0			$ 700.0
Shareholders' Equity					
Paid-in Capital	$ 300.0	$180.0	(1) 180.0		$ 300.0
Retained Earnings	400.0	120.0	(1) 120.0		400.0
Total Shareholders' Equity	$ 700.0	$300.0			$ 700.0
Total Liabilities and Equity	$1,200.0	$500.0			$1,400.0

(1) Elimination of investment in S, Inc., and shareholders' equity of S, Inc.

From P's standpoint, the cost to acquire S's net assets (by means of a purchase of S's outstanding shares) exceeds S's carrying value of the net assets by $100 million. Of this amount, $80 million can be assigned to specific assets and liabilities, and the remaining unassigned portion is considered "goodwill." **Goodwill** reflects the fact that the combination of S's recorded net assets has a value that exceeds their separate values. Though the term goodwill is widely used, the phrase "unassignable excess of cost over book value" is preferred. It is important to recognize that S, Inc., on its separate financial statements, continues to report the book values of the net assets. On P's separate financial statements, the investment in S is reported at its cost to P Company of $400 million. When the companies are consolidated, however, the excess of cost over book value is assigned to the identifiable assets and liabilities and to goodwill, as shown in Exhibit 9-7.

Exhibit 9-7 shows that the assets and liabilities of S, Inc., are revalued only as the consolidation is prepared, and any remainder is charged to goodwill. The term "goodwill arising in consolidation" is often employed to underscore

Exhibit 9-7

Post-acquisition Balance Sheets and Consolidation at Acquisition Date
100-percent Ownership; Investment Cost Exceeds Investee's Book Value

P Company and S, Inc.
January 1, 1987
(in millions)

	P Company	S, Inc.	Consolidating Adjustments		P Company Consolidated
Assets			dr.	cr.	
Current Assets	$ 100.0	$200.0	(1) 20.0		$ 320.0
Noncurrent Assets	700.0	300.0	(1) 50.0		1,050.0
Investment in S, Inc.	400.0			(1) 400.0	
Goodwill			(1) 20.0		20.0
Total Assets	$1,200.0	$500.0			$1,390.0
Liabilities					
Current Liabilities	$ 100.0	$ 50.0			$ 150.0
Noncurrent Liabilities	400.0	150.0	(1) 10.0		540.0
Total Liabilities	$ 500.0	$200.0			$ 690.0
Shareholders' Equity					
Paid-in Capital	$ 300.0	$180.0	(1) 180.0		$ 300.0
Retained Earnings	400.0	120.0	(1) 120.0		$ 400.0
Total Shareholders' Equity	$ 700.0	$300.0			$ 700.0
Total Liabilities and Equity	$1,200.0	$500.0			$1,390.0

(1) Elimination of investment in S, Inc., and shareholders' equity of S, Inc., and assignment of excess cost to specific assets, liabilities, and goodwill.

the fact that these amounts do not appear on the separate (unconsolidated) financial statements of the companies being consolidated. Of course, on P's separate financial statements the cost of investment in S implicitly includes the goodwill and other revaluations to be made in consolidation.

Case 3: Majority (80 percent) Ownership; Cost Greater than Subsidiary's Book Value

In our third case, we assume that P Company buys a controlling interest, but less than 100 percent, of the outstanding S, Inc., shares. Specifically, P buys 80 percent of the S shares at a cost of $320 million. Since the total net worth of S is $300 million, P's share of S's net worth is $240 million ($300 million × 80 percent), and the cost exceeds the book value of the net assets acquired by $80 million ($320 million cost, less $240 million book value). Twenty percent of the S, Inc., shares were not acquired by P Company, and the equity of these minority shareholders must also be shown on the consolidated financial statements. The resulting consolidation is shown in Exhibit 9-8, in which you should note the following features:

1. P Company has purchased 80 percent of S, Inc., so that only 80 percent of the difference between the market values and the book values of S's net assets is recorded in consolidation. From a consolidated perspective, only 80 percent of these items has been

Exhibit 9-8

Post-acquisition Balance Sheets and Consolidation at Acquisition Date Less than 100-percent Ownership; Investment Cost Exceeds Investee's Book Value

P Company and S, Inc.
January 1, 1987
(in millions)

	P Company	S, Inc.	Consolidating Adjustments		P Company Consolidated
			dr.	cr.	
Assets					
Current Assets	$ 180.0	$200.0	(1) 16.0		$ 396.0
Noncurrent Assets	700.0	300.0	(1) 40.0		1,040.0
Investment in S, Inc.	320.0			(1) 320.0	
Goodwill			(1) 16.0		16.0
Total Assets	$1,200.0	$500.0			$1,452.0
Liabilities					
Current Liabilities	$ 100.0	$ 50.0			$ 150.0
Noncurrent Liabilities	400.0	150.0	(1) 8.0		542.0
Total Liabilities	$ 500.0	$200.0			$ 692.0
Minority Interest				(2) 60.0	$ 60.0
Shareholders' Equity					
Paid-in Capital	$ 300.0	$180.0	(1) 144.0 (2) 36.0		$ 300.0
Retained Earnings	400.0	120.0	(1) 96.0 (2) 24.0		$ 400.0
Total	$ 700.0	$300.0			$ 700.0
Total Liabilities and Equity	$1,200.0	$500.0			$1,452.0

Adjustment explanations:

(1) Elimination of investment in S, Inc., and P's interest in the shareholders' equity of S, Inc., and assignment of cost to specific assets, liabilities, and goodwill (see page 438).
(2) Reclassification of remaining ownership of S, Inc., as minority interest.

"sold" to P. The amounts in the consolidating adjustment are computed as follows:

Difference between Market Value and Book Value (see page 434)		Percent Owned		Revaluation in Consolidation
Current assets	$ 20 ×	.80	=	$16.0
Noncurrent assets	50 ×	.80	=	40.0
Current liabilities	0 ×	.80	=	0.0
Noncurrent liabilities	10 ×	.80	=	8.0
Goodwill	20 ×	.80	=	16.0
Total	$100			$80.0

This 80 percent revaluation of S's net assets makes the interpretation of items in the consolidated balance sheet rather cumbersome. For example, consolidated current assets include (a) the current assets of P at book value and (b) 20 percent of the current assets of S at book value, plus the remaining 80 percent of the current assets of S at market value as of the acquisition date.

2. The consolidated balance sheet shows the net worth of S, Inc., applicable to the 20 percent minority interest. The amount is not a liability of the consolidated firm because it does not represent debt. Neither is it consolidated owners' equity, since only the parent company's equity is included there. Instead, the convention is to classify minority interest between liabilities and stockholders' equity in the consolidated financial statement.

   The reason that minority interest is needed to balance the statement is that *all* of the subsidiary's recorded assets and liabilities have been included in the consolidation, while the parent firm owns less than 100 percent of the outstanding shares of S. One purpose of consolidated statements is to show all of the economic resources under the control of the parent company, so it would not be suitable to include only the percentage of net assets actually owned by P.

CONSOLIDATION EFFECTS AND THE INCOME STATEMENT

The preceding section treats consolidation procedures for three separate cases, but limits discussion to the preparation of the consolidated balance sheet. This section focuses on the effects of consolidation on the income statement in those three cases.

Basic Adjustments in Computing Consolidated Net Income

We begin by considering again Case 1 and Case 2 from the previous section. In both these cases, P Company owns 100 percent of the stock of S, Inc. The cases differ from one another, however, in two important ways:

- In Case 1, the cost of P's investment in S is equal to the book value of S's net assets, while in Case 2, the cost is assumed to be greater than book value.
- In Case 1, we assume that no intercompany purchases and sales take place, and in Case 2, we will now make the additional assumption that P sells inventory to S (which S then sells to its own customers).

In Case 1 (100-percent ownership; cost equal to subsidiary's book value), if there have been no revenue and expense transactions between the parent and the subsidiary, the consolidated income statement is just the sum of the separate company income statements, as shown in Exhibit 9-9, panel (1).

Case 2 (100-percent ownership; cost exceeds subsidiary's book value; intercompany purchases and sales) requires two consolidating adjustments in computing consolidated net income. If the cost of the parent's investment is greater than the book value of the subsidiary, this excess cost must be assigned to specific assets and liabilities to the extent possible, and the unassignable difference reported as goodwill. When the revalued assets are consumed in operations, the expense from a consolidated standpoint differs from the expense reported on S's separate income statement. Referring to our earlier example for Case 2, P Company acquired a 100-percent interest in S, Inc., for $400 million, which exceeded S's book value of net assets by $100 million. In consolidation, the net assets of S were revalued upwards by $100 million (see page 434). If we assume that the revalued assets and goodwill have remaining economic lives of ten years, and we also assume a straight-line benefit pattern, $10 million of net asset cost must be expensed each year for ten years when computing consolidated net income. For this reason, consolidated net income will be $10 million lower over the ten-year period than the sum of P's and S's separate income (ignoring any tax consequences resulting from the additional expenses). This is shown in adjustment (1) in Exhibit 9-9, panel (2).

The second adjustment is necessary because of intercompany purchases and sales. Assume that during the year 1987 P Company sold $200 million worth of merchandise to S, Inc., and that S has in turn sold that merchandise to customers. From a consolidated standpoint, both the sales and cost of sales are overstated unless an adjustment is made. In consolidation, P and S are part of the same economic entity, so that a sale of goods from P to S is not a sale to an outside entity. Likewise, the cost of sales (goods sold) reported by S includes the cost of goods purchased from P, which is not correct from a consolidated standpoint. Accordingly, the overstatements of sales and cost of sales are removed by adjustment (2).

Other Adjustments in Computing Consolidated Net Income

A variety of other situations would result in additional adjustments in computing consolidated net income. Two examples involve unrealized profits in inventory and a minority interest in net income.

Exhibit 9-9

Post-acquisition Income Statements and Consolidation Subsequent to Acquisition Date

P Company and S, Inc.
Separate and Consolidated Income Statements
For the Year Ended December 31, 1987
(in millions)

Panel (1): 100-percent Owned Subsidiary; Investment Cost Equals Book Value; No Intercompany Revenue or Expense Transactions.

	P Company	S, Inc.	Consolidating Adjustments dr.	cr.	P Company Consolidated
Revenue	$3,000	$1,100			$4,100
Cost of sales	(1,400)	(600)			(2,000)
Gross margin	$1,600	$ 500	None		$2,100
Selling and administration, including taxes	(1,300)	(380)	Required		(1,680)
Net income	$ 300	$ 120			$ 420

Panel (2): 100-percent Owned Subsidiary; Investment Cost Exceeds Subsidiary's Book Value; Intercompany Purchases and Sales.

	P Company	S, Inc.	Consolidating Adjustments dr.	cr.	P Company Consolidated
Revenue	$3,000	$1,100	(2) 200		$3,900
Cost of sales	(1,400)	(600)		(2) 200	(1,800)
Gross margin	$1,600	$ 500			$2,100
Selling and administration, including taxes	(1,300)	(380)	(1) 10*		(1,690)
Net income	$ 300	$ 120			$ 410

*The other part of this adjustment is a credit to reduce the carrying value of the related costs in the consolidated balance sheet, and is not shown here because we are illustrating only the income statements of the consolidating firms.

Adjustment explanations:

(1) Straight-line amortization of $100 million of excess cost of net assets over ten years. (See page 434.)
(2) Elimination of intercompany sales and cost of sales. (See page 439.)

Unrealized profits in inventory   Unrealized profits in inventory may exist when some of the inventory included in intercompany purchases and sales remains unsold to outsiders at the balance sheet date. If this occurs, an adjustment is required to compute consolidated cost of sales. Assume that S's ending inventory includes $10 million of merchandise purchased from P Company, and that P's cost for this merchandise was $6 million. The ending inventory thus includes unrealized profits of $4 million ($10 million − $6 million), and this overvaluation is removed in computing consolidated cost of sales by means of the following entry, which is made on the consolidating worksheet.

dr. Cost of Sales   4,000,000
    cr.   Inventory   4,000,000

Minority interest in net income   The portion of a subsidiary's net income applicable to a minority interest is shown as a subtraction on the income statement. The adjustment should be viewed as an apportionment of subsidiary net income rather than as an expense. Refer again to the first case (Panel 1) in Exhibit 9-9, where we assume a 100-percent ownership for P Company in S, Inc. Now assume that there is a 20-percent minority interest in S, Inc. Consolidated net income would be computed as follows:

Net income before minority interest [see Exhibit 9-9, panel (1), on page 440] $420.0
Less: Minority interest in S's income (20% × $120 million)   (24.0)
Consolidated net income $396.0

Conversely, if the subsidiary had reported a loss, the minority interest would bear a portion of the loss, and consolidated net income would be increased (or consolidated net loss decreased) by this adjustment.

In cases where there are unrealized profits from sales by a subsidiary to the parent company (termed **upstream sales**) and a minority interest, the share of subsidiary net income apportioned to the minority interest would differ from the example shown above. In consolidation, the subsidiary's income would be *reduced* by the unrealized profit before computing the minority interest in net income.

CONSOLIDATION POLICY: CONSOLIDATION COMPARED TO THE EQUITY METHOD

If a corporation owns more than 50 percent of the common stock of another firm, it will ordinarily use the consolidation method of reporting intercorporate investments. Yet management does have some discretion over the question of whether to consolidate; it may elect not to do so if the consolidation method does not provide better disclosure.[1] The two most important criteria in deciding whether to consolidate a majority-owned subsidiary are (1) the degree of parent company control and (2) the relatedness of activities.

---

[1]As this book is being written, management has discretion over whether subsidiaries with unrelated activities (real estate, insurance, and financial subsidiaries, for example) are to be consolidated. The FASB, however, is currently preparing an exposure draft of a proposed financial accounting standard that would require consolidation of such subsidiaries.

Foreign subsidiaries are often excluded from a consolidation because of restrictions by the foreign government on the parent company's ability to control subsidiary operations or on the repatriation of dividends. Domestic subsidiaries operating under the Federal Bankruptcy Act or other legal restrictions on parent company control are often not consolidated.

Even when the criterion of control is met, the operations of a parent and a subsidiary may be so dissimilar that consolidation might conceal important differences in the structures of the companies being combined. The basic issue to be addressed in setting consolidation policy is the effect of aggregation on the usefulness of financial reports. There is presently very little evidence on the merits of aggregated versus disaggregated data related to the usefulness of accounting numbers in financial analysis.

Exhibit 9-10 includes excerpts from the footnotes of recent annual reports of three firms—Anheuser-Busch; Sears, Roebuck; and ITT. In each instance the footnotes provide management's rationale for *excluding* majority or wholly-owned subsidiaries from their firm's consolidation. Anheuser-Busch excludes subsidiaries "which are not an integral part of the company's primary operations." Sears excludes manufacturing subsidiaries, and ITT Corporation excludes its insurance and finance subsidiaries. In all cases, the majority-owned firms that are excluded from the consolidation are accounted for by using the equity method discussed earlier.

A comparison of the consolidation policies of Sears and ITT is helpful in understanding the effects of consolidation policy on the analysis of financial statements. Both of these firms have substantial finance and insurance subsidiaries; Sears chooses to include these subsidiaries in their consolidation, and ITT chooses to exclude them. Selected financial information from the December 31, 1983, financial statements of these two firms is presented in Exhibit 9-11.

Exhibit 9-11 shows that financial ratio comparisons between the two firms are quite sensitive to consolidation of the insurance and finance subsidiaries.[2] For example, using the information reported in each firm's financial statements, Sears appears to have a higher debt-to-assets ratio (78.8 percent versus 56.2 percent for ITT), a lower return-on-assets ratio (2.9 percent versus 4.8 percent), and a higher return on equity ratio (13.7 percent versus 11 percent). ITT's footnote disclosures reveal that the subsidiaries excluded from consolidation have total assets *exceeding* those of ITT, the parent company, and that those assets are financed mainly (85.3 percent) by debt. As a consequence, if the subsidiaries were to be consolidated, the primary financial statements would indicate that ITT's debt-to-assets ratio is 80 percent (rather than 56.2 percent) and that ITT's return on assets ratio is 2.2 percent (rather than 4.8 percent).

Note that if a firm were to consolidate a subsidiary that is presently accounted for using the equity method, consolidated shareholders' equity would be unaffected. This is the case because under the equity method the parent's

---

[2]A comprehensive discussion of financial ratios appears in Chapter 12. The ratios discussed in this section, however, have been encountered earlier in this text.

Exhibit 9-10
Footnotes Concerning Consolidation Policy

Anheuser-Busch Companies, Inc.

Principles of Consolidation
The consolidated financial statements include the company and all its subsidiaries. Certain subsidiaries which are not an integral part of the company's primary operations are included on an equity basis. Several operating subsidiaries of Campbell Taggart, a wholly-owned subsidiary of the company, have minority interest shareholders. Minority interest in income is not material and is recorded in other income (expense), net. The Consolidated Statement of Income includes the operations of Campbell Taggart from November 2, 1982, through year-end, 1983.

Sears, Roebuck and Co.

The consolidated financial statements include the accounts of Sears, Roebuck and Co. and all domestic and significant international companies in which the company has more than a 50% equity ownership, except those engaged in manufacturing.

ITT Corporation

Consolidation Principles: The consolidated financial statements cover the accounts of all significant majority-owned subsidiaries, after including the insurance and finance subsidiaries on an equity basis. Marketable equity securities in the insurance subsidiaries portfolios are carried at market with the after-tax difference from cost reflected in stockholders' equity. Combined statements for the insurance and finance subsidiaries are shown in support of the consolidated financial statements.

Intercompany transactions are eliminated, except for intercompany profits in certain manufacturing inventories which are transferred on an arm's-length basis and have no material effect on consolidated inventories or net income.

Other Investments: Investments in 20–50% owned companies ($461,432,000 and $388,510,000 as of December 31, 1983 and 1982) are included on an equity basis. Certain other investments ($43,501,000 and $52,834,000 as of December 31, 1983 and 1982) are carried at cost.

Sources: Anheuser-Busch Companies, Inc., *Annual Report*, 1983; Sears, Roebuck and Co., *Annual Report*, 1983; ITT Corporation, *Annual Report*, 1983.

---

share of the subsidiary's income is already fully reflected in the parent's retained earnings. In addition, consolidated net income is unaffected because under the equity method the parent's share of the subsidiary's income is included in the parent company's net income. On the other hand, consolidation causes total liabilities to increase because the subsidiary's liabilities are added to the parent's liabilities. Total assets also increase because the subsidiary's assets are added to the parent's assets, while the parent's investment in the subsidiary is eliminated as a consolidation adjustment (shown earlier on page 435). The effect of adding the subsidiary's assets and subtracting the parent company's investment is to increase total assets by an amount approximately equal to the subsidiary's liabilities.

Exhibit 9-11
Effects of Consolidation Policy on
Selected Financial Statement Relationships

Sears, Roebuck and Co. and ITT, 1983
($ in millions)

Primary Financial Statements

	Sears, Roebuck and Co. (as reported)	ITT (as reported)
Total assets	$46,176.1	$13,966.7
Total liabilities	$36,389.2	$ 7,860.7
Shareholders' equity	$ 9,786.9	$ 6,106.0
Net income	$ 1,342.2	$ 674.5
Debt-to-assets ratio	78.8%	56.2%
Return on assets ratio	2.9%	4.8%
Return on equity ratio	13.7%	11.0%

Supplementary Information for ITT

	ITT Insurance and Finance Subsidiaries	ITT Restated to Consolidate Subsidiaries
Total assets	$19,523.3	$30,611.7*
Total liabilities	$16,645.0	$24,505.7†
Shareholders' equity	$ 2,878.3	$ 6,106.0
Net income	$ 405.3	$ 674.5
Debt-to-assets ratio	85.3%	80.0%
Return on assets ratio	2.1%	2.2%
Return on equity ratio	14.1%	11.0%

Sources: Sears, Roebuck and Co., *Annual Report*, 1983; ITT Corporation, *Annual Report*, 1983.

*ITT's assets as reported ($13,966.7), plus subsidiary assets ($19,523.3), less subsidiary shareholders' equity ($2,878.3).

†ITT's liabilities as reported ($7,860.7), plus subsidiary liabilities ($16,645.0).

In sum, net income and shareholders' equity are the same under consolidation as under the equity method of accounting. Consolidation of a subsidiary increases the parent company's assets and liabilities by an amount equal to the subsidiary's liabilities, and increases the revenues and expenses on the consolidated income statement.[3] As a consequence, financial ratios may be affected substantially by the consolidation of major subsidiaries.

---

[3]There is an exception when the subsidiary's assets or liabilities are revalued in consolidation.

BUSINESS COMBINATIONS: DIFFERENT METHODS AND MOTIVATIONS

There are several different ways in which one firm may obtain control over another firm. Among the most popular methods are (1) merger, (2) consolidation, (3) acquisition of assets, and (4) acquisition of stock. These arrangements are described below.

1. **Merger.** The boards of directors of the investor firm and the investee firm approve a plan for the exchange of the investee firm's voting stock in return for the voting stock and/or other consideration paid by the investor firm. The investee firm then ceases to exist as a separate legal entity.

2. **Consolidation.** A *new* corporation is formed to acquire the stock of both firms, and both cease to exist as legal entities.

3. **Acquisition of assets.** A firm purchases a substantial portion of the assets of another firm. The other corporation continues to exist as a separate legal entity and does *not* become a subsidiary of the investor firm.

4. **Acquisition of stock.** The investor firm acquires all or part of the voting stock of the investee firm in return for stock or other valuable considerations. The acquisition of stock does not require that the boards of directors of both firms reach a formal agreement, however, as in the case of a merger. The investor firm may acquire the other firm's shares by direct purchases in the stock market, through a publicly announced "tender offer," or by other means. After the acquisition of stock, the investee firm continues to exist as a separate legal entity.

The discussion that follows concerns accounting for the controlling interest in the voting stock of another firm (the last arrangement described above).

A number of reasons may motivate firms to acquire all, or substantially all, of the voting shares of other firms. Motives may include the detection of undervalued securities; the replacement of inefficient management; the acquisition of assets at below current replacement costs; the reshaping of the buyer's capital structure; the exploitation of possible economies of scale in production, distribution, financing, or information-processing activities; the acquisition of market power by means of the absorption of competing firms; the reduction of business risk through diversification; and tax factors, such as unutilized operating loss carryovers. Even this partial listing suggests that there may be sound economic reasons for business combinations. In addition, there are important accounting consequences to business combinations, and in some cases the projected accounting results may dominate other issues in shaping the terms of an acquisition.

ACCOUNTING FOR BUSINESS COMBINATIONS

In accordance with generally accepted accounting principles, a business combination must be accounted for as either (1) a **purchase** or (2) a **pooling of interests**.[4] While both methods are acceptable, they are not to be considered as alternatives to one another for the same transaction. In its *Opinion No. 16* the Accounting Principles Board specified the conditions for a pooling of interests; if these conditions are met, the combination must be accounted for by use of the pooling-of-interests method. If the conditions for pooling of interests are not met, the purchase method of accounting must be used. This is a matter of some consequence, since the effects on the financial statements of the buyer firm can be dramatic.

Pooling-of-interests Method and Balance Sheet Effects

The most important criteria for identifying a pooling of interests are summarized below. Before attempting to apply the criteria to particular cases, however, the reader should refer to the original professional pronouncements.[5] The key criteria are the following:

1. The combination is to be accomplished in one transaction or to be the result of a plan of acquisition that is completed within a year.
2. The buyer is to issue voting common stock for at least 90 percent of the voting stock of the seller.
3. There are no contingent issuances of securities at the final date of the plan and no agreements to retire or reacquire the voting shares issued.
4. There is no plan to dispose of a major portion of the assets of the combined company within the first two years after the combination.

The pooling-of-interests method does *not* revalue the assets and liabilities of the subsidiary to reflect fair market value at the acquisition date. Instead, the *book values* of the pooled subsidiary continue to be reported. In effect, the pooling method presumes that nothing of economic substance has occurred; there has only been a change in the form of the ownership interests. Proponents of the pooling method argue that the shareholders of the buyer and seller firms could have achieved the same result by a simple exchange of shares with one another, in which case there would be no accounting revaluation of assets of either firm to reflect fair market values. The APB accepted the premise that there

---

[4]The carrying value of the investment at acquisition and subsequent to acquisition is dependent on which accounting method is used (purchase or pooling of interest). The earlier discussion of the consolidation of P Company and S, Inc., is consistent with the purchase method of accounting.

[5]There are twelve conditions for pooling that are enumerated in Accounting Principles Board *Opinion No. 16*. Listed here are *simplified* statements about *only four* of those conditions. See Accounting Principles Board *Opinion No. 16*, "Business Combinations" (New York: AICPA, 1970), paragraphs 45–48, for a complete discussion of the conditions that must be met before the pooling-of-interests method may be used.

is no acquisition of one firm by another in a pooling, because the combination is accomplished without disbursing the resources of either constituent.

To illustrate the pooling method, consider the financial statements presented in Exhibit 9-12 for companies X and Y. Assume that Company X acquires Company Y's stock on January 1, 1988, and that at the acquisition date Company X stock is selling for $80 per share and Company Y stock is selling for $40. Assume also that Company X issues 500,000 shares of stock in exchange for the 1 million Company Y shares outstanding. If Company Y is not

Exhibit 9-12

Pre- and Post-combination Balance Sheets
for Companies X and Y Using
the Pooling-of-interests Method

(in millions)

Pre-combination Balance Sheets, January 1, 1988

	X	Y
Assets	$130.0	$40.0
Liabilities	$ 35.0	$18.0
Owners' Equity		
Common Stock, $20 Par for Company X, $10 Par for Company Y	$ 40.0	$10.0
Excess over Par	30.0	5.0
Retained Earnings	25.0	7.0
Total Owners' Equity	$ 95.0	22.0
Total Liabilities and Equity	$130.0	$40.0

Post-combination Balance Sheet, Company X, January 1, 1988

	Unconsolidated	Consolidated
Assets		
Investment in Y	$ 22.0	$ 0.0
Other Assets	130.0	170.0*
Total Assets	$152.0	$170.0
Liabilities	$ 35.0	$ 53.0†
Owners' Equity		
Common Stock, $20 Par	$ 50.0	$ 50.0
Excess over Par	35.0	35.0
Retained Earnings	32.0	32.0
Total Owners' Equity	$117.0	$117.0
Total Liabilities and Equity	$152.0	$170.0

*$130.0 + Company Y's assets of $40.0.

†$35.0 + Company Y's liabilities of $18.0.

dissolved (that is, Company Y continues to exist and operate as a wholly-owned subsidiary) the entry to record the acquisition on Company X's separate books would be the following:

dr.	Investment in Company Y	22,000,000	
	cr. Common Stock at Par		10,000,000
	cr. Excess over Par		5,000,000
	cr. Retained Earnings		7,000,000

To record the issuance of 500,000 shares of Company X $20 par common shares in order to obtain Company Y shares with a total book value or net worth of $22 million.

The key balance sheet effects of the pooling of Company X and Company Y are the following:

1. The market values of the Company X and Company Y shares at the acquisition date are entirely ignored in recording Company X's investment in Company Y. Instead, Company X's carrying value of the investment in Company Y is recorded at an amount equal to the book value of net worth appearing on Company Y's balance sheet.
2. The increase to paid-in capital upon the issuance of the new Company X shares is equal to the paid-in capital of Company Y. (More complicated situations are possible, but they are beyond the scope of this text.) In addition, because Company Y's retained earnings are added to those of Company X, the retained earnings of Company X increase as a direct result of the acquisition.
3. In consolidation, the book values of Company Y's assets and liabilities are added to those of Company X. There is no revaluation to reflect market values existing at the acquisition date.

Moreover, balance sheets presented for any prior periods will be presented *as if* the companies had been combined at those dates.

Purchase Method and Balance Sheet Effects

The purchase method of accounting for the same business combination just described is illustrated in Exhibit 9-13. The purchase method recognizes that the cost of the Company Y stock is equal to the market value of the Company X stock issued to effect the combination ($40 million—500,000 shares × $80 market price per share). The entry to record the acquisition on Company X's books would be the following:

dr.	Investment in Company Y	40,000,000	
	cr. Common Stock at Par		10,000,000
	cr. Excess over Par		30,000,000

To record the issuance of 500,000 shares of Company X $20 par common shares with a total market value of $40 million.

Exhibit 9-13

**Post-combination Balance Sheets for Company X
Using the Purchase Method**

Balance Sheets at January 1, 1988
(in millions)

	Purchase Method		Pooling-of-interests Method
	X, Unconsolidated	X, Consolidated	X, Consolidated (from Exhibit 9-12)
Assets			
Investment in Y	$ 40.0	$ 0.0	$ 0.0
Other Assets	130.0	170.0 ($130.0 + 40.0)	170.0
Goodwill	0.0	18.0 (1)	0.0
Total Assets	$170.0	$188.0	$170.0
Liabilities	$ 35.0	$ 53.0 ($35.0 + 18.0)	$ 53.0
Owners' Equity			
Common Stock, $20 Par	$ 50.0	$ 50.0	$ 50.0
Excess over Par	60.0	60.0	35.0
Retained Earnings	25.0	25.0	32.0
Total Owners' Equity	$135.0	$135.0	$117.0
Total Liabilities and Equity	$170.0	$188.0	$170.0

(1) This illustration assumes that the market values of Y's individual assets and liabilities are equal to their book values. Consequently, the excess of cost (40) over the book value of Y's net assets (22, per Exhibit 9-12) is not assignable to individual assets and liabilities, and is classified as goodwill arising in consolidation.

The post-combination balance sheets of Company X are shown in Exhibit 9-13, both unconsolidated and consolidated, reflecting the purchase method of accounting. The consolidated balance sheet under pooling of interests is repeated from Exhibit 9-12 for comparison.

The balance sheet effects of the purchase and the pooling-of-interests methods are contrasted in the list below.

1. Under purchase accounting, the carrying value of the investment in Company Y reflects fair market value at the acquisition date. Consequently, any difference between this amount and the book value of Company Y's net assets must be recognized on the consolidated balance sheet. For simplicity we have assumed in our illustration that the entire excess cost is assigned as goodwill arising in consolidation. Under pooling of interests, by contrast, the carrying value of the investment in Company Y equals the book value of Company Y's net assets, so there are no such differences for which to account.

2. Under purchase accounting, the shares issued to acquire Company Y were recorded at the fair value of Company Y's net assets by a credit to Company X's paid-in capital from the issuance of common shares. Under pooling, the credits to Company X's shareholders' equity reflect the book values of Company Y's shareholders' equity.

3. Under purchase accounting, the asset revaluations arising in consolidation (in this case, goodwill) will affect the consolidated income statement when those assets are consumed or sold. In its *Opinion No. 17* the APB has required that purchased goodwill be written off over a period not to exceed 40 years.[6] As a result, the consolidated net income will be lower than would be the sum of the separate incomes of Company X and Company Y (excluding income from investments).[7] Pooling does not entail such revaluations.

Income Statement Effects of Pooling-of-interests and Purchase Methods

Exhibit 9-14 includes the separate income statements of Company X and Company Y for 1987 and 1988 and shows how the income statements would be reported in Company Y's 1988 consolidated financial statements to reflect the fact that the firms were combined on January 1, 1988. Note the following points:

1. Under the pooling-of-interests method, the incomes and expenses of both firms are merely added together. This is so because pooling does not entail the revaluation of Company Y's net assets.

2. Under the pooling-of-interests method, the operating results of both firms are combined for all periods reported in the financial statements, as if the firms had been combined at the earliest date reported. This reflects the view that pooling does not entail an actual acquisition of one firm (Company Y) by another (Company X).

3. Under the purchase method, various income statement items may require adjustments to reflect any revaluations of Company Y's assets pursuant to the acquisition cost paid by Company X. In this case, Company X's investment cost exceeds the underlying book value of Company Y's net assets by $18 million (see Exhibit 9-13, page 449), and we are assuming that this excess is written off over ten years or at a rate of $1.8 million per year. As a consequence, the earnings of the consolidated firm are less under purchase than under pooling. (Of course, if Company X had paid less than the book value of Company Y,

---

[6]Accounting Principles Board *Opinion No. 17*, "Intangible Assets" (New York: AICPA, 1970), par. 29.

[7]Assuming that Company X uses the equity method of accounting for the investment in Company Y, the net income of Company X, including investment income, would be the same as consolidated income, as was discussed earlier.

Exhibit 9-14

Pre- and Post-combination Comparative Income Statements,
for Firms X and Y
Using the Pooling-of-interests and Purchase Methods

(in millions)

Separate Income Statements*

Firm X	1988	1987	Firm Y	1988	1987
Revenues	$100	$90	Revenues	$30	$28
Expenses	(80)	(74)	Expenses	(23)	(26)
Net income	$ 20	$16	Net income	$ 7	$ 2

Combined Income Statements, Pooling-of-interests Method

	1988			1987		
	X	Y	Combined	X	Y	Combined
Revenues	$100	$30	$130	$90	$28	$118
Expenses	(80)	(23)	(103)	(74)	(26)	(100)
Net income	$ 20	$ 7	$ 27	$16	$ 2	$ 18

Combined Income Statements, Purchase Method

	1988				1987†
	X	Y	Adjustment	Combined	X
Revenues	$100	$30		$130	$90
Expenses	(80)	(23)	($1.8)‡	104.8	(74)
Net income	$ 20	$ 7	($1.8)	$ 25.2	$16

*For illustration, Firm X's income statement does not include income from the investment in Y. If X were to prepare separate financial statements after the acquisition of Firm Y's stock, the equity method of accounting would be required and X's income would include X's share of Y's income.

†As discussed in the text, the purchase method does not entail a combination of operating results prior to X's acquisition of Y.

‡Goodwill amortization over a ten-year period. See Exhibit 9-13 and text commentary.

the consolidated earnings would be higher under the purchase method.)

4. Under the purchase method, the operations of the firms are not combined for periods prior to the acquisition. This occurs because, in concept, Company X was a separate economic entity prior to the combination.

Evaluation of Purchase and Pooling of Interests

Unlike pooling of interests, the purchase method of accounting is consistent with the historical cost accounting model: assets acquired are recorded at their cost on the acquisition date. The acquisition cost is equal to the amount of cash paid plus the market value of any noncash consideration exchanged, and the total cost is then assigned to individual assets and liabilities based on the fair market values of each. Pooling of interests, on the other hand, is inconsistent with the historical cost model. Acquisition costs are ignored in favor of the seller's carrying value of assets and liabilities. There is no conceptual basis whatever for the combinations of shareholders' equity using the pooling method.

In addition to the fact that pooling violates the historical cost concept, it has been widely argued that pooling is used by managers to deliberately distort earnings results. For example, when the market value of the seller is greater than book value, the true cost of the seller's net assets is understated on the buyer's (consolidated) books. As a result, if the buyer then sells those assets at their true cost, there will be an apparent gain on the sale. In an economic sense, this "gain" was fully paid for at the acquisition date.

In an information-efficient securities market, as long as the terms of a business combination are publicly disclosed, the purchase or pooling choice should not affect securities prices. Bear in mind that there are no direct income tax implications to the purchase and pooling methods, since the I.R.S. criteria for taxable and tax-free exchanges of stock are not tied to the APB's purchase-pooling criteria. Accordingly, there is no reason to believe that the choice of purchase or pooling will have any direct impact on the cash flows, and hence, the share prices of combining firms.

This argument notwithstanding, representatives of many merger-active firms argued forcefully at the APB's public hearings preceding the issuance of *Opinion Nos. 16* and *17*. They maintained that the passage of these rules would make otherwise attractive business combinations financially unattractive, and that the merger wave of the late 1960's would come to a halt. The rules were passed in spite of these objections, and in fact, the number of large mergers dropped dramatically for several years thereafter. Those were disruptive times for the U.S. economy. The economic consequences of war coupled with rapid expansion of social programs were beginning to be felt, and it is difficult to disentangle the causes of the merger decline from among the many possible contributing factors in such an economic climate.

Interesting evidence about the effects of the purchase-pooling choice on the prices of buyer-firm shares was provided in an empirical study that examined stock-for-stock mergers. In that study, buyer firms were divided into two groups—one using the purchase method and the other using the pooling-of-interests method. The study found that management's choice of the pooling method did not appear to benefit the buyer's shareholders. Quite to the contrary, the share returns of the purchase firms were superior to those of the pooling firms. One plausible interpretation of the finding is that investors might view the willingness of managers to choose the purchase method of accounting as an implicit forecast that those firms will have economic benefits due to merger, and that the income effects of those benefits are sufficient to absorb the higher expenses associated with the purchase method.

Earnings-per-share Effects of Business Combinations

Earnings-per-share (EPS) effects of proposed business combinations are frequently employed in merger negotiations, and managers often use EPS effects as a way of demonstrating the success or failure of a given merger. The effects of a merger on EPS, however, may be a misleading gauge of success because of the fact that whenever a buyer's price-to-earnings multiple (market price per share divided by EPS) exceeds that of the seller, the EPS of the buyer must increase if there is a stock-for-stock acquisition based on relative market prices. This happens because the numerator of the EPS calculation (net income) will increase in a greater proportion than the denominator (shares outstanding).

In order to illustrate this effect, consider the following information for Firms A and B:

Firm	Shares Outstanding	Market Price	Net Income	Earnings per Share	Price-earnings Multiple	
A	1,000,000	$120	$4,000,000	$4.00	30	($120/$4)
B	600,000	$ 40	$3,000,000	$5.00	8	($40/$5)

Assume that Firm A will acquire Firm B's outstanding shares by means of a stock-for-stock exchange based on relative market values—one share of Firm A's stock with a market price of $120 will be exchanged for three shares of Firm B's stock (3 × $40 = $120). Thus, Firm A will issue 200,000 shares to acquire all of the 600,000 outstanding shares of Firm B's stock. As a result of the combination, the EPS of Firm A will increase by over 45 percent—from $4.00 per share to $5.83 per share—as follows:

Firm A's EPS *before* acquisition of Firm B:

$$\frac{\text{Net Income}}{\text{Shares Outstanding}} = \frac{\$4,000,000}{1,000,000}$$

$$= \underline{\$4.00}$$

Firm A's EPS *after* acquisition of Firm B:

$$\frac{\text{Net Income}}{\text{Shares Outstanding}} = \frac{\$4,000,000 + \$3,000,000}{1,000,000 + 200,000}$$

$$= \frac{\$7,000,000}{1,200,000}$$

$$= \underline{\$5.83}$$

EPS has increased because net income has increased by 75 percent (from $4 to $7 million), while shares outstanding have increased by just 20 percent (from 1 million to 1.2 million).

This "P/E magic" appears to have been a powerful stimulus to merger activity over the past two decades. In statistical studies of the financial characteristics of buyer and seller firms, it is usually the case that seller firms have appreciably lower price-earnings multiples than do buyer firms. Moreover, in times when the range of price-earnings ratios narrows so that buyers find it difficult to find low P/E-candidate seller firms, the pace of merger activity slows considerably.

SUMMARY

This chapter discusses accounting for intercorporate investments and business combinations. Appendix D, which follows the chapter, describes reporting standards for segments of a business. The economic entity that is meaningful to the user of financial statements may not be identical to the corporation as it is legally defined. Financial reporting for intercorporate investments generally entails *aggregating* or combining the financial statements of two or more legally separate firms. In contrast, segment disclosure entails the reporting of subentity data: total corporate operations are *disaggregated* to reveal the operating results and assets employed in various lines of business.

Depending on management's motivations, investments in the ownership shares of another company may be classified as active or passive. When an investor firm intends to influence or control the activities of another firm, the investment is regarded as active; if this is not the case, the investment is said to be passive.

There are two methods of accounting for unconsolidated intercorporate investments on the books of the investor firm: the cost method and the equity method. One method or the other will apply to a given set of circumstances, depending on whether the investment is active or passive. An ownership percentage of less than 20 percent of the voting shares is presumed to be a passive investment and requires the use of the cost method. An ownership percentage that equals or exceeds 20 percent is presumed to be an active investment and requires the use of the equity method.

All intercorporate investments are recorded initially at acquisition cost. Subsequent to the date of purchase, however, the cost and equity methods differ. Under the equity method, income earned by the investee firm is recognized on the books of the investor in the period that the investee earns the income. Under the cost method, the investor will recognize income from the investee only if it is received in the form of dividends.

Consolidated financial statements show the assets, liabilities, revenues, and expenses of legally distinct entities *as if* they were in fact a single economic entity under the control of the parent company's shareholders. Majority control, evidenced by ownership of more than 50 percent of a subsidiary's voting stock, is a necessary, though not sufficient, condition for consolidation; the usefulness of the resulting financial statements is the essential criterion. To illustrate, management may elect not to consolidate a foreign subsidiary because of restrictions imposed by a foreign government that inhibit the parent company from exercising sufficient control. The two most important criteria in deciding whether to consolidate a majority-owned subsidiary are (1) degree of parent-company control and (2) the relatedness of activities. Procedures for preparing consolidated financial statements are illustrated in the chapter.

In accordance with generally accepted accounting principles, a business combination must be accounted for as either a purchase or a pooling of interests. Accounting Principles Board *Opinion No. 16* lists specific conditions for a pooling of interests. If any of these conditions are not met, the combination must be accounted for as a purchase.

In contrast to the purchase method, the pooling-of-interests method does *not* revalue the assets and liabilities of the subsidiary to reflect fair market value at the acquisition date. Instead, the *book values* of the pooled subsidiary continue to be reported. Also, because the pooling-of-interests method does not involve revaluation of assets and liabilities, the revenues and expenses of both firms are merely added together in preparing an income statement for the combined firms.

Different methods of accounting for intercorporate investments and alternative reporting approaches for business combinations may result in marked dissimilarities in the financial statements. The effects of these differences on key financial ratios are explained in the chapter.

The chapter's appendix describes standards of reporting for segments of a business. Reporting for intercorporate investments entails reporting for an economic entity that is broader than the corporation as legally defined and usually involves an aggregation or combining of data. By contrast, segment reporting entails a disaggregation of data to reveal the separate results of different lines of business. In both cases, the reporting standards reflect a concern with economically meaningful disclosures that transcend the legal definition of the firm.

APPENDIX D
FINANCIAL REPORTING FOR SEGMENTS OF A BUSINESS

Chapter 9 deals with the aggregation or consolidation of data reported in the separate financial statements of legally distinct but economically related corporations. This appendix, in contrast, is concerned with the disaggregation of data reported in the financial statements of public corporations—a procedure referred to as **segment** or **line-of-business reporting.** Our discussion here includes the segment-reporting disclosure policies adopted by the Financial Accounting Standards Board and the Securities and Exchange Commission. Reference is also made to the Federal Trade Commission's efforts to establish line-of-business reporting requirements.

SEGMENT DISCLOSURE POLICIES OF THE FINANCIAL ACCOUNTING STANDARDS BOARD

In February 1977, following public hearings and issuance of an exposure draft, the Financial Accounting Standards Board published *SFAS No. 14*, "Financial Reporting for Segments of a Business." A summary of the salient features of this statement is presented below.

1. *Reportable segments.* Under the provisions of *SFAS No. 14*, products and services are to be grouped according to industry segments.[1] The determination of industry classifications is left essentially to the judgment of corporate management. An industry segment may include a consolidated subsidiary that prepares separate financial reports. Financial information pertaining to unconsolidated subsidiaries does not have to be disaggregated. To the extent that it is practicable, the industrial classifications of multinational companies are determined on a worldwide basis.

2. *Operating profit or loss.* Revenues reported for segments are to include sales to external customers and intersegment sales or transfers, and these are to be identified separately. Operating expenses not directly traceable to an industry segment are to be allocated among segments on a reasonable and consistent basis. However, the following items are not to be allocated to segments: general corporate expenses, corporate interest, domestic and foreign income taxes, equity in income or loss of unconsolidated subsidiaries, and extraordinary gains or losses.

3. *Intersegment sales.* Revenue from intersegment sales or transfers is to be accounted for on the basis of the transfer prices actually used by the company.

4. *Identifiable assets.* Tangible and intangible segment assets used by an industry segment must be reported. Assets used jointly by two or more segments are to be allocated on a reasonable basis. General corporate assets are not to be allocated to segments.

5. *Materiality criteria.* An industry segment is to be regarded as reportable if the following conditions are met: (a) segment revenues are 10 percent or more of the combined internal and external sales; (b) the absolute amount of the segment's operating profit or loss is 10 percent of either the combined operating profit of all industry segments that did not incur an operating loss or the combined operating loss of all industry segments that incurred losses; (c) the segment's identifiable assets are 10 percent or more of the combined identifiable assets of all industry segments; and (d) the combined revenue from sales to unaffiliated (external) customers of all reportable segments constitutes at least 75 percent of the total company sales to unaffiliated customers. If the 75-percent test is not satisfied, additional industry segments are to be identified and reported until the 75-percent test is met.

---

[1]*Statement of Financial Accounting Standards No. 14*, "Financial Reporting for Segments of a Business Enterprise" (Stamford, CT: FASB, 1976), paragraphs 9–30.

6. *Disclosure of capital expenditures and depreciation.* The amount of capital expenditures, depreciation, depletion, and amortization is to be reported for each segment.

7. *Foreign operations.* Foreign revenues, operating profit or loss, and identifiable assets are to be reported separately if (a) foreign sales to unaffiliated customers are 10 percent or more of a company's consolidated revenues or (b) identifiable foreign assets are 10 percent of consolidated total assets. If foreign operations are conducted in two or more geographical areas, the specified information shall be reported separately for each significant geographical area. An example of foreign segment disclosure appears in Exhibit D-1.

8. *Major customers.* If 10 percent or more of the revenues of an enterprise is derived from sales to any single customer, that fact and the amount of revenues from each such customer should be disclosed.

A typical presentation of segment data, pursuant to the requirements of *SFAS No. 14,* appears in Exhibit D-2.

SEGMENT DISCLOSURE REQUIREMENTS OF THE SEC

The SEC initiated segment-reporting requirements in 1969, and these reporting requirements substantially influenced the content of *SFAS No. 14.* The Commission subsequently altered its segment-reporting requirements to conform to those detailed in *SFAS No. 14.*

LINE-OF-BUSINESS REPORTING REQUIREMENTS OF THE FTC

Published financial statements are used not only by investors and creditors, but also constitute an important input for macroeconomic policy setting. By and large, the development of accounting principles and disclosure policies in the United States has been concerned with the private sector. However, in other countries — Sweden, France, and Russia, for example — accounting has been greatly influenced by national goals. In this respect, the Federal Trade Commission's actions in regard to line-of-business reports are particularly interesting. The reasons that the FTC felt impelled to impose its own segment requirements are summarized in the list that follows.

1. The segment reporting requirements instituted by the SEC and the FASB are concerned primarily with investors' interests in a total company rather than with persons attempting to evaluate the performance of various industry sectors within the economy. Therefore, SEC and FASB disclosure requirements do not demand the degree of detail necessary for this level of analysis.

2. The economy can only operate efficiently if there are clear-cut signals guiding the allocation of resources into those fields where buyers' demands are inadequately satisfied and where, as a consequence, product prices are abnormally high and profits are excessive. The presence of abnormal profit in an industry segment of a company may suggest the existence of monopolistic

Exhibit D-1

Foreign Segment Reporting

General Mills, 1983

(in millions)

	U.S.A.	Other Western Hemisphere	Europe	Other(a)	Unallocated Corporate Items(b)	Consolidated Total
Sales						
1983	$5,049.5	$219.6	$262.6	$19.1		$5,550.8
1982	4,783.1	248.7	259.1	21.2		5,312.1
1981	4,300.6	223.3	307.9	20.6		4,852.4
1980	3,649.2	191.9	308.5	20.7		4,170.3
1979	3,187.5	161.8	377.8	17.9		3,745.0
Operating Profits						
1983	490.9	36.4	15.4	2.1	$(135.1)	409.7
1982	459.9(c)	41.3	7.4	2.6	(104.5) (c)	406.7
1981	422.3	31.6	7.0	3.4	(89.9)	374.4
1980	366.5	20.4	3.9	2.6	(76.8)	316.6
1979	298.3	16.6	14.2(d)	1.3	(66.5)	263.9
Identifiable Assets						
1983	2,303.7	112.1	165.6	11.5	351.0	2,943.9
1982	2,147.9	120.8	157.6	12.3	263.1	2,701.7
1981	1,876.2	124.3	176.0	8.6	116.2	2,301.3
1980	1,561.1	118.9	189.6	14.6	128.2	2,012.4
1979	1,384.2	97.6	172.6	13.2	167.6	1,835.2

Source: General Mills, *Annual Report*, 1983.

(a) Both inter-segment sales and export sales are immaterial.

(b) Corporate expenses include interest expense, profit sharing, employee stock-ownership plan, balance sheet related foreign currency effects and general corporate expenses. Corporate assets consist mainly of cash and short-term investments, investment in tax leases and other miscellaneous investments.

(c) In Fiscal 1982, provision for estimated losses on dispositions pending as of May 30, 1982 was charged to Unallocated Corporate expense. These dispositions are now substantially completed and the estimated losses have been reclassified for 1982 to the operating profits of the applicable segment (Consumer Foods $5.6 million charge, Specialty Retailing and Other $17.4 million charge). Other variations between the data shown in these tables and similar amounts published in preceding reports are due principally to immaterial restatements and adjustments in the classification of certain items.

(d) Includes a $4.4 million gain on the sale of Smiths U.K.

practices. Intervention by antitrust agencies may then be needed to rectify this malfunctioning sector of the economy.

3. When returns of both profitable and unprofitable ventures are combined, investors receive a less precise indication of the future growth and earnings potential of industries. As a result, it is more difficult for investors to exercise the selectivity that is so important to the proper allocative functioning

Exhibit D-2
Segment Reporting

Allied Corporation, 1983
(in millions)

Note 12. Segment Financial Data

As a result of the Bendix acquisition the Company has realigned the segments by which it reports the results of its operations. Prior period results are shown on a comparable basis.

		Chemical	Oil and Gas	Automotive	Aerospace	Industrial and Technology	Unallocated and Corporate(1)	Total
Net sales	1983	$2,337	$1,989	$2,370	$1,603	$1,708	$ 15	$10,022(2)
	1982	2,143	1,992	298	48	1,392	140	6,013
	1981	2,387	2,068	371	42	963	311	6,142
Research and development expense	1983	67	—	82	114	60	71	394(3)
	1982	76	—	8	1	43	58	186
	1981	65	—	9	1	31	45	151
Depreciation, depletion, and amortization	1983	137	189	45	22	67	8	468
	1982	117	176	13	1	56	10	373
	1981	108	165	12	1	40	9	335
Income from operations(4)	1983	224	724	203	152	(44)	(154)	1,105
	1982	132	803	6	—	1	(127)	815
	1981	189	910	17	(5)	49	(89)	1,071
Income from operations (adjusted)(4)(5)	1983	227	413	203	152	(43)	(154)	798
	1982	136	486	6	—	1	(127)	502
	1981	199	570	17	(5)	49	(84)	746
Property, plant, and equipment additions	1983	112	224	86	73	91	21	607
	1982	162	249	11	2	73	27	524
	1981	189	317	11	1	48	43	609
Identifiable assets	1983	1,299	1,562	1,729	909	1,661	487	7,647
	1982	1,439	1,626	163	22	1,262	1,760	6,272
	1981	1,526	1,367	181	27	1,485	758	5,344

Source: Allied Corporation, *Annual Report*, 1983.

Intersegment sales approximate market and are not significant.

(1) The "Unallocated and Corporate" column includes amounts for businesses sold or shut down and corporate as appropriate. Included in the caption "Identifiable assets" are the investments in Bendix and Martin Marietta of $1,194 million for 1982, assets for discontinued operations of $127, $183 and $284 million, and Corporate assets of $382, $356 and $288 million for each of the respective years.

(2) Sales to the United States Government and its agencies, mainly for the aerospace segment, were $815 million in 1983.

(3) Includes Bendix engineering activities of $114 million.

(4) Operating profit as defined by *FASB Statement No. 14* would also include an allocation to segments of "Other income — net" and "Nonrecurring Items." The amounts in these captions have not been allocated to the segments in order to avoid distortions in trends and comparability among segments.

(5) Income from operations for selected businesses has been adjusted for the difference between taxes provided and ordinary United States tax rates, primarily to remove distortions created by extremely high tax rates in certain foreign countries which would have obscured comparability between segments.

of capital markets — that is, guiding capital investments into those industries with the greatest sales and earnings growth potential.

4. Profitability of industry segments is important in applied macroeconomic analysis. In predicting gross national product, the U.S. Bureau of Economic Research must calculate the profit contributions of individual industries. The projected data for these industry sectors is then aggregated for the entire economy.

The FTC required and published line-of-business data for the years 1974–1976. We shall not present a detailed description of the FTC's line-of-business reporting requirements since our primary interest in this section is to provide an illustration of the potential influence of public policy objectives on accounting standards. It is sufficient merely to indicate that the FTC's disclosure requirements were far more extensive than those of the FASB. Not only did traceable revenues, costs, and assets have to be reported for each line of business, but details, such as freight costs, payrolls, materials used, depreciation, and internal transfers, had to be disclosed for each segment. In addition, the FTC required companies to define their segments in terms of the FTC's standard industry classifications.

The FTC's proposed line-of-business reporting requirements encountered fierce opposition from corporate management, and some 400 companies filed motions to quash the Commission's "order." Management's opposition was to no avail, however, and in November 1978, the Supreme Court refused to review a lower court decision that affirmed the FTC's authority to obtain its line-of-business information. The FTC suspended data collection in 1984, following the results of a staff cost-benefit study.

SEGMENT REPORTING IN RETROSPECT

A basic question with regard to segment disclosures involves whether or not this information has actually enhanced the ability of analysts and investors to forecast company sales and earnings. In recent years, a number of research studies have been performed in an attempt to gauge the utility of segment reporting. While at least two of these studies reached negative conclusions regarding the usefulness of segment reporting, considered in the aggregate, the studies suggest that the disclosure requirements of *SFAS No. 14* do have information content.

Securities analysts apparently have little doubt about the usefulness of segment reporting. In fact, in 1984 a committee of the Financial Analysts Federation concluded that segment reports often were inadequate and inconsistent from period to period. In February 1984 the SEC proposed changes in its rules that would require the inclusion of segment information in quarterly reports submitted to the Commission. It also has given advance notice that it is considering an expansion of its segment disclosure requirements.

SUMMARY

The segment reporting requirements of *SFAS No. 14* are discussed in this appendix, as are other segment-reporting requirements that have been enacted by various government agencies at various times. In essence, public companies must now disclose operating profit and loss, identifiable assets, capital expenditures, and depreciation for each segment that conforms to stipulated materiality criteria. Securities analysts overwhelmingly support segment disclosure since it reveals information considered to be highly useful in their forecasting and evaluative functions.

QUESTIONS

1. The terms listed below were introduced in this chapter. Define or explain each of them.

active investment	parent company
consolidation	passive investment
cost method	pooling-of-interests method
equity method	purchase method
goodwill	segment reporting
merger	subsidiary company
minority interest	upstream sales
one-line consolidation	

2. Distinguish between passive and active investments. What are the major reasons that the management of one firm might make a passive investment in another firm? What are the major reasons that one firm might make an active investment in another firm?
3. "If a company owns 30 percent of the voting stock of another company, it probably uses the cost method to account for that investment." Do you agree or not? Explain.
4. Contrast how the following transactions or events would be handled on the books of the investor company under both the cost method and the equity method: (a) purchase of stock in the investee company, (b) income earned by the investee company, and (c) dividends received from the investee company.
5. Assume the investor sells merchandise to the investee at a profit. Why is it necessary to eliminate this intercompany profit when using the equity method of accounting?
6. Compare the balance sheet and income statement effects of using the cost method as opposed to using the equity method of accounting for intercorporate investments.
7. What is the difference between a one-line consolidation (which is achieved by using the equity method) and consolidated financial statements?
8. Assume that an investor firm purchases 100% of the stock of the investee firm and pays more than the book value of the investee's net assets. Describe the accounting procedures used to handle this situation.

9. Are the adjustments and eliminations that are entered on the consolidating worksheet also entered on the books of the parent company? On the books of the subsidiary company? Explain.

10. If minority interests exist, they are needed to balance the consolidated balance sheet. Explain why this is so.

11. Assume the investor sells merchandise to the investee at a profit. Why is it necessary to eliminate this intercompany profit when preparing consolidated financial statements?

12. Foreign subsidiaries are often not consolidated when preparing consolidated financial statements. Why?

13. Assume that a firm purchases 100% of the stock of another firm and uses the equity method to account for this investment. How, if at all, would the total amount of periodic net income differ under the following circumstances: (a) the firm prepared consolidated financial statements or (b) the firm did not prepare consolidated financial statements?

14. List at least three adjustments that might be necessary in preparing financial statements that consolidate the separate financial statements of the parent and subsidiary companies.

15. Explain the differences between the following methods by which one firm may obtain control over another: merger, consolidation, acquisition of assets, and acquisition of stock.

16. "The purchase method and the pooling-of-interests method may be considered as alternatives to one another in accounting for business combinations." Do you agree or not? Explain.

17. What are the key criteria for determining if the pooling-of-interests method should be used to account for a business combination?

18. "The pooling-of-interests method does not revalue the assets and liabilities of the subsidiary company to fair market value at the acquisition date." Do you agree or not? Explain.

19. Compare the balance sheet and income statement effects of using the purchase method versus the pooling-of-interests method in accounting for business combinations.

20. "The purchase method of accounting is consistent with the historical cost accounting model, but the pooling-of-interests method is not." Do you agree or not? Explain.

21. Explain why earnings-per-share numbers might lead to a misleading evaluation of the success or failure of a given merger.

EXERCISES AND PROBLEMS

22. *Cost Method: Investments.*   Limpid Pool Company purchased 10,000 shares of the FYI Corporation early in 1985 at a cost of $48 per share. In August, the FYI Corporation stock was split two for one, so that Limpid Pool received 20,000 new shares in exchange for its 10,000 old (pre-split) shares.

FYI paid dividends of $2 per share in September 1985, and had earnings per share (EPS) of $3 per share for the year ended December 31, 1985.

REQUIRED   Assume that Limpid Pool Company accounts for its investment in FYI Corporation on the cost basis, and prepare journal entries to record the events described above.

Note: Complete exercise 22 before attempting this exercise.

23. *Equity Method: Investments.*   Assume that the shares of FYI Corporation that were purchased by the Limpid Pool Company (described in exercise 22) represented 20% of FYI's outstanding shares. In addition, assume that the book value per share at the date of purchase was $48 — equal to the market value per share.

REQUIRED

   (a) Assume that Limpid Pool Company accounts for its investment in FYI Corporation by the equity method, and prepare journal entries to record the events described in exercise 22.
   (b) How would your answer to item (a) differ if the book value per share at the date of purchase was $30? (Assume that the excess of cost over book value represents goodwill and that the appropriate amortization period is ten years.)

Note: The cost and equity methods are not to be considered as alternatives. Either one or the other will be appropriate, depending on the circumstances in a given case, as discussed in the chapter. This exercise applies both methods to a single case in order to emphasize their differences.

24. *Comparison of Cost and Equity Methods: Comprehensive.*   On January 1, 1986, the Westhaven Tub Company purchased 100,000 shares (representing 20% of the outstanding common stock) of PDQ Company, at a total cost of $10 million ($100 per share). On that date, the book value of PDQ's total common equity was $30 million. The difference between book value and market value of the PDQ shares is due primarily to the fact that PDQ's fixed assets have market values in excess of book values. These assets have an average remaining life of five years, and a straight-line amortization pattern. PDQ is expected to earn net income of $10 per share and to pay dividends of $7 per share each year for the next five years.

REQUIRED

   (a) Provide journal entries to record transactions in the PDQ shares for the years 1986–1990 assuming that Westhaven Tub Company employs the cost method. What is the total investment income over the five years? What is the carrying value of the investment at December 31, 1990?

(b) Provide journal entries to record transactions in the PDQ shares for the years 1986–1990 assuming that Westhaven Tub Company employs the equity method. What is the total investment income over the five years? What is the carrying value of the investment at January 1, 1986? At December 31, 1990? Explain the change in carrying value over the five-year period.

(c) Explain the difference in the carrying values of the PDQ shares between the cost and equity methods.

(d) Explain the relationship between the book value of common equity shown on PDQ's balance sheet and the carrying value of the PDQ shares on the Westhaven Tub Company's balance sheet at December 31, 1990.

(e) Explain why the following amounts are different from each other:
  (1) 1986 investment income, cost basis, reported by Westhaven Tub
  (2) 1986 investment income, equity basis, reported by Westhaven Tub
  (3) 20% of 1986 net income reported by PDQ Company

25. *Consolidation at Date of Acquisition: Purchase of 100% of Stock at Book Value.* On January 1, 1987, RPM Corporation bought all of the outstanding shares of MPH, Inc., for $75 million in cash (an amount equal to the book value of MPH's net assets). The balance sheets of both firms immediately after the stock purchase are shown below.

Balance Sheets at January 1, 1987

	RPM Corporation	MPH, Inc.
	(in millions)	(in millions)
Assets		
Investment in MPH, Inc.	$ 75	
Other Assets	325	$250
Total Assets	$400	$250
Liabilities	$200	$175
Stockholders' Equity		
Common Stock	125	50
Retained Earnings	75	25
Total Liabilities and Stockholders' Equity	$400	$250

REQUIRED Prepare a consolidated balance sheet at January 1, 1987.

Note: Complete exercise 25 before attempting this exercise.

26. *Consolidated Balance Sheet at Acquisition: Minority Interest, at Book Value.* Assume the same facts as in exercise 25, except that RPM bought 80% of MPH's outstanding shares for $60 million in cash (an amount equal to the book value of the percentage of net assets purchased [$75 million × 80% = $60 million]; other assets of RPM are $340 instead of $325). As a result, the unconsolidated balance sheet of RPM Corporation shows the following assets on January 1, 1987:

RPM Corporation
Assets at January 1, 1987

Assets	**(in millions)**
Investment in MPH, Inc.	$ 60
Other assets	340
Total	$400

REQUIRED   Prepare a consolidated balance sheet at January 1, 1987. Explain in your own words the interpretation of the balance in "minority interest."

Note: Complete exercise 25 before attempting this exercise.

27. *Consolidations at Acquisition: Cost Exceeds Book Value.*

   (1) Assume the same facts as in exercise 25, except that RPM Corporation paid $90 million in order to acquire the MPH, Inc., shares. The assets of RPM before consolidation are as follows:

	(in millions)
Investment in MPH, Inc.	$ 90
Other assets	310
Total	$400

   Prepare the consolidated balance sheet on January 1, 1987, assuming that the excess cost of RPM's investment is due to the fact that MPH's assets have market values that exceed their book values by $15 million.

   (2) Assume the same facts as in item (1), except that the excess cost of RPM's investment is due to (a) the fact that MPH's assets are undervalued by $20 million and (b) the fact that MPH's liabilities are undervalued by $5 million. Prepare the consolidated balance sheet at January 1, 1987.

Note: Complete exercise 26 before attempting the following exercise.

28. *Consolidations at Acquisition: Minority Interest, Cost Exceeds Book Value.*

    (1) Assume the same facts as in exercise 26, except that RPM Corporation paid $80 million in order to acquire 80% of MPH's outstanding shares. The assets of RPM before consolidation are as follows:

	(in millions)
Investment in MPH, Inc.	$ 80
Other assets	320
Total	$400

    Prepare the consolidated balance sheet on January 1, 1987, assuming that the excess investment cost is due to the fact that MPH's assets have market values that exceed their book values by $25 million (80% of $25 million = $20 million excess cost).

    (2) Assume the same facts as in item (1), except that the excess cost of RPM's investment is due to (a) the fact that MPH's assets are undervalued by $20 million and (b) the fact that MPH's liabilities are overvalued by $5 million (so that MPH's net assets are undervalued by $25 million).

29. *Consolidated Balance Sheet: Various Eliminations.*   Presented below are condensed balance sheets at January 1, 1987, for DNA Corporation and its 60%-owned affiliate, NFS, Inc. DNA acquired its shares of NFS early in 1984.

    Balance Sheets at January 1, 1987

	DNA Corporation	NFS, Inc.
Assets	(in millions)	(in millions)
Current	$1,200	$ 450
Noncurrent	3,800	750
Total Assets	$5,000	$1,200
Liabilities	$2,600	$ 500
Stockholders' Equity		
Common Stock	1,500	600
Retained Earnings	900	100
Total Liabilities and Stockholders' Equity	$5,000	$1,200

Additional information:

    (1) The noncurrent assets of DNA include $420 million as the carrying value of its investment in NFS. The shares were initially purchased at

a cost equal to their underlying book value, and DNA has used the equity method to account for this investment.

(2) The current assets of NFS and the current liabilities of DNA reflect the fact that DNA has borrowed $75 million from NFS, and this amount remains unpaid at December 31, 1987.

(3) The current assets of DNA include $100 million of inventory purchased from NFS, Inc. The carrying value of $100 million represents the amount paid by DNA to NFS for the inventory. The cost of the inventory to NFS was $82 million (the gross margin earned on the sale by NFS was $18 million).

(4) The noncurrent assets of NFS include land purchased from DNA for $20 million. The cost of the land to DNA was $16 million.

REQUIRED

(a) Discuss how each of the items of additional information provided above would affect your preparation of a consolidated balance sheet.

(b) Prepare a consolidated balance sheet at December 31, 1987.

(c) Explain why the minority interest shown in your consolidated balance sheet differs from $280 million (NFS, Inc., total shareholders' equity of $700 million × 40% minority interest = $280 million).

30. *Consolidated Income Statement: Various Eliminations.* Presented below are condensed income statements for the DBL Corporation and its 60%-owned affiliate, HLX, Inc., for the year ended December 31, 1987. DBL acquired its shares of HLX early in 1984.

Income Statements
For the Year Ended December 31, 1987

	DBL Corporation	HLX, Inc.
	(in millions)	(in millions)
Sales	$20,000	$2,800
Cost of sales	11,000	1,550
Gross margin	$ 9,000	$1,250
Selling and administrative expenses, and income taxes	7,000	1,420
Other income, net of taxes	0	250
Investment income	48	0
Net income	$ 2,048	$ 80

Additional information:

(1) The investment income of DBL is 60% of HLX's reported income of $80 million (60% × $80 million = $48 million). DBL has made no

adjustments to reflect the various intercompany revenues and expenses described below.

(2) The other income reported by HLX, Inc., includes $10 million of interest earned on loans to DBL (and included in DBL's administrative expense).

(3) During 1987 HLX made sales to DBL totalling $950 million. Of this amount, $100 million remains in DBL's ending inventory; the original cost to HLX of these inventory items was $82 million (the gross margin earned by HLX on these items was $18 million).

(4) The beginning inventory of DBL included $40 million of inventory purchased from HLX, Inc., in previous years; the gross margin earned by HLX on those sales was $6 million.

REQUIRED

(a) Discuss how each of these items of additional information provided above would affect your preparation of a consolidated income statement.

(b) Prepare a consolidated income statement for the year ended December 31, 1987.

(c) Explain why the minority interest in consolidated net income differs from $32 million (HLX, Inc., separate net income of $80 million × 40% minority interest = $32 million).

31. *Consolidation Policy and Financial Ratios.*   The information provided below pertains to two legally distinct, though economically related, entities: (1) ABM Corporation, and (2) MAD Company, ABM's wholly-owned subsidiary.

The management of ABM intends to publish only separate (unconsolidated) financial statements for ABM and MAD. This intention is based on management's argument that MAD is primarily a financing subsidiary, so that its consolidation with ABM, a manufacturing company, would obscure relevant financial statement relationships. ABM uses the equity method to account for its investment in MAD.

ABM Corporation
Selected Financial Information
1987 Financial Statements
(in thousands)

Current assets (mainly inventories and securities)	$ 40,000
Noncurrent assets (mainly property, plant, and equipment)	160,000
Total assets	$200,000
Current liabilities	$ 20,000
Noncurrent liabilities	80,000
Shareholders' equity	100,000
Total liabilities and equity	$200,000
Net income, 1987	$ 20,000

MAD Company
(in thousands)

Current assets (mainly accounts receivable)	$ 60,000
Noncurrent assets (mainly installment notes)	50,000
Total assets	$110,000
Current liabilities	$ 30,000
Noncurrent liabilities	79,000
Shareholders' equity (100% owned by ABM)	1,000
Total liabilities and equity	$110,000
Net income (loss), 1987	$ (5,000)

REQUIRED   Considering both management's basis for its consolidation policy and the economic relationships among the entities described above, compute the following financial ratios:

(a) Return on assets (net income divided by assets)
(b) Return on equity (net income divided by shareholders' equity)
(c) Debt-to-equity ratio (debt divided by shareholders' equity)
(d) Current ratio (current assets divided by current liabilities)
(e) Working capital (current assets less current liabilities)

32. *Purchase Accounting for a Business Combination.*   The CAR Company intends to acquire all of the outstanding shares of the API Company in a transaction that will be interpreted as a purchase for accounting purposes. After the purchase, API will continue in existence as a subsidiary of CAR Company. Pertinent information is provided below.

Pre-merger Financial Information

	CAR Company	**API Company**
Total assets	$30,000,000	$18,000,000
Liabilities	$16,000,000	$10,000,000
Shareholders' equity		
Common stock	9,000,000	5,000,000
Retained earnings	5,000,000	3,000,000
Total liabilities and equity	$30,000,000	$18,000,000

REQUIRED

(a) Assume that CAR Company acquires all of the outstanding API stock by issuing CAR stock with a total market value of $8 million and a total par value of $5 million. Provide a journal entry to record the purchase transaction on CAR's books, and prepare a consolidated balance sheet at the acquisition date (January 1, 1988).

(b) Assume that CAR acquires all of the outstanding API stock by issuing CAR stock with a total market value of $14 million and a total par value of $5 million. Assume also that any excess of acquisition price over the book value of net assets acquired is due to goodwill. Provide a journal entry to record the purchase transaction on CAR's books, and prepare a consolidated balance sheet at the acquisition date.

(c) Assume that CAR acquires 95% of the outstanding API stock by issuing CAR stock with a total market value of $15 million and a total par value of $5 million. Assume also that any excess of acquisition price over the book value of net assets acquired is due to goodwill. Provide a journal entry to record the purchase transaction on CAR's books, and prepare a consolidated balance sheet at the acquisition date.

Note: This exercise is based on the pre-merger financial information for CAR Company and API Company provided in exercise 32.

33. *Pooling-of-interests Accounting for a Business Combination.*   Assume that the acquisition by CAR Company of the outstanding API stock qualifies as a pooling of interests for financial accounting purposes.

REQUIRED   Prepare journal entries on CAR's books to record the acquisition, and prepare a consolidated balance sheet providing for each of the following sets of circumstances.

(a) CAR acquires 100% of the outstanding API stock by issuing CAR stock with a total market value of $8 million and a total par value of $5 million.

(b) CAR acquires 100% of the outstanding API stock by issuing CAR stock with a total market value of $14 million and a total par value of $5 million.

(c) CAR acquires 95% of the outstanding API stock by issuing CAR stock with a total market value of $15 million and a total par value of $5 million.

34. *Valuation of Net Assets: Purchase of Less Than 100% of Outstanding Stock.* The assets and liabilities of SWAK Company as they appear on its balance sheet at December 31, 1987, are shown on page 471. On this date, the SWAT Company acquired SWAK in a purchase transaction.

REQUIRED   Show how the assets and liabilities of SWAK would be valued in the consolidated balance sheet of SWAT Company under each of the following independent sets of assumptions:

(a) SWAT acquires 100% of the outstanding SWAK shares for consideration of $120,000.
(b) SWAT acquires 80% of the outstanding SWAK shares for consideration of $68,000.
(c) SWAT acquires 80% of the outstanding SWAK shares for consideration of $80,000.

SWAK Company
Assets and Liabilities at Book Values
and at Fair Market Values
December 31, 1987

	Fair Market Values	Book Values
Assets		
Current assets		
Cash and receivables	$ 10,000	$ 10,000
Inventories	20,000	25,000
Total current assets	$ 30,000	$ 35,000
Noncurrent assets		
Property, plant, and equipment	$110,000	$ 90,000
Other noncurrent assets	60,000	40,000
Total noncurrent assets	$170,000	$130,000
Total assets	$200,000	$165,000
Liabilities		
Current liabilities	$ 20,000	$ 20,000
Noncurrent liabilities	80,000	60,000
Total liabilities	$100,000	$ 80,000
Net Assets	$100,000	$ 85,000

APPENDIX PROBLEMS

35. *Allocation of Joint Expenses to Segments.* The United Container Corporation manufactures four product lines (metal, glass, paper, and plastic) in one large midwestern plant. Each product line is a separate, relatively autonomous division. The income statement shown in Exhibit A was prepared by the firm's accounting department for internal purposes. However, a question arose as to how indirect manufacturing expenses should be allocated to the product lines in financial statements issued to stockholders and filed with the SEC. The following discussion took place between the president and the controller with reference to this allocation question:

Exhibit A

United Container Corporation
Income Statement
For the Year Ended December 31, 1986
(in millions)

	Metal	Glass	Paper	Plastic	Total
			Divisions		
Sales	$100	$60	$40	$20	$220
Less: Direct expenses					
Materials used	$ 27.5	$18.5	$ 7	$ 3	$ 50
Direct labor	15	8	5	2	30
Factory overhead	28	12	18	5	57
Selling and administrative	19.5	15.5	6	2	43
Total direct expenses	$ 90	$48	$30	$12	$180
Divisional direct profit	$ 10	$12	$10	$ 8	$ 40
Less: Indirect expenses—manufacturing					
Plant depreciation, repairs, insurance, property taxes, etc.					$ 16.5
Purchasing, inventory control, receiving, storing, etc.					2.6
Power plant					1.8
Machine shop					1.0
Miscellaneous expenses					2.1
Total					$ 24
Corporate					6
Total indirect expenses					$ 30
Income before tax					$ 10
Less: Income tax					4
Income					$ 6

CONTROLLER: "Last year we allocated all indirect plant expenses to the four divisions according to the relative amount of direct expenses sustained by each division. However, we could also justify allocating these expenses on the basis of either divisional sales or divisional direct profit."

PRESIDENT: "The method you used last year resulted in a loss for the metal container division and embarrassing questions were raised by stockholders at the annual meeting. I predicted that there would be no loss for the metal container division this year. Use the method that produces the highest profit for the metal container division but don't report a loss."

In calculating product costs, the cost accounting department allocates purchasing, receiving, materials, handling, and storage expenses to divisions on the basis of materials used. Miscellaneous plant expenses are charged to divisions in relation to total direct expenses. General plant maintenance expense (depreciation, plant repairs, insurance, property taxes), power plant, and machine shop expenses are allocated to divisions as follows:

Expense	Allocation Basis	Percentage Charged to Divisions			
		Metal	Glass	Paper	Plastic
General plant maintenance	space	50	22.5	17.5	10
Power plant	Kwt. hrs.	48	24	18	10
Machine shop	Est. usage	48	26	18	8

REQUIRED

(a) Assuming that a single general method is to be used to allocate joint plant expenses to product lines, what logical justification can you find to support each of the three methods mentioned by the controller? What are the shortcomings of each of these methods?

(b) Prepare an income statement that will conform to the president's instructions.

(c) If you were auditing the company's books, what would your reaction be to the income statement prepared in item (b)?

(d) Prepare an income statement that would be more acceptable to the auditor.

36. *Segment Disclosures and Financial Ratios.* A portion of the 1983 annual report of ITT Corporation, which includes business segment disclosures, is reproduced below.

ITT Corporation
Business Segment Information

(in millions)	Sales and Revenues			Operating Income			Identifiable Assets		
	1983	1982	1981	1983	1982	1981	1983	1982	1981
Telecommunications	$ 5,388	$ 6,278	$ 6,963	$ 423	$ 417	$ 558	$ 3,908	$ 4,022	$ 4,820
Industrial Technology	4,805	4,921	5,119	333	335	363	3,003	3,152	3,359
Natural Resources and Food Products	2,539	2,655	3,101	182	137	205	2,305	2,312	2,354
Diversified Services	7,517	7,347	7,203	380	456	454	21,145	19,482	18,179
Unallocated	—	—	—	(117)	(137)	(98)	251	243	291
Total	$20,249	$21,201	$22,386	$1,201	$1,208	$1,482	$30,612	$29,211	$29,003

REQUIRED

(a) Contrast the rates of growth in total sales, operating income, and assets for the entire period (1981–1983), and the end of the subperiods

(1981–1982, 1982–1983). Which measure is most pertinent in assessing the firm's growth? Why are the growth rates different across these three series?

(b) Contrast the rates of growth in sales, operating income, and assets for each of the segments disclosed, for the period 1981–1983. If these rates of growth persist, what will be ITT's total sales, operating income, and assets at the end of 1993?

(c) Determine the percentage of total sales, income, and assets in 1983 accounted for by each of the segments disclosed in the table. Assume [as in item (b)] that growth rates persist and determine the percentages of total sales, income, and assets for each segment in 1993. Evaluate the reasonableness of your projections.

(d) Calculate return on sales (operating income divided by sales) and return on assets (operating income divided by identifiable assets) for each segment, and in total, for each of the three years. Based on these calculations, which segment is the most profitable?

(e) Portions of total operating income and identifiable assets appear as "unallocated." List likely reasons for these items. Why are negative figures given for the operating income amounts?

Note: In the following problem, the assumption that Tenneco's management has considered the sale of its chemical segment has, to our knowledge, no basis in fact and is made only to illustrate the potential usefulness of segment disclosures.

37. *Calculating the Effect of Selling a Segment.* You are a securities analyst and have learned that Tenneco is about to sell its chemical segment at 150% of the book value of the assets directly involved in the operations of the segment (including investments in affiliated companies). The sale is to be for cash and the proceeds are to be used to repurchase outstanding long-term debentures with an average interest rate of 11.6%. While Tenneco is earning a good return on its stockholders' investment, the company has a high ratio of debt to total assets and you want to determine the effect of the sale on the company's earnings, cash flow, and liquidity.

Exhibit A contains Tenneco's segment disclosures as presented in its 1982 annual report. Other financial information for 1982 is included in Exhibit B. (These exhibits appear on pages 475 and 476.)

REQUIRED

(a) Calculate Tenneco's 1982 operating income from continuing operations before taxes as a percent of property, plant, and equipment, and stockholders' equity.

(b) Recalculate the ratios calculated in item (a) as if the sale of the chemical segment had occurred at the beginning of 1982. Ignore the effect of income taxes.

Exhibit A

Tenneco, Inc.
Segment Information
At December 31, 1982, and for the Year then Ended
(in millions)

			Oil Processing and Marketing, Chemicals		Manufacturing					
	Oil Exploration and Production	Natural Gas Pipelines	Oil Processing and Marketing	Chemicals	Ship-building	Construction and Farm Equipment	Automotive	Fiber, Food, Land and Other	Reclass. and Elimination	Consolidated
Net sales and operating revenues										
External	$1,419	$4,645	$2,695	$1,104	$1,324	$2,014	$850	$ 928	$ —	$14,979
Intersegment	911	80	30	4	—	—	—	11	(1,036)	—
Total	2,330	4,725	2,725	1,108	1,324	2,014	850	939	(1,036)	14,979
Operating profit from continuing operations	1,085	423	82	15	120	(23)	88	72	—	1,862
Equity in net income of affiliated companies	(6)	17	1	1	—	36	—	128	—	177
General corporate expenses	(20)	(18)	(9)	(5)	(9)	(13)	(5)	(9)	—	(88)
Income from continuing operations before interest and federal income taxes	1,059	422	74	11	111	—	83	191	—	1,951
Identifiable assets	6,869	2,796	1,343	963	568	1,605	595	1,584	(1,001)	15,422
Investments in affiliated companies	37	171	149	5	—	370	—	1,224	—	1,956
Total assets	6,906	2,967	1,492	968	568	1,975	595	2,908	(1,001)	17,378
Depreciation, depletion, and amortization	601	190	37	51	25	49	26	40	—	1,019
Capital expenditures	$1,375	$ 216	$ 236	$ 44	$ 83	$ 62	$ 30	$ 57	$ —	$ 2,103

Segment

Exhibit B

Tenneco, Inc.
Selected Financial Data from 1982 *Annual Report*
(dollars in millions)

	1982
Operating income from continuing operations before income tax	$ 1,025
Funds provided from continuing operations	2,254
Long-term debt, December 31, 1982	5,032
Stockholders' equity, December 31, 1982	5,474
Property, plant, and equipment—net, December 31, 1982	10,834

(c) Calculate the effect of the hypothetical sale of the chemical segment on Tenneco's funds flow from continuing operations.

(d) Determine the effect of the hypothetical sale on Tenneco's 1982 year-end debt-to-equity ratio.

38. *Contribution Margin Reporting by Segments.* The National Association of Accountants, in its research study entitled *External Reporting for Segments of a Business*, recommended that the expenses for each segment be discussed in three broad classifications: (1) variable (materials, labor, selling commissions); (2) programmed fixed (research, marketing, advertising); and (3) long-term committed fixed (depreciation, insurance, property taxes).

Contribution margin reporting is also supported by the FASB in its November 1981 Exposure Draft, "Reporting Income, Cash Flow, and Financial Position of Business Enterprises," wherein it is stated,

It is relevant to report separately (1) expenses that vary with volume of activity or with various components of income; (2) expenses that are discretionary, and (3) expenses that are stable over time or that depend on other factors, such as the level of interest rates and the rate of inflation. (par. 48)

Exhibit A on page 477 contains the segment disclosures included in ECA's annual report for 1985, as required by *SFAS No. 14.* You are a securities analyst and are attempting to forecast ECA's profits for 1986. The company's management has provided you with the following information.

(1)

Variable Expenses as a Percent of Sales

Segment	Materials	Labor	Overhead	Selling
A	30	20	10	16
B	25	25	6.25	15
C	30	20	10	10
D	40	30	5	10

(2) In calculating operating profit (Exhibit A), programmed fixed expenses and long-term committed fixed expenses were charged to the segments as shown below.

Segment	Programmed Fixed Expenses	Long-term Committed Fixed Expenses
A	$10,000,000	$ 4,000,000
B	8,000,000	7,000,000
C	6,000,000	8,000,000
D	2,000,000	1,000,000
Total	$26,000,000	$20,000,000

Exhibit A

ECA, Inc.
Segment Reporting
For the Year Ended December 31, 1985
(in millions)

Segment	Sales	Operating Profit
A	$100,000	$10,000
B	80,000	8,000
C	60,000	4,000
D	60,000	6,000
	$300,000	$28,000

Less: Corporate expenses	11,000
Income before income taxes	$17,000
Income taxes	6,800
Net income	$10,200

REQUIRED

(a) From the data given, prepare a contribution margin income statement for ECA for the year 1985 in the form shown below.

			Segments		
	A	B	C	D	Total
Sales	XXX	XXX	XXX	XXX	XXX
Less: Variable expenses					
Materials	XXX	XXX	XXX	XXX	XXX
Labor	XXX	XXX	XXX	XXX	XXX
Overhead	XXX	XXX	XXX	XXX	XXX
Selling	XXX	XXX	XXX	XXX	XXX
Total	XXX	XXX	XXX	XXX	XXX
Contribution margin	XXX	XXX	XXX	XXX	XXX
Less: Fixed expenses					
Programmed	XXX	XXX	XXX	XXX	XXX
Committed	XXX	XXX	XXX	XXX	XXX
Total	XXX	XXX	XXX	XXX	XXX
Operating profit	XXX	XXX	XXX	XXX	XXX
Less: Corporate expenses					XXX
Income before taxes					XXX
Income tax expense					XXX
Net income					XXX

(b) Based on your discussions with the management of ECA and other sources of information you estimate that in 1986 the following changes will take place in sales and expenses. Corporate expenses and committed fixed expenses are not expected to change. Prepare a forecast of ECA's earnings for 1986.

Percent Change over 1985 Expected in 1986

Segment	Sales	Variable Expenses	Programmed Fixed Expenses
A	+10	+2	+5
B	+15	+4	–
C	+ 3	+2	+4
D	+ 5	+3	–

(c) As a securities analyst what advantages do you find in a segmented contribution margin income statement?

(d) As a high-level corporate executive what is apt to be your reaction to a request from the securities analysis profession that a segmented contribution margin income statement be included in annual reports?

Chapter

10

Accounting for Leases and Pensions

This chapter examines two controversial areas in financial reporting: accounting for long-term leases and accounting for defined-benefit pension plans. The controversies in lease accounting focus on the distinction between completed transactions and commitments (discussed in Chapter 6), and on the importance of the economic substance, rather than the legal form, of the lease agreement.

The pension accounting debate involves the question of whether pension plans should continue to be considered as economic and reporting entities that are *distinct* from the firm that sponsors (and funds) them. Moreover, the calculation methods that firms are currently required to use in reporting pension obligations may significantly understate the present value of those obligations. Both topics—leases and pensions—entail a close examination of the liability concept in financial accounting.

ACCOUNTING FOR LEASES

Leases are agreements to rent assets for a period of time—usually for several years. Leasing has become an increasingly popular way for companies to finance the use of capital equipment and other assets due to factors such as the growing cost and complexity of capital equipment, shortages of investment funds, high interest rates, and changes in income tax and bank regulations. The owner of the asset being leased is referred to as the **lessor**; the person receiving the right to use the leased asset is referred to as the **lessee**.

Lease Financing

The U.S. Department of Commerce estimates that about 15 percent of all capital equipment purchases are made by leasing arrangements, and that leasing will continue to grow at a faster rate than other methods of business financing. For accounting purposes, the basic issue is whether leasing agreements should be interpreted as debt-financed purchases or as rentals. If a lease is interpreted as a debt-financed purchase, the present value of the lease payments should be reported by the lessee as both a noncurrent asset and a noncurrent liability at the time the lease is signed. If, on the other hand, the lease is interpreted as a rental, neither reported assets nor liabilities should be affected by the signing of the lease.

The use of lease financing to purchase an asset may seem to be an attractive alternative to the borrowing of funds for several reasons:

1. Leasing may offer tax advantages, especially if the lessor and the lessee have different tax rates or differ in their abilities to utilize accelerated depreciation. Leasing may also be viewed as a method of depreciating land. (A firm that owns a building on a parcel of land may depreciate only the building for tax purposes. If the facilities are leased rather than owned, however, the entire rental payment may be tax deductible.)
2. Leasing may shield the firm from risks, such as equipment obsolescence. This advantage assumes that the lease term is shorter than the life of the asset, with the lessee having the option of renewing the lease at a predetermined rental. For a lessor, obsolescence risk may be lower if there is a secondary market for the asset. (Remember that the economic life of an asset depends on the firm that uses its services. Propeller-driven aircraft, for example, continue to serve some regional markets.)
3. Leasing may allow the firm to avoid violating restrictions imposed by lenders in lending agreements. Bank lending arrangements sometimes impose restrictions on firms by means of selected financial ratios, dividend and capital spending policies, and various other financial actions. Lease arrangements generally do not give the lessor the power to impose such restrictions.

4. Leases may be less burdensome than other forms of debt for firms in financial distress. While default on a single bond installment may result in the entire debt becoming due and payable, a lessor may recover only three years' lease payments if the lessee declares bankruptcy.
5. Lease financing may conserve working capital. A lease typically requires no down payment and (unlike a bank loan) no compensating balance.
6. A lease that qualifies as an operating lease for financial accounting purposes (the criteria for an operating lease are described below) may have desirable effects on the balance sheet of the lessee. An operating lease allows the firm to rent an asset, but neither the asset nor the debt financing appears on the lessee's balance sheet. Off-balance-sheet financing does not explicitly raise the debt-to-equity ratio, and thus may not impair the borrowing capacity of the firm. (This alleged advantage is sometimes overstated, however, because the lease arrangement is described in a financial statement footnote, and only a naïve loan officer or investment banker would ignore the impact of the lease on the financial position of the firm.)

Accounting for Leases: an Overview

In 1976, the FASB issued a new standard involving the reporting of leases in financial statements. *Statement of Financial Accounting Standards No. 13* outlines a set of classifications for lease agreements, for both lessor and lessee. The classification of a lease, in turn, determines how it will be reported in the financial statements. Before considering the FASB's criteria for classifying leases, it is useful to contrast three different ways that a firm might obtain the use of an asset.

Case 1: Rentals

Business firms, as well as individuals, obtain the right to use assets under the terms of rental agreements and frequently rent vehicles and real estate. Rented assets remain the property of the lessor and do not appear on the balance sheet of the lessee. Rental agreements usually are for relatively short periods of time.

Case 2: Installment purchases

Assets are also frequently purchased by means of payments to be made in installments over future periods. In many cases, the seller of the asset may provide financing as a method of promoting sales and as a source of interest income. (Accounting for installment sales was discussed in Chapter 5.) Assets purchased under the installment method appear on the balance sheet of the purchaser, as does the liability for payment. Even in cases where the title to the asset is not transferred until the installment payments are completed, the buyer reports the asset (and the liability) when the asset is placed into service.

Case 3: Long-term leases

Long-term leases are rental arrangements that extend over many years, often encompassing the major part of an asset's useful life. Frequently the leased assets have been specifically constructed to meet the lessee's requirements, and the lessee has the right to purchase the asset, often at a bargain price, at the end of the lease term. In some cases, assets obtained under long-term leases do not appear on the lessee's balance sheet, which is consistent with the view that rented assets remain the property of the lessor. In other cases, assets obtained under long-term leases are *capitalized;* that is, the leased asset and the related lease obligation (liability) both appear on the lessee's balance sheet based on the assumption that *in substance*, the lease is like an installment purchase.

A key issue in accounting for leases is whether companies can still arrange off-balance-sheet financing via the leasing of assets. Purportedly, a major advantage of leases from the perspective of the lessee is that they enable the lessee to acquire an asset for an extended period of time without entering the future lease-payment obligations on the balance sheet as a liability. The ability to relegate information about lease financing to the footnotes of the financial statements may be seen as a substantial advantage by financial managers who assume that investors and lenders define debt only in terms of the amounts reported on the face of the balance sheet. Such a belief seems prevalent: subsequent to the release of *SFAS No. 13,* many leasing firms advertised their ability to create "*SFAS No. 13* Operating Leases," — leases that would still manage to qualify for off-balance-sheet treatment. Because such leases are often less attractive when evaluated from a purely financial perspective, there seems to be a prevailing view among prospective lessees that bankers and investors are naïve users of financial statement data.

SFAS No. 13 establishes criteria for classifying various kinds of leases, and provides a set of reporting standards for each class. The classifications are summarized in Exhibit 10-1. Note that from the standpoint of the lessee, all leases are either (1) capital leases or (2) operating leases. **Capital leases** meet any one (or more) of a set of explicit criteria (to be explained below) and must be "capitalized." **Capitalization** of a lease means that the lease payments, discounted at an appropriate rate of interest, must be shown as both assets and liabilities on the balance sheet of the lessee. All other leases are treated as **operating leases** and do not appear on the balance sheet as assets or liabilities. The lease payments for operating leases are interpreted simply as rental expenses.

For the lessor, the classifications of leases parallel those for the lessee, although there are some differences in the classification criteria, which will be discussed later. Generally, leases that qualify as capital leases for the lessee will be either (a) sales-type leases or (b) direct financing leases for lessor accounting purposes.

Exhibit 10-1

Classifications of Leases by Lessees and Lessors

Lessee

1. Capital lease
2. Operating lease

Lessor

1. Capital lease
   (a) Sales-type lease
   (b) Direct financing lease
2. Operating lease

As we have seen, much of the controversy surrounding accounting for leases depends on the distinction between situations in which the leased assets and related obligations must be included on the lessee's balance sheet (capital leases), and situations in which only the periodic rentals need to be reported on the lessee's income statement (operating leases). The discussion in the following sections will describe the criteria for each lease type, as well as the accounting methods associated with these lease classifications.

Accounting for Leases: Lessee

From the standpoint of the lessee, accountants must classify leases as either (1) capital leases or (2) operating leases. **Capital leases** meet one or more of the following criteria:

1. The lease transfers ownership of the property to the lessee by the end of the lease.
2. The lease contains a bargain purchase option.
3. The lease term is equal to 75 percent or more of the estimated economic life of the leased property.
4. At the beginning of the lease, the present value of the minimum lease payments equals or exceeds 90 percent of the fair value of the leased property to the lessor.[1]

Usually the lessee will compute the present value of the minimum lease payments using his or her borrowing rate. To show the accounting require-

---

[1]*Statement of Financial Accounting Standards No. 13,* "Accounting for Leases" (Stamford, CT: FASB, 1976), par. 7.

ments imposed by the criteria for capital leases, consider the following example.

Assumptions

Fair value of leased property to the lessor	$600,000
Cost of the leased property to the lessor	$550,000
Estimated economic life of equipment	15 years
Lease term	9 years
Rental, paid on last day of each year	$100,000
Estimate of residual value at end of lease	$186,150
Lessee's incremental borrowing rate	10%

The first step is to measure the lease against the four criteria for capital leases listed above.

Criterion 1. *Not met:* The equipment is not transferred to the lessee at the end of the lease term.

Criterion 2. *Not met:* There is no bargain purchase option.

Criterion 3. *Not met:* The lease term is nine years, while 75 percent of the equipment's useful life would be 11 years and three months.

In order to apply Criterion 4, it is necessary to compute the present value of the minimum lease payments. This calculation requires the use of the compound interest tables included in Appendix C at the end of Chapter 5 (see pages 258–59). The rental payments will be discounted at the lessee's borrowing rate of 10 percent. The present value of the rental payments is $575,900, computed as follows:

Rental payments, paid at the end of each year for nine years	$100,000
Present value factor for a nine-period annuity at 10% interest (from Table C-2, page 259).	5.759
Present value ($100,000 × 5.759)	$575,900

Consequently,

Criterion 4. *Met:* At the beginning of the lease term the present value of the lease payments, $575,900, exceeds 90 percent of the fair value of the leased property to the lessor ($600,000 × 90% = $540,000).

Since at least one of the requirements (in this case, Criterion 4) is met, the lease is considered a capital lease and would be recorded by the following journal entry:

dr.	Leased Equipment	575,900	
	cr. Lease Obligation		575,900

Upon signing the lease, the lessee's reported assets and liabilities have increased by $575,900. The lease obligation (credit) is measured as the present value of the series of lease payments, and the lessee's "cost" for the equipment (debit) is equal to the present value of the lease obligation. Each period of the lease term will require one entry to record amortization of the cost of the leased equipment and another to record interest expenses and periodic payments of the lease rentals. Because we have assumed a straight-line benefit pattern and a nine-year term, each period's amortization equals one-ninth of the asset's capitalized cost of $575,900.[2] Each period's interest expense equals the carrying value (book value) of the lease obligation at the beginning of the period, multiplied by the interest rate used initially in computing the present value of the lease. This is the compound interest method of accounting for borrowing costs, as discussed in Chapter 6. Exhibit 10-2 shows the expenses to be recognized each period over the life of the lease; Figure 10-1 shows some of the same information graphically. Assuming straight-line amortization of the asset's cost, entries for the first two years would be as follows:

Year 1

(1) dr. Amortization of Leased Equipment   63,989
        cr.   Leased Equipment   63,989
      To amortize one-ninth of the intangible asset cost of $575,900.

(2) dr. Lease Obligation   42,410
     dr. Interest Expense   57,590
        cr.   Cash   100,000
      To record first lease payment and interest expense, 10% of
      $575,900, the carrying value of the lease obligation at the start
      of the period. (See Exhibit 10-2.)

Year 2

(1) dr. Amortization of Leased Equipment   63,989
        cr.   Leased Equipment   63,989
      To amortize one-ninth of the intangible asset cost of $575,900.

(2) dr. Lease Obligation   46,651
     dr. Interest Expense   53,349
        cr.   Cash   100,000
      To record second lease payment and interest expense, 10% of
      $533,490, the carrying value of the lease obligation at the start
      of the period. (See Exhibit 10-2.)

Note in Exhibit 10-2 that the total expense (amortization and interest expense) over the life of the lease equals the total rental payments of $900,000. The

---

[2] If the lease qualifies as a capital lease by meeting either of the first two criteria, the appropriate amortization period would be the full 15-year economic life of the leased asset, and the residual value of the leased asset would be included in the present value calculation. Such cases are not considered in this chapter.

Exhibit 10-2
Lease Obligation and Expense
(each year for a nine-year lease term)

Period	(1) Rental Payment	(2) Lease Obligation, Beginning of Period	(3) Interest Expense at 10%	(4) Amortization Expense Straight Line	(5) Total Expense (3) + (4)	(6) Reduction of Lease Obligation (1) − (3)
1	$100,000	$575,900	$ 57,590	$ 63,989	$121,579	$ 42,410
2	100,000	533,490	53,349	63,989	117,338	46,651
3	100,000	486,839	48,684	63,989	112,673	51,316
4	100,000	435,523	43,552	63,989	107,541	56,448
5	100,000	379,075	37,908	63,989	101,897	62,092
6	100,000	316,983	31,698	63,989	95,687	68,302
7	100,000	248,681	24,868	63,989	88,857	75,132
8	100,000	173,549	17,355	63,989	81,344	82,645
9	100,000	90,904	9,096*	63,988*	73,084	90,904
Total	$900,000		$324,100	$575,900	$900,000	$575,900

Note: Column (1) shows the annual expense (equal to the rental payment) for an operating lease, and column (5) shows the annual expense for a capital lease. Both columns total $900,000 over the nine years, but the timing of the expense is quite different.
*Due to rounding

Figure 10-1
Capital Lease versus Operating Lease

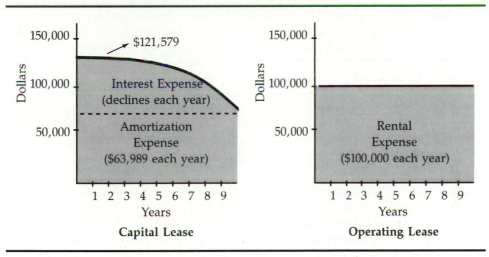

Capital Lease

Operating Lease

Note: This figure is based on the information provided in Exhibit 10–2. The annual expense for the operating lease is equal to the annual rental payment of $100,000.

timing of the expense, however, is quite different for capital and operating leases. The annual rental expense for an operating lease would be the amount paid each year—$100,000. The annual expense (amortization and interest) for the capital lease is highest in the initial period and reduces thereafter, because the interest expense is lower as the lease obligation declines.

In sum, classification of the lease as a capital lease results in the reporting of higher asset values, a greater amount of debt, and a lower net income in the earlier years of the lease, as compared to classification as an operating lease.

Accounting for Leases: Lessor

We have seen that lessors and lessees classify leases in a similar fashion. Leases that are capital leases from a lessee standpoint will be either *sales-type* or *direct financing* leases (both defined later) from a lessor standpoint, provided that two additional conditions are met. In addition to meeting at least one of the lessee's four criteria to qualify for classification as a capital lease (see page 483), sales-type or direct financing leases must meet two additional conditions:

1. Collectibility of the lease payments must be reasonably predictable.
2. No important uncertainties may surround any remaining related costs to be incurred by the lessor.

These additional conditions assure that the revenue recognition criteria discussed in Chapter 3 have been met before the lessor recognizes any profits associated with the lease.

Leases that do not meet at least one of the lessee's criteria for capital leases, or do not satisfy both of the conditions for classification from a lessor standpoint, are classified as operating leases by the lessor. Accordingly, in the majority of cases leases will be classified consistently between lessees and lessors.

The remainder of this section will discuss the accounting methods used by lessors for (1) sales-type leases, (2) direct financing leases, and (3) operating leases.

Sales-type leases   **Sales-type lease** arrangements provide a profit or loss at the point of sale to the lessors (who are manufacturers or dealers) and are normally utilized when manufacturers or dealers use leases as a means of marketing their products. In effect, the lease agreement for a sales-type lease has *two* elements. First, there is a sale of the "leased" asset. The lessor earns a profit on this transaction equal to the difference between the lessor's cost of the leased asset and the discounted present value of the rents to be received. Second, the lessor is extending financing to the lessee, and thus earns interest income over the life of the lease. The treatment of a sales-type lease for accounting purposes is similar to that of an installment sale, except for the residual value of the asset at the end of the lease term.

To illustrate accounting for a sales-type lease, we will return to the lease arrangement described earlier on page 484, but this time we will look at it from the lessor's perspective. We need to determine the following:

1. Gross investment in the lease: the sum of the lease payments and the estimated residual value of the leased asset, or

Lease payments (9 × $100,000)	$ 900,000
Estimated residual value	186,150
Total gross investment	$1,086,150

2. Net investment in the lease: the present value of the gross investment discounted using the implicit interest rate in the lease, which we will assume to be 12 percent.[3] As a result, the net investment is

Lease payments ($100,000 × 5.328)*	$532,800
Estimated residual value ($186,150 × .361)	67,200
Total net investment	$600,000

*From the present value tables on page 259 we have determined that 5.328 is the present value factor for a nine-period annuity, and .361 is the present value factor for a ninth period cash flow at 12%.

3. Unearned interest income: the difference between the gross and net investment, which must be recognized over the term of the lease using

---

[3]The implicit interest rate is the rate of discount that causes the present value of the lease payments and the residual value to be equal to the fair value of the leased asset.

the effective interest method:

Gross investment (1, page 488)	$1,086,150
Net investment (2, page 488)	600,000
Unearned interest income	$ 486,150

This unearned income will become earned income with the passage of time. For example, in the first period, interest income would be computed as 12 percent of the net investment of $600,000, or $72,000. In each subsequent period, interest income will also be computed as 12 percent of the carrying value of the net investment at the beginning of the period.

4. Gross margin from the sale of the leased property:

Present value of lease payments (2, page 488)		$532,800
Cost of leased asset (from assumption information on page 484)	$550,000	
Less: Present value of residual (2, page 488)	(67,200)	
Cost of sale		(482,800)
Gross margin		$ 50,000

In effect, the gross margin calculation assumes that a portion of the asset's economic benefits has been sold, and a portion has been retained. In this example, the lease shows a profit on the sale equal to $50,000. Of course, the lessor also will earn interest income of $486,150 over the life of the lease.

Direct financing lease   Leases in the **direct financing lease** category meet at least one of the criteria listed earlier for capital leases, but they do not provide profit to a manufacturer or dealer at inception. The accounting is identical to that just described for unearned income in sales-type leases. To illustrate, major insurance firms, pension trusts, and other financial investors often obtain title to long-lived, tangible assets for the express purpose of leasing those assets and earning interest income. In these cases, there is no manufacturer or dealer profit to be recognized at the time that the lease is signed. Instead, the income will be recognized as interest income using the implicit rate of interest in the lease. To illustrate accounting for a direct financing lease, assume that a lessor has acquired a building with a cost (and a fair value) of $14,938,000, and on January 1, 1988, has agreed to rent the building for 20 years. The annual rental is $2 million, payable at the end of each year, and the building is estimated to have no residual value at the end of the rental period.

The first step in this process is to determine the rate of interest implicit in the lease. The implicit rate of interest will satisfy the following equation:

$$\text{Fair Value of Asset when Lease Is Signed} = \text{Present Value of Lease Payments and Residual Value}$$

In this case,

$$\$14{,}938{,}000 = \$2\ \text{million} \times \begin{array}{c}\text{Present Value of}\\ \text{Annuity Factor,}\\ \text{20 periods}\end{array}$$

Reorganizing this equation,

$$\begin{array}{c}\text{Present Value of Annuity}\\ \text{Factor, 20 periods}\end{array} = \dfrac{\$14{,}938{,}000}{\$2{,}000{,}000}$$

$$= 7.469$$

The annuity table (page 259) shows that this present value of annuity factor for 20 periods occurs when the discount rate is 12 percent, so 12 percent is the rate of interest implicit in the lease. In the first year, the lessor will recognize interest income computed as 12 percent of the beginning-of-the-year carrying value of the asset, or $1,792,560 (12 percent × $14,938,000). In each subsequent period, interest income will also be computed as 12 percent of the carrying value of the net investment at the beginning of the period.

Operating leases   In the case of **operating leases,** the leased asset is accounted for by the lessor in the same manner as other fixed assets, and rental income is recorded on the accrual basis.

Implications of Lease Accounting for Financial Statement Analysis

In the years of often sharp debate preceding adoption of *SFAS No. 13*, there were dire predictions that the rules proposed for the new standard would hurt the credit worthiness of companies that leased equipment, thereby inflating their financing costs and depressing the prices of their stock. Predictions of this sort were based on the assumption that investors and lenders take a myopic look at financial accounting numbers and pay insufficient attention to other sources of information, such as the explanatory footnotes included in financial statements. Companies have long been required to include a thorough description of the cash flow consequences of significant lease contracts in footnotes. The major effect of the inclusion of capital lease criteria in *SFAS No. 13* has been to move such information from the footnotes of the financial statements to the body of those statements. For the most part, the information provided is not new; only the location of its disclosure has changed.

If the information required by *SFAS No. 13* was already known to investors, and if markets were information efficient, we would expect that securities prices already reflect the consequences of leases. A number of research studies undertaken after *SFAS No. 13* was adopted support this view. Researchers have been unable to detect any significant stock price reactions for companies affected by the new rules. It also appears that the riskiness of stock prices reflected the impact of leases prior to the new reporting requirements.

On the other hand, there may be economic consequences related to the new disclosures, even in markets that are information efficient. For example, bond indenture agreements and other debt covenants often define limits on company debt and on key financial ratios, which are computed based on the accounting numbers reported in the firm's financial statements. Management incentives and bonus plans, as well as labor contracts, may likewise be tied to financial accounting results. In such cases, the methods used for reporting leases in the financial statements may indeed affect future cash flows and the market's valuation of the firm's securities.

ACCOUNTING FOR PENSION OBLIGATIONS AND EXPENSES

Pension plans are agreements between a firm and its employees to provide payment to the employees after retirement. Pensions constitute a large and increasing share of business expense, and corporate pension obligations are substantial relative to other forms of debt. Viewed both in relation to other forms of debt or equity financing, and in relation to net income, pension obligations and expenses are often significant.

As a result of increasing pension coverage, rising benefits per employee, and an expanding labor force, pension fund assets have grown at an impressive rate. Over the decade from 1970–1980, pension fund assets increased from $138 billion to over $1.4 trillion. The pension funds of individual firms are large in relation to other resources. At the end of a recent year, the market value of pension fund assets for General Motors totaled $9.4 billion and was equivalent to 54 percent of stockholders' equity for that firm. Comparable figures for General Foods and DuPont were $0.5 billion (the equivalent of 40 percent of stockholders' equity) and $3.0 billion (the equivalent of 63 percent of stockholders' equity), respectively. A recent survey of 475 of the *Fortune* 500 companies revealed that pension costs averaged 12.5 percent of pretax profits. **Vested benefits** (benefits to which employees have irrevocable rights) in the same survey averaged 34 percent of total stockholders' equity.

Pension Agreements

This section discusses the essential elements of defined-benefit pension plans, which are used by all but a small minority of U.S. firms. **Defined-benefit pension plans** specify (1) the amount and timing of benefits that retiring employees will receive; (2) when employees become vested (that is, when they have an irrevocable right to the plan's benefits); and (3) how the plan will be funded. Each of these elements will be discussed in some detail. Exhibit 10-3 describes a pension plan just adopted by the Cradle Corporation and will be used to illustrate the points in our discussion.

Benefits and vesting   The plan adopted by the Cradle Corporation includes all full-time salaried employees (item a), and gives full credit for prior service

Exhibit 10-3

Defined-benefit Pension Plan
Provisions and Assumptions

Cradle Corporation
Pension Plan Adopted January 1, 1988

(a) Eligible employees: all full-time salaried workers.
(b) Prior service credit: full credit for all years worked prior to adoption of the plan.
(c) Benefit formula: for each year of service, 2% of maximum annual salary, to begin at age 65.
(d) Vesting: 10% for each year's service.
(e) Funding: costs will be funded at the end of each year by payments to Granite Security as plan agent.
(f) Interest rate: 8% per annum, estimated future rate of return on pension fund investments.
(g) Prior service costs, January 1, 1988: $50,000,000.
(h) Vested benefits, January 1, 1988: $16,000,000.

(item b). The benefit formula (item c) provides two percent of maximum salary for each year of service, and the vested percentage (item d) increases ten percent per year. As an example, an employee terminating after eight years would receive a pension at retirement age equal to 12.8 percent of maximum salary (2% × 8 years = 16%; 10% vesting × 8 years = 80% vested; 16% × 80% = 12.8%).

Funding of pension costs The funding of a pension plan (item e) allows considerable management discretion, although the Employee Retirement and Income Security Act of 1974 (ERISA) specifies minimum funding requirements. Usually, the sponsoring company employs a **funding agent**—often a bank or insurance company—to receive pension contributions from the employer, invest them, and disburse benefits to retirees as specified in the plan. Most firms make annual payments to the plan agent that are equal to the pension expense recognized for financial statement purposes, as follows

dr. Pension Expense   XXX
    cr. Pension Obligation   XXX
To record pension expense.

dr. Pension Obligation   XXX
    cr. Cash   XXX
To record funding of current period's pension expense.

The cash will be invested by the plan agent in order to earn returns. The Cradle Corporation plan agreement indicates that the firm expects pension fund investments to earn eight percent each year (item f). The relationships

Exhibit 10-4
Relationships between Pension Plan Sponsor, Agent, and Covered Employees

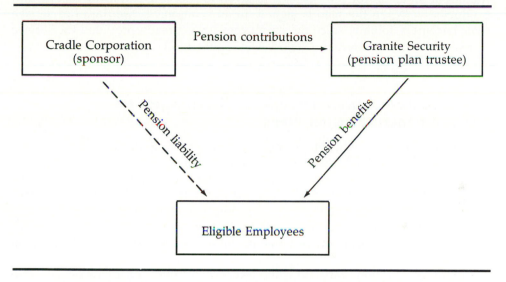

between the sponsoring firm, the pension plan trustee or agent, and the covered employees are summarized in Exhibit 10-4.

Prior service costs   When an employer allows credit for years worked prior to the adoption or amendment of a pension plan, **prior service costs** (item g) result. In concept, these costs are a liability because the benefits have already been earned by the employees covered, and the firm has agreed to pay these benefits (see the dotted line in Exhibit 10-4 for pension liability). Figure 10-2 depicts the accumulation and payment periods for pension benefits for an individual employee.

Figure 10-2
Pension Benefits: Accumulation and Payment

	Pension plan adopted	Employee retires	
	Period A	Period B	Period C
Time			
	Prior Service Costs	Pension Expenses	Retirement Benefits

When a pension plan is to be adopted, management decides whether to give prior service credit in computing employee retirement benefits. Typically, full or partial credit for prior service is given to promote employee morale and productivity. When the plan is signed, in an economic sense the prior service costs become a liability, since the employees have already provided the service to which those costs pertain (Period A in Figure 10-2).

Required Accounting Methods and Disclosures for Defined-benefit Pension Plans

The current rules for pension accounting and reporting are contained in *SFAS No. 87,* issued late in 1985 and effective at various dates through 1988. The statement specifies how pension expenses, assets, and liabilities are to be measured in the financial statements, and also requires extensive supplementary disclosures. The remainder of this chapter will describe and illustrate the method of accounting for defined-benefit pension plans and will show the supplementary disclosures contained in a recent annual report of the Allied Signal Corporation.

FASB deliberations preceding the issuance of *SFAS No. 87* caused intense debate, which centered mainly on whether pension expenses and liabilities were to be measured using projected future salary levels or salary levels earned to date. The FASB opted to base the computation of pension expense on projected salary levels and the computation of pension liability (for balance sheet purposes) on salary levels earned to date. This inconsistency was incorporated in *SFAS No. 87* by the FASB as a compromise to alleviate concern by some firms about potential undesirable economic consequences of the new reporting rules.

The discussion to follow will address (1) the measurement of pension expense and its components; (2) the measurement of pension liabilities and assets; (3) additional pension disclosures; and (4) an evaluation of *SFAS No. 87* reporting rules.

Measuring and Reporting of Pension Expense

Components of pension expense   The pension expense of an accounting period consists of several separate components, reflecting both the benefits earned by employees in the current period, and the manner in which management decides to fund the plan. Specifically, there are five separate components of pension expense:

1. Service cost
2. Interest cost
3. Return on plan assets
4. Amortization of unrecognized gains and losses
5. Amortization of unrecognized prior service cost

The income statement will report the net (combined) amount of these five components, and each of the components will be disclosed in the accompanying footnotes. Each of these cost elements will first be defined and then illustrated in a simple example.

Service cost The **service cost** component is the present value of projected benefits earned by employees in the current period. In theory, this should be the discounted value of the increase in future benefits to be received by employees as a result of services rendered during the period. The measurement of service costs depends on the assumptions used to compute the increase in future benefits (assumptions regarding mortality, employee turnover, early retirement, promotion, salary increases, and so forth) and the time value of money (the discount rate). Actuarial cost calculations are beyond the scope of this text, but the reader is well-advised to note that each actuarial assumption is an estimate and subject to revision. Revisions in actuarial assumptions can substantially affect the valuation of pension obligations.

Interest cost The **interest cost** component of pension expense is the increase in the present value of the benefits due to the passage of time. Because the firm measures the pension obligation at its present value, it is necessary to accrue interest cost at a rate equal to the assumed discount rate.

Return on plan assets Plan assets usually consist of stocks, bonds, and other investments that must be segregated and restricted (usually in a trust) in order to provide pension benefits. The **return on plan assets** *reduces* pension cost, because these investment returns represent additional funds that may be used to satisfy pension obligations. The return on plan assets is computed as an expected return, rather than the actual return realized on these assets.

Amortization of unrecognized gains and losses A variety of assumptions underlie the calculations of the pension cost components listed above, and inevitably some of these assumptions will need to be revised. As a consequence, either the present value of the pension obligations or the value of the plan assets may differ from expectations, resulting in unrecognized gains and losses. If such unrecognized gains and losses exceed ten percent of the greater of the beginning of the year present value of the pension obligations or the value of the plan assets, the gains or losses must be amortized over the remaining service lives of the covered employees.

Amortization of unrecognized prior service cost When pension plans are adopted or amended, provisions are often included that grant increased benefits based on services rendered in prior periods. Such prior service costs are recognized during future service periods of the employees affected; it is acceptable to use straight-line amortization for this purpose.

The simple example that follows illustrates the basic calculations involving the pension expense components. On January 1, 1987, the One Hoss Shay

Company was established by 40 members of the graduating MBA class of State University. The entire group plans to retire at the end of 20 years. At that time, the pension will be calculated as follows: for each year of employment, each individual will receive a lump sum pension equal to ten percent of the salary earned during the year of retirement. (An employee with 20 years of service will receive 200 percent of the final year's salary when he retires.) Presently, each employee earns $40,000 per year. Salaries are expected to grow at a rate of six percent each year, and the time value of money is eight percent per year. On January 1, 1987, the company made a $150,000 contribution to the pension plan, which has been invested in assets expected to earn eight percent each year. At the end of the first year, the plan assets have a market value of $170,000. The pertinent actuarial assumptions include the discount rate (eight percent), the rate of salary increase (six percent), and employee turnover (none).

For 1987, the interest cost and service cost components of pension expense are computed as follows:

Interest cost, 1987: Because there were no future benefits earned at the beginning of the year, there is no interest cost in this year. Interest cost for the second year of the plan will be calculated later.

Service cost, 1987:

Present salary, covered employees ($40,000 × 40)	$1,600,000
Future value factor at 6 percent, $(1.06)^{19}$ (Table C-3)	× 3.026
Salary projected for year preceding retirement	$4,841,600
Percentage earned in current period	× .10
Projected future pension benefit earned in current period	$ 484,160
Present value factor at 8 percent, $(1.08)^{-19}$ (Table C-1)	× .232
Service cost, current period	$ 112,325

The calculation has required that the projected change in future benefits due to the current period's employment ($484,160) be discounted to the present; that is, the 19 years remaining until retirement.

Return on plan assets, 1987: This negative component of pension cost is computed at the *expected* return rate of eight percent:

Beginning balance in plan assets	$150,000
Expected rate of return	× .08
Return on plan assets	$ 12,000

Amortization of unrecognized gains and losses, 1987: There is an unrecognized gain of $8,000 in the One Hoss Shay Company's pension plan, because the plan's assets of $170,000 are greater than the $162,000 ($150,000 beginning balance plus $12,000 return) that was expected. Because this gain does not exceed 10 percent of the beginning-of-the-year pension plan assets ($150,000), no amortization is required.

Amortization of unrecognized prior service cost, 1987: There are no prior service costs, because all services from covered employees are received after the date of plan adoption. If there were prior service costs, they would be recognized as expense evenly over the remaining service lives of the employees covered.

As a result of all of the preceding pension calculations, One Hoss Shay's 1987 net pension cost is $100,325, as follows:

Service cost	$112,325
Interest cost	0
Return on plan assets	(12,000)
Amortization of unrecognized gains or losses	0
Amortization of unrecognized prior service cost	0
Net pension cost	$100,325

It is useful to extend this example through the second year — 1988 — to illustrate the interest cost calculation and the change in the present value of the pension obligation. Assume that One Hoss Shay Company contributes an additional $150,000 to the pension plan on January 1, 1988, and that the plan assets have a market value of $340,000 at the end of 1988.

Second year, 1988 pension cost

Interest cost, 1988: The present value of the projected pension obligations was $112,325 at the beginning of 1988 (equal to the balance at the end of 1987). If no additional benefits were earned during 1988, the present value of the projected obligations would have increased by eight percent due solely to the passage of time.

Present value at the beginning of the year, of projected benefits earned in prior years	$112,325
Discount rate	× .08
Interest cost	$ 8,986

Service cost, 1988:

Salary projected for the year of retirement (same as that computed in 1987)	$4,841,600
Percentage earned in current period	× .10
Projected future pension benefit earned in current period	$ 484,160
Present value factor at 8 percent, $(1.08)^{-18}$ (Table C-1)	× .250
Service cost, current period	$ 121,040

The present value of the projected pension obligation at the end of 1988 may be computed in one of two ways:

Present value of present projected pension obligation at beginning of the year	$112,325
Interest cost on beginning balance	8,986
Service cost, current year	121,040
Present value of projected pension obligation	$242,351

Alternative calculation:

Salary projected for the year of retirement (same as computed in 1987)	$4,841,600
Percentage earned through end of 1988	× .20
Projected future pension benefit earned through end of 1988	$ 968,320
Present value factor at 8 percent, $(1.08)^{-18}$ (Table C-1)	× .250
Present value of projected pension obligation (slight difference due to rounding)	$ 242,080

Return on plan assets: At the beginning of 1988 the plan assets had a market value of $320,000 ($170,000 end of 1987 value, plus $150,000 additional contribution).

Beginning balance in plan assets	$320,000
Expected rate of return	× .08
Return on plan assets	$ 25,600

Amortization of unrecognized gains and losses, 1988: During 1988, there is an unrecognized loss of $5,600 because the plan's assets of $340,000 are less than the expected amount of $345,600 ($320,000 beginning balance plus $25,600 expected return). The net unrecognized gain is $2,400 ($8,000 gain in 1987, and $5,600 loss in 1988), which is not large enough to require amortization.

Amortization of unrecognized prior service costs, 1988: Not applicable.

Consequently, the net pension costs for 1987 and 1988 may be compared as follows:

Net Pension Cost	1987	1988
Service cost	$112,325	$121,040
Interest cost	0	8,986
Return on plan assets	(12,000)	(25,600)
Amortization, gains and losses	0	0
Amortization, prior service cost	0	0
	$100,325	$104,426

In general, for an employee group with little turnover and a pension plan that is funded currently (that is, employer contributions approximately match current service costs), the service cost, interest cost, and returns on plan assets will increase over time.

The remaining portion of this chapter describes the measurement and reporting of pension assets and liabilities.

Measuring and Reporting of Pension Assets and Liabilities

If management decides to contribute to the pension plan in an amount that differs from the period's net pension expense, pension assets or liabilities will result. For example, recall that the One Hoss Shay Company decided to fund its plan at the rate of $150,000 per year in 1987 and 1988. Net pension expenses (computed previously) were $100,325 in 1987 and $104,426 in 1988, and the following journal entries were recorded:

1987:	dr.	Pension Expense	100,325	
	dr.	Prepaid Pension Cost	49,675	
	cr.	Cash		150,000
1988:	dr.	Pension Expense	104,426	
	dr.	Prepaid Pension Cost	45,574	
	cr.	Cash		150,000

As a result, at the end of 1988 the company would report a balance of $95,249 ($49,675 + $45,574) as an asset on the balance sheet, reflecting the excess of its cumulative contributions over its cumulative net pension expenses. If, on the other hand, the cash funding is less than the pension expense, a liability for accrued pension cost will be created.

In many cases, the FASB's new rules require that firms recognize additional liabilities beyond those created by differences between cumulative contributions and cumulative expenses. These additional liabilities are due primarily to three factors: (1) substantial prior service costs at the time of the adoption or amendment of pension plans, (2) methods used to compute pension expenses and fund pension plans prior to the adoption of *SFAS No. 87* in late 1985, and (3) lower than expected returns on plan assets. If at the balance sheet date the **accumulated pension benefit obligation** of the pension plan exceeds the value of the plan's assets (plus or minus any pension liabilities or assets appearing on the balance sheet), an additional liability must be recorded. To illustrate, assume that Golden Harvester, Inc., provides the following information at December 31, 1987:

Pension plan assets, at fair value	$520 million
Accrued pension cost (liability)	$ 45 million
Accumulated pension benefit obligation	$600 million

In this case, Golden Harvester, Inc., would be required to recognize an additional liability of $35 million, computed in this manner:

Accumulated pension benefit obligation	$600 million
Less: Accrued pension cost (liability)	(45 million)
Unrecognized pension obligation	$555 million
Less: Pension plan assets, at fair value	(520 million)
Net pension liability	$ 35 million

If the recording of such an additional liability is required, offsetting amounts must be recorded. The offsetting amount is recorded as an intangible asset not to exceed the amount of the firm's unrecognized prior service cost. If the amount of the additional liability recorded is greater than the firm's unrecognized prior service cost, the excess of this liability over prior service cost is recorded as a negative shareholders' equity account. If Golden Harvester has unrecognized prior service costs of $21 million, the required adjustment would be

dr.	Intangible Pension Asset	21,000,000	
dr.	Excess Additional Pension Liability over		
	Unrecognized Service Cost	14,000,000	
	cr. Pension Liability		35,000,000

The rationale for recording the intangible pension asset at a value not to exceed the amount of unrecognized prior service cost is that prior service costs are intended to benefit future periods. Accordingly, the intangible pension asset will be amortized over the service life of the employee group to which it applies.[4] There is no clear interpretation of the negative shareholders' equity account, however; it is employed mainly as the result of inadequate pension funding or lower than expected returns on plan investments in previous periods.

The **accumulated benefit obligation** used in these calculations does not correspond to the present value of the projected pension benefits that was used earlier in computing the service cost component of net pension expense. The difference between these amounts stems from the fact that the accumulated benefit obligation ignores future compensation changes and instead assumes that pension benefits will be based on present salary levels. The rate used in discounting the pension benefits in order to compute the accumulated benefits obligation, on the other hand, is based on prevailing market rates of interest, which incorporate investor expectations concerning inflation. This is a basic inconsistency, because in computing the present value of the accumulated benefit obligation, the numerator of the present value calculation assumes

---

[4]This intangible asset is amortized in a unique way through the prior service cost portion of the net pension expense. There is no individual entry made to debit amortization expense and credit an intangible asset account.

no inflation, while the denominator of the calculation assumes the level of inflation reflected in prevailing interest rates. As a consequence, if prices (and salary levels) are expected to increase, then the accumulated benefit obligation will be less than the present value of the projected pension obligation.

The extent to which the accumulated benefit obligation differs from the present value of projected pension liabilities depends on both the discount rate selected and the rate of salary growth to be expected. If the accumulated benefit obligation is computed using a relatively low rate (five or six percent per annum), then the difference is likely to be minor because the rate of inflation assumed in the discount rate is low. If on the other hand, relatively high rates of discount are used, then the difference is likely to be substantial.

Supplementary Financial Statement Disclosures

The pension expense and asset and liability amounts discussed above comprise just a portion of required pension disclosures. The FASB requires that employers sponsoring defined-benefit pension plans disclose the information listed in Exhibit 10-5.

The *SFAS No. 87* disclosure requirements were to become effective at various dates in 1986 and 1988, so that we are unable to incorporate in this text a set of actual financial statements reflecting these disclosures. Allied Signal Company is one firm that elected to include many of the disclosures in its 1986 financial report, and the pension-related footnotes from that report appear in Exhibit 10-6 on page 503.

EVALUATION OF PENSION REPORTING

Reporting of pension costs and obligations has been a source of accounting controversy for many years. Critics of accounting requirements prior to *SFAS No. 87* argued that pension costs were not comparable from one firm to another, and often were not consistently calculated over time for the same firm. Moreover, substantial pension obligations and assets were not recognized in the body of the financial statements, and footnote disclosures were of questionable usefulness to financial analysts.

In framing the requirements in *SFAS No. 87*, the FASB decided to retain three features of past pension accounting: (1) delayed recognition, (2) net cost, and (3) offsetting of liabilities and assets. These features will be explained next.

1. **Delayed recognition** means that not all gains and losses are recognized in the periods in which they occur. For example, changes in actuarial assumptions or differences between the expected and actual returns on pension plan assets cause economic gains or losses which, for pension accounting purposes, are deferred and amortized over future periods. The retention of this practice may only be understood as a compromise by the FASB in an effort to reduce the potential volatility of pension expenses induced by such gains and losses.

2. **Net cost** means that a single amount, such as net pension cost, is reported in the aggregate although it is the result of disparate types of economic

Exhibit 10-5

Required Disclosures for Defined-benefit Pension Plans

(Adapted from paragraph 54 of *SFAS No. 87.*)

Disclosures

An employer sponsoring a defined-benefit pension plan shall disclose the following:

a. A description of the plan including employee groups covered, type of benefit formula, funding policy, types of assets held and significant nonbenefit liabilities, if any, and the nature and effect of significant matters affecting comparability of information for all periods presented

b. The amount of net periodic pension cost for the period showing separately the service cost component, the interest cost component, the actual return on assets for the period, and the net total of other components[1]

c. A schedule reconciling the funded status of the plan with amounts reported in the employer's statement of financial position, showing separately:
   (1) The fair value of plan assets
   (2) The projected benefit obligation identifying the accumulated benefit obligation and the vested benefit obligation
   (3) The amount of unrecognized prior service cost
   (4) The amount of unrecognized net gain or loss (including asset gains and losses not yet reflected in market-related value)
   (5) The amount of any remaining unrecognized net obligation or net asset existing at the date of initial application of this Statement
   (6) The amount of any additional liability recognized pursuant to this Statement
   (7) The amount of net pension asset or liability recognized in the statement of financial position (which is the net result of combining the preceding six items)

d. The weighted-average assumed discount rate and rate of compensation increase (if applicable) used to measure the projected benefit obligation and the weighted-average expected long-term rate of return on plan assets

e. If applicable, the amounts and types of securities of the employer and related parties included in plan assets, and the approximate amount of annual benefits of employees and retirees covered by annuity contracts issued by the employer and related parties.

---

[1]The net total of other components is the net effect during the period of certain delayed recognition provisions of this Statement. That net total includes:
a. The net asset gain or loss during the period deferred for later recognition (in effect, an offset or a supplement to the actual return on assets)
b. Amortization of the net gain or loss from earlier periods
c. Amortization of unrecognized prior service cost
d. Amortization of the unrecognized net obligation or net asset existing at the date of initial application of this Statement.

Exhibit 10-6
Pension Reporting in Accordance with *SFAS No. 87*

Allied Signal Corporation

Note 22. Pensions and Other Postretirement Benefits

The Company's pension plans, most of which are defined benefit plans and almost all of which are noncontributory, cover substantially all employees. Benefits under the plans are generally based on years of service and employees' compensation during the last years of employment or a flat dollar benefit. Benefits are paid from funds previously provided to trustees. In the Company's principal United States plans, funds are contributed to a trustee as necessary to provide for current service and for any unfunded projected benefit obligation over a reasonable period. To the extent that these requirements are fully covered by assets on hand, a contribution may not be made in a particular year. As of year-end 1986, approximately 55 percent of the assets of these plans were held in equity securities, with the balance in fixed income-type securities.

Pension expense in 1986, 1985 and 1984 was $93, $150 and $163 million, respectively. The reduction in pension expense in 1985 is attributable to a change in the interest rate assumption to reflect current and future investment returns. Effective January 1, 1986 the Company adopted the provisions of FASB No. 87 for its United States defined benefit pension plans which, along with related changes, including recognition of favorable investment experience, reduced 1986 pension expense by $55 million. The Company uses the services of enrolled actuaries to calculate the amount of pension expense and contributions to trustees of the pension plans.

Net periodic pension cost for 1986 included the following components:

	1986
Service cost–benefits earned during the period	$102
Interest cost on projected benefit obligation	307
Actual return on plan assets	(616)
Net amortization and deferral	284
Net periodic pension cost for defined benefit plans	77
Foreign plans and other	16
Net periodic pension cost	$ 93

The assumed rate of return for the Company's United States defined benefit pension plans was nine percent in 1986, nine percent for certain plans and eight percent for other plans in 1985 and eight percent for 1984. Benefits at December 31, 1986 and at December 31, 1985 were calculated based on a 8.25 percent and a nine percent assumed discount rate, respectively. In addition, the assumed annual increase in compensation over employees' estimated remaining working lives was 5.5 percent at December 31, 1986 and six percent at December 31, 1985 and 1984.

Exhibit 10-6 continued

Presented below are the plans' funded status and amounts recognized in the Company's Consolidated Balance Sheet at December 31, 1986 and 1985, for its United States defined-benefit pension plans:

December 31	1986		1985	
	Assets Exceed Accumulated Benefits	Accumulated Benefits Exceed Assets	Assets Exceed Accumulated Benefits	Accumulated Benefits Exceed Assets
Actuarial Present Value of Benefit Obligation:				
Vested	$2,480	$625	$2,206	$ 562
Nonvested	260	24	235	22
Accumulated benefit obligation	$2,740	$649	$2,441	$ 584
Projected benefit obligation	$3,295	$669	$2,925	$ 604
Less: Fair value of assets	3,575	559	3,170	466
Over (under) funded plans	280	(110)	245	(138)
Unrecognized transition (asset) liability	77	(68)	84	(74)
Unrecognized net (gain) loss	(15)	4	—	—
Tax effect of pension (asset) liability relating to purchase accounting	(189)	75	(203)	80
(Accrued) prepaid pension cost	$ 153	$(99)	$ 126	$(132)

The Company has a number of foreign defined benefit pension plans. The present value of the accumulated benefits of the plans were $67 and $64 million for vested benefits and $8 and $9 million for nonvested benefits at December 31, 1985 and 1984, respectively. The net assets held by trustees was $108 and $101 million at December 31, 1985 and 1984. The accumulated pension benefits were calculated using an eight percent rate of return for certain plans and seven percent for the balance in 1985 and 1984.

In addition to providing pension benefits, the Company provides other postretirement benefits (i.e., health care and life insurance benefits) for employees. Substantially all of the Company's employees may become eligible for those benefits if they reach normal retirement age while working for the Company. The cost of retiree health care and life insurance benefits are expensed as paid. In 1986, 1985 and 1984 the Company's cost for providing other postretirement benefits for its operations aggregated $57, $54 and $42 million, respectively.

---

activity. For example, net pension expense or cost is the aggregate of employee compensation (service cost), employer funding policy (interest cost), and investment performance (return on plan assets). For areas other than pensions, it is conventional to report the effects of such disparate activities separately.

3. **Offsetting of assets and liabilities** means that the net pension liability is computed by subtracting pension assets from pension liabilities. This is not consistent with economic reality because the liability has not been paid, the assets may be effectively controlled by the sponsoring firm, and the risks and rewards associated with both the assets and the obligations are still borne by

the sponsoring firm. Moreover, the basis used to value the liabilities is not compatible with the base used to value the assets: asset values are derived from current market prices, which reflect the discounted value of future cash flows. Liabilities, on the other hand, are valued on a basis that ignores the effect of compensation changes on future cash flows. As a consequence, the economic meaning of the net pension liabilities is unclear.

Three additional objections have been advanced by analysts with respect to the reporting of pension obligations. First, financial analysts argue that unfunded pension liabilities are not strictly equivalent to other obligations of the firm because payments to the pension plan are tax deductible. Thus, it is argued that pension obligations should be reported at their after-tax amounts. Second, analysts also suggest that the composition of the plan's assets is important in measuring the sponsoring firm's net monetary position and financial leverage; in concept the plan's monetary assets (such as investments in debt securities) should offset the sponsor's outstanding liabilities in computing debt-based financial ratios. If these arguments are accepted, then it is not clear if the highly aggregate disclosures required by the FASB will be adequate.

Finally, analysts object to the wide discretion that firms have in choosing a rate at which to discount pension obligations. In theory, the rate used to discount such obligations should equal the anticipated rate of return on the plan's investments, and so should vary with the composition of the plan's portfolio of securities and other investments. Recent surveys, however, indicate that discount rates seem unrelated either to the composition of the plan's investments or to the actual returns being earned on plan assets. Some analysts suggest that the use of a single rate by all firms, while questionable in concept, would increase the comparability of pension obligations among firms. In that case, footnote disclosures might report the effects of using other interest rates that management deems more appropriate.

This section has described the FASB's recently revised reporting rules for pension costs and obligations. Many troublesome issues remain unresolved, and pension reporting will continue to be a major area of accounting controversy among accountants, managers, regulators, and investor analysts.

SUMMARY

This chapter discusses two controversial areas in financial reporting: accounting for long-term leases and accounting for defined-benefit pension plans. The discussion of lease accounting focuses on the distinction between completed transactions and commitments, and on the importance of the economic substance, rather than the legal form, of a lease arrangement. The pension accounting controversy includes questions of whether pension plans are economic entities that are distinct from employer firms; whether past service costs are assets of the employer and if so, what constitutes an appropriate amortization period for those assets; and whether the method that firms are currently required to use in computing pension obligations produces a realistic valuation of those obligations.

QUESTIONS

1. The terms listed below were introduced in this chapter. Define or explain each of them.

   accumulated pension   operating lease
     benefit obligation   pension interest cost
   capital lease   pension plan
   defined-benefit pension plan pension service cost
   direct financing lease   prior service cost
   funding (plan) agent   return on plan assets
   lease   sales-type lease
   lessee   vested benefits
   lessor

2. Some leases may be considered to be debt-financed purchases, while other leases are more properly classified as rentals. Distinguish between these two lease categories. Give an example of a lease arrangement that fits each category.

3. List and briefly discuss some of the reasons that a firm might lease an asset rather than borrow funds to purchase the asset.

4. Describe what is meant by off-balance-sheet financing of leased assets. If a manager wishes to engage in off-balance-sheet financing, would that manager prefer that a given lease be classified as a capital lease or as an operating lease? Explain.

5. In using GAAP, how does a lessee distinguish between a capital lease and an operating lease?

6. List the criteria established by GAAP for use in determining whether a given lease arrangement is deemed to be a capital lease for financial reporting purposes.

7. From the standpoint of the lessor, leases are classified as being one of four types. List and briefly describe each of these four lease categories.

8. "Having a lease arrangement classified as an operating lease is preferred to having that arrangement classified as a capital lease because the total amount of reported expense over the life of the lease is less for operating leases than for capital leases." Do you agree or not? Explain.

9. "From the standpoint of the lessor, no income (revenue) would be recorded on the day a lease agreement is signed, if the lease is deemed to be a direct financing lease." Do you agree or not? Would your answer be the same if the lease was classified as a sales-type lease? Explain.

10. What cash flow consequences, if any, might result from the way a particular lease is classified (operating as opposed to capital lease) for financial reporting purposes?

11. "Reporting requirements under current GAAP assume that a firm's pension plan for its employees is a distinct economic entity from the firm itself." Do you agree or not? Explain.

12. Describe the journal entry sequence for a typical period to account for a pension plan in which the sponsoring company employs an outside funding agent.

13. Why would an employer give credit for prior service at the time a new pension plan is adopted?

14. *SFAS No. 87* specifies that the pension expense of an accounting period consists of five separate components. List and briefly describe each of these components.

15. It is possible to calculate pension expense by using either future salary levels or current salary levels. Which is required by the FASB in *SFAS No. 87*?

16. It is possible to calculate pension liability by using either future salary levels or current salary levels. Which is required by the FASB in *SFAS No. 87*?

17. Accountants disagree about the proper period to use to amortize a prior service cost associated with a pension plan. What two periods of time are most often suggested for the amortization of prior service costs? What is the rationale for using each of these periods?

18. Why would the return on a pension plan's assets reduce (be a negative component of) the reported amount of the pension cost?

19. One of the components of pension cost is the amortization of unrecognized gains and losses. Describe at least two different situations or events that would give rise to an unrecognized gain or loss.

20. Distinguish between the amount of pension expense shown on a firm's income statement for a particular period and the amount of funding (cash given to the funding agent) for that period. Are these two dollar amounts necessarily the same? Explain.

21. "For a given company, the accumulated pension benefit obligation is the same as the present value of its projected pension liabilities." Do you agree or disagree with this statement? Explain.

22. What supplemental footnote disclosures regarding the reporting entity's pension plan are currently required by GAAP?

23. "According to current GAAP, past service costs are not recorded as liabilities for financial reporting purposes, although such costs are obligations to pay employees for services rendered in the past." Do you agree or not? Explain.

24. In framing the requirements for *SFAS No. 87*, the FASB decided to retain three features of prior pension accounting practices: (1) delayed recognition, (2) net cost, and (3) offsetting assets and liabilities. Briefly describe each of these features of pension accounting.

EXERCISES AND PROBLEMS

25. *Lessee Accounting: General Concepts.* From the lessee's standpoint, a lease may be classified for financial reporting purposes as either (1) an operating

lease or (2) a capital lease. This distinction makes a difference in terms of accounts and amounts reflected on the balance sheet and the income statement.

REQUIRED

(a) What is difference between the nature of an operating lease and the nature of a capital lease?
(b) In accordance with GAAP, what are the criteria to be used to distinguish between an operating lease and a capital lease?
(c) Are the criteria listed in (b) consistent with your descriptions of the nature of operating and capital leases in (a)? Explain.
(d) Describe in general terms the accounting for a lease classified as an operating lease. Why is an operating lease sometimes called off-the-balance-sheet financing?
(e) Describe in general terms the accounting for a lease classified as a capital lease.

26. *Lessor Accounting: General Concepts.* From a lessor's standpoint, a lease may be classified for financial reporting purposes a number of different ways.

REQUIRED

(a) Define each of the following:
  (1) direct financing lease
  (2) sales-type lease
  (3) operating lease
(b) Contrast a direct financing lease and a sales-type lease in terms of timing of revenues (profit).
(c) Explain how the timing of revenues for a lease classified as an operating lease would differ from the timing of revenues for a lease classified as a sales-type lease.
(d) Profit (or loss) is shown at the inception of a sales-type lease. Describe how the amount of this profit is determined.
(e) Under a direct financing lease, would the lessor show depreciation expense for the asset being leased? Would depreciation expense be shown if the lease was classified as an operating lease? Explain.

27. *Equipment Purchased with Installment Debt.* On January 1, 1988, the New Bedford Company purchased a machine from the Boston Machinery Company to be paid for in five annual installments of $250,000, payable at the end of each year. New Bedford has recently borrowed money with similar terms at an interest rate of 16%. The machine is expected to last five years

and will be depreciated on the straight-line basis assuming no salvage value.

REQUIRED

(a) What is the present value of the installment note on January 1, 1988?
(b) Provide a journal entry to record the acquisition of the machine.
(c) Provide journal entries at December 31, 1988, to record interest expense, payment of the first installment, and depreciation expense for the year.
(d) Provide the same two journal entries at December 31, 1989. Explain why the interest expense for 1989 differs from that for 1988.

28. *Equipment Acquired by Leasing.* Assume that the New Bedford Company described in the previous problem decided to lease rather than purchase the machine, and that the lessor will receive rentals of $250,000 at the end of each year for five years. At the end of the lease the machine will be returned to the lessor. Assume that the relevant interest rate is 16%.

REQUIRED

(a) What is the present value of the lease obligation on January 1, 1988?
(b) Provide a journal entry to record the signing of the lease. (Assume the lease qualifies as a capital lease.)
(c) Provide journal entries at December 31, 1988, to record interest expense, and payment of the first year's rental and lease amortization expense for the year.
(d) Provide the same two journal entries at December 31, 1989. Explain why the interest expense for 1989 differs from that for 1988.

29. *Equipment Sold for Installment Notes Receivable.* On January 1, 1988, the Boston Machinery Company sold a machine to the New Bedford Company, as described in Exercise 27. The machine will be purchased for five annual installments of $250,000, to be paid at the end of each year. The cost of the machinery to the Boston Machinery Company was $600,000, and the prevailing interest rate is 16%.

REQUIRED

(a) What is the present value of the installment note receivable on January 1, 1988?
(b) Provide a journal entry to record the sale of the machine on the books of the Boston Machinery Company.
(c) Provide journal entries at the end of 1988 to record interest income and the receipt of the first payment installment.

(d) Provide journal entries at the end of 1989 to record interest income and the receipt of the second payment installment. Explain why the interest income for 1989 differs from that for 1988.

30. *Equipment Leased by a Manufacturer-Dealer.*   Assume that on January 1, 1988, the Fresno Machinery Company leased a machine to the Bakersfield Company for which Fresno will receive rentals of $250,000 at the end of each year for five years. The residual value of the leased asset at the end of the lease term is estimated to be $100,000. The cost of the machinery to Fresno was $600,000, and the prevailing interest rate is 16%. Assume that the fair value of the machine to the lessor is the same as the lessor's net investment in the lease, and that the lease qualifies as a sales-type lease.

REQUIRED

(a) What is the present value of the lease payments on January 1, 1988? What is the present value of the estimated residual value at that date?
(b) Provide a journal entry to record the leasing of the machine on January 1, 1988, on the books of the Fresno Machinery Company.
(c) Provide journal entries at the end of 1988 to record interest income and the receipt of the first payment installment.

31. *Annual and Total Expense: Capital versus Operating Lease.*   Foley Axle Company will lease a machine for six years at an annual rental of $100,000 payable at the end of each year.

REQUIRED   Determine the total expense over the lease term and the annual expense for the first and last years in each of the following situations:

(a) The lease qualifies as an operating lease.
(b) The lease is a capital lease, and the interest rate is 8%.
(c) The lease is a capital lease, and the interest rate is 14%.

32. *Annual and Total Lessor Income: Capital versus Operating Lease.*   Naroff Obstruction Company, a manufacturer and dealer, has decided to lease rather than to sell a machine to the Dayton Company. The annual rental cost of $100,000 will be payable at the end of each year for a period of six years. The machine has a cost on Naroff's books of $500,000 and is estimated to have a residual value of $90,000 at the end of the lease term. Assume that the fair value of the machine to the lessor is the same as the lessor's net investment in the lease.

REQUIRED   Determine the total income over the lease term and the annual income in the first and last years for each of the following situations:

(a) The lease qualifies as an operating lease.
(b) The lease is a sales-type lease, and the interest rate is 8%.
(c) The lease is a sales-type lease, and the interest rate is 14%.

33. *Leasing and Assessing Divisional Performance.* Ashton Lens Corporation uses a return on assets measure as one gauge of divisional operating performance. Both the Lewis division and the Libby division were newly established at the beginning of 1988, and each signed an agreement to rent lens-grinding machines for ten years at annual rentals of $1 million, payable at the end of each year. The Lewis division rental agreement qualifies as an operating lease, while the Libby division rental agreement contains a bargain purchase option that qualifies it as a capital lease. In addition to the grinding machines, each division maintains $4 million in operating assets and earns profits of $2 million before depreciation, amortization, and rental or interest expense. The interest rate is 10%.

REQUIRED: Determine the following:

(a) Total assets for each division at December 31, 1988 (that is, other assets of $4 million, plus the capitalized cost, if any, of the grinding machinery).
(b) Net income for 1988. (Ignore income tax effects.)
(c) Return on assets, 1988. (Use the asset values determined in item (a) above.)

34. *Journal Entries for Capital Leases.* In Ashland Oil's annual report for the fiscal year ended September 30, 1986, Note G, "Leases and Other Commitments," states the following with respect to capital leases.

Ashland and its subsidiaries are lessees in noncancelable (capital) leasing arrangements for office buildings, pipelines, tankers, service stations, manufacturing facilities and other equipment and properties that expire at various dates. Future minimum lease payments at September 30, 1986, follow.

Future Minimum Payments

(in thousands)

1987	$ 14,951
1988	14,525
1989	14,398
1990	14,197
1991	15,693
Later years	98,647
	$167,411

For purposes of this problem, assume the following:

(1) The minimum annual capital lease payments for "later years" are as shown below.

1992–1996 — $15,600
1997 — $15,647

(2) All of these capital assets were acquired on September 30, 1986, and the composite annual depreciation rate for these assets is 3.5%.

(3) No additional leased capital assets will be acquired through 1997 and all lease payments will be made on September 30 of each year.

(4) On September 30, 1986, the company's long-term borrowing rate for debt with similar characteristics is 8%.

REQUIRED Based on the information provided, indicate the journal entries that the company would record on September 30, 1987, to account for these leased assets.

35. *Effects of Capitalizing Leases.* *SFAS No. 13* (issued in 1976) required capitalization of defined capital leases. This problem is designed to show the effects of this requirement on Guscorp's financial position and operating results for 1985. The following selected data were taken from Guscorp's 1985 annual report for the year ending December 31, 1985.

Net income	$118,050,000
Stockholders' equity	962,500,000
Long-term debt	450,900,000

At December 31, 1984, obligations under capital leases for future minimum lease payments were as follows:

	Capital Leases
	(in thousands)
1985	$ 11,087
1986	9,899
1987	9,797
1988	9,896
1989	7,841
Thereafter	53,136
Total minimum lease payments	$101,656
Less: Amount representing interest	40,644
Present value of net minimum lease payments	$ 61,012

The following amounts applicable to capital leases are included in property and equipment on the company's balance sheets at December 31, 1985, and December 31, 1984:

| | December 31 | |
	1984	1985
	(in thousands)	
Flight equipment	$56,474	$70,105
Ground property and equipment	4,297	7,063
Total	60,771	77,168
Less: Accumulated depreciation	20,483	32,165
	$40,288	$45,003

In responding to the questions below, assume the following:

(1) The interest rate used to discount all future capital leases is 8% (actual interest rates varied from 6.99% to 11.1%).
(2) Annual lease payments are made on December 31 of each year.
(3) Income tax is not affected by noncapitalizations of leases.

REQUIRED

(a) Record the journal entry made on December 31, 1985, for the interest portion of the capital lease expense.
(b) Record the journal entry that would have been made if these leases had not been capitalized.
(c) What was the amount of depreciation taken on capitalized leases in 1985? (Assume no capital leases were terminated during 1985.)
(d) What would reported income for 1985 have been if leases were not capitalized?
(e) Compare the debt-to-equity ratio with and without capitalization of leases by Guscorp on December 31, 1985.

36. *Effects of Capitalizing Leases.* (*President of bank to vice-president in charge of commercial loans*) "I don't agree with the distinction that the FASB makes between capital and operating leases. Financial leverage is a key index in our evaluation of commercial loans. As far as I am concerned, a noncancelable operating lease is a long-term debt. Therefore, our analyses of financial statements of loan applicants that have noncancelable operating leases should presume that these leases are capitalized in the same manner as so-called 'capital leases'. As an example, let's see what effect capitalization of operating leases would have on the debt-to-equity ratio of U.S. Air on December 31, 1985."

On December 31, 1985, U.S. Air's long-term debt (net of current maturities) was $451,441,000 and total stockholders' equity was $955,523,000. At

December 31, 1984, U.S. Air's noncancelable operating leases were reported as follows:

	Minimum Lease Payments
	(in thousands)
1985	$ 31,057
1986	30,158
1987	28,157
1988	26,619
1989	26,491
Thereafter	269,215
Total minimum lease payments	$411,697

Assume that minimum noncancelable operating lease payments were $29,215,000 in 1990 and $30,000,000 per annum from 1991–1998, and that the company would use a 10% interest rate to discount these obligations.

REQUIRED

(a) Assuming that operating leases were capitalized, calculate U.S. Air's debt-to-equity ratio on December 31, 1985. The company's composite depreciation rate on flight equipment and on ground property and equipment in 1985 was 4.7%.

(b) Indicate whether current ratio or cash flow would be affected by capitalization of operating leases. If either is affected, indicate how.

(c) Do you agree with the bank president's comment about operating leases? If so, why do you think the FASB drew a distinction between noncancelable capital and operating leases?

37. *Pension Accounting: Issues.*   As discussed in the chapter, the FASB has recently mandated significant changes in the way that companies must account for pensions. In response to these changes, a national accounting firm included the following statements in a memorandum to its clients:

(1) The FASB views a defined-benefit pension plan as an exchange of the employer's promise to pay retirement benefits for employee service, much like deferred compensation. This results in the employer having an obligation to the employees for benefits that have been earned, but not yet paid. By contrast, others argue that the employer's only legal obligation is to make sufficient contributions to the plan under an acceptable actuarial cost method. Thus, if all scheduled contributions to the plan have been made, the employer has no current pension obligation.

(2) The FASB believes that the pension liability should be determined based on the assumption that the employer and the plan will continue in operation, unless there is evidence to the contrary. Opponents argue that if the pension liability is recognized, it should be limited to

the amount based on plan termination or to the amount of vested benefits, because the employer has the ability to avoid any additional amount.

(3) Some argue that actuarially determined amounts are not sufficiently accurate to be recognized in financial statements. The measure of pension obligation requires estimates of future events, including mortality, turnover, and rates of interest. These estimates of events decades in the future lead many to believe the pension obligation is not reliable enough for balance sheet presentation. The FASB, however, believes that the information is relevant enough to compensate for a lack of precision.

(4) The FASB decided that the pension plan assets should be deducted from the pension obligation because the assets must be used to pay the pension obligations; thus, a right of offset exists. The FASB also believes that the pension plan assets should be measured at fair (market) value because that provides the most relevant information.

(5) In many respects, pensions are like other executory contracts. The promise to pay benefits is given in exchange for a promise to render service. Other executory contracts, such as purchase commitments and employment contracts, generally are not reported as liabilities. Although the employer often grants past service credit to employees, it is the anticipation of future services from the employees that motivates the employer to do this.

(6) The FASB contends that a single method of estimating pension obligations among firms would serve investors by increasing comparability and understanding. But in many cases the increase in comparability would be illusory. No two companies have identical work forces and plan benefits. Actuarial assumptions, which are subjective, will differ. The increase in users' understanding would be a false sense of comprehension.

(7) The impact of the FASB's proposals on financial position and earnings could influence assessments of a company by securities and credit analysts and by bond-rating agencies. These reassessments would impair the availability of financing for some companies and could escalate borrowing costs for others. Labor unions also might be influenced by the proposed accounting to demand accelerated funding. These financial pressures could in turn affect dividend policies.

(8) Management strategies to avoid the accounting results of the FASB's proposals also could affect the structure of pension systems in our country. The new accounting would tend to inhibit plan improvements, including benefit increases to help retirees cope with inflation. . . . Undoubtedly, yet other schemes would be devised to avoid liability recognition and reduced earnings reports. Thus, the FASB proposals could create an accounting quagmire, similar to what happened with leases.

REQUIRED   Comment in detail on each of the statements listed on pages 514 and 515.

38. *Pension Expense and Liability.*   John Done presently earns $36,000 per year. He expects to retire in 20 years and to receive a pension of $60,000 per year thereafter.

REQUIRED   Answer the following questions that relate to John Done's pension.

(a) If Mr. Done has a life expectancy of 15 years beyond retirement, what is the expected present value of his pension benefits at the date of his retirement? Assume that all cash flows occur at the end of the years indicated and that the interest rate is 8%.

(b) Based on your answer to item (a), what is the present value of Mr. Done's pension benefits today (20 years prior to the date of his expected retirement)?

(c) Assume that Mr. Done's pension benefits will be equal to his salary during his last year of employment, and that his present annual salary is expected to increase at an annual rate of 5%. What is the present value of Mr. Done's pension benefits today?

39. *Pension Liability: Interest Rate and Salary Growth Assumptions.*   Murray Dotage expects to retire in 30 years and to receive pension benefits equal to 80% of his maximum annual salary each year thereafter.

REQUIRED

(a) If Mr. Dotage has a life expectancy of 20 years beyond retirement, what is the present value of his expected pension benefits today (30 years before retirement) given the following assumptions:

(1) Present salary of $30,000; interest rate of 12%; no expected growth in salary each year.

(2) Present salary of $30,000; interest rate of 12%; 5% expected growth in salary each year.

(3) Present salary of $30,000; interest rate of 6%; no expected growth in salary each year.

(4) Present salary of $30,000; interest rate of 6%; 5% expected growth in salary each year.

(b) Based on your answers to (a) above, comment on the relationships between the present value of pension obligations and the assumptions regarding interest rates and salary growth rates.

40. *Pension Calculation: Individual Employees.*   The Pearly Gates Corporation adopted a pension plan in late December 1987, and pertinent provisions are

described in the exhibit on page 517. Dee Kline and Kurt Codger are two employees covered by the plan. Ms. Kline has been employed by the firm since early January 1984, and at the end of 1987 has an annual salary of $80,000. Her salary is projected to grow at an annual rate of 8% until the expected date of her retirement 10 years hence. Mr. Codger was hired in late December 1987 at an annual salary of $50,000, which is expected to grow at an average rate of 5% until his expected retirement 20 years hence. Both employees have a life expectancy of 20 years after retirement.

Pearly Gates Corporation
Defined-benefit Pension Plan
Provisions and Assumptions

Benefit formula: for each full year of service, 1.5% of average salary in the two years preceding retirement.

Vesting: 10% for each year's service.

Prior service credit: full credit for all years worked prior to adoption of the plan.

Interest rate: 10% per annum.

Funding: net pension costs to be fully funded each year by payments to the plan agent.

REQUIRED   Determine the following amounts for each of the two employees:

(a) Projected benefit obligation at December 31, 1987.
(b) Accumulated benefit obligation at December 31, 1987.
(c) Service cost and interest cost for 1988.
(d) Projected benefit obligation at December 31, 1988.
(e) Accumulated benefit obligation at December 31, 1988.

41. *Chapter Illustration Carried One Year Further: Plan Amendment and Prior Service Costs.*   The pension plan of the One Hoss Shay Company, adopted on January 1, 1987, is described in the chapter (pages 495–96), and the calculation of net pension expense is illustrated there for the years 1987 and 1988. You are provided the following information for 1989 and 1990.

1989: Funding: $150,000 paid to the plan agent at year end.
Return on plan assets: 9% earned on fair market value at the beginning of the year.
Fair value of plan assets, end of year: $520,600

1990: In early January the plan benefit formula was revised so that the lump-sum payment will be equal to 12% of the salary earned during the year preceding retirement for each year of employment (retroactive to date of initial employment). The discount rate used in computing the present value of the pension obligation was raised to 12%.

REQUIRED

(a) Determine net pension cost for the year 1989, and provide journal entries to record the pension cost and payment to the plan agent.

(b) At December 31, 1989, before the plan amendment, determine the plan's projected benefit obligation, accumulated benefit obligation, and unrecognized prior service cost.

(c) In January, 1990, after the plan amendment, determine the plan's projected benefit obligation, accumulated benefit obligation, and unrecognized prior service cost.

42. *Pension Plan: Journal Entries and Financial Statement Disclosures.* The Tender Trap Company adopted a trusteed pension plan on January 1, 1986. Information about pension costs, funding, assets, and obligations appears below.

	(in millions)		
	1986	**1987**	**1988**
Net pension costs	$500	$580	$ 620
Pension funding (paid each year end)	500	580	750
Projected benefits pension obligation, December 31, 1988			$3,200
Accumulated benefits pension obligation, December 31, 1988			$2,600
Fair value of plan assets, December 31, 1988			$1,920
Unrecognized prior service costs, December 31, 1988			$ 410

REQUIRED

(a) Provide journal entries to record net pension cost and payments to the plan agent at the end of each of the three years. How would the cumulative difference between net pension costs and payments to the plan be reflected on the firm's balance sheet at December 31, 1988?

(b) Identify the nature and amount of all items related to Tender Trap Company's pension plan to be reported in the firm's balance sheet at December 31, 1988.

43. *Pension Plan: Interpretation of Assets and Liabilities; Consolidation of Plan and Sponsor.* The following table includes summary financial information for the Hasten Thyme Company and its trusteed pension plan.

Hasten Thyme Company	**Balance at December 31, 1988**
Total assets (includes an intangible pension asset of $2 billion).	$30 billion
Total liabilities (includes a pension liability of $3 billion).	19 billion
Shareholders' equity (net of $1 billion debit for excess of additional pension liability over unrecognized prior service cost).	11 billion

Pension Plan	Balance at December 31, 1988
Plan assets at original cost	$ 8.5 billion
Plan assets at fair market value	12.5 billion
Projected benefit obligation	17.0 billion
Accumulated benefit obligation	15.5 billion

REQUIRED

(a) Explain why the Hasten Thyme Company's balance sheet reports a pension liability of $3 billion. Explain the nature of the intangible pension asset of $2 billion.

(b) Is the $3 billion pension liability a realistic measurement of Hasten Thyme's obligation to retirees? Explain.

(c) Is Hasten Thyme's pension liability of $3 billion included as an account receivable in the assets of the pension plan? Evaluate this practice.

(d) Assume that an investor analyst desires to consolidate Hasten Thyme Company and its pension plan. Prepare the consolidated balance sheet and explain your decisions concerning the appropriate valuation of the pension benefit obligation and the plan assets.

44. *Pension Plan and Selected Financial Ratios of the Sponsoring Firm.* The exhibit below provides selected financial information for the Padded Shoals Company and for its pension plan, which is administered by a separate financial institution for the benefit of covered employees.

Padded Shoals Company
Selected Financial Information
(in millions)

December 31, 1987:	
Total assets	$2,500
Total liabilities (includes pension obligations of $12,000,000)	1,000
Shareholders' equity	1,500
For year ended December 31, 1987:	
Net income	$ 250
Pension plan, selected financial information at December 31, 1987:	
Investments and other assets, at fair market value:	
Equity securities	$ 900
Debt securities	500
Other assets	100
Total Assets	$1,500
Pension obligations, at present value based on the accumulated benefits cost method:	
Vested	$ 600
Unvested	900
Total	$1,500

REQUIRED

(a) What does the $12 million of pension obligations reported on the balance sheet of the Padded Shoals Company represent? Does the company fund all pension expenses as they are accrued? How are these pension obligations related to the amounts shown on the financial statements of the pension plan?

(b) Assume that the pension plan is to be considered as an economic entity distinct from the Padded Shoals Company and compute the following financial ratios for Padded Shoals:

   (1) Debt to equity
   (2) Debt to total assets
   (3) Return on equity
   (4) Return on total assets

(c) Assume that the pension plan and Padded Shoals Company are not distinct economic entities, and recompute the ratios listed in item (b), above.

(d) The accumulated benefits method used by the pension plan to compute the present value of pension obligations does not allow for future salary increases. How would your answers to item (c) above be revised if salaries are expected to grow at an annual rate of 4%, and the average employee has an estimated remaining service life of 25 years?

45. *Measuring Financial Leverage When Components of Debt Have Different Income Tax Effects.*   Crisis Management Company's balance sheet shows the following items of debt and equity at December 31, 1987:

Sundry current liabilities	$0.5 billion
Long-term debt	1.5 billion
Capital lease obligations	2.0 billion
Pension liability	1.0 billion
Total liabilities	$5.0 billion
Paid-in capital	1.2 billion
Retained earnings	2.4 billion
Excess of net pension liability over unrecognized prior service cost	(1.6) billion
Total liabilities and shareholders' equity	$7.0 billion

Supplementary disclosures reveal that the firm's pension plan assets have a fair market value at December 31, 1987, of $1.8 billion, the firm's accumulated pension benefit obligation is $3.0 billion, and unrecognized prior service cost is $0.4 billion. The company's income is taxed at a rate of 40%.

REQUIRED

    (a) Lease payments and payments to the firm's pension plan generally are tax deductible when paid, while repayments of other components of debt have no direct effect on the firm's income tax obligations. Evaluate the argument that lease and pension obligations should be valued net of tax effects (in this case at 60% of their before-tax present values) in order to measure financial leverage.

    (b) How would the amount reported as "excess of net pension liability over unrecognized prior service cost" affect your valuation of owners' equity in measuring financial leverage?

    (c) Based on your responses to items (a) and (b), determine Crisis Management Company's ratio of debt to total assets at December 31, 1987.

46. *Pension Accounting: Objections to FASB's Reporting Rules.* In the course of debate before the FASB's issuance of *SFAS No. 87,* "Employers' Accounting for Pensions," respondents raised a number of objections, including the following:

    (1) The uncertainties inherent in predicting future interest rates and salary levels are sufficiently great that available measures of the projected benefit obligation fail to achieve the level of reliability needed for recognition in financial statements.

    (2) The employer's only obligation is to make periodic contributions sufficient to support the plan. It is the plan, as a distinct legal entity, that has an obligation for benefits promised to employees. Moreover, the plan's assets are not the assets of the employer.

    (3) Information about pension costs and obligations would be just as useful if it were disclosed in the footnotes and, therefore, changes in the basic financial statements are not necessary.

    (4) Measuring plan assets at fair value could introduce volatility into the financial statements as a result of short-term changes in fair values. Such volatility would be meaningless because of the long-run nature of the pension commitment and the fact that pension investments are often held for long periods, thus providing the opportunity for some gains or losses to reverse.

    (5) Securities of the employer that are held by the plan should be eliminated from plan assets and from the employer's financial statements as being, in effect, treasury securities.

    (6) The FASB should not require the use by all firms of a single method to determine service cost. Choices among accounting methods are allowed in other areas, including accounting for inventory and depreciation. Also, a single method does not ensure comparability because of differences in assumptions.

(7) Based on the definition of a liability, pension benefits dependent on future increases in compensation cannot be a present obligation, and the liability measurement should be based only on actual compensation expenditures to date. Also, if the plan was terminated or if an employee with vested benefits did not render future services, the employer's obligation would be limited to amounts based on compensation to date.

(8) It is inconsistent to measure pension obligations ignoring future compensation increases that reflect inflation, and to use discount rates that reflect expected inflation rates. Discounting a benefit that does not include the effects of inflation amounts to removing the effect of inflation twice.

(9) A pension liability should be limited either to the amount that would have to be paid on plan termination or to the amount of vested benefits, because the employer has discretion to avoid any obligations in excess of those limits.

(10) Differences in assumptions, especially the discount rates and assumed compensation levels, will impair comparability. Therefore, the FASB should require all employers to use the same assumptions.

(11) Accounting requirements should be different for employers subject to rate regulation or for employers that have certain types of government contracts for which reimbursement is a function of costs incurred. In both cases a change in reported pension cost might have a direct effect on the revenues of the employer.

REQUIRED   Evaluate each of these objections.

47. *Analysis of Pension Disclosures Contained in General Electric Company Annual Report.*   Although the reporting requirements of *SFAS No. 87* did not become mandatory until 1986 and later years, General Electric elected to voluntarily report information beyond that required in 1985. General Electric's 1985 annual report included the footnote disclosures shown in Exhibit A on page 523. Selected additional information from GE's financial statements is provided in Exhibit B on page 525.

REQUIRED

(a) Note that GE reports two separate measures of pension obligations and two separate valuations of pension trust assets, which allow up to four separate measures of the firm's net pension obligation. Which measure of pension obligation most closely represents the economic value of the pension liability? Which measure(s) is currently required by GAAP in order to compute pension cost and net pension liability for balance sheet purposes? Do you consider GE's pension plan to be overfunded or underfunded? Explain.

Exhibit A
Supplementary Pension Disclosures

General Electric Company and Consolidated Subsidiaries

Pensions and Other Retiree Benefits

General Electric and its consolidated affiliates sponsor a number of pension plans. The costs of these plans were $496 million in 1985, $603 million in 1984 and $643 million in 1983.

General Electric Pension Plan (the "Pension Plan") is the most significant pension plan and substantially all employees in the United States are participants. The projected unit credit method, which recognizes the effect of future compensation and service of employees, is used to determine trust funding and pension cost. Changes in pension benefits allocable to previous service of employees give rise to prior-service costs which are amortized over 20 years. Gains and losses which occur because actual experience differs from amounts assumed are amortized over 15 years.

Pension Plan benefits are funded through the General Electric Pension Trust (the "Trust"). The "carrying value" of investments is amortized cost plus recognition of appreciation in the common stock portfolio on a systematic basis which does not give undue weight to short-term market fluctuations. Investment income of the Trust, including systematic recognition of common stock appreciation, as a percentage of the average carrying value of the portfolio was 11.5% in 1985, 10.3% in 1984 and 10.8% in 1983.

A comparison of the present value of Pension Plan benefits with carrying value of Trust assets is shown in the table below.

General Electric Pension Plan December 31 (in millions)	1985	1984	1983
Present value of benefits attributed to employee service to date, recognizing projected compensation and service	$11,598	$11,116	$10,604
Carrying value of Trust assets	10,924	9,704	8,590
Unfunded benefit obligation	$ 674	$ 1,412	$ 2,014
Persons receiving pensions at year end	111,200	103,800	97,800

The funding program and Company cost determination for the Pension Plan use 8.0% (7.5% in 1984 and 1983) as the estimated rate of future Trust income, except for the effect of a dedicated portfolio. This fixed-income portfolio, consisting of securities backed by the U.S. Treasury, was dedicated in 1984 to the payment of certain future pension benefits. The carrying value of Trust assets at the end of 1985 included $935 million for this portfolio. The 13.4% rate of return on the dedicated portfolio was a factor in determining the present value of plan benefits.

The change in the estimated rate of future Trust income, the full-year impact of the dedication, and amortization of continued favorable Trust income experience were the principal causes of the 1985 reduction in pension costs. Pension cost as a percentage of compensation was 5.9% in 1985 (6.9% in 1984 and 8.1% in 1983).

. . . In addition, the table below shows the current value of Trust assets plus accruals. General Electric believes funding comparisons for the Pension Plan shown earlier in this note are more realistic because the benefit amounts include the expected effect of future compensation and service, and because Trust assets are valued on a basis which reduces the impact of short-term market fluctuations. The interest rate assumptions used in determining the present value of benefits are the same as discussed previously for the Pension Plan.

Exhibit A continued

General Electric Pension Plan and Supplementary Pension Plan
December 31 (in millions)

	1985	1984	1983
SFAS 36 estimated present value of accumulated plan benefits:			
Vested benefits	$ 8,764	$ 8,331	$ 7,939
Non-vested benefits	744	709	557
Total accumulated benefits	$ 9,508	$ 9,040	$ 8,496
Current value of Trust assets plus accruals	$14,727	$11,695	$10,172

The change in the estimated rate of future Trust income in 1985 reduced the present value of total accumulated benefits by $457 million. Partially offsetting this reduction was the impact of 1985 Plan amendments. The current value of Trust assets includes unrecognized appreciation of $3,438 million, principally resulting from strong investment market performance during the last four years.

Condensed financial statements for the General Electric Pension Trust, which are not consolidated with those of the Company, follow.

General Electric Pension Trust
Net Assets at Current Value
December 31 (in millions)

	1985	1984	1983
U.S. government obligations and guarantees	$ 2,785	$ 2,238	$2,004
Corporate bonds and notes	1,770	1,076	1,037
Real estate and mortgages	1,660	1,976	1,341
Common stocks and other equity securities	7,541	5,782	5,180
	13,756	11,072	9,562
Cash and short-term investments	514	145	256
Other assets — net	92	133	68
Net assets	$14,362	$11,350	$9,886

Change in Net Assets at Current Value
For the Year (in millions)

	1985	1984	1983
Net assets at January 1	$11,350	$ 9,886	$8,440
Company contributions	434	503	545
Employee contributions	107	101	87
Investment income	1,176	931	857
Benefits paid	(497)	(421)	(376)
Unrecognized portion of change in current value	1,792	350	333
Net assets at December 31	$14,362	$11,350	$9,886

Source: General Electric Company, *Annual Report,* 1985.

(b) Note that the percentage relationship between pension cost and compensation expense has declined considerably over the past few years. What factors have likely caused this decline? Do you agree with

Exhibit B
Selected Financial Information

General Electric Company and Consolidated Subsidiaries

Total assets, December 31, 1985	$26.432 billion
Total liabilities, December 31, 1985	12.528 billion
Stockholders' equity, December 31, 1985	13.904 billion
Net income, 1985	2.336 billion

the suggestion by some analysts that a proper matching of pension costs would attempt to reflect a stable percentage relationship between these two elements? Explain.

(c) The rate of discount used to obtain the present value of accumulated plan benefits was raised from 7½% in 1984 to 8% in 1985, and this relatively minor increase caused the firm's obligation to be reduced by $457 million. What factors cause firms to change the rate of discount used in computing previous obligations? Should management retain discretion to change discount rates? Are pension disclosures sufficiently detailed to allow meaningful comparisons of pension costs and liabilities if the firms to be compared are using different rates of discount? Is there an economic effect on GE's shareholders when changes in discount rates affect the valuation of pension obligations? Explain.

(d) The listing of pension plan assets accompanies GE's supplementary disclosures. Although GAAP currently do not permit consolidation of the sponsoring firm and its pension plans, securities analysts often argue that consolidation would produce a more meaningful set of financial statements. Determine how each of the following financial statement relationships would change if General Electric Company and its pension plan were to be consolidated:

(1) Total assets, December 31, 1985
(2) Total liabilities, December 31, 1985
(3) Shareholders' equity, December 31, 1985
(4) Net income, 1985
(5) Return on assets (ratio of net income to assets)
(6) Return on shareholders' equity
(7) Debt-to-total assets ratio

(Note that your computations require that you make decisions concerning the valuation of pension plan assets and obligations and decisions about which items to include in measurement of pension plan income.)

11

Accounting for Price Changes and Foreign Operations

Τhis chapter consists of two related parts: accounting for price changes and accounting for foreign operations. In the United States, continuing inflation has impaired the usefulness of the data reported on company financial statements and has caused the FASB to suggest that firms make supplemental reporting disclosures to reveal the impact of changing prices on their operations. The first part of the chapter examines the methods that may be used to adjust for changes in the general price level, the methods for estimating and reporting changes in current costs, and the supplementary disclosures suggested by the FASB to deal with the effects of changing prices.

Internationally, differences in rates of inflation among nations have been a major cause of changes in foreign currency exchange rates. Foreign currency financial statements must often be translated into U.S. dollars to permit consolidation of these statements with those of U.S. firms. The second part of this chapter discusses and evaluates financial reporting practices related to the translation of foreign currency financial statements.

CHANGING PRICE DISCLOSURES

Accounting for Price Changes: Background

Until recently, the accounting profession and the Securities and Exchange Commission have clung tenaciously to the cost principle. This has occurred despite the fact that spiraling inflation has substantially lessened the significance of the data reported on company financial statements. As prices rise, the replacement of consumed assets becomes more and more costly. Because a financial reporting system based on historical costs ignores these higher prices, it may generate misleading signals that indicate that the depreciation charges to income and the rates of return on investment are sufficient to maintain the stock of capital and provide for growth. Consequently, there has been mounting pressure to adjust the traditional financial reporting system so that it will better reflect the impact of changing prices.

In 1979, the FASB began to require that large, publicly held companies that met certain size tests report supplemental financial information on both a constant dollar and a current cost basis. **Constant dollar reports** restate historical cost financial statements to adjust for changes in the *general* level of prices. Although the attribute measured (measurement base) is still historical cost, the information is expressed in terms of dollars of equal purchasing power, or constant dollars. **Current cost reports** restate historical cost financial statements to adjust for changes in *specific* prices of assets owned by a firm. The attribute measured is changed from historical cost to current cost. The FASB's requirements were intended as an experiment to determine whether companies could prepare inflation-adjusted information with reasonable reliability, and whether investors, creditors, and others would find the information useful. Late in 1984 the FASB revised the reporting rules and reduced the amount of constant dollar information that was required for disclosure. Then, in late 1986 the FASB concluded that the supplementary disclosures involving changing prices should be encouraged, but should no longer be required.

Our discussion of accounting for changing prices will begin by describing and evaluating the methods used to adjust nominal dollar amounts for changes in the general price level (inflation or deflation). Next, methods of estimating and reporting changes in current costs will be discussed and evaluated. Finally, the FASB's suggested supplementary disclosures concerning the effects of changing prices will be illustrated. The discussion ends with an overall evaluation of the impact of changing price disclosures.

Constant Dollar Accounting

Constant dollar adjustments convert the historical costs of assets to dollars having the same purchasing power. In effect, historical cost is redefined (rather than abandoned) as a basis for accounting. Under constant dollar accounting, historical cost is measured as the amount of purchasing power invested, rather than as the amount of dollars invested. The amount of dollars invested in an asset is referred to as the **nominal dollar** cost of the asset.

Constant dollar disclosures are of interest to managers for several reasons. Among those reasons is the fact that constant dollar disclosures are required in certain high-inflation economies in South America and the Middle East, either in the primary financial statements or as supplementary disclosures to those financial statements. Also, while constant dollar disclosures are no longer required for U.S. firms, they are still encouraged by the FASB, and some managers may consider constant dollar information to be a useful way of communicating the effects of inflation to investors.

The adjustment of nominal dollar accounting numbers to reflect inflation entails the use of **price indexes** that are designed to measure changes in purchasing power. In addition, it is necessary to distinguish between monetary and nonmonetary items in the financial statements because these types of items are affected differently by inflation.

Price indexes of purchasing power changes The U.S. Government publishes a number of indexes designed to measure price changes in different sectors of the economy. These indexes are of two general types: (1) highly aggregated indexes designed to measure price levels for a wide array of goods and services and (2) indexes of changes in specific, narrowly defined categories of goods or services. The **broadly based indexes** are used to gauge overall changes in the purchasing power of money—inflation or deflation. The **specific indexes,** by contrast, are designed to measure price changes for specific types of assets.

Companies use the **Consumer Price Index for All Urban Consumers (CPI-U)** to convert nominal dollar amounts into their constant dollar equivalents. The CPI-U is widely used to determine the direction and intensity of changes in the cost of living from period to period. It embodies a typical "market basket" of expenditures presumed to be representative of an average U.S. family. Exhibit 11-1 shows the average annual levels of the CPI-U over a twenty-year period, beginning in 1966.

These CPI-U annual averages depict the price level for any given year relative to the **base year** of 1967, which is represented by an index number of 100. To understand how the index works, consider an illustration. The average index for 1978 is 195.4, indicating that in 1978 it required $1.954 to purchase the same quantity of goods and services that cost $1.00 in 1967.

The formula used to adjust nominal dollar amounts to their current purchasing power under constant dollar accounting is

$$\text{Constant Dollar Amount} = \frac{\text{Nominal Dollar}}{\text{Cost}} \times \frac{\text{Current Price Index}}{\text{Price Index at}}$$

To use the formula, assume that a parcel of land is purchased in 1977 for $20,000. Adjustment of these 1977 dollars to the purchasing power of 1982 dol-

Exhibit 11-1

**Average Consumer Price Index
for All Urban Consumers (CPI-U)**

Year	Index	Year	Index
1966	97.2	1976	170.5
1967*	100.0	1977	181.5
1968	104.2	1978	195.4
1969	109.8	1979	217.4
1970	116.3	1980	246.8
1971	121.3	1981	272.4
1972	125.3	1982	289.1
1973	133.1	1983	298.4
1974	147.7	1984	311.1
1975	161.2	1985	322.2

Source: U.S. Department of Labor.
*Base year.

lars using CPI-U annual averages from Exhibit 11-1 is calculated as follows:

$$\text{Constant Dollar Amount} = \$20,000 \times \frac{289.1}{181.5}$$
$$= \$20,000 \times 1.593$$
$$= \$31,860$$

This means that $31,860 in 1982 had the same general purchasing power as did $20,000 in 1977.

Monetary versus nonmonetary items   **Monetary items** are claims (assets) or obligations (liabilities) that are fixed in dollar amount. The amount of cash to be received from a particular monetary asset (accounts or notes receivable, for example) or the amount of cash to be paid to satisfy a monetary liability (bonds payable, for instance) is not altered by changes in the value of the dollar. Examples of monetary assets include cash, demand bank deposits, accounts and notes receivable, allowances for bad debts, refundable deposits, prepaid interest, the cash surrender value of life insurance, and investments in bonds. Examples of monetary liabilities include accounts and notes payable, accrued expenses payable, bonds payable, cash dividends payable, payables under long-term leases, pension costs payable, refundable deposits, and other debts.

Nonmonetary items are those items whose prices are not fixed in numbers of dollars. Examples of nonmonetary items include inventories, plant and equipment, prepaid expenses other than interest, securities investments, capital stock, and retained earnings. Only nonmonetary items are adjusted for changes in the purchasing power of the dollar. A monetary item, such as cash, is already stated on the balance sheet in terms of the latest current purchasing power.

An important distinction between monetary and nonmonetary items is that the holding of monetary items at the time that a change in the general price level occurs results in a **monetary gain or loss,** while the holding of nonmonetary items does not. The reason for this difference is that the holding of monetary assets during a rise in the general price level means that cash, or a fixed amount of cash to be received or paid, will buy fewer goods and services as time passes. The same rise in the general price level will benefit debtors as the burden of debt shrinks, since the debt can be paid off with cheaper dollars.[1]

The carrying value of nonmonetary assets must be adjusted for changes in the purchasing power of the dollar in order to reflect the constant dollar equivalent of the purchasing power invested in those assets.

Constant dollar restatements illustrated   Exhibit 11-2 shows how the nominal dollar cost of a factory building acquired in 1978, when the price index was 195.4, would be restated to constant dollars in 1985, when the price index was 322.2.

It is important to recognize that the conversion of nominal dollars to constant dollars (as shown in Exhibit 11-2) is *not* a departure from historical cost and does not entail a revaluation of the factory building. Rather, the historical cost of the asset has merely been restated in terms of purchasing power invested; it required $2,143,700 in 1985 to purchase the "market basket" of goods and services that cost $1,300,000 in 1978. In addition, note that the accumulated depreciation also is adjusted to constant dollars, using the historical price index

Exhibit 11-2
Nominal Dollars and Constant Dollars of 1985 Purchasing Power

Factory Building and Accumulated Depreciation

	Nominal Dollars	Conversion Factor*	Constant Dollars
Factory building			
Original cost	$1,300,000	1.649	$2,143,700
Accumulated depreciation	− 550,000	1.649	− 906,950
Book value	$ 750,000		$1,236,750

$$*\frac{\text{1985 Price Index}}{\text{1978 Price Index}} = \frac{322.2}{195.4} = 1.649$$

---

[1]In an economic sense, it is only *unanticipated* increases in inflation that benefit debtors, because fully anticipated inflation is reflected in the nominal interest rate on the debt.

at the date of acquisition of the building. As will be shown below, the depreciation and amortization expenses reported on the income statement will also require adjustment to constant dollars.

Purchasing power gains and losses illustrated The impact of monetary gains and losses on a particular firm depends on two factors. The first factor is the amount of monetary assets and liabilities involved; the second factor is the change in the general price level that has occurred from the date that the asset or liability arises to the current balance sheet date. If the general price level has increased, firms with a significant amount of monetary debt outstanding (utilities or airlines) will normally have monetary gains, while firms with large cash and receivable balances and little debt (banks or finance companies) will sustain monetary losses. The method for calculating monetary gains or losses is illustrated in Exhibit 11-3.

The calculations in Exhibit 11-3 show that during inflationary periods firms with an average net monetary liability position (cases A and C) report purchasing power gains, while firms with an average net monetary asset position (case B) report purchasing power losses. If we presume that the inflation rate was steady throughout the period and that any changes in a firm's net monetary position occurred evenly throughout the year, then it is appropriate to use the average monetary position in computing the purchasing power gain or loss.

Constant dollar balance sheet The **constant dollar balance sheet** is prepared by converting the nominal dollar historical costs of all elements of the balance sheet into dollars that have the same purchasing power. Usually, the purchasing power of the dollar at the date of the latest balance sheet is used for computing constant dollar amounts. Monetary assets and liabilities at that date do not require any conversion because they are already stated in dollars of current purchasing power.

Exhibit 11-4 illustrates the conversion from a nominal dollar to a constant dollar balance sheet, using dollars of current (year-end) purchasing power. Notice that various relationships among the elements in the balance sheet are affected by constant dollar conversions. The illustration in Exhibit 11-4 is based on the assumption that the dollar has been declining in purchasing power. Consequently, the relative amounts of nonmonetary assets and paid-in capital are larger in the constant dollar balance sheet than in the nominal dollar balance sheet. Specifically, before conversion, monetary assets constituted 11.3 percent of total assets ($3,000/$26,500); after the conversion the percentage is 7.8 ($3,000/$38,221). Before conversion, debt equaled 45.3 percent of total assets ($12,000/$26,500); after conversion to constant dollars, the debt percentage falls to 31.4 ($12,000/$38,221). It is up to the analyst to decide which set of relationships (before or after conversion) is more meaningful for investment analysis.

Constant dollar income statement The **constant dollar income statement** is prepared by converting the nominal dollar amounts into dollars having a

Exhibit 11-3

Purchasing Power Gains and Losses: Three Illustrations

(In all cases, assume that the inflation rate is 9% for the year.)

CASE A: Net Monetary Liability Position throughout the Year

	1989	
	January 1	**December 31**
Monetary assets	$12,000	$ 7,000
Monetary liabilities	(14,000)	(15,000)
Net monetary position	$(2,000)	$(8,000)

Average net monetary position = 1/2 [$(2,000) + $(8,000)]
= $(5,000)
Purchasing power gain: 9% × $5,000 = $450

CASE B: Net Monetary Asset Position throughout the Year

	1989	
	January 1	**December 31**
Monetary assets	$11,000	$ 9,000
Monetary liabilities	(5,000)	(6,000)
Net monetary position	$ 6,000	$ 3,000

Average net monetary position = 1/2 [$6,000 + $3,000]
= $4,500
Purchasing power loss: 9% × $4,500 = $405

CASE C: Change from Net Monetary Asset to Net Monetary Liability Position

	1989	
	January 1	**December 31**
Monetary assets	$16,000	$24,000
Monetary liabilities	(12,000)	(32,000)
Net monetary position	$ 4,000	$(8,000)

Average net monetary position = 1/2 [$4,000 + $(8,000)]
= $(2,000)
Purchasing power gain: 9% × $2,000 = $180

---

purchasing power equal to the average level of the CPI-U index during the current year.[2]

Cost of goods sold and depreciation expense must be restated to constant dollars because they represent dollars spent in previous years, and the

---

[2]Because the constant dollar balance sheet is stated in year-end dollars, it would be more consistent to convert the revenues and expenses to year-end dollars. To reduce the number of items that require conversion, however, the FASB has recommended the use of the average level of the CPI-U index during the year. Consequently, for most firms, no adjustment is needed for revenues and expenses that are received or incurred evenly throughout the year.

Exhibit 11-4

Conversion of Nominal Dollar to Constant Dollar Balance Sheet

Background: The CPI-U at the balance sheet date is 405. The firm's plant and equipment were acquired when the CPI-U was 270, and the land was acquired when the CPI-U was 240. The inventory was purchased during the last quarter of the year, when the average CPI-U was 390. The firm's common stock was issued when the CPI-U was 180.

	Nominal Dollars (in thousands)	Conversion Factor*	Constant Dollars (in thousands)
Monetary Assets	$ 3,000	405/405	$ 3,000
Inventory	2,500	405/390	2,596
Plant and Equipment	15,000	405/270	22,500
Land	6,000	405/240	10,125
Total Assets	$26,500		$38,221
Monetary Liabilities	$12,000	405/405	$12,000
Common Stock	11,000	405/180	24,750
Retained Earnings	3,500		1,471[†]
Total Liabilities and Equity	$26,500		$38,221

*Conversion Factor = $\dfrac{\text{Price Index at the Balance Sheet Date}}{\text{Price Index When Item Originated}}$

[†]For illustrative purposes, we have elected simply to "plug in" this figure. A detailed calculation is beyond the scope of this discussion.

purchasing power of the dollar has subsequently changed. Sales revenue and most operating expenses other than depreciation and cost of goods sold involve recent receipts or expenditures of cash, and these items, therefore, are not adjusted. Exhibit 11-5 shows how income from continuing operations based on nominal dollars is converted to constant dollar income. For illustrative purposes, we have assumed that the firm had monetary assets equal to monetary liabilities for the year as a whole (that is, the firm had a zero average net monetary asset balance). If this assumption were not made, a purchasing power gain or loss would also be reported, as illustrated earlier.

Observe that constant dollar adjustments can have a substantial effect on the amount of reported income and also on key relationships within the income statement. On a nominal dollar basis, income is $300,000. Conversion to constant dollars results in a reported loss of $773,200. Because constant dollar conversions are not permitted for income tax purposes, the constant dollar income statement shows a tax expense of $200,000, even though the firm has a pretax loss on a constant dollar basis of $573,200. The major differences between the nominal dollar and the constant dollar income statements are due to depreciation and amortization of noncurrent assets (depreciation expense, in Exhibit 11-5). Generally, over periods of sustained inflation, constant dollar

Exhibit 11-5

Conversion of Nominal Dollar to Constant Dollar Income Statement

Background: The firm's plant and equipment were acquired when the CPI-U was 270. FIFO costing is used for inventories. The beginning and ending inventories were produced in the last quarter of 19X1 and 19X2, when the average CPI-U's were 360 and 390, respectively. The average CPI-U during 19X2 was 375. The tax rate on nominal dollar income is 40%.

	Nominal Dollars (in thousands)	Conversion Factor*	Constant Dollars (in thousands)
Sales	$12,000	375/375	$12,000.0
Cost of goods sold			
Beginning inventory	$ 1,500	375/360	$ 1,562.5
Additions	5,500	375/375	5,500.0
Ending inventory	(1,000)	375/390	(961.5)
Cost of goods sold	$ 6,000		$ 6,101.0
Gross margin	$ 6,000		$ 5,899.0
Depreciation expense, plant and equipment	(2,500)	375/270	(3,472.2)
Other expenses	(3,000)	375/375	(3,000.0)
Income (loss) before tax	$ 500		$ (573.2)
Income tax expense	(200)		(200.0)
Net income (loss)	$ 300		$ (773.2)

Note: If the firm had either net monetary assets or net monetary liabilities, a purchasing power loss or gain (calculated as discussed earlier) would also appear on the income statement.

$$*\text{Conversion Factor} = \frac{\text{Average Price Index in Current Period}}{\text{Price Index When Item Originated}}$$

adjustments will have the greatest effects on firms with substantial amounts of older noncurrent assets.

Impact of constant dollar adjustments on specific firms   Exhibit 11-6 compares nominal dollar and constant dollar incomes for selected U.S. firms during 1980—a year in which the United States had a high rate of inflation. All of the firms show decreases in income (or increased losses), and in some cases nominal dollar profits become constant dollar losses. Capital-intensive firms, such as American Telephone and Telegraph, show the largest declines. For several firms, constant dollar income plus monetary gains exceeds nominal dollar income. Generally, the effect of constant dollar adjustments on the profits of individual firms depends on several factors.

   1. *Capital intensity.*   Firms that use relatively high amounts of noncurrent assets in their operations are referred to as *capital intensive*. In such firms, depreciation charges are large relative to other expenses and revenues. (Because depreciation expense must be restated as a constant dollar amount, conversion to constant dollars is likely to substantially reduce net income if inflation persists.)

Exhibit 11-6

Income Reported in Nominal and Constant Dollars
for Selected Companies for the Year 1980

| | Income from Continuing Operations | | |
| | (dollars in millions) | | |
	(1) Nominal Dollars	(2) Constant Dollars*	(3) Monetary Gain (loss)
Allied Chemical	$ 289	$ 111	$ 182
American Can	86	(51)	100
American Motors	(155)	(242)	32
American Telephone and Telegraph	6,080	951	6,969
Baltimore Gas and Electric	126	50	161
Bethlehem Steel	121	(176)	171
DuPont	716	236	85
Florida Power and Light	198	36	374
Ford	(1,543)	(2,703)	675
General Electric	1,409	1,064	(209)
General Motors	2,892	1,776	182
International Telephone and Telegraph	701	313	329
Johnson and Johnson	352	298	(43)
Mead	129	114	90
Monsanto	331	170	123
National Can	93	52	26
National Cash Register	235	120	(34)
Radio Corporation of America	315	159	328
Revlon	192	135	22
U.S. Steel	607	24	268
Weyerhaeuser	321	8	178
Westinghouse	403	221	(113)

Sources: Selected annual reports, 1980.

*Excluding monetary gain or loss, which is shown in column (3).

2. *Age of property, plant, and equipment.* Even a modest rate of annual inflation will compound over time to create large differences between nominal dollar and constant dollar costs. For example, a firm with depreciable assets having an average age of 15 years and an average annual inflation rate of 7 percent would need to increase its depreciation charges by over 175 percent in reporting constant dollar amounts.

3. *Inventory costing method.* Firms that use LIFO may report large increases in inventory in making constant dollar disclosures because the LIFO layers may date back many years. The cost-of-goods-sold calculations of most firms are unlikely to be strongly affected by constant dollar adjustments, however, because both the beginning and ending inventories are restated.

4. *Monetary position.*   Firms that rely heavily on debt financing will have net monetary liabilities and, therefore, will report purchasing power gains in periods of inflation. Firms with little outstanding debt and substantial investments in monetary assets will report purchasing power losses during such periods.

Evaluation of constant dollar accounting   The practical effects of constant dollar disclosures depend on (1) the quality of accounting information provided to report users and (2) the impact such disclosures have on decisions made by firm managers, government regulators, and taxing authorities.

Constant dollar adjustments merely restate nominal dollar historical costs in terms of current purchasing power dollars. For this reason, most of the deficiencies associated with the historical cost concept persist in the constant dollar model; that is to say, constant dollar reports do little to address the controversies in accounting for inventories, fixed assets, debt, or stockholders' equity discussed in earlier chapters.

The primary effect of constant dollar disclosures is to improve the internal coherence of historical cost data by restating the dollar amounts reported to correct for general purchasing power changes. In this way, constant dollar accounting may provide a sounder basis for interperiod and intercompany comparisons than do nominal dollar reports.

Current Cost Accounting

Current cost adjustments revalue assets at current cost using one of several methods described below. Unlike constant dollar accounting, current cost accounting involves a departure from historical cost. (Recall that constant dollar accounting adheres to the historical cost concept, but redefines historical cost in terms of invested purchasing power.) The current cost of an asset may be determined using one of the following alternatives:

1. Find the present cost of a used asset that is of the same age and in the same condition as the asset owned.
2. Find the present cost of a new asset that has the same service potential as the used asset had when it was new (the present cost of the asset *as if* it were new), less an allowance for depreciation.
3. Find the present cost of a new asset with a different service potential, and adjust for the value of the differences in service potential due to differences in useful life, output capacity, nature of service, and operating costs, less an allowance for depreciation.

The approach described in alternative 1 depends on the existence of a well-functioning market for used assets. This procedure may be practical in the case of such assets as automobiles and airplanes. In most cases, however, fixed assets used in the business are so highly specialized and are used in such diverse ways that it is difficult to obtain relevant price data from the second-hand market. The methods described in alternatives 2 and 3 are referred to as reproduction cost and replacement cost, respectively. The results obtained under these two valuation methods may differ significantly.

The FASB permits current costs to be estimated using either direct prices or indexation. When index numbers are utilized to develop current costs, the nominal dollar amounts are translated into current costs by the use of the following conversion factor:

$$\text{Conversion Factor} = \frac{\text{Specific Index at Reporting Date}}{\text{Specific Index at Acquisition Date}}$$

This conversion factor is similar to that used in making constant dollar adjustments, except that the current cost conversion factor employs specific price indexes pertaining to the type of asset whose value is being restated. A variety of appropriate price indexes are currently published by trade and professional journals, leading appraisal firms, and government agencies.

Reproduction versus replacement cost   **Reproduction cost** represents the current cost to replicate an existing asset in its present condition and age. If the asset was constructed internally, the original cost inputs (labor, materials, and overhead) are restated in current cost terms. If the asset was purchased and there has been no technological obsolescence, the current cost is the cost of a potential replacement for the existing asset, less accumulated depreciation.

Replacement cost is equivalent to the cost of a new asset (one that utilizes the most advanced technology available) of the same type as an existing asset, adjusted for depreciation and any operating inferiority (obsolescence) of the existing asset. The difference between reproduction and replacement cost is due to some or all of the following factors:

1. *Improvements in technology.*   Improved technology results in increased productivity per invested dollar of newer assets. (Various indexes developed by government agencies and engineering appraisal firms reflect estimated technological improvements in different types of plants and equipment over time.)
2. *Market size.*   The market for the output of the asset may be less than originally anticipated, resulting in long-term excess capacity.
3. *Economies of scale.*   The asset may be saddled with an excessive operating cost penalty because of uneconomical size compared with newer assets.

In addition to the problems that may arise in determining the current cost of depreciable fixed assets, technical difficulties may also be encountered in adjusting the cost of goods sold amount for the excess of the current cost of inventories sold over their acquisition cost. Since numerous transactions of this sort occur throughout the year, in most cases it would be impractical to make this adjustment for each transaction. The FASB recognized this problem by accepting cost of goods sold on a LIFO basis as a reasonable approximation of the current replacement cost of inventories sold, provided there has not been a LIFO liquidation of lower-cost inventory layers purchased earlier. The current cost of inventories sold may also be estimated by the use of price indexes and statistical samples.

Current cost balance sheet The **current cost balance sheet** is prepared by revaluing each of the assets and liabilities at their present cost at the balance sheet date, using one of the approaches described earlier. Monetary assets and liabilities are valued at their market values at the balance sheet date. The market values of long-term receivables and payables will vary as interest rates change, and it is possible that market values and nominal dollar (historical cost) valuations will differ substantially. The market values of short-term receivables and payables are likely to equal their nominal dollar carrying values.

Exhibit 11-7 compares the nominal dollar and current cost balance sheets for the firm considered earlier in the discussion involving the constant dollar balance sheet (refer to Exhibit 11-4). Because current cost is a departure from historical cost, the assets and liabilities are *revalued,* not *converted* (as in the constant dollar balance sheet). The current cost amounts in Exhibit 11-7 imply that for this firm the current cost of nonmonetary assets exceeds their nominal dollar amounts. Also, the current costs (market value) of monetary assets and liabilities are below their nominal dollar values, which implies that the market rates of interest have risen since the dates on which these items originated.

For the firm described in Exhibit 11-7, the current cost valuation (in thousands) of net assets—$32,800 ($43,000 assets, less $10,200 liabilities)—exceeds the nominal dollar valuation of net assets—$14,500 ($26,500 assets, less $12,000

Exhibit 11-7

Comparison of Nominal Dollar and Current Cost Balance Sheets

	Nominal Dollars (in thousands)	Current Costs (in thousands)*
Monetary Assets	$ 3,000	$ 2,800
Inventory	2,500	2,900
Plant and Equipment	15,000	28,300
Land	6,000	9,000
Total Assets	$26,500	$43,000
Monetary Liabilities	$12,000	$10,200
Common Stock	11,000	11,000
Retained Earnings	3,500	21,800
Total Liabilities and Equity	$26,500	$43,000

*The amounts reported as current costs are simply assumed for purposes of illustration and would ordinarily be obtained by reference to current market values, or by applying other techniques described in this chapter.

liabilities). This difference — $18,300 ($32,800 less $14,500) — represents a **holding gain.** The holding gain is *unrealized* to the extent that the related assets (or liabilities) have not been sold or consumed (or repaid) at the balance sheet date. This unrealized holding gain has been *recognized* in net income, however, in the periods in which the current cost changes have occurred. The next section will illustrate the treatment of holding gains and losses in the current cost income statement.

The percentage relationships among the elements in the current cost balance sheet differ from those in the nominal dollar balance sheet and from those in the constant dollar balance sheet (Exhibit 11-4). The analyst must decide which relationships to use for purposes of investment analysis.

Current cost income statement The **current cost income statement** is prepared by restating each of the expenses on the income statement at its current cost of replacement as of the date of incurrence. This reflects the presumption that in order for a firm's operations to be profitable, revenues must be adequate to replace all resources consumed, at current costs of replacement.

Exhibit 11-8 compares the nominal dollar and current cost income statements for the firm considered earlier in connection with the constant dollar income statement (refer to Exhibit 11-5).[3] Income (loss) before tax is computed using the current costs of resources consumed in operations. In addition, income is affected by changes in the current cost of assets not yet consumed or sold and liabilities that remain outstanding at year-end. These changes in current cost are referred to as "unrealized holding gains and losses." Analysts maintain different interpretations of such holding gains and losses. Some argue that an increase in the current cost of net assets is beneficial to the firm because the net assets have been obtained at costs below their current values. Other analysts argue that such increases in current costs are potentially harmful to the firm because revenues may fail to increase sufficiently to cover the higher costs. Often, analysts attempt to remove the portion of unrealized holding gains that is due to inflation, in order to determine the "real" amount of holding gain. This diversity of treatment emphasizes the fact that there is little consensus concerning either the concept or the usefulness of current cost measurements of income.

Advantages of current cost accounting Proponents of current cost accounting contend that the calculation and reporting of the current cost of assets and expenses results in more realistic and, hence, more useful information. The various benefits attributed to current cost accounting are discussed below.

1. *Prediction.* Financial reports are used by investors and creditors to predict future earnings and cash flows. In conventional accounting, operating

---

[3]Accounting theorists have proposed a wide variety of income measurements and income statement formats to incorporate current cost concepts. We have opted in this discussion to provide a relatively simple version of current cost income, adequate to provide the reader with sufficient background to evaluate the FASB's reporting suggestions, which are discussed later in the chapter.

Exhibit 11-8

Comparison of Nominal Dollar and Current Cost Income Statements

	Nominal Dollars (in thousands)	Current Costs (in thousands)
Sales	$12,000	$12,000
Cost of goods sold	6,000	7,200
Gross margin	$ 6,000	$ 4,800
Depreciation expense, plant and equipment	(2,500)	(3,500)
Other expenses	(3,000)	(3,000)
Income (loss) before tax	$ 500	$(1,700)
Income tax expense	(200)	(200)
Current period's holding gain or loss		
Realized*	–	2,200
Unrealized†	–	7,800
Net income	$ 300	$ 8,100

*Realized holding gains represent the increase during the period of current costs of net assets that have been *consumed or sold* during the period. Note that the income (loss) before tax is $2,200 lower on the current cost income statement. This implies that the firm realized holding gains of $2,200 during the period. For simplicity, we are assuming that these current cost increases occurred in the current period.

†Unrealized holding gains represent the increase during the period of current costs of net assets that are *on hand* at the end of the period.

income emerges from a matching of revenues with historical rather than current costs. With constantly rising prices, conventional accounting will result in higher reported operating income because historical costs are below current costs. This may create false impressions about a company's earning power.

2. *The effects on income claimants.* The income reported under historical cost accounting during periods of rising prices may induce stockholders and labor unions to exert pressure on corporate management for higher dividends and wage payments, respectively. Moreover, taxing authorities base their calculations on reported income (adjusted for differences between generally accepted accounting principles and tax accounting). These demands and expectations from income claimants may impede a company's capacity to replace its consumed capital at current prices.

3. *Interfirm comparisons.* Intercompany comparisons are essential in investment decisions. However, financial data for different companies are difficult to interpret when companies have varying capital intensities and the age and condition of their plants and equipment are dissimilar. When these assets and depreciation allowances are restated at current cost, interfirm comparisons and financial ratio analysis become more meaningful. A current cost system also eliminates income statement and balance sheet variations caused by disparate inventory cost flow assumptions (LIFO versus FIFO, for example).

Disadvantages of current cost accounting   In spite of the potential advantages outlined above, some firms' managers question the usefulness of current cost disclosures. Exhibit 11-9 shows a portion of the commentary included by Allied Signal Corporation in its 1984 current cost disclosures.

It is true that current cost disclosures depend on more subjective measurements than does the transactional type of evidence associated with historical costs. Whether this subjectivity negates the advantages of current costs is a question of concern to the accounting profession and the financial community.

Present Disclosures for Changing Prices

Rather than recommend a comprehensive adjustment of conventional financial statements to reflect the effects of price changes, the FASB suggests a piecemeal approach to price change disclosures. The piecemeal supplementary disclosures may be classified as one of two types: (1) the effects of price changes on specific elements of the current year's financial statements or (2) a five-year comparison of selected financial data. Each of these types of disclosures will be illustrated using the supplementary disclosures for changing prices contained in the 1985 annual report of Safeway Stores, Inc.

Effects of changing prices on specific elements of the current year's financial statements   The FASB recommends that the following supplemental information be reported for the current year:

1. Income from continuing operations on a current cost basis.

Exhibit 11-9

Limitations of Current Cost Disclosures

Allied Signal Corporation

The Company's financial statements are presented on the basis of historical (actual) costs. Such financial statements, however, do not reflect the decline in the purchasing power of the dollar during inflationary periods. The Financial Accounting Standards Board requires the presentation of information reflecting the changes in the prices of specific goods and services (current cost method) on the Company's historical financial data. The accompanying supplemental data is set forth in accordance with this requirement and is believed by the Company to have been prepared on a reasonable basis; however, much of the FASB-mandated data in this section lacks the relevance and reliability attributes which characterize historical accounting information. The application of indexes to the Company's varied fixed assets requires numerous estimates and assumptions which raises a question as to the usefulness of the information developed. Management cautions users of this information that the data is of limited value for decision-making purposes.

Source: Allied Signal Corporation, *Annual Report*, 1984.

2. Gain or loss from the change in purchasing power of net monetary assets or liabilities.
3. Depreciation and amortization, and cost of goods sold on a current cost basis.
4. Increase during the period in the current costs of inventories and property, and an adjustment of the current cost increase for the effect of general inflation.
5. The current cost at year-end of merchandise inventories and net property.

Exhibit 11-10 contains Safeway's supplementary disclosures related to the current year's financial statements, as well as management's explanations of the items disclosed. Note the following relationships:

1. Net income reported in the firm's primary financial statements was $231 million in 1985. If expenses were restated to current cost, income would decline to $164 million, due mainly to higher current costs of depreciation and amortization.
2. The provision for income taxes is not restated because current cost adjustments are not deductible for tax purposes. Accordingly, Safeway reports an average income tax rate of 34.6 percent ($122 million/ $353 million) based on historical cost and a tax rate of 42.6 percent ($122 million/$286 million) based on current costs.
3. Because Safeway is a net monetary debtor in a period of general inflation, there is a substantial ($103 million) purchasing power gain reported.
4. Management's commentary reveals that the current costs of inventory and property increased by $418.7 million. This figure exceeds the effect of general inflation, which would have increased asset costs by $225.4 million. The difference of $193.3 million ($418.7 − $225.4) is often referred to as a **holding gain, net of inflation.**

As is apparent, the analyst may modify Safeway's reported net income of $231 million in a variety of ways in order to incorporate these supplementary disclosures. Whether to include or exclude purchasing power gains and losses, holding gains and losses, and current-cost-based expense calculations is a matter of individual judgment. At present, there is little in the way of theory to predict or evidence to indicate how these disclosures are to be used.

Note that the disclosures in Exhibit 11-10 predominantly involve current cost adjustments and do not provide for the calculation of net income or asset valuations based on constant dollars. The impact of general inflation is indicated, however, at two points: (1) the calculation of purchasing power gain or loss based on the firm's net monetary position and (2) the identification of the portion of holding gains or losses that is the result of general inflation.

Five-year comparison of selected financial data   In addition to the current-year information just described, the FASB also suggests that firms report a

Exhibit 11-10
Supplementary Disclosures for Changing Prices

Safeway Stores, Inc.

Note L—Supplementary Information on Inflation and Changing Prices (Unaudited)

The company's primary financial statements are stated on the basis of historical costs. The statements reflect the actual transactions expressed in the number of dollars earned or expended without regard to changes in the purchasing power of the dollar. The following supplementary information attempts to measure the effect of changes in specific prices on the results of operations by restating historical costs to amounts which approximate the current costs to the company of producing or replacing inventories and property.

The computed net income for 1985 under current cost accounting includes restatements of merchandise costs, depreciation and amortization expense. The effects of inflation on merchandise costs have already been recognized in the historical financial statements to the extent that the LIFO method of accounting is used for approximately 68 percent of merchandise inventories.

The provision for income taxes has not been restated to a current cost basis because inflation adjustments are not deductible for income tax purposes.

The purchasing power gain results from an excess of net monetary liabilities over monetary assets. In periods of general inflation monetary assets lose purchasing power because such assets will buy fewer goods. Conversely monetary liabilities gain purchasing power since the liabilities will be repaid with dollars of reduced purchasing power.

In 1985, the current costs of merchandise inventories and property increased by $418.7 million, whereas those assets increased by $225.4 million as a result of general inflation. Thus, the year's increase in inventories and property due to current cost exceeded the increase in general inflation by $193.3 million, indicating a greater increase in the company's specific price indices than the rate of general inflation. At year-end 1985, the current cost of merchandise inventories was $1.9 billion and the current cost of net property was $3.8 billion.

Current cost accounting methods involve the use of assumptions, estimates and subjective judgments, and the results should not be viewed as precise measurements of the effects of inflation.

Supplementary Financial Data Adjusted for the Effects of Changing Prices

(in millions)

	1985	
	As reported in the Consolidated Statement of Income (Historical Cost)	Adjusted for Changes in Specific Prices (Current Cost)
Sales	$19,650	$19,650
Cost of sales	14,872	14,903
Other expenses, net	4,425	4,461
Income before provision for income taxes	$ 353	$ 286
Provision for income taxes	122	122
Net income	$ 231	$ 164
Gain from the change in purchasing power of net monetary liabilities		$ 103
Net income including purchasing power gain		$ 267
Depreciation and amortization expense*	$ 333	$ 422

Source: Safeway Stores, Inc. *Annual Report*, 1985.

*Allocated between cost of sales and other expenses in the determination of net income.

five-year comparison of selected financial data. This comparison includes current cost information from prior years, adjusted for changes in the general purchasing power of the dollar. Exhibit 11-11 shows this information as reported by Safeway Stores in 1985.

The amounts shown in Exhibit 11-11 are stated in average 1985 dollars. This means that amounts reported in previous years have been restated using the average CPI-U index reported in the last line of Exhibit 11-11. To illustrate, in its historical-cost-based consolidated income statement in 1985, 1984, and 1983, Safeway Stores reported revenues of $19,650 million, $19,642 million, and $18,586 million, respectively. The amounts shown in the five-year comparison differ, however, because they have been adjusted for the effects of inflation. The CPI-U index was employed in the following manner to make these adjustments:

Year	Historical Cost-based Revenues	×	Conversion Factor	=	Constant Dollar-based Revenues
1983	$18,586	×	322.2/298.4	=	$20,068
1984	$19,642	×	322.2/311.1	=	$20,343
1985	$19,650	×	322.2/322.2	=	$19,650

Analysts often examine accounting numbers over time in order to estimate growth rates and to assess the volatility or riskiness of income or cash flows.

Exhibit 11-11

Five-year Comparison of Items Adjusted for the Effects of Changing Prices

Safeway Stores, Inc.
(in dollars of 1985 average purchasing power)

	1985	1984	1983	1982	1981
Sales	$19,650	$20,343	$20,068	$19,652	$19,611
Net income (loss)	164	57	22	23	(50)
Net income (loss) per share of common stock	2.72	.96	.40	.45	(.96)
Gain from the change in purchasing power of net monetary liabilities	103	100	96	93	216
Net income including gain in purchasing power	267	158	118	116	166
Increase in the current costs of merchandise inventories and property over (under) the increase due to general inflation	193	(140)	83	(161)	(280)
Net assets at year-end	3,034	2,951	3,045	2,762	2,913
Cash dividends per share of common stock	1.625	1.579	1.539	1.477	1.538
Market price per share of common stock at year-end	36.62	28.48	27.80	25.49	15.67
Average Consumer Price Index (CPI-U)	322.2	311.1	298.4	289.1	272.4

Source: Safeway Stores, Inc., *Annual Report*, 1985.

Note: Dollars in millions except per-share amounts.

Adjustment of asset values, revenues, and expenses for the effects of general and/or specific price changes may have an important effect on such assessments. For example, observe that historical cost-based revenues have increased by 5.7 percent from 1983 to 1985 (from $18,586 million to $19,650 million). On the other hand, after adjustment to constant dollars, revenue has actually decreased by 2.1 percent (from $20,068 million to $19,650 million) over the same period. In other words, the purchasing power equivalent of Safeway Stores' revenues declined over the period 1983–1985 due to one or more of the following factors: (1) the rate of general inflation exceeded the rate of price increase for the goods sold by Safeway; (2) the underlying physical quantity of goods sold by Safeway declined over the period; and/or (3) the product mix sold by Safeway shifted to lower-price items.

Overall Evaluation of Changing Price Disclosures

Theoretical basis for changing price disclosures   The preceding discussion has emphasized the absence of a strong theoretical link between the information requirements of investors and the information disclosed concerning changing prices. With respect to constant dollar disclosures, the attribute measured is historical cost, adjusted to reflect purchasing power rather than nominal dollars. Because the effectiveness of historical cost as an attribute useful to investors has yet to be proven, it is hard to demonstrate on theoretical grounds that constant dollar adjustments either improve or impair the quality of accounting reports.

Current cost disclosures, by comparison, entail a departure from historical cost. The attribute measured is the present cost of replacing either the asset or the productive capacity of the asset. Accounting theorists have long argued that historical costs be either abandoned in favor of, or augmented by, current value disclosures. Yet the advocates of current value disclosures hold widely varying views on how best to measure current values. Current costs constitute only one of a number of alternative proposals for asset valuation; other alternatives were described in this text in the discussion of the income concept in Chapter 3, and in the discussion of asset valuation in Chapter 5.

Empirical basis for changing price disclosures   There is little convincing empirical evidence to indicate the usefulness of changing price disclosures in either explaining or predicting securities market phenomena. Some researchers have compared the relative ability of nominal-dollar- and constant-dollar-based financial ratios to explain differences among firms in terms of bond yields, bond ratings, the likelihood of bankruptcy, and the riskiness of equity prices. For the most part, these studies do not indicate that the inflation-adjusted ratios improve on the performance of conventional nominal dollar ratios.

The fact that changing price disclosures are available to investors may lead managers to alter their decisions in areas such as capital structure, capital spending, and performance evaluation. For example, the fact that firms with net monetary assets or liabilities will show purchasing power losses or gains in periods of inflation or deflation may lead some managers to alter the composition of their net assets. The high reported asset values and depreciation charges for older property, plant, and equipment may provide managers with a stimulus for new capital spending, since in many cases new assets may be acquired at amounts well below the adjusted cost of older assets.

In addition, the availability of the new disclosures to investors may lead managers to revamp the measures of performance used in decentralized organizations. The relationship between income and assets employed is a widely used gauge of divisional performance. Calculations of this relationship based on either current cost or constant dollar adjustments might provide quite different pictures of the relative performance of a firm's segments and might cause the firm to alter the ways in which its assets are deployed.

The decisions of legislators and other government policy makers may also be influenced by changing price disclosures. The major impact is likely to be on income taxation. Income from continuing operations differs substantially for many firms among the different changing prices methods. Income tax payments, however, presently are based on nominal dollar calculations. After income is adjusted to reflect changing prices, there appear to be widely varying rates of income taxation for different firms. In some cases, the effective income tax rate exceeds 100 percent.

Researchers have studied the possibility that changing price disclosures may influence the decisions of managers, regulators, or others capable of affecting the firm's future cash flows. The findings of some researchers suggest that the share prices of firms do react as the probabilities of new changing price disclosures increase or decrease. This evidence is consistent with the view that investors expect that these disclosures ultimately will affect a firm's cash flows, due to effects on capital spending, debt and equity financing, methods used in performance evaluation, revisions in income tax laws, and other factors.

TRANSLATING THE ACCOUNTS OF FOREIGN SEGMENTS

The Currency Translation Problem

The accounting profession has been attempting for a long time to develop a standard procedure for translating the accounts of foreign segments into U.S. dollars. Currency translation is necessary in order to prepare consolidated financial statements that combine the accounts of domestic and foreign subsidiaries with those of a parent company. The currency translation problem almost seems to defy a satisfactory solution. However, it can hardly be ignored because the reported income of an American multinational company can be greatly affected by fluctuations in the exchange rates of different currencies.

The balance of this chapter is devoted to a discussion of methods for translating the accounts of foreign segments under the FASB's current reporting requirements. The scope of this text precludes a more comprehensive discussion of other aspects of foreign operations (such as transfer pricing, performance evaluation, taxation, and the financing of foreign operations), but extensive literature on these and other aspects of international business is now available.

There is a technical distinction between the terms "conversion" and "translation" as applied to foreign currencies. **Conversion** signifies a realized gain or loss arising from an actual transaction. For example, an American textile firm purchases lace from a French supplier at a price specified in francs. The American company will instruct its bank to convert a sufficient number of dollars into francs to reimburse its suppliers. **Translation** of foreign currency, on the other hand, represents a mere restatement of the accounts of a foreign branch or subsidiary into U.S. dollars. The gain or loss is unrealized because no actual transaction has taken place. Such unrealized gains and losses are caused by fluctuations in the rates of exchange between the U.S. dollar and foreign currencies.

The translation of foreign currency raises several difficult questions, including the following:

1. Which of several potential procedures, each with varying results, should be used to accomplish the currency translation?
2. How should gains or losses from currency translation be accounted for?
3. To what extent should currency translation recognize inflation in foreign countries?

Currency Exchange Rates

Prior to the depression of the 1930s, major world currencies were essentially supported by gold and most were convertible into gold. In 1944 the western Allies met in New Hampshire in an attempt to formulate a long-term international economic framework. At the Bretton Woods Conference a compromise was reached between proponents of fixed exchange rates and those who favored flexible rates. Par values of currencies continued to be based on gold but were allowed to fluctuate to a limited extent—plus or minus one percent of parity. The International Monetary Fund was established to provide financial assistance to member nations that temporarily incurred unfavorable trade balances.

Following World War II, currency devaluations took place in many European countries and a **gold/dollar standard** emerged under which other currencies were tied to the strong U.S. dollar. The dollar was convertible into gold on demand at a parity price of $35 an ounce. However, as the free-market price of gold rose above the parity price, other nations became reluctant to hold dollars, particularly since the United States could liquidate its international debts by simply printing more dollars. An increased demand for repayment of international debts in gold created a severe drain on the United States' gold supply. Consequently, the United States was compelled to abrogate the convertibility of dollars into gold and to devalue the dollar.

Many factors contribute to changes in exchange rates, including currency demand and supply, inflation, favorable or unfavorable trade balances, comparative interest rates, and political instability. At the present time, there is no single conversion unit (gold or silver) that supports major currencies, nor are there parity rates of exchange. Instead, most exchange rates are permitted to float freely, resulting in greater volatility in the rates.

Foreign Currency Translation

SFAS No. 8 and *SFAS No. 52* are the authoritative pronouncements on accounting for foreign currency translation. Until 1982, U.S. firms were required to comply with *SFAS No. 8*. In that year, *SFAS No. 52* established thorough changes in the objectives and procedures for translation. In certain cases, the earlier *SFAS No. 8* rules still apply. The requirements of both statements will be illustrated and compared using the Continental Company financial statements contained in Exhibit 11-12.

There are two basic issues in translating these foreign currency financial statements into dollars: (1) at what exchange rate should the various items be translated and (2) if the translated balance sheet does not balance, how should the difference be interpreted?

SFAS No. 8 translation method   *SFAS No. 8* is used to translate the financial statements of entities whose functional currency is highly inflationary.[4] *SFAS No. 8* must also be used when a foreign entity has a functional currency (other than the dollar) that is not the same currency in which its books are kept. For example, if a French firm keeps its books in francs but has a functional currency of British pounds, *SFAS No. 8* must be used to translate the statements into British pounds. *SFAS No. 52*, described in a later section, must then be used to translate the British pounds into U.S. dollars.

Exchange rates used for translation   *SFAS No. 8* aims to measure the foreign entity's transactions as though they had occurred in dollars. Each year the items in the balance sheet that are stated at historical cost are translated at the exchange rates that were in effect when those items originated. As a result, the dollar amount at which the item is stated after translation does not change from year to year, even though the exchange rate changes. Balance sheet items that are carried at current prices rather than historical costs (cash, receivables, payables, market value of inventories, and investments) are translated at current exchange rates.

For the purposes of our illustrations, we will assume the exchange rates given on page 549 (that is, the number of deutsche marks [DMs] required in exchange for one U.S. dollar at the date indicated):

---

[4]An entity's functional currency is the currency of the primary economic environment in which the entity operates. The term is more fully defined in the later discussion of *SFAS No. 52*.

Exhibit 11-12

Financial Statements Prior to Translation
Balance Sheet and Income Statement, 1988

Continental Company
Balance Sheet
December 31, 1988
(in millions of deutsche marks [DM])

Assets

Cash and Receivables	DM	2,910
Inventory		3,040
Fixed Assets (net of depreciation)		5,400
	DM	11,350

Liabilities and Owners' Equity

Accounts Payable	DM	2,350
Noncurrent Debt		3,000
Capital Stock		2,700
Retained Earnings		3,300
	DM	11,350

Continental Company
Income Statement
For the Year Ended December 31, 1988
(in millions of deutsche marks [DM])

Sales		DM	20,160
Expenses			
Cost of goods sold	DM 12,060		
Depreciation expense	1,620		
Other expenses	5,400		
Total expenses			(19,080)
Income before taxes		DM	1,080
Income tax expense			(540)
Net income		DM	540

	DMs Required for One U.S. Dollar
Historical rate when all fixed assets were acquired and capital stock was issued	2.70
Historical rate when inventory was acquired	1.90
Average rate during 1988	1.80
Rate on December 31, 1988	2.00

Interpretation of translation adjustment: Because different elements are translated at different exchange rates, *SFAS No. 8* requires a translation adjustment. Each year's change in the translation adjustment is included in income, and the cumulative effect of translation adjustments is thereby included in retained earnings. Exhibit 11-13 applies the *SFAS No. 8* method to Continental Company's financial statements.

SFAS No. 52 **translation method**   The procedures to be discussed here are used when the functional currency of the foreign entity is the currency in which its books are kept and the functional currency is not highly inflationary. *SFAS No. 52* defines an entity's **functional currency** as "... the currency of the primary economic environment in which the entity operates; normally, that is the currency of the environment in which an entity primarily generates and expends cash."[5] If the books are kept in a different currency, it is necessary to translate first to the functional currency (using the *SFAS No. 8* method described earlier) and then to translate from the functional currency to U.S. dollars. For all of the examples in this discussion (as well as the exercises at the end of the chapter), we assume that the foreign entity's books are kept in its functional currency.

SFAS No. 52 specifies that all assets and liabilities of the foreign entity are to be translated at the current exchange rate—the rate prevailing at the balance sheet date. Capital stock is translated at the rate prevailing when the stock was sold. Revenues and expenses are translated at the average rate for the period. Revenues, expenses, gains, and losses should theoretically be translated at the rate in effect at each transaction date. An acceptable substitute is to translate using a weighted-average exchange rate for the period. If revenues and expenses occur uniformly throughout the period, then the average rate for the period may be used. In the illustrations that follow, we use the period's average exchange rate to translate the income statement.

Because not all financial statement elements are translated at the same exchange rate, an adjustment is required to bring the statements into balance. For example, if a credit (or debit) adjustment is required to balance the statement of financial position, the foreign entity's shareholders' equity is increased (or decreased) by the necessary amount. The increase or decrease is not interpreted as a gain or loss (determinant of net income), however.

Exhibit 11-14 shows the translation of Continental Company's financial statements in compliance with *SFAS No. 52*. Observe the following important features:

1. Because different translation rates are used for various elements of the financial statements, the translated balance sheet does not balance until a **translation adjustment** of $500 million is added to stockholders' equity. This

---

[5]*Statement of Financial Accounting Standards No. 52,* "Foreign Currency Translation" (Stamford, CT: FASB, 1981), par. 39.

Exhibit 11-13

SFAS No. 8 Translation of Balance Sheet and Income Statement

Continental Company
Balance Sheet
December 31, 1988

	Millions of DM	Translation Rate	Millions of Dollars
Assets			
Cash and Receivables	DM 2,910	1.00/2.00	$ 1,455
Inventory	3,040	1.00/1.90	1,600
Fixed Assets (net of depreciation)	5,400	1.00/2.70	2,000
	DM 11,350		$ 5,055
Liabilities and Owners' Equity			
Accounts Payable	DM 2,350	1.00/2.00	$ 1,175
Noncurrent Debt	3,000	1.00/2.00	1,500
Capital Stock	2,700	1.00/2.70	1,000
Retained Earnings	3,300		1,380*
	DM 11,350		$ 5,055

Continental Company
Income Statement
For the Year Ended December 31, 1988

	Millions of DM	Translation Rate	Millions of Dollars
Sales	DM 20,160	1.00/1.80	$11,200
Cost of goods sold[†]	(12,060)	1.00/1.80	(6,700)
Depreciation expense	(1,620)	1.00/2.70	(600)
Other expenses	(5,400)	1.00/1.80	(3,000)
Translation adjustment (gain)			100 [‡]
Income before taxes	DM 1,080		$ 1,000
Income tax expense	(540)	1.00/1.80	(300)
Net income	DM 540		$ 700

*For this illustration, it is assumed that the Retained Earnings balance on January 1, 1988, was $680 under *SFAS No. 8*. Income for 1988 is $700, so the ending balance of Retained Earnings is $1,380 ($700 + $680).

[†]Assumes LIFO inventory and that all goods sold were produced in the current period.

[‡]This translation adjustment does not appear in the Continental Company financial statements before translation and reflects the fact here that the firm had monetary assets and liabilities denominated in DMs in a period when exchange rates changed.

translation adjustment reflects the fact that the current (December 31, 1988) exchange rate differs from historical exchange rates and the average rate used to

Exhibit 11-14
SFAS No. 52 Translation of Balance Sheet and Income Statement

Continental Company
Balance Sheet
December 31, 1988

	Millions of DM	Translation Rate	Millions of Dollars
Assets			
Cash and Receivables	DM 2,910	1.00/2.00	$ 1,455
Inventory	3,040	1.00/2.00	1,520
Fixed Assets (net of depreciation)	5,400	1.00/2.00	2,700
	DM 11,350		$ 5,675
Liabilities and Owners' Equity			
Accounts Payable	DM 2,350	1.00/2.00	$ 1,175
Noncurrent Debt	3,000	1.00/2.00	1,500
Capital Stock	2,700	1.00/2.70	1,000
Retained Earnings	3,300		1,500*
Translation Adjustment	–		500[†]
	DM 11,350		$ 5,675

Continental Company
Income Statement
For the Year Ended December 31, 1988

	Millions of DM	Translation Rate	Millions of Dollars
Sales	DM 20,160	1.00/1.80	$11,200
Cost of goods sold	(12,060)	1.00/1.80	(6,700)
Depreciation expense	(1,620)	1.00/1.80	(900)
Other expenses	(5,400)	1.00/1.80	(3,000)
Income before taxes	DM 1,080		$ 600
Income tax expense	(540)	1.00/1.80	(300)
Net income	DM 540		$ 300

*For this illustration, it is assumed that on January 1, 1988, the Retained Earnings balance was $1,200 on the translated balance sheet. Income for 1988 is $300, so the ending balance of Retained Earnings is $1,500 ($1,200 + $300).

[†]Figure needed to balance the statement. See text on page 550 for explanation.

translate the income statement for the period. The translation adjustment is *not* interpreted as a gain or loss.

2. When current exchange rates change, the translated carrying value of the firm's assets and liabilities will also change. As an example, assume that

Continental Company's net fixed assets remain at 5,400 million DMs, but that the exchange rate changes as follows:

Balance Sheet Date	Current Exchange Rate (DMs per dollar)
December 31, 1989	1.60
December 31, 1990	1.20
December 31, 1991	.80

If these changes occur, on successive balance sheets the net fixed assets would be translated using the prevailing rates, as shown below.

Net Fixed Assets	DMs	Translation Rate	Dollars
At December 31, 1989	5,400	1/1.60	3,375
At December 31, 1990	5,400	1/1.20	4,500
At December 31, 1991	5,400	1/ .80	6,750

In this case, the DM has progressively strengthened against the dollar (more dollars are required to buy a given amount of DMs), and this is reflected on the translated balance sheet as a progressive increase in the carrying value of the assets. In effect, the assets are not valued at their historical cost in dollars, because each change in the current exchange rate causes the assets to be revalued. If the DMs were to weaken against the dollar — that is, if fewer dollars were required to buy a given amount of DMs — the opposite effect would occur, and the dollar carrying value of the assets would decline on successive balance sheets.

These revaluation effects can be substantial. Consider the case of a factory in Brazil purchased for 10 million cruzeiros in January, 1970, when the exchange rate approximated one Brazilian cruzeiro as the equivalent of $ .24. The factory would have had a translated cost of $2,400,000. At December 31, 1980, when the exchange rate was one cruzeiro equals $ .0153, the translated cost of the plant would be $153,000. It is unclear how to interpret this amount. Such dramatic shifts in exchange rates are usually due to the fact that the financial statements to be translated are prepared in the currency of a highly inflationary economy. In response to this problem, the FASB requires that the financial statements of the foreign entity in such cases be restated following the rules contained in *SFAS No. 8*. The dollar cost of the assets will not be affected by exchange rate changes using *SFAS No. 8* translation rules. This requirement applies only to highly inflationary economies, defined by the FASB as those with a cumulative inflation of 100 percent or more over a three-year period.

3. Finally, Exhibit 11-14 shows that all assets and liabilities are translated at the current (year-end) rate, while all income statement items are translated at the average rate for the period. As a result, financial ratios that are calculated using elements of both statements (inventory turnover, for example) will be different before and after translation, while financial ratios that use elements of

the same statement, such as the ratio of net income to sales, will be the same before and after translation.

The translated financial statements in Exhibit 11-14, which reflect the *SFAS No. 52* requirements, differ from the financial statements in Exhibit 11-13, which reflect the *SFAS No. 8* requirements. The three main differences are the following:

1. Under *SFAS No. 8,* any gain or loss from currency translation is included in income. *SFAS No. 52* requires that the translation gain or loss be presented in a separate component of stockholders' equity.
2. Under *SFAS No. 8* all financial statement elements that are valued at historical cost on the foreign currency financial statements are translated at the rate of exchange in effect when those items originated. As a result, the translated dollar cost of those items is not affected by subsequent changes in the exchange rate. By contrast, *SFAS No. 52* translates these items at current exchange rates, so that the translated dollar cost changes as exchange rates fluctuate.
3. Because *SFAS No. 8* uses different exchange rates to translate individual elements in the financial statements, financial ratios will differ before and after translation. Under *SFAS No. 52* ratios within the same statement are generally unaffected by translation, while ratios that use elements of both the balance sheet and the income statement usually will be affected. This occurs because the assets and liabilities are translated at the year-end rate, whereas the income statement is translated at the average rate for the year. Exhibit 11-15 (which is based on the data contained in Exhibits 11-13 and 11-14) shows how several key financial ratios are affected by translation under each statement.[6]

Evaluation of Foreign Currency Translation Methods

From its inception, the FASB recognized the seriousness of the diversity in accounting procedures for foreign segments. There were considerable differences among American companies regarding methods of translation used and the treatment of translation gains or losses. The principal objective of the FASB, therefore, was to establish a uniform method of currency translation for all U.S. multinational companies that conformed to American accounting principles. After careful analysis of the problem, the FASB adopted *SFAS No. 8*. Translation gains and losses were to be reflected in both interim and annual reports. This was to be accompanied by adequate disclosure of realized and unrealized exchange gains and losses.

While *SFAS No. 8* resulted in a standard procedure for foreign currency translation, it evoked widespread opposition from multinational company management. When exchange rates fluctuated from period to period, a "yo-yo"

---

[6]Chapter 12 provides a comprehensive discussion of financial ratios. However, the ratios listed in Exhibit 11-15 have already been discussed at various points earlier in this text.

Exhibit 11-15

Selected Financial Ratios, Before and After Translation

Continental Company

	Deutsche Marks	Translation to U.S. Dollars	
		Under SFAS No. 8	Under SFAS No. 52
Long-term debt as a percentage of equity	50.00	63.03	50.00
Net income as a percentage of sales	2.68	6.25	2.68
Income before income taxes and foreign exchange gain as a percentage of assets	9.52	17.80	10.57
Income before income taxes as a percentage of assets	9.52	19.78	10.57
Net income as a percentage of assets	4.76	13.85	5.29

effect on earnings per share was produced that allegedly made investors' evaluations of the real earnings potential of a company more difficult. Whether translation gains or losses were reported depended on the mix of monetary assets and liabilities and on the relative strength or weakness of the foreign currency relative to the U.S. dollar. Some critics of *SFAS No. 8* also found it incongruous to translate foreign fixed assets at an historic rate while long-term debt incurred to finance such acquisitions was translated at a current rate.

Frequently, a foreign subsidiary may operate fairly independently of its parent company. There may be few intercompany transactions and no dividend distributions. The foreign segment may have sustained no discernible deterioration in asset values in terms of its local environment. Therefore, according to some opponents of *SFAS No. 8*, it seemed unrealistic to record any short-term gains or losses arising from currency translation.

Another disturbing consequence of *SFAS No. 8* was that many multinational companies felt impelled to engage in certain transactions (sometimes at an economic loss) in order to offset the effect on reported earnings of the FASB's pronouncement. If a particular foreign currency was expected to appreciate relative to the dollar, a firm might decide to replace a debt denominated in a foreign currency with a debt incurred in U.S. dollars. Alternatively, if a company expected a foreign currency to depreciate relative to the dollar, it might accelerate inventory turnover or otherwise reduce the average inventory of a subsidiary, as well as the level of cash and marketable securities maintained. Firms might increase or decrease net cash remittances from foreign subsidiaries to reduce their vulnerability to an adverse rate change. *SFAS No. 8* provisions also motivated managers to increase hedging transactions in foreign currencies. Such actions are legitimate when undertaken to reduce risk exposure in foreign countries. However, they are questionable when designed purely to achieve desired accounting results. Accounting should depict rather than create transactions.

The criticisms of *SFAS No. 8* were addressed by the FASB in *SFAS No. 52*. Under the new requirements provided for in the later statement, the assets and liabilities of the foreign segment are translated into dollars at the current exchange rate and the segment's revenue and expenses are translated at the average rate for the period. The translation adjustment is no longer reported in income as a gain or loss but is included on the consolidated balance sheet as a separate component of stockholders' equity. Since the translation gain or loss is unrealized, the FASB apparently felt justified in reversing its previous position.

The complexity of the currency translation issue is evidenced by the different procedures adopted by the FASB over time. The basic problem is that the accounts of a foreign entity cannot be consolidated with those of its U.S. parent without an unrealized gain or loss occurring as a consequence of fluctuations in rates of currency exchange. Yet from a conceptual standpoint, questions may arise as to how stockholders' equity can be increased or decreased, apart from additional capital investments or withdrawals, when no gain or loss has been recognized. If the dollar remains strong (or weak) for a relatively long period of time, this new balance sheet classification may become sizeable and affect key ratios used in financial analysis.

Under *SFAS No. 52* fixed assets are translated at the current exchange rate. However, an exception is made for segments operating in countries with high inflation. In such countries, the historical rate is to be used for translating fixed assets into dollars. Otherwise, as indicated previously, an unrealistic asset write-down could take place. Nevertheless, this represents an inconsistency in the translation procedure and requires an arbitrary quantitative definition of what constitutes high inflation.

SUMMARY

This chapter discusses and evaluates financial reporting practices in two different but related areas: (1) changes in the level of prices (both general price changes and changes in specific prices of assets) and (2) translating the accounts of foreign segments into U.S. dollars.

In 1979, the FASB began a five-year experiment to determine whether companies could prepare inflation-adjusted information with reasonable reliability, and whether investors, creditors, and others would find the information useful. As part of the experiment, large, publicly held companies meeting certain size tests were required to report supplemental financial information on both a constant dollar and a current cost basis. Constant dollar reports restate historical cost financial statements to adjust for changes in the general level of prices. This approach adjusts historical cost dollars to dollars of equal purchasing power. In contrast, current cost reports restate historical cost financial statements to adjust for changes in specific prices of assets owned by a firm. In the case of current cost reports, the attribute measured is changed from historical cost to current cost. These supplemental disclosures are no longer required by the FASB, but firms are encouraged to provide them on a voluntary basis.

In order to prepare consolidated financial statements that merge the accounts of foreign subsidiaries with those of the parent company, it is necessary to translate the accounts of the foreign segments into U.S. dollars. There has been much controversy in recent years regarding this process. *SFAS No. 8* and *SFAS No. 52* are the authoritative pronouncements that provide guidelines for foreign currency translation. While *SFAS No. 52* established thorough changes in the objectives and procedures for translation, *SFAS No. 8* still applies in certain situations; these include translation of financial statements of entities whose functional currency is highly inflationary and also situations in which a foreign entity has a functional currency (not the U.S. dollar) that is not the same currency as that in which its books are kept. *SFAS No. 52* applies in all other situations.

SFAS No. 8 aims to measure the foreign entity's transactions as though they occurred in U.S. dollars. Each year the items in the balance sheet that are stated at historical cost are translated at the exchange rates that were in effect when those items originated. In contrast, *SFAS No. 52* specifies that all assets and liabilities of the foreign entity are to be translated at the current exchange rate.

QUESTIONS

1. The terms listed below were introduced in this chapter. Define or explain each of them.

   constant dollar adjustments
   constant dollar balance sheet
   constant dollar income statement
   Consumer Price Index for
     All Urban Consumers (CPI-U)
   conversion (of foreign currency)
   current cost adjustments
   current cost reports
   functional currency
   gold/dollar standard
   holding gain

   holding gain, net of inflation
   monetary gain or loss
   monetary items
   nonmonetary items
   price indexes
   replacement cost
   reproduction cost
   specific price indexes
   translation (of foreign currency)
   translation adjustment

2. What is the current position of the FASB regarding the reporting of the effects of changing prices on a company's published financial statements?
3. "The Consumer Price Index for All Urban Consumers (CPI-U) is a measure of specific price changes in the economy." Do you agree or disagree? Explain.
4. Provide three different examples of a monetary item. List three different nonmonetary items.

5. During inflationary periods, would you expect companies with substantial investments in net monetary assets to report large monetary gains or large monetary losses?

6. "Conversion of nominal dollars to constant dollars is not a departure from the historical cost principle." Do you agree or disagree? Explain.

7. Distinguish between a constant dollar income statement and a current cost income statement.

8. Describe the effects of constant dollar adjustments on reported income due to each of the following factors: (a) capital intensity; (b) age of property, plant, and equipment; (c) inventory cost flow assumption used; and (d) monetary position.

9. "To date, empirical evidence supports the view that the use of constant dollar disclosures improves the decisions of investors." Do you agree or disagree? Explain.

10. List and briefly describe three alternative approaches to valuing assets at current cost.

11. Distinguish between reproduction cost and replacement cost. What factors might account for differences between these two measures of current cost?

12. List and briefly describe several of the problems that may be encountered in determining the current cost of various financial statement items.

13. Distinguish between a current cost balance sheet and a constant dollar balance sheet.

14. "An advantage of current cost adjustments over constant dollar adjustments is that adjustments in the former case are more objective." Do you agree or disagree? Explain.

15. What are the main benefits attributed to current cost accounting? What are the major disadvantages?

16. Distinguish between "conversion" and "translation" as the two terms are used in connection with a foreign currency.

17. Both *SFAS No. 8* and *SFAS No. 52* focus on foreign currency translation. What are the major differences between these two FASB statements?

18. "*SFAS No. 52* specifies that all assets and liabilities of a foreign business segment are to be translated at the exchange rate that was in effect when each of the assets and liabilities was acquired." Do you agree or disagree? Explain.

19. List and discuss several alleged disadvantages (negative economic consequences) of using *SFAS No. 8*.

20. In what ways did *SFAS No. 52* address the criticisms levelled against *SFAS No. 8*?

EXERCISES AND PROBLEMS

21. *Management's Discussion of Its Inflation-Accounting Data.*   The statements presented below were made by the managers of the Tyler Corporation in the firm's 1982 annual report.

(1) Income tax on the constant dollar and current cost/constant dollar basis represents historical expense for 1982 expressed in year-end 1982 dollars. Present tax laws do not allow deductions for the higher constant dollar and current cost amounts of depreciation due to the effects of inflation resulting in effective tax rates of 81% (constant dollar) and 95% (current cost/constant dollar), which exceed the statutory rate.

(2) The values (of property, plant, and equipment) represent the estimated current cost of existing assets and do not consider technological improvements and efficiencies associated with the normal replacement of productive capacity.

(3) In recent years, the Company has been investing substantial amounts of cash in treasury stock, utilizing a monetary asset with declining value to increasingly leverage the capital structure of the company.

REQUIRED

(a) Explain the meaning of each of these statements.
(b) What is the implication of the statement listed in item (1)?
(c) Explain the possible reasons for the strategy presented in item (3). What does this statement imply about the company's perception of the importance of a monetary gain or loss?

22. *Purchasing Power Gains and Losses.* Consider the following information concerning monetary assets and liabilities for three firms at the beginning and end of 1987:

	Monetary Assets		Monetary Liabilities	
	1987 January 1	1987 December 31	1987 January 1	1987 December 31
Firm A	$5,000	$6,000	$4,000	$3,000
Firm B	$2,000	$4,000	$3,000	$2,000
Firm C	$7,000	$2,000	$1,000	$4,000

REQUIRED   Assume that the inflation rate was 8% throughout the year, and that changes in monetary position occurred evenly.

(a) Determine the amount of purchasing power gains and losses for each of the three firms during 1987.
(b) Which of the firms was best off as the result of its holdings of monetary assets and liabilities during 1987? Which was worst off? Would the prevailing rates of interest on monetary items affect your conclusions? Explain in detail.

23. *Inflation Expectations and Purchasing Power Gains and Losses.*   On January 1, 1987, the Quandry Company issued a $5-million noninterest-bearing bond

to be repaid in a single installment five years later on January 1, 1992. The bond was issued when the market rate of interest was 12%, which was due in part to the fact that inflation was expected to average about 8% over the life of the loan.

The actual inflation rate during 1987 was only 6%. Moreover, inflation was then expected to average just 5% per annum over the next four years, and the prevailing interest rate on similar borrowing consequently had fallen to 8% by the end of the year.

REQUIRED

(a) Determine the proceeds received by Quandry Company upon issuing the note on January 1, 1987. (Use the present value tables on pages 258–59.)
(b) Determine the interest expense for 1987, as well as the carrying value of the loan on December 31, 1987.
(c) Compute the purchasing power gain or loss on the loan for 1987.
(d) Is a debtor firm better or worse off during a period of inflation? How is a debtor firm affected by changes in expected inflation and changes in interest rates? How (if at all) are these effects reflected in your calculation of Quandry's purchasing power gain or loss for 1987?
(e) What is the present value (discounted at 8%) of Quandry's debt on December 31, 1987? Is there an economic interpretation of the difference between the present value and the carrying value of the debt? Explain.

24. *Nonmonetary Items: Current Cost and Constant Dollar Adjustments.*   The composition of Elastic Yardstick's December 31, 1987, balance in the machinery account in its ledger is shown below.

Item	Date Acquired	Original Cost	Accumulated Depreciation	1987 Depreciation
		(in thousands)		
A	January 1, 1971	$1,000	$ 600	$ 50
B	January 1, 1979	3,000	1,000	200
C	January 1, 1985	2,000	400	200
		$6,000	$2,000	$450

Assume for the illustration that the following price indexes existed at the dates shown:

	General Purchasing Power (for example, CPI-U)	Construction Costs, Machinery
January 1, 1971	1.50	1.50
January 1, 1979	2.40	1.20
January 1, 1985	3.00	.90
December 31, 1987	3.20	.90

REQUIRED

(a) Determine the constant dollar and current cost amounts for the machinery's original cost and accumulated depreciation at December 31, 1987, and depreciation for the year 1987. (Note: The current cost of machinery has not changed since 1985.)

(b) Examine the percentage relationships among total original cost, accumulated depreciation, and depreciation expense, computed by using nominal dollars, constant dollars, and current costs. Which relationships are most useful to investor analysts? Explain.

25. *Analysis of Current Cost and Constant Dollar Data.* Exhibit A shows the supplemental inflation disclosures included in the 1984 annual report of Rexnord, Inc. At that time, firms were *required* by the FASB to report constant dollar as well as current cost data.

REQUIRED

(a) Compare Rexnord's four-year growth rates using historical (nominal) dollars, constant dollars, and current costs for each of the following:

(1) Net sales
(2) Net income
(3) Primary earnings per share
(4) Total net assets
(5) Return on assets (ratio of income to net assets)
(6) Market price per share

Exhibit A

Rexnord Inc.
Supplemental Inflation Disclosures
(Unaudited)
(Dollars in Thousands Except Per-share Data)

Supplemental Statement of Income Adjusted for Changing Prices

	As Reported in the Primary Statements (Historical Dollars)	Adjusted for General Inflation (Average 1984 Constant Dollars)	Adjusted for Changes in Specific Prices (Current Costs)
Net sales	$921,053	$921,053	$921,053
Costs	876,561	892,600	894,000
Provision for income taxes	16,266	16,266	16,266
Net income	28,226	12,187	10,787
Net income per share	1.37	.59	.52

Exhibit A continued

Five-Year Comparison of Selected Data Adjusted for Effects of Inflation
(Inflation-Adjusted Amounts Are Stated in Average 1984 Dollars)

	1984	1983	1982	1981	1980
Net Sales					
Historical	$921,053	$804,513	$ 936,552	$1,130,039	$1,083,690
Constant Dollars	921,053	837,820	1,007,917	1,300,449	1,383,114
Net Income (Loss)					
Historical	28,226	3,927	7,154	38,548	41,462
Constant Dollars	12,187	(23,122)	(29,237)	15,089	20,514
Current Cost	10,787	(23,246)	(31,071)	15,527	22,585
Primary Net Income (Loss) Per Share					
Historical	1.37	.19	.35	1.92	2.08
Constant Dollars	.59	(1.16)	(1.46)	.75	1.02
Current Cost	.52	(1.16)	(1.55)	.77	1.12
Net Assets at Year End					
Historical	391,484	364,652	372,085	392,509	392,007
Constant Dollars	576,333	541,342	594,852	646,805	668,299
Current Cost	581,205	540,395	590,855	648,590	734,325
Cash Dividends					
Historical	.40	.40	1.08	1.07	1.02
Constant Dollars	.40	.42	1.16	1.23	1.30
Market Price Per Common Share					
Historical	14.25	15.88	11.38	14.75	19.38
Constant Dollars	14.25	16.50	12.20	16.50	24.00
Unrealized gain from decline in purchasing power of net monetary liabilities	4,524	2,724	6,148	17,276	16,210
Excess of increase in current costs of inventories and property over increase in general inflation*	7,412	(12,822)	5,833	(36,091)	8,091
Average CPI-U	309.0	296.7	287.1	268.5	242.1

Source: Rexnord, Incorporated, *Annual Report*, 1984.

*At October 31, 1984, current cost of inventories and property was $245,959 and $412,901, respectively.

(b) Which of the growth rates calculated in item (a) is most useful to investor analysts? Explain.

(c) Is Rexnord a net monetary debtor or a net monetary creditor? Does the decline in purchasing power gains in the more recent years suggest that Rexnord is less successful in managing its monetary position? Explain.

(d) In three of the five years, Rexnord's current costs of net assets increased at a rate faster than the general inflation rate, while in the other two years inflation exceeded the rate of current cost increases. Which situation is better for Rexnord's shareholders? Explain.

26. *Calculation of Net Gain or Loss in Purchasing Power.*   Comparative balance sheets for Universal Container Corporation at December 31, 1981, and

1980, are presented in Exhibit A; Exhibit B on page 564 contains the firm's income statement for the year ended December 31, 1981.

REQUIRED

(a) Prepare a schedule showing the calculation of the net monetary gain or loss during the year 1981. The average CPI-U index during 1981 was 272. At the beginning of the year the index was 260, and it was 282 at the end of the year. Assume that all monetary transactions occurred uniformly throughout 1981.
(b) Explain what caused the net change in purchasing power during the year.
(c) Do you believe that the net gain or loss in purchasing power is a real (that is, an economic) gain or loss? Explain.

Note: part (d) of this Required material is on page 564.

Exhibit A

Universal Container Corporation
Balance Sheets
December 31, 1981, and 1980
(in millions)

Assets	1981	1980
Cash	$ 40,000	$ 38,000
Accounts Receivable	280,000	230,000
Less: Allowance for Bad Debts	(1,000)	(1,000)
Marketable Securities	30,000	30,000
Inventories	250,000	200,000
Prepaid Interest	6,000	4,000
Plant and Equipment	800,000	800,000
Less: Accumulated Depreciation	(350,000)	(290,000)
Total Assets	$1,055,000	$1,011,000
Liabilities and Stockholders' Equity		
Accounts Payable	$ 106,000	$ 148,000
Bank Loan	200,000	200,000
Refundable Deposits	30,000	22,000
Income Tax Payable	30,000	12,000
Bonds Payable	250,000	250,000
Total Liabilities	$ 616,000	$ 632,000
Common Stock Outstanding	$ 300,000	$ 300,000
Retained Earnings	139,000	79,000
Total Stockholders' Equity	$ 439,000	$ 379,000
Total Liabilities and Stockholders' Equity	$1,055,000	$1,011,000

Exhibit B

Universal Container Corporation
Income Statement
For the Year Ended December 31, 1981
(in millions)

Sales		$1,000,000
Less: Cost of sales		
Inventory, January 1, 1981	$200,000	
Purchases	700,000	
Total available	$900,000	
Less: Inventory, December 31, 1981	250,000	650,000
Gross profit		$ 350,000
Less: Other expenses		
Depreciation		$ 60,000
Selling and administrative		200,000
Total		$ 260,000
Income from operations		$ 90,000
Less: Income taxes		30,000
Net income		$ 60,000

(d) Assume that the net gain or loss in purchasing power is actually included in reported income. How might this affect management's strategies?

27. *Increases in Current Cost: Meaning and Calculation.*   The following data apply to the Artcroft Printing Company for the year 1984:

	Historical Cost	Current Cost
Inventories		
January 1, 1984	$ 180,000	$ 195,000
December 31, 1984	200,000	220,000
Net machinery and equipment*		
January 1, 1984	400,000	500,000
December 31, 1984	360,000	450,000
Depreciation	40,000	46,000
Cost of goods sold	1,000,000	1,150,000

*There were no purchases or disposals of machinery and equipment during the year.

REQUIRED   There has been considerable controversy over the accounting treatment of holding gains (increases in the current costs of assets that are still held by the reporting firm).

(a) Using the information on page 564, determine Artcroft's holding gains relating to income from continuing operations.
(b) Indicate the arguments for and against including holding gains in income from continuing operations.
(c) Indicate the arguments for and against accounting for increases or decreases in assets held during the period as adjustments to stockholders' equity.

28. *Preparation of a Constant Dollar Income Statement.*   Exhibit A contains an income statement for the Interstate Department Stores for the year ended December 31, 1981. Purchases and sales were made uniformly throughout the year. All depreciable assets were acquired on January 1, 1980. The company uses the FIFO inventory method, and the end-of-the-year inventories are assumed to have been acquired during the last quarter of the year. Relevant CPI-U index data are listed below.

Average for 4th quarter, 1980	256
Average for 4th quarter, 1981	281
Average for the year, 1981	272
January 1, 1980	233
January 1, 1981	261
December 31, 1981	282

Exhibit A

Interstate Department Stores
Income Statement
For the Year Ended December 31, 1981

Sales	$700,000
Cost of sales	
Inventory, January 1, 1981	$ 80,000
Purchases	440,000
Available for sale	$520,000
Inventory, December 31, 1981	120,000
	$400,000
Gross profit	$300,000
Less: Other expenses	
Selling and administrative	$160,000*
Depreciation	30,000
Taxes	40,000
Total	$230,000
Income	$ 70,000

*Includes $50,000 advertising expenditure on December 31, 1981.

REQUIRED   Using the CPI-U data presented on page 565, prepare an income statement showing income from continuing operations in constant dollars for 1981.

29. *Preparation of a Constant Dollar Income Statement.*   The Stern Company commenced business on January 1, 1980. At that time, it acquired machinery and equipment to be depreciated on a straight-line basis over a ten-year period. Also purchased on that date was a patent, which was to be amortized over six years. Exhibit A contains comparative balance sheets as of December 31, 1981, and 1980. Exhibit B contains a combined statement of income and retained earnings for the year ended December 31, 1981.

Exhibit A

Stern Company
Balance Sheets
December 31, 1981, and 1980
(in millions)

Assets	1981	1980
Current Assets		
Cash	$ 4,000	$ 2,100
Accounts Receivable — Net	8,000	7,000
Inventories	10,000	9,000
Total	$22,000	$18,100
Long-term Assets		
Machinery and Equipment	$15,000	$15,000
Less: Accumulated Depreciation	(3,000)	(1,500)
Patents	1,000	1,200
Total	$13,000	$14,700
Total Assets	$35,000	$32,800
Liabilities and Stockholders' Equity		
Liabilities		
Accounts Payable	$ 6,500	$ 5,000
Deferred Income Taxes	1,500	1,500
Total	$ 8,000	$ 6,500
Stockholders' Equity		
Common Stock Outstanding	$20,000	$20,000
Retained Earnings	7,000	6,300
Total	$27,000	$26,300
Total Liabilities and Stockholders' Equity	$35,000	$32,800

Exhibit B

Stern Company
Combined Income and Retained Earnings Statement
For the Year Ended December 31, 1981

Sales		$100,000
Cost of sales		
Inventory, January 1, 1981	$ 9,000	
Purchases	66,000	
Inventory available for sale	$75,000	
Less: Inventory, December 31, 1981	(10,000)	65,000
Gross margin		$ 35,000
Less: Other expenses		
Selling and administrative	$28,000	
Depreciation	1,500	
Amortization of patents	200	29,700
Pretax accounting income		$ 5,300
Less: Income tax expense		2,600
Income from continuing operations		$ 2,700
Retained earnings, December 31, 1980		6,300
		$ 9,000
Less: Cash dividend (Paid January 1, 1981)		2,000
Retained earnings, December 31, 1981		$ 7,000

Assume that sales, purchases, and selling and administrative expenses occurred uniformly throughout 1981 and that the year-end inventories were acquired uniformly during the preceding quarter. Relevant CPI-U indexes are as follows:

December 31, 1981	282
December 31, 1980	258
Average, 1981	272
Average, last quarter of 1981	281
Average, last quarter of 1980	256
January 1, 1980	230

REQUIRED

(a) Prepare an income statement for 1981 showing the income from continuing operations in constant dollars.
(b) On a separate schedule, calculate the firm's net gain or loss in general purchasing power during 1981.

30. *Determination of Cost of Goods Sold on a Current Cost Basis.* The following information relates to cost of goods sold during the year by the R.J. Harrison Company:

	Actual Cost	Current Cost
Raw materials, January 1	$ 30,000	$ 36,000
Purchases	400,000	
Raw materials, December 31	80,000	90,000
Direct labor	300,000	
Factory overhead	600,000	
Finished goods, January 1	160,000	168,000
Finished goods, December 31	180,000	

In order to facilitate the taking of the annual physical inventory at the end of each year, management completes all items in the factory prior to the inventory.

Additional information:

(1) The purchasing department estimates that the current replacement cost of materials purchased during the year is $440,000.
(2) The payroll department has calculated that the current hourly rate for direct laborers is 5% higher than the average rate during the year.
(3) Management believes that the current cost of the indirect labor component of factory overhead, which amounts to 20%, also is 5% higher than the actual wages paid, and that the current cost of the balance of factory overhead is 2% greater than the actual costs incurred.

The company uses the FIFO inventory method, and finished goods at December 31 are believed to be reflective of the factory cost inputs that were incurred throughout the year.

REQUIRED Determine the cost of goods sold during the year by R.J. Harrison Company on a current cost basis.

31. *Changing Prices Disclosures and Financial Ratios.* The financial summary included in ITT Corporation's 1983 annual report contained the following statement:

The impact of worldwide inflation and the erosion of purchasing power limits the economic conclusions that can be drawn from a review of conventional "historic cost" financial statements. These traditional presentations regain a degree of usefulness if read in conjunction with the "Effects of Inflation" disclosures included elsewhere herein.

The "effects of inflation" footnote to the financial statements included the following disclosures:

In millions	Historic Cost (As reported)	Constant Purchasing Power	Current Cost
December 31, 1983			
Inventories	2,322	2,329	2,440
Plant, property and equipment, net	5,022	7,790	8,151
Other assets (liabilities) less minority	(1,238)	(1,174)	(1,225)
Stockholders Equity	$ 6,106	$ 8,945	$ 9,366
Results for 1983			
Sales and Revenues	$20,249	$20,249	$20,249
Cost of sales and services	10,221	10,330	10,274
Depreciation	553	755	851
Other costs and expenses	8,607	8,691	8,730
Income taxes and minority equity	193	183	185
Income	$ 675	$ 290	$ 209

Comparative Data Adjusted for Inflation (Average 1983 dollars)	1983	1982	1981	1980	1979
Consumer Price Index–Average for Year	298.7	289.1	272.4	246.8	217.4
Sales and Revenues–As Reported	$20,249	$21,201	$22,386	$22,850	$21,215
–Constant purchasing power	20,249	21,905	24,547	27,655	29,149
Income–As Reported	675	572	685	668	608
–Constant purchasing power	290	103	247	76	495
–Current cost	209	97	264	277	488
Purchasing Power Gain on Net Monetary Items	106	159	309	434	475
Holding Gain Net of Inflation	(49)	(562)	(211)	(805)	(321)
Translation and Parity Adjustments					
–Constant purchasing power	(340)	(417)	(1,426)	(503)	153
Earnings Per Common Equivalent Share–As					
Reported	4.50	3.86	4.63	4.57	4.23
–Constant purchasing power	1.92	.67	1.65	.50	3.43
–Current cost	1.38	.64	1.76	1.88	3.37
Stockholders Equity–As Reported	6,106	6,083	6,084	6,324	6,015
–Constant purchasing power	8,945	9,333	9,812	11,313	10,908
Dividends Declared Per Common Share–As					
Reported	2.76	2.70	2.62	2.45	2.25
–Constant purchasing power	2.76	2.79	2.87	2.97	3.09
Market Price Per Common Share at Year End					
–As Quoted	44.75	31.25	29.75	30.00	25.50
–Constant purchasing power	43.77	31.92	31.57	34.68	33.13

REQUIRED

(a) Do the "effects of inflation" disclosures help the traditional financial statements to "regain a degree of usefulness"? Explain.

(b) Why is stockholders' equity higher than historical cost (as reported) when adjusted to constant purchasing power and to current cost? Why is stockholders' equity adjusted to current cost higher than stockholders' equity adjusted to constant purchasing power?

(c) Which of the three income numbers is most pertinent to investment analysts? Explain.

(d) Calculate the rates of growth in sales, income, dividends, and earnings per share for the four-year period under each of the methods reported ("historic cost," constant purchasing power, and current cost). Which measure provides the most useful indicator of growth in sales, income, dividends, and earnings per share?

(e) Assume that the four-year growth trends computed in item (d) continue through the decade ending December, 1993. What are the projected levels of sales, income, dividends, and earnings per share in 1993 for historical cost and constant purchasing power? What is the projected current cost earnings per share in 1993? Are these projections reasonable? Explain.

32. *Current Cost Calculations: before and after the Effects of General Price Level Changes.* The following information relates to inventory and property, plant, and equipment items owned by Wentro, Incorporated:

Data Relevant to Inventory

Current cost of inventory, January 1, 1981	$1,000,000
Current cost of inventory, December 31, 1981	900,000
Purchases during 1981 at actual cost	1,400,000
Current cost of goods sold	1,700,000

Data Relevant to Property, Plant, and Equipment

Current cost — net, January 1, 1981	$4,900,000
Current cost — net, December 31, 1981	6,000,000
Additions, at historical cost	500,000
Depreciation — current cost	350,000
Disposals — net amount realized	50,000

REQUIRED

(a) Calculate the increase or decrease in the current cost of Wentro's inventory and property, plant, and equipment during 1981.

(b) Calculate the increase or decrease in the current cost, net of general inflation, of Wentro's inventory and property, plant, and equipment during 1981. Relevant CPI-U index data are as follows:

January 1, 1981	258
December 31, 1981	282
Average for the year	272

33. *Comparisons: Historical Cost versus Current Cost Data.* The following facts apply to the Southland Company during 1985:

(1) Cost of goods sold (exclusive of depreciation and amortization) on a current cost basis exceeded cost of goods sold on a historical cost basis by $2.5 million. Moreover, the current cost of inventories and property, plant, and equipment held during the year increased by $220.4 million.
(2) The average specific price index used to convert depreciation and amortization on a historical cost basis to current cost was 1.4403. The average CPI-U rose by 3.57% during the year.
(3) The average number of common shares outstanding was 47.7 million. Dividends paid to preferred stockholders amounted to $2.2 million.
(4) The average net monetary liabilities of the company during 1985 totaled $1.902 billion.

REQUIRED

(a) Complete the following schedule, "The Impact of General Inflation and Specific Price Changes on Selected Financial Data," that is being presented by the Southland Company as supplementary information. Follow the format given.

Southland Company
The Impact of General Inflation and Specific
Price Changes on Selected Financial Data
For the Year Ended December 31, 1985

	As Reported in Financial Statements	Adjusted for Current Costs
	(in millions)	
Revenues	$12,789.6	$
Expenses		
Cost of goods sold, exclusive of depreciation and amortization	$10,502.0	$
Depreciation and amortization	186.9	
Interest expense	79.7	
Other operating expenses	1,738.8	
	$12,507.4	$
Income before income taxes	282.2	
Income taxes	69.7	
Net income	$ 212.5	$
Effective tax rate	24.7%	%
Unrealized gain from decline in purchasing power of net amounts owed	–	$

(b) Calculate earnings per share under both the historical cost and the current cost methods.

(c) What relationship, if any, exists between "net earnings adjusted for current costs" and the $220.4-million increase in current costs during 1985?

(d) What is the significance of the effective tax rate under these two methods?

(e) Is the monetary gain or loss a real (economic) gain or loss? If the gain or loss is real, why shouldn't it be included in the income statement?

34. *Different Income Measures in a Period of Changing Prices.*   Consolidated Natural Gas Company reported earnings per share of common stock of $5.15 for the year ended December 31, 1985, and cash dividends to common stockholders of $2.40 per share. Income before income taxes (in thousands) was $382,372 and income taxes totaled $169,943.

In a supplementary disclosure showing "Estimated Effects of Changing Prices," the company presented the schedule shown below (Exhibit A).

Exhibit A

Consolidated Natural Gas Company
Consolidated Statement of Income Adjusted for Changing Prices
For the Year Ended December 31, 1985
(stated in thousands of average 1985 dollars)

	Current Cost (specific prices)
Net Income Applicable to Common Stock, as Shown in the Consolidated Statement of Income	$212,429
Adjustments for changing prices:	
Increase in depreciation and amortization	287,990
Increase in operation expense	6,785
Adjusted net income (loss) applicable to common stock (excluding adjustment to net recoverable cost)	$(82,346)*
Changes in carrying values:	
Adjustment to net recoverable cost	198,508
Gain from decline in purchasing power of net amounts owed	44,894
Excess of increase in general price level ($221,799) over increase in specific prices of property, plant, and equipment held during the year[†] ($157,764)	(64,035)
Net Income Applicable to Common Stock, as Adjusted for Changing Prices	$ 97,021

*Including the adjustment to net recoverable cost, the net incomes (losses) on a current cost basis would have been $(394,959), $(535,795), $149,926, $316,305, and $116,162, respectively, for the years 1981 through 1985.

[†]At December 31, 1985, current cost of property, plant, and equipment net of accumulated depreciation was $7,514,368 while historical cost or net cost recoverable through depreciation was $2,511,152.

In its discussion of Exhibit A, the company made the following statements:

Until such time as the FASB completes its project, the changing prices data will be prepared under the "current cost" accounting methods. The company cautions that the information shown should not be used to adjust historical earnings dollars because the estimated effects of inflation are not recognized for rate-making purposes.

Because only the historical cost of certain System Properties is presently recoverable in revenues as depreciation, any difference from such historical cost has been reported in the preceding table (Exhibit A) as an "adjustment to net recoverable cost." Such adjustment has been excluded from adjusted net income applicable to common stock and combined with the "gain from decline in purchasing power of net amounts owed" to reflect the economics of rate regulation.

For restatement under the "current cost" method of the investment in System Properties at December 31, 1985, the estimated cost of replacing existing plant assets was determined in large part by indexing the surviving plant by the Handy-Whitman Index of Public Utility Construction Costs. It was assumed that replacement would be more or less in kind and in place, and technological changes would not be a material consideration.

The FASB requirement does not permit any adjustment to income taxes.

REQUIRED

(a) Identify and discuss three different concepts of income included in Exhibit A.
(b) Calculate earnings (loss) per share under each of these income concepts and relate the calculated earnings to dividends paid.
(c) Calculate the effective tax rates under each of these income concepts and discuss their implications.
(d) What is the purpose of reporting the "Excess of increase in general price level ($221,799) over increase in specific prices of property, plant, and equipment held during the year ($157,764)"?
(e) What is the difference between the current reproduction cost method and the replacement cost method for reporting the effects of price-level changes? Which method does Consolidated Natural Gas use?

35. *Usefulness of Changing Prices Disclosures to Financial Analysts.*   Early in 1983, at a time when the inflation rate had declined to a ten-year low, the Financial Accounting Standards Board held a conference to review research on the applications and effects of changing prices disclosures that had been required as supplemental information in published financial reports. While no one at the conference seemed to believe that inflation had come to a

halt, there seemed to be a consensus that there was no further need for continuing the disclosure requirement.

Mr. William C. Norby, a leading securities analyst, was commissioned to investigate the usefulness of these disclosures to the investment community. Norby's findings and personal conclusions are contained in an article published in the *Financial Analysts Journal* (March–April 1983) and are summarized below.

Despite evidence of considerable variability in current cost data as compared with (historical) reported data, the relative rankings of companies do not change much. For about 75% of industrial companies, the relative earnings trends or return on capital ranks tend to be of the same order by either accounting method.

. . . The analyst looks for insights that explain change and change in the rate of change. The current cost adjustments do not modify these quarterly or annual changes very much except in periods of rapid inflation. Therefore, it usually has not been essential to consider them in making one-year earnings and cash flow projections. . . . Current cost financial statements are most likely to provide useful incremental information over a longer time horizon and for those 25% of companies that lie at the edges of the general trend. The adverse cumulative impact of inflation may appear as an incessant need for additional debt, a pressure on dividends to meet cash requirements, a dilution of the common stockholders' interest, or an inability to grow in real terms. Low inflation-adjusted returns on capital may be a precursor of financial problems. . . . Although these adverse trends may eventually appear in historical cost statements, current cost statements may give investors and managements an early warning of impending trouble and conceivably lead to actions to preserve the company's financial integrity.

After considering his research findings, Mr. Norby made the following recommendations regarding the supplementary disclosures:

(1) Simplify the disclosures by adopting only the current cost method.
(2) Clarify current cost measurements; incorporate current cost changes in income; drop the purchasing power adjustment on monetary items; and adopt the comprehensive income concept.
(3) Expand the presentation to include more balance sheet and funds statement items for comparative purposes.
(4) Prescribe a single presentation format to make the data easier to use and to incorporate in computer data bases.
(5) Retain the five-year trend table of key items deflated to a constant-dollar basis, but add current cost data in nominal terms.
(6) Reconsider company coverage. Regulated utilities and financial organizations might be relieved of the adjustments to income, although not of the five-year constant dollar table. Additional industrial companies might be added if given the option of short-term current cost computations.

(7) Require specific information on price trends in sales and costs; these may be specific prices or narrow, relevant price indexes.

REQUIRED   Be prepared to participate in a general class discussion of the contents of this article. List the major points made by Mr. Norby and your agreement or disagreement with his conclusions.

36. *A Dissenting Vote on* SFAS *No. 33: A Case Study of the Issues Involved.*   SFAS *No. 33* was adopted by a vote of 5–2 by members of the FASB. The FASB's report of the dissent of Mr. Mosso, one of the board's members is presented in its entirety below.

Mr. Mosso dissents because he believes the statement does not bring the basic problem it addresses—measuring the effect of inflation on business operations—into focus. Because of that he doubts that it will effectively communicate the erosive impact of inflation on profits and capital and the significance of that erosion on all who have an investment stake in business enterprises. The statement seems to him to fail the cost-benefit test because potential benefits are diminished by diffusion and some costs are unnecessary regardless of benefits.

The lack of focus stems from the dual reporting requirements imposed by this statement—reporting on both historical cost/constant dollar and current cost basis—and is compounded by the ambivalence of the income concepts in both approaches. The statement offers at least four income numbers—historical cost/constant dollar or current cost, each with or without adjustments for purchasing power gains or losses on monetary items. Other income combinations are invited in the current cost approach because of the juxtaposition of the increase or decrease in current cost amounts of assets. This array of income numbers is a good reflection of the range of views existing among the Board's respondents; but a good mirror does not make a good standard.

Mr. Mosso does not share the widely held view that the historical cost/constant dollar and current cost models have different objectives. The objective is the same: to measure the effect of inflation on a business enterprise. But there are two types of inflation effects. The Board's historical cost/constant dollar model captures one type—the effect of inflation on the purchasing power of money invested in a particular business. The Board's current cost model captures both types. It incorporates some features of the constant dollar model and also the effect on the prices of goods and services that a particular business deals in. Inflation affects different specific prices in different ways. Consequently, information about changes in an index of general inflation does not provide sufficient information about the effect of inflation on a specific business enterprise. The current cost model is a more comprehensive inflation measurement approach and it makes a free-standing historical/constant dollar model superfluous.

The constant dollar approach has two uses that he would support: one, as a method of computing simple one-line adjustments of net income and owners' equity in the primary historical cost financial statements, in conjunction with current cost supplemental statements (a proposal that deserves more support than it has received so far); and two, as an integral part of a supplemental current cost model, essentially as in the current cost approach required by this Statement. As a complete model, however, the historical cost/constant dollar approach has little to recommend it except seniority.

A major criterion that the Board has established for choosing alternative disclosures is usefulness of the information for predicting earnings and cash flows. The evidence presented to the Board on usefulness in this sense was sketchy, but virtually all of it favored the current cost approach. In fact, usefulness for predicting earnings and cash flows was rarely associated with the historical cost/constant dollar approach, even by its supporters.

Beyond the investor-oriented usefulness criterion, the current cost model bears directly on an urgent national economic policy issue — that of capital formation and its corollary, productivity. The current cost model is built around the notion of maintaining operating capacity, and the distributable income concept that goes with it is triggered at the point where reduction of capacity sets in. The whole system pivots on the point where capital investment begins to rise or fall. In the historical cost/constant dollar model, reduction of operating capacity can occur without showing up in the financial statements. This is not to suggest that it is a function of the Board to design accounting standards to promote economic policy objectives. But it is a function of the Board to design standards that measure business income and investment and to be aware, in doing so, of the broader economic consequences of standards. The current cost model has the potential for measuring and communicating many effects of inflation in ways that will be useful to investors, to policy makers, and to the business community.

Much of the resistance to current cost accounting derives from two interrelated misconceptions: first, that it is a major step toward current value accounting and second, that its measurements are subjective and open to income manipulation. These are valid concerns. They should not be dismissed. But neither is an inherent concomitant of current cost accounting.

The essence of current value accounting is revenue recognition on some prerealization basis. The increases in current cost amounts of assets (so-called "holding gains") arising in a current cost model can be viewed as income equivalents, but that view is not necessary. The model can classify those items as capital maintenance adjustments necessary to keep the business on a level output trendline.

Subjectivity of measurement is also associated with the current cost model because in theory it breaks the link to historical transaction prices. In practice, this need not be a problem. Indexing can maintain a linkage to historical prices and preserve objectivity and reliability. Many other current costing techniques compare favorably in terms of objectivity with historical cost allocation techniques.

In Mr. Mosso's view, conventional accounting measurements fail to capture the erosion of business profits and invested capital caused by inflation. The urgent need is to focus attention on the basic problem. To do that effectively, it is essential to settle on a single inflation-adjusted bottom line within a framework that captures the price experience of individual firms. The door should be closed quickly and firmly on the dual approach with multiple income numbers.

REQUIRED

(a) Do you agree that there is ambiguity and a lack of focus in the variety of income measurements reported under *SFAS No. 33*?

(b) Do you believe that Mr. Mosso is correct that "a good mirror", (that is, a good reflection of the range of views existing among the Board's respondents) "does not make a good standard"?

(c) Do you agree that the objectives of historical cost/constant dollar and current cost models are the same?

(d) Do you agree that "information about changes in an index of general inflation does not provide sufficient information about the effect of inflation on a specific business enterprise"?

(e) Is Mr. Mosso consistent in supporting "one-line adjustments of net income and owners' equity in the primary historical cost financial statements, in conjunction with current cost supplemental statements . . . or as an integral part of a supplemental current cost model," while rejecting a complete constant dollar model?

(f) To what degree do you think the Board should be concerned with the extent to which "the current cost model bears directly on an urgent national economic policy issue . . ."?

(g) How do you think holding gains should be accounted for?

(h) Do you think Mr. Mosso is correct in his views on the relative subjectivity of current and historical cost systems?

37. *Foreign Currency Translation Issues.* When the FASB proposed changing the rules for translating foreign currency financial statements from those contained in *SFAS No. 8* to those prescribed in *SFAS No. 52*, a national accounting firm included the statements presented below in a memorandum sent to its clients.

REQUIRED   Comment in detail on each of these statements.

(a) The search for a solution to the problem of accounting for foreign currency translation is intertwined with another of the FASB's complex, controversial, and as yet, unresolved problems—accounting for the effects of changing prices.

(b) The proposed new rules are inconsistent with some long-standing accounting concepts, such as the consolidated entity concept and the single unit-of-measure concept.

(c) The new rules should reduce the large earnings fluctuations that some companies have reported under *SFAS No. 8* as a result of changes in foreign currency exchange rates. Some analysts and managements believe that this will help the multinational companies' stock prices.

(d) Under *SFAS No. 8* many companies used dollar debt to finance their operations even though it might be more costly than local debt. They did this to avoid having a large net monetary position that could give rise to significant reported foreign exchange gains or losses. Under *SFAS No. 52*, more companies are likely to finance their foreign operations by using foreign debt.

(e) Ratios that measure return on assets and on sales would tend to be higher under the new rules in countries with weakening economies because depreciation charges and assets would be lower. Some believe this may lead companies to allocate more resources to their operations in countries with weakening currencies.

(f) The results of translation under *SFAS No. 52* appear to be more in accord with the economic substance of the effects of changes in foreign exchange rates. For example, under *SFAS No. 8* a foreign subsidiary with a foreign currency net monetary liability position reports losses (a decrease in shareholders' equity) as the foreign currency strengthens. Under the new rules, such a loss would not be reported; rather, the foreign subsidiary's shareholders' equity would increase.

38. *Financial Analysis and Translated Financial Statements.* Hannibal Corporation is a foreign subsidiary of Empire Builders, Incorporated, a United States firm. Hannibal Corporation's functional currency is the hern (H), and its financial statements require translation from herns to U.S. dollars so that consolidated financial statements for 1988 may be prepared. The financial statements (before translation) for 1988 appear in Exhibit A. Relevant exchange rates are as follows:

	Exchange Rate (dollars per hern)
Historical rate when Hannibal's noncurrent assets were acquired and shareholders' equity originated	$2.00 per H
Historical rate when beginning inventory was acquired	$3.00 per H
Historical rate when ending inventory was acquired	$4.75 per H
Average rate during 1988	$4.50 per H
Current rate at December 31, 1988 (reporting date)	$5.00 per H

Additional information: The translated balance of Hannibal's retained earnings at December 31, 1987, was $3,000, using *SFAS No. 52* translation rules.

REQUIRED

(a) Prepare 1988 financial statements translated to U.S. dollars for Hannibal Corporation.

(b) Compute and compare the following financial ratios for Hannibal Corporation before and after translation: (1) net income to sales; (2) debt to total assets; (3) net income to assets; (4) net income to shareholders' equity; (5) sales to assets. Where the ratios differ, which ratios would be more meaningful to investor analysts? Explain.

Exhibit A

Hannibal Corporation,
Subsidiary of Empire Builders, Incorporated
Financial Statements before Translation

Balance Sheet
December 31, 1988

Monetary Assets	H 1,200
Inventory	200
Other Nonmonetary Assets	1,200
Total Assets	H 2,600
Monetary Liabilities	H 850
Shareholders' Equity	
Paid-in Capital	1,000
Retained Earnings	750
Total Liabilities and Equity	H 2,600

Income Statement
For the Year Ended December 31, 1988

Revenues		H 1,000
Cost of goods sold		
Beginning inventory	H 100	
Additions	400	
Ending inventory	(200)	(300)
Gross margin		H 700
Depreciation and amortization		(300)
Other expenses		(150)
Net income		H 250

Note: This problem should be attempted only after completion of problem 38 for the Hannibal Corporation. It is based on the set of financial statements before translation included in that problem.

39. *Financial Analysis and Translated Financial Statements in a Highly Inflationary Economy.*   Assume that Hannibal Corporation (described in the previous problem) functions in a highly inflationary economy, so that its financial statements must be translated in accordance with the requirements of *SFAS No. 8*. If *SFAS No. 8* rules had been followed in 1987, the translated balance of retained earnings at December 31, 1987 would have been $1,700.

REQUIRED

(a) Prepare 1988 financial statements for Hannibal Corporation translated to U.S. dollars in accordance with *SFAS No. 8* rules.
(b) Compute the following financial ratios for Hannibal Corporation after translation to U.S. dollars: (1) net income to sales; (2) debt to total assets; (3) net income to assets; (4) net income to shareholders' equity; (5) sales to assets.
(c) Compare the financial ratios computed above to the set of ratios computed in problem 38, which were based on *SFAS No. 52* translation rules. Which ratios would be more meaningful to investor analysts? Explain.

40. *Foreign Currency Translation under* SFAS No. 8 *and* SFAS No. 52.   The Intercontinental Corporation has a foreign subsidiary whose financial statements have been prepared in foreign currency (FC). Three transactions that affect the preparation of consolidated financial statements in this case are listed below.

(1) The foreign subsidiary purchased items for resale at the beginning of the year for 200,000 FC. These items were sold uniformly throughout the year for 300,000 FC.
(2) At the beginning of the year, a machine was purchased by the foreign subsidiary for 50,000 FC, to be depreciated on a straight-line basis over ten years.
(3) At the beginning of the year, Intercontinental advanced $100,000 to its foreign subsidiary, a loan that was still outstanding at the end of the year.

Each transaction should be regarded as independent of the others.
Foreign currency exchange rates are as follows:

At beginning of the year, 1 FC = $.50

Average rate during the year, 1 FC = $.45

At end of the year, 1 FC = $.40

REQUIRED

(a) For transaction (1), what amount of the subsidiary's gross margin should be included in the parent company's consolidated income statement under both *SFAS No. 8* and *SFAS No. 52*?
(b) For transaction (2), how much depreciation expense should be included in the parent company's consolidated income statement for the year under both *SFAS No. 8* and *SFAS No. 52*? Also, what should be the net cost (book value) of the machine to be included in

Intercontinental's consolidated balance sheet under both *SFAS No. 8* and *SFAS No. 52*?

(c) How would transaction (3) affect the consolidated financial statements of Intercontinental Corporation under both *SFAS No. 8* and *SFAS No. 52*?

41. *Foreign Currency Translation and Preparation of Consolidated Financial Statements.* On January 1, 1983, Argo Products, Inc., established a wholly owned subsidiary in Japan. The major portion of the sales of Argo Products–Japan consisted of items manufactured and sold in Japan. Exhibit A contains trial balances of the parent company and the subsidiary as of December 31, 1986. The exchange rates of yen to dollars at different times are noted below.

	Exchange Rate (dollars per yen)
At issuance of subsidiary's capital stock	.00400
At acquisition of year-end inventories	.00410
At acquisition of fixed assets	.00390
At average rate for 1986	.00405
Current rate	.00416

Exhibit A

Argo Products, Inc., U.S. and Japan
Trial Balances
At December 31, 1986

	Argo–Japan (in millions–yen)		Argo–U.S. (in thousands–dollars)	
	dr.	cr.	dr.	cr.
Cash	¥ 25		$ 10,000	
Accounts Receivable	450		9,000	
Inventories	1,000		22,000	
Fixed Assets—Net	10,000		150,000	
Investment in Argo–Japan			42,000	
Current Liabilities		¥ 600		$ 12,000
Bonds Payable				50,000
Capital Stock		10,000		120,000
Retained Earnings		575		48,000
Foreign Currency Adjustment			2,000	
Sales		5,000		100,000
Cost of Sales	3,500		70,000	
Depreciation	500		5,000	
Other Expenses	700		20,000	
Total	¥16,175	¥16,175	$330,000	$330,000

The translated dollar value of the subsidiary's retained earnings account on December 31, 1985 was $2,415,000.

REQUIRED   Prepare a pretax consolidated income statement for Argo Products, Inc., for the year 1986, and a consolidated balance sheet as of December 31, 1986.

42. *Translating the Accounts of a Foreign Subsidiary.*   Peerless Tire, Inc., established a subsidiary in Chile at the beginning of 1984. At that time, no-par common stock was issued by the subsidiary; the stock was purchased by Peerless Tire in exchange for 60 million pesos (P). Immediately thereafter, the subsidiary acquired a plant for P 30 million and machinery for P 10 million. The plant is to be written off on a straight-line basis over a 40-year period, and the machinery is to be depreciated over a ten-year period on the sum-of-the-years'-digits basis.

    The following transactions occurred relatively uniformly throughout the year. All such transactions took place within Chile.

Factory expenses incurred (other than depreciation)	P 40,000,000
Sales (90% collected by end of year)	P 50,000,000
Selling and administrative expenses	P 9,000,000
Current payables at year-end	P 6,000,000

The rates of exchange were as follows:

	Pesos in Dollars
	($ per peso)
Beginning of year	.0114
End of year	.0032
Weighted average during year	.0070
Weighted average last quarter	.0050

Year-end inventory (produced during last quarter) was P 6,000,000.

REQUIRED   Prepare a pre-closing trial balance of the subsidiary's accounts translated into U.S. dollars, using the following columnar headings.

Preclosing Unadjusted Trial Balance	Year-end Adjustments	Preclosing Adjusted Trial Balance	Conversion Factor	Trial Balance
(pesos)	(pesos)	(pesos)		(dollars)

43. *Translation of the Accounts of a Foreign Subsidiary: Adjustment to GAAP.*   Computermart, a wholly owned subsidiary of Computron, USA, was established on January 1, 1985, in West Germany. Computermart was to function

as a sales outlet for Computron, stocking and selling personal computers acquired from Computron. Selling prices and policies were set by Computron. Funds were forwarded to Computermart, and on January 1, 1985, it acquired the following fixed assets at the costs indicated.

	Deutsche Marks	Annual Rate of Depreciation
Warehouse	400,000	.02
Truck	50,000	.20
Office equipment	60,000	.10

During 1985, Computron made the following inventory shipments to Computermart:

January 15	$ 900,000
June 30	1,200,000
October 1	2,100,000

A trial balance of Computermart's accounts is presented in Exhibit A.

Exhibit A

Computermart
Trial Balance
At December 31, 1985
(in deutsche marks)

	Debit	Credit
Cash	DM 350,000	
Accounts Receivable	158,000	
Inventory	800,000	
Warehouse	440,000	
Truck	55,000	
Office Equipment	66,000	
Allowance for Depreciation — Warehouse		DM 8,800
Allowance for Depreciation — Truck		11,000
Allowance for Depreciation — Office Equipment		6,600
Accounts Payable		168,000
Common Stock		600,000
Fixed Asset Inflation Adjustment		51,000
Sales		4,800,000
Cost of Sales	3,400,000	
Selling and Administrative Expense	350,000	
Depreciation — Warehouse	8,800	
Depreciation — Truck	11,000	
Depreciation — Office Equipment	6,600	
Total	DM 5,645,400	DM 5,645,400

At the close of the year, the manager of Computermart had written up the fixed asset accounts by 10%, which corresponded to the rate of inflation in West Germany. The offsetting credit had been posted to a Fixed Asset Inflation Adjustment (equity) account. Depreciation for the year was based on the balances in the fixed asset accounts after adjustment for inflation.

Computermart uses FIFO for costing its inventory. The December 31 inventory amounted to DM 800,000.

The deutsche mark to dollar rates of exchange during 1985 were as follows:

January 1	DM 2.7 = $1
October 1	DM 2.9 = $1
December 31	DM 3.1 = $1
Average for year	DM 2.9 = $1

REQUIRED   Translate the accounts of Computermart into dollars for consolidation with Computron's accounts. For translating cost of sales, assume that the firm uses LIFO inventory costing. Also, assume that units produced during the year equals units sold.

ACCOUNTING ANALYSIS

12

Financial Statement Analysis

Users of financial accounting reports attempt to discern important relationships among the items included in the financial statements. This type of analysis entails the calculation of key financial ratios. This chapter discusses financial ratios widely used by lenders, equity investors, and other analysts of financial statements. In addition to describing how financial ratios are calculated, the chapter considers evidence concerning the usefulness of financial ratios, and the effects of certain accounting policy choices on the interpretation of financial ratios.

FINANCIAL RATIOS DEFINED

Financial ratios relate two items of accounting information — one number is divided by another to provide a percentage or a ratio. Various financial ratios (price earnings ratio, debt-to-assets ratio, return on assets ratio) were defined and used in earlier chapters. This chapter will provide a comprehensive listing and discussion of those ratios and many others that are used by financial statement analysts.

REASONS FOR RATIO ANALYSIS

Managers are concerned with financial ratio analysis for various reasons, including those presented in the paragraphs that follow.

1. *Impact of ratios on securities prices.*   Prices of equity securities are affected when investors revise their expectations about investment risks and returns. Since investors use financial ratios in assessing risks and returns, managers must consider these same ratios in making operating and financing decisions. In this manner managers may be able to predict the effect of their actions on the market value of company shares.

2. *Effect of ratios on the cost and availability of credit.*   Banks and other lenders frequently use financial ratios in making decisions involving the availability and costs of debt capital. Moreover, debt agreements often include provisions, termed **restrictive covenants,** that govern the acceptable limits for key financial ratios. If a borrowing firm's ratios violate the restrictive covenants, the loan may be in technical default, and the firm may need to rearrange its financing.

In addition to the importance of ratios in shaping the terms of new borrowings, financial ratios may affect the market value of a firm's outstanding debt securities. For example, bond ratings appear to be significantly affected by financial ratios, and the market values of outstanding bonds depend to some extent on the quality of the firm's bond ratings.

3. *Use of financial ratios in appraising management performance.*   Ratios that measure business profitability, efficiency, and liquidity are often used by shareholders and directors to assess the operating and financing policies of corporate managers. In addition, large firms often decentralize, and the performance of individual divisions or departments is frequently measured by a few summary ratios.

4. *Reliance on ratios in consumer credit-granting decisions and in choosing suppliers.*   Financial ratios are often used in reaching decisions concerning customers' credit terms (whether to extend credit, the maximum dollar amount to be extended, and the repayment period). Similarly, the choice of suppliers may be based partly on financial ratios as indicators of stability or reliability. Price negotiations with suppliers may be affected by profitability ratios.

5. *Availability of industry statistics in ratio form.*   Many industry associations publish industry averages in the form of financial ratios as well as financial ratios for individual member companies. These ratios may be used by managers

as a basis for scrutinizing their own operating and financing policies. Although it is naïve to assume that industry averages are desirable as norms or targets, managers should always be conscious of their reasons for structuring their firm differently than other firms in the industry.

METHODOLOGY OF FINANCIAL RATIO ANALYSIS

Comparisons and predictions are at the core of financial statement analysis. The analyst computes a set of key financial ratios and may compare these to (a) industry norms, (b) ratios of similar firms, and (c) past (historical) ratios for the same firm. In each case, the ratios calculated for an individual firm are compared to a benchmark set of ratios, so that the analyst may evaluate features such as profitability, liquidity, efficiency, and risk. Investor analysts use ratio comparisons in order to make predictions about changes in the market values of the firm's debt and equity securities.

Individual financial analysts often disagree concerning which financial ratios are most useful in making comparisons and predictions, how the ratios are to be computed, or the type of prediction models that should be used. This lack of agreement is due in part to the absence of an accepted theory of ratio analysis. As a consequence, an almost bewildering array of ratios is available to the analyst, and the professional journals report on many empirical studies examining the success or failure of various ratios in helping to explain or predict events.

TYPES OF FINANCIAL RATIOS

Financial ratios may be classified according to the characteristics that they are intended to measure. In Exhibit 12-1, we have classified ratios into three broad

Exhibit 12-1

Types of Financial Ratios

1. Percentage composition of financial statements
   a. Vertical analysis
   b. Horizontal analysis
2. Operating ratios
3. Financing ratios
   a. Debt-related
      (1) Liquidity
      (2) Solvency
   b. Equity-related
      (1) Intrinsic value and expected returns
      (2) Risk

groupings: (1) percentage composition of the financial statements; (2) operating ratios, which are related to how effectively the firm utilizes its assets; and (3) financing ratios, which are related to the capital structure of the firm, and resulting costs of debt and equity capital. The following sections discuss the computation of various ratios in each of the categories listed in Exhibit 12-1.

CALCULATION OF SPECIFIC FINANCIAL RATIOS

This section describes the calculation of specific financial ratios representative of the general types of ratios listed in Exhibit 12-1. To illustrate these calculations, we are using financial statements that appeared in the 1985 *Annual Report* of ITT Corporation. These statements include a balance sheet (Exhibit 12-2), an income statement (Exhibit 12-3), and a statement of changes in financial position (Exhibit 12-4). (Remember that at the time these financial statements were issued [1985], the FASB had not yet replaced the statement of changes in financial position with the statement of cash flows.) At later points in the discussion, we will also refer to selected footnote disclosures included in the published financial statements.

Observe that the financial statements included in these exhibits are consolidated statements. The balance sheet (Exhibit 12-2) shows a sizeable investment in insurance and finance subsidiaries among the noncurrent assets, however, that have not been consolidated with the parent company. The income statement (Exhibit 12-3) shows that ITT's equity in the earnings of these unconsolidated subsidiaries is equal to about 73 percent of operating income in 1985 (equity in earnings of $412.3 million, compared to operating income of $563.6 million). Although we are using the numbers included in consolidated financial statements to illustrate the ratio calculations discussed in the following pages, the reader should bear in mind that corporate consolidation policy may have a substantial impact on financial ratios. Later in the chapter we will observe how various ratios calculated for ITT would change if figures here for their subsidiaries were to be included in the consolidated financial statements.

In the sections that follow we discuss each of the types of ratios listed in Exhibit 12-1 and illustrate their calculation using the ITT financial statements contained in Exhibits 12-2, 12-3, and 12-4.

Percentage Composition Ratios: Vertical and Horizontal Analysis

As a first step in the analysis of financial statements, the statements are recast in percentage terms; all of the dollar amounts in a given statement are expressed as a percentage of the column total. This is commonly termed a **vertical analysis** of the financial statements, and Exhibits 12-2, 12-3, and 12-4 show the results of this type of analysis in columns on the right side of each exhibit. Each balance sheet item has been divided by the total assets; each income statement item has been divided by net sales; and the sources and uses of working capital have been divided by the total sources (which equal total uses).

Exhibit 12-2

Financial Statements for the Calculation of Financial Ratios

ITT Corporation
Consolidated Balance Sheets
At December 31, 1984 and 1985
(in thousands)

	1985	1984	Vertical Analysis Percent Composition 1985	Vertical Analysis Percent Composition 1984	Horizontal Analysis Percent Change
Assets					
Current Assets					
Cash	$ 200,181	$ 128,304	.01	.01	+.56
Accounts receivable	2,183,388	1,972,774	.15	.15	+.11
Inventories	2,061,708	1,883,327	.14	.15	+.09
Net assets of discontinued operations	276,662	748,372	.02	.06	−.63
Other current assets	287,767	238,659	.02	.02	+.21
	5,009,706	4,971,436	.34	.39	+.01
Investments, Deferred Receivables, and Other Assets					
Insurance and finance subsidiaries	3,077,889	2,697,861	.22	.21	+.14
Other investments	632,994	580,822	.04	.04	+.09
Receivables due subsequent to one year	516,103	264,177	.04	.02	+.95
Other assets	621,572	431,241	.04	.03	+.44
	4,848,558	3,974,101	.34	.30	+.22
Plant, Property, and Equipment	7,355,952	6,487,996	.53	.50	+.13
Less—Accumulated depreciation	2,941,717	2,412,042	(.20)	(.19)	+.22
	4,414,235	4,075,954	.33	.31	+.08
	$14,272,499	$13,021,491	1.00	1.00	+.10

Liabilities and Stockholders' Equity					
Current Liabilities					
Short-term debt					
Banks	$ 670,612	$ 545,261	.05	.04	+.23
Commercial paper	10,230	309,714	.00	.02	−.98
Current maturities of long-term debt	150,192	158,655	.01	.01	−.05
Other	53,989	48,474	.00	.00	+.12
	885,023	1,062,104	.06	.07	−.17
Trade payables	876,757	776,178	.06	.06	+.13
Other payables	321,792	210,404	.02	.02	+.53
Accrued payroll and benefits	474,355	407,951	.03	.03	+.16
Accrued taxes	297,514	191,604	.02	.01	+.55
Other current liabilities	991,505	716,417	.07	.05	+.39
	3,846,946	3,364,658	.26	.24	+.14
Reserves and Deferred Liabilities	1,199,398	900,341	.08	.07	+.33
Deferred Income Tax	23,974	54,250	.00	.00	−.55
Long-term Debt	2,576,531	2,557,545	.18	.22	+.01
Minority Equity in Subsidiaries Consolidated	155,858	112,035	.01	.01	+.38
	3,955,761	3,624,171	.27	.30	+.09
Stockholders' Equity					
Cumulative preferred stock (aggregate liquidation value $620,894 as of December 31, 1985)	321,544	321,153	.02	.02	+.00
Common stock—Authorized 200,000,000 shares, $1 par value Outstanding 140,533,317 and 139,746,601 shares	140,533	139,747	.01	.01	+.00
Capital surplus	1,240,425	1,235,273	.09	.10	+.00
Unrealized gain (loss) on equity securities, net of tax of $9,014 and $1,354	11,738	(2,110)	.00	.00	*
Cumulative translation adjustments	(652,083)	(943,007)	(.05)	(.07)	−.31
Retained earnings	5,407,635	5,281,606	.40	.40	+.02
	6,469,792	6,032,662	.47	.46	+.07
	$14,272,499	$13,021,491	1.00	1.00	+.10

Source: ITT Corporation, *Annual Report*, 1985.
*It is not meaningful to compute percentage in this case.

Exhibit 12-3

Financial Statements for the Calculation of Financial Ratios

ITT Corporation
Consolidated Income Statements
For the Years Ended December 31, 1984 and 1985
(in thousands)

	1985	1984	Vertical Analysis Percent Composition 1985	1984	Horizontal Analysis Percent Change
Results for Year					
Sales and Revenues	$11,871,150	$11,167,635	1.00	1.00	+.06
Costs and Expenses					
Cost of sales and services (including depreciation of $455,971 and $401,868)	9,618,271	8,922,930	.81	.80	+.08
Selling and general expenses	1,689,247	1,632,062	.14	.15	+.03
	11,307,518	10,554,992	.95	.95	+.07
Operating Income	563,632	612,643	.05	.05	−.08
Earnings (pre-tax) of Insurance and Finance Subsidiaries	412,345	186,464	.03	.02	+1.22
	975,977	799,107	.08	.07	+.22
Interest expense	(532,302)	(537,794)	(.04)	(.05)	−.01
Interest and dividend income	112,121	86,074	.01	.01	+.30
Special provision for product line closedowns	(160,000)	—	(.01)	—	*
Gain on issuance of capital stock by U.K. affiliate	—	54,747	—	.00	−1.00
Miscellaneous income (expense)—net	72,439	(72,710)	.01	(.01)	*
	468,235	329,424	.04	.03	+.42

Income Tax and Minority Equity					
U.S. and foreign income tax	(157,628)	(13,328)	(.01)	(.00)	*
Minority equity in net income	(24,230)	(9,777)	(.00)	(.00)	+1.49
Income from Continuing Operations	286,377	306,319	.03	.03	– .06
Discontinued Operations					
Income (loss) from operations and phaseout, net of tax (benefit) of $(10,603) and $(421)	(10,006)	624	(.00)	.00	*
Gain on disposal, net of tax of $45,653 and $60,459	17,130	141,103	.00	.01	– .88
Net Income	$ 293,501	$ 448,046	.03	.04	– .35
Earnings per Common Equivalent Share					
Continuing Operations	$1.84	$2.02			–.09
Discontinued Operations					
Operations and phaseout	(.07)	—			*
Gain on disposal	.12	.95			–.87
Net Income	$1.89	$2.97			–.36
Average Common Equivalent Shares	142,139	149,226			

Source: ITT Corporation, *Annual Report*, 1985.

*It is not meaningful to compute percentage changes in these cases.

Exhibit 12-4

Financial Statements for the Calculation of Financial Ratios

ITT Corporation
Consolidated Source and Application of Funds
For the Years Ended December 31, 1984 and 1985
(in thousands)

	1985	1984	Vertical Analysis Percent Composition 1985	1984	Horizontal Analysis Percent Change
Source of Funds					
Income from continuing operations including minority equity	$ 310,607	$ 316,096	.13	.21	– .02
Items which did not affect working capital					
Depreciation	455,971	401,868	.18	.27	+ .13
Reserves, deferred liabilities, and deferred income tax	262,481	9,993	.11	.01	*
Amortization and write-off of goodwill, computer software, and deferred business development costs	60,928	26,456	.02	.17	+1.30
Undistributed earnings of insurance and finance subsidiaries	(149,462)	(91,084)	(.06)	(.06)	+ .64
Special provision for product line closedowns (excluding $97,700 of working capital)	62,300	—	.03	—	*
Gain on issuance of capital stock by U.K. affiliate	—	(54,747)	—	(.03)	+1.00
Working capital provided from continuing operations	1,002,825	608,582	.41	.41	+ .65

Discontinued Operations

Income (loss) from operations and phaseout	(10,006)	624	(.00)	.00	*
Proceeds from sales	730,850	620,500	.30	.42	+ .18
Funds invested during the year	(242,010)	(105,730)	(.10)	(.07)	+1.28
Increase (decrease) in net assets from beginning of year	(471,710)	(373,667)	(.19)	(.25)	+ .26
Issuance of long-term debt	562,685	659,147	.23	.44	− .15
Cumulative translation adjustments	290,924	(202,517)	.12	.14	+ .44
Sales and retirements of plant, property, and equipment	140,785	91,098	.06	.06	+ .54
Minority equity	19,593	(25,694)	.00	(.02)	*
Issuance of capital stock	6,329	23,739	.00	.02	− .73
Decrease in working capital	444,018	196,304	.18	.13	+1.27
	$2,474,283	$1,492,386	1.00	1.00	+ .66

Application of Funds

Repayments and conversions of long-term debt	$ 733,103	$ 630,194	.30	.42	+ .16
Plant, property, and equipment (including $33,704 and $96,013 for companies purchased)	676,400	738,896	.27	.49	− .08
Other investments, deferred receivables, and other assets	560,457	121,833	.23	.08	+3.59
Investments in and advances from insurance and finance subsidiaries	216,718	(217,515)	.09	(.15)	*
Dividends declared	167,472	288,730	.07	.19	− .42
Exchange rate effects on plant, property, and equipment and long-term debt	120,133	(69,752)	.04	(.05)	*
	$2,474,283	$1,492,386	1.00	1.00	+ .66

Source: ITT Corporation, *Annual Report*, 1985.
*It is not meaningful to compute percentage changes in these cases.

For each item in the statements, the **horizontal analysis** of the financial statements indicates the percentage change from the previous year. This information is also included in Exhibits 12-2, 12-3, and 12-4. The vertical and horizontal analyses enable us to make the following observations:

1. In 1985 ITT Corporation's current assets comprised about 34 percent of total assets (see Exhibit 12-2, vertical analysis). The noncurrent assets consisted mainly of plant and equipment (33 percent) and investments in nonconsolidated subsidiaries (22 percent). The percentage composition of total assets changed little from the previous year (horizontal analysis).

2. The capital structure of ITT Corporation in 1985 consisted of 53 percent liabilities and 47 percent shareholders' equity. The liabilities were evenly divided between current (26 percent) and noncurrent (27 percent) categories. These percentages were also quite similar to those of the previous year.[1]

3. In 1985 the total assets and equities of ITT Corporation increased about 10 percent over the previous year (see Exhibit 12-2). This was due mainly to increases in noncurrent assets.

4. ITT's net income as a percentage of sales decreased from 4 percent in 1984 to 3 percent in 1985 (see Exhibit 12-3, vertical analysis). Although sales increased by 7 percent from 1984 to 1985, the dollar amount of profits decreased by 35 percent (horizontal analysis).

5. Several factors contributed to the lower profits in 1985, including (1) a substantial ($160 million) special charge for product line closedowns and (2) a more than tenfold increase in tax expense. (Statement footnotes, not reproduced in the exhibits here, reveal that the latter factor is due in large part to taxable gains on companies sold by ITT during 1985.)

6. Working capital from operations in 1985 comprised 41 percent of total funds sources (Exhibit 12-4, vertical analysis). Working capital provided by operations increased by 65 percent between 1985 and 1984 (horizontal analysis). This was due primarily to increases in reserves and deferred liabilities.

7. Approximately 30 percent of total funds in 1985 were received as proceeds from sales of discontinued operations. Long-term debt issuances accounted for 23 percent of the fund sources, down from 44 percent in 1984.

8. The main uses of funds by ITT Corporation in 1985 were for debt repayment (30 percent); new property, plant, and equipment (27 percent); and investments in other long-term assets (23 percent).

---

[1]These calculations are based on the classifications used in ITT Corporation's published financial statements. Some analysts may question the way that certain items are classified (deferred taxes, minority interest, translation gains, and various other items, for example). Those analysts might reclassify those amounts and compute different percentages.

Declared dividends were 42 percent lower in 1985 than in 1984. Overall in 1985, ITT Corporation was involved in selling substantial amounts of investments, discontinuing product lines, reducing long-term debt, and increasing shareholders' equity by reducing dividends to shareholders.

The preceding observations indicate just some of the relationships that are revealed by vertical and horizontal analysis of the financial statements. The specific relationships that are deemed to be of importance will vary with the purposes of the analyst. Typically, the analyst will begin with an overview of the relationships within the financial statements (vertical analysis) and changes in key items over time (horizontal analysis), and then proceed to the calculation of other specific ratios.

Operating Ratios

Operating ratios attempt to measure the profitability and efficiency with which the firm uses its resources. Profitability ratios relate the firm's income to bases such as assets employed, sales, or shareholders' equity. Efficiency ratios generally measure the "turnover" of specific assets: the carrying values of individual assets are compared to the amount of related revenues or expenses for the period.

The most widely used bases for assessing profitability are assets employed, sales, and shareholders' equity. Return on assets and return on sales ratios relate operating profit to assets employed and to sales, respectively. Return on shareholders' equity relates income from recurring operations to shareholders' equity. These ratios will be discussed in detail in the following sections.

Return on assets ratio   The return on assets ratio is calculated using the following equation:

$$ROA = \frac{\text{Operating Income}}{\text{Operating Assets}}$$

The numerator of the ROA equation is **operating income**—income before financing expenses. The denominator of this ratio is the cost of assets *employed* in providing the firm's operating income. (This means that an investment item, such as land held for future use, might be excluded from the denominator because it does not represent an asset that is currently being employed.)

Let us turn again to the ITT Corporation case. The operating income reported in Exhibit 12-3 does not include ITT's equity in the earnings of nonconsolidated finance and insurance subsidiaries nor the effect of discontinued operations. Consequently, the costs of these investments and net assets of discontinued operations must be subtracted from total assets before computing the return on assets. Information extracted from Exhibit 12-2 permits us to calculate ITT's operating assets.

	(in thousands)	
	1985	1984
Operating income (Exhibit 12-3)	$ 563,632	$ 612,643
Total assets (Exhibit 12-2)	$14,272,499	$13,021,491
Investments in insurance and finance subsidiaries	(3,077,889)	(2,697,861)
Net assets of discontinued operations	(276,662)	(748,372)
Operating assets (that is, total assets less investments in nonconsolidated subsidiaries and net assets of discontinued operations	$10,917,948	$ 9,575,258

The ROA calculation for ITT Corporation may now be made as follows:

$$\text{ROA} = \frac{\text{Operating Income}}{\text{Operating Assets}}$$

$$\text{ROA (1985)} = \frac{\$563,632 \text{ thousand}}{\$10,917,948 \text{ thousand}}$$

$$= 5.16\%$$

$$\text{ROA (1984)} = \frac{\$612,643 \text{ thousand}}{\$9,575,258 \text{ thousand}}$$

$$= 6.40\%$$

The frequent attention given to return on assets as a measure of profitability leads one to ask whether managers ought to define successful performance in terms of improvements in the return on assets ratio. Surveys of prevailing management practice consistently reveal that *return on assets is widely used as a primary means of assessing performance in decentralized organizations.* Economists, however, have demonstrated that the firm that attempts to maximize return on assets will be led to produce below the levels indicated by sound economic reasoning. Microeconomic theory tell us that investments in assets should be *expanded* when the expected returns exceed the opportunity costs of investment. Managers who are judged on the basis of return on assets, however, may often improve their firm's ROA ratio merely by *curtailing* the level of capital spending. If the net book values of assets decline more rapidly than do the profits generated by those assets, the return on assets percentage must increase. The effect is especially pronounced for older assets and, in some cases, may lead managers to act against the best interests of the shareholders.

Return on sales and asset turnover ratio   The return on assets measure can be explained in terms of the following two separate ratios:

$$\text{Return on Sales} = \frac{\text{Operating Income}}{\text{Sales}}$$

$$\text{Asset Turnover} = \frac{\text{Sales}}{\text{Operating Assets}}$$

Therefore,

$$\text{Return on Assets} = \text{Return on Sales} \times \text{Asset Turnover}$$

$$= \frac{\text{Operating Income}}{\text{Sales}} \times \frac{\text{Sales}}{\text{Operating Assets}}$$

$$= \frac{\text{Operating Income}}{\text{Operating Assets}}$$

Return on sales (ROS) indicates the percentage of each sales dollar represented by operating income. **Asset turnover** indicates the number of sales dollars produced by each dollar invested in operating assets. For ITT Corporation, the calculations for 1985 (using sales totals from Exhibit 12-3) are

$$\text{ROA} = \frac{\text{Operating Income}}{\text{Sales}} \times \frac{\text{Sales}}{\text{Operating Assets}}$$

$$= \frac{\$563,632}{\$11,871,150} \times \frac{\$11,871,150}{\$10,917,948}$$

$$= 0.0475 \times 1.0873$$

$$= 5.16\%$$

In 1984:

$$\text{ROA} = \frac{\text{Operating Income}}{\text{Sales}} \times \frac{\text{Sales}}{\text{Operating Assets}}$$

$$= \frac{\$612,643}{\$11,167,635} \times \frac{\$11,167,635}{\$9,575,258}$$

$$= 0.0549 \times 1.1663$$

$$= 6.40\%$$

The advantage of relating these ratios in this way is that it results in a depiction of the separate factors that influence the profitability of assets:

1. For a given level of sales, greater cost efficiencies will increase profits, and thereby increase return on assets.
2. For a given level of sales, a reduction of assets will increase asset turnover and thereby increase return on assets.

The difficulty with such statements rests in the implied separation of variables that are in most cases highly *interdependent.* Sales prices and quantities are affected by the firm's investments in receivables, inventories, warehouses, and other facilities. Changes in assets cause changes in expenses and thereby directly affect the income statement. There are many other direct and indirect linkages between assets, sales, and profits. Of course, the return on assets ratio may serve to remind managers that unproductive assets ought to be done away with and that sales should be produced as efficiently as possible.

For ITT Corporation, ROA decreased from 6.40 percent in 1984 to 5.16 percent in 1985. This reflects a decrease in return on sales (ROS) from 5.49 percent in 1984 to 4.75 percent in 1985 and a decrease in asset turnover from 1.166 in 1984 to 1.087 in 1985.

Although the asset turnover ratio is widely used in assessing efficiency, there are a number of troublesome issues involved with its interpretation.

1. The asset turnover ratio may be very sensitive to the firm's consolidation policy. For example, ITT accounts for various unconsolidated subsidiaries using the equity method. The carrying value of these investments was $3.078 billion at the end of 1985 (Exhibit 12-2). Supplementary footnote disclosures, however, indicated that these subsidiaries had total assets of more than $26.6 billion at the close of 1985. As a consequence, consolidation of these subsidiaries would increase ITT's reported assets by over $23.5 billion ($26.6 billion − $3.078 billion), an increase of 164 percent over the reported amount of $14.272 billion.

2. Aside from the question of which assets to include in the asset turnover measure, there is the issue of how such assets are to be measured. In the framework of historical cost, should asset values be computed before or after depreciation? In ITT's case, Exhibit 12-2 shows that accumulated depreciation was $3.2 billion at December 31, 1985, so gross assets would be larger than net assets ($14.3 billion, Exhibit 12-2) by approximately 20 percent. This type of effect is likely to vary from firm to firm depending in part on the age of the firm's assets and the depreciation methods employed.

3. Some analysts may not be satisfied with accounting measures of assets that fail to allow for changing prices and/or values. Certain analysts may adjust for inflation by updating historical costs for general price level changes. Others may consider current (replacement) costs of assets to be a more useful measure of assets employed. Another group may regard the "exit price" or current liquidating values of the assets to be a better measure of their value. Since managers forego receipt of these liquidating values if they continue to use the assets in operations, liquidating value may be a better measure of opportunity cost.

Each of these issues affecting the interpretation of the asset turnover ratio is unsettled. Consequently, different analysts of financial statements are likely to produce different measures of asset turnover.

Return on shareholders' equity ratio   The return on shareholders' equity (ROE) ratio is calculated as follows:

$$ROE = \frac{\text{Net Income from Continuing Operations}}{\text{Shareholders' Equity}}$$

The numerator of the ROE equation is net income from continuing operations, which includes the after-tax cost of interest on the firm's indebtedness. This differs from the operating income measure that was used earlier in computing ROA. This difference is due to the fact that ROE focuses on the profitability of shareholders' investment, which is the result of both operating and financing activities.

The numerical relationship of ROA and ROE depends on the firm's after-tax borrowing cost, and the firm's after-tax return on assets. If after-tax borrowing costs are below ROA, then a firm will increase its ROE by increasing its proportion of debt financing. Increasing the proportion of debt in order to increase ROE is referred to as **trading on the equity.** To illustrate the effects, consider a firm with $1 billion of operating assets, all equity financing (no outstanding debt), a 10-percent after-tax ROA, and an after-tax interest cost of 6 percent. ROE would vary with changes in the proportion of debt as follows:

Financing Percent		Net	Shareholders'	
Debt	Equity	Income*	Equity	ROE
0%	100%	$100 million	$1,000 million	10 %
30%	70%	82 million	700 million	11 5⁄7%
60%	40%	64 million	400 million	16 %
90%	10%	46 million	100 million	46 %

*Net income is $100 million, less 6 percent interest cost of outstanding debt.

In this example we assume that increasing the debt percentage does not affect the cost of additional borrowing. That is not likely to be the case. As firms rely more heavily on debt, the cost of borrowing is likely to increase substantially (as was discussed in Chapter 6). Moreover, even in cases where additional borrowing at a rate below ROA increases ROE, such an increase in ROE is not necessarily to the advantage of the equity shareholder. If investors perceive the firm's common shares to be more risky as the debt percentage increases, then the market value of the stock may actually decline while ROE increases. In summary, both the cost of borrowing and the required investor return on outstanding stock will increase when the firm relies more heavily on debt financing. ROE will increase as long as the borrowing cost is below ROA. The effect on the market value of shareholders' equity depends on investor reactions to increased investment risk.

Other turnover ratios: inventory and accounts receivable   The broad measure of asset turnover just described may be too highly aggregated to suit the analyst. The firm's overall investment in operating assets consists of many types of assets—customer accounts receivable, inventories, plant and equipment, and so on. Each of these types of assets pertains to different activities of the firm. Customer accounts receivable depend on the level of credit sales and the firm's collection policy; inventory balances are related to levels of production and sales; and plant and equipment investment depends on the technology used in production. These factors lead analysts to compute various additional turnover ratios. Two of these ratios will be discussed here: the inventory turnover ratio and the accounts receivable turnover ratio.

The **inventory turnover ratio** relates cost of sales to the average inventory balance for the period and is computed in accordance with the following formula:

$$\text{Inventory Turnover} = \frac{\text{Cost of Sales}}{\text{Average Inventory}}$$

In order to illustrate this calculation, refer to ITT's financial statements. The income statement (Exhibit 12-3) reports a "cost of sales and services." For purposes of illustration, we will assume that the entire amount represents the cost of goods sold. The figures for beginning and ending inventory appear in Exhibit 12-2. Accordingly, the calculation of ITT's inventory turnover ratio for 1985 is as follows:

$$\text{Inventory Turnover} = \frac{\text{Cost of Sales and Services}}{1/2 \text{ (beginning plus ending inventories)}}$$

$$= \frac{\$9,618 \text{ million}}{1/2 \text{ (\$1,883 million} + \$2,062 \text{ million)}}$$

$$= 4.88$$

This calculation indicates that ITT "turns over" its inventory 4.88 times a year. Stated another way, ITT has about one-fifth of a year's sales, or approximately 72 days worth of sales in the average inventory. In interpreting this ratio (as with others we have examined) a number of limitations must be recognized:

1. Inventories often fluctuate in response to seasonal movements in demand and to longer-term sales trends. Since seasonal fluctuations are entirely ignored in the computation of inventory turnover, we may not obtain an adequate measure of "average" inventory by using annual opening and closing balances.
2. Changes in inventory turnover may reflect shifts in a firm's product-line mix rather than a changed relationship between units of inventory related to sales. For example, if products that require a

higher level of inventory represent a greater proportion of total sales, this might cause a decrease in inventory turnover measures; yet within each product line the relationship between inventory and cost of sales might be stable.

3. The composition of inventory balances may be at least as important as inventory totals. For example, ITT's ending inventory balance includes completed products awaiting delivery to dealers and customers, as well as partially fabricated products at various plant locations, and warehouse stocks of raw materials and component parts. A breakdown of total inventory costs by degree of inventory completion is not available in the financial report. However, the analyst may believe that stocks of completed products provide a useful measure of inventory turnover. Analogous statistics may be useful for other inventory analyses; it is production requirements rather than expected sales that govern the amount of raw materials and components on hand. Sales and production budgets are often quite dissimilar.

4. A variety of inventory cost flow assumptions are available to management. ITT uses the FIFO costing method. If we assume that inventory replacement costs have generally been rising, then the cost of sales reported by ITT is somewhat lower than the replacement costs of those goods at the date of sale. In any event, comparison of ITT's inventory turnover with those of other "similar" firms would need to be made with a correction for any differences in inventory costing methods.

5. Since inventory management policies must be seen in the context of several related decisions, it is difficult to interpret a change in inventory turnover as unambiguously good or bad. Inventories may be promotional variables since customer convenience may be improved by higher stocks of finished goods. In some cases inventory stockpiles are increased based on anticipated price increases, possible disruptions in supply sources, or efficiencies in large block purchases and deliveries.

The **accounts receivable turnover ratio** relates credit sales to average accounts receivable for the period and is computed as follows:

$$\text{Accounts Receivable} = \frac{\text{Credit Sales}}{\text{Average Accounts Receivable}}$$

Again, to illustrate using ITT, we will assume that the entire amount of "sales and revenues" reported in Exhibit 12-3 represents credit sales. In many cases the financial analyst would attempt to separate credit sales from non-credit sales because accounts receivable arise from credit sales only. The ITT calculations (using sales figures from Exhibit 12-3 and accounts receivable totals from Exhibit 12-2) are shown on page 604.

$$\text{Accounts Receivable Turnover (1985)} = \frac{\text{Sales and Revenues}}{1/2\,(\text{beginning plus ending accounts receivable})}$$

$$= \frac{\$11{,}871 \text{ million}}{1/2\,(\$1{,}973 \text{ million} + \$2{,}183 \text{ million})}$$

$$= 5.71$$

This ratio indicates that in 1985 ITT turned over its receivables about 5.71 times. Expressed another way, it takes ITT on average about 63 days to collect its receivables; this amount is calculated by dividing the number of days in the year by the accounts receivable turnover rate (360 days ÷ 5.71).

Analysts frequently compare the average collection period to the firm's credit policy in attempting to assess the quality of the receivables. As always, however, there are a number of points to be noted in using this ratio.

1. The accounts receivable balance may not be used to compute average days' sales uncollected unless sales are at a consistent level throughout the year. For example, if ITT's credit sales slacken in the winter months, then the average age of the year-end balances is probably well in excess of the 63 days calculated above. On the other hand, for those firms with unusually large sales demand preceding the financial reporting date, the ratio would overstate the average age of the outstanding receivables.
2. Collection terms on accounts receivable are often changed as part of a firm's overall sales promotion strategies, and in these cases, changes in receivables turnover may simply reflect trade-offs between price competition, advertising expenditures, and other attempts to increase sales.
3. Another factor to be considered in using the accounts receivable turnover ratio to measure operating efficiency involves awareness of the completeness of the accounts receivable information being utilized. Footnote disclosures of financial information for ITT's unconsolidated finance and insurance subsidiaries report substantial amounts of additional accounts receivable. The effects of including these receivables in the calculation will be presented later in the chapter.

This section has described several ratios that are designed to assess operating performance. The return on assets measure (ROA) aims to reflect the ability of operating managers to profitably employ the firm's economic resources. ROA depends on both the level of earnings and on the investment in assets necessary to generate those earnings. Operating efficiency depends on control of operating expenses and amounts invested in operating assets. Analysts must keep in mind, however, that the accounting policies of the firm may have substantial effects on the level of and changes in these ratios.

Financing Ratios

We now consider those financial ratios that result from the firm's financing decisions. Financing ratios reflect the capital structure of the firm (the overall mix of debt and equity financing) and are widely used by investor analysts in assessing the potential risks and returns related to the firm's debt and equity securities. We will continue to follow the outline presented in Exhibit 12-1 and first consider ratios pertinent to present and potential lenders; then we will proceed to a discussion of ratios relevant to equity shareholders. Of course, some of the features of a firm that affect its debt quality also affect the value of shareholders' equity. The economic characteristics of a firm are interrelated and its value depends on the efficiency of its resource utilization, the manner in which it is financed, and the riskiness of its earnings and cash flows.

Debt ratios   Generally, debt ratios assess either liquidity or solvency. **Liquidity ratios** address the short-term ability of the firm to meet its debt obligations as they come due. **Solvency ratios,** on the other hand, center on the long-term ability of the firm to pay its debts.

Liquidity ratios   The two most widely used measures of the firm's ability to meet its debt obligations as they come due are the current ratio and the quick ratio. The **current ratio** is computed by dividing current assets by current liabilities and is intended to indicate the ability of the firm to pay its short-term debts at maturity. For ITT the computation at the end of 1985 (using figures from Exhibit 12-2) is

$$\text{Current Ratio} = \frac{\text{Current Assets}}{\text{Current Liabilities}}$$

$$= \frac{\$5,010 \text{ million}}{\$3,847 \text{ million}}$$

$$= 1.30$$

The wide use of this ratio to assess liquidity is the result of the accounting convention used in defining "current" assets and liabilities. **Current assets** are cash and other economic resources that can reasonably be expected to be realized in cash or sold or consumed within one year (or within the normal operating cycle of the firm, if longer than one year). **Current liabilities** require the payment of operating cash or the creation of other current liabilities within the same period. These definitions convey the impression that if current assets are large enough to meet current liabilities, the firm is sufficiently liquid. Yet the difficulties with such a ratio are easily seen:

1. Current assets do not represent the total estimated cash inflows over the coming year, nor do current liabilities represent the total budgeted cash outflows. Rather, current assets are simply those on hand at

year-end, and current liabilities are those that result from accounting transactions that occur prior to the balance sheet date.

2. The composition of current assets may change markedly, while the current ratio remains reasonably stable. The components vary in degree of liquidity. Cash and marketable securities are immediately available funds. Accounts receivable are less liquid, but can be sold or pledged without significant loss. Inventory balances can usually be expected to convert to cash at the firm's normal markup over cost, but in the event of forced liquidation, inventory balances are likely to bear significant losses. Finally, prepaid expenses generate no cash in the current period.

3. A larger current ratio is not obviously an improvement in financial position. Increases in a firm's current assets may reflect overinvestment in short-term assets financed by long-term debt or equity capital. It is also frequently a simple matter for financial managers to "window-dress" the financial statements to improve the appearance of certain ratios. If the current ratio is greater than 1.0, it increases as current assets are used to pay current liabilities, while net working capital remains unchanged. Consider the current ratio of 1.30 calculated earlier for ITT. If $1 billion of current assets were used to pay (reduce) $1 billion in current liabilities, the ITT current ratio would rise to 1.41. In contrast to the rule and example just discussed, if the current ratio is less than 1.0, it is improved not by decreasing but by increasing current assets and current liabilities in equal amounts.

The **quick ratio** compares cash and near-cash items to current liabilities. The calculation for ITT during 1985 is

$$\text{Quick Ratio} = \frac{\text{Cash} + \text{Receivables}}{\text{Current Liabilities}}$$

$$= \frac{\$200 \text{ million} + \$2,183 \text{ million}}{\$3,847 \text{ million}}$$

$$= .619$$

This ratio is unaffected by inventories or prepaid expenses, and thus avoids some of the difficulties raised earlier in connection with use of the current ratio. The problems of timing and the possibilities for window dressing, however, still remain. The difficulties with both the current ratio and the quick ratio suggest that the next period's cash budget may be a more useful indication of short-term financial liquidity. Of course, outsiders are seldom privy to such information.

Solvency ratios   With the calculation of solvency ratios the focus shifts to the long-term ability of the firm to pay its debts. The financial leverage ratio and the times-interest-earned ratio are widely used for this purpose.

The basic question involved with the **financial leverage ratio** involves how much of the firm's total economic resources reflect borrowed capital. Alternatively, the question may be reformulated to ask what percentage of total assets is available as a buffer to absorb losses in the event of a forced liquidation of company assets. Financial leverage is measured alternatively as the ratio of debt to total assets or as the ratio of debt to equity. Using data (1985 total assets, current liabilities, and long-term debt) for ITT from Exhibit 12-2, the computation is

$$\text{Financial Leverage} = \frac{\text{Debt}}{\text{Total Assets}}$$

$$= \frac{\$7,803 \text{ million}}{\$14,272 \text{ million}}$$

$$= .547$$

or

$$\text{Financial Leverage} = \frac{\text{Debt}}{\text{Stockholders' Equity}}$$

$$= \frac{\$7,803 \text{ million}}{\$6,470 \text{ million}}$$

$$= 1.21$$

The first equation indicates that 54.7 percent of ITT's capital is provided by borrowed funds. In the event of liquidation, debt holders are protected unless losses exceed 45.3 percent (100 − 54.7) of the carrying value of total assets.

There are several issues to bear in mind when interpreting the debt-to-assets ratio. To begin, consider the valuation methods that are used in reporting debt and equity. Refer to ITT's balance sheet (Exhibit 12-2). Current liabilities are obligations to be paid shortly at the dollar amounts listed. The long-term debt is recorded at adjusted book value (original proceeds modified by the amortization of bond discount). Should the dollar amount of debt be computed at book value, at the principal amount of the debt, at the current market price of the debt, or at some other figure? Observe also that a portion of ITT's financing reflects deferred taxes. Should this amount be included as an obligation? Is it useful to distinguish between debtor claims that must be paid in the event of company bankruptcy and other debts that depend on the results of future operations (such as deferred taxes)? There are no clear-cut answers to the issues raised by these questions, and each analyst must decide on an appropriate measure.

The dollar amount of equity also presents difficulties in definition and measurement. The book value of net worth for ITT Corporation is $6.5 billion. This is the total of the dollars paid to the company for outstanding shares plus retained earnings. The market (trading) value of company equity shares will usually differ from the net worth shown on the balance sheet.

Some financial writers suggest that the debt-to-assets ratio of the firm be computed using the *market values* of the related securities. This approach, however, is difficult to apply for two reasons: (1) many items that might be considered as debt, (leases and pension liabilities, for example) are not publicly traded, so market values are unavailable, and (2) the underlying purpose of debt-to-assets calculations is not served by market values because these values will change dramatically if bankruptcy becomes a likely event.

The basic question addressed by the **times-interest-earned ratio** is, How large a multiple is earnings in relation to interest charges? The ratio is computed in accordance with the following formula:

$$\text{Times-interest-earned Ratio} = \frac{\text{Net Income} + \text{Income Tax} + \text{Interest Expense}}{\text{Interest Expense}}$$

Income taxes are added back because interest is a tax-deductible expense; no tax is due unless earnings are sufficient to pay the interest expense. For ITT, which reported interest expenses of $532.3 million in 1985 (Exhibit 12-3), the calculation is as follows:

$$\text{Times-interest-earned Ratio} = \frac{\text{Net Income} + \text{Income Tax} + \text{Interest Expense}}{\text{Interest Expense}}$$

$$= \frac{\$293,501 + 157,628^2 + 532,302}{\$532,302}$$

$$= 1.85$$

This computation indicates that pretax income before interest expense is 1.85 times as large as interest expense.

The times-interest-earned ratio should be interpreted cautiously for a number of reasons, including the following:

1. The firm likely has various committed fixed costs in addition to interest expense, which must be met regardless of operating levels. There is no reason to focus solely on interest, since other claims may have equal priority against the firm's resources.
2. Although the usual purpose of the times-interest-earned ratio is to assess the firm's ability to pay interest with cash, the computation emphasizes income rather than cash flow from operations.
3. Many contractual cash flows (both receipts and disbursements) have no direct effect on the income calculation. For example, the firm may have contractual installment accounts receivable. These provide regular

---

[2]ITT's income statement includes a charge for minority equity. In some situations this amount would also need to be added back to the numerator. The calculation shown above assumes that all interest expense pertains to the parent company and its 100-percent-owned consolidated subsidiaries.

cash inflows in periods when little or no earned income is reported. Conversely, the firm may have contractual payments to bond sinking funds or to trusteed pension funds, which represent cash outflows not appearing on the income statement.

Equity Ratios   Equity ratios are used in common stock valuation and in the assessment of stock risk. Securities valuation involves an attempt by analysts to detect mispriced securities and is based on the belief that the true or "intrinsic" value of the firm might be uncovered by looking at various fundamental characteristics of the firm. Analysts engaged in securities valuation attempt to "beat the market" — to earn superior returns after adjustment for risk. Risk assessment, on the other hand, involves an attempt by analysts to predict and control the variability of investment returns.

Ratios used in securities valuation: intrinsic value and expected returns   Although no accepted theory exists to link financial ratios to the true or intrinsic value of the firm, various financial ratios are widely cited by analysts anxious to demonstrate that a given security is either overpriced or underpriced in the financial market. Exhibit 12-5 lists several ratios popularly used for this purpose.

Per-share amounts, which are listed in the upper segment of Exhibit 12-5, are used in computing the growth measures and other ratios described in the lower portion of the exhibit. The earnings-per-share (EPS) amount is computed using the weighted-average number of shares outstanding during the year. The details of the calculation were given in Chapter 7. The other per-share amounts are based on the shares outstanding at the end of the year.

For ITT Corporation, the per-share amounts for 1985 are shown below. (The figures given for market price per share and dividends per share are disclosed in portions of ITT Corporation's annual report that are not included in the exhibits in this chapter.)

Earnings per share (Exhibit 12-3)   = $1.89

Book value per share — The preferred shareholders' equity must first be subtracted from ITT's total shareholders' equity in order to compute the book value of the common stock:

Total stockholders' equity (Exhibit 12-2)	$6,469.8 million
Less: preferred stock at liquidation value (Exhibit 12-2)	620.9 million
Common stockholders' equity	$5,848.9 million

Common stock outstanding, December 31, 1985 (Exhibit 12-2)   140,533,317 shares

$$\text{Book value per share} = \frac{\$5,848.9 \text{ million}}{140,533,317}$$
$$= \$41.62$$

Market price (value) per share at December 31, 1985 = $36.00
Dividends per share during 1985   = $ 1.00

Exhibit 12-5
Financial Accounting Numbers Used in Securities Valuation

Per-share Amounts

$$\text{Earnings per Share} = \frac{\text{Net Income Available to Common Shareholders}}{\text{Weighted-average of Common Shares Outstanding}}$$

$$\text{Book Value per Share} = \frac{\text{Book Value of Total Common Equity, End of Year}}{\text{Common Shares Outstanding, End of Year}}$$

Market Value per Share = Closing Market Price at End of Reporting Period

Dividends per Share = Total Dividends Declared per Common Share for the Reporting Period

Growth Rates

$$\left.\begin{array}{l} \text{Earnings Growth} \\ \text{Asset Growth} \\ \text{Sales Growth} \end{array}\right\} \quad \begin{array}{c} \text{Average annual rates of growth} \\ \text{over time periods selected by} \\ \text{the analyst} \end{array}$$

Other Ratios

$$\text{Price-to-Earnings Ratio} = \frac{\text{Market Value per Share}}{\text{Earnings per Share}}$$

$$\text{Dividends-to-Earnings Ratio} = \frac{\text{Dividends per Share}}{\text{Earnings per Share}}$$

$$\text{Dividends-to-Price Ratio} = \frac{\text{Dividends per Share}}{\text{Market Value per Share}}$$

$$\text{Market Value-to-Book Value Ratio} = \frac{\text{Market Value per Share}}{\text{Book Value per Share}}$$

Measurement of the firm's rate of growth, which is used both in securities valuation and in risk assessment, is frequently based on earnings, assets, or sales. Using figures from Exhibit 12-2 and Exhibit 12-3, the calculations for ITT Corporation are on page 611. (Note that the resulting percentages, which have been rounded to the nearest percent, also appear in the percent change columns in Exhibits 12-2 and 12-3.)

$$\text{Earnings Growth} = \frac{1985 \text{ Net Income}}{1984 \text{ Net Income}} - 1$$

$$= \frac{\$293.5 \text{ million}}{\$448.0 \text{ million}} - 1$$

$$= -35\%$$

$$\text{Asset Growth} = \frac{\text{Total Assets, December 31, 1985}}{\text{Total Assets, December 31, 1984}} - 1$$

$$= \frac{\$14,272 \text{ million}}{\$13,021 \text{ million}} - 1$$

$$= 10\%$$

$$\text{Sales Growth} = \frac{1985 \text{ Sales}}{1984 \text{ Sales}} - 1$$

$$= \frac{\$11,871 \text{ million}}{\$11,167 \text{ million}} - 1$$

$$= 6\%$$

There is little agreement among financial analysts concerning how growth is best measured. As the various growth ratios for ITT indicate, different elements of the financial statements are likely to change at different rates. Moreover, if past growth rates are used to predict future growth rates, the selection of a "representative" time period is crucial.

The per-share amounts developed above may now be utilized to calculate the remaining ratios (the "Other Ratios") listed in Exhibit 12-5 for ITT Corporation. (Remember that some of the figures employed here for ITT have been taken from portions of the ITT Corporation annual report not included in the exhibits in this chapter.)

$$\text{Price-to-Earnings Ratio} = \frac{\text{Market Value per Share}}{\text{Earnings per Share}}$$

$$= \frac{\$36.00}{\$1.89}$$

$$= 19$$

$$\text{Dividends-to-Earnings Ratio} = \frac{\text{Dividends per Share}}{\text{Earnings per Share}}$$

$$= \frac{\$1.00}{\$1.89}$$

$$= 52.9\%$$

$$\text{Dividends-to-Price Ratio} = \frac{\text{Dividends per Share}}{\text{Market Value per Share}}$$

$$= \frac{\$1.00}{\$36.00}$$

$$= 2.7\%$$

$$\text{Market Value-to-Book Value Ratio} = \frac{\text{Market Value per Share}}{\text{Book Value per Share}}$$

$$= \frac{\$36.00}{\$41.62}$$

$$= 86.5\%$$

These ratio calculations enable the analyst to make the following observations:

1. ITT had a price to earnings ratio of 19 at the end of 1985. This was well above the average for large corporations at that date. Price to earnings ratios are expected to be positively related to growth (high-growth firms tend to have high price to earnings ratios) and negatively related to risk (high risk firms tend to have low ratios). The reciprocal of the price to earnings ratio is referred to as **earnings yield.** For ITT the earnings yield is 5.25 percent ($1.89/$36.00).

2. The dividends to earnings ratio, widely referred to as **dividend payout,** indicates that ITT paid out 52.9 percent of earnings as dividends and retained the remaining 47.1 percent (100 − 52.9 percent) for reinvestment. Based on the year-end share price, these dividends provided a return of 2.7 percent to shareholders. Of course, the shareholders' returns are also affected by changes in the market price of ITT shares. The annual report reveals that ITT shares' prices ranged from a low of $28.38 to a high of $38.88 during 1985.

3. The market to book value ratio shows that the book value per share exceeds the market price per share. The book value amount reflects the accounting methods used by ITT, and by this point, the reader is well aware that historical cost-based accounting values do not represent the economic value of the firm's net assets. Nonetheless, this ratio is frequently cited in the business press as an indicator that the shares of specific firms may be misvalued.

Ratios used in assessing risk Investors are concerned with the riskiness or variability of investment returns, and financial ratios are often used as measures of firms' characteristics that affect risk. Exhibit 12-6 lists several ratios that have been found useful for this purpose. Of the five ratios listed, three have already been discussed (financial leverage, dividends to earnings, and growth).

Exhibit 12-6

Financial Ratios Used in Assessing Risk

1. Financial leverage (debt-to-equity ratio)
2. Operating leverage
3. Earnings variability
4. Dividends-to-earnings ratio
5. Growth (in assets, sales, or earnings)

The calculation of the other two ratios (operating leverage ratio and earnings variability ratio) is discussed here.

The **operating leverage ratio** relates the percentage change in operating income to the percentage change in operating revenues and is computed in this manner:

$$\text{Operating Leverage} = \frac{\text{Percent Change in Operating Income}}{\text{Percent Change in Operating Revenues}}$$

Based on the income statement information provided in Exhibit 12-3, it would not be sensible to compute this ratio for ITT. ITT's operating revenues and operating income changed in opposite directions from 1984 to 1985: sales in 1985 increased by 6 percent, and operating income decreased by 8 percent from the previous year. Calculation of the operating leverage ratio shown above assumes that the firm's product mix, production methods, prices, and overall efficiency have remained stable over the period used in measuring operating leverage. When these assumptions cannot be made, the ratio calculation will not be useful.

An **earnings variability ratio** measures the *stability* of earnings. There are many different ways to define and measure variability. The selection of a given measure depends on the purpose of the analyst, the availability of suitable data, and statistical concerns that are outside the scope of this text. One straightforward measure of earnings variability is the percentage change in earnings. In 1985 the percentage change in earnings for ITT was 35 percent (Exhibit 12-3).

The ratios listed in Exhibit 12-6 that are used to measure risk are expected to be related to risk as follows:

1. Financial leverage is positively related to risk because debt represents a prior claim against the firm's revenues. Moreover, as a firm's debt burden increases, the likelihood of insolvency or bankruptcy also rises.
2. Operating leverage is positively related to risk because the ratio reflects the predominance of fixed expenses. Fixed expenses by definition do not vary with changes in revenues. For this reason, percentage

changes in income will exceed percentage changes in revenues if the firm has fixed expenses.

3. Earnings variability relates to the firm's ability to meet its fixed financing and operating expenses, and is positively related to risk. Earnings variability also may affect the amount of dividends that are paid to shareholders.

4. The dividends to earnings ratio reflects the proportion of earnings that are currently distributed to shareholders. There is little theoretical support for the use of this ratio to assess risk, but the literature in financial ratio analysis persistently supports its utilization. Empirically, the dividends to earnings ratio is negatively related to risk.

5. Since growth entails expansion (often into new product markets), substantial capital spending and changes in the technology of production, growth and risk are positively related.

EVIDENCE OF THE USEFULNESS OF FINANCIAL RATIOS

In the preceding sections we have illustrated the computation of various widely cited financial ratios and have stressed the absence of underlying theory tying specific ratios to users' predictions. In recent years, however, there have been a number of rigorous empirical studies that indicate that financial ratios may have some value in explaining or predicting various economic events. Although such research is in an embryonic stage, this section provides a brief summary of some of the evidence supporting the usefulness of financial ratios in the areas of (a) securities valuation, (b) securities risk assessment, (c) bond ratings, (d) bankruptcy, and (e) merger activity.

Securities Valuation

As we have seen, securities valuation involves an attempt by the analyst to identify mispriced securities. We have also seen that securities valuation is based on the belief that the true or "intrinsic" value of the firm might be uncovered by looking at various fundamental characteristics of the firm, and that the implications of such information will not yet be fully reflected in securities prices. Recent empirical evidence suggests that publicly available information is fully impounded in securities prices by the date of publication. However, certain contrary evidence also has been reported. Studies have shown that investors can "beat the market" by investing in (a) relatively small firms, (b) firms with low price-to-earnings multiples, and (c) firms with high financial leverage ratios. This evidence may indicate either that investors may earn superior returns by analysis of published accounting information, or that investors only *appear* to beat the market due to errors in the underlying models of expected securities returns. At this time, there is not sufficient evidence to reject either of these two views.

Securities Risk Assessment

Modern investment theory suggests the importance of a security's **systematic risk,** which reflects the expected co-movement of a security's returns with returns of the general market. For those who accept this investment theory, a main purpose of financial analysis is the estimation and prediction of systematic risk. Several studies have attempted to establish a relationship between various financial accounting ratios and risk and to see whether accounting ratios can be used to develop better predictions of risk. Evidence from these studies shows that some accounting ratios have information content in the sense that they explain a substantial portion of the differences in risk among firms. In particular, measures of dividend payout, financial leverage, firm size, and growth rates (measured using either sales or assets) are highly associated with market risk measures. It does not appear, however, that accounting ratios are useful in predicting systematic risk.

Bond Ratings

Typically, corporate bonds are sold to yield a return in excess of the "risk-free" rate on treasury bills or other direct obligations of the federal government. Generally, the amount of this excess interest or "risk premium" depends on the risk that the issuing firms will default on the bond obligations. A number of rating services (Moody's, Standard and Poor's, and so forth) assign quality ratings to a firm's outstanding bonds. These ratings are widely used by financial institutions and other lenders as indicators of the investment quality of available bonds.

Several studies have attempted to explain differences in risk premiums on corporate bonds by using financial ratios. In related work, researchers have attempted to explain differences in bond ratings using financial ratios. These studies indicate that financial ratios are highly associated with the pricing and the rating of corporate bonds. Ratios that appear to be useful for this task include measures of the size and age of the firm, measures of financial leverage, and measures of the total market value of the firm's bonds.

Bankruptcy

Corporate bankruptcy is a disruptive and costly event, and a series of studies suggests that financial ratios may provide useful early warnings of impending bankruptcy. Studies of the usefulness of individual financial ratios in predicting bankruptcy indicate that the ratio of cash flow to total debt has the best predictive power, followed by the ratio of net income to total assets. In general, "mixed ratios" — those with income or cash flow in the numerator and balance sheet items in the denominator — outperform the liquidity ratios, which have traditionally been used as predictors of failure. In fact, the current ratio has proven to be one of the least useful of the ratios tested for bankruptcy-prediction purposes.

Other recent studies aimed at assessing the usefulness of sets of financial ratios to predict bankruptcy employ statistical techniques that permit the simultaneous use of several financial ratios. A widely known study indicates that using data one year prior to bankruptcy, financial ratios permit the identification of impending bankruptcy with better than 95-percent accuracy. The financial ratios used in that study were net working capital to total assets; retained earnings to total assets; earnings to total assets; financial leverage; and asset turnover.

Merger Activity

Studies of corporate mergers consistently indicate that the shareholders of buyer and seller firms gain from mergers. Gains to buyers are modest (about five percent during the year preceding merger), while gains to sellers are substantial (ranging from 20–40 percent during the year preceding merger). The usefulness of financial ratios in predicting mergers has been studied in order to determine (a) the financial characteristics of seller firms that foreshadow a successful merger and (b) the possibility of earning abnormal securities returns by trading in the shares of buyer and seller firms. Generally, such studies indicate that the average seller firm has several distinguishing characteristics as compared to the average nonmerging firm, including (1) a lower price to earnings ratio, (2) lower financial leverage, (3) a higher rate of growth, and (4) smaller size.

ACCOUNTING METHODS AND FINANCIAL RATIOS

Financial ratios reflect the set of accounting methods used by the firm, and alternative accounting methods will affect the ratio calculations. Earlier chapters of this text have discussed alternative methods of accounting for inventories, noncurrent assets, changing prices, leasing, pensions, intercorporate investments, and various other items. The analyst must decide whether to base financial ratio calculations on the numbers reported in the firm's financial statements (as we have done throughout this chapter) or whether to adjust those numbers on the basis of additional information acquired from footnote disclosures and other supplementary data prior to ratio computation.

Effects of Consolidating ITT's Insurance and Financial Subsidiaries

This section will illustrate the effects on the firm's financial ratios of consolidating ITT's unconsolidated finance and insurance subsidiaries. The information concerning the finance and insurance subsidiaries is contained in the footnotes to the financial statements included in ITT's 1985 annual report. The end-of-chapter exercises include additional footnote disclosures, so that the reader may decide whether it would be useful to further revise the ratio calculations.

Exhibit 12-7 compares selected financial ratios for ITT Corporation prior to and following inclusion of the finance and insurance subsidiaries in the consolidated financial statements. (The ratio calculations excluding these subsidiaries were provided earlier in this chapter; the ratio calculations computed to include these subsidiaries are provided in the chapter appendix, Exhibit E-3) It is clear from Exhibit 12-7 that consolidation policy can have a substantial effect on financial ratios. For example,

- The return on assets ratio declines from 5.16 percent to 4.92 percent. This decline occurs because consolidation has increased total operating assets by a greater proportion than the increase in operating income.
- Financial leverage (debt to total assets) increases from 54.7 percent to 83 percent. This increase occurs because consolidation has not affected total shareholders' equity, although total debt has increased.
- Receivables turnover decreases from 5.71 to 2.22 times because the subsidiaries have large outstanding receivables balances. The extent to which these receivables on the books of the subsidiaries are related to the sales of the parent company is not clear from the financial statements.

In the case of ITT Corporation, consolidation policy is seen to have a substantial effect on selected financial ratio calculations. Yet it remains for the analyst to decide whether inclusion or exclusion of subsidiaries in the consolidation provides the "best" ratio to suit the purposes at hand. Because there is no coherent theory linking financial-accounting-based ratios to economic variables (such as liquidity, efficiency, risk, and valuation), it is difficult to provide a logically persuasive argument for or against consolidation.

Exhibit 12-7

**Selected Financial Ratios before and after Consolidation
of Insurance and Finance Subsidiaries**

ITT Corporation

Financial Ratio	Finance and Insurance Subsidiaries	
	Unconsolidated	**Consolidated**
Return on assets	5.16%	4.92%
Return on sales	4.70%	9.23%
Receivables turnover	5.71 times	2.22 times
Current ratio	1.30	2.34
Financial leverage	54.7%	83.0%

FINANCIAL RATIOS AND ACCOUNTING POLICY DECISIONS

Managers must be alert to the effects on financial ratios of their choices among alternative methods of accounting. Financial ratios may be affected substantially by the accounting methods used in accounting for inventory costs, depreciation, pension expenses and liabilities, leasing, mergers, consolidations, and many other items discussed throughout this text. To some extent, the perceived importance of these effects depends on whether managers accept the notion that securities markets are information efficient (see Chapter 1). If investors have sufficient financial disclosure information to convert readily from one accounting method to another, and if there are no direct cash flow effects due to the choice of accounting methods (such as the direct cash flow effects caused by the tax impact of inventory cost flow assumptions), then securities prices are unlikely to be affected by management's choices of accounting methods.

On the other hand, there are various instances when the impacts of accounting methods on financial ratios may have important economic consequences. Restrictive bond covenants may fail to allow for the effects of accounting method changes and a shift in accounting method might cause violation of the firm's borrowing agreements. Management bonuses or other compensation elements may depend on financial ratios and failure to adjust adequately for accounting method changes could deprive valued personnel of deserved benefits. Negotiations with labor organizations (and the attendant publicity) may be influenced by financial accounting-based measures of productivity and profitability without due allowance for the effects of accounting methods.

For several reasons, financial ratio effects are also pertinent to changes in accounting rules by the FASB and the SEC. First, accounting rules may have direct economic consequences to the extent that accounting methods affect the decisions and actions of investors, managers, and others. In presentations before the FASB and the SEC, managers often insist that the effects of accounting rules on key financial statement relationships will cause them to change operating or financial policies. There is little direct evidence with regard to this point, although surveys and interviews of managers indicate that accounting rules have affected decisions in areas such as foreign operations, oil and gas exploration, research and development, and the number and types of business combinations.

Second, the effects of differing accounting methods on the properties of financial ratios may be important information to accounting rule makers attempting to identify "better" methods of accounting. The predictive ability criterion for choosing among alternative methods of accounting (discussed in Chapter 1) rests on the premise that better accounting methods are those that facilitate better explanations and predictions of economic events. If different accounting methods produce substantially different sets of accounting ratios, then it may be possible to measure the change in predictive accuracy associated with a change in accounting method.

SUMMARY

This chapter defines financial ratio analysis, illustrates the calculations of a representative set of widely used financial ratios, and discusses some recent evidence on the usefulness of financial accounting ratios in explaining and predicting the behavior of securities prices, bond ratings, bankruptcy, and merger activity. The sensitivity of selected financial ratio calculations to accounting methods is illustrated for ITT's unconsolidated finance and insurance subsidiaries.

The discussion emphasizes the implications of financial ratio analysis for managers in terms of (a) the impact of ratios on securities prices, (b) the effects of ratios on the cost and availability of credit, (c) the usefulness of ratios in appraising the overall performance of the firm, and (d) the effects of accounting methods on the properties of financial ratios.

APPENDIX E
ITT CORPORATION: CONSOLIDATION OF FINANCE AND INSURANCE SUBSIDIARIES, AND RECALCULATION OF RATIOS

The ITT Corporation financial statements that are used as a basis for computing financial ratios in Chapter 12 do not consolidate that company's finance and insurance subsidiaries. The financial statements of these unconsolidated subsidiaries were included in ITT's footnote disclosures, however, and the analyst may choose to recast ITT's financial statements to reflect those disclosures. Various other firms with large finance and insurance subsidiaries may elect to consolidate their subsidiaries, and to make meaningful ratio comparisons between ITT and such firms, the analyst would need to adjust for differences in consolidation policy. For this reason, we will illustrate the procedures for recalculating the financial ratios.

Exhibits E-1 and E-2 consolidate ITT Corporation with its finance and insurance subsidiaries. The information for ITT Corporation is repeated from the exhibits in Chapter 12; the information for the subsidiaries was obtained from financial statement footnotes that are not reproduced in this book. It was necessary to make several assumptions in order to prepare the consolidations shown in Exhibits E-1 and E-2:

1. It is assumed that intercompany receivables and payables are zero, and that revenues and expenses do not represent transactions among the firms being consolidated. (If these assumptions are incorrect, the types of adjustments described in Chapter 9 for intercompany transactions would be required.)
2. The balance sheets of the subsidiaries do not distinguish between current and noncurrent assets and liabilities. For our purposes all items not labeled as "short-term" are classified as noncurrent. Moreover, the subsidiaries did not report the amounts of property, plant, and equipment separately, and it is likely that these amounts are included in the "other noncurrent assets" category.

Exhibit E-1
Consolidation Worksheet (Balance Sheets)

ITT Corporation and Subsidiaries
For the Year Ended December 31, 1985
(in thousands, except per-share data)

Assets	ITT Corporation 1985 (from Exhibit 12-2)	Insurance and Finance Subsidiaries	Consolidation Adjustments	Consolidated Totals
Current Assets				
Cash	$ 200,181	$ 108,818		$ 308,999
Accounts receivable	2,183,388	6,838,441		9,021,829
Inventories	2,061,708	—		2,061,708
Net assets of discontinued operations	276,662	—		276,662
Other current assets	287,767	7,456,631		7,744,398
Total Current Assets	5,009,706	14,403,890		19,413,596
Investments, Deferred Receivables and Other Assets				
Insurance and finance subsidiaries	3,077,889	—	(3,077,889)	—
Other investments	632,994	12,250,730		12,883,724
Receivables due subsequent to one year	516,103	—		516,103
Other assets	621,572	—		621,572
	4,848,558	12,250,730		14,021,399
Plant, Property and Equipment	7,355,952			7,355,952
Less—Accumulated depreciation	2,941,717			2,941,717
	4,414,235			4,414,235
	$14,272,499	$26,654,620		$37,849,230

Liabilities and Stockholders' Equity

Current Liabilities			
Short-term debt			
Banks	$ 670,612	$ 1,469,644	$ 2,140,256
Commercial paper	10,230	2,972,744	2,982,974
Current maturities of long-term debt	150,192	—	150,192
Other	53,989	—	53,989
Trade payables	885,023	—	885,023
Other payables	876,757	—	876,757
Accrued payroll and benefits	321,792	—	321,792
Accrued taxes	474,355	—	474,355
Other current liabilities	991,505	—	991,505
Total Current Liabilities	3,846,946	4,442,388	8,289,334
Reserves and Deferred Liabilities	1,199,398	15,857,959	17,057,357
Deferred Income Tax	23,974	559,753	583,727
Long-Term Debt	2,576,531	2,565,323	5,141,854
Minority Equity in Subsidiaries Consolidated	155,858	151,358	307,216
Total Long-term Debt	3,955,761	19,134,393	23,090,154
Stockholders' Equity			
Cumulative preferred stock (aggregate liquidation value $620,894 as of December 31, 1985)	321,544		321,544
Common stock—Authorized 200,000,000 shares, $1 par value		846,742	(846,742)
Outstanding 140,533,317 and 139,746,601 shares	140,533		140,533
Capital surplus	1,240,425		1,240,425
Unrealized gain (loss) on equity securities, net of tax of $9,014 and $1,354	11,738	11,738	(11,738)
		(85,125)	85,125
Cumulative translation adjustments	(652,083)	2,304,534	(2,304,534)
Retained earnings	5,407,635	3,077,889	(3,077,889)
	6,469,792		6,469,792
	$14,272,499		$37,849,230

Source: ITT Corporation, *Annual Report*, 1985.

Exhibit E-2
Consolidation Worksheet (Income Statements)

ITT Corporation and Subsidiaries
For the Year Ended December 31, 1985
(in thousands, except per-share data)

	ITT Corporation	Insurance and Finance Subsidiaries	Consolidation Adjustments	Consolidated Totals
Results for Year				
Sales and Revenues	$11,871,150	$8,136,029		$20,007,179
Costs and Expenses (including depreciation of $455,971)				
Cost of sales and services	9,618,271	5,129,011		14,747,282
Selling and general expenses	1,689,247	1,723,706		3,412,953
	11,307,518	6,852,717		18,160,235
Operating Income	563,632	1,283,312		1,846,944
Earnings (pre-tax) of Insurance and Finance Subsidiaries	412,345	—	(412,345)	—
	975,977	1,283,312	(412,345)	1,846,944
Interest expense	(532,302)	(1,057,041)		(1,589,343)
Interest and dividend income	112,121	—		112,121
Special provision for product line closedowns	(160,000)	—		(160,000)
Miscellaneous income (expense)—net	72,439	186,074		258,513
	468,235	412,345	(412,345)	468,235
Income Tax and Minority Equity				
U.S. and foreign income tax	(157,628)			(157,628)
Minority equity in net income	(24,230)			(24,230)
Income from Continuing Operations	286,377			286,377
Discontinued Operations				
Income (loss) from operations and phaseout, net of tax (benefit) of $(10,603)	(10,006)			(10,006)
Gain on disposal, net of tax of $45,653	17,130			17,130
Net Income	$ 293,501	$ 412,345	(412,345)	$ 293,501

Source: ITT Corporation, *Annual Report*, 1985.

Exhibit E-1 shows that ITT's shareholder equity is not changed by the consolidation, although assets and liabilities are increased by a substantial amount. Exhibit E-2 indicates that ITT's net income is not changed by the consolidation, although revenues and expenses are increased by substantial amounts. The reason neither shareholders' equity nor net income is changed as a result of consolidation is that ITT has used the equity method of accounting for those wholly-owned, unconsolidated subsidiaries.

Exhibit E-3 recomputes selected financial ratios that were discussed in Chapter 12, using the numbers that appear in the consolidated statements developed in Exhibits E-1 and E-2.

Exhibit E-3
Financial Ratios Based on Consolidated Statements

ITT Corporation and Its Finance and Insurance Subsidiaries
(in thousands)

$$\text{Return on Assets} = \frac{\text{Operating Income (Exhibit E-2)}}{\text{Operating Assets*}}$$

$$= \frac{\$1,846,944}{\$37,572,568} = 4.92\%$$

$$\text{Return on Sales} = \frac{\text{Operating Income (Exhibit E-2)}}{\text{Total Revenues (Exhibit E-2)}}$$

$$= \frac{\$1,846,944}{\$20,007,179} = 9.23\%$$

$$\text{Receivables Turnover} = \frac{\text{Credit Sales (Exhibit E-2)}}{\text{Accounts Receivable (Exhibit E-1)}^{\dagger}}$$

$$= \frac{\$20,007,179}{\$9,021,829} = 2.22$$

$$\text{Current Ratio} = \frac{\text{Current Assets (Exhibit E-1)}}{\text{Current Liabilities (Exhibit E-1)}}$$

$$= \frac{\$19,413,596}{\$8,289,334} = 2.34$$

$$\text{Financial Leverage} = \frac{\text{Debt (Exhibit E-1)}}{\text{Total Assets (Exhibit E-1)}}$$

$$= \frac{\$31,379,488}{\$37,849,230} = .83$$

*Consolidated total operating assets are $37,572,568 thousand ($37,849,230 thousand total assets, less $276,662 thousand net assets of discontinued operations).

†For convenience, we have used the balance in Accounts Receivable at December 31, 1985, rather than the average of the beginning and ending balances.

QUESTIONS

1. The terms listed below were introduced in this chapter. Define or explain each of them.

accounts receivable turnover	liquidity ratios
asset turnover	operating leverage
current ratio	operating ratios
debt-to-equity ratio	quick ratios
dividend payout	restrictive covenants
earnings variability ratio	return on assets
earnings yield	return on sales
equity ratio	return on stockholders' equity
financial leverage	solvency ratios
financial ratios	systematic risk
financing ratios	times-interest-earned ratio
horizontal analysis	vertical analysis
inventory turnover	

2. List and briefly discuss several reasons why managers might be concerned with financial ratio analysis.
3. What benchmarks (frames of reference) might be used by an analyst to evaluate financial ratios?
4. Distinguish between operating ratios and financing ratios.
5. "A person studying trends in financial data is more likely to use vertical analysis than horizontal analysis." Do you agree or disagree? Explain.
6. Why would return on stockholders' equity differ from return on assets?
7. List several possible problems with using return on assets as the primary means of assessing performance in decentralized organizations.
8. What are the advantages of explaining the return on assets ratio in terms of the product of the return on sales ratio times the asset turnover ratio?
9. What are some of the difficulties (limitations) of interpreting the inventory turnover ratio?
10. "Everything else being equal, one would expect a firm using LIFO to have a higher inventory turnover ratio than a firm using FIFO." Do you agree or disagree? Explain.
11. What factors might you consider in determining if an accounts receivable turnover ratio is too low?
12. Distinguish between liquidity and solvency.
13. What are some of the difficulties of interpreting the current ratio? How might the quick ratio overcome some of these difficulties of interpretation?
14. What are some of the difficulties of interpreting the times-interest-earned ratio?

15. "Price to earnings ratios are usually expected to be positively related to growth and negatively related to risk." Do you agree or disagree? Explain.
16. Which of the following ratios are positively related to risk: financial leverage, operating leverage, dividends to earnings?
17. For what reason(s) does an analyst attempt to measure the "systematic risk" of a firm's common stock? List several financial ratios that are likely to be used in this endeavor.
18. Several studies have shown that "mixed ratios" are particularly useful in predicting bankruptcy. What is a "mixed ratio"?
19. Several studies of merger activity have found that the average seller firm, as compared with the average nonmerging firm, has a number of distinguishing characteristics. List some of these distinguishing characteristics.
20. What important economic consequences, if any, might result if a firm switches its inventory costing from FIFO to LIFO?
21. It is possible that management's choice of accounting methods might have important economic consequences by virtue of the way the accounting methods affect certain financial ratios. Give one example of this phenomenon.

EXERCISES AND PROBLEMS

22. *Effects of Transactions on Ratios.* Six transactions are listed below, together with various ratios discussed in the chapter.
Transactions:

(1) Inventory is sold at a profit to customers for cash.
(2) Inventory is purchased from suppliers on account.
(3) Accounts payable are paid in cash.
(4) Dividends are declared and paid in cash.
(5) Noncurrent assets are purchased for cash.
(6) Bonds (noncurrent liabilities) are sold to investors for cash.

	Transactions					
Ratio:	(1)	(2)	(3)	(4)	(5)	(6)
Return on assets						
Current ratio						
Debt to assets						
Book value per share						

REQUIRED   Indicate the effect of each of the transactions on the ratios listed. (State any assumptions you make, where necessary.)

23. *Effects of Accounting Methods on Ratios.* As an analyst, you are attempting to compare Firm A and Firm B, using the following financial ratios:

    (1) Return on shareholders' equity
    (2) Debt to assets
    (3) Market value to book value
    (4) Earnings per share
    (5) Asset growth

REQUIRED   Indicate how your ratio comparisons would be affected by each of the following differences in accounting methods being used by the two firms. (Where necessary, state the assumptions you make to reach your conclusions.)

    (a) Firm A uses FIFO and Firm B uses LIFO to cost inventories. Inventory unit costs generally have been rising for several years.
    (b) Both firms lease substantial amounts of equipment. Firm A's leases are mainly operating leases, while Firm B's leases are mainly capital leases.
    (c) Both firms have steadily increasing expenditures on new plants and equipment. Firm A uses straight-line depreciation and Firm B uses accelerated depreciation.
    (d) Both firms have consolidated subsidiaries. Firm A's subsidiaries were acquired in pooling-of-interests transactions, and Firm B's subsidiaries were acquired in purchase transactions.
    (e) Both firms have pension plans. Firm A's footnotes disclose substantial unfunded pension obligations, and reveal that the plan discounts pension benefits at 14%. Firm B's footnotes indicate that the plan's net assets exceed the pension obligations, and that the plan discounts pension benefits at 5%.
    (f) Both firms have substantial amounts of bonds outstanding that are convertible into common stock. Firm A's stock is selling at a market price that is well below the conversion price, and Firm B's stock is selling at a market price that is well above the conversion price.

24. *Earnings Commentary and Financial Ratios.* ITT Corporation's annual report included the following statements in the financial summary.

> Net income for 1983 was $675 million or $4.50 per share, up from the $663 million or $4.47 per share for 1982. For 1981, net income amounted to $667 million or $4.51 per share. . . .
>
> . . . Also in 1983, the Corporation restated its financial statements for certain accounting changes. These changes, which are more fully described in the Notes to Financial Statements, increased (reduced) net income in 1983, 1982 and 1981 by $.05, $(.28) and $(.07) per share. . . .

REQUIRED   How, if at all, would these statements affect your calculation of earnings per share and of the rate of growth of ITT's per-share earnings?

25. *Credit Lines and Liquidity Ratios.*   The financial summary included in ITT Corporation's annual report contained the following statement:

> More than 120 U.S. and foreign banks are parties to revolving credit agreements with the ITT parent company which expire within five years and provide for commitments aggregating approximately $1.5 billion. These lines, for which ITT pays commitment fees, are used for working capital needs. At the end of 1983 borrowings under these bank lines amounted to $282 million, including $203 million by subsidiaries.

REQUIRED   How, if at all, would this disclosure affect your interpretation of the current ratio and quick ratio calculations for ITT Corporation?

26. *Pension Plans and Financial Ratios.*   Footnotes to ITT Corporation's 1983 financial statements included the following information concerning pensions:

> Benefits and asset information, including insurance and finance subsidiaries but excluding multi-employer pension plans for which allocation to participating employers is not currently available, is presented below as of January 1, 1983 and 1982 (in thousands):

	1983	1982
Actuarial present value of accumulated plan benefits		
Vested	$1,687,275	$1,490,340
Non-vested	170,470	160,918
	$1,857,745	$1,651,258
Net assets available for benefits including balance sheet reserves	$1,975,365	$1,664,045

> The weighted average assumed rate of return used in determining the above actuarial present value was 9.0% and 8.9% in 1983 and 1982.

REQUIRED

(a) How, if at all, should the pension plan assets and obligations be incorporated in your financial ratio calculations?
(b) The actuarial present value of accumulated plan benefits does not incorporate the effects of future salary increases. Is this consistent with the weighted-average return percentages disclosed above? If not, how would this affect your analysis of ITT's debt-related financial ratios?

27. *Ratio Comparisons across Industries.*   The following exhibit shows each of the financial ratios discussed in this chapter for firms in five different industries, based on financial reports for the year ended December 31, 1983.

Ratios	Levi-Strauss (Apparel)	Abbott Laboratories (Drugs)	Atlantic Richfield (Petroleum)	Family Dollar Stores (Variety)	American Motor Inns (Motels)
Return on assets	.19	.22	.20	.23	.21
Return on sales	.12	.22	.16	.09	.22
Asset turnover	1.58	1.01	1.22	2.39	.91
Inventory turnover	3.51	3.14	12.40	2.76	12.75
Receivables turnover	6.52	6.09	20.15	*	13.18
Current ratio	2.72	1.25	1.15	2.09	1.62
Quick ratio	1.83	.77	.67	.89	1.29
Financial leverage	.40	.48	.55	.36	.64
Times interest earned	6.84	6.67	5.41	1073.15	3.03
Earnings per share	3.05	2.37	6.61	1.71	3.17
Book value per share	23.36	10.73	39.01	8.75	13.00
Price per share	38.50	38.75	42.00	35.37	26.62
Dividend payout	.54	.34	.36	.19	.05
Price to earnings multiple	12.62	16.35	6.35	20.68	12.37
Market price to book value	1.64	3.61	1.07	4.03	2.04
One-year asset growth	.01	.08	.09	.20	.04
Five-year asset growth	.67	.72	.66	.91	.41
One-year net income growth	−.30	.15	.00	.16	.24
Five-year net income growth	−.02	.39	.87	.32	1.64
One-year sales growth	−.10	.10	−.04	.13	.13
Five-year sales growth	.50	.73	.88	.82	.66

*No significant receivables.

REQUIRED

(a) Explain why the return on sales varies from 9% (Family Dollar Stores) to 22% (American Motor Inns), while the return on assets for these same two firms varies over a much narrower range (from 23% to 21%).

(b) Provide likely reasons for the variations across industries in the turnover of total assets, inventory, and accounts receivable.

(c) Based on the ratios listed above, which firm appears to be the most liquid? the least liquid?

(d) Attempt to rank the firms from low to high in terms of (1) riskiness of debt securities and (2) riskiness of common stocks.

(e) Why do the firms vary so widely in their dividend payout percentages (from 5% to 54%)?

(f) Why does Atlantic Richfield sell at a price to earnings ratio of 6.4 at the same time that Family Dollar Stores has a price to earnings ratio of 20.7? In what manner, if at all, are these differences in price to earnings ratios related to the dividend payout ratio?

(g) Why does Atlantic Richfield stock trade at a price close to book value, while two of the other firms trade at close to four times book value? Which of these stocks represents the "best buy"?

(h) Explain why sales, net income, and assets may grow at different rates over the short term (one year), and over the longer term (five years). Are the one-year or five-year growth percentages more useful? Explain.

28. *Ratio Comparisons within an Industry.* The following exhibit shows each of the financial ratios discussed in this chapter for four different firms in the petroleum refining industry, based on financial reports for the year ending December 31, 1983.

Petroleum Refining Industry

Ratios	Atlantic Richfield Co.	Pennzoil Co.	Shell Oil Co.	Texaco, Inc.
Return on assets	.20	.26	.20	.18
Return on sales	.16	.29	.22	.07
Asset turnover	1.22	.70	.93	1.73
Inventory turnover	12.40	6.01	14.47	16.58
Receivables turnover	20.15	6.69	10.08	10.84
Current ratio	1.15	1.81	1.02	1.40
Quick ratio	.67	1.18	.75	1.15
Financial leverage	.55	.62	.51	.47
Times interest earned	5.41	2.75	5.09	10.31
Earnings per share	6.61	3.60	5.19	4.92
Book value per share	39.01	22.98	33.30	55.11
Price per share	42.00	35.12	37.00	31.12
Dividend payout	.36	.61	.34	.61
Price to earnings multiple	6.35	9.75	7.12	6.32
Market price to book value	1.07	1.52	1.11	.56
One-year asset growth	.09	.07	.06	.01
Five-year asset growth	.66	.45	.87	.36
One-year net income growth	.00	−.16	−.05	−.59
Five-year net income growth	.87	.49	.78	.31
One-year sales growth	−.04	−.16	−.07	−.20
Five-year sales growth	.88	.59	.62	.52

REQUIRED

(a) Explain why the return on assets figures for the four firms are approximately the same, while the return on sales figures vary widely (from 7% to 29%). Why is Texaco's return on assets below those of the other firms in the industry?

(b) Which of the firms is utilizing its assets the most efficiently? the least efficiently?

(c) Which firm appears to be the most risky? the least risky?

(d) What factors account for the differences between the price-to-earnings ratios of Texaco and Pennzoil? Support your explanation with specific financial ratios, if possible.

(e) Why is Texaco's price per share only 56% of book value per share, while Pennzoil's price per share is 152% of book value?

(f) Which firm has grown the most rapidly, and which the least rapidly, over the past five years? Which do you expect to grow most rapidly over the next several years? Explain.

(g) Which firm's shares represent the "best buy"? Explain.

29. *Ratio Comparisons within an Industry.*   The following exhibit shows each of the financial ratios discussed in this chapter for three different firms in the apparel industry, based on financial reports for the year ended December 31, 1983.

Apparel and Other Finished Products Industry

Ratios	Barco of California	Blue Bell, Inc.	Levi Strauss & Co.
Return on assets	.12	.16	.19
Return on sales	.07	.09	.12
Asset turnover	1.73	1.74	1.58
Inventory turnover	2.99	.71	3.51
Receivables turnover	3.74	5.02	6.52
Current ratio	3.41	3.37	2.72
Quick ratio	1.90	1.36	1.83
Financial leverage	.25	.41	.40
Times interest earned	10.85	4.29	6.84
Earnings per share	.37	3.35	3.05
Book value per share	5.51	33.74	23.36
Price per share	4.12	31.12	38.50
Dividend payout	.32	.53	.54
Price to earnings multiple	11.14	9.29	12.62
Market price to book value	.74	.92	1.64
One-year asset growth	.12	−.10	.01
Five-year asset growth	.22	.40	.67
One-year net income growth	.27	−.08	−.30
Five-year net income growth	.65	−.48	−.02
One-year sales growth	.16	−.09	−.10
Five-year sales growth	.23	.39	.50

REQUIRED

(a) What factors account for the difference in return on assets between Levi Strauss (19%) and Barco of California (12%)?

(b) Which firm is using its assets the most efficiently? the least efficiently?

(c) Which of the firms is the most liquid? the least liquid?

(d) Why do firms in the same industry vary widely in terms of financial leverage?

(e) Why do two of the three firms have market values that are well below book values per share? Which firm(s) represents the "best buy"?

(f) Explain why these firms in the same industry exhibit differences in price earnings ratios (from 9.29 to 12.62 times earnings). Are your reasons consistent with the financial ratios provided?

30. *Comprehensive Ratio Analysis: Abbott Laboratories.* Exhibits A, B, C, and D contain selected portions of the financial statements and footnotes of Abbott Laboratories included in that firm's 1983 annual report. Exhibit E contains a list of ratios and ratio values at December 31, 1983, for ITT Corporation.

Exhibit A
Selected Portions of Financial Statements and Footnotes

Abbott Laboratories and Subsidiaries
Consolidated Statement of Earnings
For the Years Ended December 31, 1981–1983
(in thousands, except per-share data)

	1983	1982	1981
Net Sales	$2,927,873	$2,602,447	$2,342,524
Cost of products sold	1,517,629	1,420,471	1,299,405
Research and development	184,533	136,967	113,655
Selling, general and administrative	621,435	555,140	513,913
Total operating cost and expenses	2,323,597	2,112,578	1,926,973
Operating Earnings	604,276	489,869	415,551
Interest expense	77,589	69,493	77,428
Interest and dividend income	(73,207)	(67,484)	(67,460)
Other (income) expense, net	25,273	14,494	13,071
Earnings before taxes	574,621	473,366	392,512
Taxes on earnings	227,004	184,243	145,229
Net Earnings	$ 347,617	$ 289,123	$ 247,283
Earnings per Common Share	$2.86	$2.37	$2.01

Abbott Laboratories and Subsidiaries
Consolidated Statement of Earnings Employed in the Business
For the Years Ended December 31, 1981–1983
(in thousands, except per-share data)

	1983	1982	1981
Balance at Beginning of Year	$1,188,022	$1,018,575	$ 866,897
Net earnings	347,617	289,123	247,283
Cash dividends declared — on common shares at $1.00, $.84, and $.72 per share in 1983, 1982, and 1981, respectively	(121,512)	(102,502)	(88,562)
Cost of treasury shares issued over proceeds from stock options exercised	(11,385)	(17,174)	(7,043)
Balance at End of Year	$1,402,742	$1,188,022	$1,018,575

Source: Abbott Laboratories, *Annual Report*, 1983.

Exhibit B

Abbott Laboratories and Subsidiaries
Consolidated Balance Sheet
At December 31, 1982 and 1983
(in thousands)

Assets	1983	1982
Current Assets:		
Cash and cash items (including marketable securities, at cost which approximates market, of $42,184 in 1983 and $20,015 in 1982	$ 213,035	$ 115,530
Trade receivables, less allowances of $17,934 in 1983 and $17,926 in 1982	481,820	427,653
Inventories		
Finished products	240,007	226,704
Work in process	87,623	77,209
Materials	102,208	127,194
Total inventories	429,838	431,107
Prepaid expenses and other receivables	168,147	148,805
Total Current Assets	1,292,840	1,123,095
Investment Securities Maturing after One Year, at Cost	402,371	468,453
Property and Equipment, at Cost:		
Land	27,497	22,993
Buildings	455,420	418,024
Equipment	931,942	773,022
Construction in progress	128,935	99,113
	1,543,794	1,313,152
Less: accumulated depreciation	474,594	410,040
Net Property and Equipment	1,069,200	903,112
Deferred Charges and Other Assets	59,717	72,249
Total Assets	$2,824,128	$2,566,909

Liabilities and Shareholders' Investment	1983	1982
Current Liabilities:		
Short-term borrowings	$ 145,860	$ 362,003
Trade accounts payable	169,170	145,787
Other accrued liabilities	191,868	133,733
Salaries, wages, and commissions	65,119	57,465
Dividends payable	30,344	25,642
Income taxes payable	72,048	160,820
Current portion of long-term debt	2,360	7,942
Total Current Liabilities	676,769	893,392
Long-term Debt	483,929	190,937
Other Liabilities and Deferrals:		
Deferred income taxes	157,772	107,548
Other	87,775	64,146
Total Other Liabilities and Deferrals	245,547	171,694
Shareholders' Investment:		
Common shares, without par value		
Authorized — 150,000,000 shares		
Issued at stated capital amount — 1983, 1982, and		
1981: 124,086,672 shares	183,725	180,683
Earnings employed in the business	1,402,742	1,188,022
Cumulative translation adjustments	(57,504)	—
	1,528,963	1,368,705
Less: common shares held in treasury at cost — 1983: 2,988,900 shares; 1982: 1,983,006 shares		
1981: 1,586,717 shares	111,080	57,819
Total Shareholders' Investment	1,417,883	1,310,886
Total Liabilities and Shareholders' Investment	$2,824,128	$2,566,909

Source: Abbott Laboratories, *Annual Report,* 1983.

Exhibit C

Abbott Laboratories and Subsidiaries
Footnote Disclosure Concerning Significant Accounting Policies

As required, effective January 1, 1983, the Company adopted the provisions of Financial Accounting Standards Board Statement No. 52 — "Foreign Currency Translation" (SFAS 52). Prior period financial statements have not been restated. Under SFAS 52, exchange gains and losses resulting from foreign currency transactions are recognized in income, while adjustments resulting from financial statement translations are generally included in the "Cumulative translation adjustments" component of Shareholders' Investment. Cumulative translation adjustments reduced Shareholders' Investment at December 31, 1983 by $57,504, including translation adjustments during the year of $25,024. Translation adjustments relating to operations in high inflation countries are reflected in current income.

Inventories — Inventories are stated at the lower of cost (first-in, first-out basis) or market. Cost includes material and applicable conversion costs.

Exhibit C continued

Pension Plans

A comparison of accumulated plan benefits and plan assets (at market value) for the Company's domestic defined benefit plans, at the most recent date such information is available, is presented below:

| | January 1 | |
	1983	1982
Actuarial present value of accumulated plan benefits:		
Vested	$186,206	$166,559
Nonvested	6,992	6,489
Total	$193,198	$173,048
Plan assets available for benefits	$324,914	$255,923

The weighted average assumed rate of return used in determining the actuarial present value of accumulated plan benefits was approximately 7.5 percent for each year presented above.

Leases

Portions of the Company's facilities and equipment (primarily warehouses, trucks, and computers) are rented under operating leases which generally have initial non-cancellable terms in excess of one year and contain certain renewal options. Total rental expense under these leases was approximately $19,000, $18,700, and $19,300 in 1983, 1982, and 1981, respectively. Future minimum rental commitments under these leases as of December 31, 1983 amount to approximately $33,400 in the aggregate and consist of $12,500 in 1984; $8,000 in 1985; $5,300 in 1986; $3,300 in 1987; $2,100 in 1988; and decreasing amounts thereafter.

Exhibit D

Abbott Laboratories and Subsidiaries
Footnote Disclosure Regarding Effects of Changing Prices

Current Costs
Operating Results

Year Ended December 31, 1983	As Reported in Historical Dollars	Adjusted for Specific Prices (Current Cost) (dollars in millions)
Net sales	$2,928	$2,928
Cost of products sold	1,440	1,451
Selling, research, and administrative	783	783
Depreciation	101	134
Interest, net	4	4
Other expense	25	25
Earnings before taxes	575	531
Taxes on earnings	227	227
Net earnings	$ 348	$ 304
Other Disclosures in Average 1983 Dollars		
Increase in inventory and net property and equipment due to general inflation		$79
Increase in current cost*		73
Excess of increase in general inflation over increase in current cost		$ 6

Constant Dollars

Selected Financial Data Adjusted for the Effects of Changing Prices in Average 1983 Dollars

| | Year ended December 31 | | | | |
	1983	1982	1981	1980	1979
	(dollars in millions except per share data)				
Net sales	$2,928	2,686	2,566	2,464	2,358
Net earnings	$ 304	252	211	191	188
Earnings per share	$ 2.50	2.06	1.71	1.55	1.51
Excess of increase in general inflation over increase in current cost of inventory and net property and equipment	$ 6	57	27	39	52
Increase (decrease) in purchasing power of net monetary balances	$ 3	3	2	(5)	(10)
Net assets (Shareholders' investment)	$1,771	1,690	1.626	1,574	1,534
Cumulative translation adjustments	$ 33	—	—	—	—
Dividends declared per common share	$ 1.00	.87	.79	.73	.69
Market Price per Share at Year End	$44.49	39.55	28.62	32.62	26.69
Average Consumer Price Index — Urban	298	289	272	247	217

Over the past five years the Company's sales, as reported in historical dollars, increased at a compound growth rate of 15 percent per year. Excluding the Company's net price increases during this period, which averaged approximately 3 percent per year (vs. 9 percent for the CPI-U), the compound sales growth rate was approximately 12 percent per year.

During this five year period, dividends declared in constant dollars have increased 67 percent. Simply stated, this means that the per share dividends in 1983 would purchase 67 percent more in goods and services than the per share dividend in 1979.

Source: Abbott Laboratories, *Annual Report*, 1983.

*If stated in year-end (rather than average) 1983 dollars, *current cost* (direct pricing for inventories and external cost indices for net property and equipment) for these assets would be $426 million and $1,457 million, respectively.

Exhibit E

Selected Financial Ratios

	ITT Corporation
Return on assets	8.63%
Return on sales	6.70%
Asset turnover	1.27 times
Inventory turnover	4.39 times
Receivables turnover	6.43 times
Current ratio	1.25
Quick ratio	.60
Financial leverage	56.2 %

Exhibit E continued

Selected Financial Ratios

	ITT Corporation
Times interest earned	2.58 times
Earnings per share	$ 4.50
Book value per share	$39.60
Price per share	$44.50
Dividend payout	61.3 %
Price earnings multiple	9.9 times
Market price/book value	1.13
One-year asset growth	−1.4 %
One-year net income growth	1.8 %
One-year sales growth	−7.1 %

REQUIRED

(a) The ratios listed in Exhibit E are commonly used in financial statement analysis. Calculate each of these ratios for Abbott Laboratories for the year ended December 31, 1983, and then compare the value for each calculated ratio with the corresponding ratio presented for ITT Corporation in Exhibit E.

(b) List plausible reasons for each of the differences observed between the financial ratios of the two firms.

(c) Based on these ratio comparisons, which firm utilizes its assets more efficiently? Which is the more profitable? Which firm is more liquid? Which is the riskiest firm? Which firm's common stock is the "better buy"?

(d) Consider the footnote disclosure concerning foreign currency translation shown in Exhibit C. How, if at all, do these cumulative translation adjustments affect your analysis?

(e) Consider the footnote concerning pension plans. How, if at all, does the fact that pension plan assets exceed the present value of pension plan benefits by $131.7 million ($324.9 million less $193.2 million) affect your analysis?

(f) How, if at all, would the footnote information concerning capital and operating leases affect your analysis?

(g) Would it be useful to incorporate the supplementary information concerning changing prices (current cost and constant dollar amounts) in your financial ratio calculations? If so, how would you use this information?

31. *Comprehensive Ratio Analysis: Anheuser-Busch Companies, Incorporated.*   Exhibits A, B, and C contain selected portions of the financial statements and footnotes from the Anheuser-Busch Companies' 1983 annual report. Exhibit D contains a list of ratios and ratio values at December 31, 1983, for ITT Corporation.

Exhibit A

Anheuser-Busch Companies, Inc., and Subsidiaries
Consolidated Statement of Income
For the Years Ended December 31, 1981–1983
(in millions, except per-share data)

	1983	1982	1981
Sales	$6,658.5	$5,185.7	$4,409.6
Less federal and state beer taxes	624.3	609.1	562.4
Net sales	6,034.2	4,576.6	3,847.2
Cost of products sold	4,113.2	3,331.7	2,975.5
Gross profit	1,921.0	1,244.9	871.7
Marketing, administrative, and research expenses	1,220.2	752.0	515.0
Operating income	700.8	492.9	356.7
Other income and expenses:			
Interest expense	(111.4)	(89.2)	(89.6)
Interest capitalized	32.9	41.2	64.1
Interest income	12.5	17.0	6.2
Other income (expense), net	(18.8)	(8.1)	(12.2)
Gain on sale of Lafayette plant	—	20.4	—
Income before income taxes	616.0	474.2	325.2
Provision for income taxes:			
Current	133.7	92.4	10.4
Deferred	134.3	94.5	97.4
	268.0	186.9	107.8
Net Income	$ 348.0	$ 287.3	$ 217.4
Earnings per share:			
Primary	$ 6.50	$ 5.97	$ 4.79
Fully diluted	6.50	5.88	4.61

Exhibit B

Anheuser-Busch Companies, Inc., and Subsidiaries
Consolidated Balance Sheet
At December 31, 1982 and 1983
(in millions)

Assets

	1983	1982
Current Assets:		
Cash (including certificates of deposit of $20.9 in 1983 and $8.1 in 1982)	$ 32.6	$ 21.5
Marketable securities, at cost which approximates market	185.8	—
Accounts and notes receivable, less allowance for doubtful accounts of $2.9 in 1983 and $2.7 in 1982	283.6	243.5
Inventories		
Raw materials and supplies	196.5	197.5
Work in process	61.1	67.9
Finished goods	41.2	42.4

Exhibit B continued

Other current assets	96.8	119.0
Total current assets	897.6	691.8

Investments and Other Assets:

Investments in and advances to unconsolidated subsidiaries	57.7	58.9
Investment properties	9.1	9.1
Deferred charges and other non-current assets	73.7	76.7
Excess of cost over net assets of acquired business, net	87.9	77.4
	228.4	222.1

Plant and Equipment:

Land	70.1	70.8
Buildings	1,303.6	1,256.9
Machinery and equipment	2,622.8	2,483.8
Construction in progress	311.6	158.6
Other real estate	5.8	10.3
	4,313.9	3,980.4
Less accumulated depreciation	1,109.7	991.5
	3,204.2	2,988.9
	$4,330.2	$3,902.8

Liabilities and Shareholders' Equity

	1983	1982
Current Liabilities:		
Short-term borrowings	$ —	$ 25.0
Accrued interest payable	29.9	29.8
Accounts payable	327.8	306.2
Due to customers for returnable containers	31.1	27.2
Accrued salaries, wages and benefits	142.5	131.1
Accrued taxes, other than income taxes	64.3	62.7
Estimated income taxes	48.4	26.4
Other current liabilities	78.5	37.6
Total current liabilities	722.5	646.0
Long-term Debt	961.4	969.0
Deferred Income Taxes	573.2	455.1
Minority Shareholders' Interest in Consolidated Subsidiaries	20.6	21.1
Convertible Redeemable Preferred Stock (Liquidation Value $300.0)	286.0	285.0
Common Stock and Other Shareholders' Equity:		
Preferred stock, $1.00 par value, authorized 32,498,000 shares in 1983 and 1982; none issued	—	—
Common stock, $1.00 par value, authorized 200,000,000 shares in 1983 and 100,000,000 shares in 1982; issued 48,514,214 and 48,416,087 shares, respectively	48.5	48.4
Capital in excess of par value	167.2	162.7
Retained earnings	1,555.4	1,316.4
Foreign currency translation adjustment	(3.7)	—
	1,767.4	1,527.5
Less cost of treasury stock	.9	.9
	1,766.5	1,526.6
Commitments and Contingencies	—	—
	$4,330.2	$3,902.8

Source: Anheuser-Busch Companies, Incorporated, *Annual Report*, 1983.

Exhibit C

Anheuser-Busch Companies, Inc., and Subsidiaries
Selected Footnote Disclosures

Acquisition

On November 2, 1982, the company acquired all of the outstanding common stock of Campbell Taggart, Inc. . . . . .

Assuming the acquisition of Campbell Taggart had occurred on January 1, 1981, the pro forma combined net sales would have been $5.6 billion and $5.1 billion for 1982 and 1981, respectively. The pro forma combined net income and net income per share for 1982 and 1981 would not have been materially different than that reported in the Consolidated Statement of Income.

Inventory

Approximately 75% and 74% of total inventories at December 31, 1983 and 1982, respectively, are stated on the last-in, first-out (LIFO) inventory valuation method. Had the average-cost method been used with respect to such items at December 31, 1983 and 1982, total inventories would have been $94.9 million and $83.3 million higher, respectively.

Pension Plans

The company has pension plans covering substantially all of its employees and follows the policy of funding all pension costs accrued. Total pension expense was $74.0, $52.7 and $41.7 million in 1983, 1982 and 1981, respectively. A comparison of the actuarial present value of accumulated plan benefits and plan net assets, as of the most recent actuarial date, generally January 1, for the company's salaried and hourly paid pension plans combined, is presented below:

	1983	1982
	(In millions)	
Actuarial present value of accumulated plan benefits:		
Vested	$265.6	$239.5
Nonvested	34.2	26.0
	$299.8	$265.5
Net assets available for benefits	$418.7	$325.0

The weighted average assumed rate of return used in determining the actuarial present value of accumulated plan benefits was 8.5% in 1983 and 8.2% in 1982.

Conclusions Concerning the Effect of Inflation

The methods adopted by the FASB to measure the impact of inflation are experimental in nature, and may not represent the true effect of inflation on the historical financial statements of the company. Accordingly, the resultant measurements should be viewed with caution and not as precise indicators of the effect of inflation on the company.

Exhibit C continued

Table 1   Five-year Comparison of Selected Supplementary Information Adjusted for the Effects of Inflation

(In millions, except per-share and statistical data)
(Information stated in average 1983 dollars)

	1983	1982	1981	1980	1979
Constant dollar data:					
Net income	$ 279.6	$ 212.8	$ 169.1	$ 146.9	$ 148.5
Net income per share	5.22	4.36	3.62	3.26	3.28
Shareholders' equity (net assets)	3,036.9	2,823.3	2,319.2	2,217.7	2,038.2
Current cost data:					
Net income	288.0	219.4	169.1	145.8	141.3
Net income per share	5.38	4.50	3.62	3.24	3.12
Shareholders' equity (net assets)	2,955.3	2,774.6	2,260.8	2,021.8	1,874.8
Excess of increase in general prices over increase in specific prices for inventories and plant and equipment	76.5	87.2	107.3	85.6	67.4
Other information adjusted for general inflation:					
Net sales	6,034.2	4,730.3	4,214.3	3,984.1	3,809.9
Gain from the decline in the purchasing power of net monetary items	61.8	58.3	121.4	140.8	114.8
Cash dividends per common share	1.62	1.43	1.25	1.24	1.20
Market price per share at year end	62.50	66.67	45.05	33.55	30.88
Average consumer price index	298.4	288.7	272.4	246.8	217.4

Table 2   Statement of Income Adjusted for the Effects of Inflation

(In millions, except per-share and statistical data)

	1983* Historical Dollars	1983* Constant Dollars	1983* Current Cost
Net sales	$6,034.2	$6,034.2	$6,034.2
Cost of products sold	4,113.2	4,181.6	4,173.2
Gross profit	1,921.0	1,852.6	1,861.0
Marketing, administrative and research expenses	1,220.2	1,220.2	1,220.2
Operating income	700.8	632.4	640.8
Interest expense	(111.4)	(111.4)	(111.4)
Interest capitalized	32.9	32.9	32.9
Interest income	12.5	12.5	12.5
Other expense, net	(18.8)	(18.8)	(18.8)
Income before income taxes	616.0	547.6	556.0
Income taxes[†]	268.0	268.0	268.0
Net income	348.0	279.6	288.0
Net income per share	6.50	5.22	5.38
Effective tax rate[†]	43.5	48.9	48.2
Depreciation and amortization	187.3	255.6	247.2
Gain from the decline in purchasing power of net monetary items		61.8	61.8
Increase in general price level of inventories and plant and equipment			161.4

Increase in specific prices of inventories and plant and equipment[‡]	84.9
Excess of increase in general prices over increase in specific prices	76.5

Source: Anheuser-Busch Companies, Incorporated, *Annual Report*, 1983.

*Constant dollars and current cost data for 1983 are stated in average 1983 dollars.

[†]Since the inflation adjusted elements of expense are not deductible for income tax purposes, the historical dollar income tax expense is not adjusted under the constant dollar or current cost methods. The resultant higher effective tax rate reflects the greater burden of taxes being borne by the company during inflationary periods.

[‡]The current cost of inventories and plant and equipment at December 31, 1983, is $402.7 million and $4.0 billion, respectively.

Exhibit D

Selected Financial Ratios

	ITT Corporation
Return on assets	8.63%
Return on sales	6.70%
Asset turnover	1.27 times
Inventory turnover	4.39 times
Receivables turnover	6.43 times
Current ratio	1.25
Quick ratio	.60
Financial leverage	56.2 %
Times interest earned	2.58 times
Earnings per share	$ 4.50
Book value per share	$39.60
Price per share	$44.50
Dividend payout	61.3 %
Price-to-earnings multiple	9.9 times
Market price/book value	1.13
One-year asset growth	−1.4 %
One-year net income growth	1.8 %
One-year sales growth	−7.1 %

REQUIRED

(a) The ratios listed in Exhibit D are commonly used in financial statement analysis. Calculate each of these ratios for Anheuser-Busch for the year ended December 31, 1983, and then compare the value for each calculated ratio with the corresponding ratio presented for ITT Corporation.

(b) List plausible reasons for any differences observed between the financial ratios of the two firms.

(c) Based on these ratio comparisons, which firm utilizes its assets more efficiently? Which is the more profitable? Which is more liquid? Which is the riskier firm? Which firm's common stock is the "better buy"?

(d) Consider the footnote disclosure concerning the acquisition of Campbell Taggart, Inc. (Exhibit C). How, if at all, does that disclosure affect your calculation of sales growth?

(e) How does the footnote concerning LIFO inventory costing results (Exhibit C) affect your comparisons of the two firms?

(f) Consider the footnote in Exhibit C concerning pension plans. How, if at all, does the fact that pension plan assets exceed the present value of pension plan benefits by $118.9 million ($418.7 million less $299.8 million) affect your ratio analysis?

(g) How would you incorporate the supplementary disclosures concerning changing prices (current cost and constant dollars) into your ratio calculations? Explain and illustrate.

32. *An Investment Decision in the Absence of Segment Disclosures: The Singer Company.*   You are a securities analyst in the process of evaluating the Singer Company. Exhibit A presents a condensed balance sheet at December 31, 1982 and 1981. Exhibit B contains the Singer Company's income statement for the years ended December 31, 1982, 1981, and 1980. Exhibit C reproduces certain statements extracted from the President's *Report to Stockholders* that were included in the 1982 annual report.

The U.S. economy was in a severe recession during the year 1982. Because a major portion of Singer's sales were directly to consumers, the company was significantly affected by the recession. However, a substantial improvement in the economy was widely anticipated in 1983.

The average market price per share of the company's common stock for each quarter of 1982 and 1981 is shown below.

	1982	1981
First quarter	$13.4	$14.3
Second quarter	13.4	20.1
Third quarter	12.9	17.6
Fourth quarter	16.8	15.8

Exhibit A

The Singer Company
Condensed Balance Sheet
For the Years Ended December 31, 1981 and 1982
(in millions)

Assets	1982	1981
Current assets	$ 937.2	$1,084.1
Investments	82.3	101.4
Property, plant, and equipment—net	348.9	335.6
Other assets	53.4	52.1
Total assets	$1,421.8	$1,573.2
Liabilities and Shareholders' Equity		
Current liabilities	$ 618.1	$ 713.1
Long-term debt	279.6	307.3
Other non-current liabilities	88.6	107.5
Total liabilities	$ 986.3	$1,127.9
Preferred stock	25.2	25.3
Common stock	166.2	166.1
Additional paid-in capital	37.2	37.1
Retained earnings	206.9	216.8
Total shareholders' equity	$ 435.5	$ 445.3
Total liabilities and shareholders' equity	$1,421.8	$1,573.2

Exhibit B

The Singer Company
Statement of Income
For the Years Ended December 31, 1980–1982
(in millions, except per-share data)

	1982	1981	1980
Net sales	$ 2,522.7	$ 2,703.3	$ 2,659.6
Costs and expenses:			
Cost of sales	1,895.1	1,937.9	1,844.8
Selling and administrative expenses	563.6	641.5	685.6
	2,458.7	2,579.4	2,530.4
Operating income	64.0	123.9	129.2

Exhibit B continued

Other income (expense):			
Income before tax of unconsolidated subsidiaries	6.0	3.0	7.8
Reduction of reserve for facility restructuring	10.0	—	—
Interest	(96.3)	(110.5)	(76.3)
Foreign exchange adjustments	7.9	4.5	(11.4)
Miscellaneous	22.9	37.1	49.8
	(49.5)	(65.9)	(30.1)
Income from continuing operations before income taxes	14.5	58.0	99.1
Provision for income taxes	26.0	22.2	61.3
Income (loss) from continuing operations	(11.5)	35.8	37.8
Discontinued operations	(10.3)	2.6	.3
Income (loss) before extraordinary credit	(21.8)	38.4	38.1
Extraordinary credit—gain on bond repurchases	18.9	—	—
Net income (loss)	(2.9)	38.4	38.1
Dividend requirements on preferred stock	5.3	5.0	5.0
Net income (loss) applicable to earnings per share	$ (8.2)	$ 33.4	$ 33.1
Average number of common shares and common share equivalents (000's omitted)	16,616	17,326	17,264
Earnings (loss) per share			
Income (loss) from continuing operations	$ (1.01)	$ 1.78	$ 1.90
Income (loss) before extraordinary credit	$ (1.63)	$ 1.93	$ 1.92
Net income (loss)	$ (.49)	$ 1.93	$ 1.92
Cash dividends per common share	$ .10	$ .10	$ .10

Source: The Singer Company, *Annual Report*, 1982.

Exhibit C

The Singer Company
Extracted Statements from President's Report to Shareholders*

To Our Shareholders:

Singer's results in 1982 were adversely affected by the worldwide recession, which had a severe impact on the Company's consumer activities. In addition, the multiple devaluations of the peso and general economic crisis in Mexico depressed our business in that major international market.

However, the high-technology aerospace operations on which we have focused our growth plans continued their progress and posted another year of record earnings. The Products and Services for Government Group approached $1 billion in sales and generated almost 40 percent of our total revenues.

Equally significant, while the weak economy had a negative influence on our results, it did not interrupt our program to reposition and strengthen Singer. Our strategy for 1982 centered around these actions:

*These statements are reproduced only in part.

- Priority was given to balance sheet and cash flow management, which enabled us to reduce debt. We ended the year with debt at $478.3 million, compared with $517.8 million at the beginning of 1982.

- The manufacturing restructuring and retail store conversion programs begun in 1979 to reduce operating costs in North America and Europe sewing were accelerated and essentially completed. We have actually accomplished more than planned when these efforts were conceived three years ago—and have done so at less cost than was estimated.

- Cost reductions were implemented in domestic and international consumer operations and corporate overhead. We eliminated substantial excess manufacturing capacity, reduced the work force, renegotiated supplier contracts for lower component and raw material costs, and took other measures to cut expenses.

- Programs oriented to future growth and improved efficiency were continued. We increased research and development in the aerospace area, further automated manufacturing, and pursued consumer product developments where there were marketing and/or cost-improvement opportunities.

As a result of this overall program, we are moving forward on a financially sound basis and with our operations lean.

Progress in Technology

The record sales and earnings of the Products and Services for Government Group once again demonstrated the strength of its technological base and leadership in key market areas.

Backlog remained in excess of $1 billion as new contract bookings matched sales during 1982. These new contracts included awards which have significant potential for add-on business and which also position us in technologies that can be applied to future new programs.

Singer received a major competitive award for a classified signal processing subsystem.

We are also proceeding with the development of SimuFlite Training International, Inc. This business will employ Link simulators and computer-based ground school instruction to offer complete flight training for corporate pilots. It expects to begin this program in 1984.

Our aerospace operations thus continue to show the capacity for innovation and advanced systems development that is the keystone of success in high-technology fields.

Sewing Programs Completed

While the North America and Europe sewing operation experienced lower overall results due to the recession, especially in Europe, the major development in this area was the essential completion of the programs to restructure manufacturing facilities and modify the distribution network.

In the United States, we now have converted our Singer-operated retail stores, which totaled 725 at year-end 1979, into dealerships consisting of independent sewing shops and fabric chain outlets. Our original intent was to reduce the number of U.S. stores to 200–300, but economic and market developments made it necessary to go beyond that objective.

We have largely completed the planned retail store conversions in Europe, although further action will be required there to deal with the added effects of the recession. The store conversions and closings, including those in process, have reduced the Singer-operated stores in Europe to approximately 700, compared with 1,350 in 1979.

In manufacturing, during 1982 we closed the Karlsruhe, West Germany, and Elizabeth, New Jersey, plants, although those actions were not scheduled under the original manufacturing restructuring plan. We also continued to restructure facilities in France and Italy.

In total, since 1979 we have closed or converted to dealerships approximately 1,375 retail stores, eliminated approximately 4 million square feet of manufacturing space, and reduced the work force by about two-thirds.

As a result, we entered 1983 with a substantially lower cost structure in North America and Europe sewing, which gives us much greater flexibility to manage this business in accordance with market developments and general economic trends.

Domestic Consumer Products

The emphasis in Products Manufactured for the Consumer continues to be on cost control and asset management. This has lowered costs so that a revival of domestic consumer demand will quickly benefit operating income.

Developing Nations Network

The Africa, Latin America, and Far East Group in 1982 was affected by the pervasive economic downturn and currency devaluations.

Conditions were especially severe in Latin America, our largest sewing machine market in the developing world. The major factor was the impact of the multiple devaluations of the peso in Mexico. Local government controls and the generally weak economy inhibited the pricing actions necessary to fully offset the devaluations.

In addition, demand for sewing machines was lower in Latin America as a result of the economic crisis in Mexico as well as the continuing recessions in Brazil and other countries.

The consumer durables business conducted by this Group increased both its sales and operating income during 1982. This was due to the relatively stronger economies in the Pacific and Far East regions, which are the principal markets for these products. A major objective of Singer is to continue to expand the range of consumer durables offered through our long-established marketing network in the developing world.

We have instituted cost reductions in the areas affected by the recession, and are further adjusting this Group to the realities of its environment. We are continuing to shift from retail to wholesale distribution in certain nations where economic conditions warrant. A key strategy accelerated in 1982 is to sell equity participations in this Group's businesses in selected countries, with Singer continuing to manage the operations.

This will mitigate risks and generate funds to help further reduce debt. It will also enhance the growth prospects of our developing world operations by making them more consistent with the increasing desire of many foreign governments to have local participation in multinational businesses.

Outlook for the Future

Looking forward, we will continue to stress balance sheet management and cost control. We will simultaneously foster continued expansion of the high-technology area as our primary base for growth, and maximize the contribution of other operations to our overriding goal of increased profitability.

We believe that Singer's financial results in 1983 will show significant improvement as our aerospace operations continue to grow and the benefits of the sewing restructuring and retail store conversion programs become increasingly apparent.

Although the recession has delayed the attainment of our earnings objectives, it has not eroded Singer's foundation for future profit performance. Given a more favorable environment for our consumer businesses, we believe the results of our repositioning program will assert themselves with increasing force.

Source: The Singer Company, *Annual Report*, 1982.

REQUIRED

(a) Calculate the following financial and operating ratios for those years for which data is provided.

(1) Percent growth in income from continuing operations.
(2) Percent growth in net sales.
(3) Income from continuing operations as a percent of net sales.
(4) Year-end stock price to earnings per share from continuing operations. (Use average stock price for last quarter.)
(5) Income from continuing operations as a percent of stockholders' equity.
(6) Turnover of plant, property, and equipment.

$$\frac{\text{Net Sales}}{\text{Average Property,}\atop\text{Plant \& Equipment}}$$

(7) Financial leverage

$$\frac{\text{Long-term Debt}}{\text{Shareholders' Equity}}$$

(8) Current ratio

(b) Evaluate these ratios and other information given and decide whether to advise your clients to buy or sell Singer's common stock.

(c) What other financial information would be particularly helpful to someone deciding whether to buy or sell Singer's common stock?

Glossary

absorption (full) costing (3)

The costing method required by GAAP under which *all* manufacturing costs — both fixed and variable — are assigned to each unit of production.

accelerated cost recovery system (ACRS) (4)

The system introduced in 1981 to determine allowable depreciation for tax purposes. The objective of ACRS is to simplify the procedures for tax depreciation and at the same time maintain the tax minimization features of the accelerated methods used prior to ACRS.

accelerated depreciation (4)

Any depreciation method that assigns a greater amount of depreciation expense to earlier years of an asset's life and lesser amounts to later years.

account (2)

A summary device that exists in the ledger to facilitate the recording of additions to and subtractions from an individual asset, liability, or owners' equity item (including revenues and expenses).

accounting (1)

The process of measuring and reporting economic events to provide relevant information to decision makers.

accounting cycle (2)

The series of steps repeated each accounting period by which financial statements are constructed from selected economic events. Major steps include analyzing transactions and recording them in the journal, posting from the journal into the ledger, adjusting the accounts, preparing the financial statements, and closing the accounts.

accounting entity (1)

The business enterprise or not-for-profit organization whose economic activities are reflected in the financial reports.

accounting income (1) and (3)

The excess of recorded revenues and gains over expenses and losses for a specific period of time. Accounting income is based on GAAP and uses a transaction-oriented approach.

Accounting Principles Board — APB (1)

The private sector standard-setting body in financial accounting that preceded the Financial Accounting Standards Board. The APB functioned from 1959 to 1973.

accounts payable (6)

A current liability that represents the amounts owed creditors of the reporting entity for goods or services purchased from them on credit.

accounts receivable (5)

A current asset that represents the amounts owed to the reporting entity for goods or services sold on credit to its customers.

accounts receivable turnover rate (5) and (12)

Net credit sales for the period divided by the average amount of accounts receivable.

accrual basis of accounting (2)

The accounting basis required by GAAP whereby revenues are recognized when earned (without regard to cash receipts) and expenses are recognized either in the period in which related revenues are recognized or when incurred (without regard to the timing of cash disbursements).

accrued liability (6)

A current liability, representing an expense item incurred during the period, which usually results from the passage of time.

accumulated depreciation (4) and (5)

A contra-asset account that shows the cumulative amount of depreciation expense that has been taken on a fixed asset since its acquisition.

accumulated pension benefit obligation (10)

The present value of pension benefits determined on an actuarial basis by the pension benefit formula. This amount is for employee service rendered before a specified date and is based on employee service and compensation prior to that date.

active investment (9)

An investment in the stock of another firm made for the purpose of directing or influencing the activities of the investee firm.

adjusting entries (2)

Adjustments by which previously unrecognized changes in assets, liabilities, revenues, or expenses are recorded in the accounting records at the end of the reporting period.

amortization (5)

The process of allocating the cost of an intangible asset over its estimated useful life.

appropriations of retained earnings (7)

A procedure used to indicate that a portion of retained earnings is not available for dividends.

arms-length transaction (3)

A transaction between unrelated parties in which, because both parties act in their own self-interest, the negotiated price is expected to be a fair one.

asset turnover (12)

The number of sales dollars produced by each dollar invested in operating assets; that is, sales of a period divided by average operating assets.

assets (1) and (2)

The FASB defines assets as "... probable future economic benefits obtained or controlled by a particular entity as a result of past transactions or events."

average cost (4)

An inventory cost flow assumption in which the weighted average of the costs of beginning inventory and purchases is used to value both ending inventory and cost of goods sold.

balance sheet (1)

A primary financial statement that provides information about the assets, liabilities, and owners' equity of the reporting entity at a specific point in time.

benefit pattern of a fixed asset (4)

The time pattern over which net revenues are expected to be generated by the use of a fixed asset.

bond (6)

A promise to pay a sum of money (called the principal) at a specified maturity date and to pay interest periodically, usually every six months.

book of original entry (2)

Another term for the journal—so called because it is the first place in which a complete record of transactions is formally made.

book value of accounts receivable (5)

Gross amount of accounts receivable less allowance for doubtful accounts; also referred to as the net realizable value of the receivables.

book value of a fixed asset (4) and (5)

Capitalized cost of a fixed asset less accumulated depreciation taken in earlier periods.

book value per share of common stock (7)

The excess of total stockholders' equity over preferred stockholders' equity divided by the number of common shares outstanding.

capital-intensive firm (5)

A company with an asset structure consisting of relatively more long-lived assets and relatively fewer current assets.

capital lease (10)

A lease agreement that meets any one or more of the following criteria: ownership of property is transferred to the lessee at the end of the lease term; the lease contains a bargain purchase option; the lease term is equal to 75 percent or more of the estimated economic life of the leased asset; or, at the beginning of the lease, the present value of the minimum lease payments equals or exceeds 90 percent of the fair value of the leased asset to the lessor. A capital lease is shown as an asset and a liability on the financial statements of the lessee.

capital maintenance (3)

The income measurement concept that states that the value of net assets (or capital) used in the firm's operations must be maintained before it is possible to have net income.

capital transactions (3)

Transactions involving paid-in capital (issuance of stock, buying or selling of treasury stock, and the like) or the declaring of dividends.

cash basis of accounting (2)

The accounting basis, not supported by GAAP, which links revenue and expense recognition to the timing of cash flows.

cash discount (6)

A reduction in the amount owed a creditor if cash payment is made on a timely basis (within the cash discount period).

cash flow per share (8)

Cash flow from operating activities (net income plus or minus noncash adjustments) divided by the number of common shares outstanding.

cash yield test for EPS (7)

A test performed to determine if a convertible security should be considered a common stock equivalent for purposes of calculating earnings per share. Under an arbitrary measure established by the FASB, a cash yield of less than two-thirds of the yield on high-quality corporate bonds will cause a convertible security to be classified as a common stock equivalent.

change in an accounting principle (3)

Switching from one acceptable financial accounting method or procedure to another.

closing entries (2)

Entries made at the end of each accounting cycle whereby the balances in all temporary accounts are transferred to the Retained Earnings account, resetting the balances in the temporary accounts to zero so that they are ready to measure revenues, expenses, and dividends for the next accounting period.

common stock (7)

The residual ownership shares of a corporation that always have voting rights.

common stock equivalent — CSE (7)

A security that, although not a common stock, gives its holder the right through conversion or exercise to acquire shares of common stock. Common stock equivalents are used in calculating earnings per share.

conservatism assumption (1)

A preference that possible measurement errors in financial accounting be made in the direction of understatement of net income and net assets rather than in overstatement of these amounts. Recently, the FASB has defined this assumption as "...a prudent reaction to uncertainty to try to ensure that uncertainty and risks inherent in business situations are adequately considered."

consolidated financial statements (9)

Financial statements that result from combining the financial statements of two or more legally separate firms to reflect the fact that the firms are under common control of a single parent company.

consolidation (9)

A business combination in which a *new* company is formed to acquire the stock of two existing firms, which then cease to exist as legal entities.

constant dollar adjustments (11)

Adjustments that convert the historical costs of assets to dollars of the same purchasing power.

constant dollar balance sheet (11)

A balance sheet prepared by converting the nominal dollar historical costs of all elements of the balance sheet into dollars of the same general purchasing power.

constant dollar income statement (11)

An income statement prepared by converting the nominal dollar amounts into dollars having a purchasing power equal to the average level of the CPI-U index during the year.

Consumer Price Index for All Urban Consumers—(CPI-U) (11)

A broadly based index used to convert nominal dollar amounts into their constant dollar equivalents.

contingency (6)

An existing condition or set of circumstances involving uncertainty as to possible gain or loss for the reporting firm that will be resolved in the future when one or more events occur or fail to occur.

contra asset (2) and (4)

An account that is subtracted directly from an asset on the financial statements.

convertible debt (7)

A liability that at the option of the holder may be converted into stockholders' equity (usually shares of common stock).

convertible preferred stock (7)

Preferred stock with a feature that allows the holder the option of converting preferred stock shares into shares of common stock.

cost flow assumptions for inventory (4)

Methods used in financial accounting for allocating costs between ending inventory on the balance sheet and cost of goods sold on the income statement.

cost method (9)

A method used on the books of the investor firm to account for intercorpo-

rate investments. This method is used if the investment is deemed to be a passive investment.

cost of goods manufactured (3)

The cost of all manufactured products completed by the firm during the period.

cost of goods sold (3)

Product costs that are expensed in a given period because the goods are sold in that period.

cost principle (3)

The primary basis used for determining the cost of a recorded asset. It states that the asset should be valued at the amount of cash or at the cash equivalent given up in an arms-length exchange transaction.

coupon rate of interest (6)

The rate of interest stated on the face of a bond or other interest-bearing instrument. Also referred to as the nominal (or face) rate of interest.

credit entry (2)

An entry on the right-hand side of an account wherein decreases in assets and increases in liabilities and owners' equity are shown.

cumulative preferred stock (7)

Preferred stock with a feature that states that before any dividend distributions may be made to common stockholders, all preferred dividends must be paid, including those that were missed in previous years (dividends in arrears).

current asset (5)

Cash and other economic resources that can reasonably be expected to be realized in cash or sold or consumed within one year, or within the normal operating cycle, whichever is longer.

current cost (5)

The amount of cash or its equivalent that would have to be given up today to acquire an existing asset.

current cost reports (11)

Reports that restate historical cost financial statements for changes in specific prices of assets owned by the firm.

current liabilities (6)

Obligations that will require the use of existing current assets or the creation of other current liabilities within one year or within the course of the firm's normal operating cycle, whichever is longer.

current market value (5)

The amount of cash or its equivalent that could be obtained by selling an asset in its present condition.

current ratio (12)

Current assets divided by current liabilities.

debit entry (2)

An entry on the left-hand side of an account wherein increases in assets and decreases in liabilities and owners' equity are shown.

debt ratios (12)

A group of ratios that assesses either the liquidity or the solvency of the firm.

debt securities (5)

Securities (such as government and corporate bonds) issued as evidence of a loan made for investment purposes. The investor in debt securities has the right to receive interest payments at specified intervals and to collect the principal when the loan matures.

debt-to-assets ratio (12)

A firm's long-term debt divided by total assets. This ratio is often referred to as financial leverage.

debt-to-equity ratio— financial leverage (12)

A firm's long-term debt divided by total stockholders' equity.

deferred charges (5)

A "catch-all" category in the noncurrent assets section of the balance sheet that is used to present long-term prepayments that do not fit in any of the other asset classifications.

deferred income tax (4)

A balance sheet item that shows the tax effects of the timing differences between a firm's taxable income and its financial accounting income.

defined-benefit pension plan (10)

A plan that specifies the amount of pension benefits to be provided, usually as a function of factors such as age, years of service, and so forth.

depreciation (2) and (4)

The process of allocating the cost of a fixed asset over its estimated useful life.

dilution of EPS (7)

A reduction in earnings per share that may result if convertible securities are converted or options and warrants are exercised.

direct financing lease (10)

A lease agreement that meets at least one of the four criteria for classifying a lease as a capital lease, but does not provide profit to a manufacturer or dealer at the inception of the lease.

direct labor (3)

The cost of services provided by employees of a manufacturing firm who work directly on the products being manufactured.

direct materials (3)

Materials used by a manufacturer that are included in and directly traceable to the manufactured product.

direct method (8)

An approach to calculating and reporting cash flow from operating activities. Calculation involves converting individual accrual-based revenues and expenses listed on the income statement to a cash basis. If the direct method is used, the statement of cash flows reports major categories of cash receipts and cash payments from operating activities.

discontinued operation (3)

A segment of a business that has been sold, disposed of, or abandoned. To qualify as a discontinued operation, the segment must represent a separate major line of

business or class of customer.

dividend payout (12)

The ratio of dividends to earnings for a specific period of time.

dividends (2)

Distributions of past corporate earnings to the stockholders. Dividends result in the reduction of both the net assets and retained earnings of the corporation.

dollar capital maintenance (3)

Capital maintenance concept under which capital is maintained as long as the dollar value of the firm's net assets has not diminished during the period, after adjustments for capital transactions.

double declining-balance depreciation—DDB (4)

An accelerated method of depreciation that allocates a declining amount of depreciation expense to each reporting period over the estimated life of the asset. DDB is determined by multiplying the book value of the asset by a percentage that is twice the straight-line rate.

early retirement of debt (6)

The reacquisition of any form of debt security by the issuer of the debt before its scheduled maturity.

earnings per share—EPS (3) and (7)

Net income available to common stockholders divided by the weighted average of common shares outstanding. GAAP require that earnings per share be presented on the face of the income statement.

earnings yield—E/P (7)

The reciprocal of the price-to-earnings ratio. This financing ratio is used in assessing risk.

economic consequences criterion (1)

A criterion used in assessing alternative accounting methods that recognizes the possible economic effects of different accounting rules on various groups.

economic income (1)

An increase in wealth (or well-offness) during a specific period of time. Economic income uses a valuation-based approach.

economic life of a fixed asset (4)

The length of time a firm expects to use a fixed asset in its operations. The economic life of an asset is an element considered in the depreciation process.

equity method (9)

A method used on the books of the investor firm to account for intercorporate investments. This method is used if the investment is deemed to be an active investment.

equity ratios (12)

Measures used in common stock valuation and in the assessment of stock risk. Examples include growth ratios, dividends-to-earnings and dividends-to-price ratios, and operating leverage.

exchange price (1) and (3)

A financial accounting assumption that specifies that the measurement of assets and liabilities be based on the prices inherent in the exchanges from which they originated.

exchange transaction (2)

A transfer of assets or services between the accounting entity and outside parties. Examples include buying and selling inventory, borrowing money, and paying salaries.

expected market value (5)

The net cash amount (selling cost less direct costs of disposal and collection) into which an asset is expected to be converted in the normal course of business. Also referred to as **net realizable value.**

expenses (2) and (3)

The FASB defines expenses as "outflows or other uses of assets or incurrences of liabilities (or a combination of both) during a period from delivering or producing goods, rendering services, or carrying out other activities that constitute the entity's ongoing major or central operations."

extraordinary item (3)

A transaction or event that is both unusual in nature and infrequent in occurrence. It is reported separately and net of tax effects on the income statement.

financial accounting (1)

The process of measuring and reporting economic events to provide relevant information to decision makers *outside* the firm, such as investors, creditors, customers, and suppliers. Financial accounting is governed by GAAP.

Financial Accounting Standards Board—FASB (1)

The seven-member organization within the private sector designated to make financial accounting policy decisions issued in the form of a *Statement of Financial Accounting Standards (SFAS).*

financial leverage (12)

See **debt-to-equity ratio** and **return-on-assets ratio.**

financial ratios (12)

Measures that relate two items of accounting information by dividing one number by the other number.

financing activities (8)

Activities involving creditors or owners that affect long-term liabilities and certain stockholders' equity accounts and may include borrowing or repaying long-term liabilities, issuing new stock, reacquiring outstanding stock, and paying dividends. Differentiating among operating, financing, and investing activities is important in preparing a statement of cash flows.

financing ratios (12)

Measures used to reflect the capital structure (the overall mix of debt and equity financing) of the firm. Financing ratios are widely used in assessing the potential risks and returns related to the firm's debt and equity securities.

finished goods inventory (3)
Completed goods of a manufacturer that are awaiting sale to customers. This account is one of the three inventory accounts of a manufacturing firm.

first-in, first-out — FIFO (4)
An inventory cost flow assumption that allocates the costs of the earliest purchases to cost of goods sold and the costs of more recent purchases to ending inventory.

fixed asset (4) and (5)
Long-lived, tangible assets that are employed by the enterprise in the production or sale of inventory or in the provision of services.

fixed manufacturing costs (3)
Those manufacturing costs that do not change in total in response to short-run changes in the levels of production, but vary on a per-unit basis with changes in the level of production.

free cash flow (8)
Reported income, adjusted for depreciation based on the replacement cost of assets, less dividends to stockholders. The residue, or free cash, is presumably available to reduce indebtedness and provide for growth.

front-loading (3)
Recognizing income for reporting purposes in the early stages of the overall earnings process.

fully diluted earnings per share — FDEPS (7)
The amount of earnings per share reflecting the maximum amount that would have resulted from conversion or exercise of all dilutive securities.

functional currency (11)
The currency of the primary economic environment in which the reporting entity operates. (Usually, this is the environment in which the entity generates and expends cash.)

fundamental accounting equation (2)
Expression of a basic relationship in financial accounting: assets equal liabilities plus owners' equity. *Every* recorded transaction affects this equation.

funding agent of a pension plan (10)
The entity (often a bank or insurance company) that receives contributions to the pension plan from the employer, invests those funds, and disburses benefits to retirees as specified in the pension plan.

gains (3)
The FASB defines gains as "increases in equity (net assets) from peripheral or incidental transactions of an entity and from all other transactions and other events and circumstances affecting the entity during a period except those that result from revenues or investments by owners."

general purchasing power of capital (3)
Capital maintenance concept under which capital is maintained as long as the general purchasing power of the firm's net assets has not diminished during the period, after adjustments for capital transactions.

generally accepted accounting principles — GAAP (1)
The set of rules and conventions created to ensure a certain level of uniformity in the preparation of financial reports for use by those outside the firm.

going concern (1)
A financial accounting assumption that the accounting entity will not be liquidating in the foreseeable future unless there is evidence to the contrary.

gold-dollar standard (11)
A standard involving currency exchange rates that existed following World War II, in which the U.S. dollar was convertible into gold on demand at a parity price of $35 an ounce.

goodwill (5) and (9)
The amount paid for a business entity in excess of the fair market value of the identifiable net assets that are purchased. Goodwill is presented on the balance sheet as a noncurrent asset.

gross margin (3)
The difference between reported sales revenue and cost of goods sold.

gross margin percentage (3)
Gross margin divided by sales.

historical cost (4) and (5)
The amount of consideration given (usually, cash paid) in an exchange transaction to acquire an asset.

holding gain (4) and (11)

A situation in which the cost of replacing an existing asset is greater than the historical cost of that asset.

holding gain, net of inflation (11)

The excess of the current cost valuation of an asset over the historical cost valuation of that asset.

holding loss (11)

A situation in which the cost of replacing an existing asset is less than the historical cost of that asset.

horizontal analysis (12)

Financial statement analysis that indicates the percentage change from the previous period of individual financial statement items.

income statement (1)

A primary financial statement that presents information about a reporting firm's profitability over a specific period of time.

income tax effect of a transaction (4)

The change (increase or decrease) in income taxes payable that results from including a specific transaction in the determination of taxable income.

income tax expense (3)

The tax expense associated with the income from recurring operations reported on the income statement.

indirect method (8)

An approach to calculating and reporting cash flow from operating activities. Calculation begins with net income as reported on the income statement and then by a series of adjustments converts this amount from an accrual basis to a cash basis. Thus, if the indirect method is used, the statement of cash flows reports a reconciliation of reported net income with cash flows from operating activities.

information-efficient markets (1)

Markets which, at least in terms of publicly disclosed information, do not contain overvalued or undervalued securities.

installment sales method (3)

A procedure for recognizing revenue and related costs in the periods in which the selling price is collected in cash.

intangible assets (5)

Noncurrent resources that lack physical substance and that are used in the regular operations of the business. Examples include patents, trademarks, franchises, and goodwill.

interperiod income tax allocation (4)

A special technique required by GAAP to account for income taxes when timing differences exist between financial accounting income and taxable income. This technique requires that the amount of income tax expense allocated to a particular year be related to the revenues and expenses recognized during that year for financial accounting purposes.

intrastatement income tax allocation (3)

The assignment of tax effects to major sections of the income statement.

inventory (4) and (5)

Those tangible goods that are held for sale to customers in the ordinary course of business. Such goods are called merchandise inventory (or simply, inventory) in a merchandising firm, and finished goods in a manufacturing firm.

inventory (or product) costs (3)

Manufacturing costs that are assigned initially to inventory accounts. These costs do not become expenses until the period in which the inventory is sold.

inventory turnover rate (5) and (12)

Cost of goods sold for the period divided by average inventory.

investing activities (8)

Activities that generally involve acquiring and disposing of noncurrent assets. Differentiating among operating, financing, and investing activities is important in preparing a statement of cash flows.

journal (2)

A book or other medium in which transactions — expressed in terms of increases or decreases to particular accounts — are listed in chronological order.

last-in, first-out — LIFO (4)

An inventory cost flow assumption that allocates

costs of the latest purchases to cost of goods sold and (except in a LIFO liquidation) assigns the oldest costs making up goods available for sale to ending inventory.

lease (10)

An agreement to rent assets for a period of time, often several years.

ledger (2)

A book or other medium that summarizes the cumulative effects of recorded transactions in separate accounts.

lessee (10)

The individual receiving the right to use the leased asset.

lessor (10)

The owner of the asset being leased.

liabilities (2) and (6)

The FASB defines liabilities as ". . . probable future sacrifices of economic benefits arising from present obligations of a particular entity to transfer assets or provide services to other entities in the future as the result of past transactions or events."

LIFO conformity requirement (4)

An Internal Revenue Service requirement that LIFO be used in preparing the firm's published financial statements if LIFO is used for tax purposes.

LIFO liquidation (4)

A situation in which a firm using LIFO to value inventory costs sells more units of inventory during the current period than it purchases during the pe-

riod. The effect of a LIFO liquidation is to assign some of the older inventory costs to cost of goods sold.

liquidating value of preferred stock (7)

The amount that a preferred stockholder is entitled to if the firm goes out of business.

liquidity ratios (12)

Ratios that address the short-term ability of the firm to meet its debt obligation as they come due. Examples include the current ratio and the quick ratio.

losses (3)

The FASB defines losses as "decreases in equity (net assets) from peripheral or incidental transactions of an entity and from all other transactions and other events and circumstances affecting the entity during a period except those that result from expenses or distributions to owners."

lower of cost or market— LCM (3)

An accounting rule whereby assets are carried at their acquisition price unless "market" is less than the acquisition price. Depending on the situation, "market" may mean replacement cost, selling price, or some other value.

managerial accounting (1)

The process of measuring and reporting economic events to provide relevant information to decision makers *inside* the firm. Managerial accounting is not governed by GAAP.

manufacturing overhead (3)

All manufacturing costs not classified as direct materials or direct labor. Accordingly, this cost category includes all indirect manufacturing costs.

marketable equity securities (5)

Securities representing ownership shares of a firm for which sales prices or bid-and-ask prices are currently available on a national exchange or in the over-the-counter market.

matching principle (1)

The principle that governs the timing of the recognition of expenses on the income statement. This concept requires that once specific revenues have been recognized in a given period, all applicable expenses incurred to generate those revenues be "assigned" to the same period.

measurement bases (5)

Different valuation methods that may be used in valuing assets. The five measurement bases used in financial accounting are historical cost, current cost, current market value, expected market value, and present value of expected cash flows.

merger (9)

A business combination in which the boards of directors of the investor and the investee firms approve a plan for the exchange of the investee firm's voting stock in return for the voting stock and/or other consideration paid by the investor firm. The investee firm then ceases to exist as a separate legal entity.

minority interest (9)
Ownership of less than 50 percent of the voting shares of another firm.

monetary items (5) and (11)
Claims (assets) or obligations (liabilities) that are fixed in terms of a given amount of dollars.

money measurement assumption (1)
A financial accounting assumption that specifies that all reported transactions be measured in terms of money.

net assets (2)
Assets minus liabilities.

net income (2)
The increase in net assets over a specific period of time due to a firm's own operations. This increase is measured and communicated by means of the income statement.

net realizable value (5)
The selling price of an asset less direct costs of disposal and collection. See **expected market value.**

noninterest-bearing note (5) and (6)
A note that nominally does not bear interest but in fact contains implicit interest. A note has implicit interest if the present value of the note is less than the face amount (maturity value) of the note.

nonmonetary items (11)
Assets or liabilities whose prices are not fixed in terms of a certain number of dollars.

one-line consolidation (9)
A synonym for the equity method of accounting for intercorporate investments.

operating activities (8)
All activities of a firm — generally those concerned with the typical day-to-day activities involving the sale of merchandise and provision of services to customers — not classified as investing activities or financing activities. This classification is important in preparing a statement of cash flows.

operating cycle (5)
The sequence that begins when a firm acquires inventory and ends when cash is collected from customers from the sale of that inventory.

operating lease (10)
A lease that does not qualify as a capital lease and for which lease payments are interpreted simply as rental expenses.

operating margin (4)
The difference between the selling price of inventory items and the cost of replacing those items.

operating ratios (12)
Ratios that attempt to measure the profitability and efficiency with which the firm uses its resources.

owners' (shareholders' or stockholders') equity (2) and (7)
The FASB defines owners' equity as "...the residual interest in the assets of an entity that remains after deducting its liabilities."

par value stock (7)
Stock that has an arbitrary fixed amount assigned to each share of a given class. The total par value of all issued stock constitutes the legal capital of the corporation.

parent company (9)
A firm that owns controlling interest in the voting shares of one or more other firms. (The company whose controlling interest is owned is referred to as the subsidiary company.)

participating preferred stock (7)
Preferred stock with a feature that allows the preferred stockholders in certain situations to receive dividends that are in excess of those normally paid.

passive investment (9)
An investment in stock of another company that is not made for the purpose of exerting influence or control over the investee firm.

patent (5)
An intangible asset that represents an exclusive right granted by the U.S. Patent Office that gives the owner control of the use or sale of an invention for 17 years.

pension interest cost (10)
A component of pension expense that reflects the increase in the present value of the pension benefits due to the passage of time.

pension plan (10)

An agreement between a firm and its employees to provide payments to the employees after retirement.

pension service cost (10)

A component of pension expense that reflects the present value of projected pension benefits earned by employees in the current period.

percentage of completion method (3)

A procedure for allocating income on a long-term construction project to each of the individual reporting periods, based on the estimated percentage of the contract completed.

period costs (3)

Costs that are not assigned to inventory accounts and are usually expensed in the period in which they are incurred.

permanent account (2)

A balance sheet account that is not closed at the end of an accounting period.

permanent difference (4)

Difference that arises from a transaction or event that affects financial accounting income but never affects taxable income, or vice versa. Interperiod income tax allocation does not apply to permanent differences—only to timing differences.

pooling-of-interests method (9)

A method of accounting for a business combination in which the assets and liabilities of the subsidiary are *not* revalued at the acquisition date to reflect fair market values; rather, the book values of the pooled subsidiary continue to be reported.

post-closing trial balance (2)

A trial balance that includes only the permanent accounts. It is prepared after the temporary accounts have been closed at the end of the period.

posting (2)

A procedure by which information recorded initially in the journal is transferred to the appropriate accounts in the ledger.

pre-closing trial balance (2)

A trial balance that includes all the permanent and temporary accounts before the latter are closed at the end of the period.

predictive ability criterion (1)

A criterion used in assessing alternative accounting methods on the basis of their usefulness in prediction. A better accounting method, by this criterion, permits more accurate prediction of economic events of interest to decision makers.

preferred stock (7)

A class of stock with certain priorities—usually involving the distribution of dividends and other corporate assets—over common stock.

prepaid expenses (5)

Assets in the form of prepayments made for goods or services in advance of their use or consumption. Prepaid expenses are usu-

ally classified as current assets.

present value of expected cash flows (3) and (5)

The net amount of discounted cash inflows and outflows pertaining to a particular asset or project.

price-earnings ratio—P/E (4) and (7)

The market price per share of a company's common stock divided by the earnings per share of that stock.

price indexes (11)

Indicators designed to represent changes in purchasing power relative to an arbitrarily determined base period.

primary earnings per share—PEPS (7)

The amount of earnings attributable to each share of outstanding common stock and common stock equivalents that have a dilutive effect on EPS.

principal (6)

The amount stated on the face of a financial instrument on which interest is charged or earned.

prior service cost (10)

The cost of retroactive benefits that are granted employees in an amendment to a pension plan.

promissory note (6)

A financial instrument with a fixed maturity date and an explicitly stated interest rate.

purchase method (9)

A method of accounting for a business combination in which the assets and liabilities of the subsidiary are revalued at the acquisition date to reflect fair market values.

quick ratio (12)

Cash plus receivables divided by current liabilities.

raw materials inventory (3)

Materials used by a manufacturer on which no work has been performed to date. This account is one of the three inventory accounts of a manufacturing firm.

realization principle (1) and (3)

The principle used in financial accounting for determining the timing of revenue recognition. In accordance with the realization principle, both of the following conditions must be met before revenue is recognized: (1) substantially all of the effort (and cost) necessary to generate the revenue should be complete and (2) the net amount to be received (the exchange price) should be measurable with reasonable objectivity.

replacement cost (5) and (11)

The cost of a new asset of the same type as the current one, adjusted for depreciation and changes in technology.

replacement cost of capital (3)

Capital maintenance concept under which capital is maintained as long as the net assets at the end of the period are sufficient to replace, at current costs, the firm's beginning-of-the-period net assets.

reproduction cost (11)

The current cost to replicate an existing asset in its present condition and age.

residual value of a fixed asset (4)

The proceeds the firm expects to receive upon disposing of the asset.

return on assets employed— ROA (4) and (12)

Earnings divided by assets employed. This ratio is widely used for performance evaluation.

return on pension plan assets (10)

The earnings on stocks, bonds, and other resources of the pension plan that are invested in order to provide pension benefits. The return on pension plan assets *reduces* pension cost because these investment returns represent additional resources that may be used to satisfy pension obligations.

return on sales—ROS (3) and (12)

The percentage of each sales dollar represented by operating income; that is, operating income divided by sales.

return on stockholders' equity—ROE (12)

Net income from recurring operations divided by stockholders' equity.

revenues (2) and (3)

The FASB defines revenues as "inflows or other enhancements of assets of an entity or settlements of its liabilities (or a combination of both) during a period from delivering or producing goods, rendering services, or other activities that constitute the entity's ongoing major or central operations."

sales revenue (3)

Revenues that represent assets received from customers (cash or accounts receivable) for goods sold during the accounting period.

sales-type lease (10)

A lease agreement that meets at least one of the four criteria for classifying a lease as a capital lease, and also provides profit to a manufacturer or dealer at the inception of the lease.

Securities and Exchange Commission—SEC (1)

The public sector organization created by Congress to administer the Securities Act of 1933 and the Securities Exchange Act of 1934.

selling, general, and administrative expenses (3)

All expenses, other than cost of goods sold and income taxes, that are related to the primary, recurring activities of the firm.

sinking fund (5)

A special restrictive fund used to accumulate cash or other assets and designated for a specific purpose, such as the payment of the principal due on a bond at its maturity date.

solvency ratios (12)

A group of financial ratios that focus on the long-term ability of the firm to pay its debts. Examples include the debt-to-equity ratio and the times-interest-earned ratio.

source document (2)

Media on which data from exchange transactions are captured. Examples include invoices, checks, payroll time cards, and cash register tapes.

specific identification method (4)

An inventory cost flow assumption in which cost of goods sold and ending inventory are stated at the actual costs of the specific units sold and on hand. Under specific identification, the cost flow assumption matches the physical flow of the goods.

specific price indexes (11)

Indexes that are designed to measure price changes for specific types of assets and thus contrast with a broadly based index.

stated value of stock (7)

The arbitrary fixed amount assigned by the company's board of directors to each share of stock of a given class.

statement of cash flows (1) and (8)

A primary financial statement that provides information about changes in the reporting firm's liquidity over a specific period of time. The statement of cash flows classifies cash receipts and payments by operating, investing, and financing activities.

statement of changes in financial position (1)

A financial statement required by GAAP prior to 1988 that presented the effects of inflows and outflows of a firm's funds during a specific period of time. This statement has been replaced by the statement of cash flows.

stock dividend (7)

A distribution of additional shares of stock to stockholders in proportion to their present ownership interest. However, in contrast to a stock split, a stock dividend does not reduce the par value per share of stock, and thus the total par value of outstanding shares *increases* as the additional shares are issued.

stock rights (7)

Agreements that entitle the holder to acquire shares of a particular class of stock in the future at a specified price per share.

stock split (7)

A distribution of additional shares of stock to stockholders in proportion to their present ownership interests. A stock split *increases* the number of shares outstanding, and at the same time *reduces* the par value per share so that the total par value of the outstanding shares is unchanged.

stock warrants (7)

A certificate used as evidence of stock rights that represents the right to purchase one or more shares of stock.

straight-line depreciation (4)

A method of depreciation that allocates an equal amount of depreciation expense to each reporting period over the estimated life of the asset.

subsidiary company (9)

A company with 50 percent or more of its voting shares owned by another company. (The company that owns the controlling interest in the subsidiary is referred to as the parent company.)

sum-of-the-years'-digits depreciation — SYD (4)

An accelerated method of depreciation that allocates a declining amount of depreciation expense to each reporting period over the estimated life of the asset.

systematic risk (12)

The expected co-movement of a security's returns with returns of the general market.

T account (2)

The simplest form of a ledger account, which takes the form of the capital letter T.

taxable income (4)

The amount of income subject to taxation as determined by the appropriate tax code.

temporary account (2)

An account that is closed (reduced to zero) at the end of each accounting period. Revenues, expenses, and dividends are temporary accounts.

temporary investment (5)

An investment classified as a current asset that meets two criteria: (1) it is *readily marketable* and (2) it is management's *intention* to convert the investment into cash as needed within one year or within the operating cycle, whichever is longer.

time period assumption (1)

A financial accounting assumption that recognizes the tradeoff between precision of information and timeliness of information. Because economic processes rarely fall neatly into a series of defined time intervals, the assignment of operating results to arbitrary time periods entails estimating and approximating.

times-interest-earned ratio (12)

The sum of net income, income tax, and interest expense divided by interest expense.

timing difference (4)

A situation in which a transaction affects the determination of net income for financial accounting purposes in one accounting period and the computation of taxable income in a different period.

trade receivable (5)

Accounts receivable and notes receivable that originate from sales transactions in the normal course of a firm's business.

trading on the equity (12)

Increasing the proportion of debt in the firm's capital structure in order to increase return on stockholders' equity.

translation of foreign currency (11)

The restatement of the accounts of a foreign branch or subsidiary into U.S. dollars for financial statement purposes.

treasury stock (7)

A corporation's own stock that has been issued and subsequently reacquired by the corporation, but has not yet been canceled or reissued.

trial balance (2)

A listing of all accounts in the ledger and their corresponding balances entered in the respective debit-credit columns.

units-of-production depreciation (4)

A method of depreciation that allocates the depreciable cost of a fixed asset as a function of the use or productivity activity of the asset during the period.

upstream sales (9)

A sale by a subsidiary company to its parent company.

variable manufacturing costs (3)

Those manufacturing costs that vary in total at different levels of production but remain the same on a per-unit basis with changes in the level of production.

vertical analysis (12)

Financial statement analysis in which items on a financial statement are stated as a percentage of some reference amount, such as total assets, net income, or the like.

vested benefits (10)

Pension benefits to which employees who participate in the pension plan have irrevocable rights.

work in process inventory (3)

Partially completed goods of a manufacturer. This account is one of the three inventory accounts of a manufacturing firm.

working capital (2)

Current assets minus current liabilities.

Checklist of Key Figures

Chapter Two Check Figures

2-22 No key figure

2-23 Firm A: Total assets, $225,000

2-24 Company A: Net loss, $20,000

2-25 Company A: Retained earnings, $310,000

2-26 Company A: Change in retained earnings, $40,000

2-27 (a) Net income, $40,000

2-28 (a) Net income, $20,000

2-29 No key figure

2-30 No key figure

2-31 No key figure

2-32 No key figure

2-33 No key figure

2-34 No key figure

2-35 Day 3: Insurance payment, $20,000

2-36 (a) Net income, $1,500

2-37 (b) Net income (accrual basis), $3,700

2-38 No key figure

2-39 No key figure

2-40 No key figure

2-41 No key figure

2-42 No key figure

2-43 No key figure

2-44 No key figure

2-45 No key figure

2-46 No key figure

2-47 No key figure

2-48 (d) Ending retained earnings, $203,000

2-49 (d) Net loss, $4,700

2-50 (d) Net income, $3,960

2-51 (b) Net income, $12,083

2-52 (c) Net income, $5,700

2-53 (c) Net loss, $17,000

Chapter Three Check Figures

3-35 (b) Net income, $7,000

3-36 No key figure

3-37 No key figure

3-38 No key figure

3-39 (b) Total sales revenue, $200,000

3-40 No key figure

3-41 (b) Percentage of completion: Net income for 1988, $80,000

3-42 (a) Net income (all years), $0

3-43 Net income, $100,000

3-44 (b) Net income for 1988, $66,700

3-45 Revenue recognized in 1989, $534,000

3-46 (d) Revenue recognized in 1988, $444,000

3-47 No key figure

3-48 No key figure

3-49 No key figure

3-50 (c) Ending retained earnings, $38,000

3-51 (c) Net income, $2,000

3-52 (1) Sales revenue, $12 million

3-53 (1) Cash inflow from sales, $292 million

3-54 Net income, $125.3 million

3-55 Case A: Merchandise purchases, $825

3-56 Estimated cost of inventory, $6,000

3-57 (1) Firm A: Gross margin, $1,100,000

3-58 No key figure

3-59 No key figure

3-60 Cost of goods manufactured, $1,175,000

3-61 Net income before taxes, $1,950,000

3-62 No key figure

3-63 Forecasted net income, $16,800

3-64 (c) Ending inventory—fourth quarter, $75,333

3-65 Net income for 1988, $12,450

3-66 (a) Variable costing method: Gross margin, $828,000

Chapter Four Check Figures

4-22 No key figure

4-23 Corrected net income for 1988, $33,500

4-24 (a) Ending inventory (FIFO), $1,950

4-25 (a) Gross margin in 1988 (LIFO), $96,000

4-26 (a) Net income for 1988, $48,400

4-27 No key figure

4-28 (a) Inventory at December 31, $100 million lower

4-29 (b) Holding gain, $40,000

4-30 (a) Assumption 1: Net loss, $2,200

4-31 (b) Tax savings, $640

4-32 No key figure

4-33 No key figure

4-34 No key figure

4-35 (a) Net income, $240,000

4-36 (a) Net income (LIFO), $1,189.5 million

4-37 (b) Net income, $174,000

4-38 (2) Depreciation expense (Year 2), $24,000

4-39 (3) Depreciation expense (Year 2), $26,400

4-40 No key figure

4-41 (a) Depreciation expense for 1988, $46,000

4-42 No key figure

4-43 (a) Beta Company: Depreciation (Year 2), $8,000

4-44 (a) Loss on sale of fixed asset, $17,500

4-45 (a) SYD depreciation (1987), $9,600

4-46 (a) DDB depreciation (Year 2), $216,000

4-47 (b) Deferred income tax balance at December 31, 1989, $5,333 (credit)

4-48 No key figure

4-49 (a) Depreciation expense (1989), $120,000

4-50 (a) Depreciation expense on tax return (1989), $11,760

4-51 No key figure

4-52 No key figure

Chapter Five Check Figures

5-33 No key figure

5-34 No key figure

5-35 No key figure

5-36 (a) Unrealized loss, $4,000

5-37 (b) Unrealized loss, $3,200

5-38 No key figure

5-39 No key figure

5-40 No key figure

5-41 (a) Present value of note, $10,290

5-42 (a) Present value of note (both cases), $1,000

5-43 (a) Accounts receivable turnover rate, 12

5-44 No key figure

5-45 (b) Book value of accounts receivable, $82,990

5-46 No key figure

5-47 No key figure

5-48 No key figure

5-49 (a) Ending inventory (LIFO), $1,000

5-50 No key figure

5-51 (a) Annual cash payments, $79,135

5-52 No key figure

5-53 No key figure

5-54 No key figure

5-55 No key figure

5-56 (a) Levered, Inc.'s carrying value, $742 million

5-57 (a) Sinking fund (end of fifth year), $61,050,000

5-58 No key figure

5-59 No key figure

5-60 Estimated fair market value of property, $490,600

5-61 No key figure

5-62 (a) Method 1: Implied value of goodwill, $9 million

5-63 No key figure

5-64 No key figure

5-65 No key figure

5-66 No key figure

5-67 No key figure

5-68 No key figure

5-69 No key figure

5-70 No key figure

5-71 No key figure

Chapter Six Check Figures

6-18 No key figure

6-19 No key figure

6-20 No key figure

6-21 No key figure

6-22 (a) Estimated warranty liability at December 31, 1987, $50,000

6-23 (a) Estimated warranty obligation at end of Year 3, $850,000

6-24 (b) Lowest price is $379.10

6-25 (a) Estimated profit, $11,900

6-26 (a) Effective interest rate on note, 16%

6-27 (a) Interest expense during first year (2% interest), $94,260

6-28 No key figure

6-29 (a) Present value, $312,000

6-30 No key figure

6-31 No key figure

6-32 (a) Cash proceeds of bond issue, $4,246,500

6-33 (b) Total interest expense (20 years), $1,753,500

6-34 (a) Cash proceeds of bond issue, $11,149,000

6-35 (a) Amount paid to bondholders, $22 million

6-36 (a) Present value of debt, $67,610,000

6-37 (a) Present value of debt, $130,482,000

6-38 (a) Present value of debt, $85,322,400

6-39 (a) Market rate of interest, 4.5%

6-40 (b) Amount on deposit at end of fifth year, $3,830,710

6-41 No key figure

6-42 (b) Event (3): Net proceeds, $57,371,250

6-43 No key figure

6-44 No key figure

6-45 No key figure

Chapter Seven Check Figures

7-24 No key figure

7-25 (b) Total shareholders' equity, $30,048,000

7-26 No key figure

7-27 No key figure

7-28 No key figure

7-29 Total shareholders' equity, $60 million

7-30 No key figure

7-31 (b) Total shareholders' equity, $26,400,000

7-32 (d) Cash dividend to preferred stockholders, $5 million

7-33 (b) Weighted average number of shares, 475,000

7-34 (b) Assumption 4: EPS, $9.60

7-35 (c) Interest expense for 1987, $1,079,100

7-36 No key figure

7-37 No key figure

7-38 No key figure

7-39 (a) EPS, $12.50

7-40 No key figure

7-41 (a) Increase EPS

7-42 (a) EPS, $2.07

7-43 (a) EPS, $1.75

7-44 No key figure

7-45 (a) Cash proceeds, $100 million

7-46 No key figure

7-47 (a) Debt to shareholders' equity, 60%

Chapter Eight Check Figures

8-21 No key figure

8-22 No key figure

8-23 No key figure

8-24 No key figure

8-25 (e) Cash flow from operating activities, $1,000

8-26 (b) Net cash flow used by operating activities, $200,000

8-27 (a) Net cash flow from operating activities, $1,531,000

8-28 No key figure

8-29 Net cash flow from operating activities, $2,070,000

8-30 Net cash flow from operating activities, $116,000

8-31 Net cash flow from operating activities, $12,000

8-32 Net cash flow from operating activities, $30,564

8-33 Net cash flow from operating activities, $122,000

8-34 Total assets at December 31, 1986, $3,173,000

8-35 Net cash used by operating activities, $95.8 million

8-36 No key figure

8-37 (a) Projected cash flow, $217,710

Chapter Nine Check Figures

9-22 No key figure

9-23 No key figure

9-24 (b) Investment carrying value at December 31, 1990, $7,500,000

9-25 Total assets, $575 million

9-26 Total assets, $590 million

9-27 (2) Total assets, $580 million

9-28 (2) Total assets, $590 million

9-29 (b) Total assets, $5,683 million

9-30 (b) Consolidated net income, $2,043.2 million

9-31 (a) ROA for ABM, Consolidated, 6.5%

9-32 (b) Goodwill, $6 million

9-33 (a) Total assets, $48 million

9-34 No key figure

9-35 No key figure

9-36 No key figure

9-37 No key figure

9-38 Contribution margin (total), $74,000

Chapter Ten Check Figures

10-25 No key figure

10-26 No key figure

10-27 (a) Present value of the note, $818,500

10-28 (a) Present value of lease obligation, $818,500

10-29 (c) Interest income for 1988, $130,960

10-30 (a) Present value of estimated residual value, $866,100

10-31 (b) Total first-year expense, $120,798

10-32 (b) Total income over lease term, $190,000

10-33 No key figure

10-34 No key figure

10-35 (d) Net income if leases not capitalized, $122,564

10-36 No key figure

10-37 No key figure

10-38 (c) Present value of pension benefits, $175,752

10-39 (a) (1) Present value of pension liability, $5,915

10-40 (a) Kline's projected benefit obligation, $32,796

10-41 (a) Net pension costs for 1989, $122,619

10-42 No key figure

10-43 No key figure

10-44 No key figure

10-45 No key figure

10-46 No key figure

10-47 No key figure

Chapter Eleven Check Figures

11-21 No key figure

11-22 (a) From A: Purchasing power loss, $160 million

11-23 No key figure

11-24 (a) Depreciation expense for item A, $50,000 (constant dollars)

11-25 (a) Growth rate in net income, −40.59% (constant dollars basis)

11-26 (a) Net monetary gain, $24,532

11-27 No key figure

11-28 Net income, $61,055 (constant dollar basis)

11-29 (a) Income from continuing operations, $1,562 (constant dollar basis)

11-30 Cost of goods sold, $1,295,154

11-31 (d) Growth rate in dividends, −10.68% (constant dollar basis)

11-32 (a) Increase in current costs, $1,200,000

11-33 (a) Effective tax rate, 35.3% (adjusted for current costs)

11-34 (b) EPS, $2.35 (constant dollar basis)

11-35 No key figure

11-36 No key figure

11-37 No key figure

11-38 No key figure

11-39 No key figure

11-40 (a) Included gross profit, $35,000 (under *SFAS No. 8*)

11-41 Income before taxes, $6,215,000

11-42 No key figure

11-43 Cash after translation, $112,910

Index

A 8
B 9
C 0
D 1
E 2
F 3
G 4
H 5
I 6
J 7